WORD PICTURES

IN THE

NEW TESTAMENT

CONCISE EDITION

A. T. ROBERTSON

EDITED BY JAMES A. SWANSON

HOLMAN REFERENCE

NASHVILLE

Word Pictures Concise Edition
Copyright © 2000 Holman Bible Publishers
All rights reserved.

Dewey Decimal Classification: 225.7
Subject Heading: BIBLE. N.T. COMMENTARIES
Library of Congress Card Catalog Number: 00-02565

Cover design, interior design, and typesetting by
Sam Gantt, SG Graphic Design Group

Library of Congress Cataloging-in-Publication Data
Robertson, A.T., 1863-1934.
   Word pictures in the New Testament / written by A. T. Robertson ; edited
by James A. Swanson.— Concise ed.
      p.   cm.
   ISBN 0-8054-9055-8 (alk. paper)
   1. Bible. N.T.—Commentaries. I. Swanson, James A., 1952- II. Title.

BS2341.2 .R65 2000
225.7—dc21   00-025658

Printed in the United States of America
1 2 3 4 5 6 04 03 02 01 00
D

CONTENTS

TRANSLITERATION OF THE GREEK

α	is transliterated into English with	a
β	,,	b
γ	,,	g
δ	,,	d
ϵ	,,	e
ζ	,,	z
η	,,	$\hat{e}$
θ	,,	th
ι	,,	i
κ	,,	k
λ	,,	l
μ	,,	m
ν	,,	n
ξ	,,	x
o	,,	o
π	,,	p
ρ	,,	r
σ, ς	,,	s
τ	,,	t
υ	,,	$u, v,$ or y
ϕ	,,	ph or f
χ	,,	ch
ψ	,,	ps
ω	,,	$\hat{o}$
Also:		
$\gamma\gamma$	,,	ng
$\gamma\kappa$	,,	nk

PREFACE

Young Archie Robertson arrived at Wake Forest College on his 16th birthday, November 6, 1879. He had two dollars in his pocket and was more than two months late registering for the Fall semester. In spite of this, Robertson soon led his Greek class because of "meticulous observation and a marvelous memory."

Who, seeing young Robertson arrive at Wake Forest that November day, could have guessed the multiplied influence his life would have?

A.T. Robertson studied at Wake Forest College from 1879 to 1885, graduating with an M.A. He then studied at The Southern Baptist Theological Seminary from 1885 to 1888. Upon graduation, he became a professor at Southern Seminary, serving there until his death, September 24, 1934.

A.T. Robertson was a creative, exacting teacher. He has a special interest in helping ministers who did not have the advantage of formal education. His ministry was multiplied through his students, his articles in popular periodicals, his lectures at Christian conference centers in various parts of the U.S. and abroad, and through the 45 books that he wrote.

Six of Robertson's 45 volumes is a set: *Word Pictures in the New Testament*. The last of these was published in 1933, the year before his death. Thousands of sets of *Word Pictures* have been sold since 1933. *Word Pictures* can be seen in the library of almost every minister and those who are studying for the ministry.

In 1996, Broadman & Holman made a decision to create a concise edition of *Word Pictures*. In doing so, we decided to give priority to A.T. Robertson's discussions of Greek words. Technical discussions of Greek grammar and syntax have been eliminated from this edition. Also, much of the biblical background material has been taken out in order to make possible a manageable, one volume edition of *Word Pictures*.

In publishing this concise edition of Word Pictures in the New Testament, Holman Bible Publishers hopes to make A.T. Robertson's insights available and accessible to both ministers and lay Bible teachers.

David R. Shepherd
Senior Vice-President and Publisher
Broadman & Holman Bible Publishers

WORD PICTURES

IN THE

NEW TESTAMENT

CONCISE EDITION

THE GOSPEL ACCORDING TO MATTHEW

AUTHOR: Apostle Matthew
RECIPIENTS: Jewish Christians
DATE: Between A.D. 58 and 69
THEME: Jesus is Son of David (Messiah, Son of Abraham, and King)

BY WAY OF INTRODUCTION

Matthew was a tax collector, also known as Levi, son of Alphaeus (Matt. 9:9; 10:3, also Mark 2:14 and Luke 5:27); one of the Twelve, usually listed either seventh or eighth of the Apostles. As a tax collector in Galilee, Matthew was in the habit of keeping accounts and it is quite possible that he took notes of the sayings of Jesus as he heard them. He shows that Jesus is the Messiah of Jewish expectation and hope, and so makes frequent quotations from the Old Testament by way of confirmation and illustration.

There are ten parables in Matthew not in the other Gospels: The Tares, the Hid Treasure, the Net, the Pearl of Great Price, the Unmerciful Servant, the Laborers in the Vineyard, the Two Sons, the Marriage of the King's Son, the Ten Virgins, the Talents. The only miracles in Matthew alone are the two blind men and the coin in the mouth of the fish. Matthew gives the narrative of the birth of Jesus from the standpoint of Joseph while Luke tells that wonderful story from Mary's perspective.

CHAPTER I

1. {*The Book*} (cf. Luke 3:23-38). Lit. "*the* book" refers to the genealogical table of Jesus Christ. Apparently, the genealogy in Luke is the real line of Jesus through Mary. Matthew's genealogy is the legal pedigree of Joseph, which is according to Jewish custom (Luke goes back to Adam, Matthew back to Abraham). {*Jesus Christ*} The name given by an angel. "Jesus" describes his mission (cf. Matt. 1:21). "Christ" means "anointed" and is a proper name or title "the Anointed One" to translate the Hebrew word "Messiah" (cf. John 1:41). {*The Son of David, the son of Abraham*} On the human side Jesus is the "son

[descendant] of David," a designation for Messiah. He is also "son [descendant] of Abraham."

2. {*Begat*} *Begat* itself does not always mean immediate parentage, but merely direct descent (hence it could skip a name in a generation). *Begat* in 1:16 must mean line of descent or the text has been tampered with in order to get rid of the Virgin Birth idea, but it was left untouched in 1:18-25.

18. {*The birth of Jesus Christ...*}Here the word for birth is *genesis*. {*Betrothed to Joseph*} (cf. Matt. 1:16). Now it is explained why Joseph, though the legal father of Jesus in the royal line, was not the actual father of Mary's Son. Betrothal was serious, not to be broken lightly. The man who was betrothed to a maiden was legally her husband (Gen. 29:21; Deut. 22:23). And a breach of faithfulness was treated as adultery and could be punished with death. {*Of the Holy Ghost*} The Greek wording plainly shows that it was the discovery of her pregnancy that shocked Joseph. He did not as yet know what Matthew plainly asserts—that the Holy Ghost, not Joseph and not any man, was responsible for the pregnancy of Mary.

19. {*A righteous man*} (cf. Luke. 1:6; 2:25). This is the Greek word *dikaios*, just, upright, not benignant or merciful. Though Joseph was upright, he would not seek Mary's death by stoning, and he would not show his zeal by branding her with public disgrace (Deut. 22:23). {*And yet not willing...*} "Willing" is the Greek verb *thelô*, with a focus on purpose in contrast to another Greek word for "desire." It was not Joseph's purpose to "make her a public example."

20. {*An angel of the Lord appeared unto him in a dream*} In the Old Testament, God himself is represented by the phrase *angel of the Lord*. It was in a dream, but the message was distinct and decisive for Joseph. {*Fear not*} Greek tense shows he is told to not *become* afraid.

21. {*Thou shalt call his name Jesus*} As the supposed father, Joseph is to name the child. *Jesus* is the Greek equivalent of the Hebrew *Joshua*, a contraction of *Jehoshuah* (Num. 13:16; 1 Chr. 7:27). This Jesus is another Joshua to lead the true people of God into the Promised Land. The meaning of the name, therefore, finds expression in the title *Savior* applied to our Lord (Luke. 1:47; 2:11; John. 4:42). "His people" Paul will later explain means the spiritual Israel, all who believe whether Jews or Gentiles. {*From their sins*} This includes both sins of omission and of commission. "Sin" is a translation of the Greek word *hamartia* which is from the verb *hamartanein* and means missing the mark as with an arrow.

22. {*That it may be fulfilled*} This shows purpose here, God's purpose. {*Through the prophet*} The prophet was the intermediate agent through which the message was spoken. {*All this has happened*} The context of this quote (Isa. 7:14) is a historical illustration which finds its richest fulfillment in the birth of Jesus. This historical illustration from the time of Ahaz finds its richest fulfillment in the birth of Jesus from Mary.

23. {*They shall call*} People will call his name Immanuel, God with us. The language of Isaiah has had marvelous illustration in the Incarnation of Christ (cf. John. 14:9).

25. {*And knew her not*} Greek tense shows that Joseph lived in continence continually with Mary until the birth of Jesus; after her firstborn's birth she had other children, and the natural meaning is that they were younger children of Joseph *and* Mary (cf. Luke. 2:7).

CHAPTER 2

1. {*In Bethlehem of Judea*} (cf. Luke 2:1-7). This town has a rich history, the original family home for both Joseph and Mary. It was the scene of Ruth's life with Boaz (Ruth 1:1; Matt. 1:5). David was born here and anointed king by Samuel (1 Sam. 17:12). {*In the days of Herod the King*} (cf. Luke 2:1-3). Jesus was born while Herod the Great was king; Herod died in 4 B.C. by our modern later dating system. So the birth of Jesus is probably 6 or 7 B.C., no later than 5 B.C. {*Wise men from the east*} Among the Persians there was a priestly caste of Magi like the astrologers in Babylon (Dan. 1:4). Daniel was head of such an order (Dan. 2:48). Though three gifts were given (gold, frankincense, myrrh), this does not mean there were only three of them. These men may have been Jewish proselytes and may have known of the Messianic hope.

2. {*We saw his star in the east*} That is, while they were in the east they saw the star and so headed west. It could also mean "we saw his star when it rose." This star was either a miracle or a combination of bright stars or a comet. "His" star refers to the Magi's belief that a star could be the *fravashi,* the counterpart or angel (cf. Matt. 18:10) of a great man. The Magi had their own way of concluding that the star which they had seen pointed to the birth of this Messianic king.

4. {*He inquired of them where the Christ should be born*} The Greek tense suggests that Herod inquired repeatedly, probably of one and another of the leaders gathered together. This was likely not a formal meeting but a free assembly for conference.

5. {*And they said unto him*} They give the answer that is in accord with the common Jewish opinion that the Messiah was to come from Bethlehem and of the seed of David (John 7:42, also Mic. 5:2). {*Shall be shepherd*} (cf. Heb. 13:20). Jesus calls himself the good shepherd (John 10:11) and Peter calls Christ the chief shepherd (1 Pet. 2:25).

9. {*Went before them*} Greek tense shows the star *kept on* in front of them, not as a guide to the town, but to the inn where the child was (cf. Luke 2:7). Justin Martyr says that it was in a cave. The stall where the cattle and donkeys stayed may have been beneath the inn in the side of the hill.

11. {*Opening their treasures*} Here "treasures" means "caskets," receptacles for valuables. In their caskets the Magi had gold, frankincense, and myrrh, all found at that time in Arabia, though gold was found in Babylon and elsewhere.

12. {*Warned in a dream*} The verb means to transact business, to consult, to deliberate, to make answer as of magistrates or an oracle, to instruct, to admonish.

15. {*Until the death of Herod*} From a human view, Joseph took his family to stay away from the monster Herod; but also this shows that this was in fulfillment of God's purpose to call his Son out of Egypt (cf. Hos. 11:1).

16. {*Slew all the male children that were in Bethlehem*} (cf. Jer. 31:15). Some note Augustus said that it was better to be Herod's sow (Greek word *hus*) than his son (Greek *huios*), for the sow had a better chance of life.

20. {*For they are dead*} (cf. Exod. 4:19). "They" is an idiomatic plural referring to Herod who alone sought to kill Jesus.

23. {*Should be called a Nazarene*} No single prophecy says that the Messiah was to be called a Nazarene. It may be that this term of contempt (John 1:46; 7:52) is what is meant, and that several prophecies are to be combined like Pss. 22:6,8; 69:11,19; Isa. 53:2,3,4. The name

Nazareth means a shoot or branch, but it is by no means certain that Matthew has this in mind. It is best to confess that we do not know.

CHAPTER 3

1. {*And in those days cometh John the Baptist*} (cf. Mark 1:2; Luke 3:1 and Acts 1:22). It is now some thirty years after the birth of John. He is described as "the Baptist," "the Baptizer" for that is the rite that distinguishes him. The Jews probably had proselyte baptism. But this rite was meant for the Gentiles who accepted Judaism. John is treating the Jews as Gentiles in demanding that they be baptized on the basis of repentance.

2. {*Repent*} This is the Greek verb as a command *metanoeô,* which here means to change (lit. "think afterwards") their mental attitudes and conduct, not merely "to be sorry." Sadly, we have no one English word that reproduces exactly the meaning and connotation of the Greek word. John was a new prophet with the call of the old prophets: "Turn/ return" (Joel 2:12; Isa. 55:7; Ezek. 33:11,15). {*For the kingdom of heaven is at hand*} It was a startling message that John thundered over the hills and it re-echoed throughout the land. The Old Testament prophets had said that it would come some day in God's own time. Evidently John meant this kingdom was very near, so near that one could see the signs and the proof. "The kingdom of heaven" means "the reign of God," not the political or ecclesiastical organization which the Pharisees expected. John's voice was a new one that struck terror in the hearts of the perfunctory theologians of the temple and of the synagogue.

4. {*Now John himself*} (cf. 2 Kgs. 1:8). Matthew thus introduces the man himself and draws a vivid sketch of his dress, habits, and food. John consciously took the prophet Elijah as a model.

6. {*And they were baptized*} the Greek tense shows the repetition of the act as the crowds from Judea and the surrounding country kept going out to him.

7. {*The Pharisees and Sadducees*} These two rival parties do not often unite in common action (cf. Matt. 16:1). The Pharisees represented hypocritical superstition; the Sadducees carnal unbelief. John had welcomed the multitudes, but right in the presence of the crowds he exposed the hypocrisy of the ecclesiastics. {*Ye offspring of vipers*} (cf.

Matt. 12:34; 23:33). Broods of snakes were often seen by John in the rocks and when a fire broke out they would scurry to their holes for safety. No doubt the Pharisees and Sadducees winced under the sting of this powerful indictment.

8. {*Fruit worthy of repentance*} John demanded proof from these men of the new life before he administers baptism to them.

9. {*Of these stones*} referring to the pebbles on the beach of the Jordan.

12. {*Will burn up with unquenchable fire*} The Greek form of "burning" shows it will be complete or thorough. "Fire" here probably refers to judgment by and at the coming of the Messiah

13. {*Then cometh Jesus*} He cames all the way from Galilee to Jordan. The fame of John had reached Nazareth and the hour had come for which Jesus had waited.

16. {*The Spirit of God descending as a dove*} It is not certain whether Matthew means that the Spirit of God took the form of a dove or came upon Jesus as a dove comes down (cf. "bodily form" Luke 3:22).

17. {*A voice out of the heavens*} (cf. Ps. 2:7 and Matt. 17:5). Each person of the Trinity is represented (Father, Son, Holy Spirit) at this formal entrance of Jesus upon his Messianic ministry.

CHAPTER 4

1. {*To be tempted of the devil*} This is at a definite time and place, to the same general region where John was preaching. It is surprising to be led (cf. driven, Mark 1:12) by the Spirit to be tempted by the devil. "Tempt" (cf. Matt. 4:7 as in Deut. 6:16) is the Greek verb *peirazô*, which means "to solicit to sin." The evil sense comes from its use for an evil purpose. *Peirazô* can also mean "to test."

2. {*Had fasted*} This is not a ceremonial fast, but a complete abstention from food (cf. Moses, Exod. 34:28).

3. {*If thou art the Son of God*} The Greek condition is assumed as true; "if" is better as "since." The devil challenges the words of the Father to Jesus at the baptism: "This is my Son the Beloved." Deftly, the devil wants Jesus to exercise his power to prove to himself and others that he really is what the Father called him. {*Become bread*} The picture is round smooth stones which possibly the devil pointed to or even picked up and held becoming loaves (each stone a loaf).

4. {*It is written*} Greek tense shows it stands written and is still in force. Each time Jesus quotes Deuteronomy to repel devil (cf. Deut. 8:3).

5. {*Then the devil taketh him…on the pinnacle of the temple*} Lit. "wing of the temple." It may refer to Herod's royal portico on the south of the temple court which overhung the Kidron Valley and looked down some 450 ft., a dizzy height (Josephus).

6. {*Cast thyself down…*} The devil urged reliance on God and quotes Scripture; he also misinterprets it, omits a clause, and tries to trip the Son of God by the Word of God (cf. Ps. 91:11).

9. {*All these things will I give thee*} The devil claims the rule of the whole world. Jesus does not deny the grip of the devil on the world of men, but the condition was spurned by Jesus.

10. {*Get thee hence, Satan*} (cf. Matt. 16:23). Here for the third time Jesus quotes Deuteronomy (cf. Deut. 6:13).

11. {*Then the devil leaveth him*} The leaving was swift. {*Angels came…and were ministering*} The angels could cheer him from the strain of conflict, and probably also attended with food as in the case of Elijah (1 Kgs. 19:6).

12. {*Now when he heard*} The Synoptic Gospels skip from the temptation of Jesus to the Galilean ministry, a whole year (cf. John 1:19-3:36).

13. {*Dwelt in Capernaum*} (cf. Luke 4:16-31). Rejected in his old home Nazareth, Jesus was in this large town, one of the centers of Galilean political and commercial life, a fishing mart, where many Gentiles came.

18. {*Casting a net into the sea*} Different that a large drag net (cf. Greek *sagênê* Matt. 13:47), or a general word for net (cf. Greek *diktua* Matt. 4:20-21) this is a casting-net thrown over the shoulder and spread into a circle.

23. {*Went about in all Galilee*} Jesus made three tours of Galilee, taking different persons: 1) first tour he took the four fishermen (verses 19,21); 2) second tour he took the Twelve; 3) third tour he sent the Twelve on ahead by twos and followed after them. {*Healing all manner of diseases and all manner of sickness*} In the Greek "disease" (*noson*) means the chronic or serious disease; "sickness" (*malakian*) means the occasional sickness.

24. {*Those that were sick…*} Lit. "those who had it bad," that is, cases that the doctors could not cure, often chronic. Some of the various diseases were: fever, leprosy, blindness. The diseases are listed and de-scribed in a descending scale of violence and severity (called "torments"): people possessed by demons, lunatics (meaning epileptic seizures) and finally paralytics.

25. {*Great multitudes*} Note the plural, not just one crowd, but crowds and crowds; an outpouring greater than any political campaign.

CHAPTER 5

1. {*He went up into the mountain*} The Sermon on the Mount in Matthew and the Sermon on the Plain in Luke are one and the same.

2. {*Taught them*} Jesus sat down on the mountainside as the Jewish rabbis did instead of standing.

3. {*Blessed*} This Greek word *makarios* is an adjective that means "happy." Some English interpreters have sought to draw a distinction between "blessed" and "happy," saying that "blessed" is more noble than "happy." But Jesus said "happy." The Greek word *makarios* is as old as Homer and Pindar and was used of both gods and men, but largely of outward prosperity. It is also used of the dead who died in the Lord (Rev. 14:13). The Greek translation of the OT uses *makarios* to denote a moral quality. Vincent says "shaking itself loose from all thoughts of outward good, it becomes the express symbol of a happi-ness identified with pure character." Jesus takes this word "happy" and puts it in this rich environment. This is one of the words which have been transformed and ennobled by New Testament use; by associa-tion, as in the Beatitudes, with unusual conditions, accounted by the world miserable, or with rare and difficult (Bruce). It is a pity that we have not kept the word "happy" to the high and holy plane where Jesus placed it. It will repay one to make a careful study of all the "beatitudes" in the New Testament where this word is employed (cf. Matt. 5:3-11). Jesus puts due value on these *makarioi,* collecting them, and making them as prominent as the Ten Commandments. This Ser-mon on the Mount has unity, progress, and consummation. It does not contain all that Jesus taught by any means, but it stands out as the greatest single sermon of all time, in its penetration, pungency, and power. {*The poor in spirit*} (cf. Luke 6:20). This refers to the pious in Israel, for the most part poor, whom the worldly rich despised and persecuted; this poverty is deeper than one who merely is of the ancient working class. "Poor" is applied to the beggar Lazarus in Luke 16:20,22 and suggests spiritual destitution from a word which means to crouch or cower. {*The kingdom of heaven*} This phrase here means the reign of God in the heart and life.

4. {*They that mourn*} In the Greek OT, this verb usually is used "for mourning for the dead, and for the sorrows and sins of others" (McNeile). Sorrow should make us look for the heart and hand of God and so find the comfort latent in the grief.

5. {*The meek*} "Meek" here means a virtue which is a fine blend of spiritual poise and strength; it is the gentleness of strength, not mere effeminacy. The Master and Moses are also such (Matt. 11:29 and Num. 12:3).

6. {*They that hunger and thirst after righteousness*} Here Jesus turns one of the elemental human instincts to spiritual use. There is in all men hunger for food, for love, for God. It is passionate hunger and thirst for goodness, for holiness. The word for "filled" means to feed or fatten cattle from the word for fodder or grass as in Mark 6:39.

8. {*Shall see God*} (cf. Heb. 12:14). Sin clouds the heart so that one cannot see God. Purity has here its widest sense.

9. {*The peacemakers*} Not merely peaceable themselves, these are active bringers and keepers of the peace.

10. {*That have been persecuted for righteousness' sake*} The kingdom of heaven belongs only to those who suffer for the sake of goodness, not who are guilty of wrong.

11. {*Falsely, for my sake*} Jesus sets forth two conditions for wearing a martyr's crown: the accusation must be false and it must be for Christ's sake.

13. {*Lost its savour*} Here this means for the salt to become tasteless, insipid (cf. Mark 9:50). It is common in Syria and Palestine to see salt scattered in piles on the ground because it has lost its flavor.

15. {*Under a bushel*} The bushel was an earthenware grain measure and putting a lamp under it would hide the light or put out the flame. An ancient lamp was normally set higher on a projecting stone in the wall or on the one lampstand, so the tiny light sufficed for all in the single room (Bruce).

16. {*Even so*} (cf. verse 15). Light shines to see others by, not to call attention to itself.

17. {*I came not to destroy, but to fulfil*} The verb "destroy" means to "loosen down" as of a house or tent (2 Cor. 5:1). Fulfil is to fill full.

18. {*One jot or one tittle*} The Greek letter *iota* is the smallest Greek vowel, underlying the Hebrew *yod* (jot), the smallest Hebrew letter. "Least stroke" (tittle) can mean either the Hebrew letter *vav* (sometimes hardly distinguishable from the *yod*); or the mere point or "hook" which distinguishes some Hebrew letters from others.

19. {*Shall do and teach*} Jesus puts practice before preaching. The teacher must apply the doctrine to himself before he is qualified to teach others (cf. Matt. 23:3).

22. {*But I say unto you*} Jesus assumes a tone of superiority over the Mosaic regulations and proves it in each of the six examples. He goes further than the Law into the very heart. {*Raca*} Lit. "empty," a frequent Aramaic word for contempt, with a focus on a person's head (Bruce). The words "stupid" and "dull" are fair equivalents. {*Thou fool*} This Greek word, *môre,* is a fair equivalent of "raca" with a focus on the person's heart and character, more like "scoundrel." {*The hell of fire*} Lit. "the Gehenna of fire." Gehenna is the Valley of Hinnom where the fire burned continually.

24. {*First be reconciled*} Lit. a command, "get reconciled."

25. {*Agree with*} Compromise is better than prison where no principle is involved, but only personal interest. {*The officer*} This word means "under rower" on the ship with several ranks of rowers, the bottom rower (*hupo* under and *êressô,* to row), the galley-slave, then any servant, the attendant in the synagogue (Luke 4:20).

26. {*The last farthing*} This coin has the value of 1/164th of a day's wage as an agricultural or common laborer, a vivid picture of inevitable punishment for debt.

28. {*In his heart*} This Greek word *kardia,* here means the entire inner man including the intellect, the affections, the will. Jesus locates adultery in the eye and heart before the outward act. Hence the peril of lewd pictures and films to the pure.

29. {*Causeth thee to stumble*} It is not the notion of giving offense or provoking, but of setting a trap or snare for one. These vivid pictures are not to be taken literally, but powerfully plead for self-mastery; not mutilation but control of the body.

31. {*A writing of divorcement*} (cf. Matt. 19:7; Mark 10:4). The written notice was a protection to the wife against an angry whim of the husband who might send her away with no paper to show for it.

34. {*Swear not at all*} Jesus here does not prohibit oaths in a court of justice for he himself answered Caiaphas on oath; as did Paul (1 Th. 5:27; 1 Cor. 15:31). Not splitting hairs, Jesus prohibits all forms of profanity. Modern Christians employ a great variety of vernacular "cuss-words" and excuse themselves because they do not use the more flagrant forms.

38. {*An eye for an eye, and a tooth for a tooth*} (cf. Exod. 21:24; Deut. 19:21; Lev. 24:20). "For" has the notion of exchange or substitution. This is a restriction upon unrestrained vengeance. It limited revenge by fixing an exact compensation for an injury.

39. {*Resist not him that is evil*} Jesus here meant that personal revenge is taken out of our hands. Aggressive war by nations is also condemned, but not necessarily defensive war or defense against robbery and murder. Professional pacifism may be mere cowardice. Note that Jesus protested when smitten on the cheek (John 18:22); denounced the Pharisees (Matt. 23); and fought the devil always. The language of Jesus is bold and picturesque and is not to be pressed too literally. Such statements startle and make us think.

40. {*Thy coat...thy cloke also*} "Coat" or "tunic" is a sort of shirt or undergarment. The cloke is the more valuable outer garment.

41. {*Shall compel thee...*} The word for "compel" is of Persian origin. By law, if a man is passing an official Persian post-station, an official may rush out and compel him to go back to another station to do an errand for the king. This was called impressment into service (cf. Matt. 27:32).

43. {*And hate thine enemy*} (cf. Lev. 19:18). This phrase is a rabbinical inference and not in Scripture, which Jesus repudiates bluntly. Jesus loved and prayed for his enemies, even when he hung upon the cross. By the parable of the Good Samaritan, Jesus taught that men of different, even hostile, races were to act as neighbors (Luke 10:29). Paul taught Christians to treat enemies kindly (cf. Rom. 12:20 and Prov. 25:22).

48. {*Perfect*} This is the Greek word *teleios,* from *telos,* end, goal, limit. Here it is the goal set before us, the absolute standard of our Heavenly Father.

CHAPTER 6

1. {***Take heed***} This idiom means "hold the mind on a matter," take pains, take heed. Pharisaic examples of righteousness are given: alms, prayer, fasting. {***To be seen***} "Seen" is our very word *theatrical*, spectacular performance. {***With your Father***} Lit. "beside your Father," standing by his side, as he looks at it.

2. {***Sound not a trumpet***} No actual instance of such conduct has been found in the Jewish writings, but still it is possible. It may refer to the blowing of trumpets in the streets on the occasion of public fasts. Another suggests the thirteen trumpet-shaped chests of the temple treasury to receive contributions (Luke 21:2). {***Hypocrites***} This is an old word for actor, interpreter, one who impersonates another, from the Greek verb *hupokrinomai* which came to mean to pretend, to feign, to dissemble, to act the hypocrite, to wear a mask. {***They have received their reward***} This verb is common in the papyri for receiving a receipt, "they have their receipt in full," all the reward that they will get is this public notoriety.

6. {***Into thy closet***} This is a store-house, a separate apartment, one's private chamber, closet, or "den" where he can withdraw and commune with God.

7. {***Use not vain repetitions***} (cf. 1 Kgs. 8:26 and Acts 19:34). Here this means babbling or chattering, empty repetition. The pagans thought that by endless repetitions and many words they would inform their gods as to their needs and weary them into granting their requests.

9. {***After this manner therefore pray ye***} (cf. Luke 11:2-4). "You" is in contrast with "the Gentiles." {***Our Father***} God is the Father of all men in one sense; the recognition of Him as the Father in the full sense is the first step in coming back to him in regeneration and conversion. {***Hallowed be thy name***} In the Greek the verb comes first as in the petitions in verse 10. Their grammatical form is expressing urgency.

11. {***Our daily bread***} "Daily" can mean "on the coming day," "the next day," (cf. Acts 16:12). "Daily" (Greek *epiousios*) has all the appearance of a word that originated in trade and traffic of the everyday life of the people. One source shows *epiousios* was used in a housekeeping book. So, this is a daily prayer for the needs of the next day as every housekeeper understands.

12. {*Our debts*} (cf. sins, Luke 11:4). Here this refers to moral and spiritual debts to God. We ask forgiveness in proportion as we *also* have forgiven those in debt to us, a most solemn reflection.

13. {*And bring us not into temptation*} God is never an active agent in subjecting us to temptation (cf. Jas. 1:13). But the word can also mean "trial" or "test" (cf. Jas. 1:20). God does test or sift us, though he does not tempt us to evil. Here we have a "permissive imperative" as grammarians term it. The idea is then: "Do not *allow* us to be led into temptation." There is a way out (1 Cor. 10:13), but it is a terrible risk. {*From the evil one*} This can also be an evil "thing" or refer to the devil, or any evil person who seeks to do us ill. This is the last actual phrase in this Model Prayer in the oldest and best Greek manuscripts. The doxologies were not a part of the Model Prayer as given by Jesus.

14. {*Trespasses*} Lit. "falling to one side," a lapse or deviation from truth or uprightness; commonly "slip" or "fault" (Gal. 6:1) in the New Testament.

16. {*Of a sad countenance*} (cf. Luke 24:17). The Greek word is a compound of *skuthros* (sullen) and *ops* (countenance). With a pretense of piety, these actors "put on a gloomy look" (Goodspeed).

19. {*Lay not up for yourselves treasures*} Do not have this habit. Here there is a play on the words, lit. "treasure not for yourselves treasures." {*Break through*} Lit. "dig through" which is easy to do through the mud walls or sun-dried bricks. The Greeks called a burglar a "mud-digger."

20. {*Rust*} This is something that eats, gnaws, or corrodes.

22. {*Single*} (cf. Luke 11:34). That is, "pure" and "simple." Of course this can refer to "single" in the physical sense that the eye is healthy (having *single* focus [without astigmatism]), and its opposite would be diseased, even cross-eyed. But the eye, besides being the organ of vision, is the seat of expression, revealing inward dispositions (Bruce).

24. {*No man can serve two masters... God and mammon*} Many try it, but failure awaits them all. *"Mammon"* is like a money-god (or devil). The slave of mammon will obey mammon while pretending to obey God.

25. {*Be not anxious for your life*} Don't have the habit of petulant anxiety and worry about food and clothing. The command can also mean that they must stop such worry if already indulging in it. This is not a reckless neglect of the future; the NT teaches the notion of proper care and forethought (cf. 1 Cor. 7:32; 12:25; Phil. 2:20). {*For your life*} Lit. "soul" here stands for the life principle common to man and beast and so needs both food and clothing. "Soul" does have other meanings as well: a life principle (Mark 3:4); or the seat of the thoughts and emotions (Matt. 22:37); or something higher that makes up the real self (Matt. 10:28; 16:26).

27. {*Unto his stature*} The Greek word *hēlikian* is used either of height (stature) or length of life (age). Either meaning makes good sense here, though probably "stature" suits the context best. This is no plea for idleness, for even the birds are diligent and the flowers grow.

28. {*The lilies of the field*} This word for wild flowers can refer to more than lilies: blossoms like anemones, poppies, gladioli, irises.

29. {*Was not arrayed*} Lit. "clothe himself."

30. {*The grass of the field*} This is common grass.

CHAPTER 7

1. {*Judge not*} This is the habit of critical censure, sharp, unjust, captious, prejudiced, unfair, criticism: a critic in the bad sense. There is a proper and necessary judgment of separating and distinguishing.

3. {*The mote*} This is a very small particle or piece of dried wood or chaff, even a splinter. {*The beam*} This is a log on which planks in the house rest. Probably this was a current proverb quoted by Jesus like our people in glass houses throwing stones.

5. {*Shalt thou see clearly*} (cf. Luke 6:42 and Mark 8:25). This verb means to "look through, penetrate."

6. {*That which is holy unto the dogs*} (cf. Exod. 22:31). Possibly this refers to meat offered in sacrifice; yelping dogs would jump at it. These dogs were kin to wolves and infested the streets of oriental cities. {*Your pearls before the swine*} Pearls look a bit like peas or acorns and would deceive the hogs until they discovered the deception. The wild boars haunt the Jordan Valley still and are not far removed from bears as they trample with their feet and rend with their tusks those who have angered them.

9. {*Loaf...stone*} Some stones look like loaves of bread (cf. Matt. 4:3).

10. {*Fish...serpent*} Fish, common article of food, and water-snakes could easily be substituted.

12. {*That men should do unto you*} (cf. Matt. 5:42; Luke 6:31; Tobit 4:15) The distilled essence of fulfilling the law (Matt. 5:17), this is the Golden Rule also used by Hillel, Philo, Isocrates, Confucius.

13. {*By the narrow gate...broad the way*} The figure of the Two Ways had a wide circulation in Jewish and Christian writings (cf. Deut. 30:19; Jer. 21:8; Ps. 1:1ff.).

15. {*False prophets*} As also in the OT, Jesus predicted false messiahs and false prophets (Matt. 24:24). They came in due time, posing as angels of light like Satan: Judaizers (2 Cor. 11:13ff.) and Gnostics (1 John 4:1; 1 Tim. 4:1). These are ravening wolves greedy for power, gain, self.

16. {*By their fruits ye shall know them*} "Recognize."

22. {*Did we not prophesy in thy name?*} "Yes" is the expected answer in the Greek syntax. Jesus will tear off the sheepskin and lay bare the ravening wolf.

23. {*I never knew you*} (cf. Matt. 10:32). That is, I was never acquainted with you as experimental knowledge. Success, as the world counts it, is not a criterion of one's knowledge of Christ and relation to him.

25. {*Was founded*} Greek tense shows it had been built upon the rock and it *stood*.

26. {*And doeth them not*} (cf. Matt. 5:19). Hearing sermons is a dangerous business if one does not put them into practice.

28. {*The multitudes were astonished*} Lit. "were struck out of themselves."

29. {*And not as their scribes*} The scribes quoted the rabbis' dreary sermons before them and were afraid to express an idea without bolstering it up by some predecessor.

CHAPTER 8

2. {*If thou wilt*} Knowing Jesus had the power to heal, his doubt was about his willingness; the Greek condition shows it was a hopeful doubt at any rate.

7. {*I will come and heal him*} "Heal" is the Greek verb *therapeusô*, which meant first to "serve, give medical attention," then, as here, "to cure, restore to health." There is a possible focus in some contexts of giving treatment or the practice of medicine. The centurion uses the more definite word for healing, *iathêsetai*.

9. {*For I also am a man under authority*} The Greek tense of the commands (Do this!) shows he expects instant obedience.

11. {*Sit down*} This is reclining at table on couches as Jews and Romans did.

12. {*The sons of the kingdom*} Lit. "the sons of the kingdom." This is a favorite Hebrew idiom (cf. Matt. 23:15; Luke 16:8). Mere natural birth (here Jewish descent from Abraham) did not bring spiritual sonship. {*Into the outer darkness*} Lit. "the darkness the outside." A bold, impressive phrase of thick blackness of the night, this means a place outside the limits of the lighted palace, one of the figures for hell or punishment (Matt. 23:13; 25:30).

14. {*Lying sick of a fever*} She was bedridden and burning with fever heat like a fire; possibly a sudden and severe attack (Mark 1:30). Fever itself was considered a disease.

17. {*Himself took our infirmities and bare our diseases*} (cf. Isa. 53:4). Apparently a free translation and interpretation by Matthew, the verse here may mean, "He took upon himself our pains, and bore our diseases." This verse at least must mean that Christ removed their sufferings from the sufferers. "He can hardly have meant that the diseases were transferred to Christ" (Plummer). *Bastazô* occurs freely in the papyri with the sense of lift, carry, endure, carry away (Moulton and Milligan). The passage, as Matthew employs it, has no bearing on the doctrine of the atonement (McNeile). Christ's sympathy with the sufferers was so intense that he really felt their weaknesses and pains. In our burdens Jesus steps under the load with us and helps us to carry on.

20. {*Holes*} This is a lurking hole, burrow. {*Nests*} (cf. Ps. 103:12). That is, "roosts, i.e. leafy, for settling at night habitat, not nests. {*The Son of man*} This is the first occurrence in Matthew. Often it means the Representative Man. Not often it may stand for the Aramaic *barnasha*, the man. Jesus uses it as a concealed Messianic title. This term suited his purpose exactly to get the people used to his special claim as "Messiah" when he is ready to make it openly.

21. {*And bury my father*} (cf. Tobit 4:3). Even if his father was not actually dead first.

22. {*Leave the dead to bury their own dead*} The spiritually dead are always on hand to bury the physically dead, if one's real duty is with Jesus.

24. {*But he was asleep*} (cf. Mark 4:37 and Luke 8:23). The Sea of Galilee is 680 feet below the Mediterranean Sea. These sudden squalls come down from the summit of Hermon with terrific force like an earthquake.

25. {*Save, Lord; we perish*} The Greek tense shows they want to be saved at once.

28. {*The country of the Gadarenes*} (cf. Gerasenes, Mark 5:1 and Luke 8:26). This village is in the district of the city of Gadara some miles southeastward so that it can be called after Gerasa or Gadara. {*The tombs*} Quite common, these were chambers cut into the mountain side.

29. {*Thou Son of God*} Not merely a disease, these are the devil's agents (unclean spirits) which torment. These demons (Greek word *daimonion,* in the Bible all of them evil) know that there is nothing in common between them and the Son of God and they fear torment "before the time." To worship an idol is to worship a demon (cf. 1 Cor. 10:20; 1 Tim. 4:1; Rev. 9:20; 16:13 ff.). Demons are disturbers of the whole life of man (Mark 5:2; 7:25; Matt. 12:45; Luke 13:11,16).

34. {*That he would depart*} Forgetting the healing of the demoniacs, their concern was over the loss of property. They cared more for hogs than for human souls, as often happens today.

CHAPTER 9

1. {*His own city*} That is, Capernaum (Mark 2:1; Matt. 4:13).

2. {*They brought*} Lit. "they were bringing" (cf. Mark 2:1-4 and Luke 5:17). {*Lying on a bed*} That is, stretched on a couch (cf. little bed Luke 5:19 and pallet Mark 2:4,9,11).

3. {*This man blasphemeth*} "This fellow" is a sneer at Jesus.

6. {*Take up thy bed*} Greek tense shows he was to pack up at once the rolled-up pallet.

9. {*At the place of toll*} A crossroads, this was the tax-office of Capernaum, placed strategically to collect taxes from boats that crossed the Sea of Galilee outside of Herod's territory or from people going from Damascus to the coast, a regular caravan route. {*Called Matthew*} (cf. Mark 2:14 and Luke 5:27). Also called Levi, this tax collector is one of the Twelve Apostles. Such tax collectors were detested and held in public disfavor because they practiced graft.

10. {*Publicans and sinners*} It was a social breach to recline together with tax collectors. These two groups are often coupled together in common scorn and in contrast with the righteous (cf. Matt. 9:13).

13. {*But go ye and learn*} With biting sarcasm, Jesus bids these preachers to learn the meaning of Hosea 6:6.

14. {*The disciples of John*} Surprisingly critical, perhaps they were blaming Jesus for doing nothing about John being in prison.

15. {*The sons of the bride-chamber*} (cf. John 2:9). Lit. "sons of the bridegroom," a late Hebrew idiom for the wedding guests, including the friends of the groom.

16. {*Undressed cloth*} That is, a raw piece of woolen cloth that will shrink when wet and tear a bigger hole than ever.

17. {*Old wineskins*} This is a bottle of leather found today in Palestine made of goatskin, one piece, tied-off at the legs, and the neck for the pouring. New wine will ferment and crack the dried-up old skins.

18. {*Is even now dead*} (cf. "is dying" Mark 5:23 and "was dying" Luke 8:42). The accounts of the Synoptics show it is not always easy even for physicians to tell when actual death has come.

20. {*The border of his garment*} That is, the hem or fringe of a garment, a tassel or tuft, made of twisted wool, hanging at the four corners of the outer garment; common then to wear (cf. Num. 15:38). Note that this woman had some superstition in her faith, but still Jesus honors her faith and cures her.

23. {*The flute-players...making a tumult*} Gathering in the outer court with various motives (some with true sorrow).

30. {*Strictly charged them*} (cf. Mark 1:32). This is the Greek word *enbrimaomai* (lit. to be moved with anger). It is used of horses snorting and of men fretting or being angry (Dan. 11:30). Here it has the notion of commanding sternly, a sense unknown to ancient writers.

32. {*A dumb man*} Lit. "blunted in tongue" and so "dumb." In other contexts this can means dullness of other senses such as the mind or the ear.

34. {*By the prince of the devils*} This refers to the devil himself. Unable to deny the reality of the miracles, the Pharisees are becoming desperate; they will renew this charge later (Matt. 12:24).

36. {*Were distressed and scattered...*} This is a picture of sheep torn or mangled by wild beasts.

38. {*That he send forth labourers*} Lit. "to drive out (push out) the workers." Prayer is the remedy offered by Jesus in this crisis for a larger ministerial supply.

CHAPTER 10

1. {*His twelve disciples*} Chosen before the Sermon on the Mount was delivered, the Greek article ("the") shows this was a group assumed as already in existence (cf. Mark 3:14). {*Gave them authority*} (cf. Luke 9:2). "Power" is more likely the idea here than "authority." The physical distress was great, but the spiritual even greater; they were to heal and preach (cf. Matt. 10:7). This healing ministry attracted attention and did a vast deal of good. Today the Master and Lord can still directly heal, but intelligent faith does not justify us in abstaining from the help of the physician or doctor.

5. {*Way of the Gentiles*} This means "way leading to the Gentiles."

6. {*The lost sheep*} Lit. "the sheep, the lost ones." Jesus uses the metaphor not in blame, but in pity.

9. {*Get you no gold*} The actual meaning here is "do not acquire" or "procure" gold for yourselves. The value of the metal is on a descending scale: gold, silver, copper. {*In your purses*} These were belts or girdles that were also used for carrying money.

10. {*No wallet*} This means either a traveling or bread bag, and in extrabiblical sources show that it can mean the beggar's collecting bag.

13. {*If the house be worthy*} What makes a house worthy? It would naturally be readiness to receive the preachers and their message (McNeile).

14. {*Shake off the dust*} This was a gesture of disfavor. The Jews had violent prejudices against the smallest particles of Gentile dust. If mistreated as a guest, the apostles were to treat the host(ess) as Gentiles (cf. Matt. 18:17; Acts 18:6).

16. {*As sheep in the midst of wolves*} The situation called for consummate wisdom and courage. {*Wise as serpents and harmless as doves*} Here are two figures of wariness and innocence to protect the sheep: the serpent was the emblem of wisdom or shrewdness, intellectual keenness (Gen. 3:1; Ps. 58:5); the dove of simplicity (Hos. 7:11).

17. {*Beware of men*} Lit. "Hold your [mind] away from men." Men refers to the wolves (cf. verse 16). {*To councils*} Lit. "Sanhedrin." This is the local courts of justice in every Jewish town. {*In their synagogues*} Being in every town of any size where Jews were, this is not merely the *place* of assembly for worship, but an *assembly of justice* exercising discipline (cf. John 9:35).

19. {*Be not anxious*} Greek tense shows "Do not *become* anxious" (cf. Matt. 6:31).

22. {*For my name's sake*} Lit. "Because of my name." "The name" stands for the person (Matt. 19:29; Acts 5:41; 9:16; 15:26).

23. {*Till the Son of man be come*} There are several interpretations as to when this refers: 1) before the end of this very tour; 2) the Transfiguration; 3) Holy Spirit at Pentecost; 4) the Second Coming.

25. {*Beelzebub*} (cf. Matt. 12:24). It is evidently a term of reproach; a disgraceful epithet.

28. {*Destroy both soul and body in hell*} Be afraid of God. "Destroy" here is not annihilation, but eternal punishment. "Soul" here means the eternal spirit, not just life in the body.

29. {*Two sparrows...sold for a penny*} (cf. Luke 12:6). This means any small bird, sparrows in particular. "Penny" is the Greek word *assarion,* a coin worth 1/16th (a little over six per cent) of a day's wage in common labor.

32. {*Shall confess me*} (cf. Luke 12:8). An Aramaic idiom, lit. "confess in me," indicating a sense of unity with Christ and of Christ with the man who takes the open stand for him.

33. {*Shall deny me*} The Greek syntax of the verse emphasizes complete breach.

34. {*I came not to send peace, but a sword*} "Bring" in the Greek tense means a sudden hurling of the sword where peace was expected.

35. {*Set at variance*} (cf. Mic. 7:1-6). Lit. "divide in two." Social and family ties cannot stand in the way of loyalty to Christ and righteous living.

38. {*Doth not take his cross*} With Jesus probably thinking of his own death, this is the first mention of cross in Matthew; a criminal's death. The Jews had become familiar with crucifixion for more than a hundred years. One of the Maccabean rulers had crucified 800 Pharisees.

39. {*Shall lose it*} This is one of the profound sayings of Christ that he repeated many times, in different forms (cf. Matt. 10:39; 16:25; Mark

8:35; Luke 9:24; 17:33; John 12:25; cf. also *Wisdom of Sirach* 51:26 [Hebrew text]).

41. {*Unto one of these little ones*} Simple believers who are neither apostles, prophets, or particularly righteous, just "learners" (cf. some children present, Matt. 18:2-6).

CHAPTER 11

1. {*He departed thence to teach and preach*} This is a transitional statement after a great discourse (cf. Matt. 7:28; 11:1; 13:53; 19:1; 26:1). {*Commanding*} This means to give orders in detail for each of them.

2. {*John heard in prison*} What had he heard? Probably the raising of the son of the widow of Nain; word sent by John's disciples (cf. Luke 7:18). "Prison" refers to Machaerus east of the Dead Sea, belonging to the rule of Herod Antipas.

3. {*He that cometh*} This phrase refers to the Messiah (Mark 11:9; Luke 13:35; 19:38; Heb. 10:37; Ps. 118:26; Dan. 7:13). Now, experiencing depression, John longed for reassurance.

5. {*And the dead are raised up*} (cf. Isa. 35:5; 61:1). Is this when he raised the son of the widow of Nain? The items in Jesus' list were convincing enough and clearer than mere eschatological symbolism. Note that "the poor" having the Gospel is the a climax of the list.

6. {*Whosoever shall find none occasion of stumbling in me*} This beatitude is a rebuke to John for his doubt even though in prison. John was in the fog and that is not the time to make serious decisions.

7. {*As these went their way*} This eulogy for John may almost be called the funeral oration of the Baptist, for not long afterwards Herodias had John put to death. {*A reed shaken by the wind*} John did not sway as the reeds. Reeds grew in plenty in the Jordan Valley where John preached and had many uses.

11. {*He that is but little...in the kingdom of heaven*} Lit. "lesser" (comparative) but means "least" (superlative). A bit of a puzzle, surely he means that John is greater than all others *in character,* but that the least in the kingdom of heaven surpasses him in *privilege.*

12. {*Suffereth violence*} (cf. Luke 16:16). This is the Greek verb *biazô.* There is question about the meaning of the form in the text. If passive, the idea is that the kingdom is forced, is stormed, is taken by men of violence like "men of violence take it by force" or seize it like a conquered city. If the middle voice, it may mean "experiences violence" or "forces its way" like a rushing mighty wind (Zahn).

14. {*This is Elijah*} (cf. Mal. 4:1). John is the *fulfilled promise* of Malachi, but not the return of Elijah *in person* as the people understood (cf. Matt. 17:12). John himself denied being Elijah in person (John 1:21).

17. {*Children sitting in the market places*} (cf. Luke 7:31ff.). These metaphors in the Gospels are vivid to those with eyes to see. The *agora* (market place) was the public square where the people gathered for trade (cf. Acts 17:17) as in many modern towns; so also the Roman Forum. The oriental bazaars today are held in streets rather than public squares. Even today with all the automobiles children play in the streets.

19. {*Wisdom is justified by her works*} (cf. Luke 7:35). "Proved right" means "set right." This saying means God's wisdom has planned the different conduct of both John and Jesus. He does not wish all to be just alike in everything. The plan of God is justified by results. In each case the ministries are exaggerated: John did not have a demon; Jesus was not a glutton or a drunkard.

20. {*Most of his mighty works*} Lit. "his very many mighty works." "Miracle" is the Greek word *dunamis,* which presents the notion of *power* like our *dynamite.* There are several other Greek words in the NT for such events, each with a different focus.

25. {*At that season Jesus answered and said*} (cf. verses 25 to 30; Luke 10:21-24). That is, he spoke to his Father in audible voice.

27. {*All things have been delivered unto me of my Father*} The Greek tense of "committed" points back to a moment in eternity, and implies the pre-existence of the Messiah. The Messianic consciousness of Christ is here as clear as a bell.

28. {*I will give you rest*} This is far more than mere rest, it is rejuvenation or refreshment; it is "resting-*up.*"

29. {*Take my yoke upon you and learn from me*} The rabbis used yoke for school.

CHAPTER 12

1. {*On the sabbath day through the cornfields*} "Grain" refers to wheat or even barley, not the American English word for corn.

2. {*Thy disciples do...*} (cf. Luke 6:1). A violation of Pharisaic Sabbath rules, plucking the heads of grain was reaping and rubbing them in their hands was threshing.

6. {*One greater than the temple*} Lit. "something greater than the temple." If the temple was not subservient to Sabbath rules, how much less the Messiah and his followers!

7. {*The guiltless*} (cf. Hos. 6:6) Lit. "no real ground against."

8. {*Lord of the Sabbath*} He is master of the Sabbath, and so above the Pharisaic regulations. "The Son of Man" involves a claim of Messiahship, but as the Representative Man he affirms his solidarity with mankind.

13. {*Stretch forth thy hand*} Probably the arm was not withered just the hand (verse 10), though that is not certain. He stretched it straight, I hope, towards the Pharisees who were watching Jesus (cf. Mark 3:2).

17. {*That it might be fulfilled...*} (cf. Isaiah 42:1-4). A very free reproduction, Matthew applies the prophecy about Cyrus to Christ.

20. {*A bruised reed...smoking flax*} This means a crushed reed he will not break. "Smoking flax" refers to the wick of a lamp, smoking and flickering and going out.

23. {*Is this the Son of David?*} Expecting a "no" answer, they put it so because of the Pharisaic hostility towards Jesus. The multitudes lit. "stood out of themselves"; they were almost beside themselves with excitement.

25. {*Knowing their thoughts*} Jesus knew what they were revolving in their minds. In response Jesus laid bare their hollow insincerity and the futility of their arguments: by parables; by a series of assumed true conditions; by sarcasm; by rhetorical question; by merciless logic. Jesus is found to be a powerful opponent. Satan does not cast out Satan. Christ is engaged in deathless conflict with Satan the strong man (verse 29).

30. {*He that is not with me...*} With these solemn words Jesus draws the line of cleavage between himself and his enemies then and now. Christ is the magnet of the ages. He draws or drives away. Satan is the arch-waster; Christ the collector, Savior.

31. {*But the blasphemy against the Spirit*} This is the unpardonable sin. What is the blasphemy against the Holy Spirit? These Pharisees had already committed it. They had attributed the works of the Holy Spirit by whose power Jesus wrought his miracles (Matt. 12:28) to the devil. People often ask if they can commit the unpardonable sin. Probably some do who ridicule the manifest work of God's Spirit in men's lives and attribute the Spirit's work to the devil.

36. {*Every idle word*} This is an ineffective, useless word (Greek formed by *a* privative [not] and *ergon* [work, deed]). This is a solemn thought. Jesus insists that our words form a just basis for the interpretation of a person's character. Here we have judgment by words; elsewhere judgment by deeds (cf. Matt. 25:31-46). Both are real tests of actual character.

38. {*A sign from thee*} They had accused Jesus of being in league with Satan (verse 24ff.). Now they turn round and ask for a sign; as if other miracles were not signs! The demand was impudent, hypocritical, insulting.

39. {*An evil and adulterous generation*} They had broken the marriage tie which bound them to Jehovah (cf. Ps. 73:27; Isa. 57:3; 62:5; Ezek. 23:27; Jas. 4:4, Rev. 2:20). What is "the sign of Jonah?"

40. {*The whale*} (cf. Jonah 2:1). Not the mammal "whale," this is a sea monster, huge fish. "Three days and three nights" may just mean "three days." Jesus rose "on the third day" (Matt. 16:21), not "on the fourth day."

41. {*They repented at the preaching of Jonah*} Jesus is something greater than the temple, than Jonah, than Solomon (Matt. 12:6, 41,42).

44. {*Into my house*} The demon refers to the man as his house.

46. {*His mother and his brothers*} "Brothers" refers to the younger sons of Joseph and Mary. Not believing Jesus was in league with Satan, some of his friends did think that he was beside himself because of the excitement and strain (Mark 3:21).

CHAPTER 13

1. {*On that day*} Matthew places these parables on the same day as the blasphemous accusation and the visit of the mother of Jesus. It is called "the Busy Day," for it serves as a specimen of many others filled to the full with stress and strain.

2. {*And all the multitude stood on the beach*} Lit. "had taken a stand (stood) upon the beach" where the waves break one after the other.

3. {*Many things in parables*} He spoke parables before (cf. Matt. 5:13-16; 6:26-30; 7:3-5; 7:13,15,17-19, 24-27, etc.). This is the first time that he had spoken so many parables, and some of such length; he will do so again in the future (Luke 12—18 and Matt. 24—25). There are eight parables in this chapter (cf. also Mark 4:21,26-29; Luke 8:16). The word "parable" is the Greek *parabolê* from *paraballô,* to place alongside for measurement or comparison like a yardstick. A parable here is a vivid, familiar object illustration for spiritual or moral truth. All allegories are parables, but not all parables are allegories. As a rule the parables of Jesus illustrate one main point and the details are more or less incidental, though sometimes Jesus himself explains these. When he does not do so, we should be slow to interpret the minor details.

4. {*By the wayside*} There were paths along the edge of a plowed field or even across it where the seed lies upon the beaten track.

5. {*The rocky places*} Limestone ledges of rock often jut out with thin layers of soil upon the layers of rock. {*Straightway they sprang up*} That is, "shot up at once."

8. {*Yielded fruit*} The Greek tense has a focus of continuous fruit-bearing. {*Some a hundredfold*} The only worthwhile kind, a hundredfold is not an exaggeration (cf. Gen. 26:12); the ancient world recorded even greater yields.

9. {*He that hath ears let him hear*} Often enigmatic, Jesus had to exhort people to listen and to understand his sayings.

11. {*To know the mysteries*} "Mysteries" is the Greek word *mustêrion,* from *mustês,* one initiated, and that from *mueô (muô),* to close or shut. The mystery-religions of the east had all sorts of secrets and signs as secret societies do today. But those initiated knew them. So the disciples have been initiated into the secrets of the kingdom of heaven; it is open to them (cf. Rom. 16:25; 1 Cor. 2:7).

13. {*Because seeing*} (cf. Isa. 6:9ff.; Mark 4:12 and Luke 8:10). Thus Matthew's adaptation presents a striking ironic wonder "though they see, they do not really see."

14. {*Is fulfilled*} Here Jesus points out the fulfillment directly, not normally in the style of Matthew. "Fulfill" here means that the prophecy of Isaiah is fully satisfied in the conduct of the Pharisees, and Jesus himself points it out.

15. {*Is waxed gross*} This is the Greek verb *pachunô,* from *pachus,* thick, fat, stout. Made callous or dull—even fatty degeneration of the heart. {*Dull of hearing*} Lit. "they hear heavily with their ears." {*Their eyes they have closed*} (cf. Isa. 6:10). Lit. "eyes shut down." The eyes can be smeared with wax or cataract and thus closed. "Sealing up the eyes was an oriental punishment"(Vincent) (cf. Isa. 29:10; 44:18). {*Lest*} This negative purpose as a judgment is left in the quotation from Isaiah. It is a solemn thought for all who read or hear the word of God.

18. {*Hear then ye the parable...*} (cf. Matt. 13:13). He uses parables, so he can go on preaching the mysteries of the kingdom without the spiritually-dulled Pharisees comprehending what he is saying. But wanting disciples to know, he explains in detail what he means.

19. {*When anyone heareth...*} Perhaps at that very moment Jesus observed a puzzled look on some faces, they were not getting or grasping it. {*The seed sown in his heart*} The seed in the heart is not of itself responsible, but the man who lets the devil snatch it away.

21. {*Yet hath he not root in himself*} (cf. Col. 2:7 and Eph. 3:18). Here the person has a mushroom growth and endures for a while. Quick to sprout, quick to stumble. Modern converts at revivals drop away overnight because they did not have the root of the matter in them. {*Tribulation*} This is the Greek word *thlipsis,* from *thlibô,* to press, to oppress, to squeeze (cf. Matt. 7:14).

22. {*Choke the word*} Lit. "choke together." Lust for money and care go together, and between them spoil many an earnest religious nature (Bruce); "thorns" indeed.

23. {*Verily beareth fruit*} It is the teacher's task as the sower to sow the right seed, the word of the kingdom. The soil determines the outcome.

25. {*Sowed tares also*} Lit. "sowed upon," that is, "resowed." "Weeds" in Greek is *zizania,* and here refers to the bearded darnel, a weed that resembles wheat (but with black grains), *lolium temulentum.* In its earlier stages it is indistinguishable from the wheat.

29. {*Ye root up the wheat with them*} Lit. "root out." This is easy to do with the mixed roots intermingled.

30. {*My barn*} (cf. Matt. 3:12; 6:26). This is the granary, storehouse.

32. {*A tree*} This refers to a mustard "tree" not in nature, but in size; excusable exaggeration in popular discourse.

33. {*Is like unto leaven*} Yeast has a focus on its pervasive power and fermentation, not a symbol of corruption here.

36. {*Explain unto us*} The Greek words and tense translate, "make thoroughly clear right now (with urgency)."

38. {*The field is the world*} The good seed and the weeds (darnel, verse 25) are sown and grown in the world, not in the Kingdom, not in the church. The separation comes at the consummation of the age (cf. verse 39), the harvest time.

43. {*Shine forth*} Lit. "shine out" as the sun comes from behind a cloud, driving away the darkness after the separation has come.

44. {*And hid*} The point is, for the enormous wealth of the Kingdom there is no price too great to pay: make any sacrifice, give all one has.

46. {*He went and sold*} Each verb with a different Greek tense; together they show lively action.

47. {*A net*} This means a drag-net, called a seine. Just as the field is the world, so the drag-net catches all the fish that are in the sea. The separation comes afterwards.

55. {*Is not this the carpenter's son?*} The Nazarenes knew the whole family: Joseph, Mary, Jesus, and his brothers and sisters. After leaving them, how could this boy they knew become the wise teacher before them? The people puzzled over this.

57. {*And they were offended in him*} Lit. "they stumbled at him." It was unpardonable for Jesus not to be commonplace like themselves. {*Not without honour*} This is a proverb found in Jewish, Greek, and Roman writers.

58. {*Mighty works*} Lit. "Powers." The disbelief of the townspeople blocked the will and the power of Jesus to work cures.

CHAPTER 14

1. {*Herod the tetrarch*} This is Herod Antipas ruler of Galilee and Perea, one-fourth of the dominion of Herod the Great.

2. {*His servants*} Lit. "boys," but here means the courtiers, not the menials of the palace. {*Work in him*} The King has the Baptist on the brain. John wrought no miracles, but one *redivivus* (i.e., the second "renewed" John) might be under the control of the unseen powers. So Herod argued. A guilty conscience quickened his fears.

4. {*For John said unto him*} The Greek tense probably means that John said it repeatedly. It was a blunt and brave thing that John said. It cost him his head, but it is better to have a head like John's and lose it than to have an ordinary head and keep it.

6. {*When Herod's birthday came*} Here this means a commemoration for birthday celebrations of living persons, namely Herod. {*Danced in the midst*} This was Salome, daughter of Herodias by her first marriage. It was a shameful exhibition of lewd dancing prearranged by Herodias to compass her purpose for John's death. Salome had stooped to the level of an *almeh*, or common dancer.

8. {*Put forward*} It should require a good deal of "educating" to bring a young girl to make such a grim request. {*Here*} That is, on the spot: here and now.

12. {*And they went and told Jesus*} It was a shock to the Master who alone knew how great John really was. The fate of John was a prophecy of what was before Jesus (cf. Matt. 14:13).

14. {*Their sick*} Lit. "Without strength." {*He had compassion*} This is the Greek verb *splagchnizomai,* giving the oriental idea of the bowels (Greek *splagchna*) as the seat of compassion.

15. {*When even was come*} This is the first of the two "evenings" which begins at 3 P.M. {*The place is desert*} This is a remote place, but not a desolate region.

16. {*Give ye them to eat*} "You" is emphatic in the sentence. The Greek tense of "give" has a sense of urgency, showing instant action.

18. {*And he said*} Here is the contrast between the helpless doubt of the disciples and the confident courage of Jesus. They had overlooked the power of Jesus in this emergency.

19. {*To sit down on the grass*} "Sit down" means "recline." {*Five loaves*} These were thin Jewish cakes of bread.

20. {*Broken pieces*} Not the scraps upon the ground, these are the pieces broken by Jesus and still in the "twelve baskets" and not eaten (one for each of the Twelve). {*Basketfuls*} "Basket" is the Greek word *kophinos,* a wicker-basket (ancient sources cite that they were sturdy enough to be used as make-shift furniture). A different word for basket in the feeding of the four thousand *sphuris* is used which was a sort of hamper or large provisions basket.

22. {*Constrained*} (cf. Mark 6:45). Lit. "compelled" or "forced," a strong word, but the crowd was going to make him national king (cf. John 6:15).

24. {*Distressed*} Lit. "tormented, strained." Picture the boat bobbing up and down in the choppy sea (Mark 6:48).

25. {*Walking upon the sea*} Another nature miracle, like the feeding of the thousands. This clearly in the Greek does *not* mean he was walking along the beach.

26. {*An apparition*} This is the Greek word *phantasma*, ghost or spectre, from *phantazô* (make visible) and that from *phainô* (shine). Terrified, they fearfully cried out with a little touch of sailor superstition.

30. {*Lord, save me!*} The Greek tense shows the cry was urgent and wanted quick response. He could walk on the water until he saw the wind whirl of water round him.

31. {*Didst thou doubt?*} "Doubt" is the Greek verb *distazô*, pulled two ways, and that from *dis* (twice). Peter's trust in the power of Christ gave way to his dread of the wind and waves.

32. {*Ceased*} Not a mere coincidence, the wind exhausted itself in the presence of its Master (cf. Mark 4:39).

33. {*Worshipped him*} Note that Jesus accepted the worship. They will soon be ready for the confession of Matt. 16:16. {*Son of God*} Though no article in Greek, probably this means "the" Son of God.

34. {*Gennesaret*} This is a rich plain four miles long and two miles broad.

CHAPTER 15

1. {*From Jerusalem*} Jerusalem is the headquarters of the united conspiracy against Jesus, with the Pharisees as the leaders in it, wanting to put him to death (Mark 3:6; Matt. 12:14; Luke 6:11). The Pharisees were the guardians of tradition in the capital.

2. {*The tradition of the elders*} This was the oral law, handed down by the elders of the past in *ex cathedra* fashion and later codified in the Mishna. {*They wash not their hands*} (cf. John 2:6-8). Not required in the OT, we know it is a good thing for sanitary reasons. But with detailed regulations, the rabbis made it a mark of righteousness (the more rigorous Jew did it between the courses of the meal). This issue was far more than a point of etiquette or of hygienics, the rabbis held it to be a mortal sin.

5. {*But ye say*} (cf. Exod. 20:12,16) "You" is in sharp contrast to God's command. They dodged the command of God to honor the parents through pronouncing "korban" (Mark 7:11). All one had to do to evade one's duty to father or mother was to say "korban" or "gift" with the idea of using the money for God. By giving this oath, one in effect refused to help one's parents, thus disobeyed the fifth commandment.

7. {***Well did Isaiah prophesy of you***} (cf. Isa. 29:13). "Well" is lit. "beautifully pictured" as a sarcasm. They were indeed far from God if they imagined that God would be pleased with such gifts at the expense of duty to one's parents.

11. {***This defileth the man***} Lit. "this makes unclean a person." "Unclean" here means what is common either ceremonially or in reality. One who is thus religiously common or unclean is cut off from doing his religious acts (cf. Acts 10:14 also 21:28; Heb. 9:13). Jesus draws here a profound distinction. Moral uncleanness is what makes a man common, defiles him. That is what is to be dreaded.

12. {***Were offended***} Lit. "Were caused to stumble." They took umbrage at the public rebuke and at such a scorpion sting in it all.

14. {***They are blind guides***} A graphic picture and proverbial expression in the OT; blind leaders and blind victims will land in the ditch.

18. {***Out of the mouth***} Spoken words come out of the heart and so are a true index of character. Heart is the Greek word *kardia*, means the entire man, the inward life of evil thoughts that issue in words and deeds.

24. {***I was not sent...***} Jesus makes a test case of her request. In a way she represented the problem of the Gentile world.

27. {***Even the dogs...***} Taking no offense at being called a Gentile dog, with quick wit she took Christ's very word for little dogs (Greek word *kunaria*) and deftly turned it to her own advantage.

28. {***As thou wilt***} Her great faith and keen rejoinder won her case.

29. {***And sat there***} Lit. "was sitting there"; likely to teach, though possibly to rest and to enjoy the view.

30. {***And they cast them down at his feet***} "Laid" is a very strong word, flung them down; not carelessly, but in haste.

32. {***Three days...what to eat***} (cf. Matt. 14:14). Jesus here is moved to compassion. He was concerned they may faint or collapse in an exhausted state.

35. {***On the ground***} (cf. Matt. 14:19). Now in midsummer the grass would be parched and gone, unlike before.

36. {***Gave thanks***} (cf. Matt. 14:19). Before he had spoken "grace" or "blessing."

39. {*The borders of Magadan*} (cf. Mark 8:10). Jesus now goes from the eastern to the western side of the lake (cf. Decapolis, Mark 7:31ff.). Related to Dalmanutha and Magdala in the district of Galilee, now he is in Magadan.

CHAPTER 16

1. {*The Pharisees and Sadducees*} Hate makes strange bedfellows. This is the first mention of this combination of the two parties. {*Tempting him*} Though this Greek word could be translated "testing," "tempting" is the better rendering for here their motive was bad.

2. {*Fair weather*} (cf. Luke 12:54-56). An ancient saying, this is the Greek word *eudia,* from *eu* (well) and *Zeus (dia)* as the ruler of the air and giver of fair weather. Some Greek texts omit this section.

3. {*Lowering*} This is a sky covered with clouds, a gloomy, overcast sky as a sign of a rainy day, though not necessarily a winter storm.

7. {*Why reason ye among yourselves*} Greek tense shows they kept up the discussion. Almost as pathetic dullards, the disciples had no ability to understand the parabolic warning against the leaven of the Pharisees and Sadducees.

13. {*Caesarea Philippi*} Up on a spur of Mt. Hermon under the rule of Herod Philip. {*He asked*} Greek tense shows that he began to question; he was giving them a test or examination. How much did the disciples understand? How had their faith developed? Are they still loyal?

14. {*And they said*} Popular opinion was divided about who he was (Matt. 14:1ff.). The disciples gave four different opinions.

15. {*But who say ye that I am?*} "You" is emphatic. This is what matters to Jesus.

16. {*Thou art the Christ, the Son of the living God*} Peter is the spokesman now; he had made this noble confession before (cf. John 6:69). Peter plainly called Jesus Messiah (Anointed One; "Christ" in Greek). Before Jesus had avoided "Messiah" due to the people's meaning of Messiah as a political leader.

17. {*Blessed art thou*} Jesus accepts the confession as true, and so he solemnly claims to be the Messiah.

18. {*And I also say unto thee*} The Father has revealed to you (Peter) one truth, and I also tell you (Peter) another. {*Peter...on this rock*}

His nickname, Peter is the Greek word *Petros* (same as Aramaic *Cephas*) which means "rock" or "stone." What did Jesus mean by this word-play? Jesus makes a pun, that has caused volumes of controversy and endless theological strife. His full given name was *Simon Bar-Jonah.* {*On this rock*} This is the Greek *petra*, a ledge or cliff of rock like that in Matt. 7:24 on which the wise man built his house. *Petros* (cf. Peter's name) is usually a smaller detachment of the massive ledge. But too much must not be made of this point since Jesus probably spoke Aramaic (*Cephas*) to Peter which draws no such distinction. {*I will build my church*} It is the figure of a building, undoubtedly picturing here a spiritual house in general, not local (cf. 1 Pet. 2:5-9). It is a great spiritual house: the church is Christ's Israel, not the Jewish nation, which he describes. What does "rock" refer to here? Not on Peter alone or even mainly; *Peter by his confession* was furnished with the illustration for the rock on which His church will rest. "Church" has several senses in the Bible: It can refer to congregation of Israel (cf. Deut. 18:16; 23:2 also Ps. 89:1 ff. and Acts 7:38). It can refer to a general or legal assembly (Acts 19:39). Then it can be applied to an "unassembled assembly" (cf. Acts 8:3). {*The gates of Hades*} Hades here is technically the unseen world, the Hebrew *Sheol*, the land of the departed, that is death (cf. 1 Cor. 15:55 and Hos. 13:14). Hades is then divided into Abraham's bosom and Gehenna (cf. Luke 16:25). Christ was in Hades (Acts 2:27,31), not in Gehenna. We have here the figure of two buildings, the Church of Christ on the Rock and the House of Death/Hades (cf. Isa. 38:10; Wisd. 16:3; 3 Macc. 5:51 also Pss. 9:13; 107:18; Job 38:17). It is not the picture of Hades *attacking* Christ's church, but of death's possible victory over the church. Christ's church will prevail and survive because He will burst the gates of Hades and come forth conqueror. The wealth of imagery here makes it difficult to decide each detail, but the main point is clear. The church will not cease. The gates of Hades or bars of Sheol will not close down on it.

19. {*The Keys of the kingdom*} Here again we have the figure of a building with keys to open from the outside. Peter is as "gatekeeper" or "steward." But we do not understand it as a special and peculiar prerogative belonging to Peter; the same power here given to Peter belongs to every disciple of Jesus in all the ages. Peter held the keys precisely as every preacher and teacher does. {*Binding...loosing*} This is rabbinical language "to forbid...to permit" with the teaching of Jesus as the standard for Peter and for all preachers of Christ (cf. Matt. 18:18 and John 20:23). Every preacher uses the keys of the kingdom when he proclaims the terms of salvation in Christ. The proclamation of these terms when accepted by faith in Christ has the sanction and approval of God the Father.

20. {*That they should tell no man*} Why not tell? For the very reason that he had himself avoided this claim in public; the people would take Messiah (Greek *Christos*), in a political sense.

21. {*From that time began...*} (cf. Matt. 17:22 ff. and 20:17-19). A little over six months away, it was a suitable time for the disclosure of the greatest secret of his death. Dimly, the shocked disciples grasped something of what Jesus said.

22. {*Peter took him...*} The Greek voice (middle) shows he does this of his own right. He acted with greater familiarity after the token of acknowledgment had been given. A minute ago Peter was speaking under inspiration from heaven, now under inspiration from the opposite quarter. {*This shall never be*} The Greek is the strongest kind of negation, as if Peter would not let it happen. Peter had perfect assurance.

23. {*But he turned*} Jesus quickly turned away from Peter in revulsion, and toward the other disciples (Mark 8:33). {*Get thee behind me, Satan*} Just before Peter gave noble confession and was given a place of leadership; now he is playing the part of Satan and is ordered to the rear. None are more formidable instruments of temptation than well-meaning friends, who care more for our comfort than for our character. {*A stumbling-block unto me*} Christ is saying now to Peter (stone), "you are like a stone quite out of its proper place, and lying right across the road in which I must go—lying as a stone of stumbling" (Morrison).

24. {*Take up his cross*} (cf. Matt. 10:38). Greek tense shows urgency, pick up at once. A figure of the crucifixion of criminals, Peter would do better to face squarely his own cross and to bear it after Jesus.

25. {*Save his life*} Lit. "save his soul"; paradoxical play on the word "life" or "soul, " using it in two senses.

26. {*Exchange*} This is the Greek word *antallagma*. The soul has no market price, though the devil thinks so. A man must surrender his life and nothing less to God.

28. {*Some of them that stand here...*} Does Jesus refer to the Transfiguration, the Resurrection of Jesus, the great Day of Pentecost, the Destruction of Jerusalem, the Second Coming and Judgment? We do not know, only that Jesus was certain of his final victory which would be symbolized in various ways.

CHAPTER 17

1. {*After six days*} (cf. Luke 9:28) One naturally thinks of a week as the probable time. These three disciples form an inner group who have shown more understanding of Jesus. {*High mountain*} Though not certain, probably this is Mount Hermon. The Mount of Transfiguration does not concern geography.

2. {*He was transfigured before them*} "Transfigured" is the Greek verb *metemorphoô* with the idea being change (*meta-*) of form (*morphê*). It really presents the essence of a thing as separate from the *schêma* (fashion), the outward accident (cf. Rom. 12:2). Matthew guards against the pagan idea by adding and explaining about the face of Christ "as the sun" and his garments "as the light" (not invisible).

3. {*There appeared*} There were popular expectations that Moses (Law) and Elijah (Prophecy) would reappear. Both names had mystery connected with their deaths. Jesus needed comfort and he gets it from fellowship with Moses and Elijah.

4. {*Tabernacles*} That is, "booths." The Feast of Tabernacles was not far away. Peter may have meant that they should just stay up here on the mountain and not go to Jerusalem for the feast.

10. {*Elijah must first come*} This piece of theology concerned them more than anything else (cf. Mal. 4:5). So they are puzzled.

12. {*Elijah is come already*} Jesus identifies John the Baptist with the promise in Malachi, though not the real Elijah in person (cf. John 1:21). {*They knew him not*} (cf. John 1:26). They killed John as they will Jesus the Son of Man.

15. {*Epileptic*} This is the Greek verb *selêniazomai,* lit. "moonstruck," "lunatic." The symptoms of epilepsy were supposed to be aggravated by the changes of the moon (cf. Matt. 4:24).

17. {*Perverse*} This Greek verb *diastrephô* means, distorted, twisted in two, corrupt.

20. {*Little faith*} Their faith was less than "a grain of mustard seed" (cf. Matt. 13:31). "This mountain" probably refers to the Mount of Transfiguration. But it is a parable.

24. {*They that received the half-shekel*} This temple tax amounted to an Attic drachma or the Jewish half-shekel, about two days common labor. Every Jewish man twenty years of age and over was expected to pay it for the maintenance of the temple. But it was not a compulsory tax like that collected by the government tax collectors. But the payment had to be made in the Jewish coin, half-shekel. Hence the money changers did a thriving business in charging a small premium for the Jewish coin.

25. {*Jesus spake first to him*} "The first" is the Greek verb *phthanô* (lit. to go before, to come before) with an implication of speaking with anticipation. Peter felt obliged to take the matter up with Jesus. But the Master had observed what was going on and spoke to Peter first. {*Toll or tribute*} (cf. Rom. 13:7). "Toll" means taxes on things (duty direct on customs and wares) and "tribute" as taxes on persons. Jesus claims exemption from the temple tax, since he is royalty in the temple of his Father. Subjects of the royalty pay the tax.

27. {*Lest we cause them to stumble*} Jesus does not wish to create the impression that he and the disciples despise the temple and its worship. {*A hook*} The only example in the NT of fishing with a hook. The first fish that comes up has a shekel coin, lit. "a *statera*" which is a four-drachma coin, enough for two persons to pay the tax. {*For me and thee*} "For" means here "in exchange for." Here we have a miracle of foreknowledge. Such instances have happened. It is not stated that Peter actually caught such a fish though that is the natural implication. Why provision is thus only made for Peter along with Jesus we do not know.

CHAPTER 18

2. {*Called to him...*} It may even be Peter's "little child" as it was probably in Peter's house (Mark 9:33).

3. {*Except ye turn and become...*} They will otherwise not get into the kingdom of heaven at all, let alone have big places in it. This Greek condition is one undetermined but with prospect of determination.

5. {*In my name*} (cf. Luke 9:48). "Little child" is any believer in Christ. "In my name" means "on the basis or ground of my name," "for my sake."

6. {*These little ones*} The child is the type of believers. {*A great mill-stone*} Lit. "a millstone turned by a donkey." The upper half of a mill-stone was turned by the beast of burden; a quite large stone.

10. {*Despise*} Lit. "think down on," with the assumption of superior-ity. {*Their angels*} (cf. Rev. 1:20). The Jews believed that each nation had a guardian angel (Dan. 10:13,20; 12:1). Certainly Jesus means that the Father takes special care of his "little ones" (God's people) who believe in Him (cf. Heb. 1:14).

12. {*Leave the ninety and nine*} That is, on the high pastures where the sheep graze at will (not in a fixed place); one has wandered afield (cf. Luke 15:4-7).

15. {*If thy brother sin against thee*} Lit. "commit a sin." {*Shew him his fault*} A plausible cause, such private reproof is hard to do, but it is the way of Christ; but a blessed achievement when he is won over.

17. {*Refuse to hear*} (cf. Isa. 65:12). That is, ignoring, disregarding, or hearing without heeding (Mark 5:36). {*The church*} This is the local body (cf. Matt. 16:18). Is this an actual body of believers already in existence or is speaking prophetically of the local churches later?

18. {*Shall be bound in heaven*} (cf. Matt. 16:19). First addressed to Peter, but it is here repeated for the local church.

19. {*Shall agree*} This is the Greek verb *sumphônêô,* our word "sym-phony" is this very root and so like a chorus in harmony, not in rasp-ing discord.

21. {*Until seven times?*} Peter thought that he was generous as the Jewish rule was three times (Amos 1:6).

22. {*Until seventy times seven*} Also translated "490 times," Jesus clearly means unlimited forgiveness in either case.

23. {*Make a reckoning*} This is the Greek verb *sunairô,* to cast up accounts, to settle, to compare accounts with.

24. {*Ten thousand talents*} A talent was 6,000 denarii (a denarius is a day's wage for a common laborer, hence 60,000,000 denarii), an enor-mous sum. For example, the imperial taxes of Judea, Idumea, Samaria, Galilee, and Perea paid 800 talents total.

25. {*Had not wherewith to pay...to be sold*} This was according to the law (Exod. 22:3; Lev. 25:39,47).

28. {*A hundred pence*} That is, 100 days wages of a common laborer. The focus is on the small amount not forgiven compared to the vast debt forgiven (cf. verse 24). {*Took him by the throat*} The Roman law allowed this indignity, as is documented. {*What thou owest*} Lit. "if you owe anything," however little. He did not even know how much it was.

30. {*And he would not*} Greek tense shows this was a persistent refusal.

33. {*Shouldst thou not?*} "Was it not necessary?" The king fits the cap on this wicked slave that the wicked slave put on the poor debtor.

34. {*The tormentors*} Not simply prison, he went to terrible punishment and torture. {*Till he should pay all*} (cf. verse 30). This is punitive, not purgatorial, for he could never pay back that vast debt.

CHAPTER 19

1. {*He departed*} Lit. "to lift up, change something to another place." This verse is a sort of formula in Matthew at the close of important groups of *logia* as in Matt. 7:28; 11:1; 13:53. {*The borders of Judea beyond Jordan*} Apparently, it means Jesus left Galilee to go to Judea by way of Perea as the Galileans often did to avoid Samaria.

3. {*Pharisees tempting him*} (cf. Matt. 4:1). Better "temptation" since they could not ask a question of Jesus without sinister motives. {*Is it lawful for a man to put away his wife for every cause?*} This alludes to the dispute between the two theological schools over the meaning of Deut. 24:1. The school of Shammai took the strict and unpopular view of divorce for unchastity alone while the school of Hillel took the liberal and popular view of easy divorce for any passing whim if the husband saw a prettier woman (modern enough surely) or burnt his biscuits for breakfast.

5. {*Shall cleave*} Lit. "shall be glued to." {*The twain shall become one flesh*} The language of the verse is an imitation of the Hebrew (cf. Gen. 2:24).

6. {*What therefore God hath joined together*} Not "whom," "what" is the marriage relation God has made. The word for "joined together" means "yoked together," a common verb for marriage in ancient Greek. {*Bill...of divorce*} A document of papyrus or parchment, this was some protection to the divorced wife and a restriction on laxity.

8. {*For your hardness of heart*} It is a heart dried up, hard and tough.

9. {*Except for fornication*} (cf. Matt. 5:32). Here Jesus is allowing divorce for fornication as a general term (Greek *porneia*) which is technically adultery (Greek *moicheia*). By implication, Jesus does allow remarriage of the innocent party, but not of the guilty one.

11. {*But they to whom it is given*} The idea is a voluntary renunciation of marriage for the sake of the kingdom of heaven. Jesus recognizes the severity of the demand as going beyond the capacity of all but a select number.

14. {*Forbid them not*} The Greek syntax translates, "Stop hindering them."

16. {*What good thing*} (cf. Mark 10:17). {*That I may have eternal life*} "may have" means "may acquire."

17. {*Concerning that which is good*} The man evidently had a light idea (not absolute) of the meaning of "good" (Greek *agathos*).

20. {*What lack I yet?*} His question implies dissatisfaction, though he claim to have kept all. He had an uneasy conscience. He thought of goodness as quantitative (a series of acts) and not qualitative (of the nature of God). Was this pride or despair? Likely, it was a bit of both.

21. {*If thou wouldest be perfect*} As the Greek shows, Jesus assumes that the young man really desires to be perfect (cf. Matt. 5:48). {*Thy belongings*} It was a huge demand, for he was rich.

22. {*Went away sorrowful*} Lit. "went away grieved." Too much to ask, he worshipped money more than God when put to the test. Does Jesus demand this same test of every one? Not unless they are in the grip of money.

23. {*It is hard*} Lit. "with difficulty."

24. {*It is easier for a camel to go through a needle's eye*} This proverb expresses the impossible. The Jews in the Babylonian Talmud did have a proverb that a man even in his dreams did not see an *elephant* pass through the eye of a needle. "Needle" here is the word for an ordinary sewing needle (Greek *rhaphis*), but Luke uses the word surgical needle (Greek *belonê*) (Luke 18:25). Changing "camel" to "rope" or "needle's eye" to a "narrow gate" are not right interpretations.

25. {*Were astonished*} Lit. "struck out" descriptive of their blank amazement. And Jesus saw their amazement.

28. {*In the regeneration*} This refers to the new birth of the world when Jesus sits on his throne of glory.

30. {*The last first and the first last*} Probably a rebuke to Peter, it refers to ranks in the kingdom. There are many other possible applications. See the following parable.

CHAPTER 20

2. {*For a penny a day*} (cf. Matt. 18:28). They agreed to work for a coin with the value of a day's wage, a denarius.

3. {*Standing in the marketplace idle*} It was a place of meeting for bargaining.

10. {*Every man a penny*} He began to pay off the last first and paid each one a denarius (a common man's day's wage) according to agreement.

12. {*The burden of the day and the scorching wind*} The last hired apparently worked as hard as any. The first hired were sweat-stained men who had stood also the sirocco, the hot, dry, dust-laden withering east wind (cf. Gen. 41:6; Jonah 4:8; Ezek. 17:10). They seemed to have a good case.

13. {*To one of them*} Evidently he was the spokesman of the group.

14. {*Take up*} Lit. "pick up," as if he had saucily refused to take it from the table or had contemptuously thrown the denarius on the ground. If the first hired had been paid and sent away, then there would have been no murmuring; but the murmuring is needed to bring out the lesson. {*What I will...with mine own*} This is the point of the parable, the *will* of the householder.

15. {*Is thine eye evil?*} (cf. Matt. 6:22-24). The complainer had a grudging eye while the householder has a liberal or generous eye.

19. {*And to crucify*} All the details fall on deaf ears.

20. {*Then...*} (cf. Matt. 19:28). Surely an inopportune time for such a request just after the pointed prediction of Christ's crucifixion. {*Mother of the sons of Zebedee*} Probably Salome, possibly a sister of the Master's mother (John 19:25), apparently prompted her two sons because of the family relationship and now speaks for them. {*Asking a certain thing*} The "something" put forward as a small matter was simply the choice of the two chief thrones promised by Jesus (Matt. 19:28).

23. {*Ye shall drink*} Christ's cup was death. James was the first (Acts 12:2) and John the last of the apostles to experience it.

24. {*Moved with indignation*} This is a strong word for angry resentment. The ten felt that James and John had taken advantage of their relation to Jesus.

26. {*Would become great*} Jesus does not condemn the desire to become great. It is a laudable ambition. But Christians do not "lord it over" one another, or "play the tyrant." {*Your minister*} This is the Greek word *diakonos,* from *dia* and *konis* (dust), to raise a dust by one's hurry, and so to minister. It is a general word for servant. Jesus says the way to be first is to be your slave. This is a complete reversal of popular opinion then and now.

28. {*A ransom for many*} (cf. Mark 10:45). The Son of man is not self-seeking as James and John are. "Ransom" is the price paid for a slave who is then set free by the one who bought him. It is the purchase money for liberating slaves. "For" has the notion of exchange. Jesus gave his own life as the price of freedom for the slaves of sin.

29. {*From Jericho*} (cf. Mark 10:46; Luke 18:35). But Luke places the incident as they were *drawing near* to Jericho. It is probable that Mark and Matthew refer to the old Jericho, the ruins of which have been discovered, while Luke alludes to the new Roman Jericho.

CHAPTER 21

1. {*Unto Bethphage*} (cf. Mark 11:1; Luke 19:29). It apparently lay on the eastern slope of Olivet or at the foot of the mountain, a little further from Jerusalem than Bethany.

2. {*Into the village that is over against you*} Probably this is Bethany right across the valley. {*And a colt with her*} The young of the animal was to come with the mother.

3. {*The Lord*} This is the Greek word *kurios* from *kuros,* power or authority. The word has a variety of uses, usually of lesser human authorities. Plainly Jesus applies "Lord" to himself, though one does not know how others who hear it will take the word. In the west the Roman emperors are not so termed "lord" until the time of Domitian. But the Christians boldly claimed the word for Christ. Jesus is here represented as using it with reference to himself. It seems as if already the disciples were calling Jesus "Lord" and that he accepted the appellative and used it as here.

4. {*By the prophet*} (cf. Isa. 62:11 and Zech. 9:9). John (John 12:14ff.) makes it clear that Jesus did not quote the passage himself.

7. {*And he sat thereon*} (cf. Mark 11:7 and Luke 19:35). Jesus rode the colt. Here the "them" refers to the outer garments, not the two animals.

8. {*The most part of the multitude*} This true superlative, "very large," is "*the most* of the crowd put outer garments on the road." The disciples put their garments on the two animals. The Greek tenses of "cut" and "spread" show the growing enthusiasm of the crowd. When the colt had passed over their garments, the bystanders would pick the garments up and spread them again in front of the animals.

9. {*Crying*} Greek tense shows that they *kept on* crying out. {*Hosanna to the Son of David*} They were now proclaiming Jesus as the Messiah and he let them do it. "Hosanna" means "Save, we pray thee." They repeat words from the *Hallel* (Ps. 148:1; cf. also Luke 2:14).

10. {*Was stirred*} It was more like shaken as by an earthquake.

12. {*Cast out*} He assumed authority over "the temple of God." John has a similar incident at the beginning of the ministry of Jesus (John 2:14), repeated at the close after three years with the same abuses in existence again. {*Doves*} These were the poor man's offering.

15. {*The children…*} The Greek gender shows these are probably boys who had caught the enthusiasm of the crowd.

16. {*Hearest thou*} The shouts of the boys in the temple are a desecration, which makes them try to shame Jesus, as responsible for it.

17. {*To Bethany*} The hometown of Martha, Mary, and Lazarus. Jesus may have stayed here prior to the crucifixion. His good friends were a comfort to him.

18. {*He hungered*} Greek tense shows he became hungry, felt hungry. Possibly Jesus spent the night out of doors and so had no breakfast.

19. {*A fig tree*} This was a single fig tree. {*Let there be no fruit from thee henceforward for ever*} The early figs start in spring before the leaves and develop after the leaves. The main fig crop was early autumn (Mark 11:14). There should have been figs on the tree with the crop of leaves.

21. {*Doubt not*} "Doubt" means to be divided in mind, to waver; the opposite of faith, trust, confidence. {*This mountain*} Removing a mountain is a bigger task than blighting a fig tree. The cursing of the fig-tree has always been regarded as of symbolic import, the tree being in Christ's mind an emblem of the Jewish people or the Holy City, with a great show of religion and no fruit of real godliness (cf. Zech. 4:7).

22. {*Believing*} The point of the "mountain" parable is "faith in the efficacy of prayer"(Plummer).

29. {*Repented and went*} "Repented" is the Greek verb *metamelomai,* lit. "to be sorry afterwards." Here the boy was sorry for his stubborn refusal to obey his father and went and obeyed. This Greek word is to be distinguished from a term usually translated repentance as a "change of mind and life" (*metanoian*), but mere sorrow is not repentance.

33. {*A hedge*} That is a fence as a protection against wild beasts. {*Digged a winepress*} Hewn out of the solid rock to hold the grapes and wine as they were crushed. Such wine-vats are to be seen today in Palestine. {*Built a tower*} A construction for vinedressers and watchmen (2 Chr. 26:10).

34. {*His servants*} These are slaves, distinguished from the workers of the soil who leased it (tenants).

38. {*Take his inheritance*} Greek syntax translates, "let us get his inheritance."

41. {*He will miserably destroy those miserable men*} In Greek there is a repetition of similar sounds and a pun. A common idiom in literary Greek.

42. {*The stone which...the builders rejected*} (cf. Ps. 118:22).

44. {*Shall be broken to pieces*} This verse graphically pictures the fate of the man who rejects Christ; ruin follows. {*Will scatter him as dust*} The verb was used of winnowing out the chaff and then of grinding to powder. This is the fate of him on whom this Rejected Stone falls.

CHAPTER 22

1. {*Again in parables*} Matthew alone gives this Parable of the Marriage Feast of the King's Son (cf. Luke 14:16-23).

2. {*A marriage feast*} The plural means wedding festivities (the several acts of feasting) which lasted for days (cf. seven days in Judg. 14:17).

3. {*To call them that were bidden*} It was a Jewish custom to invite a second time the already invited (Esth. 5:8; 6:14). The prophets of old had given God's invitation to the Jewish people. Now the Baptist and

Jesus had given the second invitation that the feast was ready. {*And they would not come*} The Greek tense characterizes the stubborn refusal of the Jewish leaders to accept Jesus as God's Son (John 1:11).

4. {*My dinner*} This is a noon or midday meal, and in some contexts the word can mean an early morning meal (cf. John 21:12,15). {*My fatlings*} This is grain-fed beef for slaughter.

5. {*Made light of it*} Lit. "neglecting, not caring for." To neglect an invitation to a wedding feast is a gross discourtesy. {*Another to his merchandise*} This is the Greek word *emporia,* from *emporos,* merchant, a traveling salesman (*emporeuomai*).

7. {*Armies*} These are bands of soldiers, not grand armies.

9. {*The partings of the highways*} The picture seems to be main streets leading out of the city where also side-streets may branch off, "by-ways."

13. {*Was speechless*} Lit. "was muzzled," dumb from confusion and embarrassment. It is used of the ox (1 Tim. 5:18). {*The outer darkness*} (cf. Matt. 8:12). It was all the blacker from the standpoint of the brilliantly lighted banquet hall.

14. {*For many are called, but few chosen*} There is a distinction between the called (Greek *klêtoi*) and the chosen (*eklektoi*), "called out from the called."

15. {*Took counsel*} (cf. Matt. 12:14). {*Ensnare in his talk*} "To trap" is the Greek verb *pagideuô,* from *pagis,* a snare or trap. This is a vivid picture of the effort to trip Jesus in his speech like a bird or wild beast.

16. {*Their disciples*} (cf. Mark 2:18). That is, the pupils of the Pharisees of two theological seminaries in Jerusalem: Hillel and Shammai. {*The Herodians*} (cf. Mark 3:6). Not actual family, these are the partisans or followers of Herod. {*The person of men*} Lit. "you do not look into the face of men." To do so is the sin of partiality (Jas. 2:1,9).

19. {*Tribute money*} With the figure of Caesar and a superscription, this probably is a silver coin struck for paying capitation [head-money], *tributum capitis.*

20. {*This image and superscription*} Probably a Roman coin because of the image on it. This coin was pretty certainly stamped in Rome with the image and name of Tiberius Caesar on it.

21. {*Render*} Lit. "Give back" to Caesar what is already Caesar's.

24. {*Shall marry*} (cf. Gen. 38:8; Deut. 25:5,6). The Sadducees were aiming at amusement rather than deadly mischief. It was probably an old conundrum.

33. {*They were astonished*} The Greek tense shows a continued amazement of the crowds. This is the Greek verb *exeplêssô*, lit. "they were struck out (literally)."

34. {*He had put the Sadducees to silence*} Lit. "muzzled the Sadducees." The Pharisees could not restrain their glee though they were joining (mustering forces) with the Sadducees in trying to entrap Jesus.

36. {*The great commandment in the law*} The form of "great" is normal (i.e., grammatically "positive") though the meaning is superlative, so translate "greatest." "The scribes declared that there were 248 affirmative precepts, as many as the members of the human body; and 365 negative precepts, as many as the days in the year, the total being 613, the number of letters in the Decalogue." But Jesus cuts through such pettifogging hair-splitting to the heart of the problem.

42. {*The Christ*} (cf. Ps. 110:1ff.). This is the same as the Messiah, not Christ as a proper name of Jesus. Messiah as David's son *and* Lord he really touches the problem of Jesus' Person (his Deity and his Humanity). Probably the Pharisees had never faced that problem before. They were unable to answer.

CHAPTER 23

2. {*Sit on Moses' seat*} The seat of Moses is a brief form for the chair of the professor whose function it is to authoritatively interpret Moses and make pronouncements.

3. {*For they say and do not*} Do not practice their practices.

5. {*To be seen of men*} Ostentation regulates the conduct of the rabbis. {*Phylacteries*} This is the Greek word *phulaktêrion*, an adjective from *phulaktêr, phulassô* (to guard); here "a safeguard, protecting charm or amulet." The rabbis wore *tephillin* or quite precisely made prayer-fillets, small leather cases with four strips of parchment on which were written the words of Exod. 13:1-10,11-16; Deut. 6:4-9; 11:13-21. Worn on the head between the eyes, consisting of a box with four compartments, each containing a slip of parchment inscribed with one of the four passages. The phylactery of the arm was to contain a single slip, with the same four passages written in four columns of seven lines each. The black leather straps by which they were fastened were wound seven times round the arm and three times round the hand. They were reverenced by the rabbis as highly as the scriptures, and, like them, might be rescued from the flames on a Sabbath. The size of the phylacteries indexed the measure of zeal, and the wearing of large ones was apt to take the place of obedience Hence they made them "wide."

6. {*The chief place at feasts*} Lit. "the first reclining place on the divan at the meal." {*The chief seats in the synagogues*} These chief seats were on the platform looking to the audience and with the back to the chest in which were kept the rolls of scripture. In the time of Jesus the hypocrites boldly sat up in front.

8. {*But be not ye called Rabbi*} "Ye" is emphatic, referring to an aside to the disciples. The Greek syntax may teach not *to seek* to be called Rabbi, if others call you this it will not be your fault.

9. {*Call no man your father*} He should not be understood to be condemning the title to one's real earthly father.

10. {*Masters*} This is the Greek *kathêgêtês,* teacher, with a possible focus of greater honor than another Greek word for teacher, *didaskalos.*

13. {*Hypocrites*} (cf. Matt. 6:2,5,16; 7:5; 15:7 and 22:18).

15. {*Twofold more a son of hell than yourselves*} It is a convert to Pharisaism rather than Judaism that is meant by "one proselyte." There were two kinds of proselytes: of the gate (not actual Jews, but God-fearers and well-wishers of Judaism, like Cornelius), of righteousness who received circumcision and became actual Jews. But a very small percent of the latter became Pharisees. The "son of Gehenna" means one fitted for and so destined for Gehenna (tormenting hell).

17. {*Ye fools*} (cf. Matt. 5:22). Not in a rage, Jesus so terms the blind Pharisees for their stupidity. Description of the class, not individuals.

23. {*Ye tithe*} (cf. Deut. 14:22; Lev. 27:30). All marketable commodities, the tithing of these small aromatic herbs show the Pharisaic scrupulous conscientiousness.

24. {*Strain out the gnat*} This is a filtering action. {*Swallow the camel*} That is, gulping or drinking down the camel, an oriental hyperbole (cf. Matt. 19:24; also 5:29,30; 17:20; 21:21. Both insects and camels were ceremonially unclean (Lev. 11:4,20,23,42).

25. {*From extortion and excess*} These punctilious observers of the external ceremonies did not hesitate at robbery (greed) and graft (self-indulgence).

26. {*Clean*} Note the change to singular, as if Jesus in a friendlier tone pleads with a Pharisee to mend his ways.

27. {*Whited sepulchre*} This is a tomb whitened with powdered lime dust, the sepulchers of the poor in the fields or the roadside. Recently and freshly done at the time of this speaking, these were whitewashed a month before the Passover that travelers might see them and so avoid being defiled by touching them (Num. 19:16).

29. {*The tombs of the prophets*} (cf. Luke 11:48-52). These men who professed to be so distressed at the murdering of the Prophets, were themselves compassing the death of Him who was far greater than any Prophet. In this seventh and last woe Jesus addresses the Jewish nation and not merely the Pharisees.

32. {*Fill ye up*} That is, fill up the measure of your fathers; crown their misdeeds by killing the prophet God has sent to you. Do at last what has long been in your hearts. The hour is come.

33. {*Ye serpents, ye offspring of vipers*} (cf. Matt. 3:17, also 12:34). As a climax, these are blistering words; they cut to the bone like whip-cords.

35. {*Zachariah son of Barachiah*} (cf. Gen. 4:10, also Luke 11:51). The usual explanation is that the reference is to Zechariah the son of Jehoiada the priest who was slain in the court of the temple (2 Chr. 24:20ff.). How the words, "son of Barachiah" got into Matthew we do not know.

Chapter 24

1. {*Went out from the temple*} All the discourses since Matthew 21:23 have been in the temple courts; after chapter 23 Jesus leaves it for good. His public teaching is over.

3. {*As he sat...on the Mount of Olives*} He was from here looking down on Jerusalem and the temple which he had just left. Peter, Andrew, James, and John come to Jesus here with the problem raised by his solemn words. They ask these questions about the destruction of Jerusalem and the temple, his own Second Coming and the end of the world. It is unknown if they thought they would all take place simultaneously? This discourse is a blend of apocalyptic language in the background of his death on the cross, the coming destruction of Jerusalem, his own second coming and the end of the world. He now touches one, now the other.

5. {*In my name*} Historically, false Christs caused the explosion against Rome that led to the city's destruction.

6. {*See that ye be not troubled*} Look out for the wars and rumors of wars, but do not be scared out of your wits by them. "Alarmed" is the Greek verb *throeô* which means to cry aloud, to scream, and in the passive to be terrified by an outcry (cf. 2 Thess. 2:2). {*But the end is not yet*} In spite of these words, people still set dates for the end of the world.

8. {*The beginning of travail*} This very phrase was used for the sufferings of the Messiah which were to come before the coming of the Messiah (Book of Jubilees, 23:18; Apoc. of Baruch 27-29).

9. {*Tribulation*} This is the Greek word *thlipsis,* pressure, for the oppression that the Christians received. {*For my name's sake*} This name became a byword of shame (Acts 5:41), but a name of honor for his disciples.

12. {*Love...shall wax cold*} This is the Greek verb *psuchô,* to breathe cool by blowing, to grow cold. It means spiritual energy blighted or chilled by a malign or poisonous wind (such as mutual hatred and suspicion).

14. {*Shall be preached*} That is, heralded in all the inhabited world. Note it does not say here that all will individually be saved.

15. {*The abomination of desolation*} (cf. Dan. 9:27; 11:31; 12:11). This refers or applies to more than one person or event: 1) Antiochus Epiphanes (1 Macc. 1:54,59; 6:7; 2 Macc. 6:1-5); 2) apparently the Roman army (Luke 21:20) in the temple. Both desecrated the temple by their actions. {*Let him that readeth understand*} (cf. Mark 13:14). The Gospel writers (Matthew following Mark) interjected these words for clarity.

16. {*Flee unto the mountains*} This refers to the mountains east of the Jordan; Christians have actually and literally done this in church history, fleeing for safety there.

17. {*On the housetop*} Going from roof to roof, the escape was on "the road of the roofs," as the rabbis called it. There was need for haste.

18. {*In the field*} The peasant worked in his time and left his outer coat at home then as now.

20. {*In winter nor on a sabbath*} In winter, because of the rough weather; on Sabbath, because some would hesitate to make such a journey on the Sabbath. Josephus in his *Wars* gives the best illustration of the horrors foretold by Jesus in verse 21.

22. {*Had been shortened*} "Cut short" is the Greek verb *koloboô*, from *kolobos,* lopped, mutilated, as the hands, the feet. {*For the elect's sake*} (cf. Matt. 22:14; 24:31). The siege of Jerusalem in the first century was shortened by various historical events

24. {*Great signs and wonders*} (cf. John 4:48; Acts 2:22; 4:30 2 Cor. 12:12; Heb. 2:4). "Miracles" is the Greek word *teras,* a wonder or prodigy; "sign" is the Greek word *sêmeion,* a sign (usually referring to God's purpose). But mere signs and wonders do not of themselves prove the power of God. {*If possible*} Here is the implication; it is not possible to lead astray the very elect. However, whether through spiritualistic mediums or sleight-of-hand men, some unwary people become excited, are deceived, and so are unable to judge.

26. {*In the wilderness…in the inner chambers*} Like Simon son of Gioras and John of Giscala (respectively) documented in Josephus's works.

27. {*As seen*} That is, visible in contrast to the invisibility of the false messiahs (cf. flash of lightning, Rev. 1:7).

28. {*Carcase*} This is a corpse or *cadaver,* a "fallen" person (cf. Luke 17:37 and Job 39:30; Prov. 30:17). {*Eagles*} Perhaps the griffon vulture, which was often seen in the wake of an army.

29. {*Immediately*} It is inappropriate to stress the literal time element of this word too much in this context; remember that this is a prophetic, apocalyptic panorama like that with foreshortened perspective. There can be some rather large amounts of time between these events (cf. "soon" Rev. 1:1 or Joel's prophecy as interpreted by Peter in Acts 2:16-22).

30. {*The sign of the Son of Man in heaven*} (cf. Dan. 7:13 and also Matt. 12:38; 16:1; John 2:18). It is certainly possible that Christ himself is the sign, though many other suggestions are made.

31. {*With a great sound of a trumpet*} The trumpet was the signal employed to call the hosts of Israel to march as to war and is common in prophetic imagery (Isa. 27:13, also Rev. 11:15).

34. {*This generation*} In the OT, this was reckoned as forty years. If this refers to the destruction of Jerusalem (the natural way to take it), there was a literal fulfillment. This could also refer to the Second Coming and end of the world.

36. {*Not even the Son*} The focus here is that only the Father knows the time of his Second Coming and the end of the world. Jesus admits ignorance of the date, but not of the character of the coming.

37. {*The days of Noah*} (cf. Luke 17:26-30). In Noah's day there was plenty of warning, but utter unpreparedness.

41. {*At the mill*} With a handle near the edge of the upper stone, this was the hand-mill which was turned by two women (cf. Exod. 11:5).

42. {*Watch therefore*} That is, keep awake, be on the watch.

43. {*In what watch*} (cf. Matt. 14:25). There were four watches of the night. {*Broken through*} This means to dig through the tile roof or under the floor (dirt in the poorer houses).

CHAPTER 25

1. {*Ten virgins*} The number ten is not especially significant. The scene is apparently centered round the house of the bride to which the bridegroom is coming for the wedding festivities. {*Lamps*} These are probably torches with a wooden staff and a dish on top in which was placed a piece of rope or cloth dipped in oil or pitch. Though it could be an oil lamp (cf. Acts 20:8).

3. {*Took no oil with them*} Probably no oil at all, not realizing their lack of oil until they lit the torches on the arrival of the bridegroom and his party.

4. {*In their vessels*} This is for extra supply.

5. {*They all slumbered and slept*} Greek tenses show they first nodded, and then went on sleeping.

6. {*There is a cry*} Lit. "a cry has come." The Greek word choice emphasizes the sudden outcry which has rent the air.

7. {*Trimmed*} That is, put in order, made ready.

8. {*Are going out*} When the five foolish virgins lit their lamps, the sputtering, flickering, smoking wicks were a sad revelation.

9. {*Peradventure there will not be enough for us and you*} "We are afraid that there is no possibility of there being enough for us both."

10. {*And while they went away*} A picture of their inevitable folly. {*Was shut*} Greek syntax shows it was "shut to stay shut."

11. {*Afterward*} And they find the door shut in their faces. {*Lord, Lord, open to us*} They appeal to the bridegroom who is now master whether he is at the bride's house or his own.

12. {*I know you not*} No special favors be granted them; they must abide the consequences of their own negligence.

13. {*Watch therefore*} This is the refrain with all the parables. Ignorance of the time of the second coming is not an excuse for neglect, but a reason for readiness.

14. {*Going into another country*} That is, from one's people, on the point of going abroad.

19. {*Maketh a reckoning*} This is a business idiom of the time.

21. {*The joy of thy lord*} "Joy" is the Greek word *chara* and may refer to the feast on the master's return.

24. {*That had received the one talent*} The Greek tense emphasizes the fact that he still had it. {*I knew thee*} This is experiential knowledge. {*A hard man*} This is the Greek *sklêros,* harsh, stern, rough man; This is a worse word than *austêros,* grasping and ungenerous (cf. Luke 19:21).

26. {*Thou wicked and slothful servant*} "Slothful" is the Greek word *oknêros,* from *okneô,* to be slow, poky. The reply is sarcasm.

27. {*With interest*} In the early Roman Empire legal interest was eight per cent, but in usurious transactions money was lent at twelve, twenty-four, and even forty-eight. The Mosaic law did not allow interest in dealings between Hebrews, but only with strangers (Deut. 23:19,20; Ps. 15:5).

32. {*All the nations*} That is, Jews and Gentiles, Christians and non-Christians: all. This is a majestic picture with which to close the series of parables about readiness for the second coming. Here is the program when he does come. {*As the shepherd separates*} A common figure, sheep are usually white and the goats black. The shepherd stands at the gate and taps the sheep to go to the right and the goats to the left.

34. {*From the foundation of the world*} The eternal purpose of the Father for his elect in all the nations.

46. {*Eternal punishment*} This is the Greek word *kolasis,* which comes from *kolazô,* to mutilate or prune. Some say this is age-long pruning that ultimately leads to salvation (cf. "eternal life") of the goats, as disciplinary rather than penal. But "eternal life" is the corresponding idea to "eternal punishment" suggesting a penal meaning; there is no suggestion here otherwise. We can leave all this to the King himself who is the Judge. "Eternal" is the Greek word *aiônios,* from *aiôn,* age, which means either without beginning or without end or both.

CHAPTER 26

2. {*Cometh...after two days*} This was probably our Tuesday evening (beginning of Jewish Wednesday). The Passover began on our Thursday evening (beginning of Jewish Friday). {*Is delivered up*} Thus Jesus sets a definite date for the coming crucifixion which he has been predicting for six months.

3. {*Then were gathered together the chief priests and elders of the people*} This is a meeting of the Sanhedrin as these two groups indicate (cf. Matt. 21:23). {*Unto the court*} This is the *atrium* or court around which the palace buildings were built, the place of an informal meeting with Caiaphas. He was high priest A.D. 18 to 36.

4. {*They took counsel together...to take Jesus by subtilty and kill him*} The Greek parsing is indicating their puzzled state of mind. The problem for them is how to kill him; the Triumphal Entry and the Tuesday debate in the temple revealed the powerful following that Jesus had among the crowds from Galilee.

5. {*A tumult*} Fearing an uprising, they argued to postpone until after the feast was over when the crowds had scattered.

6. {*In the house of Simon the leper*} Simon a common name, evidently he had been healed by Jesus. He gave the feast in honor of Jesus. This feast took place at the very time that the Sanhedrin was plotting the death of Jesus (Mark 14:1ff.). Who this Simon is (cf. Luke 7:36ff.) and whose house it is, are matters of speculation. {*A woman*} This woman is distinct from the account of Luke 7:1ff. Mary Magdalene, Mary of Bethany, and this woman are all distinct.

7. {*An alabaster cruse of exceeding precious ointment*} This vial or flask was used for precious ointments. As a rule it had a cylindrical form at the top, like a closed rosebud. An alabaster of nard could be a present for a king. {*She poured it upon his head*} (cf. Mark 14:3; feet, John 12:3) Head and feet were anointed.

8. {*This waste*} They considered it a dead loss; nothing but sentimental aroma; worth a year's wage (cf. Mark 14:5). It was a cruel shock to Mary of Bethany to hear this comment from Judas (John 12:4).

12. {*To prepare me for burial*} Mary alone understood what Jesus repeatedly said about his approaching death, and did this with purpose.

15. {*They weighed unto him*} This means they placed the money in the balances or scales. Coined money was in use, but the shekels may have been weighed out in antique fashion. It is not known whether the Sanhedrin had offered a reward for the arrest of Jesus or not. {*Thirty pieces of silver*} (cf. Zech. 11:12). If a man's ox gored a servant, he had to pay this amount (cf. Exod. 21:32). These thirty shekels equaled 120 days wages of a common laborer, the current price of a slave. There was no doubt contempt for Jesus in the minds of both the Sanhedrin and Judas in this bargain.

16. {*Sought opportunity*} The Greek tense shows Judas went at his business and stuck to it. He *kept on* watching for a good chance.

17. {*To eat the passover*} The Passover Meal is meant here, though Passover Feast can be meant (cf. John 18:28). Though disputed by some, Jesus ate the Passover Meal at the regular time about 6 P.M. (which is the beginning of 15 Nisan), and died on the cross the afternoon of 15 Nisan. The Passover Lamb was slain on the afternoon of 14 Nisan and the meal eaten at sunset; again, which is the beginning of 15 Nisan (cf. John 13:1,27; 18:28; 19:14,31, and the Synoptic accounts, Matt. 26:17,20; Mark 14:12,17; Luke 22:7,14).

18. {*To such a man*} This is an old idiom for "Mr. X." Jesus may have indicated the man's name. This man was carrying a pitcher of water (cf. Mark 14:13 and Luke 22:10). It may have been the home of Mary the mother of John Mark. Evidently there was no surprise in this home at the command of Jesus. It was a gracious privilege to serve him.

20. {*He was sitting at meat...*} (cf. Exod. 12:4,43). Jesaus was lying back on the left side on the couch with the right hand free. Jesus and the Twelve all reclined.

21. {*One of you*} This was a bolt from the blue for all except Judas and he was startled to know that Jesus understood his treacherous bargain.

22. {*Is it I, Lord?*} The Greek syntax expects a "no" to the question. Judas bluffed the same exact question (verse 25).

23. {*He that dipped...*} Having no knives, forks, or spoons, they all dipped their hands. {*Dish*} This is a dish or platter with the broth of nuts and raisins and figs into which the bread was dipped before eating. This language means that one of those who had eaten bread with him had violated the rights of hospitality by betraying him. Judas knew full well, though the rest apparently did not grasp it.

24. {*Good were it for that man...*} Not excusing the crime of Judas (as some today do), Jesus here pronounces his terrible doom. Judas heard it and still went on with his hellish bargain with the Sanhedrin (cf. John 13:31).

26. {*And blessed and brake it*} This is a special "Grace prayer" in the middle of the Passover Meal, "as they were eating," for the institution of the Supper. Jesus broke the bread so each might have a piece, not as a symbol of the breaking of his body. If fact, the body of Jesus was not broken (John 19:33). Bread is a symbolic *representation* of the body Jesus offered for us. This memorial is to remind us of his death for our sins.

28. {*The Covenant*} (cf. Heb. 7:22; 8:8). The covenant is an agreement or contract between two parties. It is used also for will (Latin, *testamentum*) which becomes operative at death (Heb. 9:15-17). Hence our *New Testament.* Either "covenant" or "will" makes sense here. In the Hebrew to make a covenant was to cut up the sacrifice and so ratify the agreement (Gen. 15:9-18). Jesus here uses the solemn words of Exod. 24:8 "the blood of the covenant" at Sinai. This is the New Covenant of Jer. 31:1ff. Heb. 8:1ff. {*Which is shed for many*} The act is symbolized by the ordinance (cf. Matt. 20:28). {*Unto remission of sins*} Jesus was clearly aware that the purpose of the shedding of his blood of the New Covenant was precisely to remove (forgive) sins.

29. {*When I drink it new with you*} Though not explicit, this implies that Jesus himself partook of the bread and the wine. "Fruit of the vine" does not make it obligatory to employ wine rather than pure grape juice if one wishes the other.

30. {*Sang a hymn*} This is the *Hallel,* part of Ps. 115-118.

33. {*I will never be offended*} "Offended" means "made to stumble." Ignoring the prophecy of the resurrection (verse 32), Peter was intent on showing that he was superior to all the rest. Judas had turned traitor and all were weak, Peter in particular, little as he knew it. {*Before the cock crows*} (cf. Mark 14:30) Mark says that Peter will deny Jesus thrice before the cock crows twice. When one cock crows in the morning, others generally follow. The three denials lasted over an hour. Some scholars hold that chickens were not allowed in Jerusalem by the Jews, but the Romans would have them.

35. {*Even if I must die with thee*} This was a noble speech and meant well.

36. {*Gethsemane*} The place was an enclosed plot or estate, "garden," or orchard. It was beyond the Kidron ravine at the foot of the Mount of Olives about three-fourths of a mile from the eastern walls of Jerusalem. There are now eight very old olive trees still standing in this enclosure.

38. {*Watch with me*} The Greek word and tense means "to keep awake and not go to sleep." The hour was late and the strain had been severe, but Jesus pleaded for a bit of human sympathy as he wrestled with his Father.

39. {*He went forward a little*} It is as if he could not fight the battle in their immediate presence. {*This cup*} The figure can mean only the approaching death (cf. Matt. 20:22). The Master is about to taste the bitter dregs in the cup of death for the sin of the world. He was not afraid that he would die before the Cross, though he instinctively shrank from the cup. He instantly surrendered his will to the Father's will and drank the cup to the full.

40. {*What...*} There is a tone of sad disappointment at the discovery that they were asleep. Every word struck home.

41. {*Watch and pray*} (cf. verse 38) Thus we are to understand the prayer in Matt. 6:13 about leading (being led) into temptation. Their failure was due to weakness of the flesh as is often the case. {*Spirit*} Here this is the moral life (intellect, will, emotions) as opposed to the flesh (cf. Isa. 31:3; Rom. 7:25).

42. {*If this cannot pass away...*} The Greek condition is one determined as fulfilled, assumed to be true.

45. {*Sleep on now and take your rest*} Some take it as a reproachful concession, "You may sleep and rest indefinitely so far as I am concerned; I need no longer your watchful interest." Or it may be a sad query. {*The hour is at hand*} The Master's time of weakness is past; he is prepared to face the worst.

46. {*Is betrayed...*} He is drawing near. How Jesus knew we do not know; whether sight, sound, or just feeling the proximity of the traitor. The eight disciples at the perimeter of the Garden seemed to have given no notice.

47. {*While he yet spake*} It was an electric moment as Jesus faced Judas with his horde of helpers as if he turned to meet an army. {*One* *of the twelve*} (cf. Mark 14:43; Matt. 26:47; Luke 22:47). This detail is an emphasis that one of the chosen Twelve should do this dastardly deed. {*A great multitude*} This is a band of soldiers from the garrison barracked in the fortress tower called Antonia (John 18:3) and the temple police (Luke 22:52). In spite of the full moon, they had torches and lanterns (cf. John 18:3).

48. {*Gave them a sign*} It was a prearranged sign (cf. Mark 14:44). {*Kissed*} The kiss was a common mode of greeting, here fervently (as the Greek verb *katephileô* shows). It was a revolting ostentatious kiss, a kiss of the enemy (cf. Prov. 27:6).

50. {*Do that for which thou art come*} The meaning in the Greek syntax is to take this as a question. "Friend, for what [why] have you come?" Thus Jesus exposes the pretense of Judas and shows that he does not believe in his paraded affection.

51. {*One of them that were with Jesus*} This is Peter, prudently not named until the writing of John's Gospel, at the end of the century. Evidently Peter aimed to cut off Malchus' ear (cf. John 18:10). Likely he is named then because Peter was then dead and in no danger.

52. {*Put up again thy sword*} Lit. "turn back your sword into its place." It was a stern rebuke for Peter (cf. Luke 22:38 and Matt. 5:39; also John 18:36). We learn that the sword calls for the sword. Offensive war is here given flat condemnation.

53. {*Legions*} This is a Roman army consisting of 6,100 foot soldiers and 726 horse in the time of Augustus. Roman soldiers were present in garrisons in Palestine already, full legions came later. One should recall the story of Elisha at Dothan (2 Kgs. 6:17).

55. {*As against a robber?*} This is the Greek word *lêistês,* also translated "Am I an insurrectionist?" This is a robber, not as a thief, but a robber hiding from justice.

59. {*Sought false witness against Jesus*} The Greek tense shows they *kept on* seeking. Judges have no right to be prosecutors, much less offer bribes to get a conviction.

61. {*I am able to destroy the temple of God*} (cf. John 2:19) Jesus referred to his body (temple) killed on the cross (destroyed), raised again in three days. This testimony was a perversion, and even so the two witnesses disagreed in their misrepresentation (Mark 14:59).

63. {*Held his peace*} He refused to answer the bluster of Caiaphas. {*I adjure thee by the living God*} Caiaphas put Jesus under oath in order to make him incriminate himself, unlawful tactic in Jewish jurisprudence. But Jesus did not refuse to answer under solemn oath, clearly showing that he was not thinking of oaths in courts of justice when he prohibited profanity. To refuse to answer would be tantamount to a denial. So Jesus answered knowing full well the use that would be made of his confession and claim.

64. {*Thou hast said*} (cf. Mark 14:62). Lit. "you say" but the meaning is "yes."

65. {*He hath spoken blasphemy*} Jesus had incriminated himself (verse 64). Of course, a real Messiah can make such a claim and it would not be blasphemy.

66. {*He is worthy of death*} The Sanhedrin took the vote though it was at night and they no longer had the power of death since the Romans took it away from them. Death was the penalty of blasphemy (Lev. 24:15). It was a unanimous vote, except for Joseph of Arimathea and Nicodemus; they were probably absent and not even invited.

69. {*Sitting without in the court*} Within the palace (cf. Matt. 26:58), Peter was sitting outside the hall where the trial was going on in the open central court with the servants or officers of the Sanhedrin.

70. {*I know not what thou sayest*} It deceived no one. It is suggested that Peter's word choice in Galilean Aramaean betrayed at once his Galilean residence (cf. verse 73).

71. {*Into the porch*} Peter was not safe here either, for another maid recognized him.

72. {*The man*} This expression could convey contempt, compare "the fellow."

73. {*They that stood by*} (cf. Luke 22:59). The bystanders came up to Peter. His dialect (Greek word *lalia*) clearly revealed that he was a Galilean. The Galileans had difficulty with the gutturals (sounds uttered from the throat in contrast to sounds distinguished with the teeth, lips, or nasal sounds).

74. {*Then began he to curse and to swear...*} He repeated his denial with the addition of profanity to prove that he was telling the truth.

75. Outside he went with a broken heart, and continued weeping (cf. Mark 14:72). Judas was a total wreck and Peter was a near derelict. Satan had sifted them all as wheat, but Jesus had prayed specially for Peter (Luke 22:31ff.). Will Satan show Peter to be all chaff as Judas was?

CHAPTER 27

1. {*Now when morning was come*} After dawn came the Sanhedrin that held a formal meeting to condemn Jesus and so ratify the illegal trial during the night (Mark 15:1; Luke 22:66-71).

2. {*Delivered him up to Pilate the governor*} What they had done was all a form and a farce. Pilate had the power of death, but they had greatly enjoyed condemning, beating, and binding him.

3. {*Repented himself*} Probably Judas saw Jesus led away to Pilate and thus knew that the condemnation had taken place. This Greek verb *metamelomai*, really means to be sorry afterwards, the next proper biblical step after feeling sorry is to lead to change of mind and life (Greek *metanoia*, or *metanoêô* commonly translated "repent"). Peter had sorrow that led back to Christ; But Judas had only sorrowful remorse that led to suicide.

4. {*See thou to it*} Lit. "you will see." Judas made a belated confession of his sin in betraying innocent blood to the Sanhedrin, but not to God nor Jesus. The Sanhedrin ignore their own guilt in the matter, but tell Judas to look after his own guilt.

6. {*Into the treasury*} The price of blood (blood-money) was pollution to the treasury (Deut. 23:18ff.). Splitting hairs again, they took the money out and used it for a secular purpose (cf. Mark 7:1-23; Matt. 15:1-20).

7. {*The potter's field*} Like a brickyard, it is suggested it was a small field where potter's clay was obtained.

8. {*The field of blood*} This name was attached to it here because it was the price of blood and/or (in Acts) because Judas' blood was shed (cf. Acts 1:18ff.).

11. {*Now Jesus stood before the governor*} Here is one of the dramatic episodes of history. Jesus stood face to face with the Roman governor. Representing Roman law, Pilate was technically a *legatus Caesaris,* an officer of the Emperor, more exactly *procurator,* ruler under the Emperor of a less important province than *propraetor* (as over Syria). {*Art thou the King of the Jews?*} (cf. Luke 23:2 and John 18:28-32). This is what really mattered. He could not ignore the accusation that Jesus claimed to be King of the Jews. Else he could be himself accused to Caesar for disloyalty. Rivals and pretenders were common all over the empire. {*Thou sayest*} The meaning here is Jesus confesses that he is.

14. {*And he gave him no answer, not even to one word*} He continued to be silent under the direct question of Pilate. The Greek is very precise besides the double negative. "He did not reply to him up to not even one word." This silent dignity amazed Pilate and yet he was strangely impressed.

20. {*Persuaded*} The chief priests (Sadducees) and elders (Pharisees) saw the peril of the situation and took no chances.

23. {*Why, what evil hath he done?*} A feeble protest by a flickering conscience, Pilate descended to that level of arguing with the mob now a veritable lynching fiasco.

24. {*Washed his hands*} He washed off his hands for himself as a common symbol of cleanliness and added his pious claim with a slap at them. The Jews used this symbol (Deut. 21:6; Pss. 26:6; 73:13).

25. {*His blood be upon us and upon our children*} This shows that the Jewish people recognized their guilt and were even proud of it. There is plenty of guilt to go around: Judas, Caiaphas, the Sanhedrin, the Jewish people as a whole, and Pilate, and, at bottom, the sins of all of us nailed Jesus to the Cross.

26. {*Scourged*} The flogging before the crucifixion was a brutal Roman custom. The scourging was part of the capital punishment.

27. {*Into the palace*} In Rome the *praetorium* was the camp of the *praetorian* (from *praetor*) guard of soldiers (Phil. 1:13), but in the provinces it was the palace in which the governor resided as in Caesarea (cf. Acts 23:35). So here in Jerusalem Pilate ordered Jesus and all the band of soldiers to be led into the palace in front of which the judgment-seat had been placed.

28. {*A scarlet robe*} A kind of short cloak worn by soldiers, military officers, magistrates, kings, emperors (cf. 2 Macc. 12:35). Mark has the color purple (cf. Mark 15:17). There are various shades of purple and scarlet and it is not easy to distinguish these colors or tints. This scarlet mantle on Jesus was mock imitation of the royal purple.

29. {*A crown of thorns*} They wove a crown out of thorns which would grow even in the palace grounds. It was more like a victor's garland (Greek word *stephanon*) than a royal diadem (Greek *diadêma*), but it served the purpose. {*Hail, King of the Jews*} The soldiers were familiar with the *Ave Caesar* and copy it in their mockery of Jesus.

These garments of mockery were removed before the *via dolorosa* to the cross (verse 31).

32. {*His cross*} Probably the shape of the cross is the one usually presented, though other shapes are possible. Usually the victim was nailed (hands and feet) to the cross before it was raised and it was not very high.

33. {*Golgotha*} In Latin called *Calvariae locus* (cf. Calvary), this meant "place of a skull-shaped mount," not "place of skulls." This is probably what is now called Gordon's Calvary, a hill north of the city wall which from the Mount of Olives looks like a skull, the rock-hewn tombs resembling eyes, in one of which Jesus may have been buried.

34. {*Wine mingled with gall*} (cf. Mark 15:23) This was a sour wine and myrrh gave the sour wine a better flavor and like the bitter gall had a narcotic and stupefying effect. Both elements may have been in the drink which Jesus tasted and refused to drink. Women provided the drink to deaden the sense of pain and the soldiers may have added the gall to make it disagreeable.

36. {*Watched him there*} This was to prevent the possibility of rescue or removal of the body. Casting lots by soldiers give a picture of comedy at the foot of the Cross, the tragedy of the ages.

37. {*His accusation*} (cf. John 19:19) The title or placard of the crime which was carried before the victim or hung around his neck as he walked to execution was now placed above the head of Jesus on the projecting piece (*crux immurus*). It was in three languages: Latin for law; Aramaic for Jews; Greek for everybody (John 19:20). The full inscription was: This is Jesus of Nazareth the King of the Jews.

38. {*Robbers*} They were not thieves, probably members of the band of Barabbas.

40. {*If thou art the Son of God*} (cf. Matt. 4:3) This once came from the devil, now hurled at Jesus under the devil's prompting. It is a pitiful picture of human depravity and failure in the presence of Christ dying for sinners.

41. {*The chief priests mocking*} The whole Sanhedrin mocked. The word for mocking is the Greek *empaizô*, from *en*, and *paizô*, from *pais*, "child" means acting like silly children who love to make fun of one another.

42. {*He saved others; himself he cannot save*} The sarcasm is true, though they do not know its full significance. If he had saved himself now, he could not have saved any one; a glorious, amazing irony (cf. Matt. 10:39). {*Let him now come down*} An untrue assertion, they would have shifted their ground and invented some other excuse. But Christ will not give new proofs to the blind in heart.

43. {*Let him [God] deliver him now*} (cf. Pss. 21; 22:8). This is a sneer at Christ's claim to be God's son. {*Desireth*} Lit. "wants," which may mean "love" or "cares for" as in the Septuagint (Pss. 18:20; 41:12).

45. {*From the sixth hour*} From noon. The crucifixion began at 9 A.M., darkness began at noon and lasted until 3 P.M. (Mark 15:33; Matt. 27:45; Luke 23:44). Not a three-hour eclipse, this may have been dense masses of clouds obscuring the sun's light. Nature showed its sympathy with the tragedy of the dying of the Creator on the Cross (Rom. 8:22), groaning and travailing until now.

46. {*My God, My God, why hast thou forsaken me?*} Nothing from Jesus so well illustrates the depth of his suffering of soul as he felt himself regarded as sin though sinless (2 Cor. 5:21). John 3:16 comes to our relief here as we see the Son of God bearing the sin of the world. This cry of desolation comes at the close of the three hours of darkness.

49. {*Whether Elijah cometh to save him*} "My God" *êli* in Hebrew sounds similar to *Eleias* (Elijah) so they misunderstood the words of Jesus in his outcry of soul anguish.

50. {*Yielded up his spirit*} (cf. Ps. 31:5 with Luke 23:46; also John 19:30). Jesus did not die from slow exhaustion, but with a loud cry. The other Gospels give more details. "He gave up his life because he willed it, when he willed it, and as he willed it" (Augustine).

51. {*Veil...was rent...earth did quake*} (cf. Mark 15:38 and Luke 23:45). The Talmud tells of a quaking forty years before the destruction of the temple, also Josephus in a more general reference. This veil was a most elaborately woven fabric of seventy-two twisted plaits of twenty-four threads each and the veil was sixty feet long and thirty wide. The rending of the veil signified the removal of the separation between God and the people.

54. {*Truly this was the Son of God*} Lit. God's Son. Deeply moved by the portents which he had witnessed, this centurion (ruler of a hundred) probably meant more than merely he was a "righteous man" (cf. Luke 23:47). If he was inclined now to trust in Christ, he came as a pagan and, like the robber who believed, was saved as Jesus hung upon the Cross. All who are ever saved in truth are saved because of the death of Jesus on the Cross. So the Cross began to do its work at once.

57. {*And when even was come*} It was the Preparation, the day before the Sabbath (Mark 15:42; Luke 23:54). This is a time just before 6 P.M. Little known to us, Joseph of Arimathea (his town) was a rich, secret disciple, and had not agreed to the death of Jesus.

63. {*Sir, we remember*} This was our Saturday, the Jewish Sabbath, the day after the Preparation (Matt. 27:62). The disciples forgot and the Jewish leaders remembered. Why? It is probably due on the one hand to the overwhelming grief of the disciples coupled with the blighting of all their hopes of a political Messiah in Jesus.

65. {*Have a guard*} This is a guard of Roman soldiers, not mere temple police. The curt permission to the Jews whom he despised is suitable in the mouth of the Roman official.

66. {*Sealing the stone, the guard being with them*} This was probably by a cord stretched across the stone and sealed at each end (cf. Dan. 6:17). The sealing was done in the presence of the Roman guard who were left in charge to protect this stamp of Roman authority and power. Trying to prevent theft and resurrection, they provided additional witness to the resurrection of Jesus.

CHAPTER 28

1. {*Now late on the sabbath as it began to dawn toward the first day of the week*} "After the Sabbath" really means "Late on the Sabbath (as it began to dawn toward the first day of the week)." Therefore this visit by the two women was before the Sabbath was over (before 6 P.M. our Saturday) at *sunset,* not sunrise of our Sunday morning (as in Mark). So between Mark and Matthew we learn the anxious women make more than one visit.

5. {*Unto the women*} Mary Magdalene had left (John 20:1ff.), but the other women remained and had the interview with the angel (or men, Luke) about the empty tomb and the Risen Christ.

6. {*Jesus the Risen*} (cf. 2 Tim. 2:8). This is the heart of the testimony of the angel to the women, who were afraid and dazzled by the glory of the scene. The body of the Risen Christ was no longer in the tomb.

7. {*He goeth before you into Galilee*} Twice Jesus did appear to the disciples in Galilee (cf. lake, John 21:1ff. and mountain, Matt. 28:16-20).

8. {*With fear and great joy*} Here is a touch of life as the excited women ran quickly. Anything seemed possible now. These mingled emotions of ecstasy and dread need cause no surprise when all things are considered.

9. {*Jesus met them*} Jesus allowed this act of worship, though here he forbade handling of his body by Mary Magdalene (John 20:17). It was a great moment of faith and cheer.

11. {*Told unto the chief priests*} These Roman soldiers had been placed at the disposal of the Sanhedrin. They were probably afraid also to report to Pilate and tell him what had happened. They apparently told a truthful account as far as they understood it. But were the Sanhedrin convinced of the resurrection of Jesus?

12. {*They gave large money*} The religious leaders knew full well the power of bribes. They make a contract with the Roman soldiers to tell a lie about the resurrection of Jesus as they paid Judas money to betray him.

13. {*Disciples...stole him away while we slept*} If they were asleep they would not know anything about it.

14. {*We will persuade him, and rid you of care*} They would try money also on Pilate and assume all responsibility. The soldiers lived up to their bargain and this lie lives on through the ages.

17. {*But some doubted*} (cf. Matt. 14:31). This is not the Eleven who were all now convinced after some doubt, but to the others present. Paul states that over five hundred were present, most of whom were still alive when he wrote (1 Cor. 15:6). It is natural that some should hesitate to believe so great a thing at the first appearance of Jesus to them.

18. {*All authority*} His authority or power in his earthly life had been great (Matt. 7:29; 11:27; 21:23ff.). Now it is boundless and includes earth and heaven. It is the sublimest of all spectacles to see the Risen Christ without money or army or state charging this band of five hundred men and women with winning all the nations.

19. {*All the nations*} That is, Jews and Gentiles, all peoples. This is the *Magna Charta* of missions. His Second Coming does not change this. He did promise to come, but he has never named the date. We are to be joyfully ready for his coming at any time. {*Make disciples*}

Lit. "make learners." This means evangelism in the fullest sense and not merely revival meetings. {*In the name of the Father, the Son, and the Holy Spirit*} "Name" here means "power" or "authority." Here is baptism in the name of the Trinity.

20. {*Teaching them*} Teaching is a weighty part of the work of Christians. Though not replacing conversion or regeneration, Christian education belongs in manifold places: home, church, school. {*I am with you*} So Matthew's Gospel closes in a blaze of glory. He is the Risen, all powerful Redeemer, who is with his people all the time. Jesus employs the prophetic present here. He is with us all the days until he comes in glory.

THE GOSPEL ACCORDING TO MARK

AUTHOR: John Mark, interpreter of Peter the Apostle, relative of Barnabas
RECIPIENTS: primarily Romans
DATE: A.D. 50 (quite probably)
FROM: possibly Rome
OCCASION: The writing of the memoirs of Peter, brought about by Peter's preaching and activity in Rome
THEME: Christ in action (Son of Man, Son of God, Lord of Life and Death) showing his ministry in Galilee and Last Week in Jerusalem

BY WAY OF INTRODUCTION

Though some place Matthew earlier, the framework of Mark's briefer Gospel lies behind both Matthew and Luke and nearly all of it is used by one or the other. One may satisfy himself on this point by careful use of a Harmony of the Gospels in Greek or English. Whether Mark made use of Q (a source document also called the *Logia of Jesus*) or not is not yet shown, though it is possible.

If Mark wrote in Rome, as is quite possible, his book was looked upon as the Roman Gospel and had a powerful environment in which to take root. It has distinctive merits of its own that helped to keep it in use.

It is mainly narrative and the style is direct and simple with many vivid touches, like the historical present of an eyewitness. The early writers all agree that Mark was the interpreter for Simon Peter with whom he was at one time (1 Pet. 5:13).

This Gospel is the briefest of the four, but is fullest of striking details that apparently came from Peter's discourses (cf. Mark's outline of Peter's preaching Acts 10:36-42). Also Mark has more Aramaic phrases than the other Gospels. There are also more Latin phrases and idioms than in the other Gospels, postulating then a Roman or even a Latin language connection. The Greek is distinctly vernacular *Koiné* as one would expect from both Peter and Mark.

Mark was the son of Mary of Jerusalem (Acts 12:12) and once a co-worker with Barnabas and Paul, but he deserted them at Perga (Acts 13:13). Paul refused to take him on the second mission tour, though later commends him (Col. 4:10), and asks for him in his dark hours (2 Tim. 4:11). Barnabas took Mark, his cousin, with him to Cyprus (Acts 15:39). He then appeared with Simon Peter with whom he did his greatest work (cf. 1 Pet. 5:13). Though initially failing, Mark is an example of one making good in the ministry.

The closing passage in the Textus Receptus, Mark 16:9-20, is not found in the oldest Greek Manuscripts, and is probably not genuine. A discussion of the evidence will appear at the proper place.

Mark deals with two great themes, the Ministry in Galilee (Mark 1-9) and the Last Week in Jerusalem (11-16) with a brief sketch of the period of withdrawal from Galilee (Mark 10).

The Gospel of Mark pictures Christ in action. There is a minimum of discourse and a maximum of deed. And yet the same essential pictures of Christ appear here as in the rest of the New Testament.

This Gospel is the one for children to read first and is the one that we should use to lay the foundation for our picture of Christ. Mark's Gospel throbs with life and bristles with vivid details. We see with Peter's eyes and catch almost the very look and gesture of Jesus as he moved among men in his work of healing men's bodies and saving men's souls.

CHAPTER 1

1. {*The beginning*} This heading or title may serve to introduce the paragraph about the ministry of the Baptist or as the superscription for the whole Gospel. {*Gospel of Jesus Christ*} This means the message about Jesus Christ.

2. {*In Isaiah, the prophet*} (cf. Mal. 3:1 and Isa. 40:3). Though part of the quote is from Malachi, Isaiah is mentioned as the chief of the prophets. Such *catenae* (chains of quotations) is common.

3. {*Paths straight*} Ancient Persian roads compare favorably to modern roads in quality. The Roman Empire was knit together by roads, some of which survive to this day.

4. {*John came*} The Greek for "came" shows his coming was an epoch, not a mere event. {*Wilderness*} (cf. Mark 1:5, 9) This is the deserted region of Judea and included the Jordan River. {*Preached the baptism of repentance*} (cf. Matt. 3:2). Lit. "a repentance kind of baptism," i.e., a baptism marked by repentance. English "repentance" means here to change their [Jews] minds and to turn from their sins, and so "confessing their sins" (cf. Matt. 3:16). The public confessions produced a profound impression as they would now. {*Unto remission of sins*} Not teaching baptism as the means of obtaining the forgiveness, this translates best as "with reference to the forgiveness of sins." The baptism was on the basis of the repentance and confession of sin (cf. the picture of death and resurrection Rom. 6:4). Here John is treating the Jewish nation as pagans who need to repent, to confess their sins, and to come back to the kingdom of God.

5. {*Then went out unto him*} The Greek tense shows a steady stream of people who kept coming to the baptism, a wonderful sight.

6. {*Clothed with camel's hair*} (cf. Matt. 3:4). Not the skin, it was a rough cloth woven of camel's hair. {*Locusts and wild honey*} Dried locusts are considered palatable and the wild honey was bountiful in the clefts of the rocks.

7. {*The latchet...*} The thong of the sandal which held it together. This action was performed by a slave for the guest before one enters the bath.

9. {*Rent asunder*} (cf. "opened" Matt. 3:16 and Luke 3:21; also John 1:32). This is the Greek verb *schizô*, to split like a garment.

12. {*Driveth him forth*} This is more bold and vivid than Matthew and Luke which have "was led."

13. {*With the wild animals*} Mark alone adds this touch.

14. {*Preaching the gospel of God*} Translate the Greek syntax, "the Good News that comes from God."

15. {*Repent and believe*} Repentance is the keynote in the message of the Baptist and Jesus' Gospel. Mark adds here "and believe in the Good News."

16. {*And passing along by the Sea of Galilee*} Mark shows Christ in action. {*Casting a net*} (cf. Matt. 4:18). The Greek verb is *amphiballô*, lit. "casting on both sides, now on one side, now on the other." This is fishing with a net, making a cast, a haul.

19. {*Mending their nets*} (cf. Matt. 4:21). They were getting ready that they might succeed better at the next haul.

20. {*With the hired servants*} (Matt. 4:22). This is evidence they had an extensive business in co-operation with Andrew and Simon (Luke 5:7, 10) and that the business would go on while they left all (Luke 5:11) and became permanent followers of Jesus.

21. {*And taught*} Jesus had now made Capernaum (modern *tell hum*) his headquarters after the rejection in Nazareth (cf. Luke 4:16–31 and Matt. 4:13–16). An ancient synagogue has been discovered here, and the stones are in a good state of preservation. Jesus was a preacher of over a year when he began to teach in Capernaum. His reputation had preceded him (cf. Luke 4:14).

22. {*They were astonished*} (cf. Luke 4:32) "Amazed" means lit. "to strike a person out of his senses by some strong feeling, such as fear, wonder, or even joy." {*And not as their scribes*} (cf. Luke 4:32). These quoted other rabbis and felt their function to be expounders of the traditions, ending in petty legalism and punctilious points of external etiquette to the utter neglect of the spiritual reality (Mark 7:9, 13). Jesus' authority was direct from God (cf. also Matt. 7:29). The chief controversy in Christ's life was with these scribes, the professional teachers of the oral law and mainly Pharisees.

23. {*With an unclean spirit*} This idiom is similar to the one Paul uses when he speaks of being "in Christ." This was a man in the power of the demon, with a focus on estrangement from God (Zech. 13:2). Usually physical or mental disease accompanied the possession by demons.

24. {*What have we to do with thee?*} (cf. Matt. 8:29). This question has a focus that there is nothing in common between the demon and Jesus. Note the "we"; the man speaks for the demon and himself, double personality. {*The Holy One of God*} (cf. John 6:69, also "Son of God" Matt. 8:29). The demon knew what the rabbis did not. The demon feared that Jesus came to destroy both him and the man in his power.

25. {*Hold thy peace*} "Quiet" is too tame a translation; it is a more vigorous word, better as "be muzzled" like an ox (cf. Deut. 25:4, 1 Cor. 9:9; 1 Tim. 5:18). "Shut your mouth" would be too colloquial.

26. {*Tearing him*} (cf. Luke 4:35). That is, convulsing like a spasm. Medical writers use the word for the rotating of the stomach. Screeching, it was a moment of intense excitement.

27. {*A new teaching*} The teaching was fresh, original (new) as the dew of the morning on the blossoms just blown. It is new teaching with authority behind it. The Greek phrasing also allows "authority" to go with the verb, "with authority commands even the evil [unclean] spirits." The people were accustomed to the use of magical formulae by the Jewish exorcists (cf. Matt. 12:27; Acts 19:13, cf. also Acts 8:19).

29. {*The house of Simon and Andrew*} (cf. Matt. 8:14). Peter had a wife and mother-in-law, and Andrew also lived with them. Later his wife accompanied him on his apostolic journeys (1 Cor. 9:5). Though each Synoptic account has some differences, they all mention the instant recovery and ministry without any convalescence. {*Took her by the hand*} Luke speaks of Jesus standing, bending over her like a doctor (cf. Luke 4:39). It was a tender scene.

32. {*When the sun did set*} The Sabbath ended at sunset and so the people were now at liberty to bring their sick to Jesus. The Greek shows they brought them to Jesus in a steady stream.

33. {*At the door*} This refers to Peter's house. The details of the account show again Mark is seeing with Peter's eyes again.

34. {*Suffered not*} Greek tense shows a continued refusal for the demons to speak.

35. {*In the morning, a great while before day*} This means well before 6 A.M. but not before 3 A.M. (cf. Mark 16:2).

36. {*Followed after him*} Translate "hunted him out (Moffatt) [until they found him]."

43. {*Strictly charged*} (cf. Luke 5:14) This Greek word is a strong word for the snorting of a horse and expresses powerful emotion as Jesus stood here face to face with leprosy, itself a symbol of sin and all its train of evils.

44. {*For a testimony unto them*} Without the formal testimony of the priests the people would not receive the leper as officially clean.

45. {*Began to publish it much*} (cf. Luke 5:15). One of the best ways to spread a thing is to tell people not to tell.

CHAPTER 2

1. {*In the house*} This refers to the home of Peter; another picture directly from Peter's discourse.

2. {*So that there was no longer room for them, no, not even about the door*} Another graphic detail seen through Peter's eyes, this house door apparently opened into the street, not into a court as in the larger houses. {*And he spake the word unto them*} "Preached" is lit. "speaking," here meaning the most serious kind of speech, with some emphasis on the sound and manner of speaking.

3. {*And they come*} (cf. Luke 5:18). This Greek tense is the vivid dramatic historical present, drawing the reader into the narrative. {*Borne by four*} This is another unique Markan detail.

4. {*They uncovered the roof*} Lit. "They unroofed the roof." They climbed up a stairway on the outside or ladder to the flat tile roof and dug out or broke up the tiles of the roof. {*They let down the bed*} (cf. Luke 5:19). Note the historical present again. Probably the four men had a rope fastened to each corner of the pallet or poor man's bed.

5. {*Their faith*} That is, the faith of the four men and of the man himself. There is no reason for excluding his faith. They all had confidence in the power and willingness of Jesus to heal this desperate case. {*Are forgiven*} (cf. Matt. 9:3 and Luke 5:20). Astonishing to the five, Jesus forgave his sins instead of healing him. The sins had probably caused the paralysis.

7. {*He blasphemeth*} The Greek word *blasphêmeô* means injurious speech or slander. It was, they held, blasphemy for Jesus to assume this divine prerogative. Their logic was correct. The only flaw in it was the possibility that Jesus held a peculiar relation to God which justified his claim.

12. {*Before them all*} (cf. Luke 5:25). It was an amazing proceeding and made it unnecessary for Jesus to refute the scribes further on this occasion. In ecstasy, the people could only say: "We have never seen anything like this." It was "remarkable" (Greek *paradoxa*, Luke 5:26).

14. {*And as he passed by*} Always alert for opportunities to do good, he finds Levi (Matthew), son of Alpheus, sitting at the tollgate on the Great West Road from Damascus to the Mediterranean.

16. {*The scribes of the Pharisees*} More than simply accepting Levi's invitation, these "sinners" became followers of Jesus; a motley crew from the standpoint of these young theologues. Tax collectors and sinners were regarded like Gentiles. Jews were not to eat with Gentiles (1 Cor. 5:11).

19. {*The sons of the bridechamber*} Lit. "sons of the bridegroom," this includes groomsmen and guests (cf. John 3:29). Jesus identifies himself with the bridegroom of the OT (Hos. 2:21).

23. {*Through the cornfields*} (cf. Matt. 12:1 and Luke 6:1). This is to go along beside on the edge of the field, Luke has "going through" the grain. {*Plucking the ears*} The rabbis called this action preparing food (cf. Matt. 12:1-8 and Luke 6:15).

26. {*The house of God*} This refers to a tent or tabernacle at Nob, not the temple in Jerusalem built by Solomon. {*Abiathar...*} (cf. 1 Sam. 22:20; 2 Sam. 8:17; 1 Chr. 18:16). They had the most elaborate rules for the preparation of the shewbread (loaves of presentation in the presence of God). It was renewed on the commencement of the Sabbath and the old bread deposited on the golden table in the porch of the Sanctuary. This old bread was eaten by the priests as they came and went. This is what David ate.

27. {*Sabbath was made for man*} Sabbath is subordinate to mankind's real welfare, contrary to the rabbis' way of viewing it (cf. 2 Macc. 5:19). So for the Christian, the church itself is for man, not man for the church.

CHAPTER 3

1. {*Had his hand withered*} His right hand was in a withered state (Luke 6:6); Greek syntax is showing that it was not congenital, but the result of injury by accident or disease.

2. {*They watched...*} (cf. Matt. 12:10). This is the Greek verb *paratêreô*, watching on the side (or sly); the kind of action in the Greek shows their personal interest in the proceedings. They were ready to catch him in the act if he should dare to violate their rules (as in the previous wheat fields incident).

3. {*Stand forth*} That is, step into the middle of the room where all can see. It was a bold defiance of the Christ's spying enemies.

5. {*When he had looked round on them with anger*} (cf. The "looks" of Jesus, Mark 3:5, 34; 5:37; 9:8; 10:23; 11:11, also Luke 6:10). Not inconsistent with love or pity, the eyes of Jesus swept the room all round and each felt the cut of that condemnatory glance. {*Being grieved at the hardness of their hearts*} Unique to Mark, the anger was tempered by grief (Swete); Jesus is the Man of Sorrows, constant in the state of grief in contrast to the momentary angry look. Their own "stubborn" heart or attitude was in a state of moral ossification (Greek *pôrôsis*) like calloused, hardened hands or feet (cf. Matt. 12:9-14).

7. {*Withdrew to the sea*} On eleven occasions Mark mentions the withdrawals of Jesus to escape his enemies, for prayer, for rest, for private conference with his disciples (Mark 1:12; 3:7; 6:31, 46; 7:24, 31; 9:2; 10:1; 14:34).

10. {*Pressed upon him*} Not hostile, the crowd was simply intensely eager, each to have his own case attended to by Jesus; creating a danger. {*That they might touch him*} A really pathetic scene, they hoped for a cure by contact with Christ. {*As many as had plagues*} Lit. "strokes or scourges," terms used by us today as a paralytic stroke (cf. Mark 5:29, 34; Luke 7:21 also 2 Macc. 9:11).

11. {*Whensoever they beheld him...*} Greek tenses of the verbs in this verse show that the demons *kept on* falling down before him and kept crying out who he was; but Jesus did not wish this testimony.

14. {*Whom he also named apostles*} Jesus himself gave the name apostle or missionary to this group of twelve. The word is applied in the New Testament to others besides as delegates or messengers of churches (1 Cor. 8:23; Phil. 2:25), and messenger (John 13:16). It is applied also to Paul on a par with the twelve (Gal. 1:1,11, etc.) and also to Barnabas (Acts 14:14), and perhaps also to Timothy and Silas (1 Tim. 2:6ff.). Note the two purposes: 1) to be with Jesus. 2) to send them forth (with a double ministry of preaching and healing). They were not ready to be sent forth until they had been with Jesus for some time.

16. {*Simon he surnamed Peter*} (cf. John 1:42; Luke 6:14). "Peter/Cephas" (lit. "Rock") is the surname Jesus gave Simon (cf. Matt. 16:18).

17-18. {*Boanerges, which is Sons of thunder...*} (cf. Luke 9:34). This name may refer to the fiery temperament revealed when James and John wanted to call down fire on the Samaritan villages that were unfriendly to them. Some names here are Greek, and some Hebrew; each name with a designated meaning.

20. {*And he cometh into a house*} Probably this refers to the house of Simon (cf., Mark 1:29). There has been some interval here in giving the Sermon on the Mount (Matt. 5-7), which Mark passes over to focus on the continued action of Jesus.

21. {*His friends*} Lit. "those from the side of him (i.e., Jesus); this could refer to a circle of disciples, but the idiom most likely means the kinspeople or family of Jesus. {*He is beside himself*} (cf. Acts 26:24; 2 Cor. 5:13). Mary probably felt that Jesus was overwrought and wished to take him home out of the excitement and strain that he might get rest and proper food.

23. {*In parables*} (Matt. 13:1ff.). A parable is from the Greek word *parabolê*, "placing beside for comparison."

27. {*Spoil*} This word means to plunder, to thoroughly ransack.

29. {*Guilty of an eternal sin*} This unpardonable sin can be committed today by men who call the work of Christ the work of the devil.

31. {*Standing without*} Crowded out, this is a pathetic picture of the mother and brothers outside thinking that Jesus inside is beside himself and wanting to take him home.

32. {*Was sitting about him*} They sat in a circle around Jesus with the disciples forming a sort of inner circle.

CHAPTER 4

7. {*Choked*} This is the Greek verb *sunpnigô* means squeeze together (cf. Matt. 13:7). {*Yielded no fruit*} This detail is in Mark alone.

8. {*Growing up and increasing*} This vivid detail is in Mark alone. It kept on yielding as it grew. Fruit is what matters.

10. {*When he was alone*} Unique to Mark, this is a vivid recollection of Peter. They did not want the multitude to see that they did not understand the teaching of Jesus.

11. {*Unto you is given the mystery of the kingdom of God*} (Mark 4:11; Matt. 13:11; Luke 8:10). "Secret" is the Greek word *mustêrion*, "mystery," used by Paul in the epistles and John in the Revelation. The secret is no longer hidden from the initiated. Discipleship means initiation into the secret of God's kingdom and it will come gradually to these men. {*But unto them that are without*} That is, outside our circle, the uninitiated, the hostile group like the scribes and Pharisees. Without the key the parables are hard to understand, for parables veil the truth of the kingdom being stated in terms of another realm.

12. {*Lest*} (cf. Isa. 6:9). God ironically commands Isaiah to harden the hearts of the people. Parables are used on this occasion as a penalty for judicial blindness on those who will not see. {*Haply they should turn again, and it should be forgiven them*} Jesus is pronouncing the Pharisees doom in the language of Isaiah for willful blindness and rejection of him. It sounds like the dirge of the damned.

13. {*Know ye not this parable?*} This question implies surprise at their dullness though initiated into the secret of God's Kingdom.

15. {*Satan*} (cf. "evil one" Matt. 13:19 and "devil" Luke 8:12). {*Sown in them*} This is "within [the heart]" not "among."

19. {*The lusts of other things*} That is, meaning here all the passions or longings, sensual, worldly, "pleasures of this life" (cf. Luke 8:14), the world of "sense" drowning the world of "spirit."

21. {*Not to be put on the stand?*} The lamp in the one-room house was a familiar object along with the bushel, the bed, the lampstand. The first question of the sentence in the Greek syntax, expects a "no" answer (the flame would go out or start a fire); but a "yes" in the second.

22. {*Save that it should be manifested*} (cf. Luke 8:17). Temporary concealment is for final manifestation and a means to that end.

23. {*Let him hear*} (cf. Mark 4:9). Perhaps some inattention was noted.

24. {*What ye hear*} (cf. "how" you hear, Luke 8:18) Some things should not be heard at all for they besmirch the mind and heart. What is worth hearing should be heard rightly and heeded.

27. {*He knoweth not how*}. The mystery of continual growth (regardless of the farmers' schedule) still puzzles farmers and scientists of today with all our modern knowledge.

28. {*Of herself*} This is the Greek word *automatê*, "automatically," we say (cf. automatic city gate, Acts 12:10). The secret of growth is in the seed, not in the soil nor in the weather nor in the cultivating. These all help, but the seed spontaneously works according to its own nature. So we sow the seed, God's kingdom truth, and the soil (the soul) is ready for the seed. The Holy Spirit works on the heart and uses the seed sown and makes it germinate and grow. This is the law and order of nature and also of grace in the kingdom of God. Hence it is worth while to preach and teach.

29. {*Putteth forth*} "Puts" is the Greek verb *apostellô*, "sends forth" the sickle (= reapers). The word for *apostle* comes from this verb (cf. John 4:38).

30. {*How shall we liken?*} (cf. Luke 13:18 and Matt. 13:31). The graphic question draws the interest of the hearers (*we*) by fine tact. This is probably one of Christ's favorite sayings, often repeated to different audiences.

31-32. {*Less than all the seeds*} Lit. "smaller of seeds." Though of course hyperbole, this means that from a very small seed a large plant grows, the gradual pervasive expansive power of the kingdom of God. The use of the mustard seed for smallness seems to have been proverbial and Jesus employs it elsewhere (Matt. 13:32; 17:20; Luke 17:6).

34. {*But privately to his disciples he expounded all things*} In private the further disclosures of Jesus amounted to fresh revelations concerning the mysteries of the kingdom of God.

35. {*Let us go over unto the other side*} They were on the western side and a row over to the eastern shore in the evening would be a delightful change and refreshing to the weary Christ. It was the only way to escape the crowds.

36. {*Even as he was*} That is, they take Jesus along without previous preparation. {*Other boats*} There was a crowd even on the lake.

37. {*There ariseth a great storm of wind*} (cf. Matt. 8:24 and Luke 8:23). "Came" is a vivid historical present, drawing the reader into the narrative. The storm fell suddenly from Mount Hermon down into the Jordan Valley and hit the Sea of Galilee violently at its depth of 682 feet below the Mediterranean Sea. The hot air at this depth draws the storm down with sudden power. These sudden storms continue to this day on the Sea of Galilee (cf. Jonah 1:4). Greek tense shows the waves broke over and over against the boat; a graphic description of the plight of the disciples.

38. {*They awake him, carest thou not?*} "Woke" is in the graphic present, drawing the reader into the narrative.

39. {*Rebuked the wind*} (cf. Matt. 8:26; Luke 8:24). The calm was sudden. He rebuked nature, and then rebuked the disciples for their lack of faith.

40. {*Have ye not yet faith?*} They had not yet come to feel that Jesus was really Lord of nature. They had accepted his Messiaship, but all the conclusions from it they had not yet drawn.

41. {*They feared exceedingly*} Lit. "they feared a great fear"; it was fear mixed with marvel (cf. Matt. 8:27; Luke 8:22). {*Who then is this?*} No wonder they feared this majestic Jesus! He commanded nature, demons, diseases, and revealed mysteries. They were growing in their apprehension and comprehension of Jesus Christ.

CHAPTER 5

1. {*The Gerasenes*} (cf. Luke 8:26 and "Gadarenes" Matt. 8:28). The ruins of the village Khersa (Gerasa) probably point to this site which is in the district of Gadara some six miles southeastward, not to the city of Gerasa some thirty miles away.

2. {*A man with an unclean spirit*} (cf. Luke 9:27). Matthew notes two demoniacs (Matt. 8:28).

4. {*Often bound*} "Fetters" are possibly cords or wooden stocks (not necessarily chains) and handcuff chains. {*Rent asunder*} Perhaps the neighbors who told the story could point to broken fragments of chains and fetters.

5. {*He was crying out, and cutting himself with stones*} The verb for "cutting himself" occurs here only in the NT. It means to "cut down." We say "cut up, gash, hack to pieces." Perhaps he was scarred all over with such gashes during his moments of wild frenzy night and day in the tombs and on the mountains.

6. {*Ran and worshipped*} "Running" at first perhaps with hostile intentions; then to the Twelve's surprise, he threw himself on his knees (Swete).

7. {*I adjure thee by God*} (cf. Luke 8:28; also Gen. 14:18). {*Torment me not*} The word means to test metals and then to test one by torture (cf. our "third degree").

8. {*For he said*} (cf. Matt. 8:29). Greek tense shows Jesus had already repeatedly ordered the demon to come out of the man.

9. {*My name is Legion*} (cf. Luke 8:30). A full Roman legion had 6,826 men (cf. Matt. 26:53), though this number may have been less.

13. {*And he gave them leave*} Why did Jesus not just send them back to the abyss? Better for hogs to perish than men, but this loss of property raises a difficulty. And how can a man contain so many demons; or just one demon make his abode there for that matter? Historical exaggeration is too easy an explanation (cf. multiple demon possession, Matt. 12:45). {*They were choked*} Greek tense pictures graphically the disappearance of pig after pig in the sea (cf. Luke 8:33).

15. {*And they were afraid*} Lit. "they became afraid." Once these had all been afraid of a wild, violent, naked man; now he was sitting clothed and in his right mind and they became afraid. The pagan influence of Decapolis feared the power of Jesus and wanted no further interference with their business affairs. The healing of the human and destruction of the hogs were all by this same Jesus.

19-20. {*Go to thy house unto thy friends*} Jesus had greatly blessed this man and so gave him the hardest task of all, to go home and witness there for Christ (to a people certainly needing the message).

Thousands of like cases of conversion under Christ's power have happened in rescue missions in our cities.

23. {*My little daughter*} "Little" has an implication of endearment in this tragic moment for Jairus. She was in her last stages before death.

24. {*He went with him*} The Greek tense shows Jesus promptly went. But in contrast the Greek tense shows the crowds kept on following and pressing him, so Jesus could hardly move or breathe because of the crowd (cf. Luke 8:42).

26. {*Had spent all that she had*} Lit. "all from herself," i.e., all her resources. Her money was gone, her disease was gaining on her; her one chance came now with Jesus (cf. Luke 8:43).

29. {*She felt in her body*} "Felt" is literally "She knew."

30. {*Perceiving in himself*} More exactly translate the meaning: "Jesus perceiving in himself the power from him go out." Certainly Jesus was conscious of the going out of power from himself. No real good can be done without the outgoing of power. That is true of mother, preacher, teacher, doctor.

34. {*Go in peace*} "Peace" here may have more the idea of the Hebrew *shalôm*, health of body and soul.

35. {*While he yet spake*} Chapter five well preserves the eyewitness details of Peter. The arrival of the messengers diverted attention from the woman just healed. {*Why troublest thou the master any further?*} (cf. Luke 7:11-17). They felt it was all over. People in general did not expect him to raise the dead. "Bother" is the Greek word *skullô*, from *skulon* (*skin, pelt, spoils*), means "to skin, to flay." Then it comes to mean "to cause vexation, annoy, distress" (cf. Matt. 9:36).

37. {*Save Peter, and James, and John*} Probably the house was too small for the other disciples to come in with the family. Greek syntax shows this is considered a unit; it is an inner circle of three at certain times (Mark 9:2; 13:3).

38. {*Wailing greatly*} "Wailing" is the Greek verb *alalazô*. Soldiers on entering battle cried *Alâla,* so it is a Greek word whose sound helps define its meaning (onomatopoetic). It is used here of the monotonous wail of the hired mourners.

40. {*And they laughed him to scorn*} Translate Greek tense, "they kept up jeering him." This jeering was to an intense (perfective) degree the form of the Greek word shows. The loud laughter was ill suited to the solemn occasion. {*Taketh the father of the child and her mother*} *and them that were with him*} Acting virtually as the master of the house, he removes the "mourners" in the house, using pressure and sternness. Taking these five to the chamber of death, the presence of these will not ruin the atmosphere for spiritual work (as would have the others).

41. {*Talitha cumi*} Aramaic, Peter heard and remembered and gives the words of Jesus to us. {*Damsel, arise*} (cf. Luke 8:5-9). This is a young girl (twelve years), but the form of the Greek word also implies an endearing term "little girl." Jesus took her by the hand, a touch of life, giving confidence and help.

CHAPTER 6

1. {*Into his own country*} (cf. Matt. 13:54). Obviously referring to Nazareth, this is a different visit than Luke 4:26-31. Though he was rejected both times, it is reasonable to think Jesus gave Nazareth a second chance. Bethlehem was his birthplace, not his hometown.

2. {*Began to teach*} This was now his custom in the synagogue on the Sabbath. The reputation of Jesus all over Galilee opened the door for him. {*Whence hath this man these things?*} The townsmen knew Jesus and they had never suspected that he possessed such gifts and graces. They felt that there was some hocus-pocus about it somehow and somewhere.

3. {*Is not this the carpenter?*} (cf. Matt. 13:55). Evidently since Joseph's death he had carried on the business. "Carpenter" is the Greek word *tektôn*, from *tekein, tiktô*, to beget, create, like *technê* (craft, art). It was used of any artisan or craftsman in metal, or in stone as well as in wood and even of sculpture. It is certain that Jesus worked in wood (known from an early Church writer); he may also have worked in stone and may even have helped build some of the stone synagogues in Galilee like that in Capernaum. {*And they were offended in him*} (cf. Matt. 13:56). Lit. "were made to stumble in him," trapped like game by the *skandalon* because they could not explain him, having been so recently one of them; he was a rock of offense (cf. 1 Pet. 2:7,8; Rom. 9:33).

6. {*And he marvelled because of their unbelief*} Showing a human limitation in certain things that are not clear to us. He marveled at the faith of the Roman centurion where one would not expect it (Matt. 8:10; Luke 7:9). Here he marvels at the lack of faith where he had a right to expect it, his own hometown, his kinspeople, his own home. {*He went round about the villages teaching*} An entirely new paragraph begins with these words, the third tour of Galilee, and so placed in verse seven. He resumes as a wandering preacher.

7. {*By two and two*} Six pairs of apostles could cover Galilee in six different directions. {*He gave...*} The Greek tense shows he *kept on giving* them power all through the tour, a continuous power (authority) over unclean spirits (representing disease and sickness [Matt. 10:1-7; Luke 9:1]).

8. {*Save a staff only*} Every traveler and pilgrim carried his staff. Compare that Matthew 10:10 says "nor staff" and Luke 9:3 "neither staff." This discrepancy has given trouble to commentators. Some suggest "no second staff" for the travelers is what is meant in Matthew and Luke.

9. {*Shod with sandals*} Again, Matthew 10:10 has "nor shoes." This may mean "no extra sandals," or other possible explanations. {*Two coats*} Two is a sign of comparative wealth; this "two" may give the contextual answer to the above apparent discrepancy between Mark and Matthew and Luke on the issue of staff and sandals.

11. {*For a testimony unto them*} (cf. Luke 9:5). If the conditions were met, then "shaking the dust off" was a command.

13. {*They cast out many demons and they anointed with oil*} This is the only example in the NT of "anointing with oil" used in connection with healing except in James 5:14. In both cases it is possible that the use of oil (olive oil) as a medicine is the basis of the practice. See Luke 10:34 for pouring oil and wine upon the wounds. It was the best medicine of the ancients and was used internally and externally. The only problem is whether "anointing" in Mark and James is used wholly in a ritualistic and ceremonial sense or partly as medicine and partly as a symbol of divine healing. The very word for "anointing" can be translated rub or anoint without any ceremony. Greek tense shows they did this over and over, with continued repetition. God and medicine, then and today. God through nature does the real healing when we use medicine and the doctor.

16. {*John, whom I beheaded*} Herod's fears got the best of him and so Herod settled down on this nightmare, now recognizing his guilt.

17. {*For Herod himself*} Here is a narrative of the death of the Baptist, in a close to chronological order. News of the murder of the Baptist seems to have brought the recent Galilee tour to an end. When Jesus heard it, he withdrew from there in a boat (Matt. 14:12).

18. {*Thy brother's wife*} That is, while the brother was alive (Lev. 18:16; 20:21); but a duty after death of the brother.

19. {*And Herodias set herself against him*} Lit. "had it in for him." The Greek tense aptly describes how Herodias *kept up* her hostility towards him. She never let up.

20. {*Feared John*} Greek tense shows a continual state of fear. He feared John and also Herodias. Between the two Herod vacillated. Herodias was another Jezebel towards John and with Herod. {*He heard him gladly*} This is the way that Herod really felt when he could slip away from the snares of Herodias.

22. {*The daughter of Herodias herself*} Salome was her given name. Toward the close of the banquet, when all had partaken freely of the wine, Herodias made her daughter come in and dance. Such a dance was an almost unprecedented thing for women of rank, or even respectability, customarily performed by professionals. Herodias thus degraded her own daughter in order to carry out her purpose against John. {*She pleased Herod and them that sat at meat*} The maudlin group lounging on the divans were thrilled by the licentious dance of the half-naked princess. {*Whatsoever thou wilt*} The drunken Tetrarch had been caught in the net of Herodias. It was a public promise.

23. {*And he sware unto her*} The girl was of marriageable age (cf. Esth. 2:9). The event and oath reminds one of Esther 5:3, given by Ahasuerus.

24. {*What shall I ask for?*} (cf. Matt. 14:8). The action of verb in the Greek implies Salome is thinking of something for herself. She was no doubt unprepared for her mother's ghastly reply.

25. {*Straightway with haste*} That is, before the king's rash mood passed, still under her dancing spell (cf. Matt. 14:8ff.).

30. {*And the apostles gather themselves together unto Jesus*} This is in the vivid historical present tense, drawing the reader into the narrative. {*All things whatsoever they had done and whatsoever they had taught*} The Greek tense shows the report as a summing up of it all, their first tour without Jesus (cf. Luke 9:10).

31. {*Come ye yourselves apart into a desert place and rest awhile*} Overwrought and excited, the apostles needed personal refreshment. The disciples cheerfully complied. Here is a needed lesson for all preachers and teachers: occasional change and refreshment. Even Jesus felt the need of it.

34. {*They were as sheep not having a shepherd*} Jesus had come over for rest, but his heart was touched by the *pathos* of this situation; the people needed leaders who were not spiritually blind.

35. {*When the day was now far spent*} It was after 3 p.m., sunset was approaching (cf. Matt. 14:15).

36. {*Into the country and villages round about*} Countryside is lit. "fields" and were the scattered farms. The villages may have included Bethsaida Julias (eastern side) not far away (Luke 9:10). The other Bethsaida was on the western side of the lake (Mark 6:45).

39. {*By companies*} The Greek word *sumposia*, here a party or group of guests of any kind; repeated to show distribution. {*Upon the green grass*} It was Passover time (John 6:4) and the afternoon sun shone upon the orderly groups sitting on the green spring grass (cf. Matt. 14:15). They may have been seated like companies at tables, open at one end.

40. {*They sat down in ranks*} Arranged in groups by hundreds and by fifties, they looked like garden beds with their many-colored clothes which even men wore in the Orient. Color and order were in the scene, and Peter never forgot the picture (so Mark wrote down this memory of Peter).

44. {*Men...five thousand*} (Matt. 14:21). Recorded by all four Gospels (told through the eyes of Matthew, Peter [i.e., Mark's Gospel], and John the Beloved); this is a nature miracle that only God can work. "Men" is male and not generic for human beings.

45. {*To Bethsaida*} That is, western Bethsaida (cf. Luke 9:10). {*While he himself sendeth the multitude away*} (cf. Matt. 14:22). Here Jesus is personally engaged in persuading the crowds to go away now (cf. John 6:41). The crowds had become so excited that they were in the mood to start a revolution against the Roman government and proclaim Jesus king. {*To go before him*} Jesus sends them ahead to keep the disciples from being swept into the danger of mixing a political twist to the whole conception of the Messianic Kingdom (a Pharisaic concept). Jesus needed the Father to stay and steady him.

47. {*When even was come*} This is the time from sunset on, about 6 p.m. this time of year. {*He alone on the land*} After prayer time with the Father, apparently Jesus remained some hours on the beach (cf. John 6:17).

48. {*About the fourth watch of the night*} That is, between 3 and 6 A.M. {*And he would have passed by them*} Lit. "he wished to pass by them."

49. {*And cried out*} Lit. this was a shriek of terror, or scream.

51. {*They were sore amazed in themselves*} Note here that Mark does not give the incident of Peter's walking on the water and then sinking. Perhaps Peter was not fond of telling that story.

52. {*Was hardened*} Their reasoning process (Greek *kardia*) was hardened ("heart" here is in the general sense for all the inner man).

53. {*And moored to the shore*} They cast anchor or lashed the boat to a post on shore. It was at the plain of Gennesaret several miles south of Bethsaida owing to the night wind.

54. {*Knew him*} The Greek word means they were knowing fully.

CHAPTER 7

2. {*With defiled, that is unwashen hands*} "Unclean" is the Greek word *koinos*; means here what is vulgar or profane and so ceremonially unclean (cf. Acts 10:14). For sanitary reasons, washing is proper; but the objection raised here is on ceremonial, not sanitary, grounds.

3. {*Diligently*} (cf. Matt. 15:2). Lit. "they wash with the fist." That is, wash up to the elbow, rubbing one hand and arm with the other hand clenched. The Greek word is the washing of a part of the body. There is another verb that is used of washing the whole body.

4. {*Wash themselves*} This is the Greek verb *baptizô*, (cf. baptize) dip or immerse. In context, the likely meaning of this is the hands were *always* washed before eating (verse 3), now by way of climax, *when they come from market* they take a bath before eating (Meyer). In the next verse various utensils were also ceremonially dipped.

8. {*Ye leave the commandment of God*} Driving a keen wedge, Jesus shows the Pharisees have covered up the Word of God with their oral teaching. The Talmud gives abundant and specific confirmation of the truthfulness of this indictment (the Talmud is the book consisting of codified Jewish oral tradition and a commentary on it).

11. {*Corban*} (cf. Matt. 15:5). Mark preserves the Hebrew word for a "gift" or "offering" to God (Exod. 21:17; Lev. 20:9). The mere saying of

"Corban" by an unfaithful son could prevent (and justify) the use of needed money for the support of father or mother. But he might use it for himself!

13. {*Making void the word of God by your tradition*} (cf. Matt. 15:6). They actually were invalidating, stronger than setting aside; though setting aside also does invalidate something (verse 9).

17. {*When he was entered into the house from the multitude*} (cf. Matt. 15:15). Unique detail to Mark, this probably refers to Peter's house in Capernaum. The parable referred to here is the parable of corban.

19. {*Making all meats clean*} Peter reports this comment to Mark, probably recalling the vision on the housetop in Joppa (Acts 10:14-16). Jesus did not directly say this here in the story. Peter was slow to understand this revolutionary declaration, a truly new spiritual insight, even after the coming of the Holy Spirit at Pentecost.

21-23. {*Evil thoughts...*} The inner man is the source of the following dreadful list: {*Fornications*} Usually of the unmarried. {*Adulteries*} Of the married. {*Thefts*} Stealing. {*Coveting*} Craving for more and more. {*Murders*} Growing out of the others. {*Lasciviousness*} That is, unrestrained sex instinct. {*Railing*} That is, blasphemy, hurtful speech. {*Pride*} That is, holding oneself above others; stuck up. {*Foolishness*} A lack of sense.

24. {*And he could not be hid*} Jesus craved a little privacy and rest. This was his purpose in going into Phoenicia.

25. {*Having heard of him*} (cf. Luke 6:17). Even in this heathen territory the fame of Jesus was known. When the Sermon on the Mount was preached, people were there from the coast of Tyre and Sidon.

26. {*A Greek, a Syro-Phoenician by race*} She was a Greek in religion, a Syrian in tongue, a Phoenician in race, not a Phoenician of Carthage. {*She besought*} Greek tense shows she kept up the begging for a request (not a mere question).

27. {*Let the children first be filled*} (cf. Matt. 10:5). The Jews had the first claim. Even Paul, Apostle to the Gentiles, gave the Jew the first opportunity (Rom. 2:9)

28. {*Even the dogs under the table... eat of the children's crumbs*} This is a delightful picture of little household dogs under the table. The Greek shows these are all little dogs, little scraps, little children. Probably a picture of little children purposely dropping a few little crumbs for the little dogs. With wit and faith, the Gentile (dog) woman begs for help from Jesus for her little daughter.

29. {*For this saying*} (cf. Matt. 15:28). She had great faith, and the quick and bright repartee pleased Jesus. He had missed his rest, but it was worth it to answer a call like this.

33. {*Took him aside*} The secrecy was partly to avoid excitement and partly to get the attention of the deaf and dumb demoniac. Saliva was by some regarded as remedial and was used by exorcists in their incantations; there was, of course, no virtue in the spittle; Jesus may have used it as a concession to the denseness of the man.

34. {*Ephphatha*} An Aramaic word preserved and transliterated, meaning "be opened." The deep sigh here shows that somehow he felt a nervous strain, which we do not fully know.

36. {*So much the more a great deal they published it*} (cf. Mark 1:44). The Greek tense shows they talked as a continued action. Human nature is a peculiar thing. Prohibitions always affect some people that way, especially superficial and light-headed folks. But we have to have prohibitions or anarchy.

37. {*He hath done all things well*} The Greek tense shows the settled convictions of these people about Jesus.

CHAPTER 8

1. {*Had nothing to eat*} Called the feeding of the four thousand, this event is clearly distinct from the feeding of the five thousand. It is given here and in Matthew, and Jesus later refers to both incidents as different events. (Mark 8:19; Matt. 16:9).

4. {*Here*} This is a desert region in the mountains. The disciples again feel as helpless. They do not rise to faith in the unlimited power of Jesus after all that they have seen.

10. {*Into the parts of Dalmanutha*} (cf. Matt. 15:39 where it is called "the borders of Magadan." Unknown elsewhere, apparently this is the same region of Galilee on the western side of the lake not far from Tiberias.

12. {*He sighed deeply in his spirit*} The form of the Greek word shows a deep, intense sigh, from the bottom of his heart. Jesus resented the settled prejudice of his enemies, now joining together against him.

15. {*Take heed, beware of the leaven of the Pharisees, and the leaven of Herod*} The Greek tense shows the warning was repeatedly charged, showing that the warning was needed. The disciples were steeped in the Pharisees' atmosphere. Yeast can have a good or bad sense (Matt. 13:33; cf. 1 Cor. 5:6). Here it is bad, even insidious: Herodian yeast refers to bad politics; Pharisaic yeast refers to bad theology *and* bad politics.

16. {*They reasoned one with another*} (cf. Matt. 16:7). The Greek tense shows they kept up the discussion.

22. {*Unto Bethsaida*} This is the eastern Bethsaida Julias. Note all the action in the verse is in the vivid dramatic present—"they come" and "they bring"—drawing the reader into the narrative.

25. {*He looked steadfastly*} He saw thoroughly now, completely restored; and the Greek tense shows he kept on seeing all things clearly or at a distance.

26. {*To his home*} He was not allowed to enter the village and create excitement before Jesus moved on to Caesarea Philippi.

27. {*Into the villages of Caesarea Philippi*} (cf. Matt. 16:13). This is not the town on the Mediterranean Sea. This is a district or region on a sloping spur of Mount Hermon in Iturea ruled by Herod Philip so that Jesus is safe from annoyance by Herod Antipas or the Pharisees and Sadducees.

29. {*Thou art the Christ*} (cf. Matt. 16:16; Luke 9:20). Mark omits all praise of Peter, probably because Peter had done so in his story of the incident. The disciples had confessed him as Messiah before (cf. John 1:41; 4:29; 6:69; Matt. 14:33), but Jesus had ceased to use the word "Messiah" to avoid political complications and a revolutionary movement (John 6:14).

31. {*After three days*} (cf. Matt. 16:21). This rainbow on the cloud was not seen. "After three days" does not mean "on the fourth day," but has the same sense as that in Matthew and Luke, else they are hopelessly contradictory.

32. {*Spake the saying openly*} (cf. Mark 8:29; Matt. 16:16; Luke 9:20). He held back nothing, told it all, without reserve, to all of them. The Greek tense shows Jesus did it repeatedly.

33. {*He turning about and seeing his disciples...*} (cf. Matt. 16:23). Peter had called Jesus off to himself, but Jesus quickly wheeled round on Peter. Jesus rebukes Peter in the full presence of the whole group.

Peter no doubt felt that it was his duty as a leader of the Twelve to remonstrate with the Master for this pessimistic utterance.

34. {*Deny himself* } (cf. Matt. 16:24). That is, say no *to himself*, a difficult thing to do. The shadow of Christ's Cross was already on him (Mark 8:31) and a cross faces all of Jesus' followers..

35. {*Save...lose...lose...save*} (cf. Matt. 16:25). There are two senses of "life" and "save" here.

38. {*For whosoever shall be ashamed of me and my words*} It is not a statement about the future conduct of one, but about his present attitude toward Jesus. The conduct of men toward Christ now determines Christ's conduct then. {*When he cometh...*} This refers to the second coming of Christ with the glory of the Father with his holy angels (cf. Matt. 16:27). This is a clear prediction of the final eschatological coming of Christ. Note that this verse goes with Mark 9:1 and so forms one paragraph.

CHAPTER 9

1. {*Till they see the kingdom of God come with power*} In context this may refer to the second coming (cf. Mark 8:38). But this brings a problem, since no one knows the hour of his coming (Mark 13:32). This can reasonably refer also to the next contextual event: the Transfiguration on Mount Hermon. It could also plausibly refer to the coming of the Holy Spirit on the great Day of Pentecost. Some think it refers to the destruction of the temple. It is at least open to question whether Jesus is speaking of the same event in Mark 8:38 and 9:1.

3. {*Glistering, exceeding white*} (cf. Matt. 17:2; Luke 9:29). {*So as no fuller on earth can whiten them*} This was the action of a fuller (professional cloth worker) whitening cloth. Probably the snow-capped summit of Hermon was visible on this very night.

4. {*Elijah with Moses*} Both were prophets and both dealt with law. Both had mysterious deaths. The next verse has Moses first in order.

6. {*For he wist not what to answer*} Perhaps Peter felt embarrassed at having been asleep (Luke 9:32) and the feast of tabernacles or booths was near.

8. {*Suddenly looking round about* } (cf. Matt. 17:8). This was the sudden glance around on the mountain side when the cloud with Moses and Elijah was gone. {*Jesus only with themselves*} (cf. Matt. 17:6). Mark shows their surprise at the situation.

9. {*Should have risen*} (cf. Luke 9:36). More exactly, "should rise." It was a high and holy secret experience that the chosen three had had for their future good and for the good of all.

12. {*Elijah...restoreth all things*} The Baptist is a restorer, as the promised Elijah and Forerunner of the Messiah (cf. Matt. 17:10-13). The disciples had not until now understood that the Baptist fulfilled the prophecy in Mal. 3:5.

18. {*Wheresoever it taketh him*} Lit. "Seizes him down." This is the English word *catalepsy* in the Greek; used in ancient medicine for fits. {*Dashes down*} That is, convulses, rends, tears asunder. {*Pineth away*} This is a word used elsewhere for drying or withering as of grass (cf. Jas. 1:11). The whole situation was a tragedy.

19. {*Bring him unto me*} The disciples had failed and their unbelief had led to this fiasco. Even the disciples were like and part of the *faithless, unbelieving* generation in which they lived. Jesus is not afraid to undertake this case. We can always come to Jesus when others fail us.

22. {*But if thou canst*} Jesus had asked (verse 21) the history of the case like a modern physician. The father gave it and added further pathetic details about the fire and the water. The form of the father's statement in Greek here suggests doubt whether the boy can be cured at all, though the father is not wholly without faith. It was a chronic and desperate case of epilepsy with the demon possession added. He ends his plea with a call for mercy.

23. {*If thou canst...*} The Greek has a neat idiom not preserved in the English translation, "can" (Greek *dunêi*) and "possible" (Greek *dunata*) have the same Greek root. This quick turn challenges the father's faith.

24. {*I believe; help my unbelief*} This is an exact description of his mental and spiritual state. He still had faith, but craved more. The Greek tense shows the father wants continuous help (in contrast to some kind of instant help), and the Greek mood is a respectful command to Jesus (imperative mood).

25. {*A multitude came running together...*} The Greek verb vividly describes the rapid gathering of the crowd to Jesus and the epileptic boy to see the outcome. {*Come out of him*} Regarding it as the cause of this misfortune, Jesus addresses the demon as a separate being from the boy as he often does.

28. {*Privately, saying*} Indoors the nine disciples seek an explanation for their colossal failure. They had cast out demons and wrought cures before.

29. {*Save by prayer*} Prayer is what the nine had failed to use. They were powerless because they were prayerless. Their self-complacency spelled defeat. They also had too much faith in themselves, too little in Christ (cf. Matt. 17:20).

32. {*But they understood not the saying*} The Greek tense shows they continued not to understand, even after the Transfiguration experience. They continued to be afraid to ask, perhaps with a bitter memory of the term "Satan" hurled at Peter when he protested the other time when Jesus spoke of his death (Mark 8:33; Matt. 16:23).

39. {*Forbid him not*} Greek syntax shows that John had been doing so, and he was now to stop it.

43. {*Into hell, into the unquenchable fire*} (cf. Matt. 18:8). The Greek word is not *Hades*, but *Gehenna*. "Never goes out" in the Greek is our very word *asbestos*. The "Valley of Hinnom" (lit. *Gehenna*) had been desecrated by the sacrifice of children to Molech so that as an accursed place it was used for the city garbage where worms gnawed and fires burned. It is thus a vivid picture of eternal punishment.

48. {*Their worm…*} (cf. Isa. 66:24). This animal preys upon the inhabitants of this dread realm. Gnawing worms and burning flame are two bold figures of *Gehenna*; but the dread reality is worse than these combined figures.

50. {*Have salt in yourselves*} (cf. salt of the earth, Matt. 5:13). Jesus warned them against losing the saltiness of the salt. Once gone, it is like an exploded shell, a burnt-out crater, a spent force. This is a warning for all Christians.

CHAPTER 10

1. {*Into the border of Judea and beyond Jordan*} A great deal of time has intervened (several months) between the end of chapter nine and here (cf. for these events see Matt. 18:1ff.; John 7-11; Luke 9:57-18:14 [one third of Luke's Gospel comes in here]). Jesus has begun his last journey to Jerusalem going north through Samaria, Galilee, across the Jordan into Perea, and back into Judea near Jericho to go up with the Passover pilgrims from Galilee (a long round about circuit to Jerusalem). Friendly crowds followed him in caravans, many of them actual followers.

2. {*Tempting him*} The word means either "test" or "tempt" (cf. Matt. 4:1), but their motive was evil, so "tempt" may be a better translation.

4. {*To write a bill of divorcement and to put her away*} (cf. Matt. 19:1-12). "Bill" is the Greek word *biblion*, lit. "little book." The Pharisees probably held to the liberal view of Rabbi Hillel, that is, easy divorce for almost any cause. In contrast, Jesus expounds the purpose of marriage (Gen. 2:24) and takes the stricter view of divorce, that of the school of Rabbi Shammai.

11. {*Whoever divorces his wife and marries another woman commits adultery*} (cf. except for fornication, Matt. 19:9). Mere formal divorce does not annul actual marriage consummated by the physical union. Breaking that bond does annul it.

12. {*If she herself shall put away her husband and marry another*} Greek and Roman law allowed the divorce of the husband by the wife though not provided for in Jewish law.

13. {*They brought*} The Greek tense implies repetition, i.e., bringing again and again. Note that this incident follows the discussion of marriage. These children (Greek *paidia*, Mark and Matthew; *brephê* [infants] in Luke) were of various ages. The mothers had reverence for Jesus and wanted him to touch them (but not for baptism or salvation).

14. {*He was moved with indignation*} The Greek tense shows that he *became* indignant, and is a strong word of deep emotion. {*Suffer the little children to come unto me*} Surely it ought to be a joy to parents to bring their children to Jesus; but to hinder their coming is a crime.

15. {*As a little child*} Jesus here presents the little child with trusting and simple and loving obedience as the model for adults in coming into the kingdom. Jesus does not here say that children are in the kingdom of God because they are children.

16. {*He took them in his arms*} This is a rebuke to the disciples. Tenderly, Jesus repeatedly blessed (as the Greek tense shows), laying his hands upon each of them. It was a great moment for each mother and child.

18. {*Why callest thou me good?*} (cf. Luke 18:19; Matt. 19:17). Probably, the young ruler was sincere, but Jesus challenges him to define his attitude towards him as was proper. The language is not a disclaiming of deity on the part of Jesus.

22. {*But his countenance fell*} "Face fell" is the Greek verb *stugnazô*, from *stugnos*, somber, gloomy, like a lowering cloud.

24. {*Were amazed*} The disciples gave a look of blank astonishment at this statement of Jesus. As was a common notion, they regarded wealth as a token of God's special favor. {*Children*} A tender expression of Jesus for the Twelve due to their perplexity over these difficult words.

25. {*Needle's eye*} (cf. Matt. 19:24). Luke uses a different Greek word for a surgical needle. Mark and Matthew use the Greek word for a common sewing needle, with a bored hole or "eye."

27. {*Looking on them*} (cf. Matt. 19:26). {*But not with God*} This verse shows that it is a needle in the saying of verse 25, and not other various petty theories of a gate called needle's eye.

32. {*And they were amazed...they that followed were afraid*} (cf. Luke 9:5). Going through Perea towards Jerusalem, they looked at Jesus walking ahead in solitude, solemnity, and a determination which foreboded danger. The Greek syntax may show only some of the disciples were afraid. They began to fear coming disaster as they neared Jerusalem. They read correctly the face of Jesus. {*And began to tell them the things that were to happen to him*} So Jesus tries once more; the fourth time (Mark 8:31; 9:13; 9:31, also Luke 18:34). Note in this passage the minds of two of the disciples were wholly occupied with plans of their own selfish ambition while Jesus was giving details of his approaching death and resurrection.

35. {*There come near unto him James and John*} (cf. Matt. 20:20). "Came" is in the dramatic present tense, drawing the reader into the narrative.

38. {*Or be baptized with the baptism that I am baptized with*} (cf. cup, Matt. 20:22) This (and cup) refers to death (Mark 14:36; Matt. 26:39; Luke 22:42, also Luke 12:50).

46. {*From Jericho*} Did this event happen while leaving or entering Jericho (cf. Matt. 20:29 and Luke 18:35)? The answer is there were two Jerichos: the old (Mark "leaving") and the new Roman (Luke "entering"). The new Jericho was about five miles west of the Jordan and fifteen east of Jerusalem, near the mouth of the *Wadi Kelt*, and more than a mile south of the site of the ancient town. {*Bartimaeus*} (cf.

Matt. 20:30). Matthew mentions two blind. {*Blind beggar*} (cf. Luke 18:35). A blind man begging by the side of the road was a common sight in the land of the Bible. Bartimaeus had his regular place.

48. {*Rebuked him*} Greek tense shows that they kept rebuking repeatedly (cf. Luke 18:39 and Matt. 20:31). They wanted him to become silent.

49. {*Stood still*} (cf. Matt. 20:32 and Luke 18:40). {*He calleth thee*} That was joyful news to Bartimaeus. This is in the vivid dramatic present.

50. {*Casting away his garment*} This is the outer robe which he cast aside in his haste, jumping to his feet.

51. {*Rabboni...that I may receive my sight*} (cf. John 20:16). "Rabbouni" is the Aramaic word translated "Lord" in Matthew 20:33 and Luke 18:41. The Greek word "see" shows that apparently he had once been able to see; he wanted to recover his sight. The Messiah was expected to give sight to the blind (Isa. 61:1; Luke 4:18; 7:22).

52. {*Followed...*} Greek tense shows Bartimaeus *kept on following* the caravan of Jesus into the new Jericho. {*Made thee whole*} is the Greek word commonly translated "save," and that may be the idea here.

CHAPTER 11

4. {*A colt tied at the door without in the open street*} That is, the colt was outside the house in the (apparently crooked) street, but fastened to the door.

5. {*Certain of those that stood there*} (cf. Luke 19:33). These are bystanders; called "owners" in Luke.

7. {*They bring the colt unto Jesus*} This is in the vivid historical present, drawing the reader into the narrative. "They"—evidently friends of Jesus. The owners acquiesced as Jesus had predicted.

8. {*Branches*} (cf. Matt. 21:4-9 and palm branches John 12:13). The deliberate conduct of Jesus (the Triumphal Entry) on this occasion could have but one meaning. It was the public proclamation of himself as the Messiah; the crowds fully realize the significance of it all. They think Messiah will set up his rule in opposition to that of Caesar, to drive Rome out of Palestine, to conquer the world for the Jews.

11. {*It being now eventide*} What a day it had been, this first day of the week we call Sunday! What did the apostles think now?

12. {*On the morrow*} (cf. Matt. 21:18). The time was likely before 6 A.M., our Monday morning.

13. {*If haply he might find anything thereon*} Hungry, Jesus went to a tree with promise but no performance; the fig had put out leaves as a sign of fruit. The early figs in Palestine do not get ripe before May or June.

14. {*No man eat fruit from thee henceforward forever*} (cf. Matt. 21:19). This is a wish for the future that, in its negative form, constitutes a curse on the tree. Jesus probably spoke in the Aramaic on this occasion. {*And his disciples heard it*} They were amazed, for it was not the fault of the poor fig tree that it had put out leaves. But Jesus offered no explanation at this time.

15. {*Began to cast out*} (cf. Matt. 21:12). This is the second cleansing of the temple; once in the beginning, once at the end of his ministry (cf. John 2:14).

16. {*Through the temple*} The temple authorities had prohibited using the outer court of the temple through the Precinct as a sort of short cut or by-path from the city to the Mount of Olives. But the rule was neglected and all sorts of irreverent conduct was going on that stirred the spirit of Jesus.

18. {*Sought how they might destroy him*} Greek tense shows that this was not a momentary attitude and intent but one that was continuous. Here both Sadducees (chief priests) and Pharisees (scribes) combine their resentment to Jesus and together determine to kill him. The climax has come right in the temple.

19. {*Every evening*} More exactly, "whenever it became late."

20. {*From the roots*} Mark alone gives this detail.

22. {*Have faith in God*} Here is the lesson for the disciples from the curse on the fig tree so promptly fulfilled (cf. Matt. 21:21).

23. {*Shall not doubt in his heart*} "Doubt" is the Greek verb *diakrinô*, and means a divided judgment, a wavering doubt (*dia* from *duo*, two, and *krinô*, to judge). This is not a single act of doubt. {*But shall believe*} Not a single act but continuous faith.

24. {*Believe that ye have received them*} That is the test of faith, the kind that sees the fulfillment before it happens.

25. {*Whensoever ye stand…*} Jesus does not mean by the use of "stand" here to teach that this is the only proper attitude in prayer. {*That your Father also may forgive you*} Evidently, God's willingness to forgive is limited by our willingness to forgive others. This is a solemn thought for all who pray (cf. Matt. 6:12,14).

27. {*The chief priests, and the scribes, and the elders*} Greek syntax shows these are three classes or groups in the Sanhedrin. This is a large committee of the Sanhedrin. {*By what authority...*} (cf. Matt. 21:23-27). The Greek tense of "doing" shows that "you *keep on* doing these things."

30. {*Answer me*} This sharp demand for a reply is only in Mark.

CHAPTER 12

1. {*A man planted a vineyard*} (cf. Matt. 21:33). {*A pit for the winepress*} This is the container or trough under the winepress on the hillside to catch the juice when the grapes were trodden.

2. {*At the season*} The season for the collection of the fruits.

6. {*A beloved son*} (cf. Luke 20:13). Evidently, Jesus has in mind the language of the Father to him at his baptism (Mark 1:11; Matt. 3:17; Luke 3:22).

10. {*This scripture*} (cf. Luke 4:21; John 19:37; Acts 1:16). A quotation from Ps. 118:22.

17. {*Marvelled greatly at him*} The form and tense of the Greek word show they kept on being thoroughly amazed.

18. {*There come unto him Sadducees*} Focusing now on the resurrection, the Sadducees now wanted to show their intellectual superiority to these inferior Pharisaic and Herodian theologians whom Jesus had already rebuffed (cf. Matt. 22:23-33).

19. {*Moses wrote*} (cf. Luke 20:28 [Gen. 38:8; Deut. 25:5]).

20. {*Took a wife*} Lit. "take a woman/wife" (cf. Luke 20:29). It means "to marry."

24. {*Is it not for this cause that ye err?*} The Greek expects a "yes" answer. "In error" is the Greek verb *planaomai*, to wander astray (cf. our word *planet*, wandering stars, cf. Jude 13) like the Latin *errare* (our *error*, err). {*That ye know not the scriptures...nor the power of God*} The Sadducees posed as men of superior intelligence and knowledge in opposition to the traditionalists among the Pharisees with their oral law. And yet on this very point they were ignorant of the Scriptures. How much error today is due to this same ignorance among the educated! These two kinds of ignorance generally go together (cf. 1 Cor. 15:34).

25. {*When they shall rise from the dead*} (cf. Matt. 22:30 and Luke 20:35). In error, the Pharisees regarded the future resurrection body as performing marriage functions. The Sadducees made this one of their objections, but at the same time revealed their own ignorance of the true resurrection body. {*As angels in heaven*} (cf. Matt. 22:30 and Luke 20:36). The angels are directly created, not procreated.

26. {*In the place concerning the Bush*} (cf. Exod. 3:3-6). That is, in the matter of, in the passage about the burning bush.

28. {*The first of all*} (cf. Matt. 22:36-40). That is, first in rank and importance (cf. Deut. 6:4 and Lev. 19:18).

34. {*Discreetly*} "Discreetly" is the Greek adverb *nounechôs*, from *nous* (intellect) and *echô*, to have. This has the sense of using the mind to good effect.

35-36. {*How say the scribes*} This question of Jesus points out a difficulty, the solution of which lay the key to the whole problem of His person and work. The scribes all taught that the Messiah was to be the son of David (John 7:41); Jesus was acclaimed as the son of David [showing humanity of Messiah] (Matt. 21:9). But David called the Messiah his Lord also [showing the deity of him] (cf. Ps. 110:1).

38. {*Beware of the scribes*} (cf. Matt. 23:1 and Luke 20:45-47). The scribes (teachers of the law) were the professional teachers of the current Judaism and were nearly all Pharisees. {*To walk in long robes*} This was the dress of dignitaries like kings and priests, receiving salutations in public places where people could see their dignity recognized.

40. {*Devour widows' houses*} They hoodwinked widows into giving their homes to the temple and took it for themselves; grabbing the homes of helpless widows. {*For a pretence make long prayers*} A pretense of extra piety, while robbing the widows and pushing themselves to the fore.

42. {*One poor widow*} This pauper is in extreme contrast to the rich (verse 41). {*Two mites*} Lit. "two *lepta*," a very small copper coin, which is 1/64th (less than two percent) of the day's wage of a common laborer.

43-44. {*More than all...*} It may mean, more than all the rich put together. {*All that she had...livelihood*} This means all her living or livelihood (Greek *bios*), not her life (Greek *zôê*).

CHAPTER 13

1-2. {*Master, behold, what manner of stones and what manner of buildings*} (cf. Matt. 24:1 and Luke 21:5). Josephus speaks of the great size of these stones and the beauty of the buildings. Some of these stones at the southeastern and southwestern angles survive today and measure from twenty to forty feet long and weigh a hundred tons. Jesus fully recognizes their greatness and beauty, having often observed them.

3. {*Over against the temple*} That is, in full view of the temple about which they had been speaking.

4. {*Tell us, when shall these things be?*} (cf. Matt. 24:1ff. and Luke 21:5-36). The events of this chapter (as in Matthew) are best explained that Jesus blended into one picture: 1) his death 2) the destruction of Jerusalem within that generation, 3) the second coming and end of the world (typified by the destruction of the city). The lines between these topics are not sharply drawn in the report and it is not possible for us to separate the topics clearly. This chapter in Mark may have been given in order to forewarn and forearm the readers against the coming catastrophe of the destruction of Jerusalem.

7. {*Must needs come to pass*} Jesus gave this prophecy in A.D. 30 (or 29). History is replete with documented examples of storms, famines (cf. Acts 11:28), wars, and outbreaks against the Jews, before it finally comes with the destruction of the city and temple by Titus in A.D. 70.

9. {*Councils*} Like the Sanhedrin in Jerusalem, these local Jewish councils were modeled after that one. {*Before governors and kings*} That is, Gentile rulers as well as before Jewish councils.

13. {*But he that endureth to the end*} Here Jesus means final salvation, not initial salvation.

14. {*Standing where he ought not*} (cf. Matt. 24:15-25, also 1 Macc. 1:54). This was fulfilled once by Antiochus Epiphanes (ruler of Syria who worshipped Zeus) and a second time by the armies of Rome. Mark personifies the abomination as personal (masculine).

23. {*But take ye heed*} Gullibility is no mark of a saint or of piety. "You" is emphatic here. Credulity ranks no higher than skepticism. God gave us our wits for self-protection. Christ has warned us beforehand.

24. {*The sun shall be darkened*} (cf. Isa. 13:9; Ezek. 32:7; Joel 2:1,10; Amos 8:9; Zeph. 1:14-16 Zech. 12:12). One should not forget that prophetic imagery was not always meant to be taken literally, especially apocalyptic symbols (cf. Acts 2:15-21).

27. {*Shall gather together his elect*} This is the purpose of God through the ages. {*From the uttermost part of the earth to the uttermost part of heaven*} Lit. "from the tip of earth to the tip of heaven."

32. {*Not even the Son*} (cf. Matt. 24:36). This disclaimer of knowledge naturally interpreted applies to the second coming, not to the destruction of Jerusalem.

34. {*Commanded also the porter to watch*} Our ignorance of the time of the Master's return is an argument not for indifference nor for fanaticism, but for alertness and eager readiness for his coming.

35. {*Evening...midnight...cock crowing...morning*} Note that these are the named four watches of the night.

37. {*Watch*} That is, be on the watch, be awake. Stay awake until the Lord comes.

CHAPTER 14

1. {*After two days*} This is our Tuesday evening (the beginning of the Jewish Wednesday). The Gospel of John mentions five items that superficially considered seem to contradict this definite date in Mark and Matthew, but which are really in harmony with them. Both "the Passover" and "the Unleavened Bread," cover the eight days. Sometimes "Passover" is applied to only the first day, sometimes to the whole period (cf. Matt. 26:2). No sharp distinction in usage was observed.

2. {*Not during the feast*} (cf. John 11:57). The Triumphal Entry and great Tuesday debate (this very morning) in the temple had made them decide to wait until after the feast was over (cf. Matt. 26:47).

3. {*As he sat at meat*} (cf. Matt. 26:6-13). This is a different incident from that recorded in Luke 7:36-50. {*Spikenard*} (cf. John 12:3). This is an unadulterated substance here. {*Brake*} She probably broke the narrow neck of the vase holding the ointment.

5. {*Above three hundred pence*} (cf. John 12:4-5). Lit. "three hundred denarii." A denarius was about a day's wage for a common laborer. {*And they murmured against her*} "Rebuked" is the striking word used of the snorting of horses (cf. Mark 1:43); it here has the sense of anger (cf. Dan. 11:30). Judas made this complaint against Mary of Bethany, but all the apostles joined in the chorus of criticism of the wasteful extravagance.

8. {*She hath done what she could*} Lit. "what she had she did." Mary could not comprehend the Lord's death, but she at least showed sympathy and some understanding with him. {*She hath anointed my body aforehand for the burying*} (cf. Matt. 26:12). Lit. "she took beforehand to anoint my body for the burial." She anticipated the event. This is Christ's justification of her noble deed.

9. {*For a memorial of her*} (cf. Matt. 26:13). This monument to Jesus fills the whole world still with its fragrance, greater than even permanent memorials.

10. {*He that was one of the twelve*} This phrase is not showing primacy, rather it calls attention that he was the one of the twelve who did this deed (cf. verse 20).

11. {*And they, when they heard it, were glad*} No doubt the rabbis looked on the treachery of Judas as a veritable dispensation of Providence amply justifying their plots against Jesus. {*Conveniently*} (cf. Luke 22:6). This was the whole point of the offer of Judas. He knew enough of the habits of Jesus to catch him before the Passover was over (cf. verse 2), away from the crowds (cf. Matt. 26:15 and Zech. 11:12). The amount of money offered Judas was the price of a slave.

12. {*When they sacrificed the passover*} (cf. Matt. 26:17). Greek tense shows this was the customary practice. The lamb was slain at 6 P.M., beginning on the fifteenth of the month (Exod. 12:6). Preparations were made beforehand on the fourteenth (Thursday).

13. {*Two of his disciples*} That is, Peter and John (cf. Luke 22:8).

14. {*The goodman of the house*} This means master (despot) of the house, householder. {*My guest-chamber*} (cf. Luke 2:7).

15. {*And he*} The "he" is emphatic in the Greek. {*A large upper room*} (cf. Luke 22:12). Jesus wishes to observe this last feast with his disciples alone, not with others as was often done. {*Furnished*} "With carpets and with couches properly spread" (Vincent).

17. {*He cometh*} This is a normal dinner time and date, 6 P.M., evening of our Thursday, beginning of Jewish Friday.

18. {*As they sat*} Reclined, of course. It is a pity that the verbs are not translated properly in English. Even Leonardo da Vinci in his immortal painting of the Last Supper has Jesus and his apostles sitting, not reclining. {*Even he that eateth with me*} To this day the Arabs will not violate hospitality by mistreating one who breaks bread with them in the tent.

20. {*The one dipping in the dish with me*} (cf. Matt. 26:21-24). This act escaped the notice of all, save Judas who understood perfectly.

23. {*A cup*} (cf. Matt. 26:26-29 and Luke 22:17-20 with 1 Cor. 11:23-26). This probably refers to the ordinary wine of the country mixed with two-thirds water. "Wine" is not used at this point in the Gospels. Rather, "fruit of the vine."

30. {*Twice*} This detail only in Mark. One crowing is always the signal for more. The cock crowing marks the third watch of the night (Mark 13:35).

31. {*Exceeding vehemently*} This probably preserves Peter's own statement of the remark (cf. Matt. 26:35).

33. {*Greatly amazed and sore troubled*} (cf. Matt. 26:37). "Deeply distressed" is the Greek verb *ekthambeô*, to be in amazement (*thambeô*) to a perfective degree (*ek*). The disciples felt amazement heading for Jerusalem (cf. *thambeô* Mark 10:32). Now Jesus himself feels amazement as he directly faces the struggle in the Garden of Gethsemane.

35. {*Prayed*} The Greek tense can mean either prayed *repeatedly* or, *began* to pray. Either makes good sense here.

36. {*Abba, Father*} "Abba" is Aramaic and "Father" is Greek. Both terms are purposely used, and is not a case of translation. This phrase is a probable memory of Paul's childhood prayers (cf. Gal. 4:6). Jesus was heard (Heb. 5:7) and helped to submit to the Father's will as he does instantly.

40. {*Very heavy*} "Heavy" in the form of the Greek word is "very" heavy to a perfective degree or amount.

41. {*It is enough*} Lit. "it is enough" in the impersonal use of the verb. It is used here by Jesus in an ironical sense, probably meaning that there was no need of further reproof of the disciples for their failure to watch with him. This is no time for a lengthened exposure of the faults of friends; the enemy is at the gate.

44. {*Token*} (cf. sign, Matt. 26:48). This is a concerted signal according to agreement. Here it was the kiss by Judas, a contemptible desecration of a friendly salutation (cf. also John 18:4-9).

47. {*A certain one*} This is Peter (cf. John 18:10), who really tried to kill the man, named Malchus. Jesus rebukes Peter (cf. Matt. 26:52).

48. {*Against a robber*} Highway robbers like Barabbas were common and were often regarded as heroes. Jesus will be crucified between two robbers in the very place that Barabbas would have occupied. Some Greek lexical sources translate this as a political "rebel" or "insurrectionist," and so some versions translate as such.

51. {*A certain young man*} A life-like touch, it is usually supposed that Mark himself, son of Mary (Acts 12:12) in whose house they probably had observed the Passover Meal, had followed Jesus and the apostles to the Garden.

52. {*Linen cloth*} This garment was a fine linen cloth used often for wrapping the dead (Matt. 27:59; Mark 15:46; Luke 23:53). Here it could refer to a fine sheet or even a shirt.

54. {*Peter had followed him afar off*} (cf. Matt. 26:58 and Luke 22:54). The disciples fled, and in contrast, John took an open stand with Christ; Peter remained, *but at a distance.* {*Was sitting with...*} (cf. John 18:25). Peter is making himself at home with these servants. Restless and weary, he stood and sat, alternating, one then the other. {*Warming himself in the light*} Fire has light as well as heat and it shone in Peter's face. He was not hidden as much as he supposed he was.

56. {*Their witness agreed not together*} Lit. "the testimonies were not equal." They did not correspond with each other on essential points. Here, no two witnesses bore joint testimony to justify a capital sentence according to the law (Deut. 19:15).

57. {*Bare false witness*} In desperation some attempted once more (conative imperfect).

58. {*Made with hands*} (cf. 2 Cor. 5:1; Col. 2:11 also Heb. 9:11). Lit. "this made with hands temple." Do the witnesses agree or not? (cf. Mark 14:58-59 and Matt. 26:60-61). The witnesses here mean he (falsely reported) would physically destroy the temple building. In John 2:19 he referred the saying to the temple of his body, though no one understood it at the time. In a larger sense, Jesus' death destroyed the old order, and His resurrection created the new.

62. {*I am*} This is an equivalent of the affirmative (cf. Matt. 26:64-68).

64. {*They all...*} That is, all present: Joseph of Arimathea was not present, (Luke 23:51) as also apparently Nicodemus (John 7:50).

65. {*Cover his face*} (cf. Luke 22:64). That is, put a veil around his face. {*Officers*} (cf. verse 54). That is the officers of the Sanhedrin, Roman lictors or sergeants-at-arms who had arrested Jesus in

Gethsemane and who still held Jesus (cf. Luke 22:63 and Matt. 26:67). {*With blows of their hands*} Here it means the act of slapping the face with the palm of the hands. It is possible that this whole phrase refers to beating with rods, since the lictors (guards) carried rods. At any rate it was a gross indignity.

66. {*Beneath in the court*} This implies that Jesus was upstairs when the Sanhedrin met (cf. Matt. 26:69).

71. {*Curse*} (cf. Matt. 26:74). This Greek word has the notion of calling down curses on one's self if the thing is not true.

72. {*Called to mind*} (cf. Matt. 26:75 and Luke 22:61). {*Wept*} Greek tense shows that he began to weep, burst into tears (cf. Matt. 26:75).

CHAPTER 15

1. {*In the morning...held a consultation*} (cf. Matt. 26:1-5). The action was illegal on the night before and they felt the need of this ratification after dawn (cf. Luke 22:66-71). {*Bound Jesus*} (cf. Mark 15:1; Matt. 27:2). He was bound on his arrest (John 18:12). It is implied that he was unbound while before Annas and then before Caiaphas and the Sanhedrin, then rebound going to Pilate.

2. {*Thou sayest*} This is an affirmation that he is (cf. John 18:34-37). This is the one question that Jesus answers.

3. {*Accused him of many things*} The Greek tense of "accused" shows repeated accusations besides those already made. They let loose their venom against Jesus.

5. {*Marvelled*} Amazed at the self-control of Jesus, Pilate was sure of the innocence of Jesus and saw through their envy (Mark 15:10).

6. {*Used to release*} (cf. Matt. 27:15). {*They asked of him*} The Greek tense shows that this asking was their habit also.

7. {*Bound with them that had made insurrection*} He was a leader in the insurrection, sedition, or revolution against Rome, and murderer; some wanted Jesus to lead a similar revolution (cf. John 6:15).

9. {*The King of the Jews*} (cf. Matt. 27:17). This phrase sharpened the contrast between Jesus and Barabbas.

10. {*He perceived*} The Greek tense shows Pilate's growing apprehension from their conduct. It was gradually dawning on him.

11. {*Stirred up*} (cf. Matt. 27:20). They shook them up like an earthquake. The priests and scribes had amazing success. They accused Jesus to Pilate of political ambition, and they recommended Barabbas to the people for the same reason. One explanation is, Barabbas represented a stronger popular passion—the passion for political liberty. Jesus was seen as an unworldly character.

13. {*Crucify him*} (cf. Luke 23:21 and Matt. 27:22-23). A hubbub of confused voices all demanded crucifixion for Christ; no doubt some had joined in the hallelujahs at the triumphal entry.

15. {*To content the multitude*} (cf. Matt. 27:26). This is an idiom found in a number of ancient writers. It means to do what is sufficient to remove one's ground of complaint. Pilate was afraid of this crowd now completely under the control of the Sanhedrin. He knew they would tell Caesar about him.

16. {*The Praetorium*} Lit. "the palace" (cf. Matt. 27:27). This is the palace in which the Roman provincial governor resided. "The court" is inside of the palace into which the people passed from the street through the vestibule (i.e., passageway between two areas).

19. {*Worshipped him*} That is, in mockery. The Greek tense shows they hit and spit in repeated indignities.

21. {*They compel*} (cf. Matt. 27:32). This Greek tense is in the dramatic present indicative, vividly drawing the reader into the narrative scene. "Forced" is a Persian word (cf. Matt. 5:41 and 27:32).

23. {*Mingled with myrrh*} (cf. mingled with gall Matt. 27:34). This verb means flavored with myrrh, myrrhed wine. {*But he received it not*} That is, he refused it.

25. {*The third hour*} This is Jewish time, 9:00 A.M.

26. {*The superscription*} (cf. Luke 23:38; Matt. 27:37; and John 19:19). This is the writing on the top of the cross (cf. our *epigraph*).

32. {*Now come down*} That is, now that he is nailed to the cross. {*That we may see and believe*} They use almost the very language of Jesus in their ridicule, words that they had heard him use in his appeals to men to see and believe.

33. {*The sixth hour*} (cf. Matt. 27:45 and Luke 23:44). This is Jewish time, 12 (noon).

34. {*Forsaken*} We are not able to enter into the fullness of the desolation felt by Jesus (as the Son of God) at this moment as the Father regarded him as sin (2 Cor. 5:21). This desolation was the deepest suffering. He did not cease to be the Son of God. That would be impossible.

35. {*He calleth Elijah*} Note how the sounds are similar; they misunderstood the *Elôi* or *Elei* (my God) for *Eli*jah.

37. {*Gave up the ghost*} Lit. "breathed out." (cf. "yielded up his spirit" Matt. 27:50).

40. {*And Salome*} Apparently this is the "mother of the sons of Zebedee" (Matt. 27:56).

41. {*Followed him and ministered unto him*} (cf. Matt. 27:55 and Luke 23:49). The Greek tense of "followed" and "cared," describe the long Galilean ministry of these three women and many other women in Galilee (Luke 8:1-3) who came up with him to Jerusalem. These faithful women were last at the Cross and saw the dreadful end to all their hopes.

42. {*The preparation*} (cf. Matt. 27:57). This is our Friday, which began at sunset.

43. {*A councillor of honourable estate...boldly*} This means he was a member of the Sanhedrin of high standing, and rich (cf. Matt. 27:57). {*Looking for the Kingdom of God*} (cf. Luke 23:5, also 2:25,38). He was a secret disciple of Jesus (cf. Matt. 27:57 and John 19:38), evidently now in his first public stand for Jesus; ironically becoming bold when the rest of the disciples were in terror and dismay.

44. {*If he were already dead... whether he had been any while dead*} The Greek is a kind of indirect question, just as we say "I wonder if..." Usually death by crucifixion was lingering. Pilate wanted to make sure that Jesus was actually dead by official report (cf. John 19:31-37).

45. {*Granted the corpse*} This official information was necessary before the burial. As a matter of fact Pilate was probably glad to turn the body over to Joseph else the body would go to the potter's field.

46. {*Wound*} (cf. Matt. 27:57-60; Luke 23:53; John 20:7). The body was wrapped in strips of linen cloth and the hundred pounds of spices brought by Nicodemus, folded into the strips (John 19:39). Some modern scholars think that this very tomb has been identified in Gordon's Calvary north of the city.

47. {*Beheld*} (cf. Matt. 27:61). The Greek tense pictures the two Marys sitting over against the sepulcher and (*kept on*) watching (Joseph and Nicodemus) in silence as the shadows fell upon all their hopes and dreams. These two remained after the other women who had been beholding from afar.

CHAPTER 16

1. {*When the sabbath was past*} It was therefore after sunset. {*Bought spices*} They could buy them after sundown, securing a fresh supply of spices. (cf. Nicodemus, John 19:40). If not embalming, it was to be a reverential anointing of the body of Jesus with spices at any rate.

2. {*When the sun was risen*} (cf. Luke 24:1 and John 20:1). Putting together all the Gospels as to the time in the morning, probably they started from Bethany while it was still dark and the sun was coming up when they arrived at the tomb, a two-mile walk. {*First day of the week*} This is our Sunday morning. Rising on the third day does not mean it was a full seventy-two hours; then he would have risen on the *fourth* day: (buried) Friday afternoon to Sunday morning is rising on the third day.

4. {*Looking up they see*} (cf. found, Luke 24:2). "Saw" here is a vivid dramatic present, drawing the reader into the narrative "see." Their problem is solved for the stone lies rolled back before their very eyes.

5. {*Entering into the tomb*} (cf. Luke 24:3). {*A young man*} (cf. Matt. 28:5 and Luke 24:1ff). That is, an angel. Any variations in the number and description of the messengers at the tomb show the independence of the narrative and strengthen the evidence for the general fact of the resurrection. {*They were amazed*} (cf. Luke 24:5). The form of the Greek word shows they were *utterly* amazed.

6. {*Be not amazed*} The angel noted their amazement and the Greek syntax urges the cessation of the alarm using this very word. {*The crucified one*} (cf. Matt. 28:5). This description of his shame has become his crown of glory, for Paul (Gal. 6:14), and for all who look to the Crucified and Risen Christ as Savior and Lord.

7. {*And Peter*} "Peter" is a detail only in Mark, showing again Peter's remembrances. Jesus' appearances to the disciples and Peter later in the day changed doubt to certainty with the apostles (Luke 24:34; 1 Cor. 15:5).

8. {*Trembling and astonishment...they said nothing to anyone*} (cf. Matt. 28:8). Lit. "trembling and ecstasy." Clearly and naturally their emotions were mixed. This excitement was too great for ordinary conversation. Hushed to silence their feet had wings as they flew on. {*For they were afraid*} The Greek tense shows the continued fear explains their continued silence. The two oldest and best Greek manuscripts of the New Testament stop with this verse. There are two endings added to the manuscripts: a shorter and a longer ending. The longer ending is the more usual one that is the addition to Mark's Gospel. The facts are very complicated, but they argue *strongly* against the genuineness of verses 9-20 of Mark chapter 16. There is little in these verses not in Matthew 28:1ff. It is difficult to believe "They were afraid" ended this Gospel. It is possible Mark was interrupted; or a leaf or column may have been torn off at the end of the papyrus roll.

9. {*When he had risen early on the first day of the week*} (cf. Luke 24:34; 1 Cor. 15:5). Note, one can also translate the phrasing so 'appeared' goes with the time frame, "When he rose, early on the first day of the week he appeared...."

11. {*Disbelieved*} (cf. Luke 24:11). This verb is common in the ancient Greek, but rare in the NT.

16. {*And is baptized*} The omission of baptized with "disbelieveth" would seem to show that Jesus does not make baptism essential to salvation. Condemnation rests on disbelief, not on baptism. So salvation rests on belief. Baptism is merely the picture of the new life, not the means of securing it.

20. Here is another ending; called the shorter ending of Mark. "And they announced briefly to Peter and those around him all the things enjoined. And after these things Jesus himself also sent forth through them from the east even unto the west the holy and incorruptible proclamation of the eternal salvation" (Westcott and Hort).

THE GOSPEL ACCORDING TO LUKE

AUTHOR: Luke, the beloved physician, friend of Apostle Paul
DATE: A.D. 59 to 62
RECIPIENTS: Addressed to Theophilus/ for the Gentile world
FROM: Possibly Caesarea Maritima
OCCASION: To create a certain history of the Gospel (in Paul's defense?)
THEME: Christ's Gospel is universal for all humanity, in all phases and conditions.

BY WAY OF INTRODUCTION

Luke is the first part of a two-part work, addressed to Theophilus (Luke 1:3; Acts 1:1). Luke refers to himself in both Luke and Acts. (The "we" sections of Acts begin at Acts 16:10ff.) These two books are parts of a whole. They are not merely two independent writings from the same pen; they are a single continuous work.

Luke was a doctor and uses medical terms with fondness, and has interest and comments on medical things which is shown in Luke and Acts, and corroborates authorship by him. Paul and Luke worked together on the Island of Malta (Acts 28:8-10) where many were healed and Luke shared with Paul in the appreciation of the natives there.

"Luke" is a form of *Lukios* and *Lukanos*. It is probable that Luke was a Greek, certainly a Gentile, possibly a freedman. So this man who wrote more than one-fourth of the NT was not a Jew. As a Greek physician, Luke was a university man and in touch with the science of his day. Certainly he was one who cared for humanity; a man of culture and broad sympathies, and personal charm. He was the first genuine scientist who faced the problem of Christ and of Christianity. He wrote his books with open mind and not as a credulous enthusiast.

Luke may have been written while Paul was a prisoner a little over two years in Caesarea (Acts 23:33). That period gave Luke abundant opportunity for the kind of research of which he speaks in Luke 1:1-4. In Palestine he could have access to persons familiar with the earthly life and teachings of Jesus and to whatever documents were already produced concerning such matters. Luke may have produced the Gospel towards the close of the stay of Paul in Caesarea or during the early part of the first Roman imprisonment, somewhere between A.D. 59 and 62.

In his Preface or Prologue (Luke 1:1-4) the author tells us that he had two kinds of sources, oral and written, and that they were "many." It is now generally accepted that we know two of his written sources, Mark's Gospel and Q (a source other than Mark also called the *Logia* of Jesus). There is a large portion of Luke's Gospel which is different from Mark and Matthew. Some scholars call this source *L*. But Luke expressly says that he had received help from "eyewitnesses and ministers of the word." This means in oral form. It is, then, probable that Luke made numerous notes of such data and used them along with the written sources at his command. It was likely Luke had contact with Mary or her circle during the two years at Caesarea, and so relates the birth of Jesus from her view.

Luke was a man of culture and a literary genius. This Gospel shows careful attention to detail and proportion of parts that give the balance and poise that come only from full knowledge of the subject, the chief element in good style.

This scientific physician, this man of the schools comes to the study of the life of Christ with a trained intellect, with a historian's method of research, with a physician's care in diagnosis and discrimination, with a charm of style all his own, with reverence for and loyalty to Jesus Christ as Lord and Savior. If we had only Luke's Gospel (we in fact have four), we should have an adequate portrait of Jesus Christ as Son of God and Son of Man.

Luke's Gospel is often called the Gospel of womanhood, of infancy, of prayer, of praise. We have in Luke the first Christian hymns. With Luke we catch some glimpses of the child Jesus for which we are grateful.

CHAPTER 1

1. {*Forasmuch as many*} The phrase "Forasmuch as" in Greek has an emphasis on importance. Certainly more than two or three have undertaken. {*Have taken in hand*} Luke had secured fuller information and planned a book on a larger scale and did surpass them with the result that they all perished save Mark's Gospel and what Matthew and Luke possess of the Logia of Jesus. {*To draw up, a narrative*} "To

draw up" is composed of *tassô*, a common verb for arranging things in proper order and *ana*, again. Luke means to say that those before him had made attempts to rehearse in orderly fashion various matters about Christ. The expression points to a connected series of narratives in some order (Greek *taxis*), topical or chronological rather than to isolated narratives; more than mere notes or anecdotes. {*Which have been fulfilled*} The careful language of Luke here really pays a tribute to those who had preceded him in their narratives concerning Christ.

2. {*Delivered unto us*} Not an eyewitness, Luke received this tradition along with those who are mentioned above (the many). He was a secondary, not a primary, witness of the events. His narratives are dependable and not mere wives' fables. Luke used both written and oral sources. {*Eyewitnesses*} This is the Greek word *autoptai,* meaning "seeing with one's own eyes," our medical term *autopsy.* {*From the first*} Apparently, this refers to the beginning of the ministry of Jesus (not childhood) as was true of the apostles (Acts 1:22) and of the early apostolic preaching (Acts 10:37-43).

3. {*Having traced the course of all things*} Lit. "to follow along a thing in mind, to trace carefully." Luke here claims fullness of knowledge before he began to write his book. Through the traditions of the eyewitnesses, he had *mentally* followed along by the side of these events in the smallest detail. {*From the first*} Seemingly, he refers to the infancy narratives (cf. Luke 1:52). {*In order*} This Gospel is chronological order in the main following Mark's general outline. But in Luke 9:51-18:10 the order is often topical. {*Most excellent Theophilus*} The name means god-lover or god-beloved. He may have been a believer already. He was probably a Gentile. Some think he held office (Acts 23:26 and 26:25).

4. {*Wast instructed*} This is the Greek word *katêchêthês,* from the verb *katêcheô,* to sound down, to din, to instruct, to give oral instruction (cf. 1 Cor. 14:9; Acts 21:21, 24; 18:25; Gal. 6:6).

5. {*There was*} Lit. "there arose" or came into notice. From Luke 1:5 to 2:52 we have the most Hebraistic (Aramaic) passage in Luke's writings, due evidently to the use of documents or notes of oral tradition. If the mother of Jesus was still alive, Luke could have seen her. She may have written in Aramaic an account of these great events. We have here the earliest documentary evidence of the origins of Christianity that has come down to us. {*Herod, king of Judea*} This is Herod the Great, client king of Rome who died 4 B.C. by our calendar. {*Of the course of Abijah*} This is a course of priests who were on duty for a week (1 Chr. 23:6; 28:13). There were 24 such courses and that of Abijah was the eighth (1 Chr. 24:10; 2 Chr. 8:14), on duty for eight days, Sabbath to Sabbath, twice a year. {*Of the daughters of Aaron*} A double distinction for Zechariah: a priest married to a priest's daughter (Plummer).

9. {*His lot was*} (cf. Acts 1:17; 2 Pet. 1:1). Lit. "he obtained the lot." It was only once in a lifetime that a priest obtained the lot of going into the sanctuary and burning incense on the golden altar. It was the great moment of Zechariah's life, and his heart was no doubt alert for the supernatural (Ragg). It was probably at this time that the angel appeared to Zechariah.

10. {*Were praying without*} The Greek tense is picturing the posture of the people while the clouds of incense rose on the inside of the sanctuary.

13. {*Is heard*} This was probably the prayer for a son in spite of the great age of Elisabeth; though the Messianic redemption is possible also. {*John*} Meaning "God is gracious," the mention of the name should have helped Zechariah to believe.

14. {*Gladness*} This is an LXX word for extreme exultation. {*Rejoice*} The coming of a prophet will indeed be an occasion for rejoicing.

15. {*Strong drink*} Originally a Hebrew word, this means an intoxicating drink (cf. Nazarite, Num. 6:3). {*The Holy Ghost*} That is, filled with Holy Spirit in contrast to the physical excitement of strong drink (Plummer).

17. {*In the spirit and power of Elijah*} (cf. Isa. 40:1-11; Mal. 3:15). Not Elijah in person (John 1:21), but Jesus will call him Elijah in spirit (Mark 9:12; Matt. 17:12). {*Prepared*} The Greek tense shows a state of readiness for Christ. This is a marvelous forecast of the character and career of John the Baptist.

18. {*Whereby*} Lit. "according to what?" It was too good to be true and Zechariah demanded proof and gives the reason for his doubt. He had prayed for this blessing and was now skeptical (cf. Acts 12:14).

21. {*Were waiting*} This is an old Greek verb for expecting; it denotes mental direction whether hope or fear.

22. {*Perceived*} The people clearly knew because Zechariah was not able to pronounce the benediction from the steps (Num. 6:24-26).

{*Continued making signs*} He nodded and beckoned back and forth, further proof of a vision that caused his dumbness.

24. {*Conceived*} (cf. Luke 1:24, 31, 36; 2:21). Luke has almost as many different words for pregnancy and barrenness as Hippocrates (cf. Luke 21:23; 2:5; 1:7; 20:28). {*Hid*} The Greek word means "to be completely (on all sides) hid."

26. {*Was sent*} (cf. Luke 1:19). This is the Greek verb *apostellô* from which *apostle* comes. The angel Gabriel is God's messenger to Mary as to Zechariah.

27. {*Betrothed*} Betrothal usually lasted a year and unfaithfulness on the part of the bride could be punished with death (Deut. 23:24).

28. {*Highly favoured*} (cf. v. 42). This is the Greek verb *charitoô* and means endowed with grace (*charis*), enriched with grace (cf. Eph. 1:6).

29. {*Cast in her mind*} She was both upset and puzzled.

30. {*Favour*} That is, "grace," from the notion of sweetness, charm, loveliness, joy, delight, kindness, and other like words of grace (cf. Luke 4:22; Eph. 4:29; Col. 4:6).

32. {*The Son of the Most High*} (cf. Luke 6:35). We cannot insist on deity here, though that is possible (cf. 2 Sam. 7:14; Isa. 9:7).

33. {*Shall be no end*} Though not explicitly stated, Luke here reports the perpetuity of *spiritual* Israel, as Paul taught the true meaning. Joseph and Mary were of this house (cf. Luke 1:27 and 2:5).

35. {*Shall overshadow thee*} This is a figure of a cloud coming upon her. Here it is like the Shekinah glory which suggests it (Exod. 40:38) where the cloud of glory represents the presence and power of God. {*Holy, the Son of God*} This title (like the Son of Man) was a recognized designation of the Messiah. It was used by the Father at the baptism (Luke 3:22) and transfiguration (Luke 9:35). The wonder of Mary would increase at these words.

36. {*Kinswoman*} Not necessarily cousin, but it is simply "relative."

40. {*Saluted*} With a bond of sympathy, her first glance at Elisabeth showed the truth of the angel's message.

41. {*Leaped*} An unborn child kicks (Gen. 25:22), but Elisabeth was filled with the Holy Spirit to understand what had happened to Mary.

42. {*With a loud cry*} It was a moment of ecstatic excitement. {*Blessed art thou*} A Hebraistic equivalent for, "most blessed are you."

43. {*The mother of my Lord*} (cf. Ps. 110:1). Only by the help of the Holy Spirit could Elisabeth know that Mary was to be the mother of the Messiah.

45. {*For...*} Elisabeth wishes Mary to have full faith in the prophecy of the angel. This song of Elisabeth is as real poetry as is that of Mary (Luke 1:47-55) and Zechariah (Luke 1:68-70). All three spoke under the power of the Holy Spirit.

46. {*Doth magnify*} The Latin is *magnificat*. Mary draws her material from the OT and sings in the noblest strain.

47. {*Hath rejoiced*} This is the Greek verb *agalliaô*, from the old Greek *agallô*. It means to exult (cf. Luke 1:14, 44). Mary is not excited like Elisabeth, but breathes a spirit of composed rapture.

48. {*The low estate*} This was true in a literal sense. She was the bride of a carpenter and yet to be the mother of the Messiah (cf. Luke 1:52).

51. {*Showed strength*} (cf. Ps. 118:15). Lit. "made might." {*Imagination*} This is intellectual insight, moral understanding.

52. {*Princes*} The Greek is comparable to our word "dynasty." It comes from the Greek verb *dunamai*, to be able.

58. {*Rejoiced with her*} The Greek tense and form pictures the continual, mutual, joy of the neighbors (cf. Phil. 2:18).

59. {*Would have called*} Greek tense translates, "*tried* to call or name."

62. {*Made signs*} Greek tense shows repeated action as usual when making signs. {*What he would have him called*} That is, "What would he wish him to be called?"

63. {*Tablet*} Greek word *pinakidion*, thus a "little" writing tablet, probably covered with wax. It was used also of a physician's notebook in other literature.

64. {*Opened*} A tongue cannot be "opened" (that verb goes with "mouth"). "Was loosed" is not formally in the Greek but is understood in the syntax.

66. {*What then*} With all these supernatural happenings they predicted the marvelous career of this child. {*They laid them up*} Lit. "placed in the heart" as Mary did (Luke 2:19).

67. {*Prophesied*} This is the *Benedictus* of Zechariah (Luke 1:68-79). Nearly every phrase being found in the OT; by the Spirit, he had caught the Messianic message in its highest meaning.

68. {*Hath visited*} A Hebrew-colored word meaning "to look (inspect, examine) into with a view to help." {*Redemption*} This originally referred to political redemption, but with a moral and spiritual basis (vv. 75, 77).

69. {*Horn of salvation*} (cf. 1 Sam. 2:10; 2 Sam. 23:3). The phrase represents strength like the horns of bulls (cf. Ps. 132:17).

74. {*To serve*} This is the Greek verb *latreuô*, from *latros*, for hire; this is also used for service for God so not having the bad sense.

75. {*In holiness and righteousness*} (cf. Eph. 4:24; Titus 1:8; 1 Thess. 2:10). Respectively, the Godward (eternal principles of right) and the manward (rule of conduct before men).

78. {*Tender mercy*} Lit. "bowels of mercy" (cf. 1 Pet. 3:8; Jas. 3:11). {*The dayspring from on high*} Lit. "rising from on high," like the rising sun or stars (Isa. 60:19).

79. {*To shine upon*} This is the Greek verb *epiphainô*, "to give light, to shine upon, like the sun or stars" (cf. Acts 27:20; Titus 2:11; 3:4). {*The shadow of death*} (cf. Ps. 107:10, also Isa. 9:1 [Matt. 4:16]). The light will enable them to see how to walk in a straight path that leads to "the way of peace."

80. {*Grew...waxed strong*} Greek tense shows the child kept growing in strength of body and spirit. {*His shewing*} (cf. Luke 2:42-52). Two boys of destiny, John and Jesus grew on with the years. Each one was waiting for "his appearing unto Israel."

CHAPTER 2

1. {*Decree from Caesar Augustus*} Not corroborated by Greek or Roman historians, some assumed Luke was in error. But papyri and inscriptions have confirmed Luke on every point in these crucial verses in Luke 2:1-7. {*The world*} Lit. "the inhabited" world ruled by Rome (cf. Acts 11:28; 17:6). {*Should be enrolled*} It was a census, though taxing generally followed based on the census.

2. {*The first enrolment*} Roman census was given about 14 years apart. The first given in 8 B.C. from Rome, and it would likely take a couple of years to be implemented by Herod the Great in Palestine. This then agrees with other data that Jesus was born in 6 B.C.

3. {*Each to his own city*} Each man went to the town where his family register was kept.

5. {*To enrol himself with Mary*} (cf. Luke 3:23-38). Mary's family register was in Bethlehem also, and she also belonged to the house of

David. {*Betrothed*} (cf. Luke 1:27). Here it really means "married" or "espoused" (cf. Matt. 1:24). Otherwise she could not have traveled with Joseph.

7. {*Her firstborn*} With no evidence otherwise, this naturally means that she afterwards had other children and we read of brothers and sisters of Jesus. {*Wrapped in swaddling clothes*} This is the action of wrapping in swathing bands of cloth. {*In a manger*} That is, in a crib in a stall whether in a cave (Justin Martyr) or connected with the inn we do not know. {*In the inn*} This is a lodging-house or *khan,* poor enough at best, but there was not even room in this public place because of the crowds for the census (cf. Exod. 4:24).

8. {*Keeping watch*} They were bivouacking by night and it was plainly mild weather.

9. {*Stood by them*} Lit. "stepped by their side" (cf. Acts 12:7). {*Were sore afraid*} Lit. "they feared a great fear."

10. {*I bring you good tidings of great joy*} "Bring good news" is our word "evangelize"; it is to Paul's influence that we owe their frequency and popularity in the language of Christendom (cf. Matt. 11:5 and Isa. 61:1).

11. {*Saviour*} The people under Rome's rule came to call the emperor "Savior" and Christians took the word and used it of Christ. {*Christ the Lord*} (cf. LXX, Lam. 4:20 and Song 17:36). This combination only here in the NT. Exactly how to translate its meaning is difficult in the verse, possibly "A Savior which is Christ the Lord" (Ragg).

15. {*Said to one another*} Greek tense can mean "*began* to speak," or repetition "they *kept on* saying."

16. {*Found*} The form of the Greek word itself suggests a search before finding.

19. {*Kept*} The Greek tense shows she *kept on* "keeping together" all these things. She was not astonished, but filled with holy awe. She could not forget. {*Pondering*} Lit. "placing together" for comparison. Brooding with a mother's high hopes and joy, Mary would go over each detail: Gabriel, the shepherds, and compare sayings with the facts.

22. {*The days of their purification*} The mother was Levitically unclean for forty days after the birth of a son (Lev. 12:1-8). {*To present him to the Lord*} Every firstborn son was thus redeemed by the sacrifice (Exod. 13:2-12, also Num. 18:15).

24. {*A pair of turtledoves, or two young pigeons*} This was the offering of the poor; while a lamb offering would cost about a dozen times more.

25. {*Devout*} (cf. Acts 2:5; 8:2; 22:12) It means taking hold well or carefully and so reverently, circumspectly. {*Looking for the consolation of Israel*} This is waiting with expectation (cf. Luke 2:38). "Consolation" here means the Messianic hope (Isa. 11:10; 40:1). {*Upon him*} Simeon and Anna are representatives of real piety in this time of spiritual dearth and deadness.

28. {*Then he*} The "he" is emphatic, and after the parents. {*Arms*} This Greek word means the curve or inner angle of the arm, where babies are held.

29. {*Now lettest thou*} This is the *Nunc Dimittis,* adoration and praise. It is full of rapture and vivid intensity like the best of the Psalms. The Greek verb *apoluô* was common for the release of slaves, as here of the Sovereign Lord for Simon.

31. {*Of all the peoples*} This is another illustration of the universality of Luke's Gospel seen already in Luke 1:70 in the hymn of Zechariah.

32. {*Revelation to the Gentiles*} With a worldwide mission, the Messiah is to be light for the Gentiles (nations other than Israel) in darkness (Luke 1:70) and glory for Israel (cf. Rom. 9:1-5; Isa. 49:6).

33. {*His father and his mother...were marvelling*} Stating the Virgin Birth in Luke 1:34-38, Luke employs here the language of ordinary custom (cf. parents, Luke 2:27). Why marvel here, after all, they had heard from Gabriel, Elisabeth, and the Shepherds? The answer is, every parent is astonished and pleased at the fine things others (like Simon) see in the child.

34. {*Is set for the falling and the rising up of many in Israel*} What is meant is the falling of some and the rising up of others: to some a stumblingblock (Isa. 8:14; Matt. 21:42, 44; Rom. 9:33; 1 Pet. 2:16); a cause of rising for others (Rom. 6:4, 9; Eph. 2:6).

35. {*A sword*} This is a large, long sword (1 Sam. 17:51). This parenthesis is seemingly out of place in the midst of glorious words; a veritable bittersweet. One day Mary will stand at the Cross of Christ with this Tracian javelin clean through her soul (John 19:25).

37. {*Which departed not...night and day*} The Spirit kept Anna in the temple as he led Simon to the temple. She never missed a service in the temple.

38. {*Gave thanks*} Anna was evidently deeply moved, Greek tense shows she *kept on* giving thanks. There was a nucleus of old saints in Jerusalem prepared for the coming of the Messiah, that pass away when he at last appears.

40. {*The child grew...*} (cf. Luke 1:80). He was a hearty, vigorous *little* boy. {*Filled with wisdom*} Greek syntax shows that in addition to bodily development, the process of filling with wisdom kept pace with the bodily growth. The intellectual, moral, and spiritual growth of the Child, like the physical, was real. His was a perfect humanity developing perfectly.

41. {*Every year*} Originally every male went to three festivals (Exod. 23:14-17; 34:23; Deut. 16:16). By this time, pious Palestinian Jews made a habit of going at least to the Passover, though not required by law to go (because of the distance to Jerusalem).

42. {*Twelve years old*} At twelve, a Jewish boy became a "son of the law" and began to observe the ordinances.

43. {*When they had fulfilled the days*} Lit. "and completing the days" which can refer to the full seven days (Exod. 12:15; Lev. 23:68; Deut. 16:3), or the two chief days after which many pilgrims left for home; probably the latter (see v. 46). {*The boy, Jesus*} Before called in the Greek "a little boy" (v. 40) and here "boy."

44. {*In the company*} In a caravan like this, the women usually went ahead and the men followed. It was so long that it took a whole day to look through it. Each parent thought Jesus was with the other. {*They sought for him*} The Greek verb shows that they *kept on* searching up and down, back and forth; it was a repeated, prolonged, and thorough search, but in vain.

46. {*After three days*} That is, one day out, one day back, and on the third day finding him. {*In the temple*} This is probably on the terrace where members of the Sanhedrin gave public instruction on Sabbaths and feastdays, so probably while the feast was still going on. {*Both hearing them and asking them questions*} (cf. Acts 22:3). It was his one opportunity in a theological school outside of the synagogue to hear the great rabbis expound the problems of life.

47. {*Were amazed*} Lit. "stood out of themselves." Greek tense describes their continued and repeated astonishment, as if their eyes were bulging out. {*At his understanding*} This is comparing and combining things based on grasping and comprehending (cf. Mark 12:33). {*His *answers*} Hard questions are easy, but this boy had astounding answers too, revealing his amazing intellectual and spiritual growth.

48. {*They were astonished*} This is the Greek verb *ekplêssô*, to strike out, drive out by a blow; as were Joseph and Mary. Even they had not fully realized the power in this wonderful boy.

49. {*How is it that...?*} The Greek syntax expresses the boy's amazement. His parents should know there was only one place in Jerusalem for him, in his Father's house.

50. {*They understood not*} All of Mary's previous preparation and brooding was not equal to the dawning of the Messianic consciousness in her boy (v. 19).

51. {*He was subject unto them*} Greek tense shows he continued to be subject to them. The next eighteen years at Nazareth (Luke 3:23) he remained growing into manhood and becoming the carpenter of Nazareth (Mark 6:3) in succession to Joseph (Matt. 13:55) who is mentioned here for the last time. {*Kept...*} (cf. v. 19). She kept thoroughly all these recent sayings; pondering and comparing all the things.

52. {*Jesus...advanced in wisdom and stature*} (cf. v. 40). Greek tense shows he *kept* cutting his way forward as through a forest or jungle as pioneers did; he *kept* growing in stature and in wisdom, more than mere knowledge.

CHAPTER 3

1. {*Now in the fifteenth year*} After centuries of prophetic silence, John revived the function of the prophet. The ancients did not have our modern system of chronology, the names of rulers as here being the common way, but Luke is vindicated by historical research and inscriptions.

2. {*The Word of God came unto John*} "Word of God" in the Greek has a focus of some particular utterance of God (Plummer). Luke alone tells of the coming of the word to John (cf. Mark 1:4; Matt. 3:1).

3. {*All the region round about Jordan*} The desert was John's abode so he began preaching where he was (Luke 1:80); it was the Jordan valley (El Ghor). Usually on the west side (though cf. John 10:40), his baptizing kept him near the river.

5. {*Valley*} This is Greek for a ravine or valley hedged in by precipices. {*Shall be filled*} Oriental monarchs often gave a call to clear the roads of rocks and to fill up the hollows, for their visits. A royal courier would go ahead to issue the call. So the Messiah sends his herald (John) before him to prepare the way for him.

6. {*All flesh*} This means in the NT "the human race." {*The salvation of God*} That is, the saving act of God; the message of Christ for all men. It is the universal Gospel in that sense.

7-9. {*To the multitude that went out*} Note plural (crowds) coming out here repeatedly, for the purpose of receiving baptism (cf. Pharisees and Sadducees, Matt. 3:7-10). Luke gives a summary of John's preaching to the crowds with special replies to these inquiries: the crowds (vv. 10-11), the publicans (vv. 12-13), the soldiers (v. 14).

10. {*Asked*} Greek tense shows they repeatedly asked.

11. {*Coats*} This is the Greek word *chitôn,* the inner and less necessary undergarment. The indispensable outer-wear (Greek *himation*) is not mentioned. Note that John puts his finger on the weaknesses of the people right before him.

12. {*Also publicans*} That is, "tax collectors" (cf. Matt. 5:46; 9:10; 11:19; 18:17; 21:31; Mark 11:15). The collector of taxes collected for the Romans and did it by terrible graft and extortions. {*Extort*} This is the Greek verb *prassô* which means only to "do" or "practice," but early the tax collectors learned how to "do" the public as regular "bloodsuckers."

14. {*Soldiers also*} (cf. 2 Tim. 2:4). Some of these soldiers acted as police to help the publicans. But they were often rough and cruel. {*Do violence to no man*} The Greek verb is *diaseisô,* meaning to shake (*seis*mic disturbance, earthquake) thoroughly (*dia*) and so thoroughly to terrify, to extort money or property by intimidating (3 Macc. 7:21). {*Neither exact anything wrongfully*} (cf. Luke 19:8). These soldiers were tempted to obtain money by informing against the rich. So the word comes to mean "to accuse falsely." {*Be content with your wages*} (cf. 1 Cor. 9:7). Discontent with wages was a complaint of mercenary soldiers. "Wages" are of different kinds in the NT (cf. preachers pay 2 Cor. 11:8; wages of sin Rom. 6:23).

15. {*Whether haply he were the Christ*} John wrought no miracles and was not in David's line. And yet he moved people so mightily that they began to suspect that he himself was the Messiah (cf. John 1:19).

16. {*He that is mightier than I*} (cf. Mark 1:7 and Matt. 3:11). Not turned aside by the flattery of the crowd, John was loyal to Messiah.

This whole verse is a bold Messianic picture of judgment upon the world (cf. Luke 3:17; Matt. 3:12).

18. {*Many other exhortations...preached the good news*} Lit. "many and different things did John evangelize." Luke has given a bare sample of the wonderful messages of the Baptist.

19. {*Reproved*} (cf. 2 Tim. 3:16). This is the Greek verb *elegchô,* to convict (Matt. 18:15), to expose (Eph. 5:11), to reprove as here.

20. {*Shut down*} (cf. Matt. 14:3). This Greek verb *katekleiô* lit. *shut down,* possibly with a reference to closing down the door of the dungeon, though it makes sense as a perfective use of the preposition, like our "shut up."

21. {*When all the people were baptized*} This is a general statement that Jesus was baptized in connection with or at the time of the baptizing of the people as a whole. {*And praying*} The Greek syntax has the natural meaning that the heaven was opened while Jesus was praying, though not necessarily in answer to his prayer.

22. {*In a bodily form*} This probably means that the Baptist saw the vision that the Holy Spirit (in symbolism) looked like a dove. The Holy Spirit may have deepened the Messianic consciousness of Jesus and certainly revealed him to the Baptist as God's Son. {*And a voice came out of heaven*} (cf. Mark 1:11 and Matt. 3:17). The Trinity here is manifest at the baptism of Jesus, which constitutes the formal entrance of Jesus upon his Messianic ministry: the Father's blessing; the power of the Holy Spirit upon the him; He is the Son of God (John 1:34).

23-38. {*Was about thirty years of age*} Luke avoids precision regarding the age of Christ. Jesus may have been a few months under or over thirty or a year or two less or more. {*Being son (as was supposed) of Joseph, the son of Heli*} (cf. Matt. 1:1-17). Joseph, of course, did not have two fathers; some explain that Heli would be Jesus' grandfather on Mary's side (an acceptable use of "son" in Biblical terms). Luke has already given testimony that Joseph was not the actual biological father of Jesus (cf. Luke 1:26-38). Luke finishes his genealogy of Jesus with Adam as the son of God. He did this possibly to dispose of the heathen myths about the origin of man and to show that God is the Creator of the whole human race; the Father of all men in that sense. But Jesus is the Son of God in a different sense than Adam was.

CHAPTER 4

1. {*Was led by the Spirit*} Greek tense shows he was *continuously* led. Luke affirms that Jesus was now continuously under the guidance of the Holy Spirit. Hence, in this same sentence he mentions the Spirit twice. {*During the forty days*} (cf. Mark 1:13 and Matt. 4:2). He was led in the Spirit during these forty days (cf. Deut. 8:2, forty years). These three temptations of Jesus may be merely specimens and so representative of the struggle which continued throughout the whole period (Plummer).

2. {*Being tempted...*} The devil challenged the Son of man though also the Son of God. It was a contest between Jesus, full of the Holy Spirit, and the slanderer of men. The Temptation bears all the marks of the high conception of Jesus as the Son of God found throughout the NT. {*He did eat nothing*} With probably nothing at hand to eat, Jesus' weakness from fasting gave the devil his special opportunity to tempt Jesus. {*He hungered*} Greek tense shows he "*became* hungry" at the close of the forty days (cf. Matt. 4:2).

3. {*The Son of God*} (cf. Matt. 4:3). The syntax here refers to the relationship as Son of God rather than to the office of Messiah. (cf. Luke 3:22). Greek syntax shows the devil assumes that Jesus *is* Son of God. {*This stone*} Note plural in Matthew. He is perhaps pointing to a particular round stone that looked in shape and size like a loaf of bread, common in the region. The hunger of Jesus opened the way for the diabolic suggestion designed to inspire doubt toward his Father. Jesus felt the force of each of the temptations without yielding at all to the sin involved, quoting Scripture (cf. Deut. 8:3).

5. {*The world*} That is, the inhabited world (cf. Matt. 4:8). {*In a moment of time*} "Instant" is the Greek word *stigmêi*, from *stizô*, to prick, or puncture, so a "point" or "dot" of time, like our "tick of the clock." This panorama was mental, a great feat of the imagination (a mental satanic "movie" performance) but this fact in no way discredits the idea of the actual visible appearance of Satan.

6. {*For it hath been delivered unto me*} Satan, called ruler of the world, here claims possession of world power and Jesus doesn't deny it. This may be due to man's sin and by God's permission (cf. John 12:31; 14:30; 16:11). {*To whomsoever I will*} The tone of Satan here is one of superiority to Jesus in world power. He offers him a share in it on one condition.

7. {*Wilt worship before me*} (cf. Matt. 4:9). The devil is saying, just bow the knee once up here in my presence, an act that would admit Satan's authority. {*It shall all be thine*} A tremendous grandstand play, Satan offers to turn over all the keys of world power to Jesus (as an ally).

8. {*Thou shalt worship...*} (cf. Deut. 6:13). Jesus clearly perceived that one could not worship both Satan and God.

9. {*Led him...the wing of the temple*} (cf. Matt. 4:5). It is not easy to determine precisely what place to which this refers. {*To guard thee*} (cf. Ps. 91:11, 12). Quoting correctly, Satan misapplies the Psalm and makes it mean presumptuous reliance on God.

12. {*It is said*} He is again quoting Scripture (cf. Deut. 6:16). Each time he uses Deuteronomy against the devil. Jesus points out to the devil that testing God is not trusting God (Plummer).

13. {*Every temptation*} These three temptations are kinds that exhaust the avenues of approach: the appetites, the nerves, the ambitions. Jesus was in all points tempted like as we are (Heb. 4:15). {*For a season*} That is, "until a good opportunity should return." We are thus to infer that the devil returned to his attack from time to time: as in the Garden of Gethsemane; or the devil attacked by the aid of Peter (Mark 8:33).

14. {*Returned*} Following Mark's gospel, Luke does not fill in the gap between the temptations in the wilderness of Judea and the Galilean Ministry, a year of obscurity in various parts of the Holy Land goes by. {*A fame*} That is, talk ran rapidly in every direction. It assumes the previous ministry as told by John.

15. {*And he taught*} The Greek tense here is descriptive of the *habit* of Jesus. The synagogues were an open door to Jesus before the hostility of the Pharisees was aroused.

16. {*Where he had been brought up*} Here Jesus comes back after a year of public ministry elsewhere and with a wide reputation (Luke 4:15). The Greek tense may imply that for some time now Nazareth had not been his home. {*As his custom was*} Jesus had the habit of going to public worship in the synagogue as a boy, a habit that he kept up when a grown man. {*Stood up...to read*} It was the custom for the reader to stand and publicly read (and that one giving occasional comments). This was apparently the first time that he had taught in Nazareth. He may have been asked to read by the ruler of the synagogue because of Jesus' great reputation as a teacher (cf. Acts 13:15).

17. {*The book of the prophet Isaiah...unrolled*} Apparently Isaiah was handed to Jesus without his asking for it. It was a congenial service that he was asked to perform. It may have been a fixed lesson for the day or it may have been his own choosing.

18. {*Anointed me*} This is the Greek verb *chriô* from which *Christ* derives, meaning the Anointed One. Isaiah is picturing the Jubilee year and the release of captives and the return from the Babylonian exile with the hope of the Messiah through it all. Jesus here applies this Messianic language to himself. {*To the poor*} The *Gospel* is for the poor. {*He hath sent me*} Greek tense shows he is now on that mission here. Jesus is God's *Apostle* to men (cf. John 17:3). {*Them that are bruised*} From the Greek verb *thrauô,* meaning to break in pieces, broken in heart and often in body as well, and so the "oppressed." Jesus' mission was to mend broken hearts and set people free from their limitations.

19. {*The acceptable year of the Lord*} This means Messianic age has come. Christ's ministry was more than one year in length.

20. {*He closed the book*} After doing this, he gave it back to the attendant who had given it to him. {*Sat down*} Taking a new seat; sitting was a sign that he was going to speak and teach (cf. Luke 5:3; Matt. 5:1; Mark 4:1; Acts 16:13). {*Eyes...were fastened on him*} (cf. 2 Cor. 3:7, 13). There was something in the look of Jesus that held the people spellbound.

21. {*Hath been fulfilled*} (cf. Isa. 61:1-2). Greek tense translates, "stands fulfilled." Jesus means that the real year of Jubilee had come, that the Messianic prophecy of Isaiah had come true today, and that in him they saw the Messiah of prophecy; and spoken here at Nazareth by one of their own townsmen!

22. {*Bare him witness*} Greek tense shows they all *began* to bear witness that the rumors were not exaggerations as they had supposed (cf. Luke 4:14). {*And wondered*} Again, Greek tense shows they *began* to marvel as he proceeded with his address. {*At the words of grace*} (cf. Luke 1:30; 2:52). They were "winning words." The Greek syntax shows words that came out of the mouth of Jesus in a steady stream and were marked by fascination and charm. {*Is not this Joseph's son?*} (cf. John

1:45). The people were puzzled, because they knew him as Jesus the carpenter (cf. Mark 6:3; Matt. 13:55); 'now Messiah?' they thought. It was beyond sober reflection for them.

23. {*This parable*} (cf. Luke 5:36; 6:39). This word here means a crisp saying which involves a comparison; here it had a tone of sarcasm. The proverb means that the physician was expected to take his own medicine and to heal himself (establish your claims by direct evidence), i.e., do in Nazareth (here and *now*) what they had heard him doing elsewhere. The same tone was at the Cross (cf. Matt. 27:40, 42).

25. {*Elijah...three years and six months*} (cf. Jas. 5:17). Here is the first illustration of the proverb. It rained in the third year (cf. 1 Kgs. 18:1), but the famine probably lasted still longer.

26. {*Unto a woman that was a widow*} Lit. "to a woman a widow" (cf. 1 Kgs. 17:8, 9). This is a heathen woman, from a land where Jesus himself will go later.

27. {*In the time of Elisha the prophet*} The second illustration of the proverb is Elisha. This is another heathen, a lone leper cleansed by Elisha (2 Kgs. 5:1, 14).

28. {*They were all filled with wrath*} Lit. "filled with anger." Town pride was insulted. Catching the point immediately, the Nazarenes saw from the examples (vv. 25-27) how God in two cases blessed the heathen instead of the Jewish people. The clear implication was that Jesus was under no special obligation to do unusual things in Nazareth because he had been reared there.

29. {*Unto the brow of the hill*} This is a movement towards lynching Jesus. {*That they might throw him down headlong*} Murder was in the hearts of the people. By pushing him over a cliff, they hoped to escape technical guilt.

31. {*Capernaum*} (cf. Luke 4:31-37; cf. Mark 1:21-28). Capernaum (Tell Hum) is now the headquarters of the Galilean ministry, since Nazareth has rejected Jesus. {*Was teaching them*} This refers to the people present in the synagogue on the Sabbath.

33. {*Which had...a spirit of an unclean demon*} Lit. "having spirit of a demon of uncleanness," a unique combination of words. {*With a loud voice*} This is really a scream caused by the sudden contact of the demon with Jesus.

34. {*Ah!*} It is expressive of wonder, fear, indignation. Here it amounts to a diabolical screech (cf. Mark 1:24 and Matt. 8:29).

35. {*Hold thy peace*} This is a command from the Greek verb *phimoô*, from *phimos*, muzzle: lit. 1 Corinthians 9:9, 1 Timothy 5:18; fig. Mark 1:25; 4:39; Matthew 22:12. {*Having done him no hurt*} Luke as a physician carefully notes this important detail not in Mark.

37. {*Went forth a rumour*} Greek tense shows the news *kept on* going forth. "News" is our very word *echo*, used for the roar of the waves on the shore (cf. Luke 21:25). This is a vivid picture of the resounding influence of this day's work in the synagogue at Capernaum.

38. {*Into the house of Simon*} This is Peter's house (cf. Matt. 8:14 and Mark 1:29), with a wife (1 Cor. 9:5) and so mother-in-law. This house came also to be the Capernaum home of Jesus. {*Simon's wife's mother was holden with a great fever*} The Greek tense is accenting the continuous fever, perhaps chronic and certainly severe.

39. {*He stood over her*} Not an exorcist's position, this stance is precisely that of any kindly sympathetic physician, including a touch (cf. Mark 1:31; Matt. 8:15). {*Rose up and ministered*} She rose up immediately, though a long high fever usually leaves one very weak. The cure was instantaneous and complete. She began to minister at once and kept it up.

40. {*When the sun was setting*} (cf. Mark 1:32). It was not only cooler, but it was the end of the Sabbath when it was not regarded as work to carry a sick person (John 5:10). And also by now the news of the cure of the demoniac and of Peter's mother-in-law had spread all over the town; people were being brought one after the other. {*He laid his hands on every one of them and healed them*} The Greek tense is picturing the healing one by one with a tender touch, not merely a ceremonial touch.

41. {*Thou art the Son of God*} This is a more definite statement of the deity of Jesus than the witness of the demoniac in the synagogue (Luke 4:34; Mark 1:24), like the words of the Father (Luke 3:22) and more so than the condition of the devil (Luke 4:3, 9). {*Suffered them not to speak*} The Greek tense accents the continued refusal of Jesus to receive testimony to his person and work from demons (cf. lepers, Matt. 8:4).

42. {*When it was day*} (cf. Mark 1:35). Jesus rose up after a restless night to go out to pray; no doubt, because of the excitement of the previous Sabbath in Capernaum. {*They tried to hinder him*} This is the Greek verb *katechô,* here meaning to hold back, to retain, to restrain (Phlm. 1:13; Rom. 1:18; 7:6; 2 Thess. 2:6; Luke 4:42).

43. {*I must...for therefore was I sent*} Jesus felt the urge to go with the work of evangelism to the other cities also, that is, to all, not to a favored few.

44. {*Was preaching*} This is his first tour of Galilee in accord with the purpose just stated; one must fill in details of this mass of work (cf. Mark 1:39 and Matt. 8:23-25).

CHAPTER 5

1. {*Pressed upon him*} (Luke 5:1-11; Mark 1:16-20; Matt. 4:18-22) Here Luke does not follow the chronology of Mark as he usually does. It seems reasonably clear that the renewed call of the four fishermen came before the first tour of Galilee in Luke 4:42-44. It is here assumed that Luke is describing in his own way the incident given in Mark and Matthew above, with a focus on Peter.

2. {*Two boats*} This Greek word *ploia* was used of boats of various sizes, even of ships.

3. {*To put out a little*} Here this is in the sense of leading a ship up upon the sea, to put out to sea, a nautical term.

4. {*Put out into the deep...let down...*} The verb "let down" was used for lowering anything from a higher place (Mark 2:4; Acts 9:25; 2 Cor. 11:33). {*For a catch*} This purpose was the startling thing that stirred up Simon.

5. {*Master*} Recognizing Christ's authority, this is the Greek word *epistatês,* only by Luke in the NT and always in addresses to Christ (Luke 8:24, 45; 9:33, 49; 17:13). Common in the older writers for superintendent or overseer (one standing over another). {*We toiled*} This verb is from *kopos* (work, toil), with the notion of weariness in toil. Peter's protest calls attention to the whole night of fruitless toil. {*But at thy word...*} Showing Jesus is Peter's Master, he does so; but with no confidence whatsoever in the wisdom of this particular command. Fishing was Peter's business; he really claimed superior knowledge on this occasion to that of Jesus.

6. {*They shut together. Were breaking*} The Greek word shows that the nets were actually tearing in two and so they would lose all the fish.

7. {*They beckoned*} They used signs. Possibly they were too far away for a call, being in the deep part of the lake. {*Unto their partners*} This Greek word *metochos,* from *metechô,* to have with, means participation with one in common blessings, but not necessarily personal fellowship (cf. *koinônos,* Luke 5:10). Simon was the head of this company of two pairs of brothers.

8. {*Fell down at Jesus' knees*} Typically, Peter goes from extreme self-confidence and pride (v. 5) to abject humiliation. But his impulse here was right and sincere. His confession was true. He was a sinful man.

10. {*Thou shalt catch men*} "Catch" is the Greek verb *zôgreô* meaning to catch alive, not to kill. So then Peter is to be a catcher of men, not of fish, and to catch them alive and for life, not dead and for death. Jesus foresees the possibilities in Simon and he joyfully undertakes the task of making a fisher of men out of this poor fisher of fish.

11. {*They...left all, and followed him*} They had already become his disciples. Now they leave their business for active service of Christ.

12. {*Full of leprosy*} (cf. Mark 1:40 and Matt. 8:2). Evidently this was a bad case full of sores and far advanced as Luke the physician notes (cf. Lev. 13:12).

14. {*To tell no man*} (cf. Mark 1:43; Matt. 8:4). He is directed to go to the priest to receive a certificate showing his cleansing, like our release from quarantine (Lev. 13:39; 14:2-32). It was for a testimony to them.

15. {*Went abroad*} The Greek tense shows the fame of Jesus *kept on* going. The more the report spread, the more the crowds came.

17. {*Doctors of the law*} This is the same as the scribes, usually Pharisees (Greek word *grammateis,* cf. Matt. 5:20; 23:34 and Luke 5:21; 19:47; 21:1; 22:2). Though not all the Pharisees were teachers of the law. They are here on purpose to find fault and to make charges against Jesus. {*Out of every village of Galilee and Judea and Jerusalem*} The Jews distinguished Jerusalem as a separate district in Judea. Judea had already been aroused and Jerusalem was the headquarters of the definite campaign now organized against Jesus. One must bear in mind that John 4:14 shows that Jesus had already left Jerusalem and Judea because of the jealousy of the Pharisees.

19. {*The housetop*} (cf. Mark 2:4). Able to be dug through, the flat roofs of Jewish houses were usually reached by outside stairways. One could go there for meditation (cf. Acts 10:9). {*Into the midst before*}

Jesus} The four friends probably each holding a rope to a corner of the pallet.

20. {*Man*} Possibly this man's malady was due to his sin as is sometimes true (John 5:14). The man had faith along with that of the four, but he was still a paralytic when Jesus forgave his sins.

22. {*Perceiving*} This is the common verb for knowing fully (cf. Mark 2:8; Matt. 9:4).

26. {*Amazement*} This is the Greek word *ekstasis,* something out of its place, as the mind. Here the people were almost beside themselves. {*Gave praise to God*} The Greek tense shows that they *kept on* glorifying God and at the same time were filled with fear. {*Strange things*} This is the Greek word *paradoxa,* our very word paradox, contrary to (*para*) received opinion (*doxa*).

28. {*He forsook all*} In Luke alone, we see that Matthew left his profitable business for the service of Christ. {*Followed him*} Greek tense shows he began at once to follow him and he kept it up (cf. Mark 2:14; Matt. 9:9).

29. {*A great feast*} (cf. Luke 14:13). This is the Greek word *dochê,* from *dechomai,* and means "reception." Levi made Jesus a big reception. {*Publicans and others*} (cf. Mark 2:15 and Matt. 9:10). None but social outcasts (also called "sinners") would eat with tax collectors at such a feast or barbecue.

30. {*The Pharisees and their scribes*} (cf. Mark 2:16). Some of the scribes were Sadducees. It is only the Pharisees who find fault here. {*Murmured*} This vivid Greek word *gon-guz-ô* sounds like the meaning; a late word used of the cooing of doves; like the buzzing of bees. The Greek tense shows they murmured and muttered repeatedly, and kept it up. Though uninvited, they hung on the outside and criticized the disciples of Jesus for being there.

31. {*They that are whole*} (cf. Luke 7:10; 15:27; 3 John 2). This is the usual word for good health (sound body) used by Greek medical writers.

32. {*To repentance*} (cf. Mark 2:17; Matt. 9:12). Only sinners would need a call to repentance, a change of mind and life. For the moment Jesus accepts the Pharisaic division between "righteous" and "sinners" to score them and to answer their criticism. At the other times he will show that they only pretend to be "righteous" and are "hypocrites" in reality.

33. {*But thine...*} (cf. Mark 2:18; Matt. 9:14). This reception probably was on one of the Jewish fast days, giving special edge to their criticism.

34. {*Can ye...?*} In the Greek, this question expects a "no" answer.

36. {*Rendeth*} This is the Greek verb *schizô*, splitting. Our word "schism" comes from it. {*Putteth it*} Lit. "puts on" with the meaning of sewing on (cf. Matt. 9:16 and Mark 2:21).

39. {*The old is good*} It is the philosophy of the obscurantist, that is here pictured by Christ. "The prejudiced person will not even try the new, or admit that it has any merits. He knows that the old is pleasant, and suits him; and that is enough; he is not going to change" (Plummer). This is Christ's picture of the reactionary Pharisees.

CHAPTER 6

1. {*On a Sabbath*} This is the second Sabbath on which Jesus is noted by Luke. The first was Luke 4:31-41. {*Plucked...did eat*} (cf. Matt. 12:1ff. and Mark 2:23). This is some grain (not our "maize" [corn]); the Greek tense shows they were plucking and eating as they went on through. {*Rubbing them in their hands*} According to Rabbinical notions, it was reaping, threshing, winnowing, and preparing food all at once.

4. {*Did take...*} (cf. Matt. 12:1-8; Mark 2:23-28). Jesus gives five arguments in defense of his conduct on the Sabbath: the example of David, work of the priests on the Sabbath, prophecy of Hosea 6:6, purpose of the Sabbath for man, the Son of Man lord of the Sabbath.

7. {*The scribes and the Pharisees*} (cf. Matt. 12:14 and Mark 3:6). {*Watched him...*} (cf. Mark 3:2). Here they were watching insidiously with evil intent. {*That they might find out how to accuse him*} They were determined to make a case against Jesus.

8. {*But he knew their thoughts*} In contrast to these spies, Jesus read their intellectual processes like an open book. {*His hand withered*} (cf. Mark 3:3). {*Stand forth...arise into the midst*} Christ worked right out in the open where all could see. It was a moment of excitement when the man stepped forth there before them all.

9. {*I ask you*} They had questions in their hearts about Jesus. He now asks a question that brings the whole issue into the open. {*A life*} The rabbis had a rule: one could save a life if it was a Jew whose life was in peril on the Sabbath.

10. {*He looked round about on them all*} The Greek voice (middle) gives a personal touch to the looking around; Mark adds "with anger." {*Stretch forth thy hand*} Jesus tells him to stretch it out, clean out, full length. {*Restored*} The focus of the form of the word means complete restoration to the former state.

11. {*They were filled with madness*} Lit. "filled with lack of sense." Here is rage that is kin to insanity. {*Communed*} (cf. Mark 3:6). The Greek tense pictures their excited counselings with one another and even the antagonistic Herodians. {*What they might do to Jesus*} (cf. Mark 3:6; Matt. 12:14). Already nearly two years before the end we see the set determination to destroy Jesus (cf. John 5:18).

12. {*In prayer to God*} This means actual prayer of Jesus to the Father all night long; it does not mean "place of prayer" here (cf. Acts 16:13). He needed the Father's guidance now in the choice of the Apostles in the morning.

13. {*He chose from them twelve*} There was a large group of disciples whom he called to him. From that larger group he chose *for himself* the Twelve. {*Whom also he named apostles*} (cf. Matt. 10:1-4 and Mark 3:14-19). The word "apostle" is derived from the Greek verb *apostellô*, to send; an apostle is a missionary, one sent. Having no successors, these twelve apostles stand apart from all other followers of Jesus. These Twelve were trained by Jesus himself, to interpret him and his message to the world as well as be personal witnesses to the life and resurrection of Jesus (Acts 1:22).

17. {*He came down with them*} (Mark 3:13; Luke 6:12). After a night of prayer up on the mountainside and the choice of the Twelve next morning, he came down. This place may be a level one towards the foot of the mountain, yet still at some elevation, and began to speak (cf. Matt. 5:1). Matthew and Luke report the same event, though different in some details and Matthew being longer, dealing with a proper conception of righteousness in contrast to the Jewish rabbis.

18. {*With unclean spirits...were healed*} Greek tense shows the healings were repeated as often as they came.

19. {*Sought to touch him*} Greek tense pictures the surging, eager crowd pressing up to Jesus. Probably some of them felt that there was a sort of virtue or magic in touching his garments (cf. Luke 8:43 and Mark 5:23;

Matt. 9:21). {*For power came forth from him*} Greek tense shows *continual* power coming forth and they *kept on* being healed as well, and was the reason for the continual approach to Jesus.

20. {*And he lifted up his eyes*} (cf. Matt. 5:2). Jesus looked the vast audience full in the face. He spoke out so that the great crowd could hear. {*The poor*} Differing from Matthew for unknown reasons, Luke has four blessings and four woes. Does the first blessing mean poverty itself is a blessing? Or does Luke represent Jesus as meaning what is in Matthew, poverty *of spirit?* {*The kingdom of God*} This means the same as "kingdom of heaven" (cf. Matt. 5:3). Not a political (Jewish focused) Messianic kingdom, Jesus here meant "kingdom" for the rule of God in the heart here and now. It is both present and future.

21. {*Now*} This sharpens the contrast between present sufferings and the future blessings. {*Filled*} (cf. Matt. 5:6). Originally it was used for giving fodder to animals, but here it is spiritual fodder (cf. Luke 15:16; 16:21).

22. {*When they shall separate you*} This is the Greek verb *aphorizô*, common for marking off a boundary; here meant in a bad sense. It refers to excommunication from the congregation as well as from social interaction. {*Cast out your name as evil*} Outlawed later in the first century, any name for "Christian" came to be a byword of contempt as shown in the Acts. {*For the Son of man's sake*} Both Son of God and Son of Man apply to Jesus (John 1:50-51; Matt. 26:63). Christ was a real man though the Son of God. He is also the representative man and has authority over all men.

24. {*But woe unto you that are rich*} "But" in the Greek is very sharp. The rich Pharisees and Sadducees were the chief opposers of Christ as of the early disciples later (Jas. 5:1-6).

26. {*Woe...when all men shall speak well of you*} That is, they spoke well (Greek word *kalôs*), finely of false prophets.

27. {*But I say unto you that hear*} This shows sharp antithesis between what the rabbis taught and what Jesus said. {*Love your enemies*} (cf. Matt. 5:43). Love of enemies is in the OT, but Jesus makes the word noble, Greek verb *agapaô*, and uses it of love for one's enemies.

29. {*On the cheek*} (cf. Matt. 5:39). It seems here this means an act of violence rather than contempt. {*Thy cloke...thy coat*} The first is the Greek word *himation,* the outer and more valuable garment is first taken, the under garment and less valuable (Greek *chitôn*) last.

30. {*Ask them not again*} Greek syntax shows "do not have the habit of asking back."

32. {*What thank have ye?*} Lit. "What grace or gratitude is there to you?" (cf. Matt. 5:46).

33. {*Do good...*} This is a plausible case, though not yet determined. {*Even "sinners"*} (cf. Matt. 5:46-47). Greek syntax shows this is a class or kind differentiated. Other outcasts include: tax collectors, Gentiles, harlots, and so on.

34. {*If ye lend*} This is the Greek verb *danizô* (old form *daneizô*) to lend for interest in a business transaction; whereas Greek verb *kichrêmi* (Luke 11:5) means to loan as a friendly act.

35. {*But...*} Lit. "never despairing" or "giving up nothing in despair" Jesus means that we are not to despair about getting the money back. We are to help the apparently hopeless cases.

36. {*Even as your Father*} (cf. Matt. 5:48). The perfection of the Father is placed as the goal before his children.

37. {*And judge not*} Greek syntax show that this is "forbidding the habit of criticism." We can form *opinions,* but not to form them rashly, unfairly, i.e., with prejudice. {*Condemn not*} The Greek syntax means either cease doing or do not have the habit of doing it; censoriousness is a bad habit.

38. {*I will measure their former work unto their bosom. Shall be measured to you again*} "Bosom" is the fold of the wide upper garment bound by the girdle that made a pocket in common use (Exod. 4:6; Prov. 6:27; Ps. 79:12; Isa. 65:6-7; Jer. 32:18).

39. {*Also a parable*} Parable here refers to both crisp proverbs and longer narrative comparisons. The two parables come right together: The blind leading the blind, the mote and the beam.

40. {*The disciple is not above his master*} (cf. Matt. 10:24). Often translated "disciple," lit. "a learner (or pupil) is not above the teacher." {*But everyone when he is perfected shall be as his master*} That is in the state of completion. The Greek word is common for mending broken things or nets (Matt. 4:21) or men (Gal. 6:1). So it is a long process to get the pupil patched up to the plane of his teacher.

44. {*Is known*} (cf. Matt. 7:17-20). The final test, the fruit of each tree reveals its actual character. {*Bramble bush*} Though also used of the burning bush (cf. Exod. 3:6), ancient medical writings abound in prescriptions of which briers are an ingredient. {*Grapes*} That is, a cluster of grapes.

45. {*Bringeth forth*} (cf. Matt. 12:34). "When men are natural, heart and mouth act in concert. But otherwise the mouth sometimes professes what the heart does not feel" (Plummer).

48. {*Digged and went deep*} Lit. "dug and made deep" really both combine into one thought. {*And laid a foundation*} That is the whole point. This wise builder struck the rock before he laid the foundation. {*Could not shake it*} That is, did not have strength enough to shake it.

49. {*He that heareth and doeth not*} In an antithetical case to the above, the crash of the house was like a giant oak in the forest, resounding far and wide.

CHAPTER 7

2. {*Centurion's servant*} (cf. Mark 15:39, 44). This is a slave, belonging to a commander of about fifty to one hundred soldiers (a *century*). Commanders in this rank were some of the best men of the army. {*Dear to him*} Though a mere slave, he was held in honor, prized, precious, dear (Luke 14:8; 1 Pet. 2:4; Phil. 2:29). {*Was sick*} Lit. "having it bad"; a paralytic (cf. Matt. 8:6).

3. {*Sent unto him elders of the Jews*} Though in apparent contradiction to Matthew, perhaps Matthew is merely making a summary statement without the details (cf. Matt. 8:5). Note Luke represents the centurion himself as "asking" through the elders of the Jews (leading citizens). {*That he would come and save*} Lit. "save" is "to bring safe through as in a storm," and so heal (cf. Acts 28:1, 4).

4. {*Besought...earnestly*} The Greek tense shows he began and kept on beseeching (cf. Matt. 8:5). The plea was in haste with earnest zeal, for time was short.

5. {*For...*} This shows why the elders considered him worthy. He was a Roman who had shown his love for the Jews; Greek syntax shows he built it all by himself and at his own expense, *for* the Jews.

7. {*My servant shall be healed*} "Servant" is lit. "boy," an affectionate term for the "slave" (v. 2), who was dear to him.

9. {*Turned...*} Jesus marvels at the great faith of this Roman centurion beyond that among the Jews. As a military man he had learned how to receive orders and to execute them and hence to expect obedience to his commands. He recognized Jesus as Master over disease with power to compel obedience.

10. {*Whole*} That is, "well, sound" (cf. Luke 5:31).

12. {*The only son of his mother*} The death of a widow's only son was the greatest misfortune conceivable. The mourning of a widow for an only son is the extremity of grief. {*Much people*} Some were hired mourners, but the size of the crowd showed the real sympathy of the town for her.

13. {*Had compassion*} Often love and pity are mentioned as the motives for Christ's miracles (Matt. 14:14; 15:32, etc.). {*Weep not*} Greek syntax translates, "cease weeping."

14. {*Touched the bier*} Here this means the funeral couch or bier. Jesus touched the bier to make the bearers stop.

15. {*Sat up*} (cf. Acts 9:40). Medical writers often used this word of the sick sitting up in bed. {*Gave him to his mother*} This is a tender way of putting it, for he had already ceased to belong to his mother (cf. Luke 9:42) (Bengel).

16. {*They glorified God*} The Greek tense shows that this glorying began and increased.

17. {*This report*} That is, that God had raised up a great prophet who had shown his call by raising the dead.

18. {*And the disciples of John told him*} (cf. Matt. 11:2-19). Such news (v. 17) was bound to come to the ears of the Baptist languishing in the dungeon of Machaerus (Luke 3:20).

21. {*In that hour he cured...*} Jesus gave the two disciples of John an example of the direct method. They had heard. Then they saw for themselves.

23. {*No occasion of stumbling*} This Greek verb *skandalizomai* used here has the double notion of to trip up and to entrap, and in the NT always means causing to sin.

24. {*When the messengers of John were departed*} (cf. Matt. 11:7). This suggests that Jesus began his eulogy of John as soon as the messengers were on their way.

25. {*Gorgeously apparelled*} (cf. Matt. 11:8-10). John did not live with splendid clothing, or luxurious living.

26. {*A prophet?*} A real prophet (like John) will always get a hearing, whether he tells the future or not. The main thing is for the prophet to have a message from God which he is willing to tell at whatever cost to himself (cf. Luke 3:2).

29. {*Justified God*} They considered God just or righteous in making these demands of them, even the tax collectors. This is a saying of Jesus, not a comment of Luke.

30. {*Rejected for themselves*} These legalistic interpreters of the law refused to admit the need of confession of sin on their part and so set aside the baptism of John.

32. {*And ye did not weep*} (cf. Matt. 11:17). They all did it at funerals. These children would not play wedding or funeral.

33. {*John the Baptist is come*} (cf. Matt. 11:18-19). Some say that Jesus was called the friend of sinners and of harlots because he loved *their ways* and so deserved the slur cast upon him by his enemies; no wonder the Pharisees and lawyers said it then to justify their own rejection of Jesus.

36. {*That he would eat with him*} (cf. Luke 11:37; 14:1). This is the Gospel of Hospitality to diverse groups: Jesus would dine with a Pharisee or tax collector (Luke 5:29; Mark 2:15; Matt. 9:10) and even invited himself to be the guest of Zacchaeus (Luke 19:5).

37. {*A woman which was in the city, a sinner*} (cf. v. 39). The town probably refers to Capernaum. The syntax of the phrase means the woman was of a sinful character, and was known as such (cf. Mark 14:3-9; Matt. 26:6-13; John 12:2-8). This sinful woman had repented and changed her life and wished to show her gratitude to Jesus who had rescued her. But her bad reputation as a harlot clung to her and made her an unwelcome visitor in the Pharisee's house. {*When she knew...he was sitting at meat*} "Knew" means "to know fully, to recognize." An intruder, she came in by a curious custom of the time that allowed strangers to enter a house uninvited at a feast to chat with the host or discuss business, especially beggars seeking a gift. Jesus here was reclining as he ate.

38. {*Standing behind at his feet*} The guest removed his sandals before the meal and he reclined on the left side with the feet outward. She was standing beside his feet. {*Weeping*} Drawn by gratitude to Jesus, she is overcome with emotion; her tears take the place of the ointment. {*Wiped them with the hair of her head*} Similar but distinct from Mary of Bethany, this was an act of impulse evidently and of embarrassment. Among the Jews it was a shameful thing for a woman to let down her hair in public. {*Kissed*} (cf. Luke 15:20). Greek tense shows she kissed repeatedly with continued action. Kissing the feet was a common mark of deep reverence, especially to leading rabbis. {*Anointed them with the ointment*} This anointing of ointment came after the burst of emotional excitement.

39. {*This man*} Lit. "this fellow." This phrase shows they had contempt for Jesus. {*If he were a (the) prophet...would have perceived*} The Greek condition shows *the Pharisee* assumes that Jesus is not a prophet, a false premise. The conclusion is also false.

42. {*Will love him most*} The point of the parable is the *attitude of the two debtors* toward the lender who forgave both of them.

43. {*I suppose*} Here this means to make an assumption, with an air of haughty indifference.

44. {*Seest thou...*} The Pharisee had neglected some points of customary hospitality toward Jesus his guest.

47. {*Are forgiven...for she loved much*} The basis of the forgiveness was not her love, but the love was proof of her forgiveness.

48. {*Are forgiven*} The Greek tense shows the sins *remain* forgiven, in spite of the slur of the Pharisee.

49. {*Who even forgiveth sins*} Once before the Pharisees considered Jesus guilty of blasphemy in claiming the power to forgive sins (Luke 5:21). Jesus read their inmost thoughts as he always does.

CHAPTER 8

1. {*Through cities and villages*} This is the second tour of Galilee, this time the Twelve with him.

2. {*Which had been healed*} These women all had personal grounds of gratitude to Jesus, having been healed some time before this. {*From whom seven devils (demons) had gone out*} (cf. Mark 16:9). This first mention of Mary Magdalene describes her special cause of gratitude. Seven demons in one person indicates special malignity (cf. Mark 5:9 and Matt. 12:45).

3. {*Joanna*} (cf. Luke 24:10). Her husband *Chuzâ*, steward of Herod Antipas, is held by some to be the nobleman who believed and all his house (cf. John 4:46-53). {*Who ministered unto them...of their substance*} The very fact that Jesus now had twelve men going with him called for help from others and the women of means responded to the demand.

4. {*By a parable*} (cf. Mark 4:1-34 and Matt. 13:1-53). Lit. "by a parable." Mark and Matthew name the seaside as the place where Jesus was at the start of the series of parables.

6. {*Upon the rock*} This is rocky ground or places (cf. Mark 4:5 and Matt. 13:5). {*As soon as it grew*} This Greek verb means to spring up like a sprout.

8. {*A hundredfold*} Luke omits the thirty and sixty (cf. Mark 4:8; Matt. 13:8). {*He cried*} The word means calling in a loud voice (cf. Mark 4:9; Matt. 13:9).

9. {*Asked*} (cf. Mark 4:10). The Greek tense and form shows eager and repeated questions on the part of the disciples, perhaps dimly perceiving a possible reflection on their own growth.

10. {*The mysteries*} (cf. Matt. 13:11 = Mark 4:11). Part of the mystery here explained is how so many people who have the opportunity to enter the kingdom fail to do so because of manifest unfitness. {*That...*} The principle here is that he who has shall receive more, while he who has not shall be deprived of what he seems to have. Jesus speaks in parables because the multitudes see without seeing and hear without hearing (Plummer).

11. {*The seed is the word of God*} Jesus now proceeds to interpret his own parable. The word of God is the seed. This means the word that comes from God, intricately related to the will of God (cf. Matt. 12:50 and Luke 8:21).

12. {*Those by the wayside*} (cf. Mark 4:15; Matt. 13:19). {*The devil*} That is the slanderer, referring to Satan. {*From their heart*} (cf. Matt. 13:19). It is the devil's business to snatch up the seed from the heart before it sprouts and takes root.

13. {*Which for a while believe*} To all outward appearances, they are sincere and have made a real start in the life of faith. {*They fall away*} That is, they stand off, lose interest, stop coming to church, drop out of sight.

14. {*They are choked*} (cf. Mark 4:19; Matt. 13:22). Worldly weeds choke the word while here the victims themselves are choked. Both are true.

15. {*In an honest and good heart*} This is an idiom difficult to translate. Though one can translate, "good and true," "sound and good," "right and good"; no one of which quite suits the Greek. {*In patience*} There is no other way for real fruit to come. The best fruits require time, cultivation, patience.

16. {*When he hath lighted a lamp*} This is a portable lamp that one lights. {*With a vessel*} Here a general word, compare "a bushel" (cf. Mark 4:21 and Matt. 5:15). {*May see the light*} (cf. see good works, Matt. 5:16) The purpose of light is to let one see something else, not the light. Jesus had kindled a light within them. They must not hide it, but must see that it spreads to others (Plummer).

18. {*How ye hear*} (cf. "what you hear" Mark 4:24). That is, the manner of hearing. Both content and manner are supremely important. {*For whosoever hath...*} (cf. Mark 4:25). This may mean, "keep on having" or "acquiring."

19. {*His mother and brethren*} (cf. Mark 3:31-35; Matt. 12:46-50). The language in the Greek allows for this to mean sisters were present also. In the beginning the siblings were more receptive, but as Jesus went on with his work and was rejected at Nazareth (Luke 4:16-31), there developed an evident disbelief in his claims on the part of the brothers who ridiculed him six months before the end (John 7:5); perhaps thinking that he is beside himself (Mark 3:21).

21. {*These which hear the word of God and do it*} No one is a child of God because of human parentage (John 1:13). Family ties are at best temporal; spiritual ties are eternal (Plummer).

22. {*And they launched forth*} "Launched forth" is the Greek verb *anagô,* an old verb, to lead up, to put out to sea (looked at as going up from the land). Its use is common in Luke's writings (Acts 27:2, 4, 12, 21; 28:10).

23. {*Came down...*} (cf. Mark 4:37). These wind storms rushed from Hermon down through the Jordan gorge upon the Sea of Galilee and shook it like a tempest, creating a sudden danger (Matt. 8:24). {*Were in jeopardy*} The Greek tense here is a vivid description.

24. {*Master, Master*} (cf. teacher, Mark 4:38 and Lord, Matt. 8:25). The repetition here shows the uneasiness of the disciples. {*We perish*} Lit. "we are perishing." (cf. Mark 4:38; Matt. 8:25). Linear present middle indicative. {*The raging of the water*} This was a boisterous surge, a violent agitation; Mark 4:37 uses the Greek word meaning "regular swell or wave."

26. {*The Gerasenes*} (cf. Mark 5:1). Gadarenes is the correct word in Matthew 8:28. This famous discrepancy is now cleared up by Thomson's discovery of Khersa (Gersa) on the steep eastern bank and in the vicinity of Gadara.

27. {*And for a long time...he had worn no clothes*} The Greek tense shows "long time" as a point of reference. Luke the physician would naturally note this item (cf. Mark 5:15).

28. {*Fell down*} (cf. "worship" Mark 5:6). {*The Most High God*} (cf. Mark 2:7 = Matt. 8:29). This phrase is common among heathen (Num. 24:16; Mic. 6:6; Isa. 14:14). The demoniac may have been a Gentile, but it is the demon here speaking.

29. {*It had seized*} (Luke 8:29; Acts 6:12; 19:29; 27:15). This is the Greek verb *sunarpazô,* to lay hold by force. {*Was driven*} This is the passive of the Greek verb *elaunô,* to drive, to row, to march.

31. {*Into the abyss*} This Greek word is *abussos,* "a" is from the Greek letter *alpha* privative (showing the absence of a quality) and *bathus* (deep). So "bottomless [place]," here referring to the abode of demons (cf. Rev. 9:1-11; 11:7; 17:8; 20:1, 3).

33. {*Rushed down the steep*} (cf. Mark 5:13; Matt. 8:32). "Rushed" is a vivid verb, "to hurl impetuously, to rush."

36. {*He that was possessed with devils (demons)*} Lit. a Greek verb with the article "the demonized." {*Was made whole*} This is the Greek verb *sôzô* to save from *sôs* (safe and sound). This is additional information to the news carried to them in verse 34.

38. {*From whom the devils (demons) were gone out*} The Greek tense of "had gone out" shows a state of completion in the past. {*Prayed him*} Lit. "kept on begging."

39. {*Throughout the whole city*} That is, in Decapolis (cf. Mark 5:20). The restored man had a great story to tell and he told it with power.

40. {*For they were all waiting for him*} This is the Greek verb *prosdokaô,* eager expectancy; this is a vivid picture of the attitude of the people towards Jesus. Driven from Decapolis, he is welcomed in Capernaum.

42. {*An only daughter*} "Only" is the same adjective used of the widow's son (Luke 7:12) and the epileptic boy (Luke 9:38) and of Jesus (John 1:18; 3:16). {*She lay a dying*} (cf. "just died" Matt. 9:18). {*Thronged*} This is the Greek verb *sumpnigô,* to press together, the verb used of the thorns choking the growing grain (Luke 8:14).

44. {*The border of his garment*} (cf. Matt. 9:20). This probably refers to the tassel of the overgarment; four corners: two were in front and two behind.

45. {*Press thee and crush thee*} "Crush" is the Greek verb *apothlibô*, a verb used of pressing out grapes in other literature (cf. Mark 5:31).

46. {*For I perceived that power had gone forth from me*} The Greek word is knowledge by personal experience. Jesus felt the sensation of power already gone.

47. {*Trembling*} Showing sensitive feelings, she now had to tell everybody of her cure. She faced the widest publicity for her secret cure.

49. {*From the ruler of the synagogue's house*} (cf. Mark 5:35). "House" is understood from context. The ruler himself had come to Jesus (Luke 8:41) and this is the real idea.

54. {*Called*} (cf. Mark 5:39; Matt. 9:24). "Called" is from the Greek verb *phôneô,* this calling was certainly not to wake up the dead, but to make it plain to all that she rose in response to his elevated tone of voice. The touch of Christ's hand and the power of his voice restored her to life.

55. {*Her spirit returned*} That is, the life came back to her at once.

CHAPTER 9

1. {*He called the Twelve together*} (cf. Mark 6:7; Matt. 10:1). Greek action shows he called them to himself.

2. {*To preach the kingdom of God and to heal the sick*} (cf. Matt. 10:7-8). The Greek tense shows these two functions (herald and healer) as continuous during this campaign.

6. {*Went*} Greek tense show this going as a continuous and repeated action. "Setting out," "preaching gospel," and "healing," describing the wide extent of the work through all the villages everywhere in Galilee.

7-8. {*He was much perplexed*} This is the Greek verb *diaporeô,* to be thoroughly at a loss, unable to find a way out (*dia* [completely], + *alpha* privative ["not"], *poros,* way).

9. {*He sought*} The Greek tense shows he *keep on* seeking to see Jesus. The rumors disturbed Herod because he was sure that he had beheaded John.

10. {*Declared*} This is the Greek verb *diêgeomai,* to carry a narrative through to the end. Jesus listened to it all.

11. {*Spake...he healed*} The Greek tense shows he *continued* speaking and *continued* healing.

12. {*To wear away*} Lit. "the day began to recline." The sun was turning down towards setting. {*Lodge*} (cf. Luke 19:7). This is the Greek verb *kataluô*, to dissolve, destroy, overthrow, and then of travelers to break a journey, to lodge (cf. *kataluma,* inn, Luke 2:7). {*Victuals*} (cf. Mark 6:32-44 = Matt. 14:13-21). This is the Greek word *episitismon*, from *episitizomai,* to provision oneself, *sitizô,* from *siton,* (wheat), common especially for provisions for a journey (snack).

13. {*Except we should go and buy food*} This is a conditional statement, though not determined or fulfilled. {*Food*} This is the Greek word *brôma,* meaning eaten pieces; from *bibrôskô,* to eat, somewhat like our "edibles" or vernacular "eats."

16. {*He gave...*} Greek tense shows he *kept on* giving. {*And brake*} Lit. "break down (or thoroughly)" is a single act shown by the Greek tense in contrast to the constant giving proceeding it.

20. {*But who say ye?*} "You" is emphatic in the Greek; what they thought is really what mattered now with Jesus. {*The Christ of God*} (cf. Luke 2:26; Matt. 16:17 and Mark 6:29). That is, the Anointed of God, the Messiah of God. Loyal to him, the disciples believe in Jesus as the Messiah of Jewish hope, but not yet the spiritual conception of the Messiah and his kingdom.

21. {*To tell this to no man*} "Messiah" or "Christ" had a political meaning to the Jews, so Jesus necessarily ceased using the word. Its use by the disciples would lead to revolution (John 6:15).

23. {*He said unto all*} (cf. Matt. 16:24-26; Mark 8:34-37). Jesus wanted *all,* the multitude with his disciples to understand the lesson of self-sacrifice. They could not yet understand the full meaning of Christ's words as applied to his approaching death. {*Take up his cross daily...and follow...*} The Greek tense of "take up" shows it as a definite point (and that "daily"); "following me" is another Greek tense that shows an ongoing event. The cross was rising before Jesus as his destiny.

27. {*Shall not taste of death...till they see*} (cf. Mark 9:1; Matt. 16:28). "Taste" means to "experience" something, a common figure in Rabbinical writings (cf. "this cup" Mark 14:36; Matt. 26:39; Luke 22:42). The Transfiguration follows in a week and may be the first fulfillment in the mind of Jesus. It may also symbolically point to the second coming.

28. {*Into the mountain*} This probably refers to Mount Hermon, near Caesarea Philippi (Mark 8:27; Matt. 16:13). {*His countenance was altered*} His face did shine like the sun (cf. Matt. 17:2). Luke does not use the word "transfigured" Greek *metemorphôthê* as in Mark 9:2; Matthew 17:2. He may have avoided this word because of its pagan associations.

31. {*There talked with him*} Lit. "they were talking about his exodus," referring to his death as a departure from earth to heaven. The glorious light graphically revealed Moses and Elijah talking with Jesus about the very subject that Peter had rebuked Jesus for mentioning (Mark 8:32; Matt. 16:22). {*To accomplish...*} Moses had led the Exodus from Egypt. Jesus will accomplish the exodus of God's people into the Promised Land on high. With his death approaching, the Transfiguration was to strengthen the heart of Jesus. No one on earth understood the heart of Jesus and so Moses and Elijah came. The poor disciples utterly failed to grasp the significance of it all.

32. {*But when they were fully awake*} "Fully awake" is the Greek verb *diagrêgoreô,* the *dia* can be either to *remain* awake in spite of desire to sleep or to become *thoroughly* awake; the latter is the likely meaning.

33. {*Let us make...*} (cf. Mark 9:5; Matt. 17:4). It was near the time of the feast of the tabernacles. So Peter proposes that they celebrate the feast here instead of going to Jerusalem for it as they did a bit later (John 7). {*Not knowing what he said*} Lit. "not understanding what he was saying." Peter acted according to his impulsive nature and spoke up even though he did not know what to say.

34. {*Overshadowed them*} The Greek tense shows the cloud *began* to come upon them. {*As they entered into the cloud*} All six entered into the cloud, but only Peter, James, and John became afraid.

35. {*My son, my chosen*} These disciples are commanded to hear Jesus, God's Son, even when he predicts his death, a pointed rebuke to Simon Peter as to all.

36. {*When the voice came*} Lit. "on the coming as to the voice." The Greek syntax shows that Jesus was found alone at the same time as the voice had spoken. {*They held their peace*} (cf. Mark 9:9; Matt. 17:9). Lit. "they became silent." Elsewhere we find that Jesus commanded them not to tell until His Resurrection; and they obeyed.

38. {*To look upon*} This is the Greek verb *epiblepô* (*epi*, upon, *blepô*, look), common in medical writers for examining carefully the patient. **39.** {*It teareth him that he foameth*} (cf. Mark 9:17; Matt. 17:15). Lit. "It tears him accompanied with foam," used by medical writers of sudden attacks of disease like epilepsy. **41.** {*How long shall I be with you and bear with you?*} (cf. Mark 9:19 and Matt. 17:17). "Put up" means to "hold myself from you" with a focus on the person who is holding back. {*Faithless*} That is, disbelieving and perverse. {*Perverse*} That is, twisted, turned, or torn in two. **42.** {*Dashed him*} This is the Greek verb *rêgnumi* or *rêssô*, to rend or convulse, a common verb, used sometimes in other literature of boxers giving knockout blows.

43. {*They were all astonished*} Greek tense shows their amazement continued, a picturesque description of the amazement of Jesus' victory where the nine disciples had failed. {*At the majesty of God*} The Greek word "greatness" came to be used by the emperors like our word "Majesty."

44. {*Sink into your ears*} (cf. Mark 9:31; Matt. 17:22). Lit. "Do you yourselves put into your ears." The contrasting focus is on the disciples as opposed to what others do.

46. {*A reasoning*} (cf. Mark 9:33). They were afraid to ask Jesus about that subject, and so they came to him to settle the dispute (cf. Matt. 18:1). Luke makes it plain that the dispute was not an abstract problem about greatness in the kingdom of heaven as they put it to Jesus (Matt. 18:1), but a personal problem in their own group. Rivalries and jealousies had already come and now sharp words.

47. {*Took a little child*} (cf. Mark 9:36; Matt. 18:3). Lit. "taking a little child to himself." Jesus gave the disciples an object lesson in humility which they sorely needed.

48. {*This little child*} Jesus holds the honored disciple is the one who welcomes little children upon the basis of Jesus' name and authority. It was a home—thrust against the selfish ambition of the Twelve.

49. {*And John answered*} It is as if John wanted to change the subject after the embarrassment of the rebuke for their dispute concerning greatness (Luke 9:46-48). {*Because he followeth not with us*} The man was doing the Master's work in the Master's name and with the Master's power, but did not run with the group of the Twelve.

50. {*Forbid not*} Lit. "stop hindering him," with the Greek syntax showing "stopping" him had already been occurring.

51. {*He steadfastly set his face…to go to Jerusalem*} The language here makes it plain that Jesus *himself* was fully conscious of the time of his death as near (Luke 9:22, 27, 31). Luke three times mentions Christ making his way to Jerusalem (Luke 9:51; 13:22; 17:11) and John mentions three journeys to Jerusalem (cf. John 7:10; 11:17; 12:1); naturally taken as the same journeys.

52-53. {*Sent messengers*} This unusual precaution was taken since Jesus was going to Jerusalem through Samaria. He was repudiating Mount Gerizim (symbolic of the religion of the Samaritans) by going by it to Jerusalem, hence the churlish Samaritans did not welcome him.

54. {*Dost thou wish?*} Perhaps the recent appearance of Elijah on the Mount of Transfiguration reminded James and John (these fiery Sons of Thunder) of the incident in 2 Kings 1:10-12.

55-56. {*But he turned…*} (cf. Matt. 5:17; Luke 19:10). Jesus rebuked the bitterness of James and John toward Samaritans as he had already chided John for his narrowness towards a fellow-worker in the kingdom.

57-58. {*Wherever you go*} Jesus knows the measure of the scribe's enthusiasm. The wandering life of Jesus explains this statement of enthusiasm. It was a case of inconsiderate impulse by the man.

59. {*And he said unto another…*} (cf. Matt. 8:21). Here he is not a volunteer, but instead one responding to the appeal of Jesus; some call him a "casual disciple." {*First…*} The burial of one's father was a sacred duty (Gen. 25:9), but this scribe's father probably was still alive (cf. Tobit 4:3). What the scribe apparently meant was that he could not leave his father while still alive to follow Jesus over the country.

60. {*Leave the dead to bury their own dead*} (cf. Matt. 8:22). The explanation is that the spiritually dead can bury the literally dead. The harshness of this proverb to the scribe probably is due to the fact that he was manifestly using his aged father as an excuse for not giving Christ active service.

61. {*But first…to bid farewell to them that are at my house*} This man meant to go home and set things in order there and then in due time to come and follow Jesus. Jesus then gives a response about conflicting duties.

62. {*Having put his hand to the plough*} The plowman who does not bend attentively to his work goes crooked; a good plowman strives to run a straight furrow. Looking to the things behind is fatal to a straight furrow; he then is not suited or adapted to plowing. This exchange was a case of a divided mind.

CHAPTER 10

1. {*Seventy others*} Here a mission in Judea, this is a similar yet different mission than the one in Galilee (Luke 9:1-6). The oldest MSS have "seventy-two." The seventy elders were counted both ways (that is, seventy and seventy-two) and the Sanhedrin likewise and the nations of the earth. {*Two and two*} (cf. Mark 6:7). This arrangement was for companionship. {*He himself was about to come*} Jesus was to follow after and investigate the work done.

2. {*Harvest*} This is the Greek word *therismos,* for the older *theros,* summer, harvest. The Twelve had the same need and prayer (cf. Matt. 9:37, 38). Prayer for preachers is Christ's method for increasing the supply.

4. {*Salute no man on the way*} (cf. 2 Kgs. 4:29). Such salutations might create chit-chat and delay. The King's business required haste.

5. {*First say...*} The word spoken is the usual oriental salutation.

6. {*A son of peace...shall rest*} Lit. "son of peace." It means "one inclined to peace," describing the head of the household. In this case, peace will "rest" (lit. "bend back") with blessing upon the one who spoke it.

7. {*In that same house*} Lit. "in the house itself" that is, in that *very* house. {*Go not from house to house*} The Greek syntax shows this was not to be done as a habit. To do so would waste time.

8. {*Such things as are set before you*} A lesson of common politeness, the Greek syntax shows this is "the things placed before you from time to time."

10. {*Into the streets thereof*} That is, go out of the inhospitable houses into the broad open streets.

11. {*Even the dust...cleaveth...*} (cf. Matt. 10:14; Luke 9:5). Dust is a plague in the east. Shake off even that. Dust clings, hence the Middle Eastern cultures took off the sandals on entering a house.

13. {*Sitting in sackcloth and ashes*} Sackcloth was a dark coarse cloth made of goat's hair and worn by penitents, mourners, suppliants. Here, ashes was a mode of voluntary humiliation.

15. {*Unto Hades*} (cf. Matt. 16:18 and Isa. 14:13-15). Lit. "go down unto Hades," here in contrast to Heaven. Note that Hades is not Gehenna. Note that Nazareth is omitted from this list of cities, who also rejected him (cf. Luke 4:28).

16. {*Rejecteth him that sent me*} The same fate of Korazin, Bethsaida, and Capernaum will befall those who set aside the message of these messengers of Christ.

17. {*Even the demons*} This was a real test, though demons were merely one sign of the conflict between Christ and Satan. The Twelve had been expressly endowed with this power when they were sent out (Luke 9:1), but the Seventy were only told to heal the sick (Luke 10:9).

18. {*I beheld Satan fallen...*} The Greek syntax shows he *was beholding* the fall as if a flash of lightning out of heaven, *quick and startling*. So the victory of the Seventy over the demons, the agents of Satan, forecast his downfall and Jesus pictured it as a flash of lightning.

19. {*Nothing shall in any wise hurt you*} "Nothing" is very strong in the Greek. But this is not a green light for presumption or foolhardiness; Jesus did not jump off the pinnacle of the temple (cf. Luke 4:9).

21. {*In that same hour*} Lit. "at the hour itself." {*Rejoiced in the Holy Spirit*} (cf. Mary's *Magnificat,* Luke 1:47 also Matt. 11:25). This holy joy of Jesus was directly due to the Holy Spirit. It is joy in the work of his followers, their victories over Satan, and is akin to the joy felt by Jesus in John 4:32-38 when the vision of the harvest of the world stirred his heart.

22. {*Knoweth who the Son is...*} This is a prayer of supreme fellowship with the Father in contemplation of final victory over Satan. Here is the Messianic consciousness in complete control and with perfect confidence in the outcome.

23. {*Turning to the disciples*} After the prayer (just after or slightly later), now Jesus turned and spoke privately apparently to the Twelve.

24. {*Which ye see*} "Ye" in the Greek is very emphatic in contrast with the prophets and kings of former days (v. 24).

25. {*And tempted him*} The Greek tense shows he *was trying* to tempt him. "Test" is the Greek word *peirazô* of *peiraô* and *ekpeirazô* (cf. Deut. 6:16 in Matt. 4:7; Luke 4:12 against Satan). The motive was evil, hence the lawyer wanted to tempt and entrap Jesus if possible. {***What shall I do to inherit eternal life?***} Lit. "By doing what...?" With an emphasis on "doing," the form of his question shows a wrong idea as to how to get it.

27. {***And he answering...***} Written on the phylacteries, this is the *Shema* of the Law (Deut. 6:3; 11:13). God is to be loved with all of man's four powers: heart, soul, strength, mind (cf. Mark 12:30). {***Love your neighbor...***} (Mark 12:28-34; Matt. 22:34-40). The second part is from Leviticus 19:18 and shows that the lawyer knew the law.

28. {***Do this and thou shalt live***} Greek tense shows to "keep on doing this forever" and "will live" is the natural result. Yet no one has ever "done" all the law lays down towards God. To slip once is to fail.

29. {***Desiring to justify himself***} The lawyer saw at once that he had convicted himself. In his embarrassment he asks another question to show that he did have some point at first. {***And who is my neighbour?***} This Jewish culture split hairs over this question and excluded from "neighbor" Gentiles and especially Samaritans.

30. {***Fell among robbers...stripped...beat him***} This was a vivid picture of the robbery. He was surrounded by robbers (meaning bandits, not petty thieves). He was stripped of clothing as well as of his money. They lit. were "placing strokes or blows" upon him; leaving him half-dead.

31. {***He passed by on the other side***} The Greek verb shows he came alongside, and then he stepped over to the opposite side of the road, to avoid ceremonial contamination with a stranger.

33. {***A certain Samaritan***} Of all men in the world to do a neighborly act! {***Came where he was***} Lit. "came down upon him." Having compassion, he did not sidestep or dodge him.

34. {***Bound up his wounds***} Lit. "bound down [his wounds]." This is a medical detail that interested Luke. {***Pouring on them oil and wine***} These were household remedies even for wounds (soothing oil, antiseptic alcohol wine).

35. {***On the morrow***} Lit. "towards the morrow" possibly referring to the time of dawn or early in the day (cf. also Acts 3:1; 4:5). {***Two pence***} This was about two days wages of a common laborer. And he would pay more as was necessary.

36. {*Proved neighbour to him that fell*} Lit. "Which…became a neighbor?" Jesus has changed the lawyer's standpoint: was it the priest, Levite, or Samaritan that acted like a neighbor to the wounded man?

37. {*On him*} The lawyer gave the correct answer, but refused to say "Samaritan" and instead used the more impersonal "the one." {*Do thou*} Would this Jewish lawyer act the neighbor to a Samaritan?

38. {*Received him into her house*} Mistress of the home and probably the elder sister, she welcomed him as a guest (cf. Luke 19:6; Acts 17:7; Jas. 2:25).

39. {*Which also sat*} Lit. "who also sat." Possibly the "also" may mean that Martha loved to sit here also as well as Mary. She sat beside Jesus, at his feet.

40. {*Was cumbered*} This is the Greek verb *perispaô,* an old verb with vivid metaphor, "to draw around." {*She came up to him*} An explosive act, the Greek tense here shows Martha was stepping up to or bursting in or upon Jesus. {*Dost thou not care*} This was a reproach to Jesus for monopolizing Mary, to Martha's hurt. Martha feels that Jesus is the key to Mary's help. {*Bid her…that she help me*} (cf. Rom. 8:26). "Help" is the Greek verb *sunantilambanomai,* a double compound verb (*sun,* with, *anti,* at her end of the line, and *lambanomai,* middle voice of *lambanô,* to take hold). It is a beautiful word, lit. "to take hold oneself at his end of the task together with one."

41. {*But one thing is needful*} Jesus seems to say to Martha that only one dish was necessary for the meal instead of the "many" about which she was so anxious.

42. {*The good portion*} Not salvation *per se,* the best dish on the table, so to speak spiritually, was fellowship with Jesus.

CHAPTER 11

1-4. {*Teach us to pray*} Jesus had taught the disciples prayer by precept (Matt. 6:7-15) and example (Luke 9:29). Somehow the example of Jesus on this occasion stirred them to fresh interest in the subject and to revival of interest in John's teachings (Luke 5:33).

5. {*Lend me…*} This is from the Greek verb *kichrêmi,* to lend as a matter of friendly interest as opposed to *daneizô,* to lend on interest as a business.

7. {*Trouble me not*} (cf. Matt. 26:10; Mark 14:6; Gal. 6:17). Lit. "stop furnishing troubles to me." {*The door is now shut*} Lit. "already shut to stay shut." Ancient locks are not easy to unlock. {*In bed*} Note too that often a whole family would sleep in the same room. {*I cannot*} That is, I am not willing.

8. {*Though...because he is his friend*} He will not get up because of friendship, but because of the shamelessness or impudence of the man.

11. {*And of which of you that is a father shall his son ask a loaf, and he give him a stone? or a fish, and he for a fish give him a serpent?*} A no answer is assumed. It is a very awkward piece of Greek and yet it is intelligible. Note some MSS add a comparison of asking for a loaf and giving a stone (cf. Matt. 7:9).

13. {*Know how to give*} (cf. Matt. 7:11). Only here Jesus adds the Holy Spirit as the great gift that the Father is ready to bestow.

15. {*By Beelzebub*} (cf. Mark 3:22; Matt. 12:24, 27). This was a blasphemous accusation here in Judea as in Galilee. It was useless for them to deny the fact of the miracles; so they were explained as done by Satan himself, a most absurd explanation.

16. {*Tempting him*} These "others" apparently realized the futility of the charge of being in league with Beelzebub. {*A sign from heaven*} (cf. Matt. 12:38). "Sign" here means a great spectacular display of heavenly power such as they expected the Messiah to give.

17. {*And a house divided against a house falleth*} (cf. Matt. 12:25; Mark 3:25). This phrase may mean "one tumbling house knocking down its neighbor's house," a graphic picture of what happens when a kingdom is divided against itself (Bruce).

18. {*If Satan is divided*} The Greek condition is determined as fulfilled and true (for argument's sake, from the view of those charging Jesus): "*Since* Satan is divided...."

19. {*And if I by Beelzebub...*} Again as in verse 18 the Greek condition is determined as true (for argument's sake, from the view of those charging Jesus): "*Since* I drive out demons by Beelzebub...." Jesus' conclusion is a *reductio ad absurdum*. The Jewish exorcists practiced incantations against demons (Acts 19:13).

21. {*Fully armed*} This is the Greek verb *kathoplizô,* the front part of the word (*kata*) is "perfective use" and is translated by the word "fully." {*His own court*} (cf. Mark 3:27; Matt. 12:29). Lit. "his own court," meaning "his own homestead [the house as a whole]."

22. {*Come upon him and overcome him*} The Greek tense shows here a single onset; contrast the Greek tense while the "guarding" in verse 21 is continuous. {*His whole armour*} Lit. "his whole armor" referring to all the soldier's outfit: shield, sword, lance, helmet, greaves, breastplate (cf. Eph. 6:11, 13); effective weapons he trusted. It may refer to the fact that strong as Satan is, Jesus is stronger and wins victories over him.

29. {*But the sign of Jonah*} The preaching of Jesus ought to have been sign enough as in the case of Jonah.

33. {*In a cellar*} (cf. Matt. 5:15 also 6:22). This is the Greek word *kruptên,* compare our word "crypt" which is a hidden place, from the Greek verb *kruptô,* to hide.

37. {*To dine*} (cf. Luke 14:12). The Greek tense shows this is for a single meal. The Greek verb is from *ariston* (breakfast), and here it means a morning meal (breakfast/brunch or lunch) after the return from morning prayers in the synagogue (Matt. 22:4), not the very early morning meal.

38. {*That he had not first washed before dinner*} It was the Jewish custom to dip the hands in water before eating and often between courses for ceremonial purification.

39. {*But your inward part...*} (cf. Matt. 23:25). The "you" refers to the Pharisees. They keep the external regulations, but their hearts are full of plunder and wickedness. Both inside and outside should be clean, but the inside first.

40-41. {*Those things which are within*} Probably this saying means, give as alms the things within the dishes; that is, have inward righteousness with a brotherly spirit and the outward becomes morally clean.

44. {*The tombs which appear not*} (cf. Matt. 23:27). Lit. "tombs not apparent." These hidden graves would give ceremonial defilement for seven days (Num. 19:16). Hence they were usually whitewashed as a warning. Men do not know how rotten they are. These three woes (v. 42ff.) cut to the quick and evidently made the Pharisees wince.

45. {*Thou reproachest us also*} The lawyers were usually Pharisees; they thought they were receiving outrageous treatment. So Jesus proceeds to give the lawyers three woes as he had done to the Pharisees.

48. {*Consent*} Outwardly the lawyers build tombs for the prophets whom their forefathers killed as if they disapproved what their fathers did. But in reality they neglect and oppose what the prophets teach just as their fathers did.

50. {*That...may be required...which was shed*} The Greek tense means the blood which is perpetually shed from time to time. {*From the foundation of the world*} Lit. "foundation of the world" (cf. Matt. 25:34; John 17:24; Eph. 1:4).

51. {*From the blood of Abel to the blood of Zachariah*} (cf. Matt. 23:35). The blood of Abel is the first shed in the OT (Gen. 4:10); the killing of Zechariah the last in the OT canon which ended with Chronicles (2 Chron. 24:22).

52. {*Ye took away the key of knowledge*} This is a flat charge of obscurantism on the part of these scribes (lawyers), the teachers (rabbis) of the people. They themselves refused to go into the house of knowledge and learn. They then locked the door and hid the key to the house of knowledge, hindering those who were trying to enter.

53. {*From thence*} That is, out of the Pharisee's house. The rage of both Pharisees and lawyers knew no bounds. They were stung to the quick by these woes which laid bare their hollow hypocrisy.

54. {*Laying wait for him*} (cf. Luke 20:45-47; Matt. 23:1-7). "Wait" in the Greek is a vivid picture as if he were a beast of prey, and so *lying in ambush* for him. "To catch" is the Greek verb *thêreusai,* here only in the NT, from *thêra* (cf. Rom. 11:9), to ensnare, to hunt. These graphic words show the rage of the rabbis toward Jesus.

CHAPTER 12

1. {*Many thousands*} Lit. "myriads" is probably hyperbolical as in Acts 21:20, but in the sense of "ten thousand," (cf. Acts 19:19), it means a very large crowd apparently drawn together by the violent attacks of the rabbis against Jesus. {*Unto his disciples first of all*} This long discourse in Luke 12:1ff. is really a series of separate talks to various groups in the vast crowds around Jesus. {*The leaven of the Pharisees which is hypocrisy*} (cf. Mark 8:15 and Matt. 16:6). "Yeast" is not always evil (cf. Matt. 13:33), though it is here. Hypocrisy was the leading Pharisaic vice and was a mark of sanctity to hide an evil heart.

2. {*Covered up*} This is the Greek verb *sugkaluptô,* to cover up on all sides and so completely. These sayings of Jesus he often repeated in other contexts (cf. Matt. 10:26-33).

5. {*Into hell*} (cf. Matt. 5:22). Lit. "Gehenna" which is a transliteration of *Ge-Hinnom,* Valley of Hinnom where the children were thrown to Molech. Josiah (2 Kgs. 23:10) abolished these abominations and then it was a place for refuse which burned ceaselessly and became a symbol of punishment in the other world.

10. {*But unto him that blasphemeth against the Holy Spirit*} (cf. Mark 3:28; Matt. 12:31). This statement of the unpardonable sin is given immediately after the charge that Jesus was in league with Beelzebub.

11. {*Be not anxious...*} (cf. Matt. 10:19 and Mark 13:11; Luke 21:14). The Greek syntax translates "do not *become* anxious."

12. {*How or what ye shall answer*} Lit. "what things it is necessary to say." This is a word for courage in a crisis to trust God without fear.

13-14. {*Bid my brother...*} The law (Deut. 21:17) was two-thirds to the elder, one-third to the younger. Not wishing arbitration, the brother wants a decision by Jesus against his brother (cf. Exod. 2:14). Jesus' repudiation of being arbiter shows that his kingdom is not of this world (John 18:36).

15. {*From all covetousness*} This is every kind of greedy desire for more. {*In the abundance of the things which he possesseth*} Lit. "in the abounding to one out of the things belonging to him."

17. {*Reasoned within himself*} The Greek tense is picturing his continued cogitations over his perplexity, "he *kept on* thinking to himself."

18. {*My barns*} This is a granary or storehouse, storing agricultural or other treasures (Matt. 3:12; 6:26; 13:30; Luke 3:17; 12:18, 24). {*My goods*} Lit. "my good things."

19. {*Laid up for many years*} The Greek syntax of the verse shows the man had eagerness for the lifestyle he could now lead; the man's soul here feeds on his goods. He will *keep on* resting, eat and drink to fill *at once* and *keep on* being merry.

20. {*Is thy soul required of thee*} Lit. "They are demanding your soul from you."

24. {*The ravens*} (cf. birds, Matt. 6:26). This Greek word includes the whole crow group of scavenger birds (rooks and jackdaws).

25. {*A cubit*} Lit. "one cubit" (cf. Matt. 6:27). This word can also be related to stature or time.

29. {*Seek not ye*} "Ye" is emphatic in the Greek. The Greek syntax shows that one is to *stop* seeking (cf. anxious, Matt. 6:31). {*Neither be ye of doubtful mind*} Greek syntax shows in this phrase one is to *stop* being doubtful as a command. The Greek verb "worry" is *meteôrizô*, from *meteôros* in midair, high (our *meteor*), to lift up on high, then to lift oneself up with hopes (false sometimes), to be buoyed up, to be tossed like a ship at sea, to be anxious, and here "to be in doubt."

33. {*Sell that ye have...*} (cf. Matt. 6:19). Did Jesus mean this literally and always? Jesus here does not condemn property as inherently sinful. I prefer to believe that even Luke sees in the words not a mechanical rule, but a law for the spirit (Bruce).

35. {*Be girded about...*} The long garments needed to be pulled up and tucked into the belt around the waist in order to move quickly or speedily.

36. {*When he shall return from the marriage feast*} (cf. Matt. 22:2). The Greek vocabulary suggests the wedding feast is perhaps breaking up and so the person is returning from it.

38. {*And if...*} The "if" is the Greek condition of the third class, undetermined, but with prospect of being determined.

39. {*The thief*} The Master returning from a wedding is replaced by a thief whose study it is to come to the house he means to plunder at an unexpected time.

40. {*Be ye*} Lit. "keep on becoming."

41. {*Peter said*} This whole paragraph (vv. 22-40) had been addressed directly to the disciples. Hence it is not surprising to find Peter putting in a question. Peter is certain that the Twelve are meant, but he desires to know if others are included, for Jesus had spoken to the multitude in verses 13-21.

42. {*Who then*} Jesus introduces this parable of the wise steward (42-48) by a rhetorical question that answers itself. Peter is this wise steward (i.e., house manager), each of the Twelve is; as is anyone who acts thus. {*Their portion of food*} This is the Greek word *sitometrion*, from the verb *sitometreô* (Gen. 47:12) for the Attic *ton siton metreô*, to measure the food, the rations.

45. {*Shall say...*} This is the Greek condition of an undetermined case, but with prospect of being determined. {*Delayeth*} That is, spends time or lingers. {*And the maidservants*} The Greek word here means a young female slave.

46. {*Shall cut him asunder*} The Greek verb is *dichotomeô*, from *dichotomos* and that from *dicha* and *temnô*, to cut, to cut in two; used literally here (cf. Matt. 24:51). {*With the unfaithful*} (cf. Matt. 24:51).

The meaning here is not "the unbelieving," but rather "the unreliable, the untrustworthy."

49. {*I came to cast fire*} Lit. "cast fire." The fire was already burning. Christ came to set the world on fire, and the conflagration had already begun (Plummer). The very passion in Christ's heart would set his friends on fire and his foes in opposition (Luke 11:53). It is like the saying of Jesus that he came to bring not peace, but a sword (Matt. 10:34-36). {*And what will I, if it is already kindled?*} Probably Luke means the conflagration to come by his death on the Cross, for he changes the figure and refers to that more plainly.

50. {*I have a baptism...*} (cf. Mark 10:32; Matt. 20:22). Having used the metaphor of fire, Christ now uses the metaphor of water. The one sets forth the result of his coming as it affects the world, the other as it affects himself. The world is lit up with flames and Christ is bathed in blood (Plummer).

51. {*But rather division*} (cf. Matt. 10:34-36). Peace at any price is not the purpose of Christ. Loyalty to Christ counts more than all else.

56. {*To interpret this time*} "Interpret" means to test as spiritual chemists (Greek verb *dokimazein*). No wonder that Jesus here calls them "hypocrites" because of their blindness when looking at and hearing him.

58. {*Give diligence to be quit of him*} (cf. Acts 19:12). Lit. "give pains to be reconciled." "Reconciled" is used here in a legal sense and the Greek tense emphasizes a state of completion, "to be rid of him for good."

59. {*Till thou have paid*} The Greek verb is *apodidōmi*, to pay back *in full*. {*The last mite*} (cf. widow's mite, Luke 21:2; Mark 12:42). This is a very small brass coin, one-eighth of an ounce; reckoned at 1/128th (less than one percent) of a day's wage of a common laborer.

CHAPTER 13

1. {*Whose blood Pilate had mingled with their sacrifices*} This incident is recorded nowhere else, but is in entire harmony with Pilate's record for outrages. These Galileans at a feast in Jerusalem may have been involved in some insurrection against the Roman government, the leaders of whom Pilate had slain right in the temple courts where the sacrifices were going on.

2. {*Have suffered*} The Greek tense of "suffered" notes that it is an irrevocable fact.

3. {*Except ye repent*} "Repent" is the Greek verb *metanoeô*, to change mind and conduct, linear action, *keep on* changing.

4. {*The tower in Siloam*} Jesus mentions this accident to illustrate still further the responsibility of his hearers. Jesus makes use of public events in both these incidents to teach spiritual lessons.

6. {*Planted*} The Greek syntax means "he had a fig tree, one already planted in his vineyard."

7. {*These three years I come...*} The three years are counted from the time when the fig tree would normally be expected to bear, not from the time of planting. The Jewish nation is meant by this parable of the barren fig tree. It is cut down since it bears no fruit, and uses up the soil.

8. {*Dung it*} Lit. "cast dung" around it, manure it.

9. {*And if it bear fruit thenceforth...*} The Greek syntax shows a sudden breaking off of the phrase for effect in relation to the next phrase.

11. {*A spirit of infirmity*} This is a spirit that caused the lack of strength, like a spirit of bondage (Rom. 8:15). {*She was bowed together...and could in no wise lift herself up*} "Bowed together" is the Greek verb *sunkuptô*, "to bend together," a medical word for curvature of the spine. She was unable to straighten up.

13. {*She was made straight*} (cf. Luke 13:13; Heb. 12:12; Acts 15:16), to make straight again. Here it has the literal sense of making straight the old woman's crooked back. {*She glorified God*} Greek tense shows she *began* to praise and *kept it up*.

15. {*The Lord answered him*} Jesus gave a crushing and overwhelming reply. {*Hypocrites*} Jesus addresses this pretentious faultfinder and all who agree with him. These very critics of Jesus cared too much for a beast to leave it all the Sabbath without water.

16. {*Daughter of Abraham*} This is really a triple argument that Jesus *had* to heal the woman even on the Sabbath, she was: (1) a human being (not animal); (2) A Jewess (daughter of Abraham, not Gentile); (3) an old and infirmed person (and so pitiful and not normal).

17. {*Were put to shame*} They were made to feel ashamed; they blushed with shame at their predicament.

19. {*A grain of mustard seed*} (cf. Mark 4:30-32; Matt. 13:31). This small seed could grow to twelve feet at times. A bush so large it appears as a tree. The Jews had a proverb: "Small as a mustard seed."

22. {*Journeying on unto Jerusalem*} This is the second of the journeys to Jerusalem in this later ministry corresponding to that in John 11:1ff.

23. {*Are they few that be saved?*} This was an academic theological problem with the rabbis, the number of the elect.

24. {*Strive*} (cf. Matt. 7:13). Jesus makes short shrift of the question; this command is plural to include others. {*Narrow door*} Here this refers to the entrance to the house.

25. {*Hath shut to*} The Greek form and tense shows the door is completely closed, and slammed fast. {*And to knock*} Greek aspect translates, "to *keep on* knocking." {*Open to us*} Greek tense and moods shows to open at once and with urgency.

27. {*I know not whence ye are*} (cf. Ps. 8:9 also Matt. 7:23). This blunt statement cuts the matter short and sweeps away the flimsy cobwebs. Acquaintance with Christ in the flesh does not open the door.

29. {*Shall sit down...*} Jesus does not mean that these will be saved in different ways, but only that many will come from all the four corners of the earth.

31. {*Pharisees...*} Here we see the Pharisees in a new role, warning Jesus against the machinations of Herod, when they are plotting themselves.

32. {*I am perfected*} This is the Greek verb *teleioô,* from *teleios,* to bring to perfection. Perfect humanity is a process and Jesus was passing through that, without sin, but not without temptation and suffering (cf. Heb. 2:10).

33. {*It cannot be...*} That is, it is not accepted, it is inadmissible. A severely ironical indictment of Jerusalem. The shadow of the Cross reaches Perea where Jesus now is as he starts toward Jerusalem.

34. {*O Jerusalem, Jerusalem*} Jesus could have made the lament both here (Perea) and in Jerusalem (cf. Matt. 23:37), though some consider it not an acceptable explanation. {*How often would I*} This shows Jesus made repeated visits to Jerusalem, as we know otherwise only from John's Gospel.

CHAPTER 14

1. {*When he went...they...were watching*} Lit. "They were themselves watching beside (i.e., on the sly)," with the "they" emphatic. They watched with evil intent (cf. Mark 3:2).

2. {*Which had the dropsy*} Only here in the NT, this is the Greek word *hudrôpikos,* a medical word from *hudôr* (water), one who has internal water (*hudrôps*).

3. {*Answering... lawyers and Pharisees*} Jesus answered the thoughts of those mentioned in verse 1. Here "lawyers and Pharisees" are treated in the Greek as one class.

4. {*Let him go*} Probably, he dismissed him from the company to get him away from these critics.

5. {*An ass or an ox*} The very form of the question in this verse is a powerful argument and puts the lawyers and the Pharisees hopelessly on the defensive.

6. {*Could not answer again*} Lit. "did not have strength to answer back or in turn." Helpless to argue, they hated to admit that they cared more for an ox than for this poor dropsical man.

7. {*They chose out...the chief seats*} As today, the place next to the host on the right was then, as now, the post of honor.

9. {*To take the lowest place*} Lit. "to hold down the lowest place." With all the intermediate seating places being taken, of course, this is a moment of embarrassment.

12. {*A dinner or a supper*} More exactly translate, "a breakfast [brunch] or a dinner" (cf. Luke 11:38). This saying (parable) is for the host, as the earlier for the guests (cf. v. 7). {*Call not*} The Greek syntax shows this command prohibiting *the habit of* inviting only friends; meaning the *exclusive* invitation of such guests that Jesus condemns.

13. {*When thou makest a feast*} "Banquet" means reception (cf. Luke 5:29). {*The poor...*} The Greek syntax shows this means: poor *people,* maimed *folks,* lame *people,* blind *people.*

14. {*To recompense thee*} "Recompense" means "to give back in return." The reward will come at the resurrection if not before and you shall be happy.

15. {*Blessed...*} This means "happy" (cf. Matt. 5:3). Either ignorant or a pious hypocrite, this man may mean that this coming banquet was the prerogative of the Pharisees. He assumed complacently that he will be among the number of the blessed.

16. {*Great supper*} This was a formal dinner (not a luncheon or brunch).

17. {*His servant*} That is, his bondservant, *Vocator* or Summoner (cf. Esth. 5:8; 6:14). Some say to refuse the second summons would be an insult.

18. {*With one consent...to make excuse*} It looked like a conspiracy for each one in his turn said quite similar things, begging pardon or making excuses for not doing or to beg (Luke 14:18). Three of the many (lit. "all") excuses are recorded here, each more flimsy than the other.

20. {*I cannot come*} (cf. Deut. 24:5 also 1 Cor. 7:33). This answer is less polite than the others but a more plausible pretense if he wanted to make it so. Yet the new wife would probably have been glad to go with him to the feast if asked.

21. {*Quickly*} The dinner is ready and no time is to be lost. The invitation goes still to those in the city.

22. {*And yet there is room*} Wishing the places to be filled, the Master had invited many (v. 16) who had all declined.

23. {*The highways and hedges*} The Gentiles are to take the place that the Jews might have had (Rom. 11:25). These are the public roads and smaller hedged rows outside the city (of Judaism) just as the streets and lanes were inside the city (v. 21). The heathen are to be invited this time.

25. {*And he turned...*} Such turning was a deliberate effort to check the wild enthusiasm of the crowds who followed just to be following.

26. {*Hateth not...*} This statement has a focus that one must hate family members (and one's soul) only *where the element of choice comes in* (cf. Matt. 6:24) as it sometimes does, when father or mother opposes Christ. Then one must not hesitate. {*And his own life also*} Love for Christ takes precedence over even the elemental instinct of self-preservation (Ragg).

27. {*His own cross*} Each follower has a cross which he must bear figuratively as Jesus did his literally (cf. John 19:17).

28. {*Build a tower*} This tower can refer to: city wall (cf. Luke 13:4), vineyard watchtower (Matt. 21:33), building for refuge, or ornament as here. {*Count the cost*} This means to count up and calculate, adding up and quantifying the costs.

29. {*To finish*} This is the Greek word *ekteleô,* which has a focus of "to finish out to the end." {*To mock him*} This is the Greek verb *empaizô,* to play like a child, at or with, to mock, scoff at, to trifle with.

31. {*To encounter...another king*} This means to clash or grapple in war. {*Take counsel*} Here this means to take counsel with oneself, to deliberate, to ponder. {*With ten thousand*} Lit. "in ten thousand." He is equipped in or with ten thousand. {*To meet*} That is, to oppose with a military meaning.

32. {*An ambassage*} (cf. Luke 19:14). This is the Greek word for the office of ambassador, composed of old men (allegedly) possessing wisdom. {*Asketh conditions of peace*} Lit. "things of peace." That is, that which concerns or looks towards peace, i.e., the preliminaries of peace (cf. Rom. 14:19).

33. {*All that he hath*} Lit. "all his own belongings." That is, he says good-bye to all his property. This verse gives the principle of the rash builder and rash king (v. 28-32); self-sacrifice is the point.

CHAPTER 15

1. {*All the publicans and sinners*} The Greek syntax here shows this is two separate classes of people (though cf. Luke 5:30; Matt. 9:11). The tax collectors are put on the same level with the outcasts or sinners.

2. {*Both...and*} The Greek syntax shows they are united in their complaint. {*Murmured*} The form of the Greek verbs shows they were murmuring probably *between* or *among* themselves. The Greek tense shows the murmuring spread whenever these two classes came in contact with Jesus. The outcasts got closer (v. 1) and these groups more distant to Jesus. {*This man*} The wording shows a contemptuous sneer. {*Receiveth...and eateth with them*} (cf. Luke 5:30). The Greek tense shows it was the habit of Jesus to receive such groups. He shows no sense of social superiority to these outcasts. In fact, the wording implies he prefers these outcasts to the respectable classes (cf. Luke 7:34).

3. {*This parable*} (cf. Matt. 18:12-14 also John 10:1-18). This is the Parable of the Lost Sheep (15:3-7), Christ's way of answering these trivial complainers. Jesus champions the lost and justifies his conduct by these superb stories.

4. {*In the wilderness...go after that which is lost*} It is the owner of the hundred sheep who knows and loves each one of the sheep. {*Until he find it*} Lit. "he *keeps on* going until success effectively comes."

7. {*Over one sinner that repenteth*} The joy in heaven is in contrast with the grumbling Pharisees and scribes. {*More than over...which need no repentance*} (cf. Luke 5:31). All need repentance of course. But Jesus for the sake of argument accepts their claims about themselves and by their own words condemns them for their criticism of his efforts to save the lost sheep.

8. {*Ten pieces of silver*} This has the purchasing power of about ten day's wages of a common day laborer.

10. {*There is joy...in the presence of the angels of God*} Lit. "joy arises." This means "the joy of God himself."

11. {*Had*} This is the parable of the Prodigal Son, the Lost Son (cf. vv. 11-32). In this parable or allegory is an element of self-recovery to give ethical and moral value to the rescue of the son who wandered away.

12. {*The portion*} This would be one-third of the estate at the death of the father to the younger son (Deut. 21:17); here also the elder son got his share of the estate.

13. {*Took his journey...*} The younger son burned all his bridges behind him, gathering together all that he had. {*Wasted*} Used of winnowing grain, he "scattered" his property as a contrast to gathering wealth (cf. Matt. 25:24). {*with riotous living*} That is, living dissolutely or profligately to the limit of sinful excesses. "Wild" is the Greek adverb *asôtôs,* from *asôtos* (*alpha* of negation [not] and *sôzô*), one that cannot be saved, one who does not save, a spendthrift, an abandoned man, a profligate, a prodigal.

14. {*When he had spent*} The "he" in Greek is emphatic (cf. Jas. 4:3 and Luke 14:28). {*He...to be in want*} Providence brought famine to the very land just when the boy had spent all (Plummer).

15. {*Joined himself*} This is the Greek verb *kollaô,* to glue together, to cleave to; he was glued to, was *joined to* the citizens of this foreign (Gentile) country. {*To feed swine*} This is an unspeakable degradation for a Jew.

16. {*With the husks*} Lit. "little horn" referring to the shape of the pods (like little horns) of the carob tree or locust tree. The gelatinous substance inside has a sweetish taste and is used for feeding swine and even for food by the lower classes.

17. {*But when he came to himself*} Once out of his head, he now began to see things as they really were, coming to his senses. He thinks of how his servants are surrounded by loaves like a flood; and then compares it to himself "while I on the other hand am here perishing with hunger."

18. {*I will arise and go*} This determination is the act of the will after he comes to himself and sees his real condition. {*I did sin*} A hard word to say, the son will say it first. The word means "to miss the mark."

19. {*No longer worthy*} This is a confession of the facts. He sees his own pitiful plight. The servants of his father are now above him.

20. {*To his father*} He acted *at once* on his decision. {*Yet afar off*} This shows that the father had been looking for him to come back, looking at this very moment; eager, he ran to the son. {*Kissed*} The form of the Greek word shows he kissed him *again and again.*

21. The son made his speech of confession as planned, but it is probable that the father interrupted him at this point before he could finish.

22. {*The best robe*} Lit. "a robe the first." This was a fine stately garment, the kind worn by kings (Mark 16:5; Luke 22:46).

23. {*The fatted calf*} "Fattened" is the Greek word *siteuton,* the verbal adjective of *sileuô,* to feed with wheat. The calf was kept fat for festive occasions, possibly in the hope of the son's return.

24. {*And is alive...*} Lit. "he was dead and he came back to life." {*He was found*} The Greek tense shows that he is found *after long waiting.*

26. {*Servants*} This Greek word can be either a hired servant or slave as a possession. {*He inquired*} The Greek tense shows he inquired repeatedly and eagerly.

27. {*Safe and sound*} This is the Greek verb *hugiainô* from *hugiês,* to be in good health. In spite of all that he has gone through and in spite of the father's fears.

28. {*But he was angry*} That is, he flew into a rage. This was the explosion as the result of long resentment towards the wayward brother and suspicion of the father's partiality for the erring son. {*Entreated*} The Greek tense shows he *kept on* pleading with him.

29. {*Do I serve thee*} The Greek word and tense pictures (from the elder's view) his virtual slavery in staying at home and perhaps with longings to follow the younger son.

30. {*This thy son*} The phrasing shows contempt and sarcasm; note it is not "my brother."

31. {*Son...thou...*} Lit. "child" with the "you" in the emphatic position in the Greek sentence. He had not appreciated his privileges at home with his father.

32. {*It was meet*} Lit. "it was necessary" in the father's heart and in the joy of the return that justifies the feasting. A real father could do no less. Jesus' critics were put to silence by these three parables which exposed the special faults of the Pharisees: their hard exclusiveness, self-righteousness, and contempt for others. This last parable is a graphic picture of their own attitude in the case of the surly elder brother.

CHAPTER 16

2. {*What is this that I hear?*} This question in the Greek may mean the one asking wants information, or it may be taken as an exclamation. In any event, the servant must give an accounting or report of his management.

3. {*Within himself*} That is, as soon as he had time to think the thing over carefully. He knew that he was guilty of embezzlement of the Master's funds.

4-5. {*I am resolved*} The Greek tense here is difficult to reproduce in English. "I know" is a burst of daylight to the puzzled, darkened man: "I've got it, I see into it now, a sudden solution." {*They may receive me*} That is, he wishes to put the debtors under obligation to himself.

6. {*Measures...*} Lit. "hundred baths." The Hebrew *bath,* which is between eight and nine gallons.

7. {*Measures...*} Lit. "hundred cors." The Hebrew *cor* is about ten bushels.

8. {*His lord commended...the unrighteous steward*} The steward's lord praised him though he himself had been wronged again (see v. 1 "wasting his goods"). He was dishonest as a class or kind (species) distinguished by unrighteousness as his characteristic. {*Wisely...*} Though lit. "wisely" with the better rendering of "shrewdly" or "discreetly." The master does not absolve the steward from guilt and he was apparently dismissed from his service. His shrewdness consisted in finding a place to go by his shrewdness. {*Wiser than...*} This is the moral of the whole parable. Men of the world in their dealings with men like themselves are more prudent than the children of light in their intercourse with one another (Plummer).

9. {*By the mammon of unrighteousness*} (cf. Matt. 6:24 and Luke 16:13). Jesus knows the evil power in money, but servants of God have to use it for the kingdom of God. They should use it discreetly and it is proper to make friends by the use of it. {*That they may receive you into the eternal tabernacles*} The wise way to lay up treasure in heaven is to use one's money for God here on earth.

10-12. {*Faithful in a very little...*} The man who can be trusted in a very small thing will be promoted to large responsibilities. Men who embezzle in large sums began with small sums. Earthly wealth is ours as a loan, a trust, withdrawn at any moment. It belongs to another (cf. Luke 12:21).

14. {*And they scoffed at him*} This is the Greek verb *ekmuktêrizô*, meaning to turn out or up the nose at one, to sneer, to scoff. These money-loving Pharisees were quick to see that the words of Jesus about the wise use of money applied to them. They show disdain through their body language: through their eyes, noses, face gestures.

16. {*Entereth violently into it*} (cf. Matt. 11:12). Here the meaning clearly is that everyone forces his way into the kingdom of God, a plea for moral enthusiasm and spiritual passion and energy that some today affect to despise.

18. {*Committeth adultery*} (cf. Matt. 5:32; Mark 10:11; Matt. 19:9). Adultery remains adultery, divorce or no divorce, remarriage or no marriage.

19. {*He was clothed...purple*} (cf. Mark 15:17, 20; Rev. 18:12 also Rev. 18:12; 19:8, 14). The Greek action shows clothed himself in or with the costly purple-dyed cloth (outer garments) and fine material from yellow flax (undergarments); The Greek tense shows it was his habit to dress in the wealthy, flashy, luxurious style. This parable apparently was meant for the Pharisees (v. 14) who were lovers of money.

20. {*Was laid*} Lit. "cast"; he had been flung there and was still there, as if contemptuous roughness is implied (Plummer). {*At his gate*} That is, right in front of the large portico or gateway.

21. {*With the crumbs that fell*} (cf. Luke 15:16 and Mark 7:28). That is, eat from the things that fell *from time to time*. The rich gave him only crumbs (nothing more), which was equal to dog scraps. {*Yea, even the dogs*} He lay in his helpless condition; it was a scramble between the dogs and Lazarus.

22. {*Into Abraham's bosom*} (cf. Matt. 8:11; 4 Macc. 14:17). This means to be in Paradise, as an extended meaning of reclining on the bosom area of a person, a place of special favor (cf. John 13:23).

23. {*In Hades*} (cf. Matt. 16:18). Lit. "Hades" which is a more general term for the place of the dead which include both Paradise (Abraham's bosom of special favor) and Gehenna (torment).

26. {*Gulf...is fixed*} This was a gaping opening, a permanent chasm and the chasm is there on purpose to prevent communication.

27. {*That you send him*} As if he (the rich man) had not had a fair warning and opportunity. Note that this petition to a saint is by a dead man, not one on earth.

28. {*That he may testify*} "Warn" means to "thoroughly witness." The rich man labors under the delusion that his five brothers will believe the testimony of Lazarus as a man from the dead.

29. {*Let them hear them*} Even the heathen have the evidence of nature to show the existence of God (cf. Rom. 1:20).

30. {*They will repent*} The rich man had failed to repent and he now sees that it is the one thing lacking. It is not wealth, not poverty, not alms, not influence, but repentance that is needed.

CHAPTER 17

2. {*It were well for him*} This is the Greek verb *lusiteleô,* from *lusitelês* and this from *luô,* to pay, and *ta telê,* the taxes. So it pays the taxes, it returns expenses, it is profitable. Lit. "It is profitable for him." {*If a millstone were hanged*} (cf. Mark 9:42 and Matt. 18:6). The Greek condition is determined as fulfilled.

3. {*If thy brother sin*} The Greek condition is unfulfilled, but a conceivable case.

4. {*Seven times in a day*} (cf. Matt. 18:21 and Luke 17:22). That is, seven times within the day. Seven times during the day would be hard enough for the same offender.

6. {*If ye have...ye would say*} The Greek conditions of these two phrases is mixed. Translate, "Since it is true you have faith...you could say" (and the saying is determined as unfulfilled). {*Would have obeyed*} Lit. "it *would* obey you." The saying is a fact that is determined as unfulfilled.

8. {*And will not rather say...?*} "Yes" is the expected answer implied in the Greek.

9. {*Does he thank?*} "No" is the expected answer implied in the Greek (cf. 1 Tim. 1:12; 2 Tim. 1:3; Heb. 12:28).

10. {*Unprofitable*} This Greek word means "useless" (*alpha* of negation ["not"] and *chreios* from *chraomai*, to use). The slave who only does what he is commanded by his master to do has gained no merit or credit.

16. {*And he was a Samaritan*} This touch colors the whole incident. The one man who felt grateful enough to come back and thank Jesus for the blessing was a despised Samaritan.

18. {*Save this stranger*} (cf. Acts 10:28). This Greek word *allogenês,* is the same word which occurs in an inscription from the limestone block from the Temple of Israel in Jerusalem which uses this very word and which may have been read by Jesus: "Let no foreigner enter within the screen and enclosure surrounding the sanctuary."

20. {*With observation*} "Careful observation" is a Greek word from the verb *paratêreô,* to watch closely. But close watching of external phenomena will not reveal the signs of the kingdom of God.

21. {*Within you*} What Jesus says to the Pharisees is that they, as others, are to look for the kingdom of God *within themselves, not in outward displays and supernatural manifestations.*

23. {*Go not away nor follow after them*} That is, do not rush after those who set times and places for the second advent. The Messiah was already present in the first advent (v. 21) though the Pharisees did not know it.

24. {*Lighteneth*} The second coming will be sudden and universally visible.

25. {*But first*} The second coming will be only after the Cross.

27. {*They ate, they drank, they married, they were given in marriage*} The Greek tense is one of past time, ongoing action (as also the verbs of v. 28) which is vividly picturing the life of the time of Noah. But "entered, came, destroyed" are three Greek verbs which conceive of the action as a point in time (as the verbs in v. 29).

31. {*Let him not go down...*} (cf. Mark 13:15; Matt. 24:17). There must be absolute indifference to all worldly interests as the attitude of readiness for the Son of Man (Plummer).

33. {*Shall preserve it*} "Preserve" here means "to keep alive" (cf. 1 Tim. 6:13; Acts 7:19).

34. {*In that night*} The Greek is a still more vivid "on *this* night," when Christ comes.

37. {*The eagles*} Or the vultures attracted by the carcass (cf. Matt. 24:28 also Job. 39:27-30; Heb. 1:8; Hos. 8:1).

CHAPTER 18

1. {*Not to faint*} This is the Greek verb *enkakeô*, lit. "not to give in to evil" (*en, kakeô,* from *kakos,* bad or evil), to turn coward, lose heart, behave badly.

2. {*Regarded not...*} This was a hard-boiled judge who knew no one as his superior (cf. Matt. 21:37).

3. {*Avenge me of...*} This is a Greek verb for doing justice, protecting one from another or taking just "vengeance."

4. {*He would not*} The Greek tense shows a continued refusal in response to her continual asking.

5. {*Yet*} Here, this Greek particle shows deep feeling. {*Lest she wear me out*} "Wear out" is lit. "beat him under the eye."

7. {*And he is longsuffering?*} "Yes" is the expected answer to this question. God delays taking vengeance on behalf of his people.

9. {*Set all others at naught*} "Set at naught" is the Greek verb *exoutheneô*, like *oudeneô*, from *outhen* (*ouden*), to consider or treat as nothing.

11. {*Stood*} That is, he struck an attitude ostentatiously where he could be seen. Standing was the common Jewish posture in prayer (Matt. 6:5; Mark 11:25). {*I thank thee*} His gratitude to God is for his own virtues, not for God's mercies to him. He thanks God he is in a class by himself, not common. The Pharisee cites the crimes of which he is not guilty.

12. {*Fast...twice in the week*} Only one fast a year was required by the law (Lev. 16:29; Num. 29:7); the Pharisees added others. {*I get*} He gave a tithe of his income, not of his property.

13. {*Standing afar off*} In contrast to verse 11, he was at a distance from the sanctuary, in a less noticeable position. {*Would not lift...*} Worshippers usually lifted up their closed eyes to God. {*A sinner*} Lit. "*the* sinner." "The" here shows contrast to the Pharisee who thought of others as sinners. The publican thinks of himself alone as the sinner.

14. {*They brought...their babes*} This word in Luke means "infants," where Mark 10:13-14; Matthew 19:13-14 have "little children." {*Rebuked*} The Greek tense in Luke shows they *began* to rebuke, or *continued, kept on* rebuking.

17. {*As a little child*} The child is the model for those who seek entrance into the kingdom of God.

18. {*What shall I do to inherit?*} (cf. Luke 10:25). This young man probably thought that by some one act he could obtain eternal life. He was ready to make a large expenditure for it. {*Good...*} (cf. Mark 10:17 and Matt. 19:16). No Jewish rabbi was called "good" in direct address. Whether mere flattery or a genuine putting Jesus on a par with God, the ruler must at any rate define his attitude towards Christ.

22. {*One thing thou lackest yet*} Lit. "one thing still fails you." It was an amazing compliment for one who was aiming at perfection (Matt. 19:21). The youth evidently was sincere in his claims.

25. {*Through a needle's eye*} (cf. Mark 10:25; Matt. 19:24). "Needle" here is the Greek word for a surgeon's needle; a sewing needle in Matthew and Mark. This is probably a current proverb for the impossible,

26. {*Then who*} Wealth was assumed to be mark of divine favor, not a hindrance to salvation.

27. {*The impossible with men possible with God*} "Impossible" refers to what is *humanly* impossible. God can break the grip of gold on a man's life, but even Jesus failed with this young ruler.

28. {*Our own*} Lit. "Own things" referring to home, business, etc. Not speaking in a spirit of boastfulness, Peter rather reacts in consternation at what has happened and at the words of Jesus (Plummer).

31. {*Took unto him*} (cf. Mark 10:32-33. Matt. 20:17-18). Jesus is making a special point of explaining his death to the Twelve.

34. {*And they perceived not...they understood none of these things...this saying was hid from them*} Stated three times in the verse by Luke, the words of Christ about his death ran counter to all their hopes and beliefs, utterly puzzling the apostles.

36. {*Inquired*} The Greek tense shows he repeatedly inquired as he heard the tramp of the crowd going by. {*What this meant*} Lit. "What it was." The Greek mode (view of the situation) has a focus on the potential of what was happening, a softened "what *could* happen."

38. {*Son of David*} He recognizes Jesus as the Messiah.

39. {*That he should hold his peace*} (cf. Mark 10:48). Greek tense translates, "that he should *become* silent."

40. {*Stood*} (cf. Mark 10:49; Matt. 20:32). Lit. "stood still" and so stopped.

43. {*Followed*} (cf. Mark 10:52). Greek tense translates either he *began* to follow, or descriptive, he *was following.*

CHAPTER 19

2. {*Chief publican*} As regional head or commissioner of the tax collections centered in Jericho, Zacchaeus likely had collectors under him.

3. {*He sought...Jesus who he was*} That is, he wanted to see which one of the crowd was Jesus; but clearly the Greek shows he was physically short.

5. {*Make haste and come down*} A command in Greek and the tense further shows urgency, "come down in a hurry."

6. {*He made haste and came down*} Lit. "he came down immediately."

7. {*Murmured*} This is an expressive Greek word whose very sounds are like muttering (an onomatopoetic word like the cooing doves or the hum of bees) *dia-gogguzô.* {*To lodge*} Jesus shocked the sensibilities of many in the region by inviting himself to be the guest of this notorious tax robber and sinner.

8. {*If I have wrongfully exacted aught of any man*} The Greek condition assumes this statement to be true. His own conscience was at work. He had extorted money wrongfully as they all knew. {*I return fourfold*} He says, "I offer to do it here and now on this spot." This was the Mosaic law (Exod. 22:1; Num. 5:6). Restitution is good proof of a change of heart.

12. {*To take to himself a kingdom*} Apparently this parable has the historical basis of Archelaus who actually went from Jerusalem to Rome on this very errand to get a kingdom in Palestine and to come back to it.

14-24. {*His citizens...when he was come back again...*} This is the Parable of the Minas, not the same as the Parable of the Talents (cf. Matt. 25:1-46). It is a parable of a profiteer and his servants who will increase his wealth through investment. The one who put the money in a napkin should have taken it to the tables of the money-managers, a kind of bank; there he would get proper and legal interest.

25. {*And they said unto him...*} (cf. Luke 19:11). Keenly following the parable, the eager audience interrupted Jesus at this point because of this sudden turn in the story (i.e., the ten-mina man getting one more).

28. {*Went on before*} Jesus left the parable to do its work and slowly went on his way up the hill to Jerusalem.

30. {*Colt...whereon no man ever yet sat*} This showed to the disciples that a royal progress into the city would occur.

33-34. {*The owners thereof*} (cf. Matt. 21:3 = Mark 11:3). Lit. "his lords" referring to the owners of the donkey, with no other expectation for this title in this context. {*The lord needs it*} Same word as "owner" in verse 33, but with a heightened meaning and expectation. This was the same word used for the emperor and as translation of *Elohim* in the Septuagint.

36. {*They spread*} The Greek tense shows the *continued* spreading as they went on.

37. {*At the descent...*} This refers to going by the southern slope of the Mount of Olives. As they turned down to the city, the grand view stirred the crowd to rapturous enthusiasm.

38. {*The king cometh...*} (cf. John 6:14; Deut. 18:15). The long-looked-for Messianic hopes of the people were now all ablaze with expectation of immediate realization. They are singing from the Hallel in their joy that Jesus at last is making public proclamation of his Messiahship.

39. {*Some of the Pharisees*} Pharisees were in the procession, perhaps half-hearted followers of the mob.

40. {*The stones will cry out*} A proverb for the impossible happening.

41. {*Wept*} Probably audible, the Greek tense shows he burst into tears, weeping.

42. {*If thou hadst known*} The Greek condition shows to be determined as unfulfilled, translating the implication, "if you had only known (and you don't)." The "you" is emphatic.

43-44. {*Shall cast up a bank...compass thee round...keep thee in...shall dash to the ground*} This is a vivid predictive prophecy by Jesus of the destruction of Jerusalem.

45. {*Began to cast out*} This is the second cleansing three years later; the first was at the beginning of his ministry (cf. John 2:14-22). There was abundant time for all these abuses to be revived.

47. {*Sought*} The Greek word and tense lit. translates, "were seeking, *trying* to seek." {*The principal men of the people*} Lit. "the first men of the people." The lights and leaders of Jerusalem were bent on the destruction of Jesus. The raising of Lazarus from the dead brought them together for this action (John 11:47-53; 12:9-11).

48. {*Hung upon him...*} Here is a picture of the whole nation (save the leaders in v. 47) hanging upon the words of Jesus as if in suspense in mid-air, rapt attention that angered these same leaders.

Chapter 20

1. {*On one of the days*} It was the last day of the temple teaching, Tuesday (cf. Luke 20:1-19 to Mark 11:27-12:12; Matt. 21:23-46). {*There came upon him*} The verb has the notion of sudden appearance. These leaders (cf. Luke 19:47) had determined to attack Jesus on this morning.

5. {*If we shall say...*} The Greek condition is not determined, but a conceivable case that could be fulfilled.

6. {*They be persuaded*} Lit. "is persuaded." This is the Greek verb *peithô*, to persuade, a settled state of persuasion.

11. {*He sent yet another*} Lit. "he added to send another." A clear Hebraism repeated in verse 12.

14. {*That the inheritance may be ours*} (cf. Matt. 21:39). Lit. "That the inheritance may become ours."

16. {*God forbid*} Lit. "may it not happen." This was the pious protest of the defeated members of the Sanhedrin who began to see the turn of the parable against themselves.

19. {*To lay hands on him...in that very hour*} Lit. "lay upon him the hands" (cf. Mark 12:12; Matt. 21:46). The Sanhedrin were angry enough to force the climax then, since he spoke the parable against them.

20. {*They watched him*} (cf. Luke 6:7). This is the Greek verb *paratêreô*, to watch on the side or insidiously or with evil intent. They were watching their chance. {*Spies*} This word means one who lies in wait who are suborned to spy out, one who is hired to spring a trap on one by crafty words. These spies are for the purpose of catching hold of the talk of Jesus if they can get a grip anywhere.

21. {*Rightly...*} (cf. Matt. 22:16 and Mark 12:13). The Sadducees, Pharisees, and Herodians are all involved in the plot. They are full of palaver and flattery and openly endorse the teaching of Jesus as part of their scheme (cf. Mark 12:13-17; Matt. 22:15-22).

22. {*Tribute*} this means the annual tax on land, houses, etc. The picture on the coin may well have been that of Tiberius.

23. {*Perceived...craftiness*} It was wicked, hypocritical, unscrupulous behavior. They would stoop to any trick and go the limit.

26. {*They were not able...*} Lit. "they did not have strength." These Pharisees had made an ignominious failure and were not able to make a case for the surrender of Jesus to Pilate.

27. {*There is no resurrection*} The Sadducees rally after the complete discomfiture of the Pharisees and Herodians. They had a stock conundrum with which they had often gotten a laugh on the Pharisees (cf. Matt. 22:23-33; Mark 12:18-27).

36. {*Equal unto the angels*} Angels do not marry, there is no marriage in heaven. {*Sons of God, being sons of the resurrection*} The second defines the first and is a direct answer to the Sadducees.

37. {*Even Moses*} (cf. Matt. 22:32; Mark 12:26ff.). Moses was used by the Sadducees to support their denial of the resurrection. Jesus skillfully uses Exodus 3:6 as a proof of the resurrection.

39. {*Certain of the scribes...*} Though hostile, these are Pharisees who greatly enjoyed this use by Jesus of a portion of the Pentateuch against the position of the Sadducees.

40. {*They durst not any more...*} The courage of Pharisees, Sadducees, and Herodians vanished.

42. {*For David himself...*} (cf. Mark 12:36; Matt. 22:43). Clearly, Jesus means that David is the author of Psalm 110:1ff.

44. {*David therefore...*} (cf. Matt. 22:45). The deity and the humanity of the Messiah in Psalm 110:1ff. are thus set forth.

45. {*In the hearing of all the people*} (cf. Mark 12:38 and Matt. 23:1-39). Jesus draws a portrait of the hypocrisy of the Pharisees and scribes in their presence. It was a solemn climax to this last public appearance of Christ in the temple when Jesus poured out the vials of his indignation as he had done before (Matt. 16:2; Luke 11:37-54; 12:1).

CHAPTER 21

1. {*And he looked up*} Jesus was watching (Mark 12:41) the rich put in their gifts as a slight diversion from the intense strain of the hours before.

2. {*Poor...*} She was poor enough to know hunger and begging, as the Greek root implies.

4. {*All these did cast...*} This refers to the whole crowd except the widow. {*Living...*} This is the Greek word for her *livelihood* (cf. Mark 12:44).

5. {*It was adorned*} The columns of the cloister or portico of the temple were monoliths of marble over forty feet high (Plummer).

6. {*One stone upon another*} (cf. Mark 13:2; Matt. 24:2). It was a shock to the disciples to hear this after the triumphal entry.

8. {*That ye be not led astray*} (cf. Matt. 24:4, 5, 11, 24). The Greek word for "led astray" is *planaô*, of which our word *planet* is from this word.

11. {*Famines and pestilences*} This is the Greek *loimoi* and *limoi*, a play on the two words pronounced just alike in the *Koiné*.

12. {*But before all these things*} (cf. Mark 13:8; Matt. 24:8). The meaning here may be "the beginning of travail" as priority of a point of time. {*Bringing you*} Lit. "you being brought before or led off." It was a technical term in Athenian legal language.

14. {*Not to meditate beforehand*} (cf. Mark 13:11). This is a classical word for directing a speech beforehand, not actually worry.

16. {*Shall they cause to be put to death*} This could also mean "to make to die (causative)."

17. {*Not a hair of your head shall perish*} Jesus has just said that some they will put to death. Hence it is spiritual safety here promised such as Paul claimed about death (cf. Phil. 1:21).

20. {*Compassed with armies*} This is the Greek verb *kukloô*, to circle, encircle, from *kuklos*, circle. It will be too late after the city is surrounded. This again is a predictive prophecy.

24. {*Until the times of the Gentiles be fulfilled*} Though disputable, this may mean that the punishment of the Jews has a limit (cf. Rom. 11:25).

25. {*Distress*} (cf. 2 Cor. 2:4). {*In perplexity*} The Greek word is *aporia*, that is one who is *aporos*, who has lost his way (*alpha* of negation ["not"] and *poros* ["way"]).

26. {*Men fainting*} This is the Greek verb *apopsuchô*, to expire, to breathe off or out. {*The world*} This word here means "the inhabited earth."

27. {*And then shall they see*} This refers to the Second Coming of the Son of Man in glory here (Mark 13:26; Matt. 24:30). It is pictured as not one certain of immediate realization.

28. {*Redemption*} This is the final act at the Second Coming of Christ, a glorious hope.

31. {*Nigh*} The consummation of the kingdom is here meant, not the beginning.

32. {*This generation*} Naturally people then living. {*Till all things be accomplished*} Some say these descriptions refer only to the A.D. 70 destruction of Jerusalem; others say only to the Second Coming and the end of the world. Though disputed, it is better to phrase this event as a reference to the destruction of Jerusalem regarded as the type of the end of the world (Plummer).

33. {*My words shall not pass away*} It is noteworthy that Jesus utters these words just after the difficult prediction in verse 32.

34. {*As a snare*} This is the Greek word *pagis*, from *pêgnumi*, to make fast a net or trap.

36. {*But watch ye*} This means to be sleepless and so keep awake and be ready is the pith of Christ's warning. {*To stand before the Son of man*} That is the goal. There will be no dread of the Son then if one is ready.

CHAPTER 22

1. {*The Passover*} (cf. Mark 14:1; Matt. 26:17). Though used interchangeably with "Feast of Unleavened Bread," strictly speaking the Passover was Nisan 14 and the Unleavened Bread Nisan 15-21.

2. {*How they might put him to death*} "Put to death" is the Greek verb *anaireô*, to take up, to make away with, to slay (cf. Luke 23:32). {*For they feared*} The triumphal entry and the temple speeches of Jesus had revealed his tremendous power with the people, especially the crowds from Galilee at the feast.

3. {*Satan entered into Judas*} Satan was now renewing his attack on Jesus suspended temporarily (Luke 4:13). Now Satan uses Judas (cf. John 13:27). Surrendering to Satan, Judas evidently opened the door to his heart and let Satan in, becoming a devil (John 6:70).

5. {*Were glad*} (cf. Mark 14:11). Naturally they would exult that one of the Twelve had offered to do this thing. {*Money*} This was thirty silver coins (Matt. 26:15).

6. {*Consented*} This is the Greek verb *exômologeô,* from *homologos* (*homos,* same, and *legô,* to say), to say the same thing with another and so agree. {*In the absence of the multitude*} Judas would get Jesus into the hands of the Sanhedrin during the feast in spite of the crowd. It was necessary to avoid tumult (Matt. 26:5) because of the popularity of Jesus.

7. {*The day of unleavened bread came*} (Mark 14:12). This was Nisan 14 which began at sunset.

8. {*Peter and John*} (cf. Mark 14:13 and Matt. 26:17). Passover here can refer to: the meal, the feast day, the whole period of celebration [including Unleavened Bread week, see v. 1] (John 18:28).

15. {*With desire I have desired*} (cf. John 3:29; Acts 4:17). A Hebraism common in the Septuagint.

16. {*Until it be fulfilled*} It seems like a Messianic banquet that Jesus has in mind (cf. Luke 14:15).

17. {*He received a cup*} It seems that this is still one of the four cups passed during the Passover meal, though which one is uncertain. It is apparently just before the formal introduction of the Lord's Supper. {*Had given thanks*} From the verb *eucharisteô* from which we get the word *Eucharist.*

18. {*The fruit of the vine*} This refers here to wine, though the language is more general and can also refer to other drink (cf. Mark 14:25; Matt. 26:29). {*Come*} This means the consummation of the kingdom, for the kingdom had already come.

19. {*This do*} The Greek tense of this command shows to do with repetition, *keep on* doing this.

20. {*The New Covenant*} (cf. Matt. 26:28 = Mark 14:24 also 1 Cor. 11:25). The ratification of a covenant was commonly associated with the shedding of blood; and what was written in blood was believed to be indelible (Plummer).

21. {*That betrayeth...*} The hand of Judas was resting on the table at the moment.

22. {*As it hath been determined*} But this fact does not absolve Judas of his guilt as the pronouncement of woe here makes plain.

23. {*Which of them it was*} They all had their hands on the table. Whose hand was it?

24. {*Greatest*} Lit. "greater" but the meaning here of this form is the superlative "greatest."

27. {*But I...*} (cf. John 13:1-20). Though their leader, Jesus dares to cite his own humble conduct, to prove his point and to put a stop to their jealous contention for the chief place at this very feast.

28. {*In my temptations...*} This is the tragedy of the situation when Jesus is facing the Cross with the traitor at the table and the rest chiefly concerned about their own primacy and dignity.

29. {*And I appoint unto you...*} They had on the whole been loyal and so Jesus passes on to them.

30. {*And ye shall sit*} (cf. Matt. 19:28). Though possibly not literal, there is the promise of honor for the loyal among these in the end.

32. {*I prayed*} Evidently Jesus could not keep Satan from attacking Peter. But he could and did pray for Peter's faith and his praying won in the end, though Peter stumbled and fell. {*Once thou hast turned again*} Meaning "return," this word implied that Peter would fall though he would come back.

33. {*To prison and to death*} Peter was not flattered by the need of Christ's earnest prayers for his welfare and loyalty. Hence this loud boast.

34. {*Until thou shalt thrice deny that thou knowest me*} This is a warning to Peter (Mark 14:30; Matt. 26:34; Luke 22:34; John 18:38).

36. {*Buy a sword*} The Greek word is for a defensive sword. Jesus does not mean that his disciples are to repel force by force, but that they are to be ready to defend his cause against attack.

38. {*Lord, behold, here are two swords*} The disciples took his words literally, as did Peter in taking action (Mark 14:47; Matt. 26:51; Luke 22:50; John 18:10). But Jesus rebuked Peter then and later will say: "For all that take the sword shall perish with the sword" (Matt. 26:52).

39. {*As his custom was*} Lit. "according to the custom (of him)." Jesus had the habit of going to Gethsemane at night.

40. {*At the place*} That is, the place of secret prayer which was dear to Jesus. {*Pray that ye enter not into temptation*} Jesus knew the power of evil temptation and the need of prayer (cf. Matt. 6:13 and Luke 22:46).

41. {*About a stone's throw*} Eight disciples are left at the entrance, three came further into the area. {*Kneeled down*} (cf. Mark 14:35 and Matt. 26:39).

47. {*Went before them*} Judas knew the place well (John 18:2).

48. {*With a kiss*} Jesus openly calls the act betrayal, but allows it.

49. {*What would follow...shall we smite with a sword?*} Lit. "sword" but they had the two swords already mentioned (Luke 22:38).

50. {*His right ear*} "Right" is a detail a physician like Luke would include (cf. Mark 14:47; Matt. 26:51 and John 18:10).

51. {*Healed him*} This miracle of surgery is given alone by Luke.

52. {*As against a robber?*} They were treating Jesus as if he were a bandit or rebel like Barabbas.

53. {*But this is your hour*} And so Jesus surrenders. The moral value of his sacrifice on the Cross consists in the voluntariness of his death.

54. {*Into the high priest's house*} (cf. Mark 14:53; Matt. 26:57). {*Followed*} Lit. "was following" (cf. Matt. 26:58; John 18:15 and the following conceived as a point in Mark 14:54).

55-56. {*When they had kindled a fire*} "Kindled" is the Greek verb *periaptô,* lit. "kindle *around,*" that is, make a good fire that blazes all over. It was April and cool at night.

57. {*I know him not*} This was Jesus' prediction (Luke 22:34).

58. {*After a little while another*} (cf. Matt. 26:71 and Mark 14:69). This time Peter's denial is very blunt.

59. {*Confidently affirmed*} (cf. Acts 12:15). The Greek tense shows he "*kept* affirming" and the form of the Greek word shows it was "strongly." {*For he is a Galilean*} His speech gave him away (cf. Matt. 26:73).

60. {*I know not what thou sayest*} Each denial tangles Peter more and more and then he could hear the crowing all right.

61. {*The Lord turned... looked upon Peter...remembered*} The cock crowing and the glancing look brought swiftly back to Peter's mind the prophecy of Jesus and his sad denials.

62. {*And he went out and wept bitterly*} (cf. Matt. 26:75). The Greek tense of "wept" is that he burst into tears.

63. {*That held...*} The servants or soldiers were holding this prisoner, not the Sanhedrin. {*Mocked*} Greek tense shows they *began* to mock, to play like boys.

64. {*Blindfolded*} This is the Greek verb *perikaluptô*, to put a veil around (cf. Mark 14:**65.** See Mark 14:65; Matt. 26:67).

66. {*As soon as it was day*} (cf. morning Mark 15:1 and Matt. 27:1). {*The assembly of the people*} "Assembly" is a technical word for "the eldership" or group of the elders composing the whole of the Sanhedrin (this whole of the Sanhedrin is composed of chief priests [Sadducees] and teachers of the law [Pharisees] nearly equally represented, Mark 15:1).

67. {*If thou art the Christ*} They mean Messiah. The Greek condition shows that the speaker is assuming it to be true. {*If I tell you*} The Greek condition shows he has not yet told them, but it is conceivable that he will. This is the second appearance of Jesus before the Sanhedrin (cf. Mark 15:1; Matt. 27:1). This is a so-called ratification meeting to give the appearance of legality to their vote of condemnation already taken before daybreak (Mark 14:64; Matt. 26:66).

69. {*The Son of man*} By saying this Jesus answers their question; he is the Messiah with a focus on humanity (v. 67). Next he makes claims of equality with God also which they take up.

70-71. {*Art thou the Son of God?*} (cf. vv. 67-70). Jesus admits and claims to be all three as practical equivalents: Messiah, the Son of man, the Son of God, showing both humanity and deity. {*Ye say*} This is Greek idiom for "Yes" (cf. Mark 14:62 and Matt. 26:64).

CHAPTER 23

1. {*The whole company*} Probably all but Nicodemus and Joseph of Arimathea (cf. v. 51).

2. {*Began to accuse*} Greek tense shows they went at it and kept it up. But Pilate alone has the power of life and death. {*We found*} Probably they mean that they had caught Jesus in the act of doing these things. {*Perverting our nation*} The Sanhedrin imply that the great popularity of Jesus was seditious. {*Forbidding to give tribute to Caesar*} This was a flat untruth; Jesus said to render unto Caesar... (cf. Luke

20:25). {***Saying that he himself is Christ a king***} This charge is true, but not in the sense meant by them. He was king of the spiritual kingdom of God; not a political/military rival of Caesar.

3. {***Thou sayest***} This is a Greek idiom that means "yes." (cf. Mark 15:2; Matt. 27:11; Luke 23:3; John 18:33).

4. {***The multitude***} Now after daybreak, the procession of the Sanhedrin would draw a crowd (cf. Mark 15:8). There was need of haste if the condemnation went through before friends of Jesus came. {***I find no fault***} Suddenly in the story here we see Pilate decide that Jesus is innocent. Evidently he held a careful examination before he delivered his judgment on the case (cf. John 18:33-38).

5. {***But they were the more urgent***} The Greek tense shows they *kept* insisting. Evidently Pilate had taken the thing too lightly.

7. {***Of Herod's jurisdiction***} Herod was naturally jealous of any encroachment by Pilate, the Roman Procurator of Judea. So here was a chance to respect the prerogative [authority] of Herod and get rid of this troublesome case also.

8. {***He hoped...***} He had long ago gotten over his fright that Jesus was John the Baptist come to life again (Luke 9:7-9). He wanted to see a miracle happening like a stunt magician would perform.

14. {***As one that perverteth the people***} Pilate here condenses the three charges into one: a treasonous revolutionary agitator (cf. v. 2). {***Having examined him before you***} Here this means a forensic examination.

18. {***Release***} A command from the crowd, the Greek tense shows "release *now* and *at once.*"

19. {***Insurrection***} Again, showing the very charge made against Jesus was untrue (cf. vv. 5, 14). If Jesus had raised insurrection against Caesar, these accusers would have rallied to his standard.

21. {***But they shouted***} That is, they repeatedly kept on calling and yelling. {***Crucify, crucify***} The Greek tense here shows "*go on* with the crucifixion." Mark has a different Greek tense with a different focus "Crucify *now* and *be done with it*" (cf. Mark 15:13).

24. {***Gave sentence***} The Greek word shows this is the final decision.

25. {***Whom they asked for...to their will***} This is mob law by the judge who surrenders his own power and justice to the clamor of the crowd.

26. {*They laid hold...laid on him*} (cf. Mark 15:21; Luke 27:32). Without scruples, the Greek action shows the soldiers "seized for themselves." This was a legal pressing someone into service.

28. {*Turning*} Jesus could not have made this dramatic gesture if he had been carrying the cross. {*Weep not*} Greek syntax translates "stop weeping."

29-30. {*Blessed...*} This is a beatitude to the barren, the opposite of the hopes of Jewish mothers (cf. Luke 1:25, 36).

31. {*In the green tree...in the dry*} The point of this proverb is that if they can put Jesus to death, being who he is, what will happen to Jerusalem when its day of judgment comes ?

32. {*Malefactors*} Lit. "evil doers" which were robbers, likely led by Barabbas.

33. {*The skull*} Called so probably because it looked like a skull (cf. Matt. 27:33 = Mark 15:22).

35. {*The people stood beholding*} This is a dazed multitude, some of whom may have been in the Triumphal Entry on the prior Sunday morning. {*The Christ of God*} (cf. Mark 15:31; Matt. 27:42). "He" is lit. "this one," as a contemptuous use of the pronoun, showing utter disrespect.

36-37. {*Mocked*} Even the soldiers yielded to the spell and acted like boys in their jeering "since you are king of the Jews." But to save others Jesus could not save himself.

38. {*A superscription*} It was the custom to write the accusation on which the criminal was condemned, with his name and residence here in three languages: Latin for law, in Aramaic for the Jews, in Greek for everybody (John 19:20).

40. {*Rebuking...*} Though both sneered at first (cf. Matt. 27:44), this second one came to himself and turned on his fellow robber in a rage; his argument was simple: we will all soon appear before God.

41. {*Nothing amiss*} Lit. "nothing out of place." This robber does in fact accept the claims of Jesus to be true. Jesus is dying for claiming to be Messiah, *as he is.*

42. {*In thy kingdom*} Referring to his Messianic rule, it is not clear whether he hopes for immediate blessing or only at the judgment.

43. {*Today shalt thou be with me in Paradise*} (2 Cor. 12:4; Rev. 2:7). Jesus promises him immediate and conscious fellowship after death with

Christ in Paradise (the very bliss of heaven itself, not an intermediate state [cf. Luke 16:22]).

45. {*In the midst*} Lit. "torn in the middle" so into two pieces (cf. Mark 15:38; Matt. 27:51).

46. {*Gave up the ghost*} (cf. Matt. 27:50 and John 19:30). This is the Greek verb *ekpneô*, to breathe out, to expire (cf. Mark 15:37, 39).

47. {*Glorified*} The Greek tense shows they either: *began* to glorify or *kept on* glorifying.

51. {*He had not consented to their counsel and deed*} It is fairly certain that both Joseph and Nicodemus were suspected of sympathy with Jesus and so were not invited to the trial of Jesus.

52. {*Asked for*} (cf. Mark 15:43; Matt. 27:58). The Greek action (grammatical voice) shows that Joseph of Arimathea asked for the body of Jesus *as a personal favor.*

54. {*The day of the Preparation*} This is the technical Jewish phrase for the day before the Sabbath (cf. Matt. 27:62). The day here was measured from sundown to sundown (about a twenty-four-hour day). Sabbath was about to begin at sunset.

55. {*Had come with him...followed after*} Witnessing the silent burial likely from a distance, the women saw "that" and "how" the body of Jesus was laid in this new tomb of Joseph in the rocks.

CHAPTER 24

1. {*At early dawn*} Lit. "at deep dawn." That is, while it was yet dark (cf. John 20:1). This is when they first started, for the sun was risen when they arrived (cf. Mark 16:2).

3. {*Of the Lord Jesus*} This precise combination (the Lord Jesus) is common in the Acts, but nowhere else in the Gospels.

4. {*While they were perplexed thereabout...two men*} The angel looked like a man and some remembered two. (cf. young man Mark 16:5; angel Matt. 28:5). The "men" had the garments of angels.

5. {*As they were affrighted*} Lit. "when they became frightened." They had forgotten the prediction of Jesus that he would rise on the third day.

6. {*The third day rise again*} (cf. Luke 9:22; 18:32, 33). Jesus foretold, yet they had forgotten it, for it ran counter to all their ideas and hopes.

11. {*As idle talk*} Medical writers used this Greek word for the wild talk of those in delirium or hysteria. They *kept on* distrusting the story of the women.

13. {*Sixty stadia*} That is, about seven miles.

16. {*Were holden that they should not know him*} Lit. "kept from knowing him *fully.*"

17. {*That you have with another*} This Greek verb to throw in turn, back and forth like a ball, from one to another, a beautiful picture of conversation as a game of words.

18. {*Dost thou alone sojourn?*} Lit. "has you been dwelling alone (all by yourself) as a stranger?" In Jerusalem everybody was talking about Jesus.

21. {*Redeem*} This no doubt refers to freedom from the bondage of Rome. In the mind of the speaker here, Jesus is still dead and we are still without hope.

22-23. {*Had seen*} The Greek language here shows all this information (i.e., women and angels) was too indirect and uncertain for Cleopas and his companion.

25. {*Foolish men*} Lit. "without sense, not understanding." They were dull and slow to comprehend or to act.

26. {*Behooved it not?*} Was it not necessary? The very things about the death of Jesus that disturbed them so were the strongest proof that he was the Messiah of the OT.

28. {*Made as though*} This is the Greek verb *prospoieô,* to conform oneself to, to pretend, act as if.

29. {*Constrained*} A strong verb compelling by use of force; though here it was the compulsion of courteous words.

33. {*That very hour*} Lit. "at the hour itself." They could not wait; it was at once.

34. {*Saying*} Greek grammar clearly show those saying are the eleven and those with them in verse 33. {*Indeed*} Lit. "really." Appearing to Simon is the crucial evidence that turned the scales with the disciples (cf. 1 Cor. 15:5).

35. {*Rehearsed*} This is the Greek verb *exêgeomai,* verb to lead out, to rehearse. Their story was now confirmatory, not revolutionary.

37. {*Terrified...affrighted*} Both these Greek terms of fear are strong.

38. {*Why are ye troubled?*} This is the Greek verb *tarassô,* to agitate, to stir up, to get excited.

39. {*Myself*} Jesus is patient with his proof. They were convinced before he came into the room, but that psychological shock had unnerved them all. Touch me, he says, (cf. 1 John 1:1) as proof of the actual, real human body of Jesus; he is not a ghost. Jesus was in a transition state and had not yet been glorified.

45. {*Opened he their mind*} (cf. vv. 31, 32). Jesus had all these years been trying to open their minds that they might understand the Scriptures about the Messiah and now at last he makes one more effort in the light of the Cross and the Resurrection. They can now see better the will and way of God, but they will still need the power of the Holy Spirit before they will fully know the mind of Christ.

46. {*It is written*} This refers to a quoting Scripture. Jesus now finds in the OT his suffering, his resurrection, and the preaching of repentance and forgiveness of sins to all nations.

49. {*Until ye be clothed...*} This is a figurative meaning "to experience"; used of the Greek word *enduô* or *endunô,* lit. for putting on (yourselves) a garment. This is the promise of the Father.

50. {*Over against Bethany*} This refers to Mount of Olivet, the blessed spot near where he had delivered the great Eschatological Discourse.

52. {*With great joy*} Now that the Ascension has come, they are no longer in despair. Joy becomes the note of victory as it is for all believers today.

THE GOSPEL ACCORDING TO JOHN

AUTHOR: John (son of Zebedee): Apostle, Beloved Disciple, of the Twelve
RECIPIENTS: Unknown
DATE: A.D. 81 to 96 (time of Domitian)
FROM: Ephesus
OCCASION: An apologetic (defense), against the Gnostic depreciation of Christ
THEME/PURPOSE: John writes to win others to like faith in Christ. "That you may believe that Jesus is the Christ, the Son of God; and by believing you may have life in his name" (John 20:31).

BY WAY OF INTRODUCTION

In the Fourth Gospel we find *The Heart of Christ* (cf. esp. John 14-17), so it is important to know that these are his very words, not someone else's artistic interpretation. The language of the Fourth Gospel has the clarity of a spring, but we are not able to sound the bottom of the depths.

A Jew familiar with the details of Jerusalem, the author is apparently still alive when this testimony to his authorship is given. It is manifest all through the book that the writer is the witness who is making the contribution of his personal knowledge of the Lord Jesus Christ during his earthly ministry (cf. we, John 1:14). The word "witness" is common in this Gospel (John 1:7,8,19; 3:11,26,33; 5:31; 12:17; 21:24, etc.), and illustrates well this point of view. One may note all through the book evidences of an eyewitness in the vivid details.

Some ancient and modern sources identify this as some other "John"; but there is early and clear witness to the apostle John. True, John the apostle is not named in the document directly (called the Beloved Disciple), but this is true of the other gospels (cf. Luke/Acts).

This is the last gospel written. The author supplements the Synoptic record in various ways, and mentions events not found elsewhere (cf. John 2:23; 6:4). The Synoptics give mainly the Galilean and Perean and Judean ministry, but John adds considerably to give the Jerusalem ministry. But there are also similar events which all gospels have (cf. feeding of the 5,000).

The Prologue (John 1:1-18) relates the Incarnation to God's eternal purpose as in Colossians 1:14-20 and Hebrews 1:1-3 and employs the language of the intellectuals of the time (Logos—Word) to interpret Christ as the Incarnate Son of God.

John writes in the ripeness of age and in the richness of his long experience. He gives his reminiscences mellowed by long reflection and yet with rare dramatic power. The simplicity of the language leads many to think that they understand this Gospel when they fail to see the graphic pictures as in chapters 7-11. The book fairly throbs with life.

In simple truth, if one takes the Fourth Gospel at its face value, the personal recollections of the aged John are phrased in his own way to supplement the narratives in the Synoptics, there is little left to give serious trouble.

The Fourth Gospel and the Epistles of John are written by the same man, all these show this: style, vocabulary, theological outlook. In the Epistles, John opposes Gnosticism both of the Docetic type which denied the actual humanity of Jesus (cf. 1 John 1:1-4); and the Cerinthian type which denied the identity of the man Jesus and the *aeon* Christ which came on Jesus at his baptism and left him at his death on the Cross as in 1 John 2:22. Though disputed by some, evidence allows for the Apostle John to be the author of the Gospel of John and Revelation, at about the same time period (during the reign of Domitian). There is undoubted radical difference in language between the Apocalypse and the other Johannine books, but it can be explained.

The unity of the gospel stands, though there are clearly three parts in the Gospel: prologue (John 1:1-18); main body (John 1:19-20:31); epilogue (John 21:1ff.). But there is no evidence that the prologue was added by another hand.

The author was beyond doubt a Jew (knowing Aramaic), but he wrote in the *Koiné* Greek of his time that is comparatively free from crude Semitisms, perhaps due in part to the help of the friends in Ephesus.

John gives a wonderful portrait of Christ: the deity of Christ, the One and Only, the Son of God (cf. John 1:1,18,34; cf. also 20:31). A high conception of Christ dominates the whole book. This high view of Christ is not unlike the rest of the New Testament.

CHAPTER 1

1. {*In the beginning*} (cf. Gen. 1:1). {*Was*} This Greek tense shows continuous existence, not origin. This is not "became" for the incarnation of the Logos (John 1:14). {*The Word*} This word was used by many ancient philosophies, but we must not import their meanings into this passage. John gives the *Logos* its own meaning; the standpoint is that of the Old Testament. This term suits John's purpose better than *sophia* (wisdom cf. Prov. 8:23) and is his answer to both the Gnostic camps: Docetics who denied the actual humanity of Christ; or Cerinthians who separated the *aeon* Christ from the man Jesus. Unlike these heresies, this pre-existent *Logos* "became flesh" (cf. John 1:14). The term *Logos* is applied to Christ only in John 1:1,14; Rev. 19:13; 1 John 1:1. {*And the Word was God*} Greek syntax does not allow the meaning "God was the Word." That would mean that all of God was expressed in the *logos* and the terms would be interchangeable.

3. {*All things*} (cf. John 1:10). John uses "the world" for the whole of the orderly universe, here "all things." {*Were made*} Lit. "came into being." Greek tense shows the creative activity is looked at as one event in contrast with the continuous existence. Creation is thus presented as a "becoming" in contrast with "being." {*By him*} That is, *by means of* him as the intermediate agent in the work of creation. The *Logos* is John's explanation of the creation of the universe (cf. Col. 1:16; Heb. 1:2). {*Not anything*} Lit. "not even one thing." Note that the punctuation varies in various sources.

4. {*In him was life*} "Life" is the Greek word *zôê* usually in John means spiritual life, but here the term is unlimited and includes all life, not "manner of life," but the very principle or essence of life. That is spiritual behind the physical. It is also personal intelligence and power.

5. {*Shineth*} Greek tense translates "The light keeps on giving light." {*Apprehended it not*} (cf. John 12:35). This is the Greek verb *katalambanô*, to lay hold of, to seize. Though there is a strong tradition of translating as a "knowing, understanding" meaning, "overtook" or "overcame" seems to be the idea here.

6. {*Whose name...*} (cf. Luke 1:59-63). "John" here is the Hellenized form of Jonathan, Joanan (Gift of God), used always of the Baptist in this Gospel which never mentions the name of John son of Zebedee (the sons of Zebedee once, John 21:2).

7. {*For witness*} This is the Greek verb *martureô* (from *martus*), both more common in John's writings than the rest of the NT. This the purpose of the Baptist's ministry. {*That all might believe*} This is the Greek verb *pisteuô,* translate the Greek tense, "come to believe." This is one of John's great words (about 100 times), with nine times the frequency with which it is used by the Synoptists.

8. {*He*} This refers to John. He was a light (cf. John 5:35 and Matt. 5:14), but not "the light."

9. {*The true light*} Lit. "The light the genuine," i.e., not a false light of wreckers of ships, but the dependable light that guides to the harbor of safety. {*Lighteth every man*} Not an "inner light that is a sufficient guide," but it may only mean that all the real light that men receive comes from Christ, not necessarily that each one receives a special revelation. {*Coming...*} (cf. Eph. 1:4).

10. {*He was in the world*} Greek tense shows continuous existence in the universe (cf. John 1:1,2).

11. {*Unto his own...they that were his own*} Grammatically different than the second, the first is lit. "his own things," (cf. John 19:27 "his own home"). The second has a narrower sense, "his intimates," "his own family," "his own friends" (cf. John 13:1), likely meaning the Jewish people, the chosen people to whom Christ was sent first (Matt. 15:24), but in a wider sense the whole world is "his own." {*Received him not*} (cf. John 14:3 also 1:5).

12. {*As many as received him*} Greek tense translates, "as many as did receive him," in contrast with the second "his own" of verse 11. {*The right*} Though it includes "power," this means authority, with the notion of privilege or right. {*Children of God*} This is in the full spiritual sense, not as mere offspring of God which is true of all men (Acts 17:28). "Sons of God" is not used in John (cf. Matt. 5:9; Gal. 3:26; Rev. 21:7). John prefers "Children of God" for the spiritual children of God whether Jew or Gentile (John 11:52). Regeneration is involved here (cf. John 3:3). {*On his name*} Name means "the person".

13. {*Which were born*} Lit. "who were begotten." This is by spiritual generation, not by physical.

14. {*And the Word became flesh*} (cf. John 1:3 also Matt. 1:16-25; Luke 1:28-38) "Became." The Greek verb was chosen to show the historic event of the Incarnation rather continuous state of being. The Logos did not enter, fill, or dwell in(to) a man; he "became" flesh (cf. also 2

Cor. 8:9; Gal. 4:4; Rom. 1:3; 8:3; Phil. 2:7; 1 Tim. 3:16; Heb. 2:14. {***Dwelt among us***} This is the Greek verb *skênoô,* to pitch one's tent or tabernacle (*skênos* or *skênê*). In Revelation it is used of God tabernacling with men and here of the Logos tabernacling, God's Shekinah glory here among us in the person of his Son (cf. Rev. 7:15; 12:12; 13:6; 21:3). {***As of the only begotten from the Father***} (cf. John 3:16; 1 John 4:9). Lit. "as of an only born from a father." "One and Only" is the Greek word *monogenês,* and here refers to the eternal relationship of the Logos (as in John 1:18) rather than to the Incarnation. The Logos is thus distinguished from believers as children of God.

15. {***Beareth witness***} The Greek tense is dramatic, vividly drawing the reader into the story. The witness of John is offered as proof of the glory which is full of grace and truth and has already been claimed for the Incarnate Logos. {***Crieth***} The Greek tense gives emphasis to recalling the wonderful Voice in the wilderness which the Beloved Disciple can still hear echoing through the years. {***After me***} (cf. John 1:27). "After" means later in time. {***Before me***} "Before" is not temporal, but higher rank and dignity. This superior dignity of the Messiah John proudly recognizes always (John 3:25-30). Jesus had always been before John in his Pre-incarnate state, but "after" John in time of the Incarnation, but always ahead of John in rank.

16. {***Of his fulness***} This is the only instance of the Greek word *plêrôma* in John's writings, though in Paul's Epistles (Col. 1:19; 2:9; Eph. 1:23; 3:19; 4:13). {***Grace for grace***} "for" was a preposition used of exchange in sale; here the picture is "grace" taking the place of "grace" like the manna fresh each morning, new grace for the new day and the new service.

17. {***Was given...by Moses***} That is, Moses as the intermediate agent of God. {***Grace and truth came***} That is, as an historical event, the beginning of Christianity. {***By Jesus Christ***} He is the intermediate agent of God the Father. John's theology is here pictured: "grace and truth" are supplements to one another. The two words aptly describe two aspects of the Logos.

18. {***No man hath seen God at any time***} That is, seen with the human physical eye. God is invisible (Exod. 33:20; Deut. 4:12 also Col. 1:15; 1Tim. 1:17 and John 5:37; 6:46 [yet cf. John 14:7]). {***The only begotten Son***} Some inferior MSS read "*Son*" but "the only begotten *God*" is the true reading from the best old Greek MSS. He is God (cf.

John 1:1,14,18). {***Hath declared him***} (cf. Luke 24:35; Acts 10:8; 15:12,14; 21:19). This is the Greek verb *exêgeomai,* old verb to lead out, to draw out in narrative, to recount. This word fitly closes the Prologue in which the Logos is pictured in marvelous fashion as the Word of God in human flesh, the Son of God with the Glory of God in him, showing men who God is and what he is.

19. {***When the Jews sent unto him***} In John, "the Jews" is distinct from "the Gentile world" and "followers of Christ"; "the Jews" often refers to hostile Jewish leaders.

20. {***And he confessed…and denied not***} The Baptist did not contradict or refuse to say who he was. {***I am not the Christ***} The Greek has the equal to quote marks for this answer; not a new question (cf. Luke 3:15).

21. {***Art thou Elijah?***} This is a logical next question, since Elijah had been understood to be the forerunner of the Messiah (cf. Mal. 4:5). There was an expectation that Elijah would return in person, so the Baptist had to deny it. But note Jesus identifies the Baptist as Elijah in spirit (cf. Mark 9:11). {***He saith***} The Greek tense is dramatic, drawing the reader into the scene. {***Art thou the prophet?***} Moses (Deut. 18:15) had spoken of a prophet like unto himself. Christians interpreted this prophet to be the Messiah (Acts 3:22; 7:37), but the Jews thought him another forerunner of the Messiah (John 7:40). People wondered about Jesus himself whether he was the Messiah or just one of the looked for prophets (Mark 8:28; Matt. 16:14).

23. {***I am the voice of one crying in the wilderness***} (cf. Isa. 40:3 also Mark 1:3; Matt. 3:3; Luke 3:4).

25. {***Why then baptizest thou?***} This is asked in view of his repeated denials (three here mentioned).

26. {***In the midst of you standeth…whom ye know not***} John had already baptized Jesus and recognized him as the Messiah. Not knowing him was the tragedy of the situation (cf. John 1:11). Apparently this startling declaration excited no further inquiry from the committee.

27. {***Coming after me…the latchet of whose shoe I am not worthy to unloose***} As the forerunner of the Messiah John has preceded him in time, but not in rank.

28. {***In Bethany beyond Jordan***} Variant errors in the Greek MSS came about in this text, under the mistaken notion that the only Bethany was that near Jerusalem.

29. {*On the morrow*} This is the second day of this spiritual diary (cf. John 1:19). {*Seeth Jesus coming*} The Greek tense is the dramatic present, drawing the reader into the graphic picture. {*Behold the Lamb of God*} (Cf. 1 Cor. 5:7, John 19:36, and 1 Pet. 1:19). The passage in Isa. 53:6 is directly applied to Christ by Philip in Acts 8:32. See also Matt. 8:17; 1 Pet. 2:22; Heb. 9:28. But the Jews did not look for a suffering Messiah (John 12:34) nor did the disciples at first (Mark 9:32; Luke 24:21). But was it not possible for John, the Forerunner of the Messiah, to have a prophetic insight concerning the Messiah as the Paschal Lamb, already in Isa. 53:1ff., even if the rabbis did not see it there? {*Which taketh away the sin of the world*} Note it is not plural, "sins." The future work of the Lamb of God here described in present tense as in 1 John 1:7 about the blood of Christ. He is the Lamb of God for the world, not just for Jews.

32. {*Bare witness*} (cf. John 1:7,15,19,29,35,36). {*I have beheld*} The Baptist recognized Jesus as Messiah when he came for baptism before the Holy Spirit came (Matt. 3:14). But this sight of the Spirit descending as a dove upon Jesus at his baptism (Mark 1:10; Matt. 3:16; Luke 3:22) became permanent proof to him. The Semites regarded the dove as a symbol of the Spirit.

33. {*With the Holy Spirit*} Lit. "In" the Holy Spirit. (cf. Synoptics Mark 1:8; Matt. 3:11; Luke 3:16).

34. {*This is the Son of God*} The Baptist saw the Spirit and heard the Father's voice, "my son whom I love (Mark 1:11; Matt. 3:17; Luke 3:22). "Son of God" is a phrase that means more than just "Messiah," and expresses the peculiar relation of the Son to the Father (John 3:18; 5:25; 17:5; 19:7; 20:31) like that of the Logos with God in John 1:1.

35. {*Again on the morrow*} This is the third day since verse 19. {*Two*} One was Andrew (verse John 1:40), the other the Apostle John, who records this incident with happy memories.

36. {*As he walked*} This word vividly pictures the rapture of John in this vision of Jesus, so far as we know the third and last glimpse of Jesus by John (the baptism, verse 29, and here).

37. {*They followed Jesus*} These two disciples of the Baptist (Andrew and John) took him at his word and acted on it. John the Baptist had predicted and portrayed the Messiah, had baptized him, had interpreted him, and now for the second time had identified him.

38. {*Turned*} This word is vividly picturing the sudden act of Jesus on hearing their steps behind him. {*Following*} It was Christ's first experience of this kind and the two came from the Baptist to Jesus. {*What seek ye?*} Lit. "what purpose have you." The first words of Jesus preserved in this Gospel (cf. also as a boy Luke 2:49). {*Rabbi*} This is an Aramaic title for "teacher," used not too often in Matthew, Mark, and John. "Lord" is the usual title for Jesus by his followers (cf. John 6:68; 13:6,25, etc.). Mary Magdalene says "Rabboni" (John 20:16). {*Being interpreted*} This is the Greek verb *methermêneuo,* late compound of *meta* and *hermêneuô,* to explain (John 1:42), old word from Hermes, the god of speech (cf. our word hermeneutics). John often explains Aramaic words (John 1:38,41,42; 4:25; 9:7, etc.). {*Where abidest thou?*} They wished a place for quiet converse with Jesus.

39. {*Come and ye shall see...that day*} This is a polite invitation and definite promise. They spent *all* during that day with him.

40. {*Andrew*} This is the brother of Simon Peter (cf. also John 6:8; 12:22). The more formal call of Andrew and Simon, James and John, comes later (Mark 1:16; Matt. 4:18; Luke 3:1-11).

41. {*He findeth first*} This is a Greek dramatic present drawing the reader into the scene. "First" means that Andrew sought Simon before he did anything else. {*Messiah*} This Aramaic title "Messiah" is preserved in the NT only here and 4:25, elsewhere translated into the Greek title *Christos,* Anointed One, from *chriô,* to anoint (cf. Matt. 1:1).

42. {*Looked upon him*} "Looked" is an eager gaze (cf. Luke 22:61). {*He brought him*} It is as if Andrew had to overcome some resistance on Simon's part. {*Thou shalt be called Cephas*} This is Peter's Aramaic nickname that will characterize him some day (cf. Matt. 16:17). The Aramaic *Cêphâs* (rock) was probably used in Matt. 16:18 for both the name "Peter" and the word "rock," without the Greek distinction of "stone" and "ledge" respectively.

43. {*He findeth Philip*} This is the Greek dramatic present, drawing the reader into the scene. Apparently this is not an accidental finding, possibly due to the efforts of Andrew and Peter. Both Andrew and Philip have Greek names. {*Follow me*} Often, Jesus uses this verb to win disciples (Mark 2:14; Matt. 8:22; 9:21; 19:21 ; Luke 9:59; John 21:19).

44. {*From Bethsaida*} Of two possible towns with this name, it is the one of Galilee, not in Iturea (cf. Luke 9:10), perhaps somewhere near Capernaum.

45. {*Nathaniel*} He was from Cana of Galilee (John 21:2), not far from Bethsaida and so known to Philip, also called Bartholomew; he is now united into the circle of believers. {*Moses...wrote*} (cf. Deut. 18:15 and also Luke 24:27,44). {*Jesus, son of Joseph, the one from Nazareth*} Jesus passed as son of Joseph, though the Apostle John has just described him as "the One and Only" (cf. John 1:18). These details were probably meant to interest Nathanael.

46. {*Can any good thing come out of Nazareth?*} There is a tinge of scorn in the question as if Nazareth had a bad name. Town rivalry may account to some extent for it since Cana (home of Nathanael) was near Nazareth. Clearly he had never heard of Jesus. {*Come and see*} Philip followed the method of Jesus with Andrew and John (John 1:39), probably without knowing it. Wise is the one who knows how to deal with the skeptic.

47. {*An Israelite indeed*} That is, one living up to the covenant name, Israel at its best (Rom. 2:29), without falsity. The servant of Jehovah was to be without guile (Isa. 53:9).

48. {*When thou wast under the fig tree*} The fig tree was a familiar object in Palestine, probably in leaf at this time. Greek syntax may suggest that Nathanael had withdrawn there for prayer. Jesus saw Nathanael's heart as well as his mere presence there. He saw him in his worship and so knew him.

49. {*Thou art the Son of God*} (cf. John 1:34). {*Thou art King of Israel*} To us this seems an anti-climax, but not so to Nathanael for both are Messianic titles in Ps. 2:1-12 and Jesus is greeted in the Triumphal Entry as the King of Israel (John 12:13).

50. {*Thou shalt see greater things than these*} The wonder of Nathanael no doubt grew as Jesus went on.

51. {*Verily, Verily*} Lit. "Amen, Amen." This is a Hebrew word transliterated into Greek and then into English, our "amen." This phrase is an illustration of Christ's authoritative manner of speaking. {*The heaven opened*} (cf. Gen. 28:12 also the baptism of Jesus Matt. 3:16; Luke 3:21). Here it refers to the opened heaven as the symbol of free intercourse between God and man (Isa. 64:1) and as it was later illustrated in the death of Stephen (Acts 7:56). Jesus Christ is the true Jacob's Ladder. "I am the Way," Jesus will say. He is more than King of Israel, he is the Son of Man (the race).

CHAPTER 2

1. {*In Cana of Galilee*} This is the home town of Nathanael. Some think the event was probably on Wednesday afternoon the fourth day of the week (usual day for marriage of virgins), when the party of Jesus arrived. {*And the mother of Jesus was there*} Probably because already well known in the Synoptics, no name is given. Probably Joseph was already dead. Mary may have been kin to the family where the wedding took place, an intimate friend clearly.

2. {*Jesus also was bidden*} That is, as well as his mother and because of her presence; possibly at her suggestion. {*And his disciples*} A nucleus of six; they probably were all acquaintances with the wedding party.

3. {*When the wine failed*} This is the Greek verb *hustereô*, from *husteros,* late or lacking (cf. Mark 10:21), an embarrassing circumstance, especially to Mary, if partly due to the arrival of the seven guests.

4. {*Woman*} Though not disrespectful, "woman" (not "mother") does show her she can no longer exercise maternal authority and not at all in his Messianic work. {*What have I to do with thee?*} Lit. "What is it to me and to you?" usually indicating some divergence of thought (cf. LXX Judg. 11:12; 2 Sam. 16:10; 1 Kgs. 17:18; 2 Kgs. 3:13; 2 Chr. 35:21) and in the NT (Mark 1:24; 5:7; Matt. 8:29; 27:19; Luke 8:28). {*Mine time has not yet come*} This phrase marks a crisis whenever it occurs, especially of his death (John 7:30; 8:20; 12:23; 13:1; 17:1). Here apparently it means the time (lit. "hour") for public manifestation of the Messiahship, though a narrower sense would be for Christ's intervention about the failure of the wine.

5. {*Whatsoever he saith unto you, do it*} The Greek syntax shows instant execution is desired by the speaker. Mary recognized the right of Jesus as Messiah to be independent of her. But she expected him to carry out her suggestion.

6. {*Waterpots...set there*} These were ready for festal ceremonial cleansing of the hands (2 Kgs. 3:11; Mark 7:3). {*Two or three firkins apiece*} Each water jar held about 20 gallons. In John 4:28 a much smaller water jar was used for carrying water.

8. {*Draw out now*} This verb is used elsewhere for drawing water from the well (John 4:7,15), but here referring to the stone water pots. Apparently the water was still water when it came out of the jars (verse 9), but was changed to wine before reaching the guests. The water in the jars remained water. {*Unto the ruler of the feast*} Not the toast-master, this was originally the superintendent of the dining-room who arranged the couches and tasted (cf. verse 9) the food.

9. {*Drunk freely*} This is the Greek verb *methuskô,* not meaning that these guests are now drunk (as the English translation implies), but that this is a common custom to put the inferior wine last. It is real wine and Jesus did socialize and was even criticized for it (Matt 11:19).

11. {*This beginning of his signs did Jesus*} Rather translate, "this Jesus did as a beginning of his signs." The Baptist witnessed and now Jesus' signs witness. The Apostle John selects eight in his Gospel by which to prove the deity of Christ (John 20:30) of which this is the first. {*Believed on him*} These six disciples (learners) had already believed in Jesus as the Messiah (John 1:35-51). Now their faith was greatly strengthened.

12. {*He went down to Capernaum*} On lower ground than Cana, this important city is also called Tell Hum on the north shore of Lake Galilee. Family and disciples were all in the fresh glow of the glory manifested at Cana. Surely Mary's heart was full.

13. {*The passover of the Jews*} John is writing after the destruction of the temple and for Gentile readers, hence "of the Jews."

14. {*Those that sold*} This is not in the temple proper, but the Gentile Court; yet all "his Father's house." The Synoptics record a similar incident at the end of Jesus' ministry. The Temple cleansing happened twice in Jesus' ministry, once at the beginning, once more at the end (cf. Mark 11:15-17; Matt. 21:12, Luke 10:45). Both instances are the indignant outcry of desecration.

15. {*A scourge of cords*} This is the Latin *flagellum.* {*The changers' money*} Lit. "the small pieces of money" (Greek is *kermata,* cut in pieces, change). Perhaps he took up the boxes and emptied the money.

16. {*Make not my Father's house a house of merchandise*} Greek syntax is lit. "Stop making my Father's house...a market-house." Note the clear-cut Messianic claim here (My Father cf. Luke 2:49).

17. {*Remembered*} In John often, the disciples were reminded. The disciples are helped (reminded), the traders are angered. {*Shall eat me up*} Lit. "to eat down thoroughly" ("up" we say).

18. {*What sign shewest thou unto us?*} These traders had paid the Sadducees and Pharisees in the Sanhedrin for the concession as traffickers which they enjoyed. They were within their technical rights in this question.

19. {*Destroy this temple*} (1 Cor. 3:16). The Greek syntax shows this as a command (destroy), but context softens it to a permission to do something. At this moment, all present understood the reference to be to Herod's temple; but this may have been a parable pointing to Jesus' resurrection after three days. They wouldn't have understood this at the time.

20. {*And wilt thou?*} The "you" in Greek is emphatic, an evident sneer. Jesus was an unknown upstart from Galilee, of the peasant class, not from any power group.

21. {*But he spake of the temple of his body*} This is John's view as he looks back at it, not what he understood when Jesus spoke the words.

22. {*Believed the Scripture*} This probably refers to Ps. 16:10 (cf. Acts 2:31; 13:35). {*And the word which Jesus had said*} (cf. John 2:19). Verses 21 and 22 could be construed to be in conflict. But they are not. John did not know for sure what it meant at the time Jesus said it. Verse 21 is written as he understood it at the writing of this gospel. Anyway, how do we know that Jesus wished to be understood clearly at this time? Certainly no one understood Christ when he spoke the words (verse 19).

23. {*Passover*} The Greek word can refer to just the meal or (as here) for the whole eight-day feast.

24. {*But Jesus did not trust himself to them*} Greek tense translates "But Jesus himself kept on refusing to trust himself to them."

25. {*For he himself knew*} Greek tense translate, "for he himself kept on knowing" as he did from the start. {*What was in man*} Not merely "a good reader of men," this supernatural knowledge of humanity is a mark of deity.

CHAPTER 3

1. {*Now*} Nicodemus is an instance of Christ's knowledge of men (John 2:25) and of one to whom he did trust himself (cf. John 2:24). He was a Pharisee, a member of the Sanhedrin, and wealthy.

2. {*By night*} Nicodemus had prominence, so it was remarkable he came to Jesus any time. The interest of Nicodemus was real and yet he wished to be cautious and avoid comment by other members of the

Sanhedrin. {***Rabbi***} Though not one technically, Nicodemus does recognize him as such; a long step for Nicodemus as a Pharisee to take. {***We know***} He seems to speak for others ("we") of his class. Possibly he knew of Jesus from the commission's report and interview of the Baptist (cf. John 1:19-27). {***Thou art a teacher come from God***} This is the explanation of Nicodemus for coming to Jesus, obscure Galilean peasant as he seemed, evidence that satisfied one of the leaders in Pharisaism. {***Except God be with him***} The Greek condition is that of a probability, not a definite fact. Jesus went about doing good because God was with him, Peter says (Acts 10:38).

3. {***Except a man be born anew***} It is better to translate "anew" as "from above." Nicodemus took it to mean "again" but that does not prove the meaning Jesus gave the word here. In the other passages in John (John 3:31; 19:11,23) the meaning is "from above" and usually so in the Synoptics. It is a second birth ("again"), to be sure, regeneration, but a birth from above by the Spirit ("from above").

4. {***Being old***} Nicodemus was probably familiar with the notion of re-birth for Gentile proselytes to Judaism, but not with the idea that a Jew had to be reborn. The blunder of Nicodemus (of misapprehending what Jesus was saying) is emphasized by the second question. The use of "second time" adds to the grotesqueness of his blunder. The learned Pharisee is as dull in spiritual insight as a novice. This is not an unheard of phenomenon.

5. {***Of water and the Spirit***} There are many views of what "water" refers to: baptism, physical birth-water, cleansing water, etc. By using water (the symbol before the thing signified) first and adding Spirit, he may have hoped to turn the mind of Nicodemus away from mere physical birth and, by pointing to the baptism of John on confession of sin which the Pharisees had rejected, to turn his attention to the birth from above by the Spirit. That is to say the mention of "water" here may have been for the purpose of helping Nicodemus without laying down a fundamental principle of salvation as being by means of baptism. Nicodemus had failed utterly to grasp the idea of the spiritual birth as essential to entrance into the Kingdom of God. He knew only Jews as members of that kingdom, the political kingdom of Pharisaic hope which was to make all the world Jewish (Pharisaic) under the King Messiah.

7. {*Marvel not*} Lit. "Do not begin to wonder," as clearly Nicodemus had done (cf. John 3:3).

8. {*The wind*} This is the Greek word *pneuma,* which can mean either wind or spirit as *spiritus* does in Latin (so also in Hebrew and Syriac), and some translate it as spirit; there are some good considerations for both views. Likely, it is best to understand it as "wind" as a metaphor of the (Holy) Spirit.

10. {*The teacher of Israel*} That is, the well-known or the authorized (the accepted) teacher of the Israel of God. {*And understandest not these things?*} His Pharisaic theology had made him almost immune to spiritual apprehension. It was outside of his groove: rote, rut, rot, the three terrible 'r's' of mere traditionalism.

11. {*We speak that we do know*} The "we" refers to Jesus and those who have personal experience of grace and so are qualified as witnesses. Jesus simply claims knowledge of what he has tried to make plain to the famous Rabbi without success. {*And bear witness of that we have seen*} He is not a dreamer, guesser, or speculator. He is bearing witness from personal knowledge, strange as this may seem to Nicodemus.

12. {*If I told...earthly things...if I tell you heavenly things*} Not things of an earthly nature or worldly or sinful, information about the new birth belongs to "earthly things." This was assumed to have been fulfilled and true; Jesus did say these things. Unlike the "earthly things" phrase, this condition is undetermined, unfulfilled. "Heavenly things" means the things that take place in heaven like the deep secrets of the purpose of God in the matter of redemption such as the necessity of the lifting up of Christ as shown in verse 14.

13. {*But he that descended out of heaven*} This high conception of Christ (pre-existing and incarnated) runs all through the Gospel and is often in Christ's own words as here.

14. {*Moses lifted up the serpent*} (cf. Num. 21:7). Moses set the brazen serpent upon the standard that those who believed might look and live. Jesus draws a vivid parallel between the act of Moses and the Cross.

15. {*That whosoever believeth may in him have eternal life*} Greek tense translates "that he may keep on having eternal life." It is more than endless, for it is sharing in the life of God in Christ (John 5:26; 17:3; 1 John 5:12). The interview with Nicodemus apparently closes with verse 15, as the change in the Greek tense shows.

16. {*Loved*} This is the Greek verb *agapaô,* the noble word so common in the Gospels for the highest form of love (John 14:23; 17:23; 1 John 3:1; 4:10) of God's love for man (cf. 2 Thess. 2:16; Rom. 5:8; Eph. 2:4). In John 21:15 John presents a distinction between *agapaô* and *phileô. Agapaô* is used also for love of men for men (John 13:34), for Jesus (John 8:42), for God (1 John 4:10). {*The world*} That is, the whole human race; a universal invitation (cf. 2 Cor. 5:19; Rom. 5:8). {*His only begotten Son*} (cf. John 1:14,18; 3:18).

17. {*But that the world should be saved through him*} "Save" is the Greek verb *sôzô,* the common verb "to save" (from *sôs,* safe and sound), from which *sôtêr* (Savior) comes (the Savior of the world, John 4:42; 1 John 4:14) and *sôtêria* (salvation, John 4:22 here only in John). The verb *sôzô* is often used for physical health (Mark 5:28), but here of the spiritual salvation as in John 5:34.

18. {*Hath been judged already*} Greek tense shows judgment has already been passed on the one who refuses to believe in Christ as Savior. {*Because he hath not believed*} Greek tense shows a permanent attitude of refusal.

19. {*And this is the judgment*} "Verdict" in the Greek is more precisely the process of judging, rather than the result of the judgment. {*The light is come*} This is a permanent result; Jesus is the Light of the world (John 1:4,5,9,11).

20. {*That doeth ill*} "Ill" is the Greek word *phaulos,* means first worthless and then wicked. {*Hateth the light...cometh not to the light*} (cf. verse 19). The light hurts his eyes, reveals his own wickedness, makes him thoroughly uncomfortable. Hence he does not read the Bible, he does not come to church, he does not pray. He goes on in deeper darkness.

21. {*That doeth the truth*} See 1 John 1:6 for this striking phrase. {*Comes to the light*} That is, is drawn by the light, not driven from it. {*They have been wrought in God*} He does not claim that they are perfect, only that what they have done has been done in the sphere of and in the power of God. Hence he wants the light turned on.

22. {*Baptized*} He did this through the hands of his disciples, not personally baptizing (cf. John 4:2).

23. {*John was also baptizing*} This verse shows the continued activity of the Baptist simultaneous with the growing work of Jesus. There was no real rivalry except in people's minds. {*And they came, and were*

baptized} The Greek tense is graphically picturing the long procession of pilgrims who came to John confessing their sins and receiving
baptism at his hands.

24. {*For John had not yet been cast into prison*} (cf. Luke 3:19).

25. {*With a Jew*} Probably some Jew resented John's baptism of Jesus
as implying impurity or that they were like Gentiles (cf. proselyte baptism). {*About purifying*} (cf. John 2:6). The committee from the
Sanhedrin had challenged John's right to baptize (John 1:25). The Jews
had various kinds of baptisms or dippings (Heb. 6:2), "baptisms of
cups and pots and brazen vessels" (Mark 6:4). The disciples of John
came to him with the dispute (the first known baptismal controversy,
on the meaning of the ceremony) and with a complaint.

26. {*Rabbi*} (cf. John 1:38; 3:2). {*To whom thou hast borne witness*}
Note avoidance of calling the name of Jesus. These disciples of John
are clearly jealous of Jesus as a rival of John and they distinctly blame
John for his endorsement of one who is already eclipsing him in popularity. {*And all men come to him*} The sight of the growing crowds
with Jesus and the dwindling crowds with John stirred John's followers
to keenest jealousy. What a life-like picture of ministerial jealousy in
all ages.

27. {*Except it have been given him from heaven*} This Greek condition is undetermined with the prospect of determination.

28. {*I said*} (cf. John 1:20,23). He had always put Jesus ahead of him as
the Messiah (1:15).

29. {*The bridegroom*} This is a metaphor of Jesus himself (cf. Mark
2:19; also 2 Cor. 11:2; Eph. 5:23-32 and John 19:7; 21:2), the Baptist is
only the *paranymph* ("friend of the bridegroom"). His office is to bring
groom and bride together.

30. {*Must...*} It has to be (cf. John 3:14). The Greek tense shows Jesus
is to go on growing while John goes on decreasing. These are the last
words that we have from John until the despondent message from the
dungeon in Machaerus whether Jesus is after all the Messiah (Matt.
11:2; Luke 7:19).

31. {*Is above all*} Jesus is above all, not just the Baptist.

32. {*No man...*} There were crowds coming to Jesus, but they do not
really accept him as Savior and Lord (John 1:11; 2:24). It is superficial as
time will show. But "no one" is not to be pressed too far, for it is the
rhetorical use.

34. {*By measure*} That is, God has put no limit to the Spirit's relation to the Son. God has given the Holy Spirit in his fullness to Christ and to no one else in that sense.

33. {*Hath set his seal*} (cf. Matt. 27:66). Lit. "he sealed the witness." The metaphor of sealing is a common one for giving attestation (cf. John 6:27). The one who accepts the witness of Jesus attests that Jesus speaks the message of God.

36. {*That obeyeth not*} Lit. "He that is disobedient to the Son." Jesus is the test of human life as Simeon said he would be (Luke 2:34).

CHAPTER 4

1. {*When therefore…*} This was the work of the Baptist and the jealousy of his disciples. {*How that…was making and baptizing more disciples than John*} Recall the tremendous success of John's early ministry (Mark 1:5; Matt. 3:5; Luke 3:7,15) in order to see the significance of this statement that Jesus had forged ahead of him in popular favor. Apparently, John was cast into prison before Jesus left for Galilee, though recently still free (John 3:24). With John out of the way, the Pharisees turn to Jesus with envy and hate.

2. {*Although Jesus himself baptized not, but his disciples*} (cf. John 3:22). The Greek tense shows it was not the habit of Jesus. Not mentioned again until after the resurrection (Matt. 28:19ff), it is possible that Jesus stopped the baptizing because of the excitement and the issue raised about his Messianic claims.

4. {*He must needs pass through Samaria*} It was only necessary (so "had") to pass through Samaria in going directly north from Judea to Galilee. In coming south from Galilee travelers usually crossed over the Jordan and came down through Perea to avoid the hostility of the Samaritans towards people who passed through their land to go to Jerusalem. Jesus once met this bitterness on going to the feast of tabernacles (Luke 9:51-56).

6. {*Jacob's well*} Lit. "A spring of Jacob" (cf. John 4:14). It is really a cistern 100 feet deep dug by a stranger apparently in a land of abundant springs (Gen. 26:19; John 4:11-12).

9. {*The Samaritan woman*} The Samaritans were a mixture by intermarriage of the Jews left in the land (2 Chr. 30:6,10; 34:9) with colonists from Babylon and other regions sent by Shalmaneser. They had

had a temple of their own on Mt. Gerizim and still worshipped there. {*Thou being a Jew*} Racial hostility was all the keener because the Samaritans were half Jews. {*For Jews have no dealings with Samaritans*} Perhaps she was surprised that Jesus would drink out of her waterpot.

10. {*The gift of God*} (cf. John 3:16 also Eph. 4:7). This is the inexpressible gift (2 Cor. 9:15). Naturally the gift mentioned in 3:16 (Westcott), the inexpressible gift (2 Cor. 9:15). Some take it to refer to the living water below, but that is another allusion to 3:16. {*Living water*} This refers to spring water or well water, somewhat superior to cistern or standing water (Gen. 26:19; Lev. 14:5; Num. 19:17). Of course, Jesus is symbolically referring to himself as the Living Water (cf. John 7:39 also Rev. 7:17; 22:1).

11. {*Sir*} Though usually translated "lord," this is the meaning of the Greek word here.

12. {*Art thou...?*} This question expects a "no" answer.

13. {*Every one that drinketh...*} Likely, Jesus pointed to the well (this water).

14. {*Shall never thirst*} In the Greek, "never" is the strongest possible negative. Jesus has not answered the woman's question save by the necessary implication here that he is superior to Jacob.

15. {*Sir*} See verse 11. {*This water*} This peculiar kind of water. She did not grasp the last phrase "unto life eternal," and speaks half ironically of "this water." {*That I thirst not...nor keep on coming*} This is alluding to the words of Jesus, water that will prevent thirst. She has to get water once or twice every day. She is evidently puzzled and yet attracted.

16. {*Go, call thy husband*} These two verbs are commands. Had she started to leave after her perplexed reply? Her frequent trips to the well were partly for her husband. We may not have all the conversation preserved, but clearly Jesus by this sudden sharp turn gives the woman a conviction of sin and guilt without which she cannot understand his use of water as a metaphor for eternal life.

17. {*I have no husband...five husbands...is not thy husband*} The Greek *anêr* means either "man" or "husband." She had her "man," but he was not a legal "husband." Her language veils her deceit. She has had five men, and the current is not her legal husband either.

19. {*Sir*} See verse 11. {*I perceive*} Greek tense translates, "I am beginning to see/perceive," as a mental contemplation (John 12:45; 14:17). {*That thou art a prophet*} "Thou" is emphatic. She felt that this was the explanation of his knowledge of her life. She wanted to change the subject at once and return to the theological dispute.

20. {*And ye say*} This refers to Jews. {*Ought to worship...in Jerusalem*} "Must" is "as of necessity." The woman felt that by raising this theological wrangle she would turn the attention of Jesus away from herself and perhaps get some light on the famous controversy.

21. {*The hour cometh*} (cf. John 4:34; 5:25,28; 16:2,25,32). {*Neither in this mountain nor in Jerusalem*} The worship of God will be emancipated from bondage to place. These ancient rivalries will disappear when the spirituality of true religion is fully realized.

22. {*That which ye know not*} (cf. Acts 17:23). "You know whom to worship, but you do not know him" (Westcott); nor do they have a full Scriptural revelation.

23. {*The...worshippers*} This is the Greek word *proskunêtês,* from the verb *proskuneô,* to bow the knee, to worship. {*In spirit and truth*} This is what matters, not where, but how (in reality, in the spirit of man, the highest part of man, and so in truth). All this is according to the Holy Spirit (Rom. 8:5) who is the Spirit of truth (John 16:13).

24. {*God is a Spirit*} More precisely, "God is Spirit"; but it cannot mean "Spirit is God." The non-corporeality of God is clearly stated and the personality of God also.

25. {*He will declare unto us all things*} "Explain" is the Greek verb *anaggellô,* to announce fully (*ana,* up and down). Perhaps here is light on the knowledge of her life by Jesus as well as about the way to worship God.

26. {*I that speak unto thee am he*} Jesus declares that he is the Messiah (cf. also John 9:37).

27. {*Upon this*} Apparently the woman left at once when the disciples came. {They marvelled...was speaking...} There was a rabbinical precept: Let no one talk with a woman in the street, no, not with his own wife (Lightfoot). The disciples held Jesus to be a Rabbi and felt that he was acting in a way beneath his dignity.

28. {*Left her waterpot*} She left it in her excitement and embarrassment. It was too large for speed anyhow (cf. John 2:6).

29. {*Can this be the Christ?*} Greek syntax shows the question is in a hesitant form to avoid arousing opposition, though she is convinced herself (cf. John 4:26). She does not take sides, but piques their curiosity.

30. {*They went out*} Greek tense shows this is at once and in a rush. {*And were coming to him*} The Greek tense graphically pictures the long procession as they approached Jesus.

31-32. {*Prayed him*} Greek tense translates "kept beseeching/urging him." Their concern for the comfort of Jesus overcame their surprise about the woman.

33. {*Hath any man brought him aught to eat?*} In the Greek syntax, a "no" answer is expected.

34. {*To do the will...and to accomplish his work*} The Messianic consciousness of Jesus is clear and steady (John 5:30; 6:38). He never doubted that the Father sent him. In John 17:4 (the Intercessory Prayer) he will say that he has done this task which the Father gave him to do. On the Cross Jesus will cry "It is finished." He will carry through the Father's program (John 3:16). That is his "food." He had been doing that in winning the woman to God.

35. {*Say not ye? "There are yet four months...and then cometh the harvest"*} Is this a rural proverb, or is Jesus just stating a fact? The meaning does not depend on this detail. {*Lift up your eyes...fields...white...already unto harvest*} The Samaritans could already be seen approaching and they were the ripe field. This is the meaning of Christ's parable.

37. {*The saying*} (cf. 1 Tim. 1:15; 3:1). Probably a proverb that is particularly true in the spiritual realm. {*One soweth, and another reapeth*} It is sad when the sower misses the joy of reaping (Job. 31:8) and has only the sowing in tears (Ps. 126:5). This may be the punishment for sin (Deut. 28:30; Mic. 6:15). Sometimes one reaps where he has not sown (Deut. 6:11; Jos. 24:13). It is the prerogative of the Master to reap (Matt. 25:26), but Jesus here lets the disciples share his joy.

39. {*Because of the saying of the woman who testified*} She bore her witness clearly and with discretion. She told enough to bring her neighbors to Christ. They knew her evil life and she frankly confessed Christ's rebuke to her. She had her share in this harvest. How timid and cowardly we often are today in not giving our testimony for Christ to our neighbor.

41. {*Many more*} Lit. "More by much." Jesus was reaping more rapidly than the woman did. But all were rejoicing that so many really believed.

42. {*The Saviour of the world*} (cf. Matt. 1:21 also 1 John 4:14). This title may be synonymous with Messiah and a full title of honor. The first century literature attests that such a title was possible to be attached to the Messiah, though some dispute such a fact. The Romans termed their emperors saviors and the New Testament so calls Christ (cf. Luke 2:11; John 4:42; Acts 5:31; 3:23; Phil. 3:20; Eph. 5:23 Titus 1:4; 2:13; 3:6; 2 Tim. 1:10; 2 Pet. 1:1,11; 2:20; 3:2,18).

44. {*A prophet hath no honour in his own country*} A similar proverb has been found in Plutarch, Pliny, Seneca. "Country" or "hometown" (cf. Luke 4:24; Mark 6:4; Matt. 13:57) can refer to: Nazareth the city; the region of Judea; the region of Galilee. In context, "Galilee" is probably John's meaning.

45. {*Received him*} Jesus had evidently anticipated a quiet arrival. As Orthodox Jews, Galileans had seen the miracles in Jerusalem and so Jesus was not a new figure to them (unlike the Samaritans).

46. {*Unto Cana*} (cf. John 2:1ff.). {*Nobleman*} This is one connected with the king, probably here it is one of the courtiers of Herod the tetrarch of Galilee, Cuza (Luke 8:3), Manaen (Acts 13:1), or some one else. {*At Capernaum*} A town some miles from Cana near where the Jordan enters the Sea of Galilee.

47. {*Went and besought*} The Greek tense shows that he began to beg and kept it up.

48. {*Ye will in no wise believe*} "Never" is very strong in the Greek, picturing the stubborn refusal of people to believe in Christ without miracles.

49. {*Come down...ere my child die*} The Greek tense and tone show urgency. The official only thought Jesus had power before death as even Martha and Mary felt at first (John 11:21,32). But the father's heart goes out to Jesus. "Child" is lit. "dear little child" in the Greek form showing tenderness.

50. {*Thy son liveth*} Lit. "Your son is living," and will not now die, Jesus means.

51. {*That his son lived*} This is the same tense and form that Jesus earlier spoke.

53. {*Himself believed...and his whole house*} Unlike in verse 50, this is complete faith in Jesus himself as the Messiah (cf. John 1:7). This is the first example of a whole family believing in Jesus like the later case of Crispus (Acts 18:8).

CHAPTER 5

1. {*After these things*} This is a vague phrase, not meaning something follows immediately. He is supplementing the Synoptic Gospels and does not attempt a full story of the work of Jesus.

2. {*A pool*} This is the Greek word *kolumbêthra,* a diving or swimming pool (from *kolumbaô,* to swim, Acts 27:43). {*In Hebrew*} That is, "in Aramaic" (cf. John 19:13,17,20; 20:16; Rev. 9:11; 16:16).

3-4. {*In these…withered*} "Withered" is the last authentic word of this verse. Some MSS add to this verse and insert a spurious verse four as well; it is wanting in the oldest and best manuscripts.

6. {*Wouldest thou be made whole?*} It was a pertinent and sympathetic question.

7. {*When the water is troubled*} "Troubled" is the Greek verb *tarassô,* to agitate, stir (Matt. 2:3). The popular belief was that, at each outflow of this intermittent spring, there was healing power in the water for the first one getting in. {*But while I am coming*} The "I" is emphatic in the Greek.

8. {*Arise, take up thy bed, and walk*} "Get up!" The Greek mood and tense shows a sort of exclamation. For "mat" see Mark 2:2-12; 6:55; Acts 5:15; 9:33.

9. {*Took up his bed and walked*} The action in Greek shows that he "took it up at once and went on walking." {*The sabbath on that day*} This is the first of the violations of the Sabbath rules of the Jews by Jesus in Jerusalem that led to so much bitterness (cf. John 9:14,16). This controversy will spread to Galilee on Christ's return there (Mark 2:23-3:6; Matt. 12:1-14; Luke 6:1-11).

10. {*To take up thy bed*} (cf. John 5:8). Carrying burdens was considered unlawful on the Sabbath (Exod. 23:12; Neh. 13:19; Jer. 17:21). Stoning was the rabbinical punishment. To the questioners, the healing of the man was a minor detail.

11. {*But he answered*} Blind man ("he") is emphasized "that man." He did not know who Jesus was nor even his name. He quotes the very words of Jesus.

12. {*Who is the man?*} This is a contemptuous expression. They ask about the command to violate the Sabbath, not about the healing.

13. {*Jesus... Had conveyed himself away*} This is the Greek verb *ekneô,* to swim out, to slip out, or from *ekneuô,* to turn out, to turn the head to one side (to one side with which compare *eneneuon,* they nodded, Luke 1:62).

14. {*Sin no more*} Lit. "No longer go on sinning." This is a clear implication that disease was due to personal sin as is so often the case. Jesus used the same words to the woman taken in adultery in the spurious passage (John 8:11). He had suffered for 38 years. All sickness is not due to personal sin (John 9:3), but much is and nature is a hard paymaster. Jesus is here living up to his name (Matt. 1:21).

15. {*Went away and told*} Instead of giving heed to the warning of Jesus about his own sins he went off and told the Jews that now he knew who the man was who had commanded him to take up his bed on the Sabbath Day, to clear himself with the ecclesiastics and escape a possible stoning. The man was either ungrateful and willfully betrayed Jesus or he was incompetent and did not know that he was bringing trouble on his benefactor. In either case one has small respect for him.

16. {*Persecute*} Greek tense translates, "began to persecute" and kept it up. They disliked Jesus when here first (John 2:18) and were suspicious of his popularity (John 4:1). Now they have cause for an open breach. {*Because he did*} Greek tense shows this is not just this one act, but he was becoming a regular Sabbath-breaker. The Pharisees will watch his conduct on the Sabbath henceforth (Mark 2:23; 3:2).

17. {*My Father*} Not "our Father," this shows a claim to peculiar relation to the Father. {*Worketh even until now*} Lit. "keeps on working until now" without a break on the Sabbath. Ancient commentators all point out this fact of the continuous activity of God.

18. {*Sought the more*} The Greek tenses shows a graphic picture of increased and untiring effort, possibly growing for two more years.

19. {*The Son*} This is the absolute use of the Son in relation to the Father. {*For what things soever he doeth, these the Son also doeth in like manner*} "That one" is emphatic. This sublime claim on the part of Jesus will exasperate his enemies still more.

20. {*Loveth*} This is the Greek verb *phileô,* not to be distinguished here from *agapaô. Phileô* here may present the notion of intimate friendship (*philos,* friend), fellowship, the affectionate side, while *agapaô* is more the intelligent choice. But John uses both verbs for the mystery of love of the Father for the Son.

21. {*Quickeneth whom he will*} (cf. 1 Cor. 15:45). Jesus claims the power to raise the dead and will: the widow's son (Luke 7:11-17 also Luke 7:22; Matt. 11:5); Jairus' daughter (Matt. 9:18,22-26).

22. {*He hath given all judgement unto the Son*} Greek tense show the entrusting is in a state of completion (cf. John 3:35; 6:27,29; 10:29).

23. {*That all may honour the Son*} Not merely a great teacher, Jesus claims here the same right to worship from men that the Father has. Dishonoring Jesus is dishonoring the Father who sent him (John 8:49; 12:26; 15:23; 1 John 2:23).

24. {*Hath eternal life*} That is, has now this spiritual life which is endless (cf. John 3:36 also John 5:24,25). Note the quick transition from physical life and death to spiritual (cf. John 5:21-29).

25. {*And now is...the dead*} (cf. John 4:23). Not the future resurrection (cf. John 5:28), but the spiritual resurrection here and now of the spiritually dead in sins shall come to life spiritually (cf. Eph. 2:1,5; 5:14).

26. {*In himself*} The Living God possesses life wholly in himself and so he has bestowed this power of life to the Son (cf. John 1:3).

27. {*Because he is the Son of man*} Lit. "a son of man." This is not a reference to Messiah, but his humanity, because the judge of men must partake of human nature himself (cf. Rev. 1:13; 14:14).

28. {*In the tombs*} The Greek has no focus on a notion of "burial" (cf. Matt. 23:27), but a memorial or sepulcher as a monument. Jesus claims the power to bring the dead to life at the Last Day. Then there will be a general judgment and a general bodily resurrection we have here for both good and bad (cf. Matt. 25:46; Acts 24:15; 2 Cor. 5:10).

29. {*Unto the resurrection of life...*} There are two resurrections as to result, one to life, one to judgment (cf. Da. 12:2).

30. {*I*} Note first person, after using "the Son" since verse 19.

31. {*If I bear witness of myself* } The emphasis is on "I" —I alone with no other witness.

32. {*Another*} This refers to the continual witness of the Father, not the Baptist.

33. {*Ye have sent*} The "You" is emphatic. As Jesus makes the reference, the Baptist has to be recognized as trustworthy by the Sanhedrin (cf. John 1:19-28).

34. {*But the witness which I receive*} Lit. "But I do not receive the witness" simply from a man (like John). The witness of God is greater than that of men and Jesus has this (cf. 1 John 5:9).

35. {*He...that burneth...and shineth*} Lit. "That one" referring to John of verse 33). Once a burning light, he is now consumed. The Baptist was now in prison and so Christ spoke of him as "was." His active ministry is over. {*The lamp*} This Greek word *lampas* (a torch whose wick is fed with oil) used variously: common lamp (cf. Matt. 5:15; 25:1,3); fig. of Christ (Rev. 21:23); not the Baptist (John 1:8). When the Light comes, the lamp is no longer needed (John 8:12; 9:5; 12:46).

36. {*But the witness which I have is greater than that of John*} As good as the witness of John is, Christ has superior testimony. {*To accomplish*} (cf. John 4:34). Jesus felt keenly the task laid on him by the Father (cf. John 3:35) and claimed at the end that he had performed it (John 17:4; 19:30). Jesus held that the highest form of faith did not require these "works" as in John 2:23; 10:38; 14:11. But these "works" bear the seal of the Father's approval (John 5:20,36; 10:25) and to reject their witness is wrong (John 10:25; 10:37; 15:24).

37. {*He hath borne witness...*} This is the direct witness of the Father, besides the indirect witness of the works. This testimony refers to the witness of the Father in the heart of the believers, not necessarily audible or visible manifestations (cf. 1 John 5:9,10). Though the Father also did speak in history: at baptism (Mark 1:11); transfiguration (Mark 9:7); at the visit of the Greeks (John 12:28). Jesus will say that those who have seen him have seen the Father (John 14:9), but here he means the Father's "voice" and "form" as distinct from the Son.

39. {*Ye search...*} This can be either a command (Search!) or a statement of fact (as in our translation). Only the context can decide, though the latter is preferred. "Scriptures" refer to the well-known collection in the Old Testament (Matt. 21:42; Luke 24:27). Elsewhere in John the singular refers to a particular passage (John 2:22; 7:38; 10:35). {*In them ye have eternal life*} Some believe the Greek word "think" has the built in notion that this is a mistaken opinion; certainly the rabbis did make a mechanical use of the letter of Scripture as a means of salvation.

40. {*That ye may have life*} This is Life in its simplest form as in John 3:36 (cf. John 3:16). This is the purpose of John in writing the Fourth Gospel (John 20:31). There is life only in Christ Jesus.

41. {*Glory from men*} Christ's motive is unlike the Jews (John 5:44; 12:43; Matt. 6:1) and seeks not his own glory, but the glory and fellowship of the Father (John 1:14; 2:11; 7:18).

42. {*But I know you*} Translate the Greek tense, "I have come to know and still know," the knowledge of personal experience (John 2:24). {*The love of God*} Lit. "the love toward God" (cf. Luke 11:42), a phrase common in 1 John (1 John 2:5; 3:17; 4:7,9; 5:3) and in Paul (2 Thess. 3:5; 2 Cor. 13:14; Rom. 5:5). These rabbis did not love God and hence did not love Christ.

43. {*In my Father's name*} Seven times Jesus in John speaks in this name (John 5:43; 10:25; 12:28; 17:6,11,12,26).

44. {*How can ye believe?*} The "you" is emphatic, that is you being what you are. They were not true Jews (Rom. 2:29; Esth. 9:28) who cared for the glory of God, but they prefer the praise of men (Matt. 6:1; 23:5) like the Pharisees who feared to confess Christ (John 12:43).

45. {*I will accuse you*} "I" is emphatic. "Accuse" is the Greek verb *katêgoreô* (*kata*, against, *agoreuô*, to speak in the assembly *agora*, to bring an accusation in court, a public accusation). {*Even Moses...on whom ye have set your hope*} The Greek tense shows they are in a state of repose in Moses.

46. {*For he wrote of me*} (cf. Deut. 18:18 quoted in Acts 3:22 and 7:37; cf. also John 3:14; 8:56) This was a home-thrust, proving that they did not really believe Moses. Jesus does here say that Moses wrote concerning him.

47. {*His writings*} (cf. Luke 16:31). The authority of Moses was the greatest of all for Jews. Jesus clearly states the fact that Moses wrote portions of the Old Testament, what portions he does not say (cf. Luke 24:27,44). There was no answer from the Rabbis to this conclusion of Christ.

CHAPTER 6

1. {*After these things*} (cf. John 3:22; 5:1; 6:1; 7:1). The phrase does not mean immediate sequence of events, but is indefinite. As a matter of fact, a whole year may intervene between the events of chapter 5 in Jerusalem and those in chapter 6 in Galilee. It was the Passover time (John 6:4) just a year before the end.

2. {*Followed*} The Synoptics fill in more details of the crowds (cf. Mark 6:32; Matt. 14:13). {*They beheld...*} John does not record many of these signs, found in the Synoptics (Mark 1:29; 2:1; 3:1; 6:5). The people were eager to hear Jesus again (Luke 9:11) and to get the benefit of his healing power.

3. {*Sat*} Lit. "was sitting," a picture of repose.

4. {*The feast of the Jews*} This is probably the third Passover in Christ's ministry (John 2:13 and one unmentioned unless John 5:1 be it). John is fond of notes of time. Jesus failed to go to this Passover because of the hostility in Jerusalem (John 7:1).

5. {*Lifting up his eyes*} It is a particularly expressive as Jesus looked down from the mountain on the approaching multitude. {*Whence are we to buy?*} (cf. Num. 11:13-22 and 2 Kgs. 4:42). John passes by the earlier teaching and healing of the Synoptics (Mark 6:34; Matt. 14:14; Luke 9:11) until mid-afternoon. In John, Jesus takes up the matter of feeding the multitude with Philip (from the other Bethsaida, John 1:44) whereas in the Synoptics the disciples raise the problem with Jesus.

6. {*To prove him*} This is not here in the bad sense of tempting as it is so often (Matt. 4:1). {*What he would do*} (cf. John 2:25). John explains why Jesus put the question to Philip.

7. {*Two hundred pennyworth of bread*} (Mark 6:37). Lit. "loaves of two hundred denarii." The denarius was the usual pay for a day's labor (Matt. 20:2,9,13).

8. {*Simon Peter's brother*} (cf. John 1:40). The great distinction of Andrew was precisely this— that he brought Simon to Christ. Philip and Andrew appear together again in John 12:20-22.

9. {*A lad here*} The Greek form shows it is a small child. How he came to have this small supply we do not know. {*Fishes*} The Greek form shows these are small fish.

10. {*Sit down*} Lit. "fall back," lie down, recline. {*The men*} This is "men" as distinct from women (cf. Matt. 14:21). {*About five thousand*} Note that this was a general estimate, though they were arranged in orderly groups by hundreds and fifties, "in ranks" like "garden beds" (Mark 6:40).

12. {*And when they were filled*} This is the Greek verb *empimplēmi*, to fill in, to fill up, to fill completely. They were all satisfied. {*Gather up...broken pieces*} This is not the crumbs or scraps on the ground, but pieces broken by Jesus (Mark 6:41) and not consumed.

13. {*Twelve baskets*} (Mark 6:43; Matt. 14:20; Luke 9:17; John 6:13). That is, one for each of the apostles. What about the lad? These are stout wicker baskets in distinction from the soft and frail baskets used at the feeding of the four thousand (Mark 8:8; Matt. 15:37).

14. {*The prophet that cometh*} There was a popular expectation about the prophet (cf. Deut. 18:15) as being the Messiah (John 1:21; 11:27). The phrase is peculiar to John, but the idea is in Acts (John 3:22; 7:37). The people are on the tiptoe of expectation and believe that Jesus is the political Messiah of Pharisaic hope.

15. {*Take him by force*} This is the Greek verb *harpazô,* violent seizing (Matt. 11:12; 13:19). There was a movement to start a revolution against Roman rule in Palestine by proclaiming Jesus King and driving away Pilate; even the apostles were sympathetic to the revolutionary impulse of the crowd.

16. {*When evening came*} This is real evening (with impending dark), not the early evening in mid-afternoon (Matt. 14:15).

17. {*And Jesus had not yet come to them*} Darkness had come, but Jesus had not come, while they were going over the sea. The Greek tenses in these verses are very graphic of the growing storm.

19. {*Furlongs*} Lit. "twenty-five or thirty stadia," The lake was about forty stadia (six miles) across, hence, a little over halfway across, about three and a half miles (cf. "middle" of the lake Mark 6:47). {*Drawing nigh unto the boat*} The Greek syntax shows they see Jesus slipping closer and closer to them on the water. {*They were afraid*} Here is a sudden change to the regular historical sequence, from the more vivid narrative present tense.

20. {*Be not afraid*} (cf. Mark 6:50 and Matt. 14:27). John does not tell that the disciples thought Jesus was an apparition (Mark 6:49; Matt. 14:26), nor does he give the account of Peter walking on the water (Matt. 14:28-31).

21. {*They were willing therefore*} According to Mark 6:51, both Jesus and Peter climbed into the boat.

22. {*Boat*} The Greek form shows this is a little boat (Mark 3:9).

23. {*Boats...*} This verse is an explanatory parenthesis in this long sentence.

24. {*When the multitude therefore saw...*} The thought of verse 22 now resumes. The crowd still did not understand how Jesus had crossed over, but they acted on the basis of the plain fact (that he was gone).

{*Seeking Jesus*} The crowd had a double motive: make Jesus king (John 6:15) and hopes of another bountiful meal (John 6:26).

25. {*Rabbi*} (cf. John 1:38). This is a courteous title.

26. {*Not because ye saw signs...but because ye ate of the loaves...*} (cf. John 6:2). The signs had led to wild fanaticism (John 6:14) and complete failure to grasp the spiritual lessons. They were more concerned with hungry stomachs than with hungry souls. It was a sharp and deserved rebuke.

27. {*For him the Father, even God, hath sealed*} Lit. "For this one the Father sealed, God." Sealing by God is rare in NT (2 Cor. 1:22; Eph. 1:13; 4:30). It is not clear to what item John refers when the Father set his seal of approval on the Son. It was done at his baptism when the Holy Spirit came upon him and the Father spoke to him (cf. John 5:37).

28. {*What must we do?...That we may work the works of God*} Greek tense translates, "What are we to do as a habit?" There may have been an element of vague sincerity in this question in spite of their supercilious patronizingly haughty attitude.

29. {*The work of God that ye believe*} (cf. 1 Thess. 1:3). Greek tense translates, "that you may keep on believing." Here Jesus terms belief in him as the work of God. These Jews were thinking of various deeds of the Pharisaic type and rules. Jesus turns their minds to the central fact.

31. {*Ate the manna*} The rabbis quoted Ps. 72:16 to prove that the Messiah, when he comes, will outdo Moses with manna from heaven. The key to the understanding of the whole situation is an acquaintance with the national expectation of the greater Moses. They quote to Jesus Exod. 16:15 (of. Num. 11:7; 21:5; Deut. 8:3). Their plea is that Moses gave us bread "from heaven." Can Jesus equal that deed of Moses?

32. {*The true bread out of heaven*} That is, "the bread out of heaven" as the manna and more "the genuine bread" of which that was merely a type (cf. "true" John 1:9; 4:23).

33. {*The bread of God...giveth life*} All bread is of God (Matt. 6:11). The manna came down from heaven (Num. 11:9) as does this bread. Manna gave nourishment, but not life. This is a most astounding statement to the crowd.

34. {*Lord*} (cf. John 6:25 "Rabbi"). How much the people meant by "Lord" is not clear.

35. {*I am the bread of life*} (cf. John 6:41,48,51; 8:12; 10:7,9,11,14; 11:25; 14:6; 15:1,5). This sublime sentence was startling in the extreme to the crowd. He is the bread of life in two senses: it has life in itself, the living bread (John 51), and it gives life to others like the water of life, the tree of life.

37. {*I will in no wise cast out*} "Never" in the Greek is strong. This is a definite promise of Jesus to welcome the one who comes.

38. {*Not to do*} Lit. "Not that I keep on doing." {*But the will*} Translate the sense, "but that I keep on doing the will." This is the fullness of joy for Jesus, to do his Father's will (John 4:34; 5:30).

39. {*At the last day*} (cf. John 11:24; 12:48). Here this means the day of judgment. Christ is the Agent of the general resurrection, (cf. John 5:28 and 1 Cor. 15:22) while here only the resurrection of the righteous is mentioned.

40. {*Should have eternal life*} Greek tense translates, "that he may keep on having eternal life" (cf. John 3:15,36). {*Beholdeth*} That is, with the eye of faith (cf. John 12:45).

41. {*Murmured*} This is the Greek verb *gogguzô*, its very sound in Greek is like the cooing of doves or the buzzing of bees. These Galilean Jews are puzzled over what Jesus had said (verses John 33,35) about his being the bread of God come down from heaven.

42. {*How doth he now say?*} They knew Jesus as the son of Joseph and Mary. They cannot comprehend his claim to be from heaven. This lofty claim puzzles skeptics today.

43. {*Murmur not*} There was a rising tide of protest.

44. {*Except the Father draw him*} (cf. John 6:65). The approach of the soul to God is initiated by God, the other side of verse 37 (cf. also Rom. 8:7).

45. {*Taught of God*} (cf. Isa. 54:13 [Septuagint] also 1 Thess. 4:9). {*And hath learned*} It is not enough to hear God's voice. He must heed it and learn it and do it. This is a voluntary response. This one inevitably comes to Christ.

46. {*This one has seen the Father*} With the eyes no one has seen God (John 1:18) save the Son who is "from God" in origin (John 1:1,14; 7:29; 16:27; 17:8). The only way for others to see God is to see Christ (John 14:9).

48. {*I am the bread of life*} (cf. John 6:35) after fuller explanation.

49. {*And they died*} That is, physical death. The manna did not prevent death. But this new manna will prevent spiritual death.

50. {*That a man may eat thereof, and not die*} The wonder and the glory of it all, but quite beyond the insight of this motley crowd.

51. {*The living bread*} Lit. "The bread the living" (cf. John 6:35,41,48). It is alive and can give life (cf. living water John 4:10).

52. {*Strove*} This the Greek verb *machomai,* to fight in armed combat (Acts 7:26), then to wage a war of words (cf. 2 Tim. 2:24). They were already murmuring (John 6:41), now they began bitter strife with one another over the last words of Jesus (John 43-51), some probably seeing a spiritual meaning in them. There was division of opinion about Jesus in Jerusalem also later (John 7:12,40; 9:16; 10:19).

53. {*Except ye eat...and drink his blood*} (cf. John 6:50-51). Drinking blood makes the demand of Jesus seem to these Jews more impossible, if taken literally. The only possible meaning is the spiritual appropriation of Jesus Christ by faith (cf. John 6:47). Life is found only in Christ.

54. {*He that eateth...*} Some say this refers to the Lord's Supper by prophetic forecast, so making participation in the bread and wine the means of securing eternal life. But this is an utter misrepresentation of Christ. Christ uses bold imagery to picture spiritual appropriation of himself who is to give his life-blood for the life of the world (cf. John 6:51). The language of Jesus can only have a spiritual meaning as he unfolds himself as the true manna.

56. {*Abideth in me and I in him*} "Abides" expresses continual mystical fellowship between Christ and the believer (cf. John 15:4-7; 1 John 2:6,27,28; 3:6,24; 4:12,16).

58. {*This is the bread*} This is the summary and final explanation of the true manna (John 6:32-58) as being Jesus Christ himself.

60. {*A hard saying*} Lit. "This saying is a hard one." "Hard" is the Greek word *sklêros,* rough, harsh, dried hard (from *skellô,* to dry), probably the last saying of Jesus that he was the bread of life come down from heaven and they were to eat him. It is to be hoped that none of the twelve joined the many disciples in this complaint.

63. {*Spirit...that quickeneth*} (cf. John 5:21 also John 3:6). {*The words...I have just spoken*} That is, those in this discourse (*I have just spoken*), for they are the words of God (John 3:34; 8:47; 17:8). The breath of God and the life of God are in these words of Jesus. There is life in his words today.

64. {*That believe not*} Failure to believe kills the life in the words of Jesus. {*Knew from the beginning*} From the first Jesus distinguished between real trust in him and mere lip service (John 2:24; 8:31). {*And who it was that should betray him*} Not necessarily referring to Judas at that moment, what he does say is that Jesus was not taken by surprise and soon saw signs of treason in Judas. Once Judas is termed traitor (cf. Luke 6:16). Judas had gifts and was given his opportunity. He did not have to betray Jesus.

67. {*Would ye also go away?*} A "no" answer is expected in the Greek in the question. Judas must have shown some sympathy with the disappointed and disappearing crowds. But he kept still. There may have been restlessness on the part of the other apostles.

68. {*Lord, to whom shall we go?*} Peter is the spokesman as usual and his words mean that, if such a thought as desertion crossed their minds when the crowd left, they dismissed it instantly. They had made their choice.

70. {*And one of you is a devil*} Jesus does not say that Judas was a devil when he chose him, but that he is one now (cf. John 13:2,27). One wonders if the words of Jesus here did not cut Judas to the quick.

71. {*Of Simon Iscariot*} Iscariot is lit. "man of Kerioth" (cf. Jos. 15:25 or Jer. 48:24). Judas was the only one of the twelve not a Galilean.

CHAPTER 7

1. {*Sought to kill*} The Greek tense shows a progressive attitude, "had been seeking to kill him" (cf. John 5:18).

2. {*The feast of tabernacles*} (Deut. 16:13; Lev. 23:34,43). It began on the 15th of the month Tisri (end of September) and lasted seven days and finally eight days in post-exilic times (Neh. 8:18). It was one of the chief feasts of the Jews.

3. {*His brethren*} (cf. John 7:5). Actually, they are Jesus' half-brothers. They were hostile to the Messianic assumptions of Jesus, a natural attitude as one can well see, though at first they were friendly (John 2:12).

4. {*Openly…manifest thyself*} Not in secret. It is wise advice in the abstract that a public teacher must allow inspection of his deeds, but the motive is evil. They might get Jesus into trouble.

5. {*For even his brethren did not believe on him*} Lit. "For not even were his brothers believing on him." The Greek tense shows a sad picture of the persistent refusal of the brothers of Jesus to believe in his Messianic assumptions, after the two rejections in Capernaum (Luke 4:16-31; Mark 6:1-6; Matt. 13:54-58), and also after the blasphemous accusation of being in league with Beelzebub when the mother and brothers came to take Jesus home (Mark 3:31-35; Matt. 12:46-50; Luke 8:19-21).

6. {*My time is not yet come*} This is the fitting or proper occasion for Christ's manifesting himself publicly to the authorities as Messiah (cf. John 7:8). The brothers of Jesus had the regular Jewish obligation to go up to the feast, but the precise day was a matter of indifference to them.

7. {*Cannot hate*} The brothers of Jesus here belong to the unbelieving world (Greek *kosmos*) which is unable to love Jesus (John 15:18,23,24).

8. {*Go ye up to the feast*} The "you" is emphatic. Jesus says, take your own advice (John 7:3). {*I go not up yet*} Actually the best Greek text reading is simply, "I am not going up." Jesus did not change his plans (cf. verse 10). He simply refused to fall in with his brothers' sneering proposal for a grand Messianic procession with the caravan on the way to the feast. He will do that on the journey to the last Passover.

9. {*He abode still in Galilee*} The Greek tense of this verb covers a period of some days.

11. {*The Jews*} That is, the hostile leaders in Jerusalem, not the Galilean crowds (John 7:12) or the populace in Jerusalem (John 7:25). {*Sought*} Jesus had avoided Jerusalem since the collision in chapter 5. The leaders clearly wished to attack him. {*Where is he?*} Jesus had been at two feasts during his ministry (cf. John 2:12; possibly John 5:1), but he had avoided the preceding Passover (John 6:4; 7:1). The leaders in Jerusalem had kept in touch with Christ's work in Galilee. They anticipate a crisis in Jerusalem.

12. {*Much murmuring*} This is the Greek *goggusmos,* from *gogguzô* (cf. John 6:41,61; 7:32), for secret displeasure (Acts 6:1) or querulous discontent (Phil. 2:14). {*Among the multitudes*} These different groups (plural) were visitors from Galilee and elsewhere and were divided in their opinion of Jesus as the Galileans had already become (John 6:66).

13. {*For fear of the Jews*} The crowds really feared the Jewish leaders and evidently did not wish to involve Jesus or themselves (cf. the disciples John 19:38; 20:19).

15. {*Marvelled*} Lit. a picturesque "were wondering." After all the bluster of the rulers (verse 13) here was Jesus teaching without interruption. {*Knoweth letters*} Lit. "knows letters." The marvel was that Jesus showed Himself familiar with the literary methods of the time, which were supposed to be confined to the scholars of the popular teachers.

16. {*Mine...but his that sent me*} That is, "not mine in origin." Jesus denies being self-taught or a schoolman. Jesus makes a bold claim that his teaching is superior in character and source (i.e., him who sent me) to that of the rabbis (John 4:34; 5:23,24,30,37; 6:38-40,44; 7:16,18,28).

17. {*If any man willeth to do...*} The Greek condition shows it is not currently fulfilled, with a prospect of determination. {*He shall know*} This is the Greek verb *ginôskô,* experimental knowledge from willingness to do God's will (cf. John 5:46; 18:37). There must be moral harmony between man's purpose and God's will. Those isolated or out of tune with God, like agnostic and atheistic critics, are disqualified by Jesus as witnesses to his claims.

19. {*Why seek ye to kill me?*} This is a sudden and startling question as an illustration of their failure to do the law of Moses. Jesus had previously known (John 5:39,45-47) that the Jews really rejected the teaching of Moses while professing to believe it.

21. {*One work*} A Sabbath violation, this is a direct allusion to John 5:1, though he had done others (John 2:23; 4:45).

23. {*Are ye wroth with me?*} "Angry" is the Greek verb *cholâô,* from *cholê* (bile, gall), possibly from *chloê* or *chlôros* (yellowish green), "be mad." This is a vivid picture of bitter spleen against Jesus for healing a man on the Sabbath when they circumcise on the Sabbath.

24. {*Stop judging...according to appearance*} (cf. John 11:44) This is not a righteous judgment.

25. {*Is not this?*} The Greek expects a "yes" answer.

26. {*Can it be that the rulers indeed know...that this is the Christ*} In the Greek, a "no" answer is expected. Yet there is ridicule of the rulers in the form of the question. "Christ" is the Messiah of Jewish hope.

27. {*This man...whence he is*} The Galilean Jews knew the family of Jesus (John 6:42), but they knew Jesus only as from Nazareth, not as born in Bethlehem (verse 42). {*When the Christ cometh no one knoweth whence...*} This statement is a piece of popular theology at that time. As the ancient sources said, "Three things come wholly unexpected—Messiah, a godsend, and a scorpion." The rulers knew it was Bethlehem (John 7:42; Matt. 2:5), but some even expected the Messiah to drop suddenly from the skies. The Jews generally expected a sudden emergence of the Messiah from concealment with an anointing by Elijah.

28. {*Whom ye know not*} Passing over popular notions (verse 27), Jesus points out their ignorance of God the Father who sent him.

30. {*They sought therefore*} Greek tense translates, "they began to seek." "They" refers to some of the Jerusalemites (not the leaders).

31. {*When the Christ shall come...will he do?*} The Greek expects a "no" answer. Jesus had won a large portion of the pilgrims either before this day or during this controversy. Apparently, many came to believe at this point, as close observers. "Do" in the Greek tense has the focus of summing up all the miracles of Jesus so far.

32. {*The Pharisees...heard the multitude murmuring*} "Whispering" is the vivid onomatopoetic Greek verb *gogguzô* (verse John 12) now grown louder like the hum of bees. Pharisees (intensely opposed to Jesus) and Sadducees (= chief priests) now teamed up, determined to silence Jesus by bringing him before the Sanhedrin. "Temple guards," this is the Greek word *hupêretês*. These are officers or servants, lit. "an under rower" (*hupo, eretês*), so any assistant; here meaning the temple police, (Matt. 5:25; Luke 1:2).

33. {*I go unto him that sent me*} (cf. John 16:5). "Go" is the Greek verb *hupagô*, old compound (*hupo, agô*), has the notion of withdrawing (literally, go under). *Hupagô* often in John of going to the Father or God (John 8:14,21; 13:3,33,36; 14:4,5,28; 15:16; 16:4,7,10,17).

34. {*And shall not find me*} This is no conflict with verse 33, but the essential eternal spiritual home of Christ in absolute, eternal being and fellowship with the Father (Vincent). This fellowship was beyond the comprehension of these hostile Jews (cf. John 7:36; John 8:21).

35. {*Will he go...?*} A "no" answer to this question is expected in the Greek.

37. {*Now on the last day...*} This is the eighth and so special day which was "an holy convocation," kept as a Sabbath (Lev. 23:36), apparently observed as a memorial of the entrance into Canaan. {*If any* *man thirst*} On each of the seven preceding days water was drawn in a golden pitcher from the pool of Siloam and carried in procession to the temple and offered by the priests as the singers chanted Isa. 12:3: "With joy shall ye draw water out of the wells of salvation." It is uncertain whether the libations were made upon the eighth day. If they were not made, the significant cessation of the striking rite on this one day of the feast would give a still more fitting occasion for the words.

39. {*Were to receive*} Lit. "whom they were about to receive," a clear reference to the great Pentecost.

41. {*Christ come out of Galilee?*} The Greek syntax expects a "no" answer.

44. {*Would have taken him*} Lit. "were wishing to seize him" (cf. John 7:30).

45. {*Why did ye not bring him?*} This is an indignant outburst of the Sanhedrin (both Sadducees and Pharisees) at the failure of the temple police to arrest Jesus. Apparently they were sitting in expectation of immediately questioning him (Dods). They were stunned at this outcome.

47. {*Are ye also led astray?*} Formally, the Greek expects a "no" answer, but the Pharisees really believed it (cf. John 6:67).

48. {*Hath any of the rulers believed on him?*} A "no" answer is sharply expected. These police were employed by the temple authorities (rulers); they have no right to believe on their own.

50. {*Nicodemus...being one of them*} (cf. John 3:1ff. also 19:39). Once timid before Jesus, now he boldly protests against the injustice of condemning Jesus unheard. His present act is courageous. He is ruler, Pharisee, and a member of the Sanhedrin.

51. {*Doth our law judge a man?...Except it first hear from himself?*} A "no" answer is expected in the Greek. These law advocates were violating the law of criminal procedure (Exod. 23:1; Deut. 1:16). There was no legal answer to the point of Nicodemus.

52. {*Art thou also of Galilee?*} The Greek formally expects a "no" answer, but really implies Nicodemus has lined up with this Galilean mob (verse 49). These aristocrats of Jerusalem had a scornful contempt for the rural Galileans.

53. John 7:53 to John 8:12 is certainly not a genuine part of John's Gospel, as the oldest and best manuscripts clearly attest. However, it is probably a true story for it is like Jesus, but it does not belong to John's Gospel.

CHAPTER 8

1. {*But Jesus went...*} Apparently, Jesus was lodging in the home of Mary, Martha, and Lazarus.

2. {*Early in the morning*} This is the Greek word *orthros* meaning daybreak (cf. Luke 24:1; Acts 5:21). {*He came again into the temple*} If the paragraph is genuine, the time is the next day after the eighth and last day of the feast. If not genuine, there is no way of telling the time of this apparently true incident.

3. {*Bring*} This is the Greek tense showing a vivid dramatic scene, drawing in the reader to the story. {*Taken in adultery*} Lit. "to seize" (Mark 9:18), to catch, to overtake (John 12:35), to overcome or over-take (cf. John 1:5).

4. {*Hath been taken*} (cf. verse 3). Greek tense shows one has been caught and is still guilty. {*In the very act*} This is the Greek *autophôros, autos*, self, and *phôr*, thief) caught in the act of theft, then extended to any crime in which one is caught.

6. {*Tempting him*} This is a "test" in the evil sense (Mark 8:11; 10:2, etc.). This laying of traps for Jesus was a common practice of his en-emies, and now a habit with these Rabbis (cf. Luke 11:16). {*Wrote on the ground*} This is to write on the sand as every one has done some-times. It is uncertain if these were words or signs; He certainly had the ability to do either. There is a tradition that Jesus wrote down the names and sins of these accusers. That is not likely. They were written on their hearts. Jesus alone on this occasion showed embarrassment over this woman's sin.

8. {*Wrote on the ground*} (cf. verse 6).

9. {*Went out...one by one...beginning from the eldest*} The elder first, as was natural for they had more sins of this sort which they recalled. They are summoned to judge themselves rather than the woman (Dods); conscience stricken, they left.

11. {*No man, Lord*} She makes no excuse for her sin. "Lord" can also mean "Sir" here; is this what she means? {*Henceforth sin no more*} (cf. John 5:14). Lit. "Henceforth no longer go on sinning." One can only hope that the woman was really changed in heart and life. Jesus clearly felt that even a wicked woman can be saved.

13. {*Of thyself...*} This technical objection was according to the rules of evidence among the rabbis, "no man can give witness for himself (Mishnah)." They were still in the region of pedantic rules and external tests." But note the witness he had: the Baptist, the Father, his works and Scriptures (Moses in particular).

16. {*For I am not alone*} Jesus now takes up the technical criticism in verse 13 after justifying his right to speak concerning himself. {*But I and the Father that sent me*} (cf. John 16:32) Jesus gives the Father as the second witness.

19. {*Where is thy Father?*} The testimony of an unseen and unheard witness would not satisfy them. In the question is possibly a double meaning or reference (both hostile references): either God the Father; or a human father (and so a possible allusion to Jesus being of illegitimate origin). {*Ye would know my Father also*} (cf. John 5:36-38). Jesus will again on this occasion (John 8:55) deny their knowledge of the Father and Son (John 16:3). The Pharisees are silenced for the moment.

21. {*And ye shall die in your sin*} (cf. Ezek. 3:18; 18:18; Prov. 24:9). Note singular "sin" meaning "sin in its essence, sin in its acts."

22. {*Will he kill himself?*} (cf. John 7:31). Formally, the Greek calls for a "no" to the question, but there is a manifest sneer in the query.

24. {*That I am he...*} Though some translations fill in the sense after "I am," there are several different senses that could follow this brief sentence. Or more likely, it may mean the absolute "I am" used of Jehovah (cf. Isa. 43:10). Jesus seems to claim absolute divine being (cf. John 8:58).

25. {*Even that which I have also spoken unto you from the beginning*} Though here a statement, this can also be translated a question. "All along" means "at all," "essentially," "primarily," so translate "Primarily what I am telling you."

28. {*When ye have lifted up the Son of man*} This is used of the Cross of Christ (John 3:14; 8:28; 12:32,34). In Acts 2:33 the verb is used of the Ascension.

30. {*Many believed on him*} Lit. "came to believe" (cf. John 2:23). But the tension was keen and Jesus proceeded to test the faith of these new believers from among the Pharisees.

31. {*Who had believed in him*} They believed (cf. John 6:30) his claims to being the Messiah with their own interpretation (John 6:15), but they did not commit themselves to him. {*If ye abide in my word*} Your future loyalty to my teaching will prove the reality of your present profession. Also today, we accept church members on *profession* of trust in Christ. Continuance in the word (teaching) proves the sincerity or insincerity of the profession. It is the acid test of life.

32. {*And ye shall know the truth*} Jesus is the Truth (cf. John 1:14; 14:6). By doing God's will, the disciples will learn truth (John 7:17). {*And the truth shall make you free*} (cf. Rom. 6:18; Gal. 5:1). Sanctified in truth, the believer's freedom of which Jesus here speaks is freedom from the slavery of sin (cf. Rom. 8:2 also John 17:19). Freedom (intellectual, moral, spiritual) is only attainable when we are set free from darkness, sin, ignorance, superstition and let the Light of the World shine on us and in us.

35. {*The bondservant…the son*} (cf. Gen. 21:10 and Gal. 4:30). The slave has no footing or tenure and may be cast out at any moment while the son is the heir and has a permanent place (cf. also Heb. 3:5 [Num. 12:7]).

36. {*Ye shall be free indeed*} "Indeed" is the Greek adverb *ontôs,* an old and common adverb from participle *ontôn,* actually, really (cf. Luke 24:34). But this spiritual freedom was beyond the concept or wish of these Jews.

39. {*If ye were*} This is a condition assumed true in the Greek.

42. {*For I came forth from God*} The Greek tense shows this to be a definite historical event (the Incarnation). Note the definite consciousness of pre-existence with God (cf. John 17:5).

43. {*My speech…my word*} "Speech" is the Greek word *lalia,* from *lalos* (talk), means here more manner of speech than just story (John 4:42), while *logos* (say) refers rather to the subject matter. They will not listen to the substance of Christ's teaching and hence they are impatient with the way that he talks.

44. {*Father of lies*} Lit. "father of him" or "father of it." Both are possible in the Greek. This means either the father of the lie or of the liar, both of which are true as already shown by Jesus.

46. {*Which of you convicteth me of sin?*} (cf. John 3:20; 16:8). This means sin in general, not particular sins. They have no answer (cf. Heb. 4:15). Some suggest that Jesus paused before going on. {*Why do* *ye not believe me?*} This question drives home the irrationality of their hostility to Jesus. It was based on prejudice.

51. {*If a man keep my word*} This is a condition not currently fulfilled, but which might be fulfilled. (John 8:51,52,55; 14:21,23,24; 15:20; 17:6; 1 John 2:5). {*He shall never see death*} (cf. Ps. 89:48 and Luke 2:26; Heb. 11:5). "Never" is very strong in the Greek syntax. "To see death" means dying.

52. {*Now we know*} (cf. John 8:48). {*He shall never taste of death*} Again, "never" is very strong in the Greek syntax. As similar in the last verse, this is another Hebraism for dying (cf. Heb. 2:9 also Matt. 16:28; Mark 9:1; Luke 9:27). The Pharisees did not misquote Jesus as to the meaning, though they misunderstood him.

53. {*Art thou greater than our father Abraham?... Whom makest thou thyself?*} "No" is the expected answer in the Greek. The question was designed to put Jesus in a difficult position. They suspect that Jesus is guilty of blasphemy, in making himself equal with God (cf. John 5:18 also 10:33; 19:7).

55. {*And ye have not known him*} "Know" is the Greek verb *ginôskô*, the verb for experiential knowledge (cf. John 17:23,25). {*But I know him*} This peculiar intimate knowledge Jesus had already claimed (John 7:29). Though a different Greek word than used above, no undue distinction can be drawn here.

58. {*Before Abraham was*} This means "before Abraham came into existence or was born."

59. {*They took up stones therefore*} This is a vivid picture of a mob ready to kill Jesus, already beginning to do so. {*Hid himself*} This is not "vanishing," but quietly and boldly Jesus went out of the temple. His hour had not yet come (cf. John 10:39).

Chapter 9

2. {*Who did sin?...that he should be born blind*} (cf. Acts 3:2; 14:8). This is the only example of congenital blindness healed. It is not clear that the disciples expected Jesus to heal this case. They are puzzled by the Jewish notion that sickness was a penalty for sin. The Book of Job had shown that this was not always the case and Jesus shows it also (Luke 13:1-5). If this man was guilty, it was due to prenatal sin on his part, a curious notion surely.

3. {*But that the works of God should be made manifest in him*} Personal sin of an individual can cause disease (cf. John 5:14). Parents can hand on the effects of sin to the third and fourth generations, but there are cases free from blame like this.

5. {*When I am in the world...I am the light of the world*} Literally, "I am light to the world, whenever I am in the world." Jesus here refers to the historic Incarnation (John 17:11) and to any previous visitations in the time of the patriarchs, prophets, etc.

7. {*In the pool of Siloam*} "Pool" is a common word for swimming pool (cf. John 5:2,7). This pool was situated south of the temple area. {*Washed*} That is, apparently bathing and not merely washing his eyes.

10. {*How then were thine eyes opened?*} Accepting the fact, the neighbors want to know the manner of the cure.

11. {*The man that is called Jesus*} He does not yet know Jesus as the Messiah the Son of God (John 9:36). He received sight for the first time here, not "again."

13. {*They bring him*} Lit. "bring" with the Greek showing a vivid dramatic present, drawing the reader into the story.

16. {*Because he keepeth not the sabbath*} Since Jesus violates our rules about the Sabbath, hence he is not from God. {*How can a man that is a sinner do such signs?*} This was the argument of Nicodemus, himself a Pharisee and one of the Sanhedrin, long ago (John 3:2). It was a conundrum for the Pharisees. No wonder there was "a division" (cf. John 7:43; 10:19).

18. {*The Jews*} Probably, this refers to a hostile section of the Pharisees (cf. verse 16). {*Did not believe*} That is, did not believe the facts told by the seeing man. Then, they called out loud for his parents to throw light on this grave problem to cover up their own stupidity.

20. {*We know that this is our son, and that he was born blind*} The two questions of verse 19 the parents answer clearly and thus cut the ground from under the disbelief of these Pharisees as to the fact of the cure (verse 18). So these Pharisees failed here.

22. {*Because they feared the Jews*} The Greek tense shows this is a continuing fear and not without reason. See already the whispers about Jesus because of fear of the Jews (John 7:13). {*If any man should confess him to be Christ*} (cf. John 12:42). This is the Greek verb *homologeô*. Confession before people was made the test of discipleship and denial the disproof (Matt. 10:32; Luke 12:8). {*That he should be put out of the synagogue*} (cf. John 12:42; 16:2). This is a purely Jewish word naturally. There were three kinds of excommunication (for thirty days, for thirty more, indefinitely).

25. {*Whereas I was blind, now I see*} Lit. "Being blind I now see." It must be borne in mind that the man did not at this stage know who Jesus was and so had not yet taken him as Savior (John 9:36-38).

27. {*Would ye also become his disciples?*} (John 9:17). Formally a "no" answer is expected in the Greek, but there is the keenest irony in this gibe. It cut to the bone.

28. {*They reviled him*} This is the Greek verb *loidoreô*, from *loidoros* (reviler, 1 Cor. 5:11), in NT only here, Acts 23:4; 1 Cor. 4:12; 1 Pet. 2:23. {*Thou art his disciple*} The Greek pronoun, "This fellow" is probably an instance of disrespect. He had called him a prophet (John 9:17) and became a joyful follower later (John 9:36-38).

29. {*But as for this man, we do not know whence he is*} "This" is in the emphatic position in the Greek syntax. Some of the people did (John 7:27), but in the higher sense none of the Jews knew (John 8:14). These Pharisees neither knew nor cared.

30. {*Why, herein is the marvel*} Lit. "Why in this very point is the wonder." The man is angry now and quick in his insight and reply. His miracle of sight is a stubborn fact that stands.

32. {*Since the world began*} Lit. "from the age," "from of old." {*Of a man born blind*} congenitally blind, this is the chief point and the man will not let it be overlooked; in fact, he almost rubs it in.

34. {*Thou wast altogether born in sin*} Lit. "In sins you were born all of you." This teaches total depravity in this case beyond controversy, the Pharisees being judges.

35. {*Dost thou believe on the Son of Man?*} "Son of Man" is almost certainly the best text reading here. This is a distinct Messianic claim quite beyond the range of this man's limited knowledge, keen as he is.

38. {*Lord, I believe*} Same Greek word as "sir" in verse 36, now said in reverence "Lord." A short creed, but to the point. {*And he worshipped him*} In John (see John 4:20) this verb is always used to express divine worship. He accepted worship from this new convert as he later did from Thomas (John 20:28).

39. {*For judgment...*} The Father had sent the Son for this purpose (John 3:17). This world is not the home of Jesus. {*They which see not*}

The spiritually blind as well as the physically blind (Luke 4:18; Isa. 42:18). This man now sees physically and spiritually. {*And that they which see may become blind*} (cf. Matt. 11:25; Luke 10:21). Another part of God's purpose is the curse on those who blaspheme and reject the Son. Pharisees profess to see, but are really blind (cf. Matt. 23:16). They are complacent and satisfied with their dim light.

40. {*Are we also blind?*} "No" is the expected answer in Greek. And yet these Pharisees who overheard the words of Jesus to the new convert vaguely suspected that Jesus was referring to them by the last clause. Up in Galilee Jesus had called the Pharisees blind guides who stumble into the pit (Matt. 15:14).

41. {*If ye were blind...*} Here this is moral blindness. If the Pharisees were born morally blind, they would, like the severely mentally challenged, be without responsibility. Instead, they arrogantly asserted superior knowledge.

CHAPTER 10

1. {*Verily, Verily I say unto you*} Lit. "Amen, amen, I say to you." This is a solemn prelude by repetition (cf. John 1:51). Jesus shows he is an authoritative guide of the people also (John 9:24,29). So Jesus has a direct word for them.

2. {*The shepherd of the sheep*} (cf. John 10:16). It is used of Christ in 1 Pet. 2:25; Heb. 13:20. Paul applies it to ministers in Eph. 4:11 (also cf. John 21:16 and 1 Pet. 5:2). Paul uses it for bishops (elders) in Acts 20:28.

3. {*The porter*} (Mark 13:34; John 10:3 also John 18:16). This is Greek for "doorkeeper" (*thura,* door, *ôra,* care, carer for the door); one in charge of the sheep in the fold at night and opens the door in the morning for the shepherd.

5. {*A stranger*} Lit. "One belonging to another," this is a shepherd of another flock, it may be, not necessarily the thief and robber. Well-trained sheep will not follow such a man or woman.

6. {*This parable*} This is the Greek word *paroimia,* from *para* (beside) and *oimos,* way, a wayside saying or saying by the way: a proverb (2 Pet. 2:22 [Prov. 26:11]); symbolic saying (cf. John 16:25,29); allegory (cf. John 10:6). Here clearly *paroimia* means an allegory which is one form of the parable.

7. {*I am the door of the sheep*} Jesus is the legitimate door of access to the spiritual Fold of the House of Israel, the door by which a true shepherd must enter (Bernard). Obviously a metaphor, not a literal meaning, any more than bread being the literal body of Christ (cf. Mark 14:22); Jesus is the entrance to the Kingdom of God (John 14:6). **9.** {*By me if any man enter in*} "Through me" is in the emphatic position in the Greek. Offered to anyone (whoever), still one can call this narrow intolerance, if he will, but it is the narrowness of truth. **10.** {*But that he may steal, and kill, and destroy*} Note the order of the verbs. Stealing is the purpose of the thief, but he will kill and destroy if necessary just like the modern bandit or gangster. {*And may have it abundantly*} Lit. "to have a surplus or overflow" (cf. of grace Rom. 5:20). Jesus gives abundance of life and all that sustains life. **11.** {*I am the good shepherd*} The Greek word "good" is *kalos* and calls attention to the beauty in character and service (cf. 1 Pet. 4:10 and 1 Tim. 4:6). "Beauty is as beauty does." That is *kalos*. **12.** {*He that is a hireling...leaveth the sheep, and fleeth...and the wolf snatcheth them and scattereth them*} "Hired hand" is the Greek word *misthôtos,* from verb *misthoô,* to hire (Matt. 20:1), from *misthos* (hire, wages, Luke 10:7), in NT only in this passage. The hireling here is not necessarily the thief and robber of verses 1,8. Without the shepherd heart that loves the sheep, he may conceivably be a nominal shepherd (pastor) of the flock who serves only for the money, a sin against which Peter warned the shepherds of the flock "not for shameful gain" (1 Pet. 5:2 also Ezek. 34:5). **16.** {*Other sheep*} Not only the Jewish fold, Christ's horizon takes in all men of all races and times (John 11:52; 12:32). God loved the world and gave his Son for the whole human race (John 3:16). {*Them also I must bring*} Amazing to the Pharisees and disciples, missions in Christ's mind takes in the whole world. This is according to prophecy (Isa. 42:6; 49:6; 56:8) for the Messiah is to be a Light also to the Gentiles. Christ died for every man. {*And they shall hear my voice*} (cf. Rom. 9:1-11:36 and Acts 28:28). Jesus means that the Gentiles will hearken if the Jews turn away from him. {*And they shall become one flock, one shepherd*} (cf. Matt. 8:11). All (Jews and Gentiles) will form one flock under one Shepherd. There may be many folds (in different sheep pens) yet of the one flock (cf. Eph. 2:1-22). There is only the one Great Shepherd of the sheep (Heb. 13:20), Jesus Christ our Lord.

18. {*Of myself*} The voluntariness of the death of Jesus repeated and sharpened. The Father gave the Son who was glad to be given and to give himself (John 3:16; Rom. 5:8). {*I have power to lay it down*} (cf. John 1:12). Again, this is restatement of the voluntariness of his death for the sheep. He did not mean that he will raise himself from the dead independently of the Father as the active agent (Rom. 8:11). {*I received from my Father*} Here in the command of death and resurrection, he always follows the Father's command in all things (John 12:49; 14:31).

21. {*Can a demon open the eyes of the blind?*} "No" is the expected answer in the Greek. Demons would more likely put out eyes.

24. {*If thou art the Christ...tell us plainly*} (John 8:25). This condition is assumed to be true for the sake of argument. The demand seemed fair enough on the surface. But "Christ" or "Messiah" was a politically loaded term, so Jesus declined to use the word. When Jesus does confess he is Christ the Son of God (Mark 14:61; Matt. 26:63), the Sanhedrin instantly vote him guilty of blasphemy and accuse him before Pilate as a rival to Caesar. Jesus knew their minds too well to be caught now.

28. {*And they shall never perish*} "Never" is very strong in the Greek. The sheep may feel secure (John 3:16; 6:39; 17:12; 18:9).

30. {*One*} This is the Greek neuter, so meaning one essence or nature (not person). This crisp statement is the climax of Christ's claims concerning the relation between the Father and himself (the Son).

31. {*Took up stones again*} "Stoning" means to pelt or overwhelm with stones.

32. {*Do ye stone me*} The Greek tense translates, "are you *trying* to stone me." They had the stones in their hands stretched back to fling at him, a threatening attitude.

34. {*Ye are gods*} (Exod. 21:6; 22:9,28). The judges of Israel abused their office and God is represented in Ps. 82:6 as calling them "gods" (Greek *theoi,* Hebrew *elohim*) because they were God's representatives.

35. {*If he called them gods*} This condition is assumed as true. Jews (and rabbis) are now shut out from charging Jesus with blasphemy because of this usage in the OT (it cannot be broken). Jesus is not disclaiming his own deity, he is simply stopping the mouths of the rabbis from the charge of blasphemy.

36. {*Because I said...I am the Son of God*} Jesus had implied this long before (cf. John 2:16; 5:18-30; 9:35; 10:30). They will make this charge against Jesus before Pilate (John 19:7). There is no answer to this question with its arguments.

37. {*Believe me not*} The Greek syntax means either "cease believing me" or "do not have the habit of believing me." Jesus rests his case on his doing the works of "my Father," repeating his claims to sonship and deity.

38. {*That ye may know and understand*} Greek tense translates, "that you may come to know and you may keep on understanding." This is Christ's deepest wish about his enemies who stand with stones in their uplifted hands to fling at him.

39. {*They sought again to seize him*} Greek tense translates, "They kept on seeking to seize." Overawed but angry, they had tried repeatedly (John 7:1,30,44; 8:20), but in vain. They gave up the effort to stone him.

41. {*Many came to him*} Jesus was busy here and in a more congenial atmosphere than Jerusalem. Jesus did signs here (Matt. 19:2).

42. {*Many believed on him there*} (cf. John 1:12; 2:11). This is a striking witness to the picture of the Messiah drawn by John. When Jesus came they recognized the original (cf. John 1:29-34).

CHAPTER 11

3. {*Thou lovest*} This is the Greek verb *phileô* and means to love as a friend (see *philos* [friend] in verse 11) and so warmly, while *agapaô* (akin to *agamai,* to admire, and *agathos,* good) means high regard; though the distinction is not always maintained.

4. {*But for the glory of God*} (cf. John 9:3). Lit. "in behalf of God's glory." The death of Lazarus will illustrate God's glory.

5. {*Now Jesus loved*} The Greek tense is picturing the continued love of Jesus for this noble family (Luke 10:38-42; John 12:1-8). The sisters expected him to come at once and to heal Lazarus.

6. {*Two days*} It was long enough for Lazarus to die and seemed unlike Jesus to the sisters.

7. {*Let us go into Judea again*} They had but recently escaped the rage of the Jews in Jerusalem (John 10:39) to this haven in Bethany beyond Jordan (John 10:40).

10. {*But if a man walk in the night*} An unfulfilled but plausible condition in the Greek. It is spiritual darkness that Jesus here pictures, but the result is the same (cf. John 12:35 [1 John 2:11]).

11. {*That I may awake him out of sleep*} "Wake" is lit. "out of [state of] sleep."

12. {*He will recover*} This is the Greek verb *sôzô* (cf. "I save") used in its original sense of being or getting well (safe and sound).

14. {*Is dead*} Greek tense translates, "died" as in a past point of time.

16. {*Didymus*} Thomas (in Aramaic) and Didymus (Greek) both mean "twin"; so he had a twin brother or sister (cf. John 20:24; 21:2).

17. {*That he had been in the tomb four days already*} In Jewish custom, burial took place on the day of death (Acts 6:6,10).

18. {*About fifteen furlongs off*} Lit. "about fifteen stadion off." A *stadios*, is variously reckoned at about two American football fields (c. 200 yards), so less than two full miles by about 500 yards.

19. {*To console them*} Lit. "to put in a word beside," i.e., to offer consolation (cf. verse 31 also 1 Thess. 2:11; 5:14 and Job 2:13).

20. {*But Mary still sat in the house*} This is a graphic picture of Mary, "while Mary was sitting in the house" (Both Mary and Martha are true to form, cf. Luke 10:38-42).

21. {*Lord, if thou hadst been here, my brother had not died*} Clearly they had said so to each other with wistful longing if not with a bit of reproach for his delay. But busy, practical Martha comes to the point (see next verse).

22. {*Whatsoever thou shalt ask of God...God will give*} Martha uses a different Greek for "ask" than when Jesus asks of his Father, but the distinction is not to be pressed. Martha still has courageous faith in the power of God through Jesus (cf. verse 41).

25. {*I am the resurrection and the life*} This reply is startling enough. They are not mere doctrines about future events, but present realities in Jesus himself. The Resurrection is one manifestation of the Life: it is involved in the Life. Jesus had taught the future resurrection often (John 6:39), but here he means more, even that Lazarus is now alive. {*Though he die...yet shall he live*} That is, spiritual life even in physical death.

26. {*Shall never die*} "Never" is strong in the Greek syntax. "Die" here refers to spiritual death, eternal death.

28. {*The Master*} Lit. "the Teacher" (cf. John 13:13).

31. {*To weep there*} This is the Greek verb *klaiô,* to weep. Sometimes to wail or howl in oriental style of grief, but surely not that here.

33. {*He groaned in the spirit...was troubled*} "deeply moved" is the Greek verb *embrimaomai,* old verb (from *en,* and *brimê,* strength) to snort with anger like a horse (cf. Da. 11:30). The notion of indignation is present here (cf. Mark 1:43; 14:5; Matt. 9:30, also John 11:38). Mary weeping and the whole situation of Lazarus' death all greatly agitated the spirit of Jesus.

34. {*Where have ye laid him?*} This is a simple, polite question for information. Though not knowing his purpose, the people invite him to come and see (cf. John 1:46).

35. {*Jesus wept*} Never meaning "wail," this is the Greek verb *dakruô,* from *dakru* or *dakruon,* a tear (Acts 20:19). These tears were a reaction from the severe strain in verse 33, but chiefly it was the sheer human sympathy (Heb. 4:15).

37. {*Could not this man*} Though three months ago, the events of the Blind man (cf. John 9:1ff.) had made a lasting impression on these. These Jews share the view expressed by Martha (verse 21) and Mary (verse 32) that Jesus could have prevented the death of Lazarus.

38. {*Cometh to the tomb*} This is the vivid historical present, drawing the reader into the story.

39. {*For he hath been dead four days*} Lit. "for he is a fourth-day man." A Jewish tradition says to the effect that the soul hovers around the tomb for three days hoping to return to the body, but on the fourth day leaves it. But there is no suggestion here that Martha held that notion. Her protest is a natural one in spite of her strong faith in verses 22-27.

41. {*I thank thee that thou heardest me*} With thanksgiving, Jesus had prayed to the Father for raising Lazarus: clearly, simply, without pomp of incantation nor wrestling in prayer.

42. {*That they may believe*} Greek tense translates, "that they may come to believe."

43. {*He cried with a loud voice*} (cf. Matt. 24:31; Mark 15:34,37; Rev. 1:10; 21:3). The loud (lit. "great") voice was not for the benefit of Lazarus, but for the sake of the crowd.

44. {*He that was dead came forth*} Lit. "Came out the dead man." He came just as he was and at once. {*With grave-clothes*} Lit. "bands" or strips of cloth (cf. Prov. 7:16).

45. {*Beheld that which he did...believed on him*} (cf. John 7:31).

47. {*Gathered a council*} (cf. Matt. 5:22). Here this is a sitting or session of the Sanhedrin. Both chief priests (Sadducees) and Pharisees combine in the call (cf. John 7:32). From now on the chief priests (Sadducees) take the lead in the attacks on Jesus, supported by the Pharisees. {*Doeth...*} He is active and we are idle. There is no specific mention of raising Lazarus.

48. {*If we let him thus alone*} Translate the Greek condition, "Suppose we leave him thus alone." Suppose also that he keeps on raising the dead right here next door to Jerusalem! {*And take away both our place and our nation*} Note "place" (job) is put before nation (patriotism), for all the world like modern politicians who make the fate of the country turn on their getting the jobs which they are seeking.

50. {*That it is expedient for you*} "It is better" means to bear together, to be profitable. It is to your interest and that is what they cared most for. {*That one man die...for the people... and that the whole nation perish not*} (cf. John 16:7; 18:7). "For" means "instead of" here (cf. Gal. 3:13, also 2 Cor. 5:14; Rom. 5:6). What Caiaphas has in mind is the giving of Jesus to death to keep the nation from perishing at the hands of the Romans.

53. {*So from that day*} Lazarus' raising brought matters to a head; it brought fresh energy to the enemy's old purpose (John 5:18; 7:19; 8:44,59; 10:39; 11:8). It was now apparently not more than a month before the end. {*They took counsel*} The Sanhedrin took the advice of Caiaphas seriously and plotted the death of Jesus.

56. {*That he will not come to the feast?*} The form of the question assumes strongly that Jesus will not dare to come this time (cf. verse 57).

57. {*The chief priests and the Pharisees...that he should shew it*} That is, the Sanhedrin. They were to report formally (Acts 23:30), for the purpose of arresting (lit. "seize") Jesus.

CHAPTER 12

1. {*Six days before the passover*} (cf. Amos 1:1). As seems certain, if the crucifixion was on Friday, then this refers probably to the week previous, on Friday afternoon, since Jesus would most likely arrive before the Sabbath. {*Came to Bethany, where Lazarus was, whom Jesus raised from the dead*} With a crowd of eager spectators to see both Lazarus and Jesus here, this was now a town of danger after that great miracle and the consequent, intensifying rage of the Sanhedrin (John 12:9-11).

3. {*A pound*} This is the Greek word *litran*, with a weight of about 12 ounces (cf. John 19:39, also [in an alabaster jar] Mark 14:3; Matt. 26:7. {*Of ointment of spikenard*} (cf. John 11:2, also Matt. 26:7). Nard is the head or spike of an East Indian plant, very fragrant. "Pure" probably means "genuine" (Greek *pistikos,* from *pistos,* reliable).

4. {*Judas Iscariot*} (cf. John 6:71; 13:1). "Iscariot" means "man of Kerioth" (a city) in the tribe of Judah (Jos. 15:25). Judas is the only one of the twelve not a Galilean.

5. {*For three hundred pence*} (cf. Mark 14:5; Matt. 26:9). Lit. "300 denarii," a common laborer's wages for a year.

6. {*And having the bag took away what was put therein*} This is the Greek word *glôssokomon,* for the earlier *glôssokomeion* (from *glôssa,* tongue, and *komeô,* to tend) was originally a receptacle for the tongues or mouth-pieces of wind instruments. Here it means "money-box."

8. {*Ye have always…*} Jesus does not discredit gifts to the poor at all; but there is relativity in one's duties. {*But me ye have not always*} (cf. Mark 14:9; Matt. 26:13). With keen sympathetic insight, Mary perceived what the apostles repeatedly failed to understand. Again, not related to Luke 7:35 of the sinful woman.

9. {*The common people*} John's use of "crowd" is usually the common crowd as "riff-raff." Here this crowd is not at all hostile to Jesus (cf. John 5:10; 6:41), but included some who were friendly (cf. John 12:11).

11. {*And believed on Jesus*} From the Sanhedrin's perspective (esp. the Sadducees), there was danger of a mass movement of the people to Jesus.

12. {*A great multitude*} (cf. John 12:9). Translate, "the common people." {*Was coming*} This is a vivid picture, "Jesus is coming into Jerusalem." He is defying the Sanhedrin with all their public advertisement for him.

13. {*The branches of the palm-trees*} (cf. 1Macc. 13:51 [also 2 Macc. 10:7]) Lit. "the palm branches of the palm trees." To carry palms was a mark of triumphant homage to a victor or a king (cf. Rev. 7:9). Palm trees grew on the Mount of Olives (cf. Mark 11:8) on the road from Bethany to Jerusalem. {*Hosanna*} This is a transliteration of the Hebrew word meaning "Save now."

15. {*Daughter of Zion*} (cf. Zech. 9:9). {*Thy King cometh*}The donkey was ridden in peace as the horse was in war (Judg. 10:4; 12:14; 2 Sam. 17:23; 19:26). Zechariah pictures one coming in peace. So the people here regarded Jesus as the Prince of Peace in the triumphal entry.

17. {*Bare witness*} This crowning triumph of Jesus gave an added sense of importance to the crowds (cf. John 11:45; 12:1,9-11).

19. {*The Pharisees therefore said among themselves*} A predicament of the Pharisees, they are standing off and watching the enthusiastic crowds sweep by. They blame each other for the defeat of their plots against Jesus.

21. {*Sir*} Lit. "Lord." Here a most respectful and courteous title. {*We would see Jesus*} Lit. "we desire to see Jesus," though not abrupt, but perfectly polite. They wish an interview with Jesus.

22. {*Cometh...telleth*} The Greek tense is a vivid present, drawing the reader starkly into the narrative.

24. {*A grain of wheat*} Rather translate, "the grain of wheat."

27. {*My soul*} "Soul" here is synonymous with spirit (here and John 13:21). {*Is troubled*} (cf. John 11:33; 13:21). While John proves the deity of Jesus in his Gospel, he assumes throughout his real humanity as here (cf. John 4:6, also Ps. 6:4; 42:7). John does not give the agony in Gethsemane which the Synoptics have (Mark 14:35; Matt. 26:39; Luke 22:42). {*And what shall I say?*} The request of the Greeks called up graphically to Jesus the nearness of the Cross. {*Father, save me from this hour*} Jesus began his prayers with "Father" (John 11:41). Here as in Gethsemane, the heart of Jesus instinctively and naturally shrinks from the Cross, but he instantly surrenders to the will of God in both experiences. It was only a moment of human weakness as in Gethsemane.

30. {*Not for my sake, but for your sakes*} (cf. verses 28-29). This is best taken as a figure of exaggerated contrast, so translate, "not merely for my sake, but also for yours"?

32. {*And I, if I be lifted from the earth*} (cf. John 3:14; 8:28). Surely not the ascension, this refers to the Cross. {*Will draw all men unto myself*} (cf. John 14:6). This is the Greek verb *helkuô*, late form of *helkô*, to draw, to attract. The magnetism of the Cross is now known of all men, however little they understand the mystery of the Cross.

33. {*Signifying*} (cf. John 18:32; 21:19). This is the Greek verb *semainô*, to give a sign (*sêmeion* Acts 25:27). The kind of death is the Cross (lifted up) as the kind of death before Christ.

35. {*Yet a little while is the light among you...*} Jesus turns to the light of the world metaphor (cf. John 8:12). {*That darkness overtake you not*} (cf. John 1:5; also 1 Thess. 5:4). {*Knoweth not whither he goeth*} (cf. John 11:10, also 1 John 2:11). The ancients did not have our electric street lights. The dark streets were a terror to travelers.

36. {*That ye may become sons of light*} Note not "were" or "are" but "become." "Sons of light" = "enlightened men" and is a Hebrew idiom (cf. John 17:12; Luke 16:8, also 1 Thess. 5:5; Eph. 5:8).

37. {*Yet they believed not on him*} Greek tense translates "they kept on not believing on him," that is, a stubborn refusal in face of the light (verse 35).

40. {*He hath blinded*} (cf. 2 Cor. 4:4; 1 John 2:11). {*He hardened...*} (cf. Isa. 6:10). This is the Greek verb *pôroô*, a late causative verb (from *pôros*, hard skin) [cf. Mark 6:52].

42. {*Nevertheless even...*} Recall the lonely shyness of Nicodemus in John 3:1; and also Joseph of Arimathea. This is a remarkable statement as to the effect that Christ had in Jerusalem as the Sanhedrin plotted his death. {*But because of the Pharisees...*} How like the cowardly excuses made today by those under conviction who refuse to step out for Christ. {*Lest they should be put out of the synagogue*} (cf. John 9:22). This ostracism from the synagogue was dreaded by the Jews and made cowards of these "believing elders."

47. {*But to save the world*} (cf. John 3:17). Jesus does judge the world inevitably (John 8:15; 9:39), but his primary purpose is to save the world (John 3:16).

CHAPTER 13

1. {*Knowing*} (cf. John 12:23). This Greek tense is emphasizing the full consciousness of Christ. He was not stumbling into the dark as he faced "his hour."

2. {*During supper*} The meal was still going on. {*The devil having already put*} "prompted" is lit. "to put in the heart" (cf. Luke 22:3) says that Satan entered Judas when he offered to betray Jesus (cf. also John 6:70).

4. {*Riseth from supper...layeth aside*} These are the Greek tense of a vivid dramatic present, drawing the reader into the narrative story. {*His garments*} This is the outer robe *tallith* (Greek *himation*) and with only the tunic (*chitôn*) on "as one that serves" (Luke 22:27). {*A towel*} This is a linen cloth. {*Girded himself*} (cf. John 13:4,5; 21:7). Lit. "to gird all around." Did not Peter recall this moving event (cf. 1 Pet. 5:5)?

5. {*Began to wash*} The Greek verb *niptô* was common for washing parts of the body like the hands or the feet.

6. {*So he cometh*} This is the Greek tense of a vivid present, drawing the reader into the scene.

7. {*But thou shalt understand hereafter*} This is the Greek verb *ginôskô* (instead of the verb *oida*) to know by experience (even if slowly).

8. {*Thou shalt never wash my feet*} "Never" is very strong in the Greek, and "my" is also emphasized. Peter's sudden humility should settle the issue, he felt.

9. {*Not my feet only, but also my hands and my head*} Peter's characteristic impulsiveness that does not really understand the Master's act. A moment ago he told his Master He was doing too much: now he tells Him He is doing too little (Dods).

10. {*He that is bathed*} This is the Greek verb *louô,* to bathe the whole body (Acts 9:37). The guest was supposed to bathe (*louô*) before coming to a feast and so only the feet had to be washed (*niptô*) on removing the sandals (cf. verse 5). "Bath" and "cleansing" does not refer to the cleansing power of his blood or to baptism.

11. {*For he knew him that should betray him*}Jesus had known for a year at least (John 6:64,70) and yet he treated Judas with his usual courtesy.

12. {*Sat down again*} This is the Greek verb *anapiptô,* to fall back, to lie down, to recline. {*Know ye what I have done to you?*} That is, "Do you understand the meaning of my act?" A question particularly to Peter and Judas.

13. {*Ye*} The Greek syntax is emphatic. {*Master*} Lit. "Teacher," this is one title for the Jewish *Rabbi* (cf. John 20:28 also 1:38; 11:28). {*Lord*} (cf. John 9:36,38). This is another and separate title, for the Jewish *Mari;* he is both in the full sense.

14. {*If I then*} The first part of this sentence is the Greek condition as true and fulfilled; he did wash.

15. {*An example*} Lit. "to show under the eyes" here as an illustration. Peter uses a different Greek word *tupoi* ("type, model" 1 Pet. 5:3) with this incident in mind.

17. {*If ye know...if ye do*} Lit. "if ye keep on doing." Just knowing does not bring happiness nor just occasional doing.

19. {*That ye may believe*} (cf. Isa. 48:5). Greek tense translates, "that ye may keep on believing."

21. {*He was troubled in the spirit*} (cf. John 11:33; 12:27) This is the agitation of Christ's spirit; though one with God (John 5:19); yet he was fully human (John 1:14). {*One of you shall betray me*} (cf. Mark 14:18; Matt. 26:21; also Luke 22:21). Though he had known (John 6:70), now it was a bolt from the blue sky as Jesus swept his eyes around and looked at the disciples.

22. {*Looked one on another*} Greek tense translates, "began to glance at one another (in bewilderment, doubting)." {*Doubting*} This is the Greek verb *aporeô,* to be at a loss, to lose one's way (*a* "not" and *poros,* "way"). They recalled their strife about precedence and Judas betrayed nothing.

23. {*Breast*} Lit. "reclining in the bosom of Jesus." This position means John was on the right of Jesus lying obliquely so that his head lay on the bosom of Jesus. The focus is being in the center, the place of honor, which Jesus occupied; not any other focus.

24. {*Beckoneth*} Lit. "nod" (cf. Acts 24:10). They were all looking in surprise at each other. {*Leaning back*} Lit. "reclining on the breast" i.e., the place of the "bosom" (cf. verse 23).

26. {*For whom I shall dip the sop*} This "dipping the sop" was and is in the orient a common token of intimacy to allow a guest to dip his bread in the common dish (cf. Ruth 2:14 also Mark 14:20).

27. {*Then Satan entered into him*} This is the only time the word "Satan" occurs in the Gospel (cf. John 6:70).

29. {*The bag*} (cf. "money bag," John 12:6).

31. {*Now*} Now at last, the crisis has come with a sense of deliverance from the presence of Judas and of surrender to the Father's will. {*Is glorified*} That is, consummation of glory in death both for the Son and the Father (cf. John 7:39; 12:16; 13:31 and 17:3.)

34. {*That ye love one another...*} Greek tense translates, "keep on loving." The measure of our love for another is set by Christ's love for us.

35. {*By this*} (cf. John 17:23). Lit. "In this way," namely, "if you have love."

CHAPTER 14

1. {*Ye believe...believe also*} "Trust" in the Greek could be a verb merely stating a fact, or as likely, a command. Translate the Greek tense and form, "keep on believing in God and in me."

2. {*Mansions*} These are abiding places, resting places in the Father's house. Christ's picture of heaven here is the most precious one that we possess. It is our heavenly home with the Father and with Jesus. {*For I go...to prepare a place for you*} It was customary to send one forward for such a purpose (Num. 10:33) also for the Passover meal (cf. Mark 14:12; Matt. 26:17). Jesus is thus our Forerunner (cf. Heb. 6:20).

6. {*I am the way, and the truth, and the life*} Any of these statements are profound enough to stagger any one, but here all three together overwhelm Thomas. He is the only way to God, the personification of truth, the center of life. There are several "I am" statements in John: 8:12; 10:7; 11:25.

12. {*Shall he do also...greater works than these*} This is not necessarily greater miracles and not greater spiritual works in quality, but greater in quantity (as with Peter and Paul in Acts). The reason for this expansion made possible by the Holy Spirit as Paraclete (John 16:7).

15. {*If ye love me...ye will keep...*} (cf. John 8:51; 14:23,24; 14:20; 1 John 2:5). Continued love prevents disobedience.

16. {*Another Comforter*} This is another of like kind, besides Jesus who becomes our Paraclete [Counselor], Helper, Advocate, with the Father (1 John 2:1, Cf. Rom. 8:26). So the Christian has Christ as his Paraclete with the Father, the Holy Spirit as the Father's Paraclete with us (John 14:16,26; 15:26; 16:7; 1 John 2:1).

17. {*Ye know him...with you...in you*} Note "you" is emphatic, in contrast to the world. At this time he was "by their side" and "at home with them"; the Spirit will be in their hearts.

18. {*Orphans*} This is the Greek word *orphanos,* old word (*orphos,* Latin *orbus*), bereft of parents, and of parents bereft of children. It is common in papyri of orphan children, here with a possible focus on their helplessness (without the other Paraclete, the Holy Spirit).

19. {*But ye behold me*} "You" is emphatic in the sentence, in contrast to the blind, unseeing world (cf. John 13:33; 16:10,16).

22. {*Not Iscariot*} So this Judas is Thaddaeus or Lebbaeus (Mark 3:17; Matt. 10:3 also "of James" (John 6:15; Acts 1:13). This is the fourth interruption of the talk of Jesus (by Peter, John 13:36; by Thomas, John 14:5; by Philip, John 14:8; by Judas, John 14:22). {*And not to the world*} (cf. John 5:27). This Judas seems to suspect a change of plan on the part of Jesus.

23. {*If a man love me*} Greek tense translates, "if one keep on loving me." That is key to the spiritual manifestation.

25. {*While yet abiding with you*} Lit. "while remaining beside you"; that is, before departing for the coming of the other Paraclete.

26. {*Whom*} The Father will send the Holy Spirit (John 14:16; Luke 24:49; Acts 2:33), but so will the Son (John 15:26; 16:7) as Jesus breathes the Holy Spirit upon the disciples (John 20:22). There is no contradiction in this relation of the Persons in the Trinity (the Procession of the Holy Spirit). Here the Holy Spirit (full title as in Mark 3:29; Matt. 12:32; Luke 12:10) is identified with the Paraclete. {*He...shall teach you all things*} The Holy Spirit knows the deep things of God (1 Cor. 2:10). {*Bring to your remembrance*} After Pentecost the disciples will be able better to recall and to understand what Jesus had said (how dull they had been at times) and to be open to new revelations from God (cf. Peter at Joppa and Caesarea).

27. {*My peace*} This is Christ's bequest to the disciples before he goes, the *shalom* of the ancient near east. Here in the sense of spiritual peace such as only Christ offers and can give (Luke 2:14). {*Neither let it be fearful*} (cf. John 14:1). This is the Greek verb *deiliaô*, like the palpitating of the heart (from *deilos*).

28. {*If ye loved me*} The Greek syntax is implying that the disciples are not loving Jesus as they should.

30. {*The prince of the world*} (cf. John 12:31). This refers to Satan.

31. {*Arise, let us go hence*} (cf. John 11:7,16). Apparently the group arose and walked out into the night and the rest of the talk (chs. 15 and 16) and prayer (ch. 17) was in the shadows on the way to Gethsemane.

CHAPTER 15

1. {*The true vine*} This is the "genuine" vine. After the institution of the Lord's Supper, the metaphor of the vine is naturally suggested by "the fruit of the vine" (Mark 14:25; Matt. 26:29). Jesus uses various metaphors to illustrate himself and his work: light, door, shepherd, vine. Jesus is the genuine Messianic vine. {*The husbandman*} (cf. Mark 12:1; Jas. 5:7; 2 Tim. 2:6, also 1 Cor. 3:9).

2. {*In me*} There are two kinds of connection with Christ as the vine: the merely cosmic which bears no fruit, the spiritual and vital which bears fruit.

4. {*Abide in me*} The only way to continue to bear fruit is to maintain a vital spiritual connection with Christ (the vine).

5. {*Ye the branches*} (cf. verse 1). {*Apart from me*} (cf. Eph. 2:12). There is nothing for a broken off branch to do but wither and die. For the cosmic relation of Christ see John 1:3.

6. {*He is cast forth*} "Servants of the vine-dresser" is the unexpressed subject of the sentence.

7. {*Ask whatsoever ye will*} This astounding command and promise is not without conditions and limitations. It involves such intimate union and harmony with Christ that nothing will be asked out of accord with the mind of Christ and so of the Father (cf. John 15:16; also 14:13; 16:23).

9. {*Abide...in my love*} Greek tense shows this as summing up the whole. Translate the meaning, "remain in the love that I have for you." Our love for Christ is the result of Christ's love for us and is grounded at bottom in the Father's love for the world (John 3:16).

11. {*That my joy may be in you...and that your joy be fulfilled*} This is Christ's permanent absolute joy in the disciples as a consummation of the process preceding.

12. {*That ye love one another*} Lit. "that ye keep on loving another" (cf. John 13:34).

13. {*That a man lay down his life*} (cf. John 10:11, also 1 John 3:16; Rom. 5:7). Translate, "in behalf/in place of his friends." Self-sacrifice is the high-water mark of love.

14. {*If ye do*} (cf. verse 10). Lit. "if you keep on doing," not just spasmodic obedience. Obedience to Christ's commands is a prerequisite to discipleship and fellowship (spiritual friendship with Christ).

15. {*No longer*} (cf. John 13:16). He was their Rabbi (John 1:38; 13:13) and Lord (John 13:13). Paul gloried in calling himself Christ's slave. {*I have called you friends*} This shows a permanent state of new dignity. Abraham was called the Friend of God (Jas. 2:23). Are we friends of Christ?

16. {*But I chose you*} Jesus recognizes his own responsibility in the choice after a night of prayer (Luke 6:13).

17. {*That ye may love one another*} (cf. John 13:34; 15:12). This very night the disciples had been guilty of jealousy and wrangling (Luke 22:24; John 13:5,15).

18. {*If the world hateth you*} This Greek condition is determined or fulfilled. "The world certainly does hate you."

19. {*But because ye are not of the world*} This is the definite and specific reason for the world's hatred of real Christians whose very existence is a reproach to the sinful world (cf. John 7:7; 17:14; 1 John 3:13). Does the world hate us? If not, why not? Has the world become more Christian or Christians more worldly?

20. {*If they persecuted me*} The Greek condition shows this is a fact. They certainly did persecute Jesus (John 5:16). They will persecute those like Jesus (cf. John 16:33; Mark 10:30; Luke 21:12; 1 Cor. 4:12; 2 Cor. 4:9; Gal. 4:29; 2 Tim. 3:12).

21. {*A servant is not greater than his lord...*} See this same warning and language of this verse in Matt. 10:22; Mark 13:13; Matt. 24:9; Luke 21:17. Loyalty to the name of Christ will bring persecution as they will soon know (Acts 5:41; Phil. 1:29; 1 Pet. 4:14).

23. {*My Father also*} Because Christ reveals God (John 14:9) and to dishonor Christ is to dishonor God (John 5:23). The coming of Christ has revealed the weight of sin on those who reject him.

24. {*They have both seen and hated*} The Greek tense shows this is a permanent attitude and responsibility. The "world" and the ecclesiastics (Sanhedrin) had united in this attitude of hostility to Christ and, in reality, to God.

25. {*In their law*} (cf. John 8:17; 10:34). Law refers here to the whole of Scripture (cf. John 12:34; alluding to Ps. 69:4 or Ps. 35:19). The hatred of the Jews toward Jesus the promised Messiah (John 1:11) is part of the mysterious purpose of God.

26. {*When the Comforter is come...whom I will send unto you from the Father...He shall bear witness of me*} (cf. John 16:7). This is similar to the Father sending in the name of Jesus (cf. John 14:16,26 and Luke 24:49; Acts 2:33). Here, this is the procession of the Holy Spirit from the Father and from the Son. Witness is the mission of the Paraclete (John 16:14) as it should be ours.

27. {*And ye also bear witness*} That is, you as well as the Holy Spirit when you are filled with and taught by the Holy Spirit the things concerning Jesus.

CHAPTER 16

1. {*That ye should not be made to stumble*} (cf. Matt. 13:21). "Astray" is the Greek verb *skandalizô*, i.e., the stumbling blocks which trip up a disciple (cf. John 6:61 and 1 John 2:10).

2. {*They shall put you out of the synagogues*} Translate, "they will make you outcasts from the synagogues" (cf. John 9:22; 12:42).

4. {*Have I spoken*} (cf. John 15:11; 16:1). This is a solemn repetition. {*From the beginning*} (cf. John 15:27). While Christ was with them, he was the object of attack (John 15:18).

5. {*And none of you asketh me*} Now that they realize that Jesus is going, the thoughts of the disciples turn on themselves and they cease asking the question of where Jesus was going (John 13:36).

6. {*Sorrow hath filled*} "Grief" is the Greek word *lupê* (cf. in Gospels John 16:6,20,21,22; Luke 22:45). They do not see their way to go on without Jesus.

7. {*It is expedient for you*} This is the Greek verb *sumpherô,* to bear together (cf. John 11:50). {*If I go not away...*} The "not" is quite strong in the Greek syntax. The Holy Spirit was, of course, already at work in the hearts of men, but not in the sense of witnessing as Paraclete which could only take place after Jesus had gone back to the Father.

8. {*And he...will convict the world*} "Convict" is the Greek verb *elegchô,* word for confuting, convicting by proof already (cf. John 3:29; 8:46). Jesus had been doing this (John 7:7), but this is pre-eminently the work of the Holy Spirit.

9. {*Because they believe not on me*} Without this conviction, people actually have a pride of intellectual superiority in refusing to believe on Jesus.

10. {*And ye behold me no more*} That is, with the bodily eyes, and without the Holy Spirit they are unable to behold Jesus with the spiritual vision (John 14:19). Without Christ they lose the sense of righteousness. This results in a lowering of standards in individuals and throughout society.

11. {*Because the prince of this world hath been judged*} (cf. John 12:31; 14:31). The Greek tense show that he stands condemned. The sinful world is in his grip, but he will be cast out (John 12:31).

12. {*But ye cannot bear them now*} Here it means a figurative "bearing" (cf. Acts 15:10). The untaught cannot get the full benefit of teaching (1 Cor. 3:1; Heb. 5:11-14).

13. {*When he, the Spirit of truth, is come*} (cf. John 15:26 also Ps. 24:5). Note *ekeinos* "he" is masculine, though followed by neuter "Spirit" which is in apposition. Christ is both the Way and the Truth (John 14:6) and the Holy Spirit is the Guide who shows the way to the Truth (John 16:14).

14. {*He shall glorify me*} The glory of the Holy Spirit is to glorify Jesus Christ. {*For he shall take of mine*} This is a definite promise of the Spirit's guidance in interpreting Christ. The NT itself is a witness to see how under the tutelage of the Holy Spirit the disciples grew into the fullness of the knowledge of God in the face of Christ (2 Cor. 6:4). The Holy Spirit as Guide and Teacher will teach them what they can only receive and understand after the resurrection and ascension of Jesus.

16. {*A little while...again a little while*} This refers to the brief period now until Christ's death, from Friday afternoon until Sunday morning (cf. John 7:33; 13:33; 14:19).

17. {*Some of the disciples*} Jesus seemed to contradict himself, for the disciples took both verbs in the same sense and were still puzzled over the going to the Father of John 14:3. But they talk to one another, not to Jesus.

21. {*A woman...when she is in travail*} This is a common O.T. image for pain; she has grief, for she knows giving birth is like a living death.

22. {*And ye therefore now*} The metaphor continues of the birth pains as fleeting sorrow and the permanent joy of the baby. So now compare the resurrection of Jesus where fleeting grief of the disciples was changed to the permanent possession of gladness or joy.

23. {*Ye shall ask me nothing*} This asking can mean one of two things: 1) ask a question 2) ask in the sense of request or favors. Either view is supported by NT examples, and either makes sense here.

24. { *Joy...may be fulfilled* } The Greek tense has a focus on the em- phasizing the abiding permanence of joy.

25. {*In proverbs*} That is, in figures of speech (cf. John 10:6). {*Plainly*} (cf. John 7:13).

26. {*I say not...*} Christ did pray for the disciples before his death (John 14:16; 17:9,15,24) and he prays also for sinners (Luke 23:34; 1 John 2:1). Here it is the special love of God for disciples of Jesus (John 14:21,23; 17:23; 1 John 4:19).

27. {*Loveth*} This is the Greek verb *phileô,* used in the whole verse as the word for warm and friendly love, here used of God's love for the disciples, while in John 3:16, *agapaô* occurs of God's love for the world.

28. {*I came out from the Father...*} This refers to the definite act of the Incarnation. The Incarnation is now a permanent fact, once only a blessed hope (John 11:27). His leaving the world and going to the Fa- ther does not set aside the fact of the Incarnation.

30. {*Now know we*} They had failed to understand the plain words of Jesus about going to the Father heretofore (John 16:5), but Jesus read their very thoughts (John 16:19) and this fact seemed to open their minds to grasp his idea.

31. {*Do ye now believe?*} Note that this could be a question in the Greek.

32. {*Cometh*} (cf. John 17:1). The long-looked-for hour is so close that it has virtually begun (the arrest of Jesus is near). {*Ye shall be scat- tered*} (cf. John 10:12). This is used of sheep scampering from the wolf (cf. also Matt. 12:30; Luke 11:33).

33. {*That in me ye may have peace*} Translate the Greek tense and mood, "that ye may keep on having peace in me," even when I am put to death, peace to be found nowhere save in me (John 14:27). {*Be of good cheer*} (cf. Acts 28:15). This is a word for courage in the face of danger (cf. also Matt. 9:2,22; Mark 10:49).

CHAPTER 17

1. {*Father*} (cf. John 5,11; 11:41). Christ is addressing him, as a usual way of beginning his prayers. The prayer is similar in spirit to the

Model Prayer for us in Matt. 6:9-13. The hour for his glorification has come as he had already told the disciples (John 13:31; 12:23). No one is putting words in Jesus' mouth; this is his prayer. Jesus had the habit of prayer (Mark 1:35; 6:46; Matt. 11:25; Luke 3:21; 5:16; 6:12; 9:18,28 Luke 11:22,42; 23:34,46; John 11:41; 12:27). He prayed here for himself (John 17:1-5), for the disciples (John 17: 6-19), for all believers (John 17:20-26). {*Glorify thy Son*} This is the only personal petition in this prayer, it carries us into the very depths of Christ's own consciousness. Christ asks for the power to glorify the Father by his death and resurrection and ascension.

2. {*Authority over all flesh*} This is a stupendous claim impossible for a mere man to make (cf. Matt. 11:27; Luke 10:22).

3. {*Should know*} Greek tense translates, "should keep on knowing." {*Even Jesus Christ*} (cf. John 1:17). This is used only twice in this Gospel. Possibly the solemnity of this occasion explains Jesus referring to himself in the third person.

4. {*Having accomplished...thou hast given*} (cf. John 4:34). That was Christ's food and joy. Now as he faces death he has no sense of failure as some modern critics say, but rather fullness of attainment (cf. John 19:30).

5. {*With thine own self*} Lit. "By the side of thyself." Jesus prays for full restoration to the pre-incarnate glory and fellowship (cf. John 1:1) enjoyed before the Incarnation (John 1:14).

6. {*I manifested*} This is another word for claiming successful accomplishment of his task (cf. verses 4 and 26). {*Whom*} Jesus regards the apostles as the Father's gift to him. Recall the night of prayer before he chose them. {*They have kept*} Though not perfect (John 6:67-71; Matt. 16:15-20), Jesus claims loyalty and fidelity in these men with the one exception of Judas (verse 12).

7. {*Now they know*} They have come to know, not as fully as they felt (John 16:30), and yet in a real sense.

8. {*The words*} The plural shows *each* word of God (cf. John 3:34), and of Christ (cf. John 5:47; 6:63,68); a singular would show *the whole* of a message (cf. John 17:6,14).

9. {*I pray*} Formally, "ask," though here a request, not question (cf. John 16:23). {*Not for the world*} Christ prays this phrase meaning "here, at this point in the prayer." Later in the prayer, he does pray for them (cf. verse 19).

10. {*Are*} Lit. "is" as a singular emphasizing the unity of the whole (cf. John 16:15). {*I am glorified in them*} The Greek tense translates, "I stand glorified [in the disciples]"; glory stands in spite of all their shortcomings and failings.

11. {*That they may be one*} Greek tense translates, "that they may keep on being." The Greek grammatical genders shows this is oneness of will and spirit (for unity), not one person (for organic union). The disciples lacked unity or oneness of spirit (cf. Luke 22:24; John 13:4-15). Jesus offers the unity in the Trinity (three persons, but one God) as the model for believers.

12. {*But the son of perdition*} Lit. "the son of perdition." This is the very phrase for antichrist (2 Thess. 2:3). It means the son marked by final loss, not annihilation, but meeting one's destiny (Acts 2:25).

13. {*That they may have my joy fulfilled in themselves*} Greek tense translates, "that they may keep on having Christ's joy in their faithfulness realized in themselves" (cf. John 15:11; 16:24; Phil. 2:2).

14. {*Not of the world*} These verses (14-19) picture the Master's ideal for believers and go far towards explaining the failure of Christians in winning the world to Christ. Too often the world fails to see the difference or the gain by the change.

15. {*From the evil one*} The grammatical markers for gender in Greek shows this can refer to either: 1) evil man, 2) Satan, or 3) evil deed. This ambiguity is also elsewhere (cf. Matt. 6:13).

17. {*Sanctify*} This is an urgent pleading request, or command of the verb *hagiazô*, to consecrate or set apart persons or things to God (cf. Exod. 28:41; 29:1,36; 40:13, also 1 Thess. 5:23).

18. {*Sent I them*} (cf. Mark 3:14, also Luke 9:2). This special commission to the disciples is renewed after the resurrection (John 20:21).

19. {*That they themselves also may be sanctified in truth*} The act of Christ helps us, but by no means takes the place of personal consecration on the part of the believer.

20. {*Through their word*} Lit. "word." That is, through the agency of conversation and preaching, blessed privilege open to all believers thus to win men to Christ, but an agency sadly limited by the lives of those who speak in Christ's name.

22. {*And the glory*} Lit. "And I the glory" with the "I" emphatic. It is the glory of the Incarnate Word (cf. John 1:14; 2:11), not the glory of the Eternal Word mentioned in John 17:24.

24. {*I will*} There is perfect identity of his will with that of the Father in this moment of spiritual exaltation, though in Gethsemane Jesus distinguishes between his human will and that of the Father (Mark 14:36). {*Where I am*} This refers to heaven (cf. John 12:26; 13:36; 14:3; Rom. 8:17; 2 Tim. 2:11). {*Before the foundation of the world*} (cf. Eph. 1:4; 1 Pet. 1:20 also Matt. 25:34; Luke 11:50; Heb. 4:3; 9:26; Rev. 13:8; 17:8). Here we find the same pre-incarnate consciousness of Christ seen in John 17:5.

26. {*And will make it known*} This is the perpetual mission of Christ through the Spirit (John 16:12,25; Matt. 28:20) as he himself has done heretofore (John 17:6).

CHAPTER 18

1. {*Over*} Lit. "beyond" (cf. John 6:22,25). {*Brook...Kidron*} Lit. "Brook of the Cedars" (cf. 2 Sam. 15:23). This "wadi" (valley of a stream) was always dry except after a heavy rain. The brook of the cedars had many unhallowed associations (1 Kgs. 2:37; 15:13; 2 Kgs. 23:4; 2 Chr. 29:16; Jer. 31:40). {*A garden*} This is also named Gethsemane. (cf. Mark 14:32; Matt. 26:36; Luke 13:19, also verse 26).

2. {*Resorted thither*} Judas knew the place, and the habit of Jesus to come here at night for prayer (Luke 22:39). Hence his offer to catch Jesus while the feast was going on, catch him at night and alone in his usual place of prayer (the very spirit of the devil).

3. {*The band of soldiers*} (Matt. 27:27; Acts 10:1). Latin *spira*, this Greek word *speira* here is a small band secured from the Tower of Antonia. The Synoptics show there is both this Roman guard and "officers" or temple police of the Sanhedrin present; likely both with weapons (cf. Matt. 26:58; Mark 14:54,65).

4. {*Knowing all the things that were coming upon him*} (cf. John 13:1). He was not taken by surprise. The surrender and death of Jesus were voluntary acts, though the guilt of Judas and the rest remains.

5. {*Was standing*} The Greek tense is a vivid picture of Judas in the very act of betraying Jesus.

8. {*Let these go their way*} Lit. "Let these men withdraw" (John 11:44). Jesus shows attentive care for the eleven as he had warned them and prayed for them (Luke 22:31). He is trying to help them.

9. {*That might be fulfilled*} (cf. John 18:32). Though a common formula for Scripture, here applied to the prophecy of Jesus (John 17:12). John treats the saying of Jesus as on a par with the O.T.

10. {*Having a sword*} (cf. Luke 22:49ff.). With actually two swords present (Luke 22:38), it was unlawful to carry a weapon on a feast-day. But Peter had become alarmed at Christ's words about his peril. Missing the head straight-on, Peter with his usual impulsiveness jerked out his sword and cut off the right ear of Malchus (John 18:10); it would later that night bring him peril (John 18:26).

11. {*Shall I not drink?*} The Greek syntax expects a "yes" answer.

12. {*Seized*} This is the Greek verb *sullambanô,* to grasp together, to arrest (technical word) in the Synoptics in this context (Mark 14:48; Matt. 26:55).

15. {*Followed*} The Greek tense is picturesque and vivid here.

16. {*Unto her that kept the door*} Lit. "[female] door-keeper." This is the Greek word *thurôros* (*thura,* door, *ôra,* care), either male or female: male in John 10:3; female here.

17. {*Art thou also?*} "No" is the formally expected answer in the Greek syntax, though she really believed he was. {*This man's*} This is a contemptuous use of the Greek pronoun with a gesture toward Jesus. She made it easy for Peter to say "no."

18. {*A fire of coals*} (cf. John 21:9). This is a heap of burning coals (cf. Greek *anthrax,* coal, cf. English "anthracite."

20. {*Openly*} This was not in secret or hiding (cf. John 7:4; 8:26; 10:24,39; 16:25,29). {*I ever taught*} He taught in the temple (cf. John 2:19; 7:14,28; 8:20, 19:23; Mark 14:49) and he taught in the synagogue (cf. John 6:59 and often in the Synoptics). Jesus also taught in private: Nicodemus (John 3:1-21); Samaritan Woman (John 4:4-42). Jesus ignores the sneer at his disciples, but challenges the inquiry about his teaching as needless.

21. {*Ask them that have heard me*} "Ask" in Greek has the features of urgency and instant action. There were abundant witnesses to be had.

22. {*Struck Jesus with his hand*} (Mark 14:65; John 18:22; 19:3). This is the Greek word *rapisma,* from *rapizô,* to smite with a rod or with the palm of the hand (cf. Matt. 26:67). Probably he struck with the palm of the hand to give the most insulting manner hitting; though possibly a rod was used (cf. 2 Cor. 11:20). But Jesus had in fact answered in a way that was a dignified protest.

23. {*Smitest*} "Strike" is the Greek verb *derô*, to flay, to skin, to beat, here referring to an insulting blow in the face as here (cf. Matt. 21:35; Luke 22:63; 2 Cor. 11:20).

25. {*Was standing and warming himself*} (cf. verse 17). The Greek tense shows a vivid renewal of the picture drawn there. John alone gives the examination of Jesus by Annas (John 18:19-24) which he places between the first and the second denials by Peter. Each of the Four Gospels gives three denials, but it is not possible to make a clear parallel as probably several people joined in each time. This time there was an hour's interval (Luke 22:59). The question and answer are almost identical with John 18:17 and put in a form which almost *suggested* that Peter should say "no" a favorite device of the devil in making temptation attractive.

26. {*Did not I see thee in the garden with him?*} "Yes" is the expected answer in the Greek; a staggering and sudden thrust (cf. verses 17,25).

28. {*They lead*} The Greek tense is a dramatic historical present, drawing the reader into the story (Luke 23:1). {*Into the palace*} This is the Latin based word, *praetorium* (cf. Matt. 27:27; Acts 23:35; Phil. 1:13). Here it is probably the magnificent palace in Jerusalem built by Herod the Great for himself and occupied by the Roman Procurator (governor) when in the city.

29. {*Pilate...went out*} He came outside, since the Sanhedrin would not come into Pilate's palace. Apparently on a gallery over the pavement in front of the palace (John 19:13). {*Accusation...against this man*} (cf. 1Tim. 5:19; Titus 1:6). This is a proper legal inquiry.

30. {*If this man were not an evil-doer*} The idea of "criminal" is a Greek construction meaning Jesus was a habitual evil-doer. It was an insolent reply to Pilate.

31. {*Yourselves*} "Yourselves" is emphatic. Pilate shrewdly turns the case over to the Sanhedrin in reply to their insolence, who have said nothing whatever about their previous trial and condemnation of Jesus.

32. {*By what manner of death*} (cf. John 12:32). This is concerning the Cross and here treated as prophecy (Scripture).

33. {*Thou*} The "thou" is emphatic. Jesus did claim to be the spiritual king of Israel as Nathanael said (John 1:49) and as the ecstatic crowd hailed him on the Triumphal Entry (John 12:13), but the Sanhedrin wished Pilate to understand this in a civil sense as a rival of Caesar as some of the Jews wanted Jesus to be (John 6:15) and as the Pharisees expected the Messiah to be.

35. {*Am I a Jew?*} With Gentile scorn he asks; and "no" is the vehement implication to the question in the Greek. {*What hast thou done?*} This is a blunt and curt question. "What is your real crime?" John's picture of this private interview between Pilate and Jesus is told with graphic power.

36. {*My servants*} "Servants" is lit. "under-rowers." Here it is the officers of a king (cf. Prov. 14:35; Isa. 32:5; Da. 3:46). Christ had only a small band of followers who could not fight against Caesar.

37. {*Art thou a king then?*} This question is clearly ironical, expecting "yes" for an answer.

38. {*What is truth?*} This famous sneer of Pilate reveals his own ignorance of truth, as he stood before Incarnate Truth (John 14:6). Not finding any basis for the charge, Pilate therefore should have set Jesus free at once.

39. {*A custom*} (cf. 1 Cor. 8:7; 11:16). This custom (cf. Mark 15:6; Matt. 27:15), is termed necessity in Luke 23:17. {*Will ye therefore that I release?*} There is contempt and irony in Pilate's use of the phrase "the king of the Jews."

40. {*Not this man*} "This" is a contemptuous use of this pronoun. The priests put the crowd up to this choice (Mark 15:11) and Pilate offered the alternative (Matt. 27:17).

CHAPTER 19

1. {*Took and scourged*} Pilate did not actually scourge Jesus, he simply ordered it done; perhaps to see if the mob would be satisfied with this penalty on the alleged pretender to royalty (Luke 23:22) whom Pilate had pronounced innocent (John 18:38), an illegal act therefore. It was a preliminary to crucifixion, but Jesus was not yet condemned.

2. {*Plaited a crown of thorns*} (cf. Mark 15:17; Matt. 27:19). It is not impossible for the mock coronation to be repeated. {*Arrayed him*} (cf. Mark 15:17,20 also Rev. 18:16). Jesus had been stripped of his outer garment (Matt. 27:28) and the scarlet cloak of one of the soldiers may have been put on him (Matt. 27:28).

3. {*They came...*} Greek tense is a repeated action, "they kept coming and saying" in derision and mock reverence with *Ave* (Hail!) as if to Caesar.

4. {*I bring him out to you*} This phrase vividly pictures Pilate leading Jesus out of the palace before the mob in front. {*That ye may know*} Greek syntax translates, "that you may come to know," by this mockery the sincerity of Pilate's decision that Jesus is innocent (John 18:38).

5. {*Wearing*} Jesus bore the mockery with kingly dignity as part of the shame of the Cross (Heb. 12:2). {*Behold, the man*} *Ecce Homo!*, is said by Pilate. This exclamatory introduction of Jesus in mock coronation robes to the mob was clearly intended to excite pity and to show how absurd the charge of the Sanhedrin was that such a pitiable figure should be guilty of treason. Pilate failed utterly in this effort and did not dream that he was calling attention to the greatest figure of history, the Man of the ages.

6. {*Crucify him, crucify him*} (cf. Matt. 27:31). Greek tense and mood shows a note of urgency. They were led to say this by the chief priests and the temple police until the whole mob takes it up (Matt. 27:22).

7. {*Because he made himself the Son of God*} Here at last the Sanhedrin gives the real ground for their hostility to Jesus, one of long standing for probably three years (John 5:18) and the one on which the Sanhedrin voted the condemnation of Jesus (Mark 14:61-64; Matt. 27:23-66), but even now they do not mention their own decision to Pilate, for they had no legal right to vote Christ's death before Pilate's consent which they now have secured.

8. {*He was the more afraid*} Pilate was already afraid because of his wife's message (Matt. 27:19). The claim of Jesus to deity excited Pilate's superstitious fears.

9. {*Whence art thou?*} Pilate knew that Jesus was from Galilee (Luke 23:6). He is really alarmed (cf. John 8:25). {*Gave him no answer*} (cf. John 1:22). The silence of Jesus, like that before Caiaphas (Mark 14:61; Matt. 26:63) and Herod (Luke 23:9), irritates the dignity of Pilate in spite of his fears.

10. {*Unto me*} "Me" is emphatic in the sentence. It amounted to contempt of court with all of Pilate's real "authority."

11. {*From above*} This means "from God" (cf. John 3:3).

12. {*Sought*} Greek tense translates, "kept on seeking," "made renewed efforts to release him." He was afraid to act boldly against the will of the Jews. {*If thou release this man*} The Greek condition is a currently unfulfilled, but a hypothetical case. This was a direct threat to Pilate. He knew all the time that the Sanhedrin might tell Caesar on him.

13. {*Sat down on the judgement seat*} This seat was the *bêma* (the raised platform for the judge outside the palace as in Acts 7:5). The examination is over and Pilate is now ready for the final stage. {*The Pavement*} This was a mosaic or tessellated pavement, spread with stones (cf. 2 Chr. 7:3). The Aramaic name *Gabbathâ,* meaning "an elevation," was apparently given because of the shape.

14. {*The Preparation of the passover*} (cf. John 31,42; Mark 15:42; Matt. 27:62; Luke 23:54). This is Friday of Passover Week, i.e., the preparation day before the Sabbath of Passover Week (or Feast). {*About the sixth hour*} Pilate rendered his final decision a little after 6 a.m.. Mark (Mark 15:25) notes that the crucifixion began when it was the third hour (Jewish time), which is 9 a.m. After A.D. 70, the Jewish state has passed away; this is evidence that he is writing for Greek and Roman readers. {*Behold your king*} The sarcasm of Pilate is aimed at the Jews, not at Jesus.

15. {*Away with him, away with him*} This is the repeated Greek word *âron,* a form of command of the verb *airô* (cf. *aire* in Luke 23:18). This thing has gotten on the nerves of the crowd.

16. {*He delivered*} (John 18:30,35). Sanhedrin handed Jesus over to Pilate; now Pilate hands Jesus back to the Sanhedrin with full consent for his death (Luke 23:25). {*To be crucified*} John does not give the dramatic episode in Matt. 27:24 when Pilate washed his hands and the Jews took Christ's blood on themselves and their children. But it is on Pilate also.

17. {*Golgotha*} Luke has simply *Kranion* (Skull), a skull-looking place (cf. Mark 15:22; Matt. 27:33; Luke 23:33).

18. {*They crucified*} That is, the soldiers did this. {*And Jesus in the midst*} A "robber" (not a "thief" which is a distinct Greek word) was on each side of Jesus (Mark 15:27; Matt. 27:38) like Barabbas (John 18:40) and probably members of his band, malefactors ("evil doers," "criminals") Luke terms them (Luke 23:32).

19. {*Pilate wrote a title also*} The Greek action of John tells us that Pilate himself wrote it and John alone uses the technical Latin word *titlon,* for the board with the name of the criminal and the crime in which he is condemned; Mark (Mark 15:26) and Luke (Luke 23:28) use "superscription." Matthew (Matt. 27:37) has simply "accusation." The inscription in John is the fullest of the four and has all in any of them save the words "this is" in Matt. 27:37.

20. {*Read*} This board was meant to be read. Latin was the legal and official language; Aramaic (Hebrew) was for the benefit of the people of Jerusalem; Greek was for everybody who passed by who did not know Aramaic.

21. {*But that he said...*} The chief priests were uneasy for fear that the joke in the mock title was on them instead of on Jesus. They were right in their fear.

22. {*What I have written I have written*} The Greek tense has emphasis on the permanence of the accusation on the board. Pilate has a sudden spirit of stubbornness in this detail to the surprise of the chief priests. Technically he was correct, for he had condemned Jesus on this charge made by the chief priests.

23. {*Four parts*} There were four soldiers, the usual *quaternion* (Greek *tetradion*, Acts 12:9) besides the centurion (Mark 15:39; Matt. 27:54; Luke 23:47). {*The coat was without seam*} This is the inner garment (cf. Matt. 5:40). This garment was lit. "unsewed together."

24. {*Let us not rend it*} It was too valuable to ruin. {*Cast lots*} This is the Greek verb *lagchanô*, the usual meaning is to obtain by lot (Luke 1:9; Acts 1:17), though historical citation is disputed by some scholars.

25. {*Were standing by the cross of Jesus*} This scene is a vivid contrast to the rude gambling of the soldiers. This group of four (or three) women interests us more. Matthew (Matt. 27:55) spoke of women beholding from afar and names three (Mary Magdalene, Mary the mother of James the less and of Joses, and the mother of the sons of Zebedee). Mark also (Mark 15:40) names three (Mary Magdalene, Mary the mother of James the less and of Joses, and Salome). They have clearly drawn near the Cross by now. John alone mentions the mother of Jesus in the group. It is not clear whether the sister of the mother of Jesus is Salome the mother of the sons of Zebedee or the wife of Clopas. If so, two sisters have the name Mary and James and John are cousins of Jesus. The point cannot be settled with our present knowledge.

26. {*Standing by*} The Greek tense shows a vivid and picturesque scene. The dying Savior thinks of the comfort of his mother. There is no disrespect in the use of "woman" (Greek is case of address, *gunai*) here as there was not in John 2:4. This trust is to John, though Salome, John's own mother, was standing there.

27. {*Unto his own home*} (cf. John 1:11; 16:32; Acts 21:6). John had a lodging in Jerusalem, whether a house or not, and the mother of Jesus lived with him there.

28. {*Are now finished*} (cf. John 13:1). Jesus here is fully conscious (knowing) of the meaning of his atoning death. {*Might be accomplished*} John sees the thirst of Jesus in Scripture (cf. Ps. 69:21). Jesus, of course, did not make the outcry in any mechanical way. Thirst is one of the severest agonies of crucifixion. Messiah was "perfected" by physical suffering (cf. Heb. 2:10; 5:7).

29. {*Was set*} John, as eyewitness, had noticed it there. {*Of vinegar*} This is not vinegar drugged with myrrh (Mark 15:23) and gall (Matt. 27:34) which Jesus had refused just before the crucifixion. {*Sponge*} (cf. Mark 15:36; Matt. 27:48) {*Upon hyssop*} Mark and Matthew call it a "reed." The reed of the hyssop bush was only three or four feet long.

30. {*Had received*} Jesus took the vinegar (a stimulant), though he had refused the drugged vinegar. {*It is finished*} (cf. verse 28). A cry of victory in the hour of defeat (cf. John 16:33). Jesus knew the relation of his death to redemption for us (Mark 10:45; Matt. 20:28; 26:28). {*Bowed his head*} This vivid detail only in John. {*Gave up his spirit*} Luke fills in a detail, (Luke 23:46 [cf. Ps. 31:5]) "Father, into thy hands I commend my spirit" (the last of the seven sayings of Jesus on the Cross that are preserved for us). Jesus died with the words of this Psalm upon his lips. The apostle John had come back to the Cross.

31. {*A high day*} Lit. "great Sabbath." It is called "great" since the Sabbath day following synchronized with the first day of Unleavened Bread which was a "great" day. A double reason therefore for wanting the bodies removed before sunset when the Sabbath began. {*That their legs might be broken*} This *crurifragium* (i.e., Latin for leg breaking action) was done with a heavy mallet and ended the sufferings of the victim.

33. {*Already dead*} So then, Jesus died before the robbers, died of a broken heart. They then did not break the legs.

34. {*Pierced his side*} (cf. John 20:20,25,27). {*Blood and water*} Dr. W. Stroud writes that this fact proves that the spear pierced the left side of Jesus near the heart and that Jesus had died literally of a broken heart since blood was mixed with water.

35. {*He that hath seen*} John the Apostle was there and saw (and Greek tense shows he still sees, in fact). {*He knoweth*} (cf. John 9:37). It is possible that "he" (Lit. "that one") may be a solemn appeal to God as in John 1:33 or Christ as in 1 John 3:5. The true focus of this phrasing (i.e., not first person) is that John is rather referring to himself as still alive.

36. {*Be broken*} (cf. lit. lamb of Exod. 12:46). This is the Greek verb *suntribô*, to crush together.

38. {*But secretly for fear of the Jews*} This is an example of the rulers described in John 12:41-43 who through cowardice feared to own their faith in Jesus as the Messiah. But it must be put down to the credit of Joseph that he showed courage in this darkest hour when the majority had lost heart. {*That he might take away*} Had he not taken it, the body of Jesus might have gone to the potter's field. Pilate gladly consented.

39. {*Seventy-five pounds*} (cf. John 12:3). Lit. "100 *litras* [about 12 ounces]." A hundred 12-ounce pounds equals about seventy-five American 16-ounce pounds.

40. {*In linen cloths*} (cf. Luke 24:12). This is the Greek word *othonion*, The form shows diminutive (designated smallness) for *othonê*, used for ships' sails.

41. {*A garden*} (cf. John 18:1,26). {*New*} This is a fresh, unused tomb. {*Was never yet laid*} It was Joseph's mausoleum, a rock tomb hewn out of the mountain side (Mark 15:46; Matt. 27:60; Luke 23:53), a custom common with the rich then and now. For royal tombs in gardens see 2 Kgs. 21:18,26; Neh. 3:16.

42. {*Was nigh at hand*} This tomb was outside of the city, near a road as the Cross was, and in a garden. The hill looked like a skull and was probably Gordon's Calvary seen from the Mount of Olives today.

CHAPTER 20

1. {*Now on the first day of the week*} Lit. "on the first of the Sabbaths" (cf. Mark 16:2; Luke 24:1); the plural "Sabbaths" here means "the week" (cf. Acts 20:7); the singular can also mean "the week," (cf. Luke 18:12; Mark 16:9). {*Cometh Mary Magdalene*} "Went" is in the dramatic and vivid historical present ("comes"), drawing the reader into the story.

2. {*Runneth*} This is the vivid dramatic present drawing the reader into the narrative. {*Loved*} This is *phileô* (cf. John 5:20; 11:3); in distinction from *agapaô* (cf. John 11:5; 13:23; 21:7,15,17).

3. {*They went*} Lit. "they were going." The Greek tense shows the two started instantly.

4. {*Outran Peter*} This is the Greek verb *protrechô,* to run on before (ahead). He ran ahead more swiftly (cf. John 13:27) than Peter; John won the race.

5. {*Stooping and looking in*} "Bent over" just means to "peep in." (cf. Gen. 26:8; Judg. 5:28; 1 Kgs. 6:4).

6. {*Entered and beholdeth*} The Greek tenses show Peter impulsively (instantly) went on in and beholds (in the vivid present, drawing the reader to the scene of the story). The Greek verb "saw" *theôreô,* is to give careful notice. John in verse 5 gave a mere glance ("looked" the Greek verb *blepô*).

7. {*The napkin*} (cf. John 11:44). This napkin for the head was in a separate place. {*Rolled up…by itself*} Lit. "to roll up" (cf. Matt. 27:59; Luke 23:53). It was arranged in an orderly fashion, separately placed. There was no haste.

8. {*And he saw and believed*} Peter saw more after he entered than John did in his first glance, but John saw into the meaning of it all better than Peter. Peter had more sight, John more insight. John was the first to believe that Jesus was risen from the tomb even before he saw him. According to Luke 24:12 Peter went away "wondering" still. John was evidently proud to be able to record this great moment when he believed without seeing in contrast to Thomas (John 20:29). Peter and John did not see the angels.

9. {*The Scripture*} (cf. Prob. Ps. 16:10). Jesus had repeatedly foretold his resurrection, but that was all forgotten in the great sorrow on their hearts. Only the chief priests and Pharisees recalled the words of Jesus (Matt. 27:62). {*Must*} This was concerning Christ's death and resurrection (cf. Mark 8:31; Matt. 26:54; Luke 9:22; 17:25; 22:37; 24:7,26,44 John 3:14; 12:34; Acts 1:16). Jesus had put emphasis on both the fact and the necessity of his resurrection which the disciples slowly perceived.

10. {*Unto their own home*} (Luke 24:12). Lit. "to themselves." John had taken the mother of Jesus to his home (John 19:27); and so he now hurried home to tell her the glorious news as he believed.

11. {*At the tomb*} This position the Greek makes clear as in front of the tomb. Pathetic and common picture of a woman weeping by the tomb (cf. John 11:31). {*As she wept*} Greek tense translates, "as she was weeping." {*She stooped and looked*} (cf. verse 5). Mary also "peeped into" the tomb, but did not enter.

12. {*Beholdeth*} This Greek tense is the historical present, drawing the reader into the narrative.

14. {*She turned herself back*} This verb and phrase is intransitive (i.e., she didn't turn another) and almost reflective sense (hence "around").

15. {*Sir*} Though this is the Greek word normally translated "Lord," here it is merely a word of human respect. She thought him to be the gardener. {*If thou hast borne him hence*} This Greek condition is assumed as determined or fulfilled. "You" here is emphatic. A new idea struck Mary as mistaken as the other one. Jesus had repeated the question of the angels, but she did not recognize him. {*And I*} This is emphatic.

16. {*Mary*} Lit. *Mariam,* the Aramaic form here and *Maria* in John 19:25. Clearly the old familiar tone of Jesus was in the pronunciation of her name. {*Rabboni*} (cf. Mark 10:51). This is Aramaic again for "my Teacher." This is practically the same as *Rabbi* (cf. John 11:28).

17. {*Touch me not*} Greek syntax translates, "Cease clinging to me" rather than "Do not touch me." Jesus allowed the women to take hold of his feet and worship (cf. Matt. 28:9). The prohibition (to stop touching) here reminds Mary that the previous personal fellowship by sight, sound, and touch no longer exists and that the final state of glory was not yet begun. Jesus checks Mary's impulsive eagerness.

18. {*And telleth*} Lit. "announcing." {*I have seen the Lord*} The Greek tense focuses on the fact that she will always carry in her heart that vision (picture) of the Risen Christ. She tells this fact before she delivers and recites Christ's message to the brethren of Christ.

19. {*When therefore it was evening on that day*} John's wording in the Greek proves that John is using Roman time, not Jewish, for here evening follows day instead of preceding it.

20. {*Showed*} This is the Greek verb *deiknumi.* This body, not yet glorified, retained the marks of the nails and of the soldier's spear, ample proof of the bodily resurrection against the modern view that only Christ's "spirit" arose and against the Docetic notion that Jesus had no actual human body. Luke (Luke 24:39) adds feet to hands and side.

{*Were glad*} Jesus had said (John 16:22) that they would have joy. Luke adds (Luke 24:41) that they "disbelieved for joy." It was too good to be true, though terror had first seized them when Jesus appeared (Luke 24:37).

22. {*Receive ye the Holy Ghost*} (cf. John 14:26). Here the Holy Spirit is treated as a proper name with or without the article.

23. {*Whosesoever sins ye forgive...are forgiven...are retained*} (Matt. 16:19; 18:18). "Not forgive" is the Greek verb *krateô*, to retain (keep, hold, seize).

24. {*Didymus*} (cf. John 11:16; 21:2). Another name for Thomas, meaning "twin," he was the pessimist of the apostolic band.

25. {*We have seen the Lord*} This is the very language in the plural that Mary Magdalene had used (John 20:18) when no one believed her. {*The print*} This is the Greek word *tupos,* the mark or stamp made by the nails, here the original idea. Clearly the disciples had told Thomas that they had seen the *tupon* of the nails in his hands and the spear in his side. {*I will not believe*} The "not" is a strong refusal in the Greek.

26. {*Cometh*} The Greek tense is in the vivid dramatic present, drawing the reader into the story. All the same, but now Thomas was with them (cf. verse 19).

27. {*Then saith he to Thomas*} Jesus turns directly to Thomas as if he had come expressly for his sake. He reveals his knowledge of the doubt in the mind of Thomas and mentions the very tests that he had named (verse 25). {*Be not faithless*} That is, stop a currently true action. The doubt of Thomas in the face of the witness of the others was not a proof of his superior intelligence. Thomas had carried his incredulity too far.

28. {*My Lord and my God*} This is not an exclamation, but the Greek form shows this is an address to someone. Thomas was wholly convinced and did not hesitate to address the Risen Christ as Lord and God. And Jesus accepts the words and praises Thomas for so doing.

29. {*Thou hast believed...and yet...*} This is probably a question in the Greek. Thomas made a noble confession, but he missed the highest form of faith without the evidence of the senses (cf. 1 Pet. 1:8).

30. {*Many other signs...are not written...*} That is, others miraculous signs in the Synoptic Gospels and this Fourth Gospel (John 2:23; 4:45; 12:37). John selected from a vast number of signs given.

31. {*Are written...that ye may believe*} This is the purpose of the book. Greek tense translates, "that you may keep on believing." The book has had precisely this effect of continuous and successive confirmation of faith in Jesus Christ through the ages. {*And that believing ye may have life in his name*} Greek tense translates, "continuing to believe," and "keep on having."

CHAPTER 21

1. {*Manifested himself* } Jesus was only seen during the forty days now and then (Acts 1:3), ten instances being recorded. The word "manifested" is often used of Christ on earth (John 1:31; 2:11; 1 Pet. 1:20; 1 John 1:2), of his works (John 3:5), of the second coming (1 John 2:28), of Christ in glory (Col. 3:4; 1 John 3:2).

2. {*There were together*} Seven total were there: Peter, Thomas, Nathanael, the sons of Zebedee, and two others (possibly Andrew and Philip). We know that the sons of Zebedee were James and John (Matt. 4:21), mentioned by name nowhere in John's Gospel, apparently because John is the author. This incident is not related to Luke 5:1-11; there are a few points of similarity, but the differences are too great for such identification even with a hypothetical common source.

3. {*I go a fishing*} Peter's proposal was a natural one. He had been a fisherman by practice and they were probably waiting in Galilee for the appointed meeting with Christ on the mountain. Andrew and Peter, James and John were fishermen also. Peter's proposition met a ready response from all.

4. {*When day was now breaking*} In Matt. 27:1 the same Greek tense of the verb suggests that dawn had come.

5. {*Children*} It is unique in Jesus addressing his disciples. It is a colloquial expression like "my boys." The aged Apostle John uses it in 1 John 2:13,18. {*Have ye aught to eat?*} "No" is the expected answer by this polite inquiry (cf. John 4:29). The rare and late Greek word *prosphagion* from the root *phag* (*esthiô,* to eat) and *pros* (in addition) was used for a relish with bread and then for fish as here.

7. {*It is the Lord*} John's quick insight appears again. {*Girt his coat about him*} (cf. John 13:4). Apparently, Peter threw on the upper garment or linen blouse worn by fishers over his waistcloth and tucked it under his girdle (i.e., belt or sash).

8. {*In the little boat*} This is a larger boat (cf. verses 3,6) and so could come no closer to shore, elsewhere "boat" and "little boat" seem interchangeable (cf. John 6:17,19,21,22,24).

9. {*Got out*} (cf. Luke 5:2). {*They see*} This is the vivid historical present, drawing the reader into the narrative.

13. {*Taketh the bread, and giveth them*} This tense is a vivid present. Jesus acts as host at this early breakfast, his last meal on earth with these seven faithful followers.

15. {*Lovest thou me more than these?*} "Love" is the Greek verb *agapaô*. Peter had even boasted that he would stand by Christ though all men forsook him (Mark 14:29). We do not know what passed between Jesus and Peter when Jesus first appeared to him (Luke 24:34). But here Christ probes the inmost recesses of Peter's heart to secure the humility necessary for service. {*I love thee*} This is the Greek verb *phileô*. Peter makes no claim here to superior love and passes by the "more than these" and does not even use Christ's word *agapaô* for high and devoted love, but the humbler word *phileô* for love as a friend. He insists that Christ knows this in spite of his conduct.

16. {*Lovest thou me?*} Again, "love" is the Greek verb *agapaô,* but this time Jesus drops the "more than" and challenges Peter's own statement. Peter repeats the same words in reply.

17. {*Lovest thou me?*} This time Jesus picks up the word *phileô* used by Peter and challenges that. These two words (*agapaô* and *phileô*) are often interchanged in the NT, but here the distinction is preserved. Peter was cut to the heart because Jesus challenges this very verb (*phileô*), and no doubt the third question vividly reminds him of the three denials in the early morning by the fire. He repeats his love for Jesus with the plea: "You know all things."

18. {*Thou girdest thyself*} The Greek tense shows this action is one of customary action.

19. {*By what manner of death*} Undoubtedly John, who is writing long after Peter's death, seems to mean that Peter was to die (and did die) a martyr's death. There is a tradition that Peter met death by crucifixion and asked to be crucified head downwards, but that is not made plain here.

21. {*And what shall this man do?*} Lit. "But this one ... what?" The abrupt ellipsis is intelligible.

22. {*Follow thou me*} Greek tense and mood translates, "you do keep on following me."

23. {*That that disciple should not die*} Peter or others misunderstood what Jesus meant as John now carefully explains. He was rebuking Peter's curiosity, not affirming that John would live on until the Master returned. John is anxious to set this matter right.

24. {*We know*} The plural here seems intentional as the identification and endorsement of a group of disciples who know the author and wish to vouch for his identity and for the truthfulness of his witness.

25. {*If they should be written every one*} Translate, "if they should be written one by one" (in full detail). {*I suppose*} Note the change back to the first person singular by the author.

THE ACTS OF THE APOSTLES

AUTHOR: Luke the Beloved Physician, friend of Apostle Paul
RECIPIENTS: To Theophilus/ for Romans and Jews
DATE: About A.D. 63
FROM: Finished in Rome (started in Caesarea Maritima?)
OCCASION: Partly a defense of Paul before the Romans, and to have him be set right with the Jews in Rome; the whole purpose is not known.
THEME: A selected account of the birth and early growth of the church

BY WAY OF INTRODUCTION

A cts is important because it has historical worth; without it we would have only the Epistles for historical information. Acts was written as part two, and continuation of the Gospel according to Luke; they are a unity (Luke 1:3; Acts 1:1). They are not merely two independent writings from the same pen; they are a single, continuous work (even the "we" sections of Acts 16:10-40; 20:6-28:31). Acts is neither an appendix nor an afterthought. The traditional view that Luke is the author holds the field with those who are not prejudiced against it (see Luke Introduction in this work). Luke and Acts have the same style; and this can be conclusively defended. The effort to disprove the unity of the Acts has failed. It stands as the work of the same author as a whole and the same author who wrote the Gospel.

Beyond a doubt Luke employed a variety of sources (including himself in the "we" sections and also Paul) for this great history as he did for the Gospel (Luke 1:1-4). Luke's Gospel used the same historical method for Acts. He had great opportunity for documentation in Jerusalem and Palestine, besides contacts in Antioch. He could have contacted sources such as Peter, Philip, Barnabas, and of course Paul.

Acts was once decried as wholly untrustworthy, not above the legendary stage. But the spade of history and archaeology has done well by Luke, for inscriptions and papyri have brought remarkable confirmation for scores of points where Luke once stood all alone and was discounted because he stood alone. In every instance where discoveries have been made they have confirmed the testimony of Luke.

The book is not a history of all early Christianity. Peter (beginning to Acts 15) and Paul (Acts 8 to the end) dominate the atmosphere of the book with Paul as the great hero of Luke.

It is possible that the book was given no title at all by Luke, for it is plain that usage varied greatly even in the same writers. If there is a title, the manuscript evidence may suggest *The Acts of the Apostles,* as probably correct.

But one can easily see that the work is done with consummate skill. The author is a man of culture, of Christian grace, of literary power. The book pulses with life today.

CHAPTER I

1. {*Which Jesus began...*} Here we see the life and teachings of Jesus grammatically bound together, as if to say that Jesus is still carrying on from heaven the work and teaching of the disciples which he started while on earth before his ascension.

2. {*Until the day in which...was received up*} (cf. Luke 24:51). This refers to the Ascension of Jesus to heaven (Mark 16:19; Acts 1:2, 11, 22; 1 Tim. 3:16). This same verb is used of Elijah's translation to heaven in the LXX (2 Kgs. 2:11). {*Had given commandment*} This is the Greek verb *entellô* (from *en* and *tellô*, to accomplish), to enjoin. This special commandment refers directly to what we call the commission given the apostles before Christ ascended on high (John 20:21-23; Matt. 28:16-20; Mark 16:15-18; 1 Cor. 15:6; Luke 24:44-49).

3. {*By many proofs*} Lit. "in many proofs." Luke does not hesitate to apply the definite word "proofs" to the evidence for the Resurrection of Christ after full investigation on the part of this scientific historian. {*By the space of forty days*} During this time there were ten appearances known to us. The Ascension was ten days before Pentecost when the Holy Spirit came. Moses was in the mount forty days (Exod. 24:18) and Jesus fasted forty days (Matt. 4:2). {*The things concerning the Kingdom of God*} "Kingdom" applies to the present and the future and covers so much that it is not strange that the disciples with their notions of a political Messianic kingdom (Acts 1:6) were slow to comprehend the spiritual nature of the reign of God.

4. {*Being assembled together with them*} An alternate rendering of this Greek verb *sunalizô,* is "eating with them." Jesus did on occasion eat with the disciples (Luke 24:41-43; Mark 16:14) and there is other evidence that this might be translated so. Still the alternate rendering is likely better. {*To wait for the promise of the Father*} Greek tense translates, "to keep on waiting for" the promise which refers to the Holy Spirit.

5. {*Baptized with water…and with the Holy Ghost*} This baptism of the Holy Spirit was predicted by John (Matt. 3:11) as the characteristic of the Messiah's work. Now the Messiah himself in his last message before his Ascension proclaims that in a few days (ten to be exact) the fulfillment of that prophecy will come to pass.

6. {*They therefore*} The Greek particle is resumptive and refers to the introductory verses (Acts 1:1-5), which served to connect the Acts with the preceding Gospel. The narrative now begins.

7. {*Times or seasons*} Lit. "periods or points" of time. It is curious how eager people have always been to fix definite dates about the second coming of Christ. The sovereign Father keeps all such matters to himself.

8. {*Power*} Not military power, this is Holy Spirit *enablement* to grapple with the spread of the gospel in the world. {*My witnesses*} (cf. Luke 24:48 and Acts 1:22; 10:39). This key verse to the book shows the expanding sphere of their witness when the Holy Spirit comes upon them is to the ends of the earth. Once they had been commanded to avoid Samaria (Matt. 10:5), but now it is included in the world program as already outlined on the mountain in Galilee (Matt. 28:19; Mark 16:15). Jesus is on Olivet as he points to Jerusalem, Judea, Samaria, the last part of the earth. The program still beckons us on to world conquest for Christ.

9-10. {*As they were looking…*} There is a grammatical emphasis of the fact that they were looking directly at Jesus. {*Received*} "hid" is lit. "took under him." He seemed to be supported by the cloud (cf. 1 Tim. 3:16). They saw him slipping away from their eyes as the cloud bore him away.

11. {*Why?*} Jesus had told them of his coming Ascension (John 6:62; 20:17) so that they should have been prepared.

13. {*Into the upper chamber*} (cf. Mark 14:15; Luke 22:12). This is a room up under the flat roof for retirement or prayer (Acts 9:37, 39), sometimes a large third story room suitable for gatherings (Acts 20:9). It was in a private house as in Luke 22:11 and not in the temple as Luke

24:53 might imply. {*They were abiding*} The Greek word shows they were abiding permanently for prayer (though constant residence is also possible). It is possible that this is the house of Mary the mother of John Mark where the disciples later met for prayer (Acts 12:12).

14. {*They were abiding*} They "stuck to" the praying for the promise of the Father until the answer came. {*And Mary the mother of Jesus*} A delicate touch by Luke that shows Mary with her crown of glory at last. She had come out of the shadow of death with the song in her heart and with the realization of the angel's promise and the prophecy of Simeon. It was a blessed time for Mary. {*With his brethren*} Once disbelieving (John 7:5), Jesus had appeared to James (1 Cor. 15:7) and now it is a happy family of believers including the mother and half-brothers.

16. {*It was needful...*} (cf. Ps. 69:25; 109:8). Peter here assumes that Jesus is the Messiah and finds scripture illustrative of the treachery of Judas. The Holy Spirit has not yet come upon them, but Peter feels moved to interpret the situation. He feels that his mind is opened by Jesus (Luke 24:45).

17. {*Received his portion*} Lit. "obtain the lot." The focus here is persons chosen by divine appointment (1 Pet. 5:3), a divine lot. The Master chose Judas and gave him his opportunity.

18. {*Falling headlong*} Lit. "became flat on the face" as opposed to being on the back. Judas hung himself (Matt. 27:5) and, the rope breaking, fell flat on his face and burst open like the crack of a falling tree.

19. {*Akeldama...the field of blood*} Is it so named because "blood money" bought it (cf. Matt. 27:7); or because literally Judas' blood poured out there (Acts 1:18)?

22. {*Beginning...*} The ministry of Jesus began with the baptism of John and lasted until the Ascension. {*A witness with us of his resurrection*} The essential thing about a successor was to pick one to be a personal witness who can speak from his own experience of the ministry, resurrection, and ascension of the Lord Jesus.

23. {*They put forward two*} Somebody nominated two names, Justus and Matthias.

24. {*Show us the one whom thou hast chosen*} That is, Lord make it plain who you (God) have picked. In this prayer they assume that God has made a choice. They only wish to know his will.

25. {*Apostolic*} This means the office and dignity of an apostle (Acts 1:25; Rom. 1:5; 1 Cor. 9:2; Gal 2:8). {*To his own place*} This is a bold and picturesque description of the destiny of Judas worthy of Dante's *Inferno.*

26. {*He was numbered...*} Not gambling, this is an OT method of learning the will of Jehovah. The two nominations made a decision necessary and they appealed to God in this way.

CHAPTER 2

1. {*Was now come*} This may mean that the day of Pentecost was not yet over, was still going on, though some take it for the interval (fifty days) between Passover and Pentecost. Apparently this day of Pentecost fell on the Jewish Sabbath (our Saturday).

2. {*A sound...*} It was not wind, but a roar or reverberation *like* a rushing, mighty wind. The Greek word for wind here is *pnoê*, uncommon in the NT, but used here probably because of the use of *pneuma* for both wind and Spirit might confuse the work of the Spirit which now follows.

3. {*Parting asunder*} The fire-like appearance presented itself at first "in a single body, and then suddenly parted in this direction so that a portion of it rested on each of those present" (Hackett). It was not real fire, but looked like fire. The audible sign is followed by a visible one. It was a symbol of the Divine presence (cf. Exod. 3:2; Deut. 5:4).

4. {*With other tongues*} That is, other than their native tongues. Each one began to speak in a language that he had not acquired and yet it was a real language and understood by those from various lands familiar with them. It was not jargon, but intelligible language. This is a third miracle: the sound, visible fire-tongues, now the untaught languages.

6. {*When this sound was heard*} The meaning seems to be that the excited "other tongues" of Acts 2:4 were so loud that the noise drew the crowd together. {*In his own language*} Every one that came heard somebody speaking in his native tongue.

7. {*Were amazed*} Lit. "to stand out of themselves," a wide-open astonishment; and the wonder grew and grew.

9. {*Parthians...*} The lists in verses 9-11 are not linguistic, but geographical and merely illustrate how widespread the Dispersion of the

Jews was as represented on this occasion. The list shows four main divisions: (1) the Eastern or Babylonian, like the Parthians, Medes, Elamites, Mesopotamians; (2) the Syrian like Judea, Cappadocia, Pontus, Asia, Phrygia, Pamphylia; (3) the Egyptian like Egypt, Libya, Cyrene; (4) the Roman.

11. {*Cretes and Arabians*} The point is not that each one of these groups of Jews spoke a different language, but that wherever there was a local tongue they heard men speaking in it.

12. {*Were perplexed*} "Perplexed" is the Greek verb *diaporeô* (*dia,* + *alpha* of negation, + *poros*) to be wholly at a loss. The Greek tense shows they *continued* to be amazed and puzzled.

13. {*New wine*} This refers to sweet wine, but intoxicating. Sweet wine kept a year was very intoxicating. They were thought to be drunk with new wine, in a state of fullness.

15. {*As ye suppose*} "You" is decidedly emphatic here. {*The third hour*} This is three o'clock in the day Jewish time, nine Roman. Drunkenness belongs to the night (1 Thess. 5:7).

16. {*This is that which hath been spoken by the prophet Joel*} (cf. Joel. 2:28-32). Peter's mind is now opened by the Holy Spirit to understand the Messianic prophecy (like in Joel) and the fulfillment right before their eyes. Giving the first formal apology for Christianity to a public audience, Peter now has spiritual insight and moral courage.

17. {*I will pour forth...of my Spirit*} The meaning in the LXX is likely the Spirit in his entirety remains with God. {*Yea and...*} What follows from "Yea" is an emphatic addition in the Greek syntax. *Even* the humblest classes like slaves will receive the Spirit of God (cf. 1 Cor. 1:26-31).

19. {*Wonders*} *Terata,* apparently akin to the verb *têreô,* to watch like a wonder in the sky.

20. {*Shall be turned...*} These are the signs and wonders of verse 19. Peter interprets these portents as fulfilled on the Day of Pentecost. Clearly Peter does not interpret the symbolism of Joel in literal terms. {*Before the day of the Lord come, that great and notable day*} The Greek syntax shows this day is a definite conception.

22. {*Hear these words...*} A command in the Greek, the aspect here means, "Listen—and do it now." Peter has found the key to God's work on this day in his words through Joel—the truth concerning Jesus the Nazarene working among this very group preached to.

23. {*Being delivered up*} That is, delivered up by Judas. {*By the determinate counsel and foreknowledge of God*} God had willed the death of Jesus (John 3:16) and the death of Judas (Acts 1:16), but that fact did not absolve Judas from his responsibility and guilt (Luke 22:22). He acted as a free moral agent. {*Ye did crucify*} Lit. "fastened to the cross" a graphic picture (cf. Col. 2:14). Note Peter's boldness now under the power of the Holy Spirit. He charges the people to their faces with the death of Christ.

24. {*God raised up...the pangs of death*} Apparently this is the first public proclamation to others than believers of the fact of the Resurrection of Jesus. {*The agony of death*} In the Hebrew language, Psalm 18:4 has "snares" or "traps" or "cords" of death where *Sheol* and death are personified as hunters laying snares for prey.

25. {*Concerning him*} (cf. Ps. 16:8-11). The quote is with reference to the Messiah (cf. Acts 13:36). David is giving his own experience which is typical of the Messiah. {*On my right hand*} The Lord Jehovah like a defender or advocate stands at David's right hand as in trials in court (Ps. 109:31).

26. {*Was glad...rejoiced*} The Greek tense of these verbs has no regard to a time element here; it is timeless in focus. {*Shall dwell...in hope*} That is, "shall tabernacle, pitch a tent, make one's abode" (cf. Matt. 13:32). The hope is of the resurrection.

27. {*In Hades*} (cf. Ps. 16:1-11). "Hades" is the unseen world of the dead as a general term, Hebrew *Sheol*. It does not mean the place of punishment, though both heaven (also called Paradise) and the place of torment (Gehenna) are in Hades (Luke 16:23).

29. {*The patriarch...was buried...*} Here David is a patriarch in the sense that he is head of the family from whom the Messiah comes.

31. {*Foreseeing...of the Christ*} David knew that in Psalm 16:1-11 he was describing the resurrection of the Messiah.

32. {*This Jesus*} Many were named Jesus, hence "this" Jesus the Nazarene, predicted Messiah, Anointed, raised from the dead—this Jesus Christ (Acts 2:24, 32, 36; 10:38; 18:5; 24:24). {*Whereof...*} All present at the sermon, this refers to the whole 120 as personal witnesses to the fact of the Resurrection of Jesus (cf. 500 witnesses in 1 Cor. 15:6). The evidence for the resurrection thus piles up in cumulative force.

33. {*He hath poured forth*} Jesus has fulfilled his promise. They heard the rushing wind and the different languages spoken by the 120; they saw the tongues like fire on each of them. They experienced demonstrations that Jesus is the Messiah.

35-36. {*Till I make*} This dominion of Christ as Mediator will last until the plan of the kingdom is carried out (1 Cor. 15:23-28). Complete subjugation will come, perhaps referring to the custom of victorious kings placing their feet upon the necks of their enemies (Josh. 10:24).

37. {*They were pricked in their heart*} "Cut" is the Greek verb *katanussô*, to pierce, to sting sharply, to stun, to smite.

38. {*Repent ye*} A command in the Greek, the tense shows "change your mind and your life." Turn right about and do it now. You *crucified* this Jesus. Now *crown* him in your hearts as Lord and Christ. {*And be baptized, every one of you*} Rather, "And let each one of you be baptized." First make a complete change of heart and life, then let each one be baptized after this change has taken place; and this in the name of Jesus (cf. in the name of the Trinity, Matt. 28:19). {*Unto the remission of your sins*} My view is decidedly against the idea that Peter, Paul, or any one in the New Testament taught baptism as essential to the remission of sins or the means of securing such remission. So I understand Peter to be urging baptism on each of them who had already turned (repented)

39. {*The promise*} (cf. Acts 1:4 and 2:18). {*To you*} This refers to the Jews (cf. v. 17). {*To all that are afar off*} This refers to Gentiles or heathen (cf. Isa. 49:1; 57:19; Eph. 2:13, 17). {*Shall call*} The Lord God calls men of every nation anywhere whether Jews or Gentiles.

40. {*And exhorted*} The Greek tense shows he *kept on* exhorting. {*Crooked*} This is the Greek word *skolias*, opposite of *orthos*, straight and here refers to a perversity for turning off from the truth (cf. Luke 9:41; Phil. 2:15).

41. {*There were added...souls...*} Luke means that the 3,000 were added to the 120 already enlisted. Did only apostles baptize? Was it all on the same day? The text implies yes to the questions, but it is not for certain.

42. {*They continued steadfastly*} "Continued" in the Greek is in a tense that shows they *kept on being* devoted to. {*Fellowship*} (cf. Phil. 1:5; 2:1; 2 Cor. 8:4; 9:13). This is the Greek word *koinônia*, from *koinônos* (partner, sharer in common interest) and this from *koinos* what is common to all. This partnership involves participation in, as the blood of

Christ. {*The breaking of bread*} (cf. 1 Cor. 11:20). This means a meal. But does it refer to: (1) the ordinary meal (cf. Luke 24:35); (2) the Lord's Supper (cf. Luke 22:19)? The possible answer is that it referred to both: the Lord's Supper following the ordinary meal. {*The prayers*} (cf. Acts 1:14). There were prayer services in the temple (Acts 3:1) and in their homes (Acts 4:23).

43. {*Came...were done*} The Greek tense shows that awe *kept on* coming on all and signs and wonders *kept on* coming through the apostles. The more wonders there were, the more fear.

44-45. {*Were together...and had...common*} They held all their property ready for use for the common good, selling and distributed as it was needed (Acts 4:32). This situation appears nowhere else except in Jerusalem and was evidently due to special conditions there which did not survive permanently.

46. {*With one accord in the temple*} (cf. Acts 1:14). They were still worshipping in the temple for no breach had yet come between Christians and Jews. Note that the first churches met in homes, and even had "worship rooms."

47. {*Added*} Greek tense shows the Lord *kept on* adding. {*Those that were being saved*} Better translated, "those saved from time to time." It was a continuous revival, day by day. Here they were saved in the sense of the present tense.

CHAPTER 3

1. {*Were going up*} That is, they were ascending the terraces to the temple courts. {*The ninth*} This is the time of the evening sacrifice, our three o'clock in the afternoon; the time in which Peter and John were still engaged in such activities.

3. {*Asked*} Greek tense shows he *began* to ask; it was his chance.

4. {*Fastening his eyes*} Peter fixed his eyes on the beggar and invited him to look on them.

6. {*In the name*} Healing power is in that name and Peter says so (cf. Luke 9:49; 10:17; Acts 4:7, 10; 19:27; 16:18). {*Walk*} A command in the Greek, the tense shows, *begin to* walk and then *go on* walking. But the beggar does not budge. He knows that he cannot walk.

8. {*Leaping up*} The Greek tense shows the beggar leaping out *repeatedly* after Peter pulled him up. {*Walking...jumping...praising*} Greek tense shows again that he *went on* repeating these new exercises.

10. {*They took knowledge of him*} The Greek tense shows they *began to* perceive.

13. {*His servant Jesus*} This phrase occurs in Isa. 42:1; 52:13 about the Messiah except the name "Jesus" which Peter adds, the first part of the quotation is from Exod. 3:6; 5:30. "Servant" can be used of many senses, but here Peter is using it in a Messianic sense (cf. Acts 3:26; 4:27, 30).

14. {*But ye*} "Ye" here is in contrast with Pilate. {*Murderer*} That is, in contrast with the Holy and Righteous One.

15. {*But the Prince of life ye killed*} Here is a magnificent antithesis, they chose a murderer to live and killed the Author of life. {*Whereof we are witnesses*} Peter had boldly claimed that all the 120 have seen the Risen Christ. There is no denial of that claim.

16. {*Through him*} That is, through Jesus, the object and source of faith.

17. {*In ignorance*} (cf. Phlm. 14 and Luke 23:34). "They had sinned, but their sin was not of so deep a dye that it could not have been still more heinous" (Hackett). If they had known what they were doing, they would not knowingly have crucified the Messiah (1 Cor. 2:8).

18. {*Foreshewed*} This is the Greek verb *prokataggellô*, to announce fully beforehand (cf. Acts 3:18; 7:52). {*That his Christ should suffer*} (cf. 1 Pet. 4:13; 5:1). Their crime, though real, was carrying out God's purpose (Acts 2:23; John 3:16 also Acts 17:3; 26:23). This immense irony was a stumbling block to these Jews as it is yet (1 Cor. 1:23).

19. {*That your sins may be blotted out*} This is the Greek verb *exaleiphô*, to wipe out, rub off, erase, smear out (cf. Col. 2:14). {*Seasons of refreshing*} From a Greek work that means to cool or to refresh. Used only here in the NT.

20. {*And that he may send the Christ, who hath been appointed for you, even Jesus*} The reference is naturally to the second coming of the Messiah, Jesus as verse 21 shows. Jesus promised to be with the disciples all the days (Matt. 28:20), and certainly repentance with accompanying seasons of refreshing help get the world ready for the coming of the King, also called the Parousia or Second Epiphany (cf. 1 Tim. 6:15).

21. {*Restoration*} This can refer to something like the new heaven and the new earth, like a new birth or renewal (cf. Rev. 21:1 also Matt. 19:28); or it can refer to moral and spiritual restoration wrought by the Baptist as Elijah (Matt. 17:11; Mark 9:12).

22. {*Like unto me...*} (cf. Deut. 18:14-18). This prophet refers to a greater one who will come, the Messiah. The Jews understood Moses to be a type of Christ (John 1:21).

25. {*Ye*} "Ye" is emphatic. {*The covenant which God made*} (cf. Matt. 26:28). This refers to the covenant (lit. "agreement between two") with Abraham (Gen. 12:1-3) and repeated at various times (Gen. 18:18; 22:18; 26:4, etc.).

CHAPTER 4

1. {*The Sadducees*} Taking the lead against Peter and John, most of the priests and all the chief priests were Sadducees. {*Came upon them...*} The Greek tense shows they burst upon them suddenly or stood by them in a hostile attitude here (Luke 20:1; 24:4; Acts 6:12; 17:5; 22:20; 23:11).

2. {*Being sore troubled*} This is the Greek verb *diaponeô,* to be worked up to a high or perfect degree, indignant.

4. {*Men*} Lit. "adult males," but this can sometimes mean men and women (cf. Luke 11:31).

5. {*Rulers and elders and scribes*} These are the three usual classes composing the Sanhedrin: rulers = Sadducees; teachers of the law = Pharisees; the elders not in either class.

6. {*Annas... Caiaphas*} Annas was one of the rulers or high priests, actually an ex-high priest (A.D. 7-14) and father-in-law of Caiaphas. Caiaphas was the actual high priest at that time. Roman law recognized the latter, and the Jews the former as high priest.

9. {*Concerning a good deed done to an impotent man*} (cf. 1 Tim. 6:2). It was a "good work," as a benefactor, not a malefactor. It was a skillful turn made by Peter. {*Is made whole*} Lit. "stands whole."

10. {*Whom ye crucified*} It was too good a chance to miss, and so Peter boldly charges the Sanhedrin with responsibility for the death of Jesus. God's answer to them was to raise him from the dead.

11. {*Of you the builders...*} The expert architects had rejected Jesus for their building (Ps. 118:22) as Jesus himself had pointed out (Matt.

21:42; Luke 21:17). {*Head of the corner*} This Rejected Stone (Messiah) is from the base meaning either of the highest corner stone right under the roof [so, "capstone"], or a foundation corner stone under the building [so, "cornerstone"] (cf. Isa. 28:16 and 1 Pet. 2:6).

12. {*Salvation...*} This is Messianic salvation (cf. Acts 5:31; 17:11 and John 4:22). It is amazing to see Peter speaking thus to the Sanhedrin and proclaiming salvation in the name of Jesus Christ.

13. {*The boldness*} Greek word is a combination which literally means "telling it all." {*They were unlearned...and ignorant*} That is, unlettered laymen without technical training in the professional rabbinical schools of Hillel or Shammai; as was Jesus (cf. John 7:15).

15. {*They conferred among themselves*} With Peter and John and the lame man outside, they began to compare notes and take stock of their predicament.

16. {*What shall we do?*} The Greek tense shows urgency in the question. {*We cannot deny it*} It was useless and would do no good to deny the sign.

17. {*That it spread no further...that they speak henceforth to no man in this name*} The phrasing "this name" by the Sanhedrin is a contemptuous use of the Greek pronoun "this."

20. {*For we cannot but speak...*} Lit. "For we are not able not to speak...." "We" is emphatic in the Greek syntax. This defiance here was justified, for the authorities stepped in between the conscience and God.

21. {*Glorified God*} The Greek tense translates, "they *kept on* glorifying God" while the Sanhedrin were threatening Peter and John. The praise was as if to laugh at the helplessness of the Sanhedrin.

24. {*With one accord*} This was a concert of voices, a word common to Acts (cf. Acts 1:14; 2:46 and later in 5:12; 7:57; 15:25). {*O Lord*} This is the Greek title *Despota,* cf. our word *despot,* a word for relation of master to slaves or household servants (1 Tim. 6:1; 2 Tim. 2:21; Titus 2:9; 1 Pet. 2:18).

25. {*By the mouth of...our father David*} (cf. Ps. 2:1ff.). The whole company may have sang the second Psalm and then Peter applied it to this emergency.

26. {*Against his Anointed*} This is the Greek word *Christos,* that is his Messiah, his Christ.

29. {*And now...grant...to speak thy word with all boldness*} The Greek tense of "enable" shows a respectful pleading command which has a sense of urgency: Do it now.

30. {*And that signs and wonders may be done*} They ask for a visible sign or proof that God has heard this prayer for courage to be faithful even unto death.

31. {*The place was shaken*} (cf. Acts 16:26) An answer to the request of verse 30, the earthquake was a token of God's presence and power (Ps. 114:7; Isa. 2:19, 21; Heb. 12:26); and very words of the prayer (for boldness) in verse 29 describes their conduct here.

32. {*Of one heart and soul*} "Mind" is lit. "soul." That is, there was a harmony in thought and affection; though the Greek words for "mind and heart" are not sharply distinguished here.

34-35. {*Sold them and brought*} Lit. "selling they brought from time to time," as there was occasion by reason of need. Hence the wants were kept supplied.

36. {*Barnabas*} Though several different meanings for this name are offered, Luke gives the popular use: Barnabas = Encourager. He was even called apostle along with Paul (Acts 14:14), but limited to the broad sense of that word.

CHAPTER 5

1-2. {*Sold...kept back*} The praise of Joseph was too much for Ananias. He sold property, but was not willing to turn it all over.

3. {*Filled*} Satan the adversary is the father of lies (John 8:44). He had entered into Judas (Luke 22:3; John 13:27) and now he has filled the heart of Ananias with a lie.

4. {*How is that thou hast conceived?*} Lit. "what you placed in the heart...?" The devil filled his heart (v. 3), but all the same Ananias did it too and is wholly responsible.

5. {*Hearing...fell down...gave up the ghost*} Ananias brought the end upon himself. It was the judgment of God. Physically the nervous shock could have caused his collapse.

6. {*Wrapped him round*} The young men enshrouded Ananias. It is a Greek word frequent in medical writers. They may have used their own overcoats. The time for burial was short in Jerusalem for sanitary reasons and to avoid ceremonial defilement.

9. {*Ye have agreed together...to tempt the Spirit of the Lord*} "Both souls were allured together" (Vincent) respecting this deceit; it was close to the unpardonable sin. {*The feet*} Graphically, Peter heard the steps of the young men at the door.

10. {*Immediately*} Her death was also supernaturally caused.

11. {*Upon the whole church*} "Church" is the Greek word *ekklêsia*, here not merely an "assembly" but "the church" consisting of scattered saints hiding in their separate homes. It was already a dangerous thing to be a follower of Christ unless one was willing to walk straight.

13. {*Durst*} Imperfect active of *tolmaô*, old verb, not to fear or shun through fear, boldly to take a stand. The fate of Ananias and Sapphira continued to hold many in check. {*Join*} From *kollaô*, old verb, to cleave to like glue as in Luke 15:15. The outsiders (the rest) preferred, many of them, to remain outside for the present, especially the rulers.

14. {*Were the more added*} The Greek tense shows they *kept on* being added.

15-16. {*As Peter came by...at the least his shadow might overshadow...*} There was, of course, no power in Peter's shadow. That was faith with superstition, just as similar cases in the Gospels occur (Matt. 9:20; Mark 6:56; John 9:5) and the use of Paul's handkerchief (Acts 19:12). God honors even superstitious faith if it is real faith in him.

17. {*Which is the sect of the Sadducees*} Lit. "the sect which is of the Sadducees," Already Luke has stated that the Sadducees started the persecution of Peter and John (Acts 4:1). Now the persecution is extended to "the apostles" as a whole.

18. {*With jealousy*} This is the Greek word *zêlos*, from *zeô*, to boil, compare our English word "zeal." In itself it means only warmth, ardor, zeal, but for a bad cause or from a bad motive, jealousy, envy, rivalry results (Acts 13:45).

20. {*All the words of this life*} Probably "this life" refers to that which the Sadducees deny and of which the angel is now speaking, this eternal life. (John 6:63, 68; 1 Cor. 15:19).

21. {*About daybreak*} Lit. "under the dawn." The temple doors would be open for early worshippers and traffickers (John 2:14). {*The senate*} This is the Greek word *gerousia*, from *gerôn*, an old man, just as the Latin *senatus* is from *senex*, old. Apparently this senate of the people was also part of the Sanhedrin, though some sources disagree.

22. {*The officers*} Lit. "under-rowers" (cf. Matt. 5:25). The servants or officers who executed the orders of the Sanhedrin.

24. {*They were much perplexed...whereunto this would grow*} Greek tense shows they *continued* puzzled. If they had only known how this grain of mustard seed would grow into the greatest tree on earth (cf. Matt. 13:32).

26. {*For they feared...lest they be stoned*} The Greek tense shows they *continued* to fear. They handled the apostles gently for fear of being pelted with stones themselves by the people (Acts 14:19; John 10:31-33).

29. {*We must...obey*} Moral necessity left them no choice.

30. {*Ye slew...hanging him upon a tree*} Peter refers to Deut. 21:23 (cf. Gal. 3:13); the curse pronounced on every one who hangs upon a tree.

32. {*And so is the Holy Ghost*} The word for "is" is not in the Greek, but this is plainly the meaning. Peter claims the witness of the Holy Spirit to the raising of Jesus Christ, God's Son, by the Father.

33. {*Were cut to the heart*} This is the Greek verb *diapriô* (*dia, priô*), to saw in two (*dia*), to cut in two (to the heart). Here it is rage and fury that cuts into their hearts, not conviction of sin (cf. Acts 2:37).

34. {*Gamaliel*} Here Gamaliel champions the cause of the apostles as a Pharisee to score a point against the Sadducees. He acts as a theological opportunist, not as a disciple of Christ.

36. {*Were dispersed*} From an old verb meaning to disolve, to go to pieces. Use only here in the NT.

38-39. {*Refrain from...*} Gamaliel gives an "if—then" scenario which demonstrates that this Christian movement will be overthrown if of human origin. But if of God, then Gamaliel warns the Sanhedrin that they cannot overthrow God.

40. {*To him they agreed...not to speak*} The Sanhedrin repeated the prohibition of Acts 4:18 which the apostles had steadily refused to obey. The Sanhedrin stood by their guns, but refused to shoot. It was a "draw" with Gamaliel as tactical victor over the Sadducees. Clearly now the disciples were set free because only the Sadducees had become enraged while the Pharisees held aloof.

41. {*They were counted worthy to suffer dishonour for the Name*} An irony, even an oxymoron, the apostles felt *honored* by *dishonor.*

With Jews, "the Name" meant Jehovah. The Christians now apply it to Jesus.

CHAPTER 6

1. {*A murmuring of the Grecian Jews…against the Hebrews*} The Greek word for "murmur" is onomatopoetic—a buzzing sound. "Grecian Jews" are members of the church in Jerusalem who are Jews from outside of Palestine, having points of contact with the Gentile world (like speaking the Greek language) without having gone over to the habits of the Gentiles. The "Hebraic Jews" were the Aramaean Jews of the Eastern Dispersion, and are usually classed with the Hebrew (speaking Aramaic) as contrasted with the Grecian group.

2. {*The twelve…said, It is not fit that we should forsake the word of God, and serve table*} That is, they should not leave behind their ministry. The tables here were for the common daily distribution of the food (cf. Acts 2:43-47). "Wait on" is the quite similar word in the Greek for deacon (cf. Phil. 1:1; 1 Tim. 3:8-13). Likely the office of deacon as separate from bishop or elder grew out of this incident in Acts 6:1-7.

3. {*Of good report*} Lit. "to bear witness to." That is, men with a good reputation as well as with spiritual gifts (the Holy Spirit and wisdom).

4. {*The ministry of the word*} This was the special ministry of preaching (cf. 2:42).

5. {*They chose…*} Each one was a Hellenist (Grecian Jew), not an Aramaean Jew (Hebraic Jew). Wisely chosen, for the murmuring had come from the Hellenists.

6. {*They laid their hands on them*} Laying on of hands was a symbol of the imparting "of the gifts and graces which they needed to qualify them for the office. It was a prayer that God would bestow the necessary gifts, rather than a pledge that they were actually conferred" (Hackett).

8. {*Stephen…wrought…*} Greek tense shows he repeatedly did such signs. Stephen would not confine his ministry to serving tables. He was a whirlwind of power in the realm of Peter and John and the rest.

9. {*The synagogue of the Libertines*} Once Jewish slaves of Rome, these people are now set free and settled in Jerusalem and numerous enough to have a synagogue of their own. Stephen appeared as a Hellenist preaching Jesus as the Messiah and he met opposition there.

10. {*They were not able to withstand*} They *continued* unable (without strength enough) to take a stand against Stephen. He was like a battery charged and in action.

11. {*Then they suborned men...*} One recalls the plight of Caiaphas in the trial of Jesus when he sought false witnesses (also v. 13). They put these men forward in an underhanded way. {*Blasphemous words against Moses and God*} The punishment for blasphemy was stoning to death (cf. Matt. 12:31). Though untrue, the purpose of this charge is to stir the prejudices of the people in the matter of Jewish rights and privileges.

12. {*They stirred up the people*} This is the Greek verb *sunkineô*, to throw into commotion. This is the first record of the hostility of the masses against the disciples.

14. {*We have heard him say...*} The accusation was really a distortion of the ideas Jesus communicated to the woman at Sychar (cf. John 4:1-42) that God is spirit and to be worshipped by men anywhere.

15. {*As if the face of an angel*} (cf. Moses' face Exod. 34:30 and 2 Cor. 3:7). Alone, (though cf. Acts 7:56) there was little that Peter and John could have done for Stephen if they had been present. Where were they?

CHAPTER 7

1. {*Are these things so?*} Two charges had been made against Stephen (1) speaking against the holy temple, (2) changing the customs which Moses had delivered. Stephen could not give a yes or no answer to these two charges. There was an element of truth in each of them and a large amount of error all mixed together. So he undertakes to explain his real position by a rapid survey of God's dealing with the people of Israel and the Gentiles.

2. {*Hearken*} A command, the tense translates, "give me your attention *now*." {*The God of glory*} That is, the God characterized by glory, the visible radiance of God (cf. Exod. 25:22; 40:34; Lev. 9:6; Heb. 9:5). By these words Stephen refutes the charge of blasphemy against God (cf. Acts 6:11). This glory appeared before there was temple or tabernacle and away over in Mesopotamia (Ur of the Chaldees, Gen. 11:31), even before he dwelt in Haran.

5. {*Not so much as to set his foot on*} (cf. Deut. 2:5). Lit. "Stepping of a foot." {*When as yet he had no child*} Greek syntax emphasizes actual absence of a child. He had only the promise of God about the land and the child.

7. {*Will I judge*} "I" is emphatic here in the Greek. {*In this place*} (cf. Exod. 3:12). This refers to Mount Sinai or Horeb, but Stephen applies it to the Promised Land.

8. {*The covenant of circumcision*} (cf. Gen. 17:9-14). That is, a covenant marked by circumcision as a sign (Rom. 4:11).

11. {*Found no sustenance*} This is the Greek word *chortasma,* from *chortazô,* here including grass [fodder] or food plants for both men and animals.

14. {*Three-score and fifteen souls*} Apparently this number (Seventy-five) counts grandchildren of Joseph. Sixty-six is the biblical number mentioned (cf. Gen. 46:26-27), and the next verse seventy including Jacob and Joseph with his two sons.

16. {*They were carried over unto Shechem*} Jacob and Joseph were buried in the cave of Machpelah (Gen. 50:13). {*Which Abraham bought*} Abraham had built an altar at Shechem when he entered Canaan (Gen. 12:6). It is possible, of course, that Abraham also bought the ground on which the altar stood.

19. {*Dealt subtilly*} This is the Greek verb *katasophizomai,* from *kata* and *sophizô,* "to be quite wise [shrewd]" here with a reference to a "wisdom" that uses fraud, craft, and deceit.

20. {*Exceeding fair*} (cf. Exod. 2:2). Lit. "fair to God" as God looked at him.

21. {*Took up...nourished him for her own son*} (cf. Exod. 2:5). That is, Moses was adopted and raised by her. The tradition is that she designed Moses for the throne as the Pharaoh had no son (Josephus).

22. {*Was instructed*} This is the Greek verb *paideuô,* here meaning to train a child (*pais*). The priestly caste in Egypt was noted for their knowledge of science, astronomy, medicine, and mathematics. Moses, like Paul, was a man of the schools.

23. {*When he was well-nigh forty years old*} Lit. "When a forty year old time." The life of Moses is divided into three periods of forty years each, totaling 120: (1) Egypt, (2) Midian, (3) As Israel's leader (cf. Deut. 34:7).

25. {*That his brethren understood*} The people did not yet realize who their deliverer would be. With great rhetorical power Stephen is building a comparison to his situation and the message of Messiah.

26. {*Appeared*} The Greek shows that this was a sudden or unexpected appearance before the men actually fighting.

28. {*Wouldest thou kill me?*} (cf. Exod. 2:14). "No" is the expected answer in the Greek syntax.

30. {*In a flame of fire in a bush*} (cf. Exod. 3:1). Lit. "in the flame of fire of a bush." In Exodus 3:20 it is Jehovah who speaks, hence this is understood to be the Angel of the Presence, the Eternal Logos of the Father, the Angel of Jehovah.

31. {*A voice of the Lord*} Here the angel of Jehovah of verse 30 is termed Jehovah himself.

33. {*Sandal*} The priests were barefooted when they ministered in the temple. Moslems enter their mosques barefooted today (cf. Josh. 5:15).

34. {*I have surely seen*} (cf. Exod. 3:7) Lit. "seeing I saw" as mimicking the Hebrew style (cf. Heb. 6:14).

35. {*This Moses*} Clearly, Stephen means to draw a parallel between Moses and Jesus. They in Egypt *denied* Moses as now you (the Jews) *denied* Jesus. Those in Egypt scouted Moses as ruler and judge (vv. 27, 35) and God has sent Moses both a ruler and a deliverer as Jesus was to be (Luke 1:68; 2:38; Heb. 9:12; Titus 2:14).

37. {*Like unto me*} (cf. Acts 3:22). Stephen argues that Moses was predicting the Messiah as a prophet like himself who is no other than Jesus so that these Pharisees are in reality opposing Moses.

38. {*In the church in the wilderness*} "Church" is the Greek word *ekklêsia,* normally translated "church" but here is better rendered "congregation" or assembly here as in Hebrews 2:12 (Ps. 22:22), the people of Israel gathered at Mt. Sinai, the whole nation. {*Living oracles*} (Acts 7:38; Rom. 3:2; Heb. 5:12; 1 Pet. 4:11). "Words" in the Greek is *logia* (lit. "little words"), from *logos,* referring to words from God to Moses which are still living today.

39. {*Turned back*} They yearned after the fleshpots of Egypt and even the gods of Egypt.

40. {*Gods which shall go before us*} (cf. Exod. 32:1). The gods would be as guides and protectors, perhaps with some allusion to the pillar of fire and of cloud that had gone before them (Exod. 13:21).

41. {*They made a calf...the idol*} (cf. Exod. 32:3). Aaron made the calf, but so did the people (Exod. 32:35). The people said the idol was their way of worshipping Jehovah! So the Egyptians worshipped the bull Apis at Memphis as the symbol of Osiris (the sun).

42. {*To serve the host of heaven*} This kind of worship is Sabaism or worship of the host of heaven (sun, moon, and stars) instead of the Lord of hosts (Deut. 17:3; 2 Kgs. 17:16; 21:3; 2 Chr. 33:3, 5; Jer. 8:2; 19:13). This star-worship greatly injured the Jews.

43. {*The tabernacle of Moloch*} Lit. "tent of Moloch" which they took up after each halt instead of the tabernacle of Jehovah. Moloch was the god of the Amorites to whom children were offered as live sacrifices.

44. {*The tabernacle of the testimony*} This first sanctuary was not the temple, but the tent in the wilderness. Stephen passes on from the conduct of the Israelites to his other argument that God is not necessarily worshipped in a particular spot.

45. {*With Joshua*} Lit. "with Jesus" as the Greek form of Joshua (cf. Matt. 1:21 and Heb. 4:8).

46. {*A habitation*} This is the Greek word *skênôma*, here it means a more permanent abode.

48. {*Howbeit*} That is, by contrast with what Solomon did and David planned. "Not" is emphatic in the Greek syntax (cf. 1 Kgs. 8:27; 2 Chron. 6:18). {*In houses made with hands*} Lit. "In things made with hands" (cf. Acts 7:24; Heb. 9:11, 24; Eph. 2:11).

49. {*What manner of house...?*} The temple was not meant to confine God's presence, and so here it is proven that Jesus had rightly shown that God is a spirit and can be worshipped anywhere.

51. {*Uncircumcised in heart*} (Exod. 32:9; 33:3, 5; 34:9; Lev. 26:41; Deut. 9:6; Jer. 6:10). No epithet could have been more galling to them. {*Ye always resist...*} Stephen has shown how God had revealed himself gradually, the revelation sloping upward to Christ Jesus. Stephen's countrymen were repeating the old mistake—treating the Messiah as the patriarchs had treated Joseph, and the Hebrews Moses.

53. {*As it was ordained by angels*} "Ordained" is the Greek word *diatagê* (from *diatassô*, to arrange, appoint). This was "at the appointment" of angels). {*And kept it not*} Like a whipcracker these words cut to the quick. They gloried in possessing the law and openly violated it (Rom. 2:23).

54. {*They were cut to the heart*} Here Stephen had sent a saw through the hearts of the Pharisees. They began to gnash their teeth in fury at him just like a pack of hungry, snarling wolves.

55. {*And Jesus standing*} Jesus is standing as if he had risen to cheer the brave Stephen. Elsewhere he is pictured as sitting at the right hand of God (cf. Matt. 26:64; Acts 2:34; Eph. 1:20; Col. 3:1; Heb. 1:3).

57. {*Stopped their ears*} Lit. "They held their ears together" with their hands. They yelled he was guilty of blasphemy (cf. Matt. 26:65). {*Rushed upon him with one accord*} No more formalities: no vote, no question of rights of the accused. It was like a modern lynching, taking the law into their own hands. {*Out of the city*} As would later be the case with Paul, they went out to keep from defiling the place with blood (cf. Acts 21:30). {*The witnesses*} (cf. Acts 6:11, 13). Suborned by the Pharisees, these false witnesses had the privilege of casting the first stones (Deut. 13:10; 17:7). {*At the feet of a young man named Saul*} Though a pupil of Gamaliel (Acts 22:3), Saul does not seem to be aware that he is going contrary to the views of his master.

59. {*Receive my spirit*} The Greek tense showing urgency, many have followed Stephen into death with these words upon their dying lips (cf. Acts 9:14, 21; 22:16).

60. {*Kneeled down*} Jesus was standing at the right hand of God and Stephen knelt before him in worship and called on him in prayer. {*He fell asleep*} A common metaphor for death, such language may have been used here to give a word picture of rest and calmness in dramatic contrast to the violence of the scene.

CHAPTER 8

1. {*Saul...was consenting*} This is the Greek verb *suneudokeô*, from Greek *sun* (with), *eu* (good), and *dokeô* (to think). This word well describes Saul's pleasure in the death of Stephen, coolly applauding the murder of Stephen (cf. Acts 22:20). {*A great persecution*} The Pharisees and Sadducees are now united in a general persecution. {*Except the apostles*} Did the Pharisees spare the apostles due to the advice of

Gamaliel (cf. Acts 5:34-40)? Or was it the courage (or popularity) of the apostles?

3. {*Laid waste*} This is the Greek verb *lumainomai,* to dishonor, defile, devastate, ruin and this from *lumê,* injury. This was like the laying waste of a vineyard by a wild boar (Ps. 79:13); Saul lead the havoc in the persecution. {*The church*} Here this means "the church" not merely an "assembly." Though scattered it was still an organized body.

4. {*They therefore...went about...preaching the word*} Saul's work unwittingly now pushes the Great Commission to the world.

5. {*Philip*} This is Philip the deacon and evangelist, not the apostle (cf. Acts 6:5; 21:8 and Mark 3:18). {*To the city of Samaria*} This refers to the name of this city here. Formerly forbidden to go into a Samaritan city (Matt. 10:5), that temporary prohibition to the Twelve was withdrawn before Jesus ascended on high (Acts 1:8).

6. {*Gave heed*} The Greek tense shows they *kept on* giving heed or holding the mind on the things said by Philip.

7. {*For many...*} The servant Philip was reaping where the Master had sown. Samaria was the mission field white for the harvest (John 4:35). The Samaritans who had been bewitched by Simon are now carried away by Philip.

9. {*Simon*} In Simon's person Christianity was for the first time confronted with superstition and religious imposture.

10. {*That power of God which is called Great*} Apparently here is already the oriental doctrine of emanations or eons so rampant in the second century. This "power" was considered a spark of God himself. Simon claimed to *impersonate God.*

12. {*They were baptized*} The Greek tense shows they were baptized *from time to time,* while a different Greek tense for "believed" shows that this belief was *constant,* not from time to time.

13. {*And Simon also himself believed*} Simon was determined to get this new power, but had no sense of personal need of Jesus as Savior for his sins. Though baptized, he was still unsaved.

14. {*That Samaria had received*} This "Samaria" refers to the district here, not the city (cf. v. 5). {*They sent Peter and John*} The sending of Peter and John was no reflection on Philip, but the mission needed the status of Peter and John to sanction acceptance of the social outcast Samaritans.

15-16. {*That they might receive*} The Samaritans had been baptized on the assumption that the Holy Spirit had given them new hearts. The coming of the Holy Spirit with obvious signs (cf. Acts 10:44-48) as in Jerusalem would make it plain.

17. {*Laid they their hands...*} The laying on of hands was not required for imparting the Spirit; there are numerous cases where the Spirit came apart from the laying on of hands (cf. not in Acts 2:4, 33; 4:31; 10:44 nor 1 Cor. 12; 14).

18-19. {*When Simon saw...*} "Saw" is evidence that it means he saw them speak with tongues. Power is what Simon determined he wanted. He took Peter to also be a performer, selling his tricks for money.

20. {*Perish with thee*} Lit. "be with you for destruction." The Greek syntax shows a future wish, revealing Peter's indignation at the base offer of Simon. Almost a curse, Simon was on the road to destruction.

21. {*Matter*} Lit. "in this word" or subject (cf. Luke 1:4; Acts 15:6). {*Straight*} "Straight" here means "right" in moral rectitude (cf. Ps. 78:37).

22. {*If perhaps*} The Greek condition is determined as fulfilled, yet minimizes the chance of forgiveness (cf. Mark 11:13). Peter may have thought that his sin was close to the unpardonable sin (Matt. 12:31), but he does not close the door of hope.

23. {*That thou art...in the gall of bitterness*} Lit. "to the bile consisting of bitterness..." (cf. Heb. 12:15; Rom. 3:14; Eph. 4:31). Peter describes Simon's offer as *poison* and a *chain*.

24. {*Pray ye for me*} "Ye" is emphatic in the Greek. Simon is thoroughly frightened by Peter's words, but shows no sign of personal repentance or change of heart. He wants to escape the penalty for his sin and hopes that Peter can avert it.

25. {*They therefore...*} Peter and John now carried on the work of Philip to the Samaritans. It would no longer be an issue to preach to Samaritans and accept them in the Lord.

27. {*A eunuch of great authority*} Eunuchs were often employed by oriental rulers in high posts. Eunuchs were not allowed to be Jews in the full sense (Deut. 23:1), but only proselytes of the gate.

28. {*Was reading...*} That is, he was reading out loud. He had probably purchased this roll of Isaiah in Jerusalem and was reading the LXX Greek text (cf. v. 32).

29. {*Join thyself*} Lit. "be glued to." Philip probably jumped on the running board on the side of the chariot.

30. {*Understandest thou what thou readest?*} A play on words in the Greek. "Read" in Greek is *anaginôsko* lit. "know [*ginôskô*] again [*ana*]." So the phrase is "do you know what you *know again* [are reading]?"
31. {*How can I, except some one shall guide me?*} Not sure at all that the outcome will be understanding ("how can I?"), the eunuch felt the need of someone to guide.
35. {*Beginning from this Scripture*} Philip needed no better opening than this Messianic passage in Isaiah. Jesus found himself as Messiah in the OT (Luke 24:27) as Philip does here.
39. {*Out of the water*} That is, out of the water altogether, not from the edge of the water (cf. Mark 1:10). {*Caught away*} A miraculous catching up or carrying off, the Greek verb *harpazô*, like the Latin *rapio* [cf. *rapture*] (cf. 2 Cor. 12:2; 1 Thess. 4:17).

CHAPTER 9

1. {*Breathing threatening and slaughter*} Lit. "breathing *in* threatening and slaughter" like a war-horse who sniffed the smell of battle. Saul "breathed on" the remaining disciples the murder that he had already "breathed in" from the death of the others.
2. {*Letters*} This authority is from the estate of the elders, that is the Sanhedrin (cf. Acts 22:5 and 26:10). {*To Damascus*} (cf. 2 Cor. 11:32). This old city is the most enduring in the history of the world. It is some 150 miles Northeast from Jerusalem. Here the Jews were strong in numbers, and here some disciples had found refuge from Saul's persecution in Judea and still worshipped in the synagogues. {*That he might bring them bound*} Three times (8:3; 9:2; 22:4) this fact of persecuting is mentioned as a special blot in Paul's cruelty and one of the items in his later calling himself "chief of sinners" (cf. 1 Tim. 1:15).
3. {*Shone round about him*} Though the broad outline and essentials agree in all three accounts, there are slight variations in this event even by the one to whom it happened (cf. Acts 22:6-16 and 26:12-20). The appearance of Jesus to Paul changed his whole life (1 Cor. 15:8; Gal. 1:16).
4. {*Saul, Saul*} Jesus was speaking Aramaic language (cf. Acts 26:14). For the repetition of names by Jesus see Luke 10:41; Luke 22:31. {*Me?*} In persecuting the disciples, Saul was persecuting Jesus (cf. Matt. 10:40;

25:40, 45; John 15:1-5). Jesus had spoken of the union that exists between him and his disciples.

5. {*Lord*} Here Paul likely means merely "sir" though the same Greek word means "Lord" when Paul later addresses Jesus (cf. Acts 22:10). Saul instantly surrendered his will, as Thomas did (John 20:28) and as little Samuel (1 Sam. 3:9). This surrender of the will to Christ was the conversion of Saul. He saw a real Person, the Risen Christ, to whom he surrendered his life. On this point he never wavered for a moment to the end.

7. {*Hearing the voice, but beholding no man*} The other accounts clear up the details: the men saw the light but did not discern the person; they heard the sound but did not understand the words (cf. Acts 22:9).

8. {*He saw nothing*} No hallucination, the blindness was proof he had seen the Risen Christ. {*They led him by the hand*} A pathetic picture, the persecutor and conqueror of the disciples was now helpless as a child.

9. {*Not seeing...*} Paul had weakness of the eyes later; either from natural glaring strain of the Syrian sun (as is common there), or the weakness of the eyes from this experience (cf. Gal. 4:15).

10. {*Ananias*} This Ananias had the respect of both Jews and Christians in Damascus (cf. Acts 22:12). {*In a vision*} Not a literary device of providential ordering of events, this vision event really happened, as yet another supernatural aspect of Christianity.

11. {*To the street...Straight*} Most city lanes were crooked, but this lane in Damascus still runs in a direct line from the eastern to the western gate of the city, probably a modern layer of street covering the very line of the ancient street Ananias walked several feet below.

13. {*To thy saints*} "Saints" means "God's people" with the special feature that they are "set apart" for God (Luke 1:70; 2:23; Rom. 1:7, etc.). Ananias in his ignorance saw in Saul only the man with an evil reputation while Jesus saw in Saul the man transformed by grace to be a messenger of mercy.

15. {*A chosen vessel*} That is, a vessel of choice or selection. Jesus chose Saul before Saul chose Jesus. He felt of himself that he was an earthen vessel unworthy of so great a treasure (cf. 2 Cor. 4:7). {*Before the Gentiles*} Saul was to be an apostle to the Gentiles (cf. Eph. 3:6-12).

17. {*Brother Saul*} All suspicion has vanished and Ananias takes Saul to his heart as a brother in Christ. It was a gracious word to Saul now under suspicion on both sides. {*Be filled with the Holy Spirit*} This endowment of special power he will need as an apostle and as promised by Jesus (Acts 1:8; Gal. 2:7).

18. {*Fell off...as if it were scales*} Luke does not say that actual "scales" fell from the eyes of Saul, but that it felt that way to him as his sight returned, "something like." {*Was baptized*} Apparently it was by Ananias (Acts 22:16) as a symbol of the new life in Christ already begun.

20. {*He proclaimed Jesus...that he is the Son of God*} This is Paul's new platform as a Christian preacher, a complete reversal. He preached it in the very synagogues in which he was originally intending to raise havoc.

21. {*Were amazed*} This is the Greek verb *existêmi.* They *continued* to "stand out of themselves" in astonishment at this reversal in Saul.

22. {*Increased the more*} (cf. Phil. 4:13; 1 Tim. 1:12; 2 Tim. 2:1; 4:17; Rom. 4:20). Christ, the dynamo of spiritual energy, was now pouring power (Acts 1:8) into Paul who is already filled with the Holy Spirit (Acts 9:17). {*Proving*} Here Saul took the various items in the life of Jesus of Nazareth and found in them the proof that he was in reality the Messiah; he continued to use this method (Acts 17:3).

23. {*When many days were fulfilled*} Probably at this point Saul went into Arabia for several years (Gal. 1:12-24). We are at liberty to supplement the narrative in the Acts with items from Paul's Epistles. So we must assume the return of Saul from Arabia at this juncture, between verses 22, 23, when Saul resumed his preaching in the Jewish synagogues with renewed energy after the period of reflection and readjustment in Arabia. {*Took counsel together...to kill him*} Things had reached a climax. It was worse than before he left for Arabia. Paul was now seeing the fulfillment of the prophecy of Jesus about him (Acts 9:16). He may even have been scourged here (2 Cor. 11:24).

24-25. {*Through the wall...in a basket*} Compare Joshua 2:15 (cf. 1 Sam. 19:12) for the way that Rahab let out the spies by a cord through the window. Here "basket" was a larger basket of braided reeds. Other baskets were smaller and still others made of ropes.

26. {*Were all afraid of him*} Paul had left Jerusalem a conquering hero of Pharisaism. He returns distrusted by the disciples and regarded by the Pharisees as a renegade and a turncoat. He had escaped the plots of the Jews in Damascus only to find himself the object of suspicion by the disciples in Jerusalem.

27-28. {*Barnabas took him...*} Barnabas was convinced that Jesus had changed the heart of Saul and he used his great influence (Acts 4:36; 11:22) to win the favor of the apostles, Peter in particular (Gal. 1:19) and James the half-brother of Jesus. {*To the apostles*} Barnabas and James are termed apostles in the general sense, though not belonging to the twelve. Although Paul was not one of the twelve, he was later viewed as being an apostle in that sense. The fear of the disciples vanished.

29. {*Disputed...*} Paul preached mainly in the synagogues of the Hellenists as Stephen had done (Acts 8:9). As a Cilician Jew he knew how to speak to the Hellenists. {*But they went about to kill him*} "Went about" is the Greek verb *epicheireô,* to put the hand to, to try (cf. Luke 1:1; Acts 9:29; 19:3). They offer to Saul the same conclusive answer that he gave to Stephen, death.

30. {*Sent forth...to Tarsus*} It takes little imagination to picture the scene at home when this brilliant young rabbi returns home a preacher of the despised Jesus of Nazareth whose disciples he had so relentlessly persecuted. What will his family think of him now?

31. {*Had peace*} Greek tense and words are lit. "*kept on* having peace" because the persecution had ceased. Many of the disciples came back to Jerusalem and the apostles began to make preaching tours out from the city. {*In the comfort of the Holy Spirit*} The Holy Spirit had been promised by Jesus as "another Paraclete" and now this is shown to be true (cf. John 14:16ff.).

34. {*Healeth*} The Greek tense shows that he is healed *here and now.* {*Make thy bed*} A command to do for himself what others have done for eight years.

36. {*Dorcas*} Her name means "Gazelle," the creature with the beautiful look.

37. {*In an upper chamber*} (cf. Acts 1:13 and 9:39). Unlike Ananias and Sapphira, interment unhurried was to place the body in upper room, usually washed by the women.

39. {*Stood by him*} A heart-breaking scene, the verse is a vivid picture of this group of widows weeping and pointing with pride to the very inner garments and outer garments which she made from time to time.

40. {*Put them all forth*} (cf. Mark 5:40-41). Peter's praying alone reminds one of Elijah (cf. 1 Kgs. 17:20) and the widow's son and Elisha for the Shunammite's son (cf. 2 Kgs. 4:33).

43. {*With one Simon a tanner*} The more scrupulous Jews regarded such an occupation as unclean, and avoided those who pursued it. The conduct of Peter here shows that he did not carry his prejudices to that extent.

CHAPTER 10

1. {*Centurion*} (cf. Matt. 8:5). Lit. "ruler of a hundred." These Roman centurions always appear in a favorable light in the NT (Matt. 8:5; Luke 7:2; 23:47; Acts 10:1; 22:25; 27:3).

2. {*Devout*} (cf. Acts 10:22, 35). Here this means a God-fearing proselyte at the gate, a term for the Gentile seekers after God (Acts 13:16, 26; 17:4, 17). He and the family were worshipping at the synagogue without circumcision, and were not strictly proselytes and still regarded as outside the pale of Judaism (Acts 10:28, 34; 11:1, 8; 15:7). They had seats in the synagogue, but were not Jews.

4. {*Lord*} Cornelius recognizes the angel of God (v. 3) as God's messenger. {*For a memorial*} His prayers and his alms proved his sincerity and won the ear of God.

6. {*By the seaside*} Lit. "along by the sea." It was outside the city walls to secure water for his trade.

10. {*Hungry*} This probably means "very hungry" from the form of the Greek word. {*He fell into a trance*} Lit. "an ecstasy came upon him," in which trance he passed out of himself and from which one came to himself (Acts 12:11). It is different from a vision as in Acts 10:3.

11. {*By four corners*} The picture is the sheet held up by four cords to which the sheet is fastened. Israel would be gathered from the four corners of the earth (cf. Isa. 11:12).

12. {*All manner of...*} Fish are not mentioned, perhaps because the sheet had no water, though they were clean and unclean also (Lev. 11:9; Deut. 14:9).

14-15. {*Not so, Lord*} The Greek is somewhere between a mild protest and a polite refusal with a reason given; it is not a blunt refusal. {*Common and unclean*} (cf. Mark 7:18). Here this means ceremonially unclean, of course. Peter had been reared from childhood to make the distinction between clean and unclean food and this new proposal even from the Lord runs against all his previous training. This symbol of the sheet was to show Peter ultimately that Gentiles could be saved without becoming Jews.

17. {*Was much perplexed in himself*} "Perplexed" is the Greek verb *diaporeô, dia,* [thoroughly], and *alpha* of negation [not], and *poros* [way], to be completely at a loss to know what road to take.

18. {*Called*} That is, in a loud voice that those inside the house might hear.

19. {*Thought*} A Greek verb of great "motion" of thought, Peter was revolving in his mind, in and out, to find the meaning of the vision.

20. {*For I...*} The Holy Spirit assumes responsibility for the messengers from Cornelius and thus connects their mission with the vision which was still troubling Peter.

22. {*Was warned*} This is the Greek verb *chrêmatizô,* here with the meaning of being divinely warned (cf. Matt. 2:12, 22; Luke 2:26; Heb. 11:7).

23. {*Accompanied him*} The wisdom of having these half dozen Jewish Christians from Joppa with Peter in the house of Cornelius in Caesarea becomes manifest in Jerusalem (cf. Acts 11:12).

24. {*Near*} The first refers to blood relations (kinsmen) here; the second to necessary friends. All Gentiles close to Cornelius and predisposed to hear Peter favorably.

27. {*Findeth...come together*} This refers to an expectant group of Gentiles eager for Peter's interpretation of the vision of Cornelius.

28. {*How that it is an unlawful thing...*} (cf. Acts 11:3; Gal. 2:12). There is no OT regulation forbidding such social contact with Gentiles, though the rabbis had added it and had made it binding by custom.

29. {*Without gainsaying*} Lit. "without answering back." That is true after the Holy Spirit expressly told Peter to go with the messengers of Cornelius (Acts 10:19-23). Peter's objections were made to the Lord in the vision which he did not understand.

31. {*Is heard*} The Greek tense here has no regard as to the time of the event.

33. {*And thou hast well done that thou art come*} Lit. "and you did well in coming," a regular formula for expressing thanks (cf. Phil. 4:14; 3 John 6; 2 Pet. 1:19). Cornelius commends Peter for his courage in breaking away from Jewish custom and takes no offense at the implied superiority of the Jews over the Gentiles. Cornelius reveals an open mind for the message of God through Peter.

34. {*I perceive...respecter of persons*} It had been a difficult thing for Peter to grasp, but now the light has cleared away the fogs. It was not until Peter had crossed the threshold of the house of Cornelius in the new environment and standpoint that he sees this new and great truth.

35. {*Acceptable to him...*} That is to say, a Gentile would not have to become a Jew in order to become a Christian. Evidently Peter had not before perceived this fact. On the great Day of Pentecost when he spoke of the promise "to all those far off" (Acts 2:39) Peter understood that they must first become Jews and then Christians.

36. {*Preaching good tidings of peace through Jesus Christ...*} Lit. "Gospelizing peace through Jesus Christ." There is no other way to have real peace between individuals and God, between races and nations, than by Jesus Christ (cf. Eph. 2:17).

37. {*Ye know*} "You" is emphatic in the Greek syntax. Peter reminds his Gentile audience that the main facts concerning Jesus and the gospel were known to them. {*Beginning*} The story began with a skip to Galilee after the baptism just like the Gospel of Mark. This first message of Peter to the Gentiles (Acts 10:37-44) corresponds in broad outline with Mark's Gospel. Mark heard Peter preach many times and evidently planned his Gospel (the Roman Gospel) on this same model.

38. {*Jesus of Nazareth*} Lit. "Jesus the one from Nazareth"; the phrase is before the verb "anointed" in the Greek for emphasis. {*God anointed him*} This can refer to: the Incarnation (Luke 1:35), the Baptism (Luke 3:22), the Ministry at Nazareth (Luke 4:14). Why not to the life and work of Jesus as a whole? {*And healing...*} Luke does not exclude other diseases (cf. Luke 13:11, 16), but he lays special emphasis on demon possession (cf. Mark 1:23).

39. {*And we are witnesses*} Peter thus appeals to what the audience knows and to what the disciples know. He made the same claim about personal witnesses of the Resurrection of Jesus at Pentecost (Acts 2:32).

41. {*Chosen before*} This is the Greek verb *procheirotoneô,* to choose or designate by hand (*cheirotoneô, cheir,* hand, and *teinô,* to stretch, as in Acts 14:23; 2 Cor. 8:19), beforehand (*pro*). Peter is evidently stating the thing as it happened and not trying to make a convincing story by saying that both friends and foes saw him after his resurrection. It is the historian's candor in Luke here that adds to the credibility of the narrative. {*To us who did eat and drink with him*} (cf. Luke 24:41-3). Such behaviors show Jesus was no hallucination or ghost, but the real Jesus himself.

42. {*Ordained...judge*} Peter's claim for Jesus is that he is the Judge of Jew and Gentile (living and dead).

43. {*Every one that believeth*} "Every one" shows it is God's plan and no distinctions are drawn according to race (cf. Acts 2:38). Gentiles do not have to become Jews, but have only to believe in Jesus as Messiah and Judge as foretold by the prophets.

44-45. {*The Holy Ghost fell...*} (cf. Acts 8:16; 10:44; 11:15). Peter was interrupted in his sermon by this remarkable event. The Jews had received the Holy Spirit (Acts 2:4), the Samaritans (Acts 8:17), and now Gentiles. This was indubitable proof of the conversion of these Gentiles who had accepted Peter's message and had believed on Jesus Christ.

46. {*Speak...with tongues*} (cf. Acts 2:4, 11). These are new and strange tongues (cf. Acts 19:6; 1 Cor. 14:4-19). This sudden manifestation of the Holy Spirit's power on uncircumcised Gentiles was probably necessary to convince those of the circumcision.

47. {*Can any man forbid the water?*} Lit. "Can any one cut off the water from the being baptized as to these?" "No" is the expected answer in the Greek. These Gentiles were converted and so entitled to be baptized.

48. {*In the name of Jesus Christ*} This is the essential name in Christian baptism (cf. Acts 2:38; 19:5); "In the name" has a focus on the *authority* for the act, not the formula that was employed.

CHAPTER 11

1. {*In Judea*} This probably refers to all Palestine. The news from Caesarea spread like wildfire among the Jewish Christians. The case of the Samaritans was different, for they were half Jews, though disliked. But here were real Romans even if with Jewish affinities.

2. {*They that were of the circumcision*} (cf. Acts 10:46). Lit. "those of circumcision (on the side of circumcision, of the circumcision party)." This refers to a larger Jewish group than the six present with Cornelius; such kinds of groups later had a narrower sense of the Judaizing or Pharisaic wing of the disciples (Acts 15:5) who made circumcision necessary for all Gentile converts (cf. Gal. 2:12).

3. {*Men uncircumcised*} Lit. "Men having uncircumcision." It is a contemptuous expression. They did not object to Peter's preaching to the Gentiles, but to his going into the house of Cornelius and eating with them, violating his supposed obligations as a Jew (cf. Jesus with "sinners" Luke 15:12).

4. {*Began*} So Peter is at once put on the defensive as the contention went on. Peter began at the beginning and gave the full story of God's dealings with him in Joppa and Caesarea.

6. {*When I had fastened my eyes...I considered*} Lit. "gazing, I was pondering." {*And saw*} The Greek tense shows "I saw *in a flash.*"

12. {*We entered into the man's house*} Peter and the other six. Note he avoids mention of Cornelius's name and office.

13. {*Fetch Simon*} (cf. Acts 10:5, 22; 11:13). Under God's direct orders, Peter did not enter a Gentile house on his own authority.

15. {*Even as on us at the beginning*} Referring to Pentecost, this is the speaking with tongues and all. "He rests his defense on what God did" (Furneaux).

16. {*I remembered*} Peter recalls the very words of Jesus, which he now understands (cf. Acts 1:5). Peter clearly sees that the water baptism is merely the symbol or picture of the spiritual baptism in the heart.

17. {*The like gift*} It was a gift equal in quality, rank, or measure. Both classes (Gentiles and Jews) trusted in Christ, and both received the Holy Spirit. {*Who was I...that I could withstand God?*} Lit. "able to hinder God."

18. {*Held their peace*} They were now quiet, and the wrangling ceased.

19. {*They therefore that were scattered abroad*} This phrase shows another sequence of events. From the events of Acts 8:4ff. Luke followed Saul through his conversion and back to Jerusalem and to Tarsus (chapter 9ff.). Then he showed the activity of Peter outside of Jerusalem (chapter 10ff.) as a result of the cessation of the persecution from the conversion of Saul with the Gentile Pentecost in Caesarea and the outcome in Jerusalem. Now Luke starts over again from the same persecution by Saul and runs a new line of events up to Antioch. {*Antioch*} This metropolis of Syria ranked next to Rome and Alexandria in size, wealth, power, and vice. There were many Jews in Antioch. It was destined to supplant Jerusalem as the center of Christian activity.

20. {*Spake...unto the Greeks also*} The correct reading of the Greek text is "Greeks" at least in part pure heathen (and not God-fearers like

Cornelius). Another inferior reading of the Greek text here is "Helle-nists" referring to Grecian *Jews* as Christians (cf. Acts 6:1ff.; also 9:29). At any rate, the preachers to these pure pagan Greeks were Hellenist Jewish Christians who were laymen outside of the circle of official leaders.

21. {*The hand of the Lord was with them...turned unto the Lord*} The first "Lord" refers to Jehovah, the second to Jesus (cf. Acts 11:20). Jesus is deity on par with Jehovah.

22. {*Of the church which was in Jerusalem*} Note the group of dis-ciples in Antioch is not yet referred to as a "church" (cf. Acts 11:26; 13:1). {*They sent forth...*} Barnabas already had a position of leader-ship in Jerusalem because of his generosity (Acts 4:36) and his champi-onship of Saul after his conversion (Acts 9:27).

23. {*He exhorted*} The Greek tense shows a *continuous* encourage-ment from Barnabas. {*Cleave unto the Lord*} Lit. "to *keep on* remain-ing loyal." Persistence was needed in such a pagan city.

24. {*For...*} This is the explanation of the conduct of Barnabas; he was good. Barnabas rose above racial narrowness which had characterized Jewishness of this time.

25. {*To seek for Saul*} The Greek verb is *anazêteô,* to seek up and down (*ana*), back and forth, to hunt up, to make a thorough search until success comes. Barnabas knew his own limitations and knew where the man of destiny for this crisis was, the man who already had the seal of God upon him. Barnabas brought Saul to Antioch.

26. {*Even for a whole year*} This is probably the year A.D. 44, the year preceding the visit to Jerusalem (Acts 11:30), the year of the famine. {*And that the disciples were called Christians first in Antioch*} The pattern of formation of the word "Christians" gives the meaning as "follower of Messiah" or "belonging to Messiah." The name was evi-dently given to the followers of Christ by the Gentiles to distinguish them from the Jews since they were Greeks, not Grecian Jews.

29. {*Every man according to his ability...*} The sentence is a bit tangled in the Greek from Luke's rush of ideas. Lit. "Of the disciples, as any one was able (or well off), they determined each of them to send relief to the brethren who dwelt in Judea." The worst of the famine came A.D. 45. The warning by Agabus stirred the brethren in Antioch to send the collection on ahead.

30. {*To the elders*} This is the first reference to Christian preachers (cf. Acts 20:17, 28). A Christian elder is the same as a Christian overseer (bishop) as in Titus 1:5, 7.

CHAPTER 12

1. {*About that time*} This is the early part of A.D. 44 since that is the date of Herod's death. {*Herod the king*} This is Herod Agrippa I, grandson of Herod the Great (ruled A.D. 42 to 44), the only Herod to formally reign as king since the death of the grandfather Herod (the Great). Archelaus "reigned" in a more general sense or as a popular title (cf. Matt. 2:22). {*To afflict*} Lit. "to do harm or evil." It had been eight years or more since the persecution over the death of Stephen ceased with the conversion of Saul. But the disciples were not popular in Jerusalem with either Sadducees or Pharisees.

2. {*James, the brother of John*} This "son of thunder," son of Zebedee, was predicted by Jesus to have a bloody death (Mark 10:38; Matt. 20:23). James is the first of the apostles to die and his brother John probably the last.

3. {*Proceeded to seize*} Lit. "he added to seize"; he seized Peter in addition to James. {*The days of unleavened bread...*} This refers to the Passover, a total of eight days of celebration.

4-5. {*To four quaternions of soldiers*} Sixteen total: Two chained to him and two on the outside; four in six hour shifts. Herod took no chances on Peter's escaping (Acts 5:19). A desperate case for Peter, the disciples prayed the more earnestly.

7. {*In the cell*} Lit. "habitation" but refers to the room in the prison. {*He smote Peter on the side*} Lit. "struck the side of Peter" from a sound asleep and yet not rouse the two guards. It was probably between 3 A.M. and 6 A.M., hours when changes in the guards were made.

8. {*Gird thyself*} The girdle was worn round the *chitôn* or undergarment; then he put on his "overcoat." {*Sandals*} This consisted of a sole made of wood or leather covering the bottom of the foot and bound on with thongs (cf. Mark 6:9). It was not a hurried flight.

9. {*Thought he saw a vision*} In distinction, Peter has had a vision before (cf. Acts 10:10), but here the event is objective fact.

10. {*The first and the second ward*} Not the two soldiers in the cell, probably the "first guard" refers to other two soldiers stationed by the door; the "second guard" refers to some other soldiers not part of the sixteen. {*Of its own accord*} This is the Greek word *automatê*, cf. "automatic." It was the first automatic door opener!

11. {*Now I know of a truth...*} There was no more confusion; it was all real. But he was still in peril, the change of guards was at about 6 A.M.

12. {*When he had considered...*} This is the Greek verb *sunoraô*, to see together, to grasp as a whole. Peter's mind worked rapidly and he decided what to do. {*To the house of Mary*} Possibly a widow of good character and of some means, she is the mother of John Mark (the scribe or author of the Gospel of Mark). {*Were gathered together and were praying*} Since this was likely just pre-dawn, the praying apparently had been going on all night with a large number of the disciples there.

13. {*When he knocked at the door of the gate*} He knocked from the gateway or passageway from the door that leads to the house. {*A maid...Rhoda*} That is, a female slave (close to the family) whose name meant "rose."

14. {*For joy*} The maid left Peter standing outside.

15. {*Thou art mad*} Though excited, it was a curious rebuff to the girl from those who had been praying all night for Peter's release. Festus used this same word of Paul (26:24). {*She confidently affirmed*} An old word of vigorous and confident assertion, originally to lean upon. Here only in the NT. The girl stuck to her statement.

16-17. {*Continued knocking*} Now all heard the knocking. {*When they had opened*} The whole group rushed out to the courtyard this time to make sure. Peter told them the wonderful story. {*Unto James and the brethren*} This James refers to the Lord's brother, not an apostle in the technical sense as one of the Twelve, but is called an apostle in the general sense (cf. Gal. 1:19). The leadership of James is here recognized due mainly to his own force of character. {*To another place*} Probably Luke did not know the place, but out of the city; a prudent thing to do.

18. {*No small stir*} Probably all sixteen soldiers were agitated over this remarkable escape. They were responsible for the prisoner with their lives (cf. Acts 16:27; 27:42).

19. {*He examined...that they should be put to death*} After a forensic investigation, they were put to death as ordinary Roman routine and not a proof of special cruelty on the part of Herod Agrippa.

21. {*Upon a set day*} It was the second day of the festival in honor of the Emperor Claudius, possibly his birthday. Josephus also records the following event, and Luke and he supplement each other with no contradiction. {*Arrayed himself in royal apparel*} Other sources report it was a robe of silver tissue. The rays of the sun shone on this brilliant apparel and the vast crowd in the open amphitheater became excited as Herod began to speak.

22. {*Shouted*} The heathen crowd repeated their flattering adulation to gain Herod's favor. {*The voice of a god*} That is, in the pagan sense of emperor worship, not as the Supreme Being. But it was pleasing to Herod Agrippa's vanity.

23. {*Smote him…he was eaten of worms*} Lit. "becoming worm-eaten." (cf. Dan. 4:30). Pride went before a fall. He was struck down in the very zenith of his glory. He accepted the impious flattery instead of giving God the glory. Josephus says that Herod Agrippa lingered for five days and says that the rotting of his flesh produced worms, an item in harmony with the narrative in Luke. Herod was carried out of the theater a dying man and lingered only five days.

CHAPTER 13

1. {*In the church that was there*} "In" is possibly translated "distributed throughout" the church. The church is not merely an "assembly" but now a strong organization. {*Prophets and teachers*} The Greek syntax shows there are three prophets (Barnabas, Simeon, Lucius) and two teachers (Manaen and Saul). Note that Barnabas heads the list and Saul comes last. These are clearly the outstanding men in the great Greek church in Antioch.

2. {*Barnabas and Saul*} (cf. Acts 13:1). Again, Barnabas is named before Saul. Both had been called to ministry long ago, but now this call is to the special campaign among the Gentiles.

3. {*Laid their hands upon them*} This is not ordination to the ministry, but a solemn consecration to the great missionary task to which the Holy Spirit had called them.

4. {*So they…*} Luke again refers to the Holy Spirit as the source of their authority for this campaign rather than the church at Antioch.

5. {*Proclaimed…*} This was Paul's rule of procedure, "to the Jew first" (cf. Rom. 1:16; Acts 13:46; 17:2; 18:4, 19; 19:8). {*As their attendant*}

This is the Greek word *hupêretês,* lit. "under-rower" (*hupo, êretês*) in the trireme. Probably here this term refers to the "minister" (*chazzan*) or assistant in the synagogue (cf. Luke 4:20).

6. {*Unto Paphos*} The new Paphos at the other end of the island, reached by a fine Roman road, some eight miles north of the old Paphos famous for the worship of Venus. {**A *certain sorcerer, a false prophet, a Jew*}** Elymas the sorcerer (or Magian) was probably his professional title (cf. Acts 13:8). These charlatans had great influence with the un-educated (cf. Acts 19:13).

7. {*With the proconsul, Sergius Paulus*} An inscription of this very man has been found naming Paulus as Proconsul. {*A man of under-standing*} He had given up idolatry and was eager to hear Barnabas and Saul.

8. {*Withstood them*} This is the Greek verb *anthistêmi,* to stand against (face to face). He persisted in his opposition and was unwilling to lose his great prize.

9. {*But Saul, who is also called Paul*} As a Jew and a Roman citizen, he had both names all the time: Saul (among Jews); Paul (among Gentiles).

10. {*Thou son of the devil...*} Paul denounces Elymas as one of the class or characteristic (lit. "son") of the Devil (cf. John 8:44), and a trickster. {*The right ways of the Lord*} Prophets and preachers are to make crooked paths straight and to get men to walk in them (cf. Isa. 40:4; 42:16; Luke 3:5).

11. {*Upon thee...not seeing...*} Though the hand of the Lord can be a kind touch, here it is the hostile hand of judgment. Elymas has not humbled himself under the mighty hand of God (1 Pet. 5:6). A judicial infliction, this was external darkness to match willful darkness within.

12. {*Believed*} The Roman proconsul was amazed at the teaching about the Lord. His conversion is not mentioned in other ancient sources and so some question if he was converted since his position required official patronage of idolatrous worship. Maybe he was not publicly baptized (cf. Cornelius Acts 10:47); even if he was, I believe he could have been both a Roman official and a Christian.

13. {*Paul and his company*} Now Paul ranks first, though before second (Acts 9:27; 11:30; 13:1). {*Departed from them*} This is Mark (cf. Acts 15:39) also called John Mark (cf. 12:12, 25). Why did he leave? Possible reasons are: dislike of the change in leadership; a change in plans; the perils of this route taken (cf. 2 Cor. 11:26); malaria; personal dislike of Paul's aggressive attitude toward the heathen.

14. {*Sat down*} That is, they took their seats as visiting Jews, possibly in the seats of the rabbis. Whether they expected to be called on or not, they were given the opportunity as prominent visitors.

15. {*After the reading of the law and the prophets*} This refers to reading from different sections of the Hebrew Scriptures (OT). The reading was followed by the sermon (cf. Luke 4:16). It was the duty of the rulers of the synagogue to select the readers and the speakers for the service (Mark 5:22, 35-38; Luke 8:49; 13:14; Acts 13:15; 18:8, 17). Any rabbi or distinguished stranger could be called on to speak.

16. {*Paul stood up*} Paul is the more gifted speaker (Acts 14:12), so that he responds to the courteous invitation of the rulers. {*Beckoning*} (cf. Acts 12:17). Speaking Greek, Paul's sermon may have been based on the just completed readings of the Law and Prophets.

17. {*With a high arm*} Lit. "high forearm" as a vivid picture of great power (cf. Exod. 6:1, 6; Deut. 5:15; Ps. 136:12).

19-20. {*For about four hundred and fifty years*} (cf. 1 Kgs. 6:1). This number runs from the birth of Isaac to the actual conquest of Canaan and does not cover the period of the Judges (cf. Acts 7:6). Then the time of the Judges began (cf. Judg. 2:16). {*Until Samuel the prophet*} He was the last of the judges, first of the prophets, God's selector of the first king.

21. {*They asked...*} They were tired of a theocracy (cf. 1 Sam. 8:5; 10:1). Paul was of Saul's tribe, and speaks it with proper pride.

22. {*A man after my heart*} (cf. Ps. 89:20, 21; 1 Sam. 13:14). David was a man who did God's will in spite of the gross sin of which he repented (Ps. 51:1).

23. {*Of this man's seed*} "This man" is emphatic in the Greek. {*A Saviour Jesus*} This title at the end of the sentence is in contrast with "this man" (David) at the beginning. Paul goes no further than David because he suggests to him Jesus, descendant in the flesh from David.

24. {*When John had first preached*} (cf. Mal. 3:1 and Luke 7:27). Lit. "John heralding beforehand," as a herald before the king [Jesus] (cf. Luke 3:3).

25. {*As John was fulfilling his course*} "Course" is the Greek word *dromos* (the course) of his own race (Acts 20:24; 2 Tim. 4:7).

26. {*To us*} That is, both Jews and Gentiles, both classes in Paul's audience. {*The word of this salvation*} That is, the message of Jesus as Savior (v. 23), long ago promised and now come to us as Savior.

27. {*Because they knew him not*} This ignorance mitigated the degree of their guilt, but it did not remove it, for it was willing ignorance and prejudice.

28. {*Though they found no cause of death*} Though Jesus was charged with blasphemy, they could not prove it (Matt. 26:65; 27:24; Luke 23:22).

30. {*But God raised him from the dead*} This crucial fact Paul puts sharply as he always did.

31. {*Was seen for many days*} He was seen for forty days by the very men and women who knew him best and who could not be easily deceived about the reality of his resurrection. (1 Cor. 15:1-8 and Acts 1:3).

32. {*We bring you good tidings of the promise...*} This verse is the heart of Paul's message on this occasion.

34. {*The holy and sure blessings of David*} (cf. 2 Sam. 7:13). The next verse tells what the "holy things" are.

35. {*Thou wilt not give thy holy one to see corruption*} (cf. Ps. 16:10). Jesus did not see corruption in his body; he was resurrected.

36. {*Was laid*} "Laid with his fathers" is a figure for death, which probably arose from the custom of burying families together (Gen. 15:15; Judg. 2:10).

38. {*Through this man...*} As with Peter at Pentecost, this is the glorious keynote of Paul's message (cf. 2:38; 5:31; 10:43 and 26:18).

39. {*And by him every one that believeth is justified from all things, from which ye could not be justified by the law of Moses*} This verse is the argument of the Epistle to Galatians and Romans in a sentence. One's relation to Mosaic law fails to bring the kind of righteousness that God demands. Real righteousness will come (Rom. 6:1-8:39) to those whom God treats as righteous (Rom. 3:1-5:21) though both Gentile and Jew fall short without Christ (Rom. 1:1-3:31). This is the doctrine of grace that will prove a stumbling block to both the Jews and the Greeks.

41. {*If one declare it unto you*} Paul hurled a thunderbolt at the close.

42. {*They besought...the next Sabbath*} Here both Jews and Gentiles asked for the repetition of the sermon.

43. {*Of the devout proselytes*} Lit. "God-fearing proselytes" which here probably refers to proselytes of the gate who had not yet become circumcised. Jews and proselytes followed Paul and Barnabas to hear more without waiting until the next Sabbath.

44. {*The whole city*} The whole city could hardly all gather in the synagogue. Perhaps Paul spoke in the synagogue and Barnabas to the overflow outside (see v. 46).

45. {*With jealousy*} Probably many of the Jews that were then favorably disposed to Paul's message had reacted against him under the influence of the rabbis during the week. These rabbis boiled with jealousy when they saw the crowds gathered to hear Paul and Barnabas.

46. {*Spake out boldly*} Both Paul and Barnabas accepted the challenge of the rabbis. They would leave their synagogue, but not without a word of explanation. {*It was necessary to you first*} This position Paul as the apostle to the Gentiles will always hold, the Jew first in privilege and penalty (Rom. 1:16; 2:9, 10). {*Lo, we turn to the Gentiles*} It is a dramatic moment as Paul and Barnabas turn from the Jews to the Gentiles, a prophecy of the future history of Christianity (cf. Rom. 9:1-11:36).

47. {*For so hath the Lord commanded us*} (cf. Isa. 49:6 and Luke 2:32). Paul is carrying out the will of God in turning to the Gentiles. He will still appeal to the Jews elsewhere as they allow him to do so, but not here.

48. {*As the Gentiles heard this they were glad*} It was the gospel of grace and liberty from legalism that Paul had proclaimed (cf. Gal. 4:13?). {*As many as were ordained to eternal life*} Here the Jews had voluntarily rejected the word of God. On the other side were those Gentiles who gladly accepted what the Jews had rejected. Paul had shown that God's plan extended to and included Gentiles. Certainly the Spirit of God moves upon the human heart to which some respond, as here, while others push him away.

49. {*Was spread abroad...*} This would seem to indicate a stay of some months with active work among the Gentiles that bore rich fruit.

50. {*Urged on...*} (cf. 2 Tim. 3:11 and 2 Cor. 11:25-26). The Jews were apparently not numerous in this city as they had only one synagogue, but they had influence with people of prominence, like the female proselytes of high station. Women often had high positions in this culture. {*The chief men of the city*} The rabbis were shrewd enough to reach these men (not proselytes) through the women of distinction who were proselytes. Probably the Jews succeeded in making the Roman officials look on Paul and Barnabas as disturbers of the peace.

51. {*But they shook off the dust of their feet against them*} It is a dramatic gesture that forbids further interaction. It was a protest against the injustice which cast them out. The sandal was taken off and the dust shaken out as a symbolic token that the very soil of the country was defiling.

52. {*And the disciples...*} That is, the Gentile Christians in Antioch in Pisidia. Persecution had precisely the opposite effect to the intention of the Jews. These Gentile Christians were now being filled with joy and the Holy Spirit (cf. Acts 4:31; 8:4; 9:31; 12:24).

CHAPTER 14

1. {*So spake that...*} The actual result was the belief of the hearers; it was a tremendous first meeting.

2. {*That were disobedient*} Here the meaning is probably the Jews that disbelieved, rather than that disobeyed. {*Made them evil affected*} An old verb from *kakos*, to do evil, to ill-treat, then in later Greek as here, to embitter, to exasperate.

3. {*Long time therefore*} After the persecution and vindication there was a season of great opportunity which Paul and Barnabas used to the full, speaking boldly (cf. Acts 13:46).

4. {*But the multitude of the city was divided*} This division was within the Gentile populace. The Jewish leaders made some impression on the Gentiles as at Antioch in Pisidia and later at Thessalonica (cf. Acts 17:4).

5. {*An onset*} This is the Greek word *hormê*, a rush or impulse. It probably denotes not an actual attack so much as the open start, the cooperation of both Jews and Gentiles (the disaffected portion). {*With their rulers*} This refers to the rulers of the Jewish synagogue (cf. Acts 13:27). {*To stone*} (cf. Acts 7:58 and Matt. 21:35). This detail shows the Jews were in the lead and followed by the Gentile rabble.

6. {*Fled*} Paul and Barnabas had no idea of remaining to be stoned (lynched) by this mob. They were following the directions of the Lord Jesus given to the Twelve on their special tour of Galilee (Matt. 10:23).

8. {*At Lystra*} Here apparently was no synagogue nor many Jews. So they had open-air preaching and language barriers. Paul could heal like Peter could heal, even one crippled (lit. "impotent") from birth (cf. Acts 3:1-11).

9. {*Heard*} This was either at the gate or in the market place (cf. Acts 17:17) Paul was preaching to such as would listen or could understand his Greek. {*To be made whole*} This is the Greek word *sôzô*, same word as "to be saved," but here clearly it means to be made whole or well as in Luke 7:50 (cf. Acts 3:16; 4:10).

10. {*Upright*} Lit. "rise up straight." Paul spoke in a loud voice so that all could hear. {*He leaped up and walked*} The picture in Greek is that of the man leaping up with a single bound and starting to walk.

11. {*In the speech of Lycaonia*} Paul was speaking in Greek, of course, but the excitement of the crowd over the miracle made them cry out that Paul and Barnabas were gods. But Paul and Barnabas did not understand how the people of Lystra viewed them.

12. {*Barnabas, Jupiter*} Barnabas called Jupiter (Zeus) because he was the older and the more imposing in appearance. {*And Paul, Mercury*} Paul was called Mercury (Hermes), because he was the messenger of the gods, and the spokesman of Jupiter.

13-14. {*Oxen and garlands*} Probably garlands were put on the oxen before they were slain. It was common to sacrifice bullocks to Jupiter and Mercury. What was unclear before by speaking Lycaonian (v. 11) is now plain by such elaborate preparation. The tearing of the clothes was a signal that an act of sacrilege was about to be committed.

15. {*We also are men of like passions with you*} Their conduct was more serious than the obeisance of Cornelius to Peter (Acts 10:25). They are evangelists, not gods. Here Paul alters his message a little to reach the Gentile crowds, in contrast to his approach in the Jewish crowds (cf. Acts 17:21-32; Rom. 1:18-23). {*Unto the living God*} A live God and not a dead statue (cf. 2 Cor. 6:16; Rom. 9:26, also 1 Thess. 1:9).

17-18. {*In that he did good*} Lit. "doing good." This witness to God (his doing good, giving rains and fruitful seasons, filling your hearts with food and gladness) they could receive without the help of the OT revelation (Rom. 1:20). {*Rain...crops*} Jupiter was the god of rain. Mercury the god of dispensing food. Paul sees the living God behind the drama of the physical world.

19-20. {*But there came thither Jews from Antioch and Iconium*}
They had driven them out of Antioch and out of Iconium and now
appear at Lystra at an opportune moment for their work. {*They stoned
Paul*} (cf. 2 Cor. 11:25). They stoned Paul as the chief speaker (Hermes).
{*Supposing that he were dead*} Note that Luke does not say that Paul
was actually dead. The would-be murderers left and a group of disciples gathered round to see if Paul was dead or alive and, if dead, to
bury him. {*With Barnabas*} That is with the assistance of Barnabas,
shaken and bruised as was Paul.

21. {*They returned to Lystra and to Iconium, and to Antioch*} Derbe
was the frontier city of the Roman empire. The quickest way to return
to Antioch in Syria would have been by the Cilician Gates or by the
pass over the Taurus Mountains by which Paul and Silas will come to
Derbe in the second tour (Acts 15:41—16:1), but this route is difficult
to travel in winter.

22. {*To continue in the faith...we must...*} These recent converts
from heathenism greatly needed encouragement if they were to hold
out. Paul warned these new converts in this heathen environment of
the many tribulations through which they must enter the Kingdom of
God (cf. Acts 20:20 also John 16:33).

23. {*And when they had appointed for them elders in every church*}
They needed also some form of organization, though there were already churches. Most likely, the people selected the elders in each
church. Teaching was a normal function of these leaders (1 Tim. 3:2;
Titus 1:9; 1 Cor. 12:28, 30; Eph. 4:11). {*Had prayed with fasting*} It
was a serious matter, so it was done in a public meeting with prayer
and fasting.

25. {*When they had spoken the word in Perga*} Apparently this is the
first time preaching here. We do not know why they did not revisit
Cyprus, perhaps because no permanent Gentile churches were founded
there.

26. {*They sailed away to Antioch*} They had been gone some eighteen months. {*They had been committed*} The grace of God had been
with them. They had fulfilled the work to which they had been set
apart by the Holy Spirit.

27. {*Gathered the church together*} It was the first missionary meeting in history. It was not hard to get the church together when the
news spread that Paul and Barnabas had returned. {*He had opened a*

door of faith unto the Gentiles} This work in Galatia gained a large place in Paul's heart (Gal. 4:14).

28. {*And they tarried no little time*} It was a happy time of fellowship. A new corner has been turned in the history of Christianity. There is a new center of Christian activity, a Gentile center. What will Jerusalem think of the new developments at Antioch?

CHAPTER 15

1. {*And certain men came down from Judea*} The echoes of jubilation in Antioch certainly reached Jerusalem. The Judaizers in Jerusalem were obscurantists who were unable and unwilling to receive new light from the Lord on a matter that involved their racial and social prejudices. They argued that Christ had not repealed circumcision as a requirement for salvation. {*Except ye be circumcised after the custom of Moses, ye cannot be saved*} This doctrine of required circumcision denied the efficacy of the work of Christ.

2. {*When Paul and Barnabas had no small dissension and questioning with them*} Paul and Barnabas were not willing to see this Gentile church treated as heretics by these self-appointed regulators of Christian orthodoxy from Jerusalem. {*Certain others of them*} Lit. "certain others of them." Certainly included is Titus, possibly Luke himself (Gal. 2:1, 3).

3. {*They therefore...being brought on their way by the church*} "Sent" is the Greek verb *propempô,* to send forward under escort as a mark of honor (cf. Acts 20:38; 21:5; 3 John 6). They were given a grand send-off by the church in Antioch.

4. {*Were received*} This refers to a public reception for Paul and Barnabas provided by the whole church (cf. Gal. 2:2).

5. {*But there rose up...*} Though believers in Christ, this group evidently still held to the Pharisaic narrowness shown in the attack on Peter (Acts 11:2). At any rate they have brought up the issue in open meeting at the height of the jubilation. It then adjourned.

6. {*Were gathered together...*} It is here that the private conference of which Paul speaks in Galatians 2:1-10 took place. It was Paul's chance to see the leaders in Jerusalem (Peter, James, and John) and he won them over to his view of Gentile liberty from the Mosaic law so that the next public conference (Acts 15:6-29) ratified the views of Paul, Barnabas, Peter, James, and John.

7. {*When there had been much questioning*} Evidently the Judaizers were given full opportunity to air their grievances and objections. {*Peter rose up*} He was the usual spokesman for the apostles and his activities in Jerusalem were well-known. In particular his experience at Caesarea (Acts 10:24-48) had caused trouble here in Jerusalem from this very same party of the circumcision (Acts 11:1-18). It was fitting for him to speak.

8-9. {*Giving them the Holy Spirit*} This was the Lord's doing. In the matter of faith and conversion God treated Jews and heathen alike.

10. {*A yoke upon the neck*} This is an image of bondage (cf. Gal. 5:1). Standing boldly with Paul and Barnabas, Peter speaks here as the spiritual emancipator.

11. {*That we shall be saved...*} This thoroughly Pauline note shows that whatever hopes the Judaizers had about Peter were false. His doctrine of grace is as clear as a bell.

12. {*Rehearsing...*} Paul gives the facts about their mission work, facts more eloquent than argument.

13. {*After they had held their peace*} Lit. "after the becoming silent as to them." {*James answered*} It was expected that James, as President of the Conference, would speak last. But he wisely waited to give every one an opportunity to speak. This half brother of the Lord Jesus (also known as James the Just) was asked to preside likely because of his gifts and character.

14. {*Hearken unto me*} The Judaizers had doubtless counted on him as a champion of their view and did later wrongfully make use of his name against Peter at Antioch (Gal. 2:12). {*First*} (cf. Acts 15:7). James notes, as Peter did, that this experience of Barnabas and Paul is not the beginning of work among the Gentiles. {*To take from the Gentiles a people for his name*} Lit. "for his name" referring to the God of Israel. But such a claim of God's purpose called for proof from Scripture to convince Jews (cf. Gal. 3:1-29; Rom. 9:1—11:36).

15. {*To this agree*} This is the Greek verb *sumphôneô,* voice together with, symphony with, harmonize with.

17. {*That the residue of men may seek after the Lord*} The main point of the quotation is that the Gentiles are referred to. {*Upon whom call my call*} This is a Jewish way of speaking of "worshipers of God."

18. {*From the beginning of the world*} (cf. Isa. 45:21). God has an Israel beyond the Jewish race, whom he will make his true "Israel" and so there is no occasion for surprise in the story of God's dealings with the Gentiles as told by Barnabas and Paul (cf. Rom. 16:25; Eph. 3:9).

19. {*Wherefore...my judgment is*} James sums up the case as President of the Conference in a masterly fashion and with that consummate wisdom.

20. {*But that we write unto them...that they abstain from*} James agrees with Peter, Paul, and Barnabas that though ceremonial law is not in effect, still the moral code applies to all such as idolatry, fornication, murder (lit. "blood"). This solution of James is not a compromise, though there is a wise concession to Jewish feeling.

21. {*For Moses...*} A reason why these four necessary things (v. 28) are named. In every city are synagogues where rabbis proclaim these matters. Hence the Gentile Christians would be giving constant offense to neglect them.

22. {*Then it seemed good...with the whole church*} Apparently a vote was taken which was unanimous, the Judaizers probably not voting. The apostles and the elders probably all vocally expressed their position.

23. {*And they wrote*} This committee of four (Judas, Silas, Barnabas, Paul) carried the letter which embodied the decision of the Conference.

24-25. {*Certain which went from us...*} The phrasing is a direct blow at the Judaizers, put in delicate language as if only at Antioch (Acts 15:1), and not also in Jerusalem in open meeting (Acts 15:5). The whole verse is a flat disclaimer of the whole conduct of the Judaizers in Antioch and in Jerusalem, a complete repudiation of their effort to impose the Mosaic ceremonial law upon the Gentile Christians.

26. {*Have hazarded their lives*} Lit. "to hand over to another their lives." The sufferings of Paul and Barnabas in Pisidia and Lycaonia were plainly well-known.

27. {*Who themselves also shall tell you the same things by word of mouth*} Lit. "they themselves also by speech announcing the same things." Judas and Silas are specifically endorsed as bearers of the epistle who will also verbally confirm the contents of the letter.

28. {*To the Holy Spirit and to us*} Here is a definite claim that the church in this action had the guidance of the Holy Spirit (cf. John 16:13).

29. {*Than these necessary things...*} See verses 20-21. It was such a concession as any converted Gentile would be glad to make even if "things strangled" be included. This "necessity" was not a matter of salvation but only for fellowship between Jews and Gentiles. {*It shall be well with you*} The peace and concord in the fellowship of Jews and Gentiles will justify any slight concession on the part of the Gentiles.

30. {*The multitude*} This refers to a public meeting of the church as in verses 1-3.

31. {*When they had read it...they rejoiced*} This is a public reading. They burst into exultant joy. To them it was not a weak compromise, but a glorious victory of Gentile liberty.

35. {*Tarried...with many others also*} This was a time of general revival and naturally so after the victory at Jerusalem. The Galatians Epistle may fill in a sad detail here (cf. Gal. 2:11-21). The Judiazers would see the misconduct of Peter as an opening.

36. {*Let us return now and visit the brethren*} Paul is anxious to go back to the fields, city by city. {*How they fare*} Lit. "how they have it." New converts in pagan lands have a precarious life.

37. {*Barnabas...was minded to take with them*} Mark had gone before (cf. Acts 12:25). It was a simple, pointed proposal.

38. {*But Paul thought not good to take with them...*} The Greek tense shows Paul felt an ongoing lively realization of the problem of having a quitter on his hands. At Perga Mark had faced the same task that Paul and Barnabas did, but he flinched and flickered and quit. Paul declined to repeat the experiment with Mark (cf. Acts 13:13).

39. {*A sharp contention*} This is the Greek word *paroxusmos,* from *paroxunô,* to sharpen (*para, oxus*) as of a blade and of the spirit (Acts 17:16; 1 Cor. 13:5). Barnabas "Son of Encouragement" loses his temper in a dispute over his cousin and Paul uses sharp words toward his benefactor and friend. One's judgment may go with Paul, but one's heart goes with Barnabas. They later continue their relationships and do not hold a grudge (cf. 1 Cor. 9:6; Col. 4:10; 2 Tim. 4:11). {*And Barnabas took Mark with him and sailed away to Cyprus*} From the harbor of Antioch, Barnabas goes to his home. Paul and Barnabas parted in anger and in sorrow.

40. {*Paul chose Silas*} Silas had influence in the church in Jerusalem (v. 22) and was apparently a Roman citizen (Acts 16:37) also. He is the Silas of the epistles (1 Thess. 1:1; 2 Thess. 1:1; 2 Cor. 1:19; 1 Pet. 5:12).

41. {*Went through Syria and Cilicia*} He took the opposite course from the first tour, leaving Cyprus to Barnabas and Mark.

CHAPTER 16

1. {*Timothy*} Apparently a native of Lystra, half Jewish (on his mother's side), he knew the Scriptures (cf. 2 Tim. 1:5; 2 Tim. 3:15). Probably Timothy was about eighteen years of age here, a convert of Paul's former visit a few years before (1 Tim. 1:2) and still young twelve years later (1 Tim. 4:12). Paul loved him devotedly (1 Tim. 1:3; Phil. 2:19).

2. {*Was well reported of* } Timothy was already known for his gifts and graces for the ministry.

3. {*He took and circumcised him*} Paul had stoutly resisted circumcision in the case of Titus, a pure Greek (Gal. 2:3, 5), because the whole principle of Gentile liberty was at stake. But Timothy was both Jew and Greek and would continually give offense to the Jews with no advantage to the cause of Gentile freedom.

5. {*Churches…increased*} The blessing of God was on the work of Paul, Silas, and Timothy in the form of a continuous revival.

6-7. {*The region of Phrygia and Galatia*} Strictly speaking Derbe and Lystra, though in the provice of Galatia, were no Phrygian, and so Luke would here be not resumptive of the record in verses 1-5; but a reference to the country around Iconium and Antioch in Pisidia in North Galatia is not included. {*And the Spirit of Jesus suffered them not*} That is, the same Spirit who in verse 6 had forbidden going into Asia now closed the door into Bithynia.

8. {*To Troas*} This is the seaport town of the district of Mysia, the place to take ship for Philippi.

9. {*A vision*} This hindrance and call to Macedonia Paul had little dreamed of when he left Antioch. Note how he did not go home at such a rebuff from the Holy Spirit, as most men might have. {*A man of Macedonia*} Some hold this man was Luke with whom Paul had conversed about conditions in Macedonia, conjecturing that Luke's home might be Philippi. {*Help us*} Note the plural "us." It was the cry of Europe for Christ.

10. {*We sought...*} The calling of God compelled them to go. Note the sudden use of the first person plural "we." section of Acts. This sudden use of the plural, dropped in Acts 17:1 when Paul leaves Philippi, and resumed in Acts 20:5 when Paul rejoins Luke in Philippi.

11. {*Setting sail...we made a straight course*} This is the Greek word *euthudromeô*, from *euthudromos*, running a straight course (*euthus, dromos*). It is a nautical term for sailing before the wind.

12. {*To Philippi*} Named after Philip, the father of Alexander the Great, this colony of Rome was situated about a mile east of the small stream, on a militarily strategic plain. It was a city on the Roman highway system, a military outpost and a miniature of Rome itself. Here Paul is face to face with the Roman power and empire in a new sense. Its citizens had the privileges of Roman citizenship. Being a leading city of this district of Macedonia, it was now a city of destiny for the Gospel.

13. {*By a river side*} This is called today little river Gangites (or Gargites) situated today about one mile west of the town. Philippi had few Jews, and evidently no synagogue inside the city. A place of prayer could be either a synagogue (3 Macc. 7:20) or more often an open air enclosure near the sea or a river where there was water for ceremonial washings. You needed ten adult males to constitute a synagogue, but here were gathered only a group of women at the hour of prayer. {*We sat down and spake*} The speaking was likely conversational preaching of an historical and expository character. Note Luke and the rest of the group also spoke, though Paul the main speaker.

14. {*Lydia*} Lydia possibly was a former female slave, now freed. Thyatira was famous for its purple dyes and had a guild of dyers. {*A seller of purple*} Lydia was a female seller of purple fabrics, evidently a woman of some means to carry on such an important enterprise. {*One that worshipped God*} Lydia probably became a Jewish proselyte in Thyatira, though the other women may or may not have been. {*Opened*} Old word, double compound meaning to open up wide or completely like a folding door. {*To give heed*} In a wonderful irony, the first convert in Europe was a woman who was from a province in the very Asia where they had been forbidden to preach (v. 6).

15. {*And when she was baptized...and her household*} There at the same river they prayed at, she and the house members obeyed the ordinance and made public declaration of her faith in Jesus Christ. "Household" can include family and servants: in context these "household members" refer to the other women slaves, servants, or employees of hers at the place of prayer by the river (cf. Euodia and Syntyche and the other women Phil. 4:2, 3). {*And she constrained us*} The Greek makes clear some moral force or hospitable persuasion was required (cf. 1 Sam. 28:23), but Lydia was a convincing woman.

16. {*A spirit of divination*} This was a spirit of *puthôna*. Python was the name given to the serpent that kept guard at Delphi, slain by Apollo, who was called *Puthios Apollo* and the prophetess at Delphi was termed *Pythia*. {*Soothsaying*} Not a "prophet," this is similar to the Greek verb *mainomai,* to be mad, like the howling dervishes of later times. {*Her masters*} Lit. "lords" this refers to joint owners of this poor slave girl who were exploiting her calamity for selfish gain.

18. {*She did...*} The strange conduct gave Paul and the rest an unpleasant prominence in the community. Paul became grieved, annoyed, indignant at the development. Note Paul distinguishes the spirit from the person possessed.

19. {*Laid hold on...dragged...into the marketplace*} The owners of the slave girl grabbed Paul and Silas and dragged them to Roman forum (like our courthouse square) to the leaders.

20. {*Unto the magistrates*} This refers to the civic governor, preferring the Latin name *praetores;* they had the power to punish. {*Being Jews*} The people of Philippi (unlike Antioch Acts 11:26), did not recognize any distinction between Jews and Christians; "Jew" used by the accusers may have had disparaging connotations, subtly encouraging punishment by racial association.

21. {*Customs which it is not lawful for us to receive, or to observe, being Romans*} "Jew" and "Romans" are sharply contrasted. It is love of money that moves these masters far more than zeal for Rome. The magistrates made their judgments on the issues of breach of the peace and the formation of secret sects and organizations, "unlawful customs."

22. {*Rose up together...*} There was no actual attack of the mob, but a sudden and violent uprising of the people, the appeal to race and national prejudice having raised a ferment.

23. {*Many stripes*} Jewish law was forty stripes save one (2 Cor. 11:24). The Roman custom depended on the caprice of the judge and was a terrible ordeal. It was the custom to inflict the stripes on the naked back.

24. {*Into the inner prison*} The Roman public prisons had a vestibule and outer prison and behind this the inner prison, a veritable dungeon with no light or air save what came through the door when open. {*Made their feet fast...in the stocks*} This was a refinement of cruelty and torment, since the cell was safe from escape already. This "stock" refers here to a log or timber with two holes to shackle the feet stretched apart (Job. 33:11).

25. {*About midnight*} (cf. Mark 13:35; Luke 11:5). {*Were praying and singing*} Paul and Silas probably used portions of the Psalms (cf. Luke 1:39, 67; 2:28) with occasional original outbursts of praise. The other prisoners listened to this music and recitation.

26. {*Earthquake*} (cf. Acts 4:31). This event was an answer to prayer, strong enough to raise from sleep. If the prison was excavated from rocks in the hillside, as was often the case, the earthquake would easily have slipped the bars of the doors loose and the chains would have fallen out of the walls.

27. {*Being roused out of sleep...drew his sword...*} The jailor was responsible for the prisoners with his life (cf. Acts 12:19; 27:42). None of the prisoners had escaped probably because they were so panic stricken by the earthquake.

28. {*Do thyself no harm*} The Greek syntax here means "do not *begin* to do harm." {*He called for lights*} The jailer was at the outer door and he wanted lights to see what was inside in the inner prison.

29. {*Trembling for fear...fell down*} Lit. "becoming terrified." Not stumbling, this is an intentional act.

30. {*Brought them out*} He left the other prisoners inside, superstitiously feeling that he had to deal first with these men whom he had evidently heard preach. {*To be saved?*} This salvation he inquires of is more than safety from the earthquake or escaped prisoners; it is the way of salvation (cf. v. 17).

32. {*They spake the word of God*} This refers to a fuller exposition of the way of life to the jailer. {*And was baptized, he and all his, immediately*} This includes the warden, his family, and slaves.

33-34. {*He brought them up...*} The event of washing the parts of the body here is seen in the Greek as a succinct point of time. The jailer washed Paul and Silas, then they washed (baptized) them all, and it was done *at once* apparently in the pool or tank in which he bathed that Paul and Silas found within the walls of the prison, though there are other possibilities of the details of the scene.

35. {*The serjeants*} This refers to the ones carrying the rods or sticks that prisoners were beaten with, officers of the "court."

37-39. {*Unto them*} To punish a Roman citizen without due process was a very serious offense. The magistrates did not know, of course, that Paul and Silas were Roman citizens. Paul wanted public acknowledgment that they had wronged and mistreated Paul and Silas. {*Themselves*} It was a bitter pill to the proud *praetors*. But they became frightened for their own lives when they saw what they had done to Roman citizens.

40. {*Into the house of Lydia*} The four missionaries were guests of Lydia (cf. v. 15) and probably the church now met in her home.

CHAPTER 17

1. {*When they had passed through...Amphipolis...Apollonia*} They took the Egnatian Way, one of the great Roman roads over 500 miles long on the Adriatic Sea. The two cities are a long day's walk apart, about 32 miles. Paul and Silas may have spent only a night here or longer. {*To Thessalonica*} Originally called Therma, this was at this time a great commercial city. The Jews were not very numerous in this town. It was a strategic center for the spread of the gospel (cf. 1 Thess. 1:8).

2. {*As his custom was*} Paul's habit was to go to the Jewish synagogue to use the Jews and the God-fearers as a springboard for his work among the Gentiles. {*For three Sabbaths*} This probably means the first three Sabbaths when Paul had a free hand in the synagogue. Paul was actually in Thessalonica a much longer period than three weeks. The rest of the time he spoke, of course, outside of the synagogue.

3. {*Opening and alleging*} Lit. "opening [the Scriptures] and setting forth alongside [the doctrine]." Paul was expounding and propounding the Scriptures, all in the midst of heated discussion with the rabbis. {*That it behoved the Christ to suffer*} Paul's major premise was the suffering Messiah according to the Scriptures (cf. Luke 24:25-27, also Isa. 52:13ff.; also Acts 3:18; 26:23). {*To rise again from the dead*} A minor premise to the argument, the actual resurrection of Jesus was also a necessity as Paul says he preached to them (1 Thess. 4:14) and argued always from Scripture (1 Cor. 15:3-4).

4. {*Some of them…*} This refers to a small group of Jews given to Paul and Silas by God's grace. {*And of the devout Greeks a great multitude*} Less under the rabbis control, this refers to a large group of Gentiles. The church here is mainly Gentile (cf. 1 Thess. 1:9; 2:14). {*And of the chief women not a few*} Lit. "And of women the first not a few." This refers to women openly friendly to Paul's message, whether proselytes or Gentiles or Jewish wives of Gentiles.

5. {*Moved with jealousy*} The success of Paul was entirely too great in both places to please the rabbis. {*Certain vile fellows of the rabble…set the city on an uproar*} (cf. Matt. 20:4) The *agora* was a hangout for people with nothing to do. {*Gathering a crowd*} Lit. "making or getting a crowd" probably this mob formed right in the *agora* itself where the rabbis could tell men their duties and pay them in advance.

6. {*They dragged…before the rulers of the city*} (cf. Acts 8:3; 16:19). "Officials" is the Greek word *politarchas*. The use of this word is now proven to show the historical accuracy of Luke in small matters of detail. {*These that have turned the world upside down*} "World" means "inhabited earth" and refers here to the whole of the Roman Empire, hyperbole to be sure (cf. Luke 2:1). It is possible that news had come to Thessalonica of the expulsion of the Jews from Rome by Claudius.

7. {*Whom Jason hath received…these all*} This is Jason's crime and he is the prisoner before the politarchs. {*Contrary…the decrees of Caesar*} This was a charge of treason and was a sure way to get a conviction. {*Saying that there is another king, one Jesus*} Paul preached Jesus as the Messiah in a spiritual kingdom that would not threaten the Roman Empire. But the Jews here turn his language to his hurt as they did with Jesus (cf. 1 Thess. 4:13-5:4; 2 Thess. 2).

8. {*They troubled the multitude and the rulers*} Lit. "they agitated the…." To the people it meant a revolution, to the politarchs a charge of complicity in treason if they let it pass. They had no way to disprove the charge of treason and Paul and Silas were not present.

9. {*When they had taken security*} Probably the demand was made of Jason that he see to it that Paul and Silas leave the city not to return (cf. 1 Thess. 2:17).

10. {*Immediately by night*} Paul and Silas had been in hiding in Thessalonica and were in real danger. Possibly an escort of Gentile converts went with them the 50 miles to Berea on this night journey.

11. {*Bereans...more noble than those...whether these things were so*} They received the message with eagerness. In Thessalonica many of the Jews out of pride and prejudice refused to listen. Here the Jews joyfully welcomed the two Jewish visitors. {*Examining the Scriptures daily*} This is the Greek verb *anakrinô*, to sift up and down, make careful and exact research as in legal processes (cf. Acts 4:9; 12:19) in the Scriptures for themselves. The Bereans were eagerly interested in the new message of Paul and Silas but they wanted to see it for themselves. What a noble attitude.

12. {*Also of the Greek women of honourable estate...*} These were women of rank, and by implication the men were also noble Greeks.

13. {*Stirring up and troubling the multitudes*} That is, shaking the crowds like an earthquake (Acts 4:31) and disturbing like a tornado (Acts 17:8). Success at Thessalonica gave the rabbis confidence and courage. The attack was sharp and swift. A church was established here (cf. Acts 20:4).

14. {*As far as to the sea*} Also one can lit. translate "upon the sea" (cf. Rev 10:2). Paul was grieved to cut short his work in Macedonia, probably not over six months in all. But the work in Macedonia spread widely (1 Thess. 1:7).

16. {*Now while Paul waited for them in Athens...*} (cf. 1 Thess. 3:1, 6 also Acts 18:5; 2 Cor. 11:8). Without these two Paul felt lonely in Athens (cf. 1 Thess. 3:1). Though at this time Athens was not politically significant, the city was still the university seat of the world with all its rich environment and traditions. {*The city full of idols*} Like any stranger, Paul was looking at the sights as he walked around. The city was full of beautiful statues, but it was not mere art, but idolatry and sensualism (Rom. 1:18-32). An ancient traveler in his diary says that Athens had more images than all the rest of Greece put together.

17. {*So he reasoned...*} Again, first to the Jew and God-fearer, then daily in the marketplace for more casual interaction with strangers and street preaching. Philosophers and rhetoricians also met here from time to time.

18. {*And certain also of the Epicurean and Stoic philosophers encountered him*} Stoicism believed in self-mastery and hardness. They had a distinctly selfish and unloving view of life and with a pantheistic philosophy. Epicureanism believed gods were unconcerned with the life of humans, and so some called them "atheists." It denied a future life and claimed pleasure as the chief thing to be gotten out of life. {**What would this babbler say?**} Lit. "seed-picker" or "picker up of seeds" like a bird in the marketplace hopping about after chance seeds. In a contemptuous tone and phrase of supreme ridicule, they were saying Paul was a rhetorician who picked up scraps of wisdom from others. To them Paul was a charlatan or quack. {**He seemeth to be a setter forth of strange gods**} Lit. "gods" is "demons," the Greek word *daimonion*. This is the only time in the NT when it means a deity or divinity whether good or bad (from the Greek religion view). All the other occurrences in the NT this term means demon. Roman law did not allow the introduction of a new religion (*religio illicita*). Paul was walking on thin ice. {**Because he preached Jesus and the resurrection**} These philosophers thought there were two gods, "Jesus" and "Resurrection."

19-20. {**Unto the Areopagus**} Lit. "Hill of Mars" this is an elevated rock area or the court itself which met elsewhere as well. This likely refers to the Court of Areopagus meeting here, and the meeting was for examination concerning his new teaching in this university city whether it was strictly legal or not.

21. {**Some new thing**} Lit. "something newer" than the new, the very latest. The new soon became stale with these frivolous Athenians.

22. {**Stood in the midst of the Areopagus**} The place is either Mars Hill or the Stoa Basilica before the Areopagus Court. Paul does not speak as a man on trial, but as one trying to get a hearing for the gospel of Christ. {**Somewhat superstitious**} This is the Greek word *deisidaimôn*, from *deidô*, to fear, and *daimôn*, deity. It can mean either pious (positive) or superstitious (negative). The Athenians had a tremendous reputation for their devotion to religion.

23. {**To an Unknown God**} If an altar was dedicated to the wrong deity, the Athenians feared the anger of the other gods. Quickly, Paul uses this "unknown god" confession on the part of the Athenians to introduce his message. He is not introducing a new god, for they already worship him, though he is not yet known by the Athenians. So any notion of violation of Roman law is brushed aside.

24-25. {*The God that made the world...and all things therein*} This is the God who is self-sufficient, yet interacting with his creation. This Supreme Personal God is the source of life, breath, and everything. {*Dwelleth not in temples made with hands*} (cf. Acts 7:48). No doubt Paul pointed to the wonderful Parthenon, supposed to be the home of the patron god of Athens.

26. {*And he made of one...*} The human race is a unity, with a common origin and with God as the Creator. This view runs counter to Greek exclusiveness which treated other races as barbarians and to Jewish pride which treated other nations as heathen or pagan. {*Having determined*} Paul here touches God's Providence. His hand appears in the history of all men as well as in that of the Chosen People of Israel.

27. {*That they should seek God...if haply they might feel after him*} That is, not turn away from him as the nations had done (Rom. 1:18-32). They might reach out like the blind groping after God.

28. {*As certain even of your own poets*} This verse quotes Aratus' work in *ta Phainomena* and Cleanthes' work in *Hymn to Zeus*. Paul quotes or alludes to pagan poets occasionally (cf. 1 Cor. 15:32 Menander and Titus 1:12 Epimenides).

29. {*That the Godhead is like*} Strictly "the divine" nature (cf. Rom. 1:20). A more general term, Paul may have used the Greek word *theion* here to get back behind all their notions of various gods to the real nature of God.

30. {*Overlooked*} This is the Greek verb *huperoraô* or *hupereidô,* to see beyond, not to see, to overlook; it is not the notion of condoning. God has all the time objected to the polytheism of the heathen, and now he has made it plain.

31. {*By the man whom he hath ordained*} This refers to Jesus Christ (cf. Matt. 25:1). Even here Paul is giving the simple gospel and not trying to philosophize. {*In that he hath raised him from the dead*} Lit. "having raised him from the dead" (cf. v. 18). This is the heart of his message, strange to the ears of his audience.

32. {*The resurrection of the dead*} The Greeks believed that the souls of men lived on, but they had no conception of resurrection of the body. They had listened with respect until Paul spoke of the actual resurrection. Now some mocked, others were polite.

34. {*Clave unto him and believed*} No sermon is a failure which leads a group of people to believe in Jesus Christ. {*Dionysius the Areopagite*} He was one of twelve judges of the Court of the Areopagus. That of itself was no small victory. {*A woman named Damaris*} This is an aristocratic woman, but her education is unknown. The sermon in Athens was not a failure, but it was not Paul's largest success either.

CHAPTER 18

1. {*To Corinth*} Fifty miles north of Athens, this is the restored city "new Corinth." It was a boom town, chief commercial city of Greece, and Roman colony, now the capital of the province of Achaia. It had a cosmopolitan population. In the "old Corinth" "to corinthianize" was a Greek verb that meant immorality. What could he expect in licentious Corinth?

2. {*He found*} But we do not know how Paul found Aquila. Possibly since the Jewish guild always kept together whether in street or synagogue so that by this bond they probably met. {*Aquila...with his wife Priscilla*} (cf. Rom. 16:3; 1 Cor. 16:19). Aquila may have been a freedman like many Jews in Rome. Her name comes before his in Acts 18:26; Romans 16:3; 2 Timothy 4:9.

3. {*Because he was of the same trade*} They made portable tents of leather or of cloth of goat's hair. So Paul lived in this home with this noble man and his wife, all the more congenial if already Christians which they soon became at any rate. They worked as partners in the common trade.

5. {*Was constrained by the word*} Paul held himself together or completely to the preaching instead of just on Sabbaths in the synagogue (v. 4). He was now also assisted by Silas and Timothy (2 Cor. 1:19). {*Testifying to the Jews that Jesus was the Christ*} Perhaps daily now in the synagogue he spoke to the Jews who came. The message was 'Jesus is the Messiah.'

6. {*From henceforth...to the Gentiles*} Paul's fresh activity roused the rabbis to opposition as it had before elsewhere. So he dramatically shook out his clothing as a very exasperating gesture. Now he will devote himself to the Gentiles, though Jews will be converted there also.

8. {*Crispus*} With a Latin name, he was Jew and ruler of the synagogue (cf. Acts 13:15) Paul baptized him (1 Cor. 1:14) himself, perhaps because of his prominence. {*Hearing believed and were baptized*} The Greek tense shows it was a continual revival after Silas and Timothy came and a great church was gathered here during the nearly two years that Paul labored in Corinth.

9. {*Be not afraid, but speak, and hold not thy peace*} Lit. "stop being afraid, but go on speaking and do not become silent." With signs of a gathering storm, Paul had doubts and so came the vision.

11. {*A year and six months*} He was in Corinth probably a couple of years in all. His work extended beyond the city (2 Cor. 11:10) and there was a church in Cenchreae (Rom. 16:1).

12. {*When Gallio was proconsul of Achaia*} Luke alone among writers says that Gallio was proconsul, but Seneca speaks of his being in Achaia where he caught fever, a corroboration of Luke. But now an inscription from the *Hagios Elias* quarries near Delphi (a letter of Claudius to Delphi) has been found which definitely names Gallio as proconsul of Achaia; this inscription would definitely fix the time of Paul in Corinth as A.D. 50 and 51 (or 51 and 52). {*Before the judgment seat*} The proconsul was sitting in the basilica in the forum or *agora*. So for the second time Paul faces a Roman proconsul (Sergius Paulus, Acts 13:7) though under very different circumstances.

13. {*Contrary to the law*} They bring the same charge here that the owners of the slave-girl brought in Philippi (Acts 16:21). Perhaps they fear to go too far with Gallio, for they are dealing with a Roman proconsul, not with the politarchs of Thessalonica.

14. {*When Paul was about to open his mouth*} Before Paul could speak, Gallio cut in and ended the whole matter. According to their own statement Paul needed no defense. The Greek condition ("if") shows the Jews had no case against Paul in a Roman court.

15. {*Questions...and your own law*} Since the Jews had a parcel of questions related to words (in contrast to facts), it was a matter of Jewish, not Roman, law. Gallio refused to allow a religious question to be brought before a Roman civil court. This decision opened the door for Paul's preaching all over the Roman Empire.

16. {*He drave them...*} The Jews were stunned by this sudden blow from the mild proconsul and wanted to linger to argue the case further, but they had to go.

17. {*They all laid hold on Sosthenes...beat him*} The beating did Sosthenes good for he too finally became a Christian (1 Cor. 1:1), a coworker with Paul whom he had sought to persecute. Gallio looked the other way with a blind eye while Sosthenes got the beating which he richly deserved. That was a small detail for the police court, not for the proconsul's concern.

19. {*To Ephesus*} On the Cayster river, it was the capital of the Province of Asia, the home of the worship of Artemis with a temple.

22. {*He went up and saluted the church*} Not Caesarea, this likely refers to going to the church in Jerusalem, which is literally "up." It was the fourth of his five visits (Acts 9:26; 11:30; 15:4; 18:22; 21:17). Paul had friends in Jerusalem now.

23. {*He departed*} Thus simply and alone Paul began the third mission tour without a Barnabas or a Silas. {*Went through...the region of Galatia and Phrygia*} (cf. Acts 16:6). It is apparently A.D. 52 when Paul set out on this tour.

24. {*Apollos*} With a great university and library in Alexandria, Apollos was undoubtedly both learned (mighty in the Scriptures) and eloquent.

25. {*A learned man...mighty in the Scriptures*} The doctrines about the Lord echoed in his mind from the repetitions of it, and he boiled hot with zeal for the Lord. {*Only the baptism of John*} Apollos knew only what the Baptist knew when he died, but John had preached the coming of the Messiah, had baptized him, had identified him as the Son of God, had proclaimed the baptism of the Holy Spirit, but had not seen the Cross, the Resurrection of Jesus, or the great Day of Pentecost.

26. {*Expounded...more carefully...*} Instead of abusing the young and brilliant preacher for his ignorance they (particularly Priscilla) gave him the fuller story of the life and work of Jesus and of the apostolic period to fill up the gaps in his knowledge.

27. {*Encouraged him*} This is the Greek verb *protrepô*, to urge forward, to push on. Priscilla and Aquila were well known in Corinth and their approval would carry weight, hence the letter. But they did not urge Apollos to stay longer in Ephesus.

28. {*Powerfully*} Adverb from *eutonos* (*eu*, well, *teinô*, to stretch), well-strung, at full stretch. {*Confuted*} To confute with rivalry in a contest.

Apollos did not convince these rabbis, but he had the last word. {***Publicly***} And it was in open meeting where all could see the victory of Apollos who was mighty in Scriptures while the rabbis were focused on oral tradition (Mark 7:8-12). {***That Jesus was the Christ***} He is in Corinth building on the foundation laid so well by Paul (1 Cor. 3:4-17).

CHAPTER 19

1. {***Paul...having passed through the upper country***} This refers to the highlands and means that Paul did not travel the usual Roman road west by Colosse. Instead he took the more direct road through the Cayster Valley to Ephesus in the Roman province of Asia minor. {***To Ephesus***} Here was the power of Rome and the splendor of Greek culture and the full tide of superstition and magic. The Temple of Artemis was one of the seven wonders of the world.

2-4. {***Did ye receive the Holy Spirit when ye believed?***} Apparently Paul was suspicious of the looks or conduct of these professed disciples. They had been dipped in baptism, but they had not grasped the significance of the ordinance. Note that this is the last mention of John the Baptist in the NT.

5. {***The name of the Lord Jesus***} This rebaptizing is unique in that no other examples of a second baptism are in the NT. The first time these people did not really know why or what they did. So this second baptism was really their first with proper understanding of the gospel.

6. {***They spake with tongues...prophesied***} Greek tense translates, "they *began* to with tongues" (cf. Acts 2:4; 10:46). The speaking with tongues and prophesying was external and indubitable proof that the Holy Spirit had come on these twelve.

8. {***Spake boldly...persuading***} Nowhere else had Paul apparently been able to speak so long in the synagogue without interruption unless it was so at Corinth (cf. Acts 18:30).

9. {***Speaking evil of the Way***} This is the Greek verb *kakologeô*, from *kakologos* (speaker of evil) for the old *kakôs legô* (cf. Mark 7:10; 9:39; Matt. 15:4). Paul now made a separate church as he had done at Thessalonica and Corinth. {***In the school of Tyrannus***} It was probably a public building or lecture hall with this name whether hired by Paul or loaned to him. Here Paul had great freedom and a great hearing.

10. {*For two years*} (cf. Acts 20:31). Paul said to the Ephesian elders at Miletus that he labored with them for the space of "three years." Two years in the lecture hall, and several months in the synagogue (v. 8), and then Paul may have preached thereafter in the house of Aquila and Priscilla for some months (v. 22), and so the two figures would be in general agreement. {*So that all they which dwelt in Asia heard*} Apparently Paul remained in Ephesus, but the gospel spread all over the province even to the Lycus Valley including the rest of the seven churches of Revelations 1:11; 2:1; 3:1.

11-13. {*Special miracles*} Lit. "powers not the ones that happen by chance," a figurative understatement. Here in Ephesus exorcists and other magicians had built an enormous vogue of a false spiritualism and Paul faces unseen forces of evil. His tremendous success led some people to superstitious practices thinking that there was power in Paul's person: personal articles (handkerchiefs) and linen work aprons became vehicles of the wonders of God. There is no power in superstition or in magic, but in God.

14. {*Seven sons of Sceva*} This bit of information shows how Judaism had fared poorly in this superstitious city. Did they imagine there was special power in the number seven?

15-17. {*Jesus I know...and Paul*} The Greek uses two different words for know here. "Jesus I *recognize* and Paul I am *acquainted with.*" {*Naked...wounded*} This is probably referring to torn garments and trauma from a beating. Jesus was held in high honor after this event.

18. {*Came...confessing*} The black arts were now laid bare in their real character. Even some of the believers were secretly under the spell of these false spiritualists. Judgment was beginning at the house of God.

19-20. {*Not a few of them that practised curious arts*} That is, a considerable number of the exorcists who knew they were frauds were led to renounce their evil practices. {*Burned them in the sight of all*} The scrolls here burned were just like the Magic Papyri now recovered from Egypt. These Magical Papyri were worn as amulets or charms. The Greek verb *katakaiô*, has a focus of complete consumption of the scrolls. {*Fifty thousand pieces of silver*} Lit. "five units of ten thousand silver" This probably refers to the Greek *drachmae* or the Latin *denarius*, reckoned at about 50,000 days' wages of a common laborer.

21. {*Purposed in the spirit...I must also see Rome*} A new stage in Paul's career begins here, a new division of the Acts which begins with

Rome in the horizon of Paul's plans and the book closes with Paul in Rome. Paul's great work in Asia had stirred afresh in him the desire to do his part for Rome (cf. Acts 23:11).

22. {*He himself stayed in Asia for a while*} The reason for Paul's delay is given elsewhere (cf. 1 Cor. 16:8). May was the month of the festival of Artemis when great multitudes would come to Ephesus, a time of opportunity to sell religious crafts.

23. {*Concerning the Way*} (cf. Acts 9:2; 19:9; 24:22). He would fight the figurative wild beasts in Ephesus (cf. 1 Cor. 15:32), referring to the violent opponents of Christ in Ephesus.

24. {*Demetrius, a silversmith*} Demetrius probably organized a guild and provided the capital for the enterprise of crafting shrines. {*Shrines*} These small models of the temple with the statue of Artemis inside would be set up in the houses or even worn as amulets. The real temple was considered one of the seven wonders of the world. Artemis was worshipped as the goddess of fertility, a figure with many breasts.

25-26. {*Whom he gathered together...with the workmen of like occupation*} Apparently all those who made the shrines would be affected, and so they gathered protest against the preaching of Paul, not for a strike. Their livelihood was at stake. Paul had cut the nerve of their business.

27. {*Of the great goddess Artemis*} This goddess was generally known as "the Great." {*Divine majesty*} This is the Greek word *megaleiotês,* which refers elsewhere in the NT to the majesty of the true God and his Son (cf. Luke 9:43; 2 Pet. 1:16). {*All Asia and the world*} Though an exaggeration to be sure, an ancient traveler says that no deity was more widely worshipped.

28. {*Cried out*} In great anger they *kept up* the shouting. Such repetition of a phrase was characteristic of the orgiastic exercises.

29-30. {*They rushed...into the theatre*} The riot poured out like a flood. They made an impetuous dash into the theater, a case of mob psychology. This amphitheater can be sat in today in the ruins of the ancient city of Ephesus. It was the place for large public gatherings. {*Having seized Gaius and Aristarchus men of Macedonia*} They wanted some victims for this "gladiatorial" show. But Paul's fellow believers refused to allow him to go or to be seized, at the risk of their own lives.

31. {*Certain also of the chief officers of Asia...being his friends*} These Asiarchs were ten officers elected by cities in the province to supervise the funds connected with the worship of the emperor, to preside at games and festivals even when the temple services were to gods like Artemis. Some Asiarchs had a high opinion of Paul and were unwilling for him to expose his life to a wild mob during the festival of Artemis.

32. {*For the assembly was in confusion*} It was really not an assembly at all, but a disorganized, illegal mob gathering in a state of confusion. Demetrius who was responsible for the mob preferred now to keep in the background.

33. {*And they brought Alexander out of the crowd*} Evidently some of the Jews grew afraid that the mob would turn on the Jews as well as on the Christians. This may be Alexander the coppersmith who did Paul much evil (2 Tim. 4:14).

34. {*All with one voice cried out...*} Lit. "one voice arose from all crying."

35. {*The town-clerk*} This was the most influential person in Ephesus: who helped draft decrees, managed the city's money, presided over counsels and assemblies, and communicated directly with the proconsul. His very presence as the city's chief officer had a quieting effect. {*Temple-keeper*} It was the boast of Ephesus, and since the temple of Artemis was in this city, not an empty boast. {*And of the image which fell down from Jupiter*} Lit. "fallen from Zeus," who was the lord of the sky or heaven and so a gift from a god.

37. {*Neither robbers of temples*} This would be a sacrilege to rob a temple. Heathen temples often had vast treasures. The ancients felt as strongly about temple-robbing as westerners used to feel about a horse-thief. {*Nor blasphemers of our goddess*} Gaius and Aristarchus as Christians had so conducted themselves that no charge could be placed against them (cf. Col. 4:5). The Ephesians had done a rash thing since these men are innocent.

38-39. {*Have a matter against any one...the courts are open*} The craftsmen were held responsible for the riot, and the clerk appealed to the mob for orderly legal procedure, not mob violence.

40. {*For indeed we are in danger to be accused concerning this day's riot*} They were in danger of being accused of insurrection. There was nothing that concerned the Romans more than a tumultuous meeting.

41. {*Dismissed the assembly*} The town-clerk thus gave a semblance of law and order to the mob by formally dismissing them.

CHAPTER 20

1-2. {*Departed for to go into Macedonia...into Greece*} Lit. "to go proceeding to Macedonia" The setting out in the Greek is a single act and the proceeding as a process. Luke condenses a whole year of Paul's life and work. Paul stayed in Troas (2 Cor. 2:12), met Titus in Macedonia (2 Cor. 2:13-7:16), visited Illyricum (Rom. 15:19), and visited Corinth.

3. {*And a plot was laid against him by the Jews*} Note that this plot is by the Jews, not the Judaizers (cf. 2 Cor. 10-13). These Jews were Paul's old enemies in Corinth who had cherished all these years their defeat at the hands of Gallio (cf. Acts 18:5-17). {*He determined...*} The Jews had heard of Paul's plan to sail for Syria and intended to kill him at the docks in Cenchrea or to push him overboard from the crowded pilgrim ship bound for the Passover. Fortunately Paul learned of their plot and so eluded them by going through Macedonia.

4-5. {*Accompanied him*} A delegation of seven from various churches, possibly starting from Corinth, accompany Paul. Luke is again with Paul now until Rome is reached.

6. {*After the days of unleavened bread*} Though a Christian, Paul observed the Jewish feasts (cf. Gal. 4:10; Col. 2:16). Paul was hoping now to reach Jerusalem by Pentecost.

7. {*Upon the first day of the week*} For the first time here we have services mentioned on the first day of the week (the Day the Lord rose from the dead). {*Discoursed...*} Since he was leaving the next day, he spoke late into the night.

8. {*Many lights*} It was three weeks since a full moon, and the room was filled with the flickering lights and smoking wicks.

9. {*Sat...in the window*} Eutychus (a common slave name) was sitting on the window sill of a latticed window (cf. 2 Kgs. 1:2). The verse describes the gradual process of going into deep sleep. {*Was taken up dead*} The people considered him dead and Luke the physician seems to agree with that view.

11. {*Had broken bread...and eaten*} This probably refers to the Eucharist, though a regular meal is also possible. {*And had talked with them a long while...so he departed*} This second discourse was from midnight until dawn and was probably more informal and conversational. He had much to say before he left.

12. {*They brought the lad alive*} Some cite this as evidence Eutychus had been actually dead, and was now alive. This reading pictures the joyful scene over the lad's restoration as Paul was leaving.

13. {*To the ship*} This may have been a chartered vessel, stopping when and where Paul wished. {*To go by land*} It was about twenty miles over a paved Roman road. It was a beautiful, enjoyable, spring-time walk.

14. {*To Mitylene*} A capital city, it was about thirty miles from Assos, an easy day's sailing.

15. {*We came over against Chios*} An island about eight miles off the mainland, they probably lay off the coast (anchoring) during the night instead of putting into the harbor. {*To Miletus*} Four days later the party is at this city, about twenty-eight miles south of Ephesus.

17. {*To Ephesus*} Ephesus was about thirty miles, a stiff day's journey each way. {*The elders of the church*} Also called "overseers" in verse 28, one of two classes of church officers. It was a noble group of preachers. Here Paul bears his soul to these dear ministers of the church in Ephesus where he had spent three years. It is his farewell discourse (cf. John 13:1-17:26). It is a fitting time and occasion for Paul to take stock of his ministry at the close of the third mission tour.

18. {*From the first day that*} Now it was four years ago he went to Ephesus, spring of A.D. 54 or 55. {*After what manner I was with you*} Paul had devoted himself with consecration to the task in Ephesus.

20. {*How that I shrank not*} This is the Greek verb *hupostellô*, to draw under or back and so here to withdraw oneself, to cower, to shrink, to conceal (cf. Heb. 10:38). {*And from house to house*} The greatest of preachers preached from house to house. He was doing kingdom business all the while as in the house of Aquila and Priscilla (1 Cor. 16:19).

22. {*Bound in the spirit*} "Spirit" here is in contrast to his own "spirit" (cf. v. 23). His own spirit was under the control of the Holy Spirit (Rom. 8:16).

24. {*So that I may accomplish my course*} (cf. 2 Tim. 4:7). He will run the race to the end.

26. {*I am pure from the blood of all men*} Paul was sensitive on this point as in Corinth (Acts 18:6).

28. {*Hath made...bishops*} Paul evidently believed that the Holy Spirit calls and appoints ministers. {*To shepherd*} This is the Greek verb *poimainô*, to feed or tend the flock (*poimnê, poimnion*), to act as shepherd (*poimên*). {*He purchased...with his own blood*} "He" most naturally refers to "God" in the prior phrase, which is in the best manuscripts. Yet Jesus gave his blood.

29. {*Grievous wolves*} (cf. false teachers John 10:12; also Matt. 7:15; Luke 10:3). Does this refer to Judaizers who had given him so much trouble? (cf. 1 Tim. 1:20).

30. {*From among your own selves...*} False philosophy, immorality, asceticism will lead some astray (Col. 2:8, 18; Eph. 4:14; 5:6); antichrists who went out from us (1 John 2:18). {*To draw away...*} The pity of it is that such leaders of dissension can always gain a certain following.

31. {*Wherefore watch ye*} (cf. Mark 13:35). Paul is saying, "Stay awake." Paul *kept up* the warnings with tears (v. 19).

32. {*The word of his grace...which is able to build up*} God works through the word of his grace and so it is able to build up (edify); a favorite Pauline word (1 Cor. 3:10-14; 3:9; 2 Cor. 5:1; Eph. 2:20-22; 2 Tim. 3:15; etc.), and Jas. 1:21.

33. {*No man's silver or gold or apparel*} One of the slanders against Paul was that he was raising this collection, ostensibly for the poor, really for himself (2 Cor. 12:17). Paul did not preach just for money.

34. {*These hands...*} (cf. 1 Cor. 4:12). Paul was not above manual labor. He pointed to his hands with pride as proof that he toiled at his trade of tent-making as at Thessalonica and Corinth for his own needs.

35. {*So labouring ye ought to help...*} (cf. 1 Thess. 5:14). This noble plea to help the weak is the very spirit of Christ (1 Thess. 5:14; 1 Cor. 12:28; Rom. 5:6; 14:1).

36-37. {*He kneeled down...*} (cf. Acts 7:60). Certainly kneeling in prayer is a fitting attitude (cf. Jesus, Luke 22:41), though not the only proper one (Matt. 6:5). Paul apparently prayed aloud.

37-38. {*They all wept sore...kissed him*} The Greek shows they *kept on* kissing or kissed *repeatedly*, probably one after the other falling on his neck (cf. Matt. 26:49).

CHAPTER 21

2. {*Having found a ship*} Paul had used a small coasting vessel (probably hired) that anchored each night at Cos, Rhodes, and Patara. He was still some four hundred miles from Jerusalem. But at Patara Paul caught a large vessel that could sail across the open sea.

3. {*When we had come in sight of Cyprus*} Cyprus is visible, rising up out of the sea into view. {*Landed at Tyre*} They unloaded the ship of its cargo, probably a grain or fruit ship. It took seven days to unload and reload.

4. {*Having found...*} It was a large city, still the numbers of church members may not have been large. Some of those that fled from Jerusalem who came to Phoenicia (Acts 11:19) may have started the work here. {*Through the Spirit*} Paul interpreted the action of the Holy Spirit as *information and warning* although the disciples at Tyre gave it the form of a *prohibition.* Duty called louder than warning to Paul.

5. {*That we had accomplished the days*} They finished their exact seven days (cf. v. 4).

6. {*Beach*} This scene is in public as at Miletus, but they did not care. {*Bade each other farewell*} Though a tender scene, there are none of the bonds of long comradeship, none of the clinging love seen at Miletus (cf. Acts 20:37).

7. {*Ptolemais*} Thirty miles south of Tyre, this is the modern city of Acco, with the best harbor in the region and is surrounded by mountains (cf. Judg. 1:31).

8. {*Unto Caesarea*} Caesarea is the political capital of Judea under the Romans where the procurators lived and a city of importance, built by Herod the Great and named in honor of Augustus. It had a magnificent harbor built. Most of the inhabitants were Greeks. {*Into the house of Philip the evangelist*} This is not Philip the apostle (cf. Acts 6:5) His evangelistic work followed the death of Stephen (Acts 8:1-40). An Evangelist means one who told the gospel story, here it is a traveling missionary (a special class of ministers) who "gospelized" communities (cf. 2 Tim. 4:5. In Eph. 4:11).

9. {*Virgins which did prophesy*} Philip had the honor of having in his home four virgin daughters with the gift of prophecy which was not necessarily predicting events, though that was done as by Agabus here.

It was more than ordinary preaching (cf. Acts 19:6) and was put by Paul above the other gifts like tongues (1 Cor. 14:1-33).

10. {*A certain prophet named Agabus*} Here, Agabus predicted again (cf. Acts 11:28).

11. {*Binding…his own feet and hands*} OT prophets often employed symbolic deeds (1 Kgs. 22:11; Jas. 2:2; Jer. 13:1-7; Ezek. 4:1-6). Though Agabus knew the feeling in Jerusalem against Paul, the Holy Spirit revealed it to him as he claims. Paul has been warned before. Now it is a chorus of warning in verses 10 and 11 (cf. Acts 20:23; 21:4).

12-13. {*Not to go up…*} Paul sees duty above danger, and he ignores the warnings (v. 4). The stature of Paul rises here to heroic proportions for the name of the Lord Jesus.

14. {*We ceased…the will of the Lord be done*} Note again, this is "we" including Luke. Since Paul would not let his friends have their way, they were willing for the Lord to have his way.

16. {*One Mnason of Cyprus, an early disciple, with whom we should lodge*} Originally from Cyprus, he is now in Caesarea. "Early" may refer to the fact that he was one of the original disciples at Pentecost (Acts 2:4ff.).

17. {*Received…gladly*} Perhaps the warm reception was from Paul's personal friends in Jerusalem.

18. {*James…and all the elders were present*} James (not the son of Zebedee) is the leading elder and the others are his guests in a formal reception to Paul (cf. Acts 15:13). Apostles are not mentioned, possibly they are away on preaching tours. The whole church was not called together probably because of the known prejudice against Paul created by the Judaizers.

19. {*He rehearsed…one by one…*} Paul takes his time to tell this great story, updating what had happened since they saw him last.

20. {*Glorified*} The Greek tense translates, "they *began* to praise." {*How many thousands*} Lit. the plural of "ten thousand" like our "myriads." An allowable hyperbole, here is a very large indefinite, impressive number.

21-22. {*They have been informed concerning thee…that thou teachest all the Jews which are among the Gentiles to forsake Moses*} Judaizers were the ones orally passing on this distorted information. They had failed in their attacks on Paul's world campaigns; now they try to undermine him at home. Paul had been long absent from Jerusalem, since Acts 18:22. Here James and the rest of the elders (representing the church) do not believe this false charge, but they wish Paul to set it straight for them.

23-24. {*Do therefore this*} The elders had thought out a plan by which Paul could set the whole matter straight. {*We have...which have a vow on them*} These Jerusalemite Christians made a voluntary Nazirite vow, with several offerings and shaving of the head (cf. Num. 6:1-21). Paul is to incur their expenses as a work of piety to relieve needy Jews. Paul is to take the vow with them. Paul does what James and the elders ask, even to the smallest detail (v. 26).

25. {*We wrote...*} (cf. Acts 15). As James again reminds through reference to the letter issued at the Jerusalem Conference of which he presided, Gentile believers can be free of Jewish ceremonial law, and Jewish Christians have the right to keep on observing the Mosaic law. James has put the case squarely and fairly, and Paul concurs.

26. {*Until the offering was offered for every one of them*} Paul probably went into the temple one day for each of the brethren and one for himself. There was no absolute moral principle here. Paul could act in an expedient manner to placate the situation in Jerusalem. In participating in these ceremonies, Paul acted wisely according to his own principle of accommodation (cf. 1 Cor. 9:20).

27. {*The seven days*} It was on the last of the seven days when Paul was completing his offerings about the vows for all five that the incident occurred. {*When they saw him in the temple*} It is ironic that in the very act of honoring the temple, he is accused of dishonoring it. Jews in Ephesus knew him only too well, even better than by Jerusalem Jews. These Jews of the province of Asia had plotted against him in Ephesus to no purpose (Acts 19:23-41; 20:19), but now a new opportunity had come. {*Stirred up all the multitude*} One is reminded of the Ephesian riot activated by Demetrius (cf. Acts 19); Jews from Ephesus had learned it from that pagan silversmith. Paul was attacked even before a charge was made.

28. {*This is the man that teacheth all men everywhere against the people, and the law, and this place*} Like the charges against Stephen and Jesus before him, truth and falsehood are mixed. Paul had said that being a Jew would not save a person. He had taught the law of Moses was not binding on Gentiles. He did hold, like Jesus and Stephen, that the temple was not the only place to worship God. But Paul gloried himself in being a Jew, considered the Mosaic law righteous for

Jews, and was honoring the temple at this very moment. {*And more-over also he brought Greeks also into the temple...hath defiled this holy place*} There was a court for Gentiles, but here the Jews maintained that Paul brought Greeks beyond this court into the court of Israel.

29. {*They supposed*} Trophimus came along (cf. Acts 20:4) and the Ephesian Jews knew him by sight. The accusers had facts, but did not put them together, making false inferences without the basis of evidence.

30. {*Dragged...*} The cry spread like wildfire over the city and there was a rush to get to the place of the disturbance. Seizing him, the mob thought they were saving the temple by dragging Paul outside. {*Straightway the doors were shut*} This refers to the doors between the inner court and the court of the Gentiles. It was preparation for the real work of the mob, blood and death.

31-32. {*To the chief captain...of the band...Roman*} During festivals especially, a large force of Roman soldiers were stationed for just such events. They responded to the disturbance, saving Paul from mob violence. The Jewish mob that had begun the work of killing Paul stopped before the job was over because of the sudden onset of the Roman soldiers.

33. {*Laid hold on him...with two chains*} Two chains was the number a violent and seditious person would be bound with. The commander is making assumptions that he is a leader of a band of assassins (cf. v. 38).

36. {*Away with him!*} Cheated of their purpose to lynch Paul, the mob was determined to have his blood.

37. {*May I say something unto thee?*} The calm self-control of Paul in the presence of this mob is amazing. His courteous request to Lysias was in Greek to the officer's amazement. {*Art thou not then the Egyptian?*} The Greek syntax shows this was a well-known character who had given the Romans so much trouble. {*Of the Assassins*} This is a Greek word transliterated from the Latin word *sicarius,* one who carried a short sword *sica* under his cloak, a cutthroat. Paul's fluent Greek shows Lysias that he was not this revolutionary.

39. {*I am...a Jew...of Tarsus in Cilicia*} Paul clearly identifies himself by race, country, and city, one of the great cities of the empire with a great university. Strangely, Paul wishes to speak to this mob howling for his blood.

40. {*In the Hebrew language*} People in Jerusalem knew this better than Greek. Paul was fluent in both languages. His enemies in Corinth had said that "his bodily presence was weak and his speech contemptible" (2 Cor. 10:10). But surely even they would have to admit that Paul's stature and words reach heroric proportions on this occasion. With majestic poise Paul faces the outraged mob.

CHAPTER 22

1. {*Brethren and fathers*} (cf. Acts 7:2) Used by Stephen, this introduction shows courtesy and dignity. {*The defence which I now make unto you*} This is the Greek word *apologia* (cf. apology), not "to apologize" but to defend oneself through reasoning and words (cf. Acts 25:16 and then also in 1 Cor. 9:3; 2 Cor. 7:11; Phil. 1:7, 16; 2 Tim. 4:16; 1 Pet. 3:15). Paul first recounts the well-known story of his zeal for Judaism in the persecution of the Christians and shows why the change came. Then he gives a summary of his work among the Gentiles and why he came to Jerusalem this time. He answers the charge of enmity to the people and the law and of desecration of the temple.

3. {*I am a Jew*} The "I" is emphatic in the Greek. Paul has a proper pride in his Jewishness (cf. Acts 26:4; 2 Cor. 11:22; Gal. 1:14; Phil. 3:4-7). {*At the feet of Gamaliel*} Paul was nourished in Pharisaic Judaism as interpreted by Gamaliel, one of the lights of Judaism (cf. Acts 5:34). He was one of the seven Rabbis to whom the Jews gave the highest title Rabban (our Rabbi). {*Being zealous for God*} Paul puts himself by the side of the mob in their zeal for the law, mistaken as they were about him. He was generous surely to interpret their fanatical frenzy as zeal for God.

5. {*Doth bear me witness*} Caiaphas was no longer high priest now, though he may be still alive. {*All the estate of the elders*} Lit. "eldership" referring to the Sanhedrin (cf. Acts 4:5) of which Paul was probably then a member (Acts 26:10). Possibly some of those present were members of the Sanhedrin then (some twenty odd years ago).

9. {*But they heard not the voice*} (cf. Acts 9:7). Lit. "hear the voice." There are some apparent discrepancies in details between the words of Paul and his own record already in chapter 9. This actually shows Luke is reporting factually by not ironing out all the differences in the accounts.

12. {*Ananias...a devout man according to the law*} Paul shows the fact that he was introduced to Christianity by a devout Jew and no law-breaker.

14. {*Hath appointed thee...to know...to see...to hear*} Note the three verbs and their objects which God chose for Paul.

15. {*Thou hast seen and heard*} "Seen" in the Greek tense means "you have seen (in the past) and continue (durative) to see." This properly shows that Paul has an enduring witness (cf. enduring apostleship in 1 Cor. 9:1). "Heard" on the other hand in the Greek tense is "heard" in a point of time (in the past time).

16. {*Be baptized*} Baptism can be a picture of death, burial and resurrection (cf. Rom. 6:4-6). So here baptism pictures the change that had already taken place when Paul surrendered to Jesus on the way (v. 10). Baptism here pictures the washing away of sins by the blood of Christ.

18. {*Saw him saying*} This is the first visit after his conversion when they tried to kill him in Jerusalem (Acts 9:29).

20. {*Was shed*} The Greek tense translates, "was being shed." {*Witness*} (cf. Rev. 2:13; 17:6). {*I also was standing by...consenting*} (cf. Acts 8:1). "Approval" means "being pleased at the same time with" (cf. Luke 11:48). Paul adds here the item of guarding the clothes of those who were slaying Stephen.

21-22. {*I will send thee forth far hence unto the Gentiles*} The word came through Ananias (cf. Acts 9:15). Paul had up until now avoided the word "Gentiles," but at last it had to come, the fatal word. This word caused an explosion of pent-up indignation.

23. {*Shouting...throwing...flinging*} The present tense of these participles give a lively picture of the uncontrolled excitement of the mob in their spasm of wild rage.

24. {*That he be examined by scourging*} Bound with thongs and tied to a post, it was a kind of third degree applied to Paul by the use of scourges and whips (cf. Heb. 11:36). But this way of beginning an inquiry by torture (inquisition) was contrary to Roman law.

25-26. {*Unto the centurion that stood by*} This is merely the soldier carrying out the order (cf. Matt. 27:54). The centurion gives the commander a sharp warning.

27. {*Art thou a Roman?*} "Thou" is emphatic in the Greek. It was unbelievable.

28-29. {*With a great sum*} Lysias was probably a Greek and so had to buy his citizenship. Emperors sold Roman citizenship as a means of filling the treasury. {*But I am a Roman born*} Lit. "But I have been even born one," (i.e., born a Roman citizen). There is calm and simple dignity in this reply and pardonable pride. Paul's citizenship was due to his personal ancestry, not the city he was born in.

30. {*To know the certainty...*} Lysias is determined to find out the truth about Paul, more puzzled than ever by the important discovery that he has a Roman citizen on his hands in this strange prisoner.

CHAPTER 23

1. {*I have lived before God*} This is the Greek verb *politeuô*, to manage affairs of city (*polis*) or state, to be a citizen, behave as a citizen (cf. Phil. 1:27). He had lived as God's citizen, as a member of God's commonwealth. {*In all good conscience unto this day*} Paul is saying to the Sanhedrin that he persecuted Christians as a conscientious, though mistaken, Pharisee; just as he followed his conscience in turning from Judaism to Christianity. Paul is no renegade Jew, no opponent of the law, the people, or the temple. The golden thread of consistency runs through his life now and then as a good citizen in God's commonwealth.

2. {*Ananias*} A man of bad character, this is different from the Ananias of Luke 3:2; John 18:13; Acts 4:7. {*To smite him on the mouth*} (cf. John 18:22). Ananias was provoked by Paul's self-assertion while on trial before his judges. The act was illegal and peculiarly offensive to a Jew at the hands of a Jew.

3. {*Thou whited wall*} (cf. Matt. 23:27). This is a figure of speech for a hypocrite. It was not a tactful thing for a prisoner to say to his judge.

4. {*Of God*} That is, as God's representative in spite of his bad character (Deut. 17:8). Here was a charge of irreverence, to say the least. The office called for respect.

6-7. {*Paul perceived...one part Sadducees...others Pharisees*} His verbal attack sunk his chances for a fair hearing. Paul also knew the two groups were nearly equal in number in the group. So Paul with great tact, seeks to bring the two parties of the council into collision with each other. {*I am a Pharisee, a son of Pharisees*} (cf. Phil. 3:5). {*Touching the hope and resurrection of the dead I am called in question*} (cf. Acts 24:21). Resurrection was a chief point of difference between Pharisees and Sadducees.

8. {*There is no resurrection, neither angel, nor spirit*} These points constitute the chief doctrinal differences between the Pharisees and the Sadducees.

9. {*Strove*} This is the Greek verb *diamachomai,* to fight it out (between, back and forth, fiercely). It was a lively scrap.

10. {*The soldiers...to go down...take him by force*} Fearing he would be torn in pieces, the band of soldiers seized and so saved Paul. Lysias was as puzzled as ever.

11. {*The Lord*} Paul never needed Jesus more than now. Paul's hopes (Acts 19:21) of going to Rome will not be in vain. He can bide Christ's time now. And Jesus has approved his witness in Jerusalem.

12-13. {*Bound themselves under a curse*} They secretly combined their plans together, and placing themselves under a curse, devoted themselves to God (cf. Lev. 27:28; 1 Cor. 16:22). {*Till they had killed*} Lit. "Until they *should* kill" [possibility in contrast to actuality]. The Greek mood here shows failure is a possibility, so the forty felt that the rabbis could find some way to absolve the curse if they failed.

14. {*Came to the chief priests and the elders*} This refers to the Sanhedrin (cf. Luke 22:4). {*With a great curse*} Lit. "With a curse we have cursed" a phrasing of Hebrew style.

15. {*Ye*} "You" is in the emphatic in the Greek syntax. {*Signify*} The authority is with the chiliarch not with the Sanhedrin, but he had appealed to the Sanhedrin for advice. So the plot of the forty to kill unfolds.

16. {*Told Paul*} Perhaps some Pharisee insider told Paul's nephew of the plot. This nephew ran the risk of death if discovered.

18. {*Paul the prisoner*} Paul was bound to a soldier, but not with two chains (cf. Acts 21:33), and with some freedom to see his friends. This was better than *custodia publica* (public custody), the common prison, but more confining.

20. {*The Jews...*} The young man recounts the details of the plot with little variation, using terminology as if the whole nation was in the conspiracy (cf. v. 12). The conspirators may have belonged to the Zealots.

21. {*Looking for the promise from thee*} All standing between the slayers and Paul's death is his consent. The wording by the young man implies the commander's complicity if he fails to heed the warning.

24. {*Unto Felix the governor*} Lit. "leader Felix." Felix married Drusilla the daughter of Herod Agrippa I with the hope of winning the favor of the Jews. He was one of the most depraved men of his time. Tacitus says of him that "with all cruelty and lust he exercised the power of a king with the spirit of a slave."

25. {*And he wrote*} The contents of the letter here are a dexterous mixture of truth and falsehood with the stamp of genuineness. It puts things in a favorable light for Lysias and makes no mention of his order to scourge Paul.

27. {*Rescued him, for he was a Roman*} With the order for scourging omitted, Lysias simply reversed the order of the facts. It was to put himself in proper light with Felix his superior officer.

29-30. {*But to have nothing laid to his charge worthy of death or of bonds*}Lysias expresses the opinion that Paul ought to be set free and the lenient treatment that Paul received in Caesarea and Rome (first imprisonment) is probably due to this report of Lysias. Every Roman magistrate before whom Paul appears declares him innocent (Gallio, Lysias, Felix, Festus).

33. {*And they...*} What would Paul's friends in Caesarea (Philip and his daughters) think of the prophecy of Agabus now so quickly come true (cf. Acts 21:9-10)?

34. {*Of what province he was*} Strictly, "of what kind of" province: senatorial or imperial. Cilicia, like Judea, was under the control of the *propraetor* of Syria (imperial province). Paul's arrest was in Jerusalem and so under the jurisdiction of Felix unless it was a matter of insurrection when he could appeal to the *propraetor* of Syria.

CHAPTER 24

1. {*And with an Orator, one Tertullus*} This was a representative deputation of elders, not the whole Sanhedrin. The Sadducees (chief priests and the like) now take the lead in the prosecution of Paul. As was customary, it was necessary for the Jews to hire a Roman lawyer, since they were not familiar with Roman legal procedure, probably arguing legality in Latin.

2-4. {*Seeing that by thee we enjoy much peace...*} Lit. "obtaining much peace by you." A regular piece of flattery, *captatio benevolentiae,* to ingratiate himself into the good graces of the governor. It sounded more like a campaign speech, but it doubtless pleased Felix.

5. {*For we have found...a pestilent fellow*} "Troublemaker" is the Greek word *loimon,* pest, plague, pestilence. Paul is branded a pest by a contemporary hired lawyer. {*A mover of insurrections...throughout the world*} That is, all over the Roman empire, a forgivable hyperbole. This was an offense against Roman law if it could be proven. {*A ringleader of the sect of the Nazarenes*} Paul is accused of being the front-rank man, a chief, a champion of this sect. The phrasing is a sneer to Jesus' followers.

6-7. {*Assayed to profane...we seized*} This is a flat untruth, but the charge of the Asian Jews (Acts 21:28-30). Remember, a mob tried to do violence without law, and the Romans arrested him, saving him.

8. {*By examining him thyself*} This means to thoroughly hear the case and its defense by Paul. This was not examination by torture, since Paul was a Roman citizen.

10. {*When the governor had beckoned to him...*} The governor gave the nod to Paul. Paul goes as far as he can in the way of a compliment.

12. {*Disputing*} Common verb in old Greek—means simply discussing, conversing, arguing. {*Stirring up a crowd*} *Epistasis*—a late word only used twice in the NT. So Paul denies the two charges that were serious and the only one that concerned Roman law—insurrection.

13. {*Prove...*} These charges are merely unproven assertions. Paul has no hired lawyer to plead for him, but he has made a masterly plea for his freedom.

14. {*I confess*} The only charge left was that of being a ringleader of the sect of the Nazarenes. This Paul frankly confesses is true. {*After the Way...*} Paul claims Christianity to be the real Judaism, not a sect of it. But he will show that Christianity is not a deviation from Judaism, but the fulfillment of it as he has already shown (cf. Gal. 3:1ff.; Rom. 9:1ff.).

16. {*Herein...do I also exercise myself...void of offence*} Paul strives to please God and not be a cause of stumbling to any. Ananias is here listening; it must have galled him, since he ordered Paul to be struck on the mouth (Acts 23:1).

17. {*To bring alms...*} (cf. Matt. 6:1, 4 and Acts 10:2). These alms were for the poor saints in Jerusalem (1 Cor. 16:1-4; 2 Cor. 8; 9; Rom. 15:26) who were none the less Jews. He does not state his whole purpose for coming, which included worship and participation in Pentecost (cf. Acts 18:18; 24:11; 20:16).

18. {*They found me...purified in the temple*} Paul was in a state of completion of the Jewish sacrifices which had gone on for seven days (Acts 21:27), the very opposite of the charges made.

19. {*But certain Jews from Asia...*} The accusers who were present had not witnessed the alleged offense: those who could have given evidence at first-hand were not present. There was no case.

22. {*Having more exact knowledge*} As a Roman official, Felix knew perfectly well the accusers had no case. Felix adjourned the case without a decision under a plausible pretext, that he required the presence of Lysias in person, which was not the case.

23. {*His friends*} Lit. "his own" This refers to Luke, Aristarchus, Trophimus, Philip the Evangelist, and likely others.

24. {*With Drusilla his wife*} Connected with a family of infamy, she was one of three daughters of Herod Agrippa I (Drusilla, Mariamne, Bernice).

25. {*Felix...was terrified*} Paul expounded the faith in Christ Jesus as it applied to Felix and Drusilla. Felix was under conviction, but apparently not Drusilla. Felix then dodged the issues by excusing Paul. The presentation took too personal a turn.

26. {*He hoped withal...*} Paul had mentioned the alms (Acts 24:17) and that excited the greed of Felix for money. Roman law demanded exile and confiscation for a magistrate who accepted bribes, but the law was lax in the provinces. Felix had doubtless received them before.

27. {*But when two years were fulfilled*} Paul lingered on in prison in Caesarea, waiting for the second hearing under Felix which never came. It is probably that during this period Luke secured the material for his Gospel and wrote part or all of it before going to Rome. {*Porcius Festus*} History fills in the details. During these two years the Jews and the Gentiles had an open fight in the market-place in Caesarea. Felix put the soldiers on the mob and many Jews were killed. The Jews made formal complaint to the Emperor with the result that Felix was recalled and Porcius Festus sent in his stead. Paul faired no better under Festus. He exhibits the same insincerity and eagerness to please the Jews as Felix. {*Left Paul in bonds*} Just as Pilate surrendered to the Jews about the death of Jesus, so Festus wanted to grant a favor to the Jews.

CHAPTER 25

2. {*The principal men*} Lit. "the first men." This was the leading men of the city, besides the chief priests who were paying their respects to the new Procurator on his first visit to Jerusalem.

3. {*Laying wait*} (cf. Acts 23:16). Two years before the Sanhedrin had agreed to the plot of the forty conspirators. Now they propose one on their own initiative. There would be plenty of opportunity between Caesarea and Jerusalem for ambush and surprise attacks.

4. {*Howbeit...*} Festus was clearly suspicious (v. 6) and was wholly within his rights to insist that they make their charges in Caesarea where he held court. {*Shortly*} Lit. "in quickness, in speed." An unimportant detail to Luke, eight or ten days of stay is merely estimated.

5. {*You go down with me, and if there is anything amiss in the man, let them accuse him*} It was a fair proposal. He is not ready to commit himself as to the merits of the case.

6. {*Sat on the judgment seat*} Lit. "sitting upon the Bema Seat." Losing no time, he sits in the judgment chair as a legal formality to give weight to the decision.

7. {*Stood round about him...bringing against him*} The accusers have no lawyer this time, but they mass their forces so as to impress Festus.

8. {*Neither against the law of the Jews, nor against the temple, nor against Caesar, have I sinned at all*} He had not sinned against the law. Paul sums up the charges under the three items of law of the Jews, the temple, the Roman state (Caesar).

9. {*Desiring to gain favour with the Jews*} Festus, like Felix, falls a victim to fear of the Jews. {*Before me...*} Festus now makes the very proposal to Paul that the rulers had made to him in Jerusalem (v. 3). Festus adds "before me" to guarantee Paul justice. But Festus had no more courage to do right than Felix.

10. {*I am standing before Caesar's judgment-seat*} Paul is a Roman citizen before a Roman tribunal. Festus was the representative of Caesar and had no right to hand him over to a Jewish tribunal.

11. {*No one has the right to hand me over to them...where I ought to be judged*} Paul is a Roman citizen and not even Festus can make a free gift of giving Paul to the Sanhedrin. {*I appeal unto Caesar*} It was the right of every Roman citizen. This is a technical phrase like

Latin *Caesarem appello.* Paul had crossed the Rubicon on this point and so took his case out of the hands of dilatory provincial justice (really injustice). Roman citizens could make this appeal in capital offenses. There would be expense connected with it, but better that with some hope than delay and certain death in Jerusalem.

12. {*When he had conferred with the council*} Apparently this refers to the chief officers and personal retinue of the procurator, his assessors (*assessores consiliarii*). Some discretion was allowed the governor about granting the appeal. If the prisoner were a well-known robber or pirate, it could be refused. Since Festus refused to acquit Paul, he must formulate charges against him to go before Caesar.

13. {*Agrippa the King*} This is Herod Agrippa II, son of Agrippa I of Acts 12:20-23. He was the last Jewish king in Palestine, though not king of Judea. He angered the Jews by building his palace so as to overlook the temple and by frequent changes in the high priesthood. {*Bernice*} He was her brother and yet she lived with him in shameful intimacy in spite of her marriage to her uncle Herod King of Chalcis and to Polemon King of Cilicia whom she left.

14. {*Laid Paul's case...*} Festus talked with Agrippa since Agrippa had an interest in and responsibility for Jewish worship in the temple in Jerusalem.

16. {*It is not the custom of the Romans*} There is a touch of disdain or scorn in the tone of Festus.

19. {*And of one Jesus...who was dead...whom Paul affirmed to be alive*} This is the climax of supercilious scorn toward both Paul and Jesus. However, Festus has here correctly stated the central point of Paul's preaching about Jesus as no longer dead, but living.

20. {*Being perplexed...to Jerusalem*} This is the Greek verb *aporeô* (*alpha* privative [not] and *poros* [way]), to be in doubt which way to turn. Festus did not know how to proceed, so this is given as the reason for changing the court venue.

21. {*When Paul had appealed...for the decision of the emperor*} Referring to Nero, "Emperor" is the Greek title *Sebastos* "the Augustus." It was a title meaning "the Revered One."

22. {*I also could wish...*} The Greek tense of this indirect request is keen enough and yet polite enough to leave the decision with Festus if inconvenient for any reason.

23-25. {*When Agrippa was come and Bernice...*} With showy parade, Festus decided to gratify the wish of Agrippa by making the "hearing" of Paul the prisoner (v. 22) an occasion for paying a compliment to Agrippa by a public gathering of the notables in Caesarea.

26. {*No certain thing...*} There is nothing definite or reliable here. All the charges of the Sanhedrin slipped away or were tripped up by Paul. Festus confesses that he had nothing left and thereby convicts himself of gross insincerity in his proposal to Paul in verse 9 about going up to Jerusalem. By his own statement he should have set Paul free. The various details here bear the marks of the eyewitness, Luke. {*That I may have somewhat to write...*} Festus makes it plain that this is not a trial, but an examination for his convenience to help him out of a predicament.

27. {*Unreasonable...signifying...the charges*} This naive confession of Festus reveals how unjust his whole treatment of Paul has been. He had to send along with the appeal of Paul *litterae dimissoriae* which would give a statement of the case.

CHAPTER 26

1. {*Thou art permitted...for thyself*} This situation is as if Agrippa were master of ceremonies instead of Festus. Agrippa as a king and guest presides at the grand display while Festus has simply introduced Paul. {*Stretched forth his hand*} This signal was for a dramatic oratorical effect, not silence (cf. Acts 12:17; 13:16) with the chain still upon it (Acts 26:29) linking him to the guard.

2. {*I think myself happy*} (cf. Matt. 5:3). Paul, like Tertullus, begins with *captatio benevolentiae,* but said only to what he could truthfully speak.

3. {*Especially because thou art expert...customs and questions*} Agrippa had the care of the temple, the appointment of the high priest, and the care of the sacred vestments. Agrippa was qualified to give Paul an understanding and a sympathetic hearing. Paul desires here to get a fresh hearing for his own case, though it seems a slim hope.

4. {*My manner of life*} Paul's early life in Tarsus and Jerusalem was an open book to all Jews.

5. {*I lived a Pharisee*} From the beginning of Paul's public education in Jerusalem, Paul had a reputation before his conversion for zeal in

Jerusalem. "I lived" here is emphatic in the Greek. Paul knew the rules of the Pharisees and played the game to the full (Gal. 1:14; Phil. 3:5).

6. {*And now*} Here is a sharp comparison between his youth and the present. {*To be judged for the hope*} That is, the hope of the resurrection and of the promised Messiah (Acts 13:32 also v. 8).

7. {*Our twelve tribes*} Paul's use of this word for the Jewish people (cf. Jas. 1:1). Paul had no knowledge of any "lost ten tribes." There is a certain national pride and sense of unity in spite of the dispersion.

8. {*Incredible with you...*} Paul turns suddenly from Agrippa to the audience, most of whom were probably Gentiles and scouted the doctrine of the resurrection as at Athens (cf. Acts 17:32). {*If God doth raise the dead*} The Greek condition here is assuming that God does raise dead people as a fact (from the speaker's view). Only God can do it.

9. {*I verily thought with myself...I ought*} Necessity and a sense of duty drove Paul on even in this great sin (see on Acts 23:1).

10. {*Having received authority from the chief priests*} Paul was the official persecutor of the saints under the direction of the Sanhedrin. He mentions chief priests (Sadducees), though a Pharisee himself. Both parties were cooperating against the saints.

11-12. {*I persecuted*} The Greek verb *diôkô* was used to run after or chase game and then to chase enemies. The word "persecute" is the Latin *persequor,* to follow through or after. It is a vivid picture that Paul here paints of his success in hunting big game, a grand heresy hunt. The Greek tense shows he did this over and over.

13. {*At midday...*} (cf. Acts 9:1ff.; Acts 22:1ff.). Paul again gives his testimony, differing slightly in some details and phrasing, such as blending direct and indirect communication with Jesus (v. 16 and Acts 9:15).

14. {*It is hard for thee to kick against the goad*} This was a common proverb. Basically, an ox that poked with a goad then reacts to the stinging pain and kicks with the heel, but then receives a severer wound.

16. {*And of the things wherein I will appear unto thee*} This also can be translated "I will be seen by you" referring to visions. The best understanding here though may be the transitive, "I will show you."

17. {*Delivering thee*} This is the Greek verb *exaireô,* which can mean either deliver or choose (cf. LXX Isa. 48:10). God was continually rescuing Paul, a chosen vessel, out of the hands of Jews and Gentiles. (Acts 9:15).

18. {*Sanctified by faith in me*} These important words of Jesus to Paul give his justification to this cultured audience for his response to the command of Jesus. This was the turning point in Paul's career.

19. {*I was not disobedient...unto the heavenly vision*} Lit. "I did not *become* disobedient...." Only time Paul uses *vision* to talk about seeing Christ on the Damascus road, but no reflection on the reality of the event.

22. {*Having therefore obtained...the help that is from God*} "Help" is the Greek word *epikouria,* from the verb *epikoureô,* to aid, and that from *epikouros,* ally, one who assists. God is Paul's ally. All of the plots of the Jews against Paul had failed so far.

23. {*How that the Christ must suffer...how that he first by the resurrection of the dead...both to the people and to the Gentiles*} Paul is speaking from the Jewish point of view. The Cross of Christ was a stumbling-block to the rabbis. The mention of "resurrection" and "Gentiles" (from the Jewish view) again cause an uproar.

24-26. {*Thou art mad*} Lit. "you are raving" (cf. John 10:20; Acts 12:15; 1 Cor. 14:23). The enthusiasm of Paul was too much for Festus and then he had spoken of visions and resurrection from the dead (v. 8). Festus thought Paul's great learning (lit. "many letters") of the Hebrew Scriptures was turning his head to madness (wheels in his head) and he was going mad right before them all.

27-28. {*I know that thou believest...*} Paul had cornered Agrippa by this direct challenge. As the Jew in charge of the temple he was bound to confess his faith in the prophets. But Paul had interpreted the prophets about the Messiah in a way that fell in with his claim that Jesus was the Messiah risen from the dead. Agrippa had listened with the keenest interest, but he slipped out of the coils with adroitness and a touch of humor. {*Thou wouldest fain make me a Christian*} The tone of Agrippa is ironical, but not unpleasant. He pushes it aside with a shrug of the shoulders.

29. {*I would to God...whether with little or with much...such as I am*} The Greek condition of "I pray" is one undetermined with less likelihood of fulfillment. It was a polite and courteous wish. Paul takes kindly the sarcasm of Agrippa. "What I am" is just a way not to repeat the word "Christian."

31. {*They spake one to another...nothing worthy of death or bonds*} This is the unanimous conclusion of all these dignitaries (Romans,

Jews, Greeks) as it was of Festus before (Acts 25:25). But Paul had not won any of them to Christ.

32. {*This man might have been set at liberty...if he had not appealed unto Caesar*} But Paul *only* appealed to Caesar after Festus had tried to shift him back to Jerusalem and had refused to set him free in Caesarea (cf. Acts 25:3). Festus comes out with no honor in the case. Since Agrippa was a favorite at court, perhaps Festus would be willing to write favorably to Caesar.

CHAPTER 27

1. {*That we should sail...*} Note the reappearance of "we" in the narrative. Had Luke been absent for a time? The great detail and minute accuracy of Luke's account of this voyage and shipwreck throw more light upon ancient seafaring than everything else put together. Though so accurate in his use of sea terms, yet Luke writes like a "landlubber," not a sailor.

2. {*In a ship of Adramyttium*} This is a city in Mysia in the province of Asia. They probably sailed on a small coasting vessel on its way home for the winter stopping at various places. Julius would take his chances to catch another ship for Rome. The usual way to go to Rome was to go to Alexandria and so to Rome, but no large ship for Alexandria was at hand. {*Aristarchus, a Macedonian of Thessalonica, being with us*} Luke and Aristarchus may have had to accompany Paul as his slaves, since they would not be allowed to go as his friends. But Luke was Paul's physician and may have gained permission on that score.

4. {*We sailed under the lee of Cyprus...because the winds were contrary*} Cyprus was thus on the left between the ship and the wind from the northwest, under the protection of Cyprus. The Etesian winds were blowing from the northwest so that they could not cut straight across from Sidon to Patara with Cyprus on the right. They must run behind Cyprus and hug the shore of Cilicia and Pamphylia.

5. {*We came to Myra of Lycia*} This town was two and a half miles from the coast of Lycia. The port Andriace had a fine harbor and did a large grain business.

6. {*Sailing for Italy*} Of Alexandria, this grain ship was bound for Rome (v. 38) out of its course because of the wind. Such grain ships usually carried passengers.

7. {*We sailed under the lee of Crete*} (cf. v. 4). Instead of going to the right of Crete as the straight course would have been they sailed southwest with Crete to their right and got some protection against the wind there.

8. {*Fair Havens*} This is a small bay two miles east of Cape Matala. This harbor would protect them for a time from the winds.

9. {*And the voyage was now dangerous...because the Fast was now already gone by*} This refers to the great day of atonement of the Jews (cf. Lev. 16:29) occurring about the end of September; this year on October 5th. The ancients considered navigation on the Mediterranean unsafe from early October until the middle of March. {*Paul admonished them*} The Greek tense show he *began* to admonish and *kept on at* it. It is remarkable that a prisoner like Paul should venture to give advice at all. Paul had clearly won the respect of the centurion and officers and also felt it to be his duty to give this unasked for warning. {*I perceive that the voyage will be with injury and much loss, not only of the lading and the ship, but also of our lives*} Fortunately no lives were lost, though all else was. But this outcome was due to the special mercy of God for the sake of Paul (v. 24), not to the wisdom of the officers in rejecting Paul's advice.

11. {*The centurion...gave more heed...*} Outranking the pilot and owner [who likely also acted as captain of the vessel], the military officer was responsible for the soldiers, the prisoners, and the cargo of wheat. It was a government ship. The centurion probably feared to risk criticism in Rome for timidity when the wheat was so much needed in Rome.

12. {*The more part advised*} Lysias held a council of the officers of the ship on the issue raised by Paul. {*If by any means they could reach Phoenix and winter there*} Phoenix is the town of palms, the modern Lutro, the only town in Crete on the southern coast with a harbor fit for wintering.

13. {*When the south wind blew softly*} This wind is in marked contrast to the violent northwest wind that they had faced so long. They were so sure of the wisdom of their decision that they did not even draw up the small boat attached by a rope to the vessel's stern (v. 16).

14-15. {*A tempestuous wind which is called Euraquilo*} "Euroquilo" means "North-easter" and can be transliterated in Greek as "Euracylon." The nature of the wind was typhoon, a violent whirlwind or squall. The suddenness of the hurricane gave no time to furl (roll up) the great mainsail. They helplessly were carried along.

16. {*Running under the lee of...Cauda*} The protection of the small island did allow the hoisting of the little waterlogged boat because of the smoother water on the lee side of the island. {*Used helps*} In context "helps" refers to ropes, cables, or chains, no doubt. Probably cables or ropes were used under the hull of the ship laterally or even longitudinally, tightly secured on deck. This "frapping" was more necessary for ancient vessels because of the heavy mast. {*The Syrtis*} Syrtis refers to two quicksand bars between Carthage and Cyrenaica, this clearly being the Syrtis Major most dangerous because of the sandbanks. The wind would drive the ship right into this peril if something were not done. {*They lowered the gear*} They slackened or reduced sail, especially the mainsail, but leaving enough to keep the ship's head as close to the wind as was practicable. {*So were driven*} The ship was now fixed as near to the wind (ENE) as possible (seven points). That would enable the ship to go actually west by north and so avoid the quicksand bars.

18-20. {*They began to throw overboard...*} This was to lighten the ship by throwing overboard the cargo. The grain in the ship would shift and make it list and so added to the danger. Day by day Luke observes the throwing off the cargo, until all that is left is the "furniture" (tackling) of the ship which also must go. Despair was beginning to settle like a fog on all their hopes.

21. {*When they had been long without food*} Lit. "there being much abstinence from food." The focus here is on their appetite, not actual quantity of food. They had plenty of grain on board, but no appetite to eat (sea-sickness) and no fires to cook it. {*Ye should have hearkened unto me*} This was a reference to the wisdom of his former counsel in order to induce acceptance of his present advice. {*And have gotten this injury and loss*} Lit. "to gain this injury and loss." A person is said in Greek 'to gain a loss' when, being in danger of incurring it, he by his conduct saves himself from doing so.

22-23. {*No loss of life...*} (cf. v. 10). He had foretold such loss of life as likely, but he now gives his reason for his changed view. An angel of the God whom Paul serves is the reason for his present confidence.

24. {*Thou must stand before Caesar*} (cf. Acts 23:11). {*God...hath granted thee*} The lives of those who sailed with Paul God had spared as a gift to Paul.

25. {*For I believe God*} This is Paul's reason for his own good cheer and for his exhortation to confidence in spite of unfavorable circumstances. Paul had doubtlessly prayed for his own life and for the lives of all. He was sure that he was to bear his witness in Rome.

27. {*Fourteenth night*} The fourteenth night is reckoned from the time they left Fair Havens. {*Surmised...that they were drawing near to some country*} Luke writes from the sailor's standpoint that a certain land was drawing near to them. The sailors heard the sound of breakers and grew uneasy.

28-29. {*They sounded...*} To heave lead into the water with a rope and see how deep it is. {*Twenty fathoms...fifteen fathoms*} A fathom means the distance from one outstretched middle finger tip to the other likewise out-stretched.

29. {*Four anchors...from the stern*} The usual practice was and is to anchor by the bows. With a view to running the ship ashore, anchoring from the stern would be best. {*Wished for the day*} The Greek tense translates *kept on* praying for day to come before the anchors broke under the strain of the storm or began to drag.

30. {*The sailors...under colour...seeking to flee out of the ship*} They pretended to need the small boat to stretch out or lay out the anchors in front.

31. {*Except these abide in the ship...*} Paul has no hesitancy in saying this in spite of his strong language in verse 24 about God's promise. He has no notion of lying supinely down and leaving God to do it all. Without the sailors the ship could not be properly beached.

32. {*The ropes...*} Paul is now savior of the ship and the soldiers quickly cut loose the skiff and let her fall off rather than be the means of the escape of the sailors who were needed.

33. {*Paul besought them all...*} That is Paul *kept on* exhorting or beseeching them until dawn began to come on. Paul wanted them to be ready for action when day really came.

35. {*Gave thanks to God*} This is the Greek verb *eucharisteô* from which our word "Eucharist" comes. It was saying grace like the head of a Hebrew family and the example of Paul would encourage the others to eat.

36. {*Then were they all of good cheer*} Lit. "then all becoming cheerful" because of Paul's words and conduct. His courage was contagious.

37-38. {*Two hundred three-score and sixteen souls*} The ancient grain ships were of considerable size. An ancient historian says that there were 600 on the ship that took him to Italy. The number included sailors, soldiers, and prisoners.

39. {*They knew not...*} The Greek tense probably means they *tried* to recognize and could not. The island was well-known (cf. Acts 28:1), but St. Paul's Bay where the wreck took place was some distance from the main harbor Malta.

40. {*Casting off...*} Lit. "Having taken away from around [the anchors]." The Greek word could mean they just let the anchors go and the ropes fell down into the sea, instead of cutting. {*At the same time loosing the bands of the rudders*} Ancient ships had a pair of paddle rudders like those of the early northmen, one on each quarter. The paddle rudders had been fastened while the ship was anchored. {*Hoisting up the foresail to the wind*} It is not clear what sail is meant by the Greek word, though an example in Latin writings shows "foresail" is probably correct.

41. {*But lighting upon...*} There is a current on one side of St. Paul's Bay between a little island (Salmonetta) and Malta which makes a sand bank between the two currents. Unexpectedly the ship stuck in this sandbar, and the stern was breaking to pieces by the opposing waves lashing on both sides. It was a critical moment.

42. {*Counsel was to kill...*} The soldiers did not relish the idea of the escape of the prisoners. Hence there came this plan.

43. {*To save Paul...*} And no wonder that he wanted this, for this centurion knew now how much they all owed to Paul. "Swim for shore" was a wise command to those who could swim.

44. {*Some on planks...*} The breaking of the ship gave scraps of timber which some used. Everyone was safe, and Paul's promise was fulfilled (v. 24).

CHAPTER 28

2. {*Showed us*} The Greek tense translates, they *kept on* showing kindness. "Kindness" is the Greek word *philanthrôpia* (*philos, anthrôpos*), love of mankind (cf. Titus 3:4).

3. {*A viper...fastened on his hand*} The natives look on Paul as a doomed man as good as dead, swelling up and falling down dead (vv. 4-6).

4. {*The beast*} Lit. "the little beast" (cf. Mark 1:13). Aristotle and the medical writers apply the word to venomous serpents, the viper in particular, as Luke does here. {*Hanging from his hand*} The Greek tense is a vivid picture of the snake *continuing to be* dangling from Paul's hand. {*No doubt...*} "Must" is lit. "by all means." They *knew* that he was a prisoner being taken to Rome on some grave charge, and *inferred* that the charge was murder. {*Yet Justice*} This is the Greek word *dikê*, here an abstraction personified like the Latin *Justitia*. The natives speak of *Dikê* as a goddess, but we know nothing of such actual worship in Malta.

6. {*But when they were long in expectation and beheld nothing amiss came to him, they changed their minds, and said that he was a god*} When he did not die or swell up, they did a turn about and decided he was a god.

7. {*To the chief man of the island...Publius*} Lit. "by name *first of the island*," an official title correct in Malta. A similar inscription has actually been found there. This official entertained Paul and his entourage (Luke and Aristarchus).

8-10. {*Paul...laying his hands on him healed him...*} (cf. Mark 1:30; John 5:6). The man had intermittent attacks of fever and our very word *dysentery*. Ramsay argues that *iaomai* is employed here of the miraculous healing by Paul while *therapeuô* ("cure") is used of the cures by Luke the physician (v. 9). {*Came and were healed...with many honours*} It is a picture of a regular stream of patients who came during these months. Luke had his share in the honors (cf. "us") and no doubt his share in the cures. "Honors" was often applied to payment for professional services as we today speak of an honorarium.

11. {*Which had wintered*} Navigation in the Mediterranean usually opened up in February (always by March), spring beginning on February 9. {*Whose sign was the Twin Brothers*} This refers to mythological twin sons of Zeus and Leda, namely, Castor and Pollux. They were the tutelary deities of sailors whose figures were painted one on each side of the prow of the ship. This sign was the name of the ship. So they start in another grain ship of Alexandria bound for Rome.

12. {*At Syracuse*} The chief city of Sicily and eighty miles from Malta. Perhaps open weather and a southerly wind helped them across.

13. {*We made a circuit*} Lit. "casting loose." The ship had to tack to reach Rhegium and was not able to make a straight course. {*A south wind sprang up*} (cf. Acts 27:13). Weather was plainly treacherous at this early season, but here no bad consequence. {*To Puteoli*} It was 182 miles from Rhegium and would require 26 hours. It was eight miles northwest from Neapolis (Naples) and the chief port of Rome, the regular harbor for the Alexandrian ships from Rome.

14. {*Where we found brethren*} There was a large Jewish quarter, so finding Christian brothers here is no stranger than finding them in Rome. {*And so we came to Rome*} Luke is exultant, "*Paulus Romae captivus: triumphus unicus*" [Paul the Roman captive: an unparalleled triumph]. This simple phrase is *the climax of the book of Acts* (cf. Acts 19:21; 23:11), but not the close of Paul's career. A new paragraph should begin with verse 15. The great event is that Paul reached Rome, but not as he had once hoped (Rom. 15:22-29).

15. {*When they heard of us…to meet us*} Good news had its way of travel even before the days of mass media. Possibly Julius had to send on special couriers with news of his arrival after the shipwreck; or the Puteoli brethren at once (beginning of the week) sent on news to the brethren in Rome. {*As far as the Market of Appius*} It was 90 miles from Puteoli, 40 from Rome, on the great Appian Way. The Censor Appius Claudius had constructed this part of the road, 312 B.C. Paul probably struck the Appian Way at Capua. {*Three Taverns*} This place was about 30 miles from Rome. Two groups of the disciples came (possibly one Gentile, one Jewish), one to Appii Forum, the other to Three Taverns. It was a joyous time and Julius would not interfere. {*Paul…took courage*} Jesus himself had exhorted Paul to be of good courage (cf. Acts 23:11) as he had done the disciples (cf. John 16:33).

16. {*Paul was suffered to abide by himself…with the soldier that guarded him*} Surely Julius would give a good report of Paul to this officer (whoever he is) who would be kindly disposed and would allow Paul comparative freedom.

17. {*Those that were the chief of the Jews*} Lit. "Those that were first among the Jews." Paul could not go to the synagogue, as was his custom. So he invited the Jewish leaders to come to his lodging and hear his explanation of his presence in Rome as a prisoner with an appeal to Caesar. He is anxious that they may understand that this appeal was forced upon him by Festus following Felix and not because he has come to make an attack on the Jewish people.

18. {*When they had examined me*} (cf. Acts 24:8; 25:6, 26) This refers to the judicial examinations by Felix and Festus. They found no basis for guilt or punishment.

19. {*When the Jews spake against it*} "Spake against" is a mild word to describe the bitter enmity of the Jews. {*I was constrained...*} Paul was compelled to appeal to Caesar (see Acts 25:11, 12), unless Paul was willing to be the victim of Jewish hate when he had done no wrong.

20. {*Because of the hope of Israel*} That is, the hope of the Messiah is his point (cf. Acts 26:6). {*I am bound with this chain*} Lit. "I am laid around (passive) with this chain." Strictly, Paul does not lie around the chain, but the chain lies around him, a curious reversal of the imagery.

21. {*Nor did any of the brethren come hither and report or speak any harm of thee*} These Jews do not mean to say that they had never heard of Paul. It is hardly likely that they had heard of his appeal to Caesar, for how could the news have reached Rome before Paul?

22. {*Concerning this sect*} Paul had identified Christianity with Judaism (v. 20) in its Messianic hope. The language seems to imply that the number of Christians in Rome was comparatively small and mainly Gentile. If the edict of Claudius for the expulsion of the Jews from Rome (Acts 18:2) was due to disturbance over Christ (*Chrêstus*), then even in Rome the Jews had special reason for hostility toward Christians.

23-24. {*Expounded*} This is the Greek verb *ektithêmi*, to set forth (cf. Acts 11:4; 18:26). He did it with detail and care and spent all day at it, from morning until evening. {*Persuading them concerning Jesus*} It was only about Jesus that he could make good his claim concerning the hope of Israel (v. 20). It was Paul's great opportunity. So he appealed both to Moses and to the prophets for proof as it was his custom to do. The response was mixed: only some believed.

25. {*Holy Spirit spoke... well...to your fathers*} By mentioning the Holy Spirit, Paul shows that they are resisting God (cf. Acts 7:52).

26-28. {*Say...*} (cf. Isa. 6:9, 10). This very passage is quoted by Jesus (Matt. 13:14, 15; Mark 4:12; Luke 8:10) in explanation of his use of parables and in John 12:40 the very point made by Paul here, the disbelief of the Jews in Jesus: it is a solemn dirge of the doom foreseen so long ago by Isaiah. The conclusion is God's salvation has been sent to the Gentiles, and they will listen.

30. {*Two whole years*} During these busy years in Rome Paul wrote Philippians, Philemon, Colossians, Ephesians; Epistles that would immortalize any man. Luke wrote as well. Luke wrote the Acts during this period of two years in Rome and carried events no further because they had gone no further. Paul was still a prisoner in Rome when Luke completed the book.

31. {*Preaching...teaching*} These two things concerned Paul most, doing both as if his right hand was not in chains, to the amazement of those in Rome and in Philippi (Phil. 1:12-14).

The Epistle to the Romans

Author: Paul, Servant of Jesus Christ, called Apostle
Recipients: The church of Rome (Jews and Gentiles)
Date: Spring of A.D. 57 or 58
From: Corinth
Occasion: Paul sends this Epistle that the Romans may really know what is Paul's gospel, dealing with Judaizing issues (Rom. 1:15; 2:16). Paul's aim may be to make the Romans complete in knowledge (of the gospel) and competent to instruct one another (Rom. 15:14).
Theme: A presentation of the content of the gospel of God as Paul understands it (Rom. 1-8), with a core presentation of justification by faith (Rom. 3:21-5:21)

By Way of Introduction

Paul wrote Romans from Corinth because he sent it to Rome by Phoebe of Cenchrea (Rom. 16:2) if chapter 16 is acknowledged to be a part of the Epistle. Though theories and discussions abound, modern knowledge leaves the Epistle intact with occasional variations in the MSS. on particular points as is true of all the NT.

It was written in the spring between Passover at Philippi (Acts 20:6) and Pentecost in Jerusalem (Acts 20:16; 21:17). The precise year is not quite so certain, but we may suggest A.D. 57 or 58 with reasonable confidence.

Romans is full of the issues raised by the Judaizing controversy as set forth in the Epistles to Corinth and to Galatia. So in a calmer mood and more at length he presents his conception of the Righteousness demanded by God (Rom. 1:17) of both Gentile (Rom. 1:18-32) and Jew (Rom. 2:1-3:20) and only to be obtained by faith in Christ who by his atoning death (justification) has made it possible (Rom. 3:21-5:21). This new life of faith in Christ should lead to holiness of life (sanctification, chapters Rom. 6-8).

Nowhere does Paul's Christian statesmanship show to better advantage than in this greatest of his Epistles. Here Paul is seen in the plenitude of his powers with all the wealth of his knowledge of Christ and his rich experience in mission work.

CHAPTER 1

1. {*Servant*} This is a slave *doulos* (cf. Gal. 1:10; Phil. 1:1). {*Separated*} Paul is saying he is a spiritual Pharisee (etymologically), separated not to the oral tradition, but to God's gospel, a chosen vessel (Acts 9:15); by man also (Acts 13:2).

3. {*Concerning his Son…according to the flesh*} Jesus is found in the OT (Luke 24:27, 46). The deity [Son] and humanity [of David] of Christ here stated (Matt. 1:1, 6, 20; Luke 1:27; John 7:42; Acts 13:23).

4. {*Who was declared*} This is the Greek verb *horizô* (cf. Luke 22:22; Acts 2:23). He was the Son of God in his preincarnate state (2 Cor. 8:9; Phil. 2:6) and still so after his Incarnation (Rom. 1:3). {*Resurrection*} This is what definitely marked Jesus off as God's Son because of his claims about himself as God's Son and his prophecy that he would rise on the third day.

7. {*From God our Father and the Lord Jesus Christ*} Paul's theology holds to the Divinity of Christ.

8. {*First*} The rush of thoughts crowds out the balanced phraseology as in Romans 3:2; 1 Corinthians 11:18. {*Your faith*} This refers to "Your Christianity." {*Is proclaimed*} This is the Greek verb *kataggellô*, to announce (*aggellô*) up and down (*kata*). See also *anaggellô*, to bring back news (John 5:15), *apaggellô*, to announce from one as the source (Matt. 2:8), *prokataggellô*, to announce far and wide beforehand (Acts 3:18). {*Throughout all the world*} This is natural hyperbole (cf. Col. 1:6; Acts 17:6). But it means that it was widely known because the church was in the central city of the empire.

9. {*I serve*} Here this means to serve in general gods or men, whether sacred services (Heb. 9:9; 10:2) or spiritual service as here (cf. Rom. 12:1; Phil. 3:3).

11. {*Impart*} Lit. "to share with one" (Luke 3:11; 1 Thess. 2:8).

12. {*That is*} This is an explanatory correction (Denney). Instead of saying that he had a spiritual gift for them, he wishes to add that they also have one for him. {*That I with you may be comforted*} Lit. "my being comforted in you together with you."

13. {*Oftentimes I purposed*} This is the Greek verb *protithêmi*, to place, to propose to oneself (cf. Rom. 3:25; Eph. 1:9).

14. {*Both to Greeks and to Barbarians*} This is the whole human race from the Greek point of view, Jews coming under Barbarians (cf.

Acts 18:2, 4; 1 Cor. 4:11; Col. 3:11). The Greeks called all others barbarians and the Jews termed all others Gentiles.

16. {*It is the power of God*} This Paul knew by much experience. He had seen the dynamite of God at work. {*To the Jew first, and also to the Greek*} The Jew is first in privilege and in penalty (Rom. 2:9).

17. {*A righteousness of God*} Translate, "a God kind of righteousness," one that each must have and can obtain in no other way save "from faith the starting point and faith the goal." {*Is revealed*} This is the Greek verb *apokaluptô*. It is a revelation from God, this God kind of righteousness, that man unaided could never have conceived or still less attained. {*Righteousness...righteous shall live by faith*} Paul grounds his position on Habakkuk 2:4 (quoted also in Gal. 3:11). A keynote term of the Epistle, by "righteousness" we shall see that Paul means both "justification" and "sanctification." Here Paul claims that in the gospel, taught by Jesus and by himself there is revealed a God kind of righteousness with two ideas in it (the righteousness that God has and that he bestows). The Greek word for "righteous" is an old word for quality from *dikaios*, a righteous man, and that from *dikê*, right or justice (called a goddess in Acts 28:4), and that allied with the Greek verb *deiknumi*, to show, to point out. Other allied words are *dikaioô*, to declare or make *dikaios* (Rom. 3:24, 26), *dikaiôma*, that which is deemed *dikaios* (sentence or ordinance as in Rom. 1:32; 2:26; 8:4). *Dikaiosunê* and *dikaioô* are easy to render into English, though we use justice in distinction from righteousness and sanctification for the result that comes after justification (the setting one right with God).

18. {*For the wrath of God is revealed*} (cf. Rom. 1:17). God reveals righteousness and wrath (an unwritten revelation). It is the temper of God towards sin, not rage, but the wrath of reason and law (Shedd). {*Unrighteousness*} This is the lack of right conduct toward men, injustice (Rom. 9:14; Luke 18:6). {*Hold down the truth*} So to speak, wicked men put truth in a box and sit on the lid and "hold it down in unrighteousness."

20. {*The invisible things of him*} This means either unseen or invisible (Col. 1:15). {*Deity*} This is the Greek word *theiotês,* from *theios* (from *theos*) quality of God (cf. Col. 2:9). {*Since the creation of the world*} Paul means by God and unto God as antecedent to and superior to the world (cf. Col. 1:15. about Christ). {*Being perceived...that* *they may be without excuse*} Likely translate, "so that [as a result] they are without excuse" (cf. Rom. 2:1).

21. {*Knowing God*} This is to know by personal experience. {*Glorified not as God*} They knew more than they did. This is the reason for the condemnation of the heathen (Rom. 2:12-16), the failure to do what they know. {*Their senseless heart*} The Greek word *kardia* (heart) is the most comprehensive term for all our faculties whether feeling (Rom. 9:2), will (1 Cor. 4:5), intellect (Rom. 10:6). It may be the home of the Holy Spirit (Rom. 5:5) or of evil desires (Rom. 1:24). So darkness settled down on their hearts.

22. {*Professing themselves to be wise...became fools*} Their wisdom is empty reasonings as often today. This is an oxymoron or sharp saying, true and one that cuts to the bone. {*For the likeness of an image*} Translate, "a likeness which consists in an image or copy" (Lightfoot).

24. {*Wherefore God gave them up*} (cf. Rom. 1:24, 26, 28). These people had already willfully deserted God who merely left them to their own self-determination and self-destruction, part of the price of man's moral freedom (cf. "overlooked" Acts 17:30). {*That their bodies should be dishonoured*} Christians had a new sense of dignity for the body (1 Thess. 4:4; 1 Cor. 6:13). Heathenism left its stamp on the bodies of men and women.

25. {*Exchanged*} This is the Greek verb *metallassô*, meaning exchanging trade (cf. Rom. 1:26). Truth for lies: this is the price of mythology (Bengel). {*Rather than the Creator*} "Rather" is lit. "placed side by side" (Creator and creature); they preferred the creature.

26. {*Unto vile passions*} Lit. "passions of dishonor" (cf. 1 Thess. 4:5; Col. 3:5). {*That which is against nature*} This refers to the degradation of sex, the results of Heathenism (the loss of God in the life of man).

27. {*Unseemliness*} This is the Greek word *aschêmosunê*, from *aschêmon* deformed (cf. Rev. 16:15). {*Recompense*} This debt will be paid in full (cf. Luke 6:34, and due as in Luke 23:41). Nature will attend to that in their own bodies and souls.

28. {*And even as they refused*} Lit. "and even as they rejected" after trial just as *dokimazô* is used of testing coins. {*Unto a reprobate mind*} This is a play on the rejection just mentioned. They rejected God and God rejected their mental attitude and gave them over (Rom. 1:24,

26, 28). {***To do those things which are not fitting***} a technical term with Stoics (2 Macc. 6:4).

29. {***Being called with***} The Greek tense has a focus of a state of completion, "filled to the brim with" four vices. Note in Greek Paul lists the items with no connective "ands" or "ors" for a dramatic effect. {***Full of***} Here is another word for "to fill full, stuffed full" followed by various evil things.

30. Paul changes the construction again to twelve substantives and adjectives that give vivid touches to this composite photograph of the God-abandoned soul. {***Haughty***} Lit. "to appear above others," and so arrogant in thought and conduct, "stuck up." {***Inventors of evil things***} These are inventors of new forms of vice as Nero was. {***Disobedient to parents***} (cf. 1 Tim. 1:9; 2 Tim. 3:2). This is an ancient and a modern trait.

31. {***Covenant-breakers***} (cf. Jer. 3:7 LXX), these are men "false to their engagements," who treat covenants as "a scrap of paper." {***Without natural affection***} Lit. "not + love of kindred" (cf. 2 Tim. 3:3). {***Unmerciful***} Lit. "not + merciful." It is a terrible picture of the effects of sin on the lives of men and women.

32. {***The ordinance of God***} The heathen knows that God condemns such evil practices.

CHAPTER 2

1. {***Wherefore***} (cf. Rom. 1:24, 26) Lit. "because of which thing." {***Whosoever thou art that judgest***} Lit. "every one that judges." Paul begins his discussion of the failure of the Jew to attain to the God-kind of righteousness (Rom. 2:1-3:20) here beginning with a general statement.

3. {***And doest the same***} Translate "and do them occasionally." {***That thou shalt escape***} "You" is emphatic, referring to the conceited Jew expecting to escape God's judgment, based on nationality (cf. Matt. 3:8). Alas, some Christians affect the same immunity.

4. {***Or despiseth thou?***} This is the Greek verb *kataphroneô,* to think down on (Matt. 6:24; 1 Cor. 11:22). {***Leadeth thee to repentance***} The Greek tense suggests that the very kindness of God is trying to lead a change of mind and attitude instead of a complacent self-satisfaction and pride of race and privilege.

5. {*After thy hardness*} This is the Greek word *sklêrotês,* from *sklêros,* hard, stiff. {*And impenitent heart*} (cf. Rom. 2:4) Translate as, "Your unreconstructed heart," "with no change in the attitude of thy heart." {*Treasurest up for thyself* } Lit. "treasure," and ironic touch (Matt. 6:19; Luke 12:21; 2 Cor. 12:14). {*Wrath*} (cf. Rom. 1:18). Paul looks to the judgment day as certain (cf. 2 Cor. 5:10-12), the day of the Lord (2 Cor. 1:14), for Jew here as earlier for Gentile.

9. {*Every soul of man*} This means "individual" (cf. Rom. 13:1). First not only in penalty as here, but in privilege (Rom. 2:11; 1:16).

12. {*Without law*} Here this means in ignorance of the Mosaic law (or of any law). {*Shall also perish without law*} The heathen who sin are lost, because they do not keep the law which they have, not because they do not have the Mosaic law or Christianity. {*By the law*} The Jew has to stand or fall by the Mosaic law.

13. {*Before God*} Lit. "by God's side," that is, as God looks at it. {*Shall be justified*} This is the Greek verb *dikaioô,* to declare righteous, to set right (cf. Jas. 1:22-25).

14. {*By nature*} The Gentiles are without the Mosaic law, but not without some knowledge of God in conscience and when they do right "they are a law to themselves."

15. {*Written in their hearts*} When their conduct corresponds on any point with the Mosaic law they practice the unwritten law in their hearts. {*Their conscience bearing witness therewith*} The Greek word *suneidêsis* means co-knowledge by the side of the original consciousness of the act. This second knowledge is personified as confronting the first. All men have this faculty of passing judgment on their actions. It can be over-scrupulous (1 Cor. 10:25) or "seared" by abuse (1 Tim. 4:12).

17. {*Bearest the name*} Lit. "to put a name upon," translate, "You are surnamed Jew" (Lightfoot). Jew as opposed to Greek denoted nationality while Hebrew accented the idea of language. {*Restest upon the law*}(cf. Luke 10:6). "Rely" means to lean upon, to refresh oneself back upon anything. It is the picture of blind and mechanical reliance on the Mosaic law. {*Gloriest in God*} The Jew gloried in God as a national asset and private prerogative (2 Cor. 10:15; Gal. 6:13).

18. {*Approvest the things that are excellent*} Originally, "You test the things that differ," and then as a result comes the approval for the excellent things (cf. Phil. 1:10). {*Instructed out of the law*} This is the

Greek verb *katêcheô,* a rare verb to instruct, though occurring in the papyri for legal instruction (cf. Luke 1:4; 1 Cor. 14:19).

19. {*A guide of the blind*} "Guide" is lit. "to lead, one who leads the way." The Jews were meant by God to be guides for the Gentiles.

20. {*A corrector of the foolish*} "Foolish" refers here to Gentiles, but it is the Jewish standpoint that Paul gives. Each termed the other "dogs." {*The form*} (cf. 2 Tim. 3:5). The Greek word is *morphôsis* as "the rough sketch, the penciling of the *morphê,*" the outline or framework. This is Paul's picture of the Jew as he sees himself drawn with consummate skill and subtle irony.

23. {*Through thy transgression of the law*} Lit. stepping across a line, for a variety of sins.

24. {*Because of you*} (cf. Isa. 52:5 LXX). Jews would not speak the very name of God, but acted in a way so that the Gentiles blasphemed that very name.

25. {*If thou be a doer of the law*} The Greek syntax has the meaning to do as a habit. {*Is become uncircumcision*} Circumcision was simply the seal of the covenant relation of Israel with God, so no advantage to the Jew.

27. {*If it fulfill the law*} Lit. "to finish," continually fulfilling to the end (as would be necessary).

29. {*Who is one inwardly*} Lit. "the in the inward part Jew." That is, circumcision of the heart (cf. Col. 2:11), in the spirit (cf. 2 Cor. 3:3, 6). This inward or inside Jew who lives up to his covenant relation with God is the high standard that Paul puts before the merely professional Jew described above.

CHAPTER 3

1. {*What advantage then hath the Jew?*} What does the Jew have over and above the Gentile?

2. {*The profit*} This refers to "much advantage," from every angle. {*First of all*} Here he singles out one privilege of the many possessed by the Jew. {*The oracles of God*} (cf. Acts 7:38, also Rom. 3:2; Heb. 5:12; 1 Pet. 4:11). This is the Greek word *logion,* probably a diminutive of *logos,* word, though the adjective *logios* also occurs (Acts 18:24).

3. {*Some were without faith*} (cf. Luke 24:11, 41; Acts 28:24; Rom. 4:20). Lit. "to disbelieve," or the meaning may be to be unfaithful to one's trust (cf. 2 Tim. 2:13); either makes sense here.

4. {*Let God be found true*} Greek tense translates, "let God continue to be true." {*But every man a liar*} This really means, "though every man be found a liar (cf. Ps. 116:12). {*That thou mightest be justified*} Here, this verb has to mean "declared righteous," not "made righteous." {*Mightest prevail*} Lit. "to win a victory."

5. {*Commendeth*} This is the Greek verb *sunistêmi*, to send together, occurs in the NT in two senses, either to introduce, to commend (2 Cor. 3:1; 4:2) or to prove, to establish (2 Cor. 7:11; Gal. 2:18; Rom. 5:8). Either makes good sense here. {*I speak as a man*} (cf. Gal. 3:15). Showing Rabbinic style, it is as if to say, "pardon me for this line of argument."

9. {*Are we in worse case than they?*} The American revisers render is: "Are we in worse case than they? There is still not fresh light on this difficult and common word though it occurs alone in the New Testament. Possibly translate contextually, "are we preferred?"; though this meaning is uncertain.

10. {*As it is written*} (2 Cor. 6:16; Rom. 9:25, 27; 11:26, 34; 12:19). Paul here uses a chain of text quotations (compound quotations) to prove his point in Romans 3:9 that Jews are in no better fix than the Greeks for all are under sin. {*There is none righteous, no, not one*} This sentence is like a motto for all the rest, a summary for what follows.

11. {*That understandeth*} Lit. "to send together," to grasp, to comprehend.

12. {*They are together become unprofitable*} Lit. "not + useful" (cf. Luke 17:10; Matt. 25:30). The Hebrew word means to go bad, become sour like milk (Lightfoot).

13. {*Open sepulchre*} Their mouth (words) are like the odor of a newly opened grave. {*They have used deceit*} This is the Greek verb *dolioô*, from the common adjective *dolios*, deceitful (2 Cor. 11:13).

17. {*The way of peace*} Wherever they go they leave a trail of woe and destruction.

19. {*That every mouth may be stopped*} Stopping mouths is a difficult business (cf. Titus 1:11). Paul seems here to be speaking directly to Jews, the hardest to convince. With the previous proof on that point he covers the whole ground for he made the case against the Gentiles in Romans 1:18-32.

20. {*By the works of the law*} Lit. "out of works of law." Mosaic law and any law as the source of being set right with God (cf. Ps. 43:2 and Gal. 2:16). {*The knowledge of sin*} (Gal. 3:19-22). The effect of law universally is rebellion to it (1 Cor. 15:56). He has now proven the guilt of both Gentile and Jew.

22. {*Through faith in Jesus Christ*} (Gal. 2:16). Jesus is the object of our faith. {*Distinction*} (cf. 1 Cor. 14:7, also Rom. 10:12). The Jew was first in privilege as in penalty (cf. Rom. 2:9), but justification or setting right with God is offered to both on the same terms.

23. {*Sinned*} The Greek tense gathers up the whole race into one statement. {*And fall short*} Greek tense translates, "still fall short."

24. {*Being justified*} Lit. "to set right," repeated action in each case, each being set right. {*Through the redemption*} This is a releasing by ransom. God did not set men right out of hand with nothing done about men's sins. We have the words of Jesus that he came to give his life a ransom for many (Mark 10:45; Matt. 20:28).

25. {*A propitiation*} This is the Greek word *hilastêrion*. The only other NT example of this word is in Heb. 9:5 where we have the "cherubin overshadowing the mercy seat" (*to hilastêrion*). In Hebrews the adjective is used as a substantive or as "the propitiatory place." But that idea does not suit here. *Hilastêrion* is an adjective from *hilaskomai,* to make propitiation (Heb. 2:17) and is kin in meaning to *hilasmos,* propitiation (cf. 1 John 2:2; 4:10). God gave his Son as the means of propitiation (1 John 2:2). {*To show his righteousness*} (cf. 2 Cor. 8:24). That is, a God-kind of righteousness. God could not let sin go as if a mere slip. God demanded the atonement and provided it. {*Because of the passing over*} Late word from *pariêmi,* to let go, to relax. {*Done aforetime*} This refers to the sins before the coming of Christ (Acts 14:16; 17:30; Heb. 9:15). {*Forbearance*} This is the holding back of God (cf. Rom. 2:4).

26. {*Just and the justifier of*} (cf. Rom. 4:5) This is the key phrase which establishes the connection between the "righteousness of God" and the righteousness out of faith. Nowhere has Paul put the problem of God more acutely or profoundly. To pronounce the unrighteous righteous is unjust by itself (Rom. 4:5). God's mercy would not allow him to leave man to his fate. God's justice demanded some punishment for sin; hence the only possible way to save some was the propitiatory offering of Christ and the call for faith on man's part.

27. {*It is excluded*} "It is completely shut out." {*Nay; but by a law of faith*} The "no" is strong. "Law of faith," by the principle of faith in harmony with God's love and grace.

28. {*We reckon therefore*} (cf. Rom. 3:21). Translate "my fixed opinion" is (cf. Rom. 2:3; 4:3; 8:18; 14:14).

30. {*If so...*} It means "if on the whole." {*By faith*} This translates, "out of faith," i.e., springing out of. {*Through faith*} This translates, "by means of the faith" (just mentioned).

CHAPTER 4

2. {*But not towards God*} Abraham deserved all the respect from men that came to him, but his relation to God was a different matter. He had *in relation to God* no ground of boasting at all.

3. {*It was reckoned unto him for righteousness*} This is the Greek verb *logizomai,* to set down accounts (literally or metaphorically). It was set down on the credit side of the ledger "for" righteousness. What was set down? His believing God.

4. {*But as of debt*} This is an illustration of the workman who gets his wages due him, not grace.

5. {*That justifieth the ungodly*} This is the impious, irreverent man (cf. Rom. 1:25). This is a forensic figure. (Shedd) The man is taken as he is and pardoned.

7. {*Blessed*} (cf. Matt. 5:3ff., also Ps. 32:1). This confirms Paul's interpretation of Genesis 15:6. {*Iniquities*} This is violations of law, a more specific than general words for sin.

8. {*Will not reckon*} The "never" is a strong negation.

9. {*Is this blessing then pronounced?*} Paul now proceeds to show that Abraham was said in Genesis 15:6 to be set right with God by faith *before* he was circumcised.

11. {*A seal of the righteousness of the faith*} The Greek word "seal" *sphragis* is an old word for the seal placed on books (Rev. 5:1), for a signet ring (Rev. 7:2), the stamp made by the seal (2 Tim. 2:19), that by which anything is confirmed (1 Cor. 9:2) as here.

12. {*The father of circumcision*} This is likely "a father of a circumcised progeny," though other interpretations are out there. {*But who *also walk*} (cf. 2 Cor. 12:18). "Walk" is the Greek verb *stoicheô,* a military term, to walk in file (cf. Gal. 5:25; Phil. 3:16).

13. {*That he should be the heir of the world*} (cf. Gen. 12:7). But where is that promise? It is the whole chain of promises about his son, his descendants, the Messiah, and the blessing to the world through him.

15. {*Worketh wrath...neither is there transgression*} That is, because of disobedience to it. There is no responsibility for the violation of a nonexistent law.

16. {*Of faith according to grace*} Faith is the source, grace the pattern. {*Sure*} This is the Greek word *bebaian,* stable, fast, firm; from verb *bainô,* to walk.

17. {*Calleth the things that are not as though they were*} Lit. "summons the nonexisting as existing." Abraham's body was old and decrepit. God rejuvenated him and Sarah (Heb. 11:19).

18. {*In hope believed against hope*} Translate "past hope in (upon) hope he trusted." This is a graphic picture.

19. {*Without being weakened in faith*} Translate the Greek tense, "not becoming weak in faith." {*Now as good as dead*} Greek tense translates, "now already dead." He knew he was too old to become father of a child.

20. {*He wavered not through unbelief*} This is the Greek common verb *diakrinô,* to separate, to distinguish between, to decide between, to desert, to dispute, and the sense here "to be divided in one's own mind" (Matt. 21:22; Mark 11:23; Rom. 14:23; Jas. 1:6).

21. {*Being fully assured*} Lit. "to bear or bring full (full measure), to settle fully" (cf. Luke 1:1; Rom. 14:5).

25. {*For our justification*} (cf. Isa. 53:12). Paul does not mean to separate the resurrection from the death of Christ in the work of atonement, but simply to show that the resurrection is at one with the death on the Cross in proof of Christ's claims.

CHAPTER 5

1. {*Being therefore justified by faith*} This is the Greek verb *dikaioô,* to set right and expressing antecedent action to the verb "we have." The "therefore" refers to the preceding conclusive argument (chapters 1 to 4) that this is done by faith. {*Let us have peace with God*} "Let us have" is the correct text, not "we have." "Let us have" is in the volitive subjunctive mode (the speaker has a desire to move the recipient to continue along to the conclusion, yet not quite as a command).

2. {*We have had*} The Greek tense has a focus that we "still have it." {*Wherein we stand*} Grace is here present as a field into which we have been introduced and where we stand and we should enjoy all the privileges of this grace about us. {*Let us rejoice*} (cf. Rom. 5:1) The exhortation is that we keep on enjoying peace with God and keep on exulting in hope of the glory of God.

3. {*But let us also rejoice in our tribulations*} "Rejoice," is extended to mean "glory," "exult." The "let us" exhortations of verses one to three hold up the high ideal for the Christian because of his being set right with God. It is one thing to endure tribulations without complaint, but it is another to find ground of glorying in the midst of them.

4. {*Knowing*} This gives the reason for the previous exhortation to glory in tribulations. He gives a linked chain, one linking to the other (tribulation, patience, experience, hope) running into verse 5.

6. {*For the ungodly*} "For" means "in behalf, instead of " (cf. Gal. 3:13 and Rom. 5:7).

7. {*Scarcely*} This is the Greek adverb *molis,* from *molos,* toil (cf. Acts 14:18). {*Righteous...good*} As Greek usage shows, the righteous man being absolutely without sympathy while the good man is beneficent and kind.

8. {*While we were yet sinners*} This is not because we were Jews or Greeks, rich or poor, righteous or good, but plain sinners (cf. Luke 18:13).

9. {*Much more then*} This is an argument from the greater to the less. The great thing is the justification in Christ's blood.

10. {*We were reconciled to God*} (cf. 2 Cor. 5:18). Paul does not conceive it our task to reconcile God to us. God has attended to that himself (Rom. 3:25).

11. {*Through whom we have now received the reconciliation*} This is "now" in contrast with the future consummation and a sure pledge and guarantee of it.

12. {*Therefore*} Lit. "for this reason," referring to the argument of Romans 5:1 to 11; justification, joy, reconciliation, future salvation, etc. {*As through one man*} The effects of Adam's sin are transmitted to his descendants. Paul does not say that the whole race receives the full benefit of Christ's atoning death, but only those who do. Christ is the head of all believers as Adam is the head of the race. {*Sin entered into the world*} Though modern notions deny true sin, this is a personification of sin and represented as coming from the outside into the world of humanity. {*And so death passed unto all men*} This means both physical death (cf. Gen. 2:17; 3:19) and eternal death (Rom. 5:17, 21). {*For that all sinned*} The Greek tense is one of a summary as of the history of the race as committing sin.

13. {*Until the law*} This refers to Mosaic law. Sin was there before the Mosaic law, for the Jews were like Gentiles who had the law of reason and conscience (Rom. 2:12-16). {*Sin is not imputed*} Lit. "to put down in the ledger to one's account." {*When there is no law*} This means, "no law of any kind."

14. {*Even over them that had not sinned after the likeness of Adam's transgression*} Adam violated an express command of God and Moses gave the law of God clearly. And yet sin and death followed all from Adam on until Moses, showing clearly that the sin of Adam brought terrible consequences upon the race. {*A figure*} (cf. Acts 7:43; 1 Thess. 1:7; 2 Thess. 3:9; 1 Cor. 10:6). Adam is a type of Christ in holding a relation to those affected by the headship in each case, but the parallel is not precise as Paul shows.

16. {*Through one that sinned*} Lit. "Through one having sinned." That is, Adam. {*Of one...of many trespasses...justification*} Note the contrast. Adam's one transgression brought condemnation, yet out of the many trespasses grew the gift by Christ-justification.

17. Note the balanced words in the contrast (transgression/grace; death/life; Adam/Jesus Christ (the verb "to reign" in both).

18. {*So then*} This is the conclusion of the argument (cf. Rom. 7:3, 25; 8:12). Paul resumes the parallel between Adam and Christ begun in Romans 5:12 and interrupted until now.

20. {*Came in beside*} Lit. "[Law] came in beside" (cf. Gal. 2:4 and also Rom. 5:12). The Mosaic law came into this state of things, in between Adam and Christ. {*That the trespass might abound*} "So that" expresses result. This increase was the actual effect of the Mosaic law for the Jews, the necessary result of all prohibitions. {*Did abound more exceedingly*} This is the Greek word *huperperisseuô* (cf. 2 Cor. 7:4), a strong word which in effect goes the superlative one better (cf. also I Tim. 1:14). The flood of grace surpassed the flood of sin.

CHAPTER 6

1. {*What shall we say then?*} This is a debater's phrase and an echo of the rabbinical method of question and answer, but also an expression of exultant victory of grace versus sin. {*Shall we continue in sin?*} (cf. I Cor. 16:8). The practice of sin as a habit is here raised. {*That grace may abound*} This means to set free the superfluity of grace alluded to like putting money in circulation. This is a horrible thought and yet Paul faced it. The very thought is false piety.

2. {*Died to sin*} This occurred when we surrendered to Christ and took him as Lord and Savior. {*How*} This is a rhetorical question.

3. {*Were baptized into Christ*} Better "in" (the sphere/relation of) Christ. Baptism is the public proclamation of one's inward spiritual relation to Christ attained before the baptism. {*Into his death*} Translate "in relation to his death," which relation Paul proceeds to explain by the symbolism of the ordinance.

4. {*In newness of life*} The picture in baptism points two ways, backwards to Christ's death and burial and to our death to sin (cf. Rom. 6:1), forwards to Christ's resurrection (and also ours) from the dead and to our new life pledged by the coming out of the watery grave to walk on the other side of the baptismal grave.

5. {*For if we have become united with him by the likeness of his death*} "United" is lit. "to grow together." Baptism as a picture of death and burial symbolizes our likeness to Christ in his death.

6. {*Was crucified with him*} (cf. Gal. 2:19). This took place not at baptism, but only pictured there. It took place when "we died to sin" (cf. Rom. 6:1). {*The body of sin*} Translate, "the body of which sin has taken possession," that is, the body marked by sin. {*That so we should no longer be in bondage to sin*} "That" shows purpose. The Greek tense translates, "[not] continue serving sin (as slaves)."

7. {*Is justified*} The Greek verb is *dikaioô*, stands justified, set free from, adding this great word to death and life (cf. Rom. 6:1, 2).

9. {*Dieth no more*} Christ's particular death occurs but once (cf. Heb. 10:10). This is a refutation of the "sacrificial" character of the "mass."

10. {*Once*} Translate, "Once and once only" (Heb. 9:26).

11. {*Reckon ye also yourselves*} This is a plea to live up to the ideal of the baptized life.

12. {*Reign*} Greek tense translates "let not sin continue to reign" as it did once (cf. Rom. 5:12).

13. {*Neither present*} Lit. " not + to place beside" Greek tense translates "stop presenting your members or do not have the habit of doing so." {*Instruments*} This is an old word for tools of any kind for shop or war (John 18:3; 2 Cor. 6:7; 10:4; Rom. 13:12). Possibly here figure of two armies arrayed against each other (Gal. 5:16-24).

14. {*Shall not have dominion*} Lit. "shall not lord it over you," even if not yet wholly dead (cf. 2 Cor. 1:24).

15. {*Shall we sin?*} Here the focus is on occasional acts of sin as opposed to the life of sin (cf. Rom. 6:1). {*Because*} (cf. Rom. 6:1 and 14). Surely, the objector says, we may take a night off now and then and sin a little bit "since we are under grace."

16. {*His servants ye are whom ye obey*} Just as we are dead to sin and alive to Christ, Paul uses slavery against the idea of occasional lapses into sin. Loyalty to Christ will not permit occasional crossing over to the other side to Satan's line.

17. {*Whereas ye were*} Imperfect but no "whereas" in the Greek. Paul is not grateful that they were once slaves of sin, but only that, though they once were, they turned from that state.

19. {*I speak after the manner of men*} (cf. Rom. 3:5; Gal. 3:15) Lit. "I speak a human word." This discussion of being slaves to righteousness is a good word, especially for our times when self-assertiveness and personal liberty bulk so large in modern speech. {*Because of the infirmity of your flesh*} That is, because of defective spiritual insight largely due to moral defects also. {*Servants to uncleanness*} This is patently true in sexual sins, in drunkenness, and all fleshly sins, absolutely slaves like drug addicts. {*So now*} That is, now that you are born again in Christ. {*Unto sanctification*} This is the goal, the blessed consummation that demands and deserves the new slavery without occasional lapses or sprees (cf. Rom. 6:15). This is a life process of consecration, not an instantaneous act.

23. {*Wages*} This is the Greek word *opsônion,* late Greek for wages of soldier, here of sin (cf. Luke 3:14; 1 Cor. 9:7; 2 Cor. 11:8). Sin pays its wages in full (eternal death) with no cut. But eternal life is God's gift, not wages.

CHAPTER 7

1. {*To men that know the law*} The Romans, whether Jews or Gentiles, knew the principle of law. {*A man*} Lit. "the person" (generic).

2. {*Is bound*} The Greek tense translates "stands bound." This is a condition considered not actually fulfilled, but is a supposable case. {*She is discharged*} The Greek verb is *katargeô,* to make void. She stands free from the law of the husband (cf. Rom. 6:6).

4. {*Ye also were made to the law*} "Die" is the Greek verb *thanatoô,* to put to death (Matt. 10:21) or to make to die (extinct) as here and Rom. 8:13. The analogy calls for the death of the law, but Paul refuses to say that. He changes the structure and makes them dead to the law as the husband (Rom. 6:3-6). {*That we should be joined to another*} This is the first mention of the saints as wedded to Christ as their Husband (cf. 1 Cor. 6:13; Gal. 4:26). {*That we might bring forth fruit unto God*} He changes the metaphor to that of the tree used in Romans 6:22.

5. {*In the flesh*} Lit. "flesh" in the sense as in Romans 6:19 and 7:18, 25. The "flesh" is not inherently sinful, but is subject to sin. It is what Paul means by being "under the law." {*Sinful passions*} Lit. "Passions of sins" or marked by sins. {*To bring forth fruit unto death*} This is a vivid picture of the seeds of sin working for death.

6. {*In newness of spirit*} The death to the letter of the law (the old husband) has set us free to the new life in Christ. So Paul has shown again the obligation on us to live for Christ.

7. {*I had not known coveting*} The law is not itself sin nor the cause of sin. Men with their sinful natures turn law into an occasion for sinful acts.

8. {*Finding occasion*} "Occasion" is a starting place from which to rush into acts of sin, excuses for doing what they want to do. {*Wrought in me*} This is the Greek verb *katergazomai,* to work out (to the finish). The command not to lust made me lust more. {*Dead*} That is, sin is inactive-not nonexistent. Sin in reality was there in a dormant state.

9. {*Sin revived*} Sin came back to life, waked up, the blissful innocent stage was over, the commandment having come. {*But I died*} My seeming life was over for I was conscious of sin, of violation of law. I was dead before, but I did not know. Now I found out that I was spiritually dead.

10. {*This I found unto death*} Lit. "the commandment the one for (meant for) life, this was found for me unto death."

11. {*Beguiled me*} Lit. "completely made me lose my way," (cf. 1 Cor. 3:18; 2 Cor. 11:3). {*Slew me*} Lit. "killed me off" and made a clean job of it. Sin here is personified as the tempter (Gen. 3:13).

12. {*Holy, and righteous, and good*} This is the conclusion to the question of Romans 7:7, 'Is the law sin?'. The commandment is God's and so like Him.

13. {*Become death unto me?*} This is a new turn to the problem. Admitting the goodness of God's law, did it issue in death for me? No, sin became death for me. {*Might become exceedingly sinful*} "Utterly" is the Greek word *huperbolê,* which is our word *hyperbole.* The excesses of sin reveal its real nature. Only then do some people get their eyes opened.

14. {*But I am carnal*} (cf. 1 Cor. 3:1). Lit. "fleshen" a relatively emphatic word expressing such a thought. {*Sold under sin*} (cf. Matt. 13:46; Acts 2:45). The Greek tense shows a state of completion. Sin has closed the mortgage and owns its slave.

15. {*I know not*} Lit. "I do not recognize" in its true nature. My spiritual perceptions are dulled, blinded by sin (2 Cor. 4:4). The dual life pictured here by Paul finds an echo in us all.

16. {*I consent unto the law*} Lit. "I speak with [the law]." My wanting to do the opposite of what I do proves my acceptance of God's law as good.

17. {*But sin that dwelleth in me*} Translate "but the dwelling in me sin." Not my true self, my higher personality, but my lower self due to my slavery to indwelling sin. Paul does not mean to say that his whole self has no moral responsibility by using this paradox.

18. {*The wishing*} What the better self wants, the lower self cannot do.

20. {*It is no more I that do it*} (cf. Rom. 7:17). That is the real Ego, my better self, and yet there is responsibility and guilt for the struggle goes on.

21. {*The law*} That is, the principle already set forth accordingly in verses 18, 19. This is the way it works, but there is no ceasing in the stings of conscience.

22. {*For I delight in*} Translate "I rejoice with the law of God," my real self, the inner being of the conscience as opposed to "the outward man" (cf. 2 Cor. 4:16; Eph. 3:16).

23. {*Warring against*} This is the rare Greek verb *antistrateuomai*, carry on a campaign against. {*The law of my mind*} This is the reflective intelligence of the inner being (cf. Rom. 7:22). It is this higher self that agrees that the law of God is good (cf. Rom. 7:12, 16, 22). {*Bringing me into captivity*} This is a vivid verb for capture and slavery (cf. Luke 21:24; 2 Cor. 10:5).

24. {*O wretched man that I am*} This is the Greek word *talaipôros*, from *talaô*, to bear, and *pôros*, a callus (cf. Rev. 3:17). This is a heart-rending cry from the depths of despair. {*Out of the body of this death*} (cf. Rom. 7:13). Paul is not exaggerating, he calls himself chief of sinners (cf. 1 Tim. 1:15).

25. {*I thank God*} Note of victory over death through Jesus Christ our Lord. {*So then I myself*} His whole self in his unregenerate state gives a divided service as he has already shown above.

CHAPTER 8

1. {*No condemnation*} As sinners we deserved condemnation in our unregenerate state. But God offers pardon to those in Christ Jesus, so one can now lead the consecrated, the crucified, the baptized life.

2. {*The law of the Spirit of life*} This is the principle or authority exercised by the Holy Spirit which bestows life and which rests "in Christ Jesus." {*Made me free*} (cf. Rom. 7:7-24). We are pardoned, we are free and able by the help of the Holy Spirit to live the new life in Christ.

3. {*That the law could not do*} (cf. Rom. 7:7-24). Lit. "the impossibility of the law." {*It was weak*} The Greek tense shows it as continued weak as already shown. {*Condemned sin in the flesh*} He condemned the sin of men and the condemnation took place in the flesh of Jesus.

4. {*Might be fulfilled*} The Greek syntax shows this as the purpose of the death of Christ. Christ met it all in our stead (Rom. 3:21-26). {*Not after the flesh, but after the Spirit*} There are two laws of life (flesh, Rom. 7:7-24; Spirit, Rom. 8:1-11). Most likely this refers to the Holy Spirit or else the renewed spirit of man.

5. {*Do mind*} (cf. Gal. 5:16-24). This is the Greek verb *phroneô*, to think, to put the mind on (cf. Matt. 16:23; Rom. 12:16).

7. {*Is not subject*} This is the Greek verb *hupotassô*, a military term for subjection to orders, the present tense here means continued insubordination. {***Neither indeed can it be***} This is the helpless state of the unregenerate man Paul has shown above apart from Christ. Hope lies in Christ (Rom. 7:25) and the Spirit of life (Rom. 8:2).

8. {***Cannot please God***} Though the unsaved is still responsible and can be saved by the change of heart through the Holy Spirit.

9. {***But in the spirit***} This refers here probably to the Holy Spirit. It is not Pantheism or Buddhism that Paul here teaches, but the mystical union of the believer with Christ in the Holy Spirit.

13. {***Ye must die...Ye shall live***} Lit. "You are on the point of dying." This refers to eternal death and life.

14. {***Sons of God***} Comparable to "children of God" (cf. Rom. 8:16), this refers here to those born again (the second birth) both Jews and Gentiles in the full sense, "the sons of Abraham" (Gal. 3:7), the children of faith.

15. {***The spirit of adoption***} (cf. Gal. 4:5). Both Jews and Gentiles receive this "adoption" into the family of God with all its privileges." {***Whereby we cry, Abba, Father***} This is a double use of "father" as a child's privilege (cf. Gal. 4:6).

16. {***The Spirit himself***} (cf. John 16:13, 26). Though "himself" is lit. the grammatical neuter "itself," it is a grave mistake to use the neuter "it" or "itself" when referring to the Holy Spirit, he is a person.

17. {***Joint-heirs with Christ***} This is the Greek word *sunklêronomos* (cf. Rom. 8:29). (Note all that we "share" and are "with" in this verse.)

19. {***The earnest expectation of creation***} (cf. Phil. 1:20) Lit. "to watch eagerly with outstretched head." {***The revealing of the sons of God***} (cf. 1 John 3:2; 2 Thess. 2:8; Col. 3:4). This mystical sympathy of physical nature with the work of grace is beyond the comprehension of most of us.

20. {***Was subjected***} (cf. Rom. 8:7). {***To vanity***} This is from the Greek *mataios,* empty, vain (cf. Eph. 4:17; 2 Pet.2:18). {***Not of its own will***} (cf. 1 Cor. 9:27). It was due to the effect of man's sin.

22. {***Groaneth and travaileth in pain***} Nature is pictured in the pangs of childbirth.

23. {***The first fruits of the Spirit***} The Holy Spirit came on the great Pentecost and his current blessings: spiritual gifts (1 Cor. 12-14); moral/spiritual gifts (cf. Gal. 5:22), and greater ones are to come (1 Cor. 15:44).

24. {***For by hope were we saved***} This can be translated also "by" hope or "for" hope (of the redemption of the body).

26. {*Helpeth...*} (cf. Luke 10:40). This is the Greek verb *sunanti-lambanomai,* "to lend a hand together with, at the same time with one." The Holy Spirit takes hold at our side at the very time of our weakness and before it is too late. {*As we ought*} Lit. "as it is necessary." How true this is of all of us in our praying. {*Maketh intercession*} This is a picturesque word of rescue by one who "happens on" one who is in trouble and "in his behalf" pleads. This is work of our Helper, the Spirit himself.

27. {*According to the will of God*} The Holy Spirit does more than plead our cause before God here, for the Holy Spirit interprets our prayers to God in the intercession.

28. {*According to his purpose*} (cf. Rom. 3:24). Paul accepts fully human free agency but through it all runs God's sovereignty as here and on its gracious side (Rom. 9:11; 3:11; 2 Tim. 1:9).

29. {*Foreknew*} (cf. Acts 26:5, also Ps. 1:6 (LXX) and Matt. 7:23). This foreknowledge and choice is placed in eternity in Ephesians 1:4. {*He foreordained*} Lit. "to appoint beforehand [for eternity]," (cf. Acts 4:28; 1 Cor. 2:7). {*Conformed to the image*} (cf. 2 Cor. 4:4; Col. 1:15). This is an inward and not merely superficial conformity. Here "form" and "likeness" express the gradual change in us until we acquire the likeness of Christ the Son of God so that we ourselves shall ultimately have the family likeness of sons of God. This is a glorious destiny. {*First born among many brethren*} Here he is first born from the dead (cf. Col. 1:18), the Eldest Brother in this family of God's sons, though at the same time a "Son" in a sense not true of us.

30. {*Called...justified...glorified*} Glorification is stated as already consummated (constative aorists, all of them), though still in the future in the fullest sense.

33. {*Who shall lay anything to the charge of God's elect?*} This is the Greek verb *egkaleô,* to come forward as accuser (forensic term) in case in court, to impeach (cf. Acts 19:40; 23:29; 26:2). Satan is the great Accuser of the brethren. {*It is God that justifieth*} God is the Judge who sets us right according to his plan for justification (Rom. 3:21-31).

34. {*Shall condemn*} (cf. 1 John 2:1). Our Advocate paid the debt for our sins with his blood. The score is settled. We are free (Rom. 8:1).

36. {*Even as it is written*} (cf. Ps. 44:23). {*We are killed*} (cf. Rom. 7:4). The Greek tense has the idea of continuous martyrdom (cf. 1 Cor. 15:31).

37. {*Nay*} Translate "on the contrary." {***We are more than conquerors***} We gain a surpassing victory through the one who loved us.

38. {***For I am persuaded***} The Greek tense translates, "I stand convinced." The items mentioned are those that people dread (life, death, supernatural powers, above, below, any creature to cover any omissions).

39. {***To separate us***} (cf. Rom. 8:35). God's love (in Christ) is victor over all possible foes.

CHAPTER 9

2. {***Sorrow***} Because the Jews were rejecting Christ the Messiah. {***Unceasing pain in my heart***} This is consuming grief (cf. 1 Tim. 6:10).

3. {***I could wish***} Translate "I was on the point of wishing."

4. {***Israelites***} This is the covenant name of the chosen people. {***The glory***} This is the Shekinah Glory of God (Rom. 3:23) and used of Jesus (cf. Jas. 2:1). {***The covenants***} Note the plural because they are renewed often (Gen. 6:18; 9:9; 15:18; 17:2, 7, 9; Exod. 2:24).

5. {***As concerning the flesh***} Paul limits the descent of Jesus from the Jews to his human side (cf. Rom. 1:3). {***Who is over all, God blessed for ever***} A clear statement of the deity of Christ following the remark about his humanity.

6. {***Hath come to nought***} Lit. "to fall out." {***For they are not all Israel, which are of Israel***} (cf. Rom. 4:1ff). This contrasts a literal nation and a spiritual entity. This startling paradox is not a new idea with Paul, that those of faith are the true sons of Abraham (Gal. 3:7-9).

7. {***Seed of Abraham***} (cf. Gen. 21:12). This is physical descent here, but spiritual seed in next verse.

8. {***The children of the promise***} The promise is not through Ishmael, but through Isaac. He is not speaking of Christians here, but simply showing that the privileges of the Jews were not due to their physical descent from Abraham (cf. Luke 3:8).

9. {***A word of promise***} Lit. "this word is one of promise." Paul combines Genesis 18:10, 14 from the LXX.

10. {***Having conceived of one***} Lit. "having a marriage bed from one" husband. One father and twins.

11. {***The children being not yet born***} There is no word for children nor even the pronoun "they" in the Greek phrase. {***According-to election***} This is the Greek verb *eklegô,* to select, to choose out (cf. 1 Thess.

1:4). Here it is the purpose of God which has worked according to the principles of election.

12. {*But of him that calleth*} (cf. Gen. 25:33 [LXX]). The source of the selection is God himself.

13. {*But Esau I hated*} (cf. Mal. 1:2). This language sounds a bit harsh to us. It is possible that the Greek word *miseô* did not always carry the full force of what we mean by "hate" (cf. Matt. 6:24; Luke 14:26; John 12:25). There is no doubt about God's preference for Jacob and rejection of Esau.

14. {*Is there unrighteousness with God?*} The Greek emphasizes God cannot be near (lit. "beside") injustice.

17. {*To Pharaoh*} (Exod. 9:16). There is a national election (choice of God) as seen in verses 7-13, but here Paul deals with the election of individuals.

19. {*Why doth he still find fault?*} (cf. Heb. 8:8). Paul's imaginary objector picks up the admission that God hardened Pharaoh's heart. {*Withstandeth his will*} This is the Greek verb *anthistêmi*, to stand, and the Greek tense translates "maintains" a stand.

20. {*The thing formed*} (cf. Isa. 29:16). This is the Greek word *plasma*, from *plassô*, to mold, as with clay or wax. The absolute power of God as Creator like the potter's use of clay (Isa. 44:8; 45:8-10; Jer. 18:6).

21. {*One...another*} (cf. Mark 11:16). Here is a strong contrast. Paul thus claims clearly God's sovereign right to use men (already sinners) for his own purpose.

22. {*Vessels of wrath*} (cf. Jer. 50:25 [LXX Jer. 27:25], cf. also Eph. 2:3). {*Fitted*} This is the Greek verb *katartizô*, to equip (see Matt. 4:21; 2 Cor. 13:11), a state of readiness. Paul does not say here that God did it or that they did it. They are responsible (cf. 1 Thess. 2:15). {*Unto destruction*} This is endless perdition (Matt. 7:13; 2 Thess. 2:3; Phil. 3:19), not annihilation.

23. {*Afore prepared*} Lit. "to make ready before" (cf. Eph. 2:10, also Rom. 8:28-30).

25. {*In Hosea*} (cf. Hos. 2:23). Hosea refers to the ten tribes and Paul applies the principle stated there to the Gentiles. Hosea had a son named *Lo-ammi* = not people of me (not my people). {*Which was not beloved*} This is the LXX rendering of *Lo-ruhamah* (not mercy, without mercy or love [*not* is emphatic]), name of Hosea's daughter.

26. {*Ye are not my people*} (cf. Hos. 1:10 [LXX Hos. 2:1]). {*There*} This is Palestine in the original, but Paul applies it to scattered Jews and Gentiles everywhere.

27. {*It is the remnant that shall be saved*} Isaiah cries in anguish over the outlook for Israel, but sees hope for the remnant.

28. {*Finishing it and cutting it short*} (cf. Isa. 28:22). Lit. "finishing it and cutting it short," with a focus that these two Greek verbs have a perfective use, "finishing completely," "cutting off completely" (cf. Luke 4:13).

29. {*Had left*}This condition in Greek is determined as unfulfilled, from the view of the speaker, referring to the remnant of verse 27.

30. {*Attained*} This carries out the figure in "pursue." It was a curious paradox, those "not pursuing" seize or grasp righteousness.

31. {*Did not arrive at that law*} This is the Greek verb *phthanô*, to anticipate (1 Thess. 4:15), now just to arrive as here and 2 Corinthians 10:14. Israel failed to reach legal righteousness, because to do that one had to keep perfectly all the law.

32. {*They stumbled at the stone of stumbling*} (cf. Isa. 8:14). The Jews found Christ a *skandalon* [a cause of snaring] (1 Cor. 1:23).

33. {*Rock of offense*} (cf. Isa. 8:14 and 28:16). Lit. "a rock of snare," i.e., a rock which the Jews made a cause of stumbling (cf. 1 Pet.2:8).

CHAPTER 10

1. {*Supplication*} This is the Greek word *deêsis*, from *deomai*, to want, to beg, to pray. It is noteworthy that, immediately after the discussion of the rejection of Christ by the Jews, Paul prays so earnestly for the Jews unto salvation. Paul would not have prayed if they had been absolutely reprobate.

2. {*But not according to knowledge*} They had knowledge of God and so were superior to the Gentiles in privilege (Rom. 2:9-11), but they sought God in an external way by rules and rites and missed him (Rom. 9:30-33).

4. {*The end of the law*} Paul's main idea is that Christ ended the law as a method of salvation for every one that believes whether Jew or Gentile.

6. {*Say not in thy heart*} This means "to think," (cf. Matt. 3:9). {*That is, to bring Christ down*} This is *Midrash* or interpretation as in Robring Christ down to earth.

7. {*Into the abyss*} (cf. Luke 8:31) This is a place bottomless like sea (Ps. 106:26), of torment (cf. Rev. 9:1). Paul seems to refer to Hades or Sheol (Acts 2:27, 31).

8. {*But what saith it?*} That is, "the from faith righteousness." {*Which we preach*} Paul seizes upon the words of Moses with the orator's instinct and with rhetorical skill, and applies them to the Incarnation and Resurrection of Christ.

9. {*If thou shalt confesss and shalt believe*} Faith precedes confession, of course. The Greek condition is that which is not necessarily a fact or fulfilled, but nevertheless a potential condition. {*With thy mouth Jesus as Lord*} "Lord" is the Greek *Kurios* (cf. 1 Cor. 12:3; Phil. 2:11). No Jew would do this who had not really trusted Christ, for *Kurios* in the LXX is used of God. No Gentile would do it who had not ceased worshipping the emperor as *Kurios*. The word *Kurios* was and is the touchstone of faith.

10. {*Man believeth*} Lit. "it is believed." (cf. Rom. 10:9). The order is reversed in this verse and the true order (faith, then confession). {*Confession is made*} Lit. "it is confessed."

14. {*Except they be sent?*} This is the Greek verb *apostellô*, to send, from which verb *apostolos* apostle comes, which here are assumed to have been sent.

15. {*How beautiful*} (cf. Isa. 52:7) This quotation is picturing the messengers of the restoration from the Jewish captivity.

16. {*But they did not all hearken*} (cf. Isa. 53:1). They heard, but did not heed.

18. {*Did they not hear?*} Translate, "Did they fail to hear?" expecting the negative answer. {*Sound*} This is used as the vibration of a musical string (cf. 1 Cor. 14:7). {*The world*} This is the inhabited earth (cf. Luke 2:1).

19. {*Did Israel not know?*} Translate again, "Did Israel fail to know?" {*First*} (cf. Deut. 32:21). Moses, before anyone else. {*With that which is no nation*} The Jews had worshipped "no-gods" and now God shows favors to a "no-nation" (people).

20. {*Is very bold*} (cf. Isa. 65:1). This is the Greek verb *apotolmaô,* to assume boldness. He uses this in support of his own courage against the prejudice of the Jews (cf. Rom. 9:30-33).

CHAPTER II

1. {*Did God cast off?*} The Greek calls for an emphatic "No!" Himself proof, Paul refers to the promise in the OT made three times: 1 Samuel 12:22; Psalm 94:14 (Ps. 93:14 LXX); Psalm 94:4.

2. {*Whom he foreknew*} (cf. Rom. 8:29). The nation of Israel was God's chosen people and so all the individuals in it could not be cast off. {*He pleadeth*} Lit., "to plead [against]." (cf. Rom. 8:27, 34).

3. {*They have digged down*} This is the Greek verb *kataskaptô,* to dig under or down (cf. 1 Kgs. 19:10, 14, 18). {*Life*} Lit. "soul," used here (like "Spirit") for the personality and for the immortal part of man.

7. {*Obtained*} This is the Greek verb *epitugchanô,* to hit upon (cf. Rom. 9:30-33 for the failure of the Jews). {*Were hardened*} Lit. "to cover with thick skin" (cf. 2 Cor. 3:14; Mark 3:5).

8. {*A spirit of stupor*} (cf. Deut. 19:4 and Isa. 29:10; 6:9). The Greek word *katanuxis* is a late and rare word from *katanussô,* to prick or stick (Acts 2:37). The torpor seems the result of too much sensation, dulled by incitement into apathy.

9. {*A snare...trap...stumbling-block*} Three words for traps: first means a snare for birds and beasts (cf. Luke 21:34-35); the last is a snare, trap stick or trigger over which they fall (cf. 1 Cor. 1:23; Rom. 9:33). {*A recompense*} This is to repay here in a bad sense.

10. {*Bow down*} Lit. "to bend together" as of captives whose backs were bent under burdens.

11. {*By their fall*} Lit. a falling aside or a false step (cf. Rom. 5:15-20). {*For to provoke them to jealousy*} (cf. 1 Cor. 10:22). As an historical fact Paul turned to the Gentiles when the Jews rejected his message (Acts 13:45; 28:28).

12. {*Their loss*} Possibly this means "defeat" here (cf. 1 Cor. 6:7 and Isa. 31:8). {*Fulness*} Perhaps the meaning here is "completion," though other senses are possible (1 Cor. 10:26, 28, also Eph. 1:23).

14. {*If by any means*} This is showing purpose or aim, and is a kind of indirect discourse.

15. {*The casting away of them*} Lit. to throw off (Mark 10:50, also Acts 27:22). {*Life from the dead*} Already the conversion of Jews had become so difficult. Many think that Paul means that the general resurrection and the end will come when the Jews are converted. Possibly so, but it is by no means certain. His language may be merely figurative.

16. {*First fruit*} (cf. 1 Cor. 15:20, 23). The metaphor is from Numbers 15:19, first of the dough as a heave offering. {*The lump*} (cf. Rom. 9:21). Apparently the patriarchs are the first fruit. {*The root*} Perhaps this is Abraham singly here. The metaphor is changed, but the idea is the same. Israel is looked on as a tree. But one must recall and keep in mind the double sense of Israel in Romans 9:6. (the natural and the spiritual).

17. {*Being a wild olive*} The ancients used the wild olive graft upon an old olive tree to reinvigorate the tree precisely as Paul uses the figure here and that both the olive tree and the graft were influenced by each other, though the wild olive graft did not produce as good olives as the original stock.

18. {*Glory not over the branches*} The Greek syntax translates "stop glorying" or "do not have the habit of glorying over the branches." "You [do not support the root]" is quite emphatic in the Greek.

19. {*Thou wilt say then*} This refers to a presumptuous Gentile speaking, showing contempt for the castoff Jews.

21. {*Be not highminded*} Greek syntax translates, "Stop thinking high (proud) thoughts." {*Of God spared not*} This a condition assumed to be true or fulfilled.

22. {*The goodness and the severity of God*} (cf. kindness Rom. 2:2). "Sternness" is the Greek word *apotomia*, from *apotomos*, cut off, abrupt, and this adjective from *apotemnô*, to cut off.

24. {*Contrary to nature*} This is the gist of the argument, the power of God to do what is contrary to natural processes. He put the wild olive (Gentile) into the good olive tree (the spiritual Israel) and made the wild olive (contrary to nature) become the good, garden olive.

25. {*Wise in your own conceits*} This is said, to prevent self-conceit on the part of the Gentiles who have believed. They had no merit in themselves. {*A hardening*} (cf. Rom. 11:7). It means obtuseness of intellectual discernment, mental dullness (cf. Mark 3:5; Eph. 4:18). {*Until the fulness of the Gentiles be come in*} (cf. Rom. 11:12), the complement of the Gentiles.

26. {*And so*} That is, by the complement of the Gentiles stirring up the complement of the Jews (cf. Rom. 11:11). {*All Israel*} (cf. Isa. 59:20; 27:9). The spiritual Israel (both Jews and Gentiles) may be his idea in accord with Romans 9:6 (Gal. 6:16) as the climax of the argument. {*The Deliverer*} (cf. 1 Thess. 1:10; 2 Cor. 1:10). The Hebrew *Goel*, the Avenger, the Messiah, the Redeemer (Deut. 25:5-10; Job 19:25; Ruth 3:12). Paul interprets it of Jesus as Messiah.

27. {*My covenant*} (cf. Jer. 31:31). Lit. "the from me covenant." This is not a political deliverance, but a religious and ethical one.

28. {*Enemies*} This is in passive sense, because of their rejection of Christ (cf. Rom. 11:10). {*As touching the election*} This is the principle of election, not as in verse 5 "the elect."

29. {*Without repentance*} (cf. 2 Cor. 7:10). This is the Greek *ametamelêtos,* formed of *a* privative and *metamelomai,* [not] to be sorry afterwards. God is not sorry for his gifts to and calling of the Jews (Rom. 9:4).

30. {*Ye in time past*} This refers to the Gentiles (cf. Rom. 1:18-32).

31. {*By the mercy shown to you*} God's purpose is for the Jews to receive a blessing yet.

32. {*Hath shut up*} This is the Greek verb *sunkleiô,* to shut together like a net (Luke 5:6). See Galatians 3:22 for this word with the phrase "under sin." The Greek tense has a focus on the result or effect because of the disbelief and disobedience of both Gentile (Rom. 1:17-32) and Jew (Rom. 2:1-3:20).

33. {*Past tracing out*} This is the Greek word *anexichniastos,* another verbal adjective from *a* privative and *exichniazô,* [not] to trace out by tracks (*ichnos* Rom. 4:12). Paul obtains from Job (Job 5:9; 9:10; 34:24, cf. also Eph. 3:8). Some of God's tracks he has left plain to us, but others are beyond us.

35. {*Shall be recompensed*} Lit. "to pay back," here is good sense (cf. Luke 14:14; 1 Thess. 3:9).

36. {*Of him...through him...unto him*} Through these three relational words, Paul ascribes the universe with all the phenomena concerning creation, redemption, providence to God as the source [from], agent [through], goal [to].

CHAPTER 12

1. {*To present*} (cf. Rom. 6:13). This is a technical term for offering a sacrifice in other ancient lit. (though not in the O.T). {*Bodies*} Here literally the body (cf. Rom. 6:13, 19; 2 Cor. 5:10) and in contrast with the mind (cf. Rom. 12:2). {*A living sacrifice*} Not as slain Levitical propitiatory sacrifices. {*Which is your reasonable service*} (Rom. 9:4). Lit. "Your rational (spiritual) service (worship)." The phrase means here "worship rendered by the reason (or soul)."

2. {*Be not fashioned... according to this world*} (1 Cor. 7:31; Phil. 2:7 and also 1 Pet.1:14). Greek syntax translates, "stop being fashioned or do not have the habit of being fashioned." Do not take this age as your fashion plate. {*Be ye transformed*} This is the Greek verb *metamorphoô*, to transfigure (cf. Matt. 17:2; Mark 9:2; 2 Cor. 3:18). There must be a radical change in the inner man for one to live rightly in this evil age.

3. {*Not to think of himself more highly than he ought to think*} (cf. Mark 5:15; 2 Cor. 5:13). Self-conceit is here treated as a species of insanity. {*A measure of faith*} Each has his gift from God (1 Cor. 3:5; 4:7). There is no occasion for undue pride.

6. {*According to the proportion of our faith*} This is the Greek *analogia* (our word "analogy") from *analogos* (analogous, conformable, proportional).

7. {*Or he that teacheth...*} There is no verb in the Greek, and an action verb of general or specific "doing" of some kind must be supplied.

8. {*He that ruleth*} Lit. "The one standing in front" (cf. 1 Thess. 5:12). {*With diligence*} Lit. "in haste" as if in earnest (Mark 6:25; 2 Cor. 7:11, 8:8, 16). {*With cheerfulness*} This is the Greek word *hilarotês,* from *hilaros* (2 Cor. 9:7) cheerful, hilarious.

9. {*Without hypocrisy*} (cf. 2 Cor. 6:6). Hypocritical or pretended love is no love at all (cf. 1 Cor. 13:1ff). {*Abhor*} This is intensive dislike (cf. 1 Cor. 6:17)

10. {*Tenderly affectioned*} This Greek word is from *philos* and *storgê* (mutual love of parents and children).

11. {*Slothful*} Lit. "to hesitate, to be slow, "poky" (cf. Matt. 25:26).

13. {*Communicating*} Lit. "contributing" (cf. 2 Cor. 9:13). Paul had raised a great collection for the poor saints in Jerusalem. {*Given to* *hospitality*} Lit. "pursuing (as if in a chase or hunt) hospitality" (cf. 1 Tim. 3:2, also Heb. 13:2).

16. {*Be of the same mind*} Lit. "thinking the same thing." {*Set not your mind on high things*} (cf. 1 Cor. 13:5). Lit. "not thinking the high things." {*Be not wise*} Greek syntax translates, "do not have the habit of becoming wise in your own conceits."

17. {*Render to no man...evil for evil*} Lit. "Giving back to no man." This is directly opposite to the law of retaliation (cf. Matt. 5:39; 1 Thess. 5:15; 1 Cor. 13:5).

19. {*But give place unto wrath*} (cf. Deut. 32:35). Lit. "Give room for the wrath" of God instead of taking vengeance in your own hands (cf. Eph. 4:27).

20. {*Feed him*} (cf. Prov. 25:21 [LXX]). This is the Greek verb *psômizw*, from *psômos*, a morsel, and so to feed crumbs to babies, then to feed in general (cf. 1 Cor. 13:3). {*Thou shalt heap coals of fire*} That is, burning or live coals (cf. our "anthracite"). This is a metaphor for keen anguish. Such kindness may lead to repentance also.

21. {*Be not overcome of evil...*} Greek syntax translates entire verse, "Stop being conquered by the evil (thing or man), but keep on conquering the evil in the good."

CHAPTER 13

1. {*Every soul*} Lit. "every soul" a Hebraism (cf. Rom. 2:9; Acts 2:43). {*To the higher powers*} (cf. Mark 2:10). The Greek verb is *huperechô*, to have or hold over, to be above or supreme (cf. 1 Pet.2:13). {*The powers that be*} Paul is not arguing for the divine right of kings or for any special form of government, but for government and order.

2. {*He that resisteth*} Lit. "to range in battle against" (cf. Acts 18:6). {*The ordinance of God*} (cf. Acts 7:53).

3. {*A terror*} (cf. Isa. 8:13). Paul does not approve all that rulers do, but he is speaking generally of the ideal before rulers.

4. {*A minister of God*} This is the general sense of the Greek *diakonos*. {*Sword*} This is a symbol of authority as today policemen carry clubs or pistols.

5. {*Ye must needs*} Lit. "there is necessity," both because of the law and because of conscience, because it is right (Rom. 2:15; 9:1).

6. {*Tribute*} This is the Greek word *phoros*, from *pherô*, to bring, especially the annual tax on lands, etc. (Luke 20:22; 23:1). Paying taxes recognizes authority over us. {*Ministers of God's service*} This refers here to a public servant, used of military servants, servants of the king, and temple servants (Heb. 8:2).

7. {*Tribute...tribute...custom...custom*} This Greek word is the tribute paid to a subject nation (Luke 20:22), while "custom" is tax for support of civil government (Matt. 17:25).

8. {*Save to love one another*} Lit. "Except the loving one another." This debt can never be paid off, but we should keep the interest paid up. {*His neighbor*} Lit. "The other man," "the second man." God set aside law for faith, so humans should set aside law for love (Matt. 22:37-40).

9. {*It is summed up*} This is a literary word or "rhetorical term," quite common for sum or summary (cf. Eph. 1:10). {*Thy neighbour*} This is a Greek adverb and with the article, it means "the one near you" (cf. Matt. 5:43).

10. {*The fulfilment of the law*} Lit. "The filling up or complement of the law" (cf. 1 Cor. 13).

11. {*The season*} This is a critical period, not time in general. {*High time*} This is like our "the 'hour' has come." {*Nearer to us*} Paul means final salvation, whether it comes by the second coming of Christ as they all hoped or by death. It is true of us all.

12. {*Is far spent*} This is the Greek verb *prokoptô*, to cut forward, to advance, old word for making progress (cf. Luke 2:52; Gal. 1:14; 2 Tim. 2:16; 3:9). {*Is at hand*} Lit. "has drawn nigh." This is a vivid picture for daybreak. {*Let us therefore cast off...let us put on the armour of light*} (cf. Col. 3:8-12). That is, to put off from oneself "the works of darkness" as we do our nightclothes, and put on weapons of light, that belong to the light, to the day time (cf. 1 Thess. 5:8; 2 Cor. 6:7; Rom. 6:13; Eph. 6:13).

13. {*Honestly*} Lit. "walk graceful" (cf. 1 Thess. 4:12; 1 Cor. 14:40).

CHAPTER 14

1. {*Receive ye*} Lit. "take to yourselves." {*Yet not to doubtful disputations*} Lit. "not for decisions of opinions." That is, discriminations between doubts or hesitations. The strong brother is not called upon to settle all the scruples of the weak brother. But each takes it on himself to do it.

2. {*Herbs*} This is the Greek word *lachana,* from *lachanô,* to dig. Hence, garden herbs or vegetables.

3. {*Set at nought*} This is a command of the Greek verb *exoutheneô,* to treat as nothing and so with contempt (Luke 23:11; 1 Thess. 5:20). {*Judge*} That is, the meat eaters despise the vegetarians, while the vegetarians criticize the meat eaters.

4. {*The servant of another*} This means another's household servant (cf. Luke 16:12; 2 Cor. 10:15).

5. {*One day above another*} Lit. "Day beyond day" in a comparison (cf. Rom. 1:25; Luke 13:2).

6. {*Regardeth*} This is the Greek verb *phronô,* thinks of, esteems, observes, puts his mind on, from *phrên,* mind. {*Unto the Lord*} Paul's principle of freedom in nonessentials is most important. The Jewish Christians still observed the Seventh day (the Sabbath). The Gentile Christians were observing the first day of the week in honor of Christ's Resurrection on that day. Paul pleads for liberty.

8. {*Whether—or*} Lit. "both if and if." Both living and dying are "to the Lord."

9. {*And lived again*} Greek tense translates, "he came to life." {*Might be lord of*} This is the Greek verb *kurieuô,* "become Lord of" (cf. Luke 22:25; Rom. 6:9).

10. {*But thou, why dost thou judge?*} This refers to the weak brother of Rom. 14:3. {*Or thou again*} This refers to the strong brother. {*Shall stand before*} Lit. to stand beside (cf. Acts 27:24, also 2 Cor. 5:10).

11. {*Shall confess to God*} Lit. "to confess openly" (cf. Matt. 3:6). Here the idea is to give praise to, to give gratitude to (Matt. 11:25).

12. {*Shall give account*} This is the common use of the Greek word *logos* for account (bookkeeping, ledger) as in Luke 16:2.

13. {*Let us not therefore judge one another any more*} Greek tense translates, "Let us no longer have the habit of criticizing one another."

14. {*I know and am persuaded in the Lord Jesus*} Lit. "I know and am persuaded—but in the sphere of the Lord Jesus (cf. Rom. 9:1), not by mere rational processes. {*Unclean of itself*} (cf. 1 Cor. 8:4). So Paul takes his stand with the "strong," but he is not a libertine. Paul's liberty as to food is regulated by his life in the Lord.

15. {*In love*} Lit. "According to love" as the regulating principle of life.

16. {*Your good*} This refers to the liberty or Christian freedom which you claim.

17. {*The kingdom of God*} This is not the future kingdom of eschatology, but the present spiritual kingdom, the reign of God in the heart (cf. 1 Cor. 4:21).

20. {*Overthrow not*} This extends the word picture of "edification," the Greek word *oikodomê*, lit. "building." {*With offence*} (cf. Rom. 14:13) The strong brother is not to cause a stumbling block by the way he eats and exercises his freedom.

22. {*Have thou to thyself before God*} "You" is very emphatic. This principle applies to both the "strong" and the "weak." {*In that which he approveth*} This beatitude cuts both ways. After testing and then approving (Rom. 1:28; 2:18) one takes his stand which very act may condemn himself.

23. {*He that doubteth*} Lit. to judge between, to hesitate (cf. Jas. 1:6, also Rom. 4:20; Mark 11:23). {*Is condemned*} Greek tense translates, "stands condemned." {*Whatsoever is not of faith is sin*}The Greek word *pistis* (faith) here is subjective, one's strong conviction in the light of his relation to Christ and his enlightened conscience.

CHAPTER 15

1. {*We the strong*} Paul identifies himself with these the morally strong (cf. 2 Cor. 12:10; 13:9, not the mighty as in 1 Cor. 1:26). {*The infirmities*} (cf. Rom. 14:1, 2). Again this refers to the scruples "of the not strong."

3. {*Pleased not himself*} (cf. Ps. 69:9). This is the supreme example for Christians (cf. Rom. 14:15).

4. {*We might have hope*} Greek tense translates, "that we might keep on having hope." This is one of the blessed uses of the Scriptures.

5. {*Grant you*} (cf. 2 Thess. 3:16; Eph. 1:17; 2 Tim. 1:16, 18; 2:25). The Greek form expresses the action or state as a wish ("may") for the future. {*According to Christ Jesus*} Translate, "According to the character or example of Christ Jesus" (2 Cor. 11:17; Col. 2:8; Eph. 5:24).

6. {*With one accord...with one mouth*} This is a vivid expression of the unity of feeling. {*May glorify*} Greek tense translates "that you may keep on glorifying."

9. {*And that the Gentiles might praise*} Thus the Gentiles were called through the promise to the Jews in the covenant with Abraham (Rom. 4:11, 16), proven by a chain of quotations from the OT.

10. {*Rejoice, ye Gentiles*} This is a command of the Greek verb *euphrainô*, from *eu,* well and *phrên,* mind (cf. Luke 15:32). Quotation is from Deuteronomy 32:43 (LXX).

12. {*The root*} (cf. Rev. 5:5; 23:16). Here is meant the sprout from the root (cf. Isa. 11:10).

13. {*Fill you*} The Greek form expresses the action or state as a wish ("may") for the future.

14. {*Full of goodness*} Paul gives the Roman Christians (chiefly Gentiles) high praise. The "complete in knowledge" is not to be pressed too literally. {*To admonish*} This is the Greek verb *nouthetô,* to put in mind (from *nouthetês* and this from *nous* [mind] and *tithêmi* [to place]), cf. 1 Thessalonians 5:12, 14. Is this Paul's purpose for the Epistle? The strategic position of the church in Rome made it a great center for radiating and echoing the gospel over the world as Thessalonica did for Macedonia (1 Thess. 1:8).

15. {*In some measure*} Perhaps he is referring to some portions of the Epistle where he has spoken plainly (Rom. 6:12, 19; 8:9; 11:17; 14:3, 4, 10, etc.).

16. {*Ministering*} This word means to work in sacred things, to minister as a priest. Paul had as high a conception of his work as a preacher of the gospel as any priest did.

18. {*By word and deed*} Lit. "word and deed," that is, by preaching and life (Luke 24:19; Acts 1:1; 7:22; 2 Cor. 10:11).

19. {*Round about even unto Illyricum*} Probably this refers to a journey when Paul left Macedonia and waited for Second Corinthians to have its effect before coming to Corinth (cf. 2 Cor. 13:1ff.; Acts 20:13). Illyricum seems to be the name for the region west of Macedonia, and thus be the extreme limits of Paul's mission journeys so far.

20. {*Making it my aim*} This is the Greek verb *philotimeomai,* to be fond of honor (*philos, timê*), cf. 1 Thessalonians 4:11; 2 Corinthians 5:9. {*Not where*} Paul was a pioneer preacher pushing on to new fields.

22. {*I was hindered*} This is the Greek verb *enkoptô,* to cut in, to cut off, to interrupt (cf. Acts 24:4; 1 Thess. 2:18; Gal. 5:7).

23. {*Having no more any place in these regions*} Paul is now free to come to Rome because there is no demand for him where he is.

24. {*Into Spain*} Spain was a Roman province with many Jews in it. The Greek name was *Iberia,* the Latin *Hispania.* {*In my journey*} Paul planned only a brief stay in Rome since a strong church already existed there. {*If first in some measure I shall have been satisfied with your company*} This is the Greek verb *empimplêmi,* to fill up, to satisfy, to take one's fill (cf. Luke 6:25). This is a delicate compliment for the Roman church.

25-26. {*Ministering unto the saints*} This collection had been one of Paul's chief cares for over a year now (see 2 Cor. 8 and 9, esp. 8:4). Many, not all the saints of Jerusalem were poor (cf. Acts 4:32-5:11; 6:1-6; 11:29; Gal. 2:10).

27. {*Their debtors*} Gentiles are debtors to the Jews (cf. Rom. 1:14; 8:12). {*For if*} This is a condition assumed as true. {*In carnal things*} That is, things which belong to the natural life of the flesh (Greek *sarx*), not the sinful aspects of the flesh at all.

28. {*Have sealed*} This is the Greek verb *sphragizô,* from *sphragis,* a seal (Rom. 4:11), to stamp with a seal for security (Matt. 27:66) or for confirmation (2 Cor. 1:22) and here in a metaphorical sense. Paul was keenly sensitive that this collection should be actually conveyed to Jerusalem free from all suspicion (2 Cor. 8:18-23).

30. {*That ye strive together with me*} This is the Greek verb *sunagônizomai,* compound verb, the simplex Greek verb is *agônizomenos,* occurring in Colossians 4:12 of the prayers of Epaphras.

31. {*That I may be delivered*} Paul foresaw trouble all the way to Jerusalem (Acts 20:23; 21:4, 13). {*May be acceptable to the saints*} Translate the Greek tense, "may become acceptable to the saints." The Judaizers would give him trouble. There was peril of a schism in Christianity.

33. {*The God of peace*} This is one of the characteristics of God that Paul often mentions in benedictions (1 Thess. 5:23; 2 Thess. 3:16; 2 Cor. 13:11; Phil. 4:9; Rom. 16:20).

CHAPTER 16

1. {*I commend*} Phoebe carries the Epistle (cf. 2 Cor. 3:1, also Rom. 3:5). {*Who is a servant of the church*} Is this "deaconess" (office, Phil.

1:1; 1 Tim. 3:8-13) or a more general servant? Most likely, in favor of "deaconess" is a discussion of "women" in 1 Timothy 3:8-13, though it could also mean "wives" of deacon-husbands.

2. {*A succourer*} This is the Greek word *prostatis,* old and rare feminine form for the masculine *prostatês,* from *proistêmi* (*prostateô,* common, but not in the NT). The word illustrates her work as "servant."

3. {*Prisca and Aquila*} This order always (Acts 18:18, 26; 2 Tim. 4:19, and here) save in Acts 18:2; 1 Corinthians 16:19, showing that Prisca was the more prominent. She may have been a noble Roman lady, but her husband was a Jew of Pontus and a tentmaker by trade.

4. {*Laid down their own necks*} This is the Greek verb *hupotithêmi,* to place under [the axe of the executioner] (cf. 1 Tim. 4:16).

7. {*Junias*} This name can be either masculine or feminine in the Greek. {*Fellow prisoners*} (Phlm. 23; Col. 4:10). Lit. "fellow captives in war." Perhaps they had shared one of Paul's numerous imprisonments (2 Cor. 11:23). {*Among the apostles*} This is in the general sense, true of Barnabas, James, the brother of Christ, Silas, and others, or just well known among the technical Apostles (Peter, John, etc.).

11. {*Herodion*} Probably one belonging to the Herod family. {*Them of the household of Narcissus*} There was a famous freedman of this name who was put to death by Agrippa. Perhaps members of his household.

12. {*Tryphaena and Tryphosa*} Probably sisters, possibly twins.

13. {*Rufus*} This is a common slave name (cf. Mark 15:21).

15. {*Philologus*} This is another common slave name. {*Julia*} This is the most common name for female slaves in the imperial household because of Julius Caesar. Possibly these two were husband and wife.

16. {*With a holy kiss*} This is the nearest mode of salutation as handshaking in the Western (1 Thess. 5:26; 1 Cor. 16:20; 2 Cor. 13:12).

18. {*Of the innocent*} Lit. "without evil or guile," (cf. Heb. 7:26).

20. {*Shall bruise*} This is the Greek verb *suntribô,* to rub together, to crush, to trample underfoot. Blessed promise of final victory over Satan by "the God of peace."

22. {*I Tertius*} This is the amanuensis (secretary) to whom Paul dictated the letter (cf. See 2 Thess. 3:17; 1 Cor. 16:21; Col. 4:18).

25. {*To stablish*} Lit. "to make stable." {*According to my gospel*} (cf. Rom. 2:16; 2 Tim. 2:8). Not a book, but Paul's message as here set forth.

26. {*By the scriptures of the prophets*} Cf. "law and the prophets" (Rom. 3:21), this thread runs all through Romans. {*According to the command of the eternal God*} Paul conceives that God is in charge of the redemptive work and gives his orders (Rom. 1:1-5; 10:15).

27. {*To the only wise God*} Better translate "to God alone wise" (cf. 1 Tim. 1:17).

The First Epistle to the Corinthians

Author: Paul of Tarsus, the Apostle to the Gentiles
Recipients: Believers in Corinth
Date: Possibly the early spring (before Pentecost) of A.D. 54 or 55
From: Ephesus (cf. 1 Cor. 16:8)
Occasion: Put an end to factions in the church and deal with specific problems and questions.
Theme: Let there be no divisions in the church of Jesus Christ: in doctrine or practice.

By Way of Introduction

It is beyond all doubt that this Epistle is genuine and Paul wrote it. The occasion is thus: some of the household of Chloe had heard or come from Corinth with full details of the factions in the church over Apollos and Paul, clearly the reason why Apollos left (1 Cor. 1:10-12).

Paul had sent Timothy over to Corinth to put an end to the factions (1 Cor. 4:17), though he was uneasy over the outcome (1 Cor. 16:10ff.). This disturbance was enough of itself to call forth a letter from Paul.

But it was by no means the whole story. Paul had already written a letter, now lost to us, concerning a peculiarly disgusting case of incest in the membership (1 Cor. 5:9); also issues of lawsuits, marriage (1 Cor. 7:1), eating meat offered to idols (1 Cor. 8:1), spiritual gifts (1 Cor. 12:1), the doctrine of the resurrection (1 Cor. 15:12); finally, the collection for the poor saints in Jerusalem (1 Cor. 16:1).

The church in Corinth had sent a committee (Stephanas, Fortunatus, Achaicus) to Paul in Ephesus. He hopes to come himself after passing through Macedonia (1 Cor. 16:5ff.). It is possible that he had made a short visit before this letter (2 Cor. 13:1), though not certain as he may have intended to go one time without going as he certainly once changed his plans on the subject (2 Cor. 1:15-22). Probably Timothy returned to Ephesus from Corinth shortly after the epistle was sent on, possibly by the committee who returned to Corinth (1 Cor. 16:17), for Timothy and Erastus were sent on from Ephesus to Macedonia before the outbreak at the hands of Demetrius (Acts 19:22).

It is clear therefore that Paul wrote what we call 1 Corinthians in a disturbed state of mind. He had founded the church there, had spent two years there (Acts 18), and took pardonable pride in his work there as a wise architect (1 Cor. 3:10) for he had built the church on Christ as the foundation. He was anxious that his work should abide.

It is plain that the disturbances in the church in Corinth were fomented from without by the Judaizers whom Paul had defeated at the Jerusalem Conference (Acts 15:1-35; Gal. 2:1-10). They were overwhelmed there, but renewed their attacks in Antioch (Gal. 2:11-21).

CHAPTER I

1. {*Called to be an apostle*} Lit. "a called apostle," (Rom. 1:1), an office due not to himself or men, but to God (Gal. 1:1). {*Through the will of God*} (cf. God's command [1 Tim. 1:1]). Paul knows that he is not one of the twelve apostles, but he is on a par with them because, like them, he is chosen by God. {*Our brother*} Lit. "the brother" but regular Greek idiom for our brother.

2. {*Which is in Corinth*} Julius Caesar restored Corinth from destruction about a hundred years before this epistle. The city had become wealthy and exceedingly corrupt. The very word "to Corinthianize" meant to practice vile immoralities in the worship of Aphrodite (Venus). {*That are sanctified...called saints*} Paul is called to be an apostle; they are called to be holy. {*With all that call upon*} This phrase occurs in the LXX (Gen. 12:8; Zech. 13:9) and is applied to Christ as to Jehovah (2 Thess. 1:7, 9, 12; Phil. 2:9, 10). Paul heard Stephen pray to Christ as Lord (Acts 7:59).

4. {*I thank my God for the grace of God which was given to you in Christ Jesus*} (cf. Rom. 1:8; Phil. 1:3; Phlm. 4; also 1 Thess. 1:2; Col. 1:3). Even in the church in Corinth he finds something for which to thank God, overriding the specific causes of irritation.

5. {*Ye were enriched in him*} (1 Cor. 1:5; 2 Cor. 6:10, 11). This is the Greek verb *ploutizô*, from *ploutos*, wealth. The Christian finds his real riches in Christ. {*In all utterance and all knowledge*} Here is one detail in explanation of the riches in Christ; speaking is outward expression, knowledge is inward.

6. {*Was confirmed in you*} This is the Greek verb *bebaioô*, from *bebaios* and that from *bainô*, to make to stand, to make stable. These special gifts of the Holy Spirit which they had so lavishly received (cf. 1 Cor. 12:1ff.) were for that very purpose.

7. {*So that ye come behind in no gift*} Later Paul will have to complain that they have not paid their pledges for the collection, pledges made over a year before, a very modern complaint (cf. 2 Cor. 8:7-11; 9:1-7).

8. {*Unto the end*} That is, until Jesus comes, the final preservation of the saints. {*That ye be unreproveable*} That is, unimpeachable, for none will have the right to impeach (cf. Rom. 8:33; Col. 1:22, 28).

9. {*Into the fellowship*} This is the Greek word *koinônia*, from *koinônos*, partner for partnership, participation (cf. 2 Cor. 13:13; Phil. 2:1; 3:10). Elsewhere the word has more focus on intimacy.

10. {*All speak*} Lit. "You all keep on speaking." Paul has the divisions in mind. {*There be no divisions among you*} The Greek translates, "that divisions may not continue to be (they already had them)." The Greek word *schisma* is from *schizô*, to split or rend, and so means a rent (Matt. 9:16; Mark 2:21). Papyri use it for a splinter of wood and for plowing. Here we have the earliest instance of its use in a moral sense of division, dissension (cf. 1 Cor. 11:18). These divisions were over the preachers (1 Cor. 1:12-4:21), immorality (1 Cor. 5:1-13), going to law before the heathen (1 Cor. 6:1-11), marriage (1 Cor. 7:1-40), meats offered to idols (1 Cor. 8:1 to 10:33), conduct of women in church (1 Cor. 11:1-16), the Lord's Supper (1 Cor. 11:17-34), spiritual gifts (1 Cor. 12-14), the resurrection (1 Cor. 15:1ff.).

11. {*For it hath been signified unto me*} Lit. "it was signified to me." {*By them of Chloe*} Lit. "those of Chloe." Whether the children, the relatives, or the servants of Chloe we do not know. Already Christianity was working a social revolution in the position of women and slaves. {*Contentions*} These are unseemly wranglings (as opposed to discussing, *dialegomai*) that were leading to the divisions (schisms).

12. {*Apollos*} Apollos refused to be a party to this strife and soon returned to Ephesus and refused to go back to Corinth (1 Cor. 16:12). {*Cephas*} Aramaic for *Petros* (Peter) in Greek (cf. Gal. 2:7, 8). He had already taken his stand with Paul in the Jerusalem Conference (Acts 15:7-11; Gal. 2:7-10), and had cordial relations (2 Pet. 3:15, also 1 Cor. 9:5). But there is no evidence that Peter himself visited Corinth. {*And I of Christ*} A fourth faction in recoil from the partisan use of Paul, Apollos, Cephas, with "a spiritually proud utterance" that assumes a relation to Christ not true of the others (Ellicott). In scouting the names of the other leaders they lowered the name and rank of Christ to their level.

13. {*Was Paul crucified for you?*} Using himself as an example, the Greek demands an indignant "No!"

14. {*Save Crispus and Gaius*} The prominence and importance of these two may explain why Paul baptized them: Crispus was the ruler of the synagogue in Corinth before his conversion (Acts 18:8) Gaius was probably the host of Paul and of the whole church in Corinth (Rom. 16:23, cf. poss. 2 John 5, 6).

15. {*Lest any man should say*} Some in Corinth were laying emphasis on the person of the baptizer; note that Jesus himself baptized no one (John 4:2) to avoid this very kind of controversy. Paul clearly denies here that he considers baptism essential to the remission of sin.

16. {*Also the household of Stephanas*} This is mentioned as an afterthought. Paul calls him a first-fruit of Achaia (1 Cor. 16:15) and so earlier than Crispus and he was one of the three who came to Paul from Corinth (16:17), clearly a family that justified Paul's personal attention about baptism.

17. {*Not in wisdom of words*} Preaching was Paul's forte, but it was not as a pretentious philosopher or professional rhetorician that Paul appeared before the Corinthians (1 Cor. 2:1-5). {*Lest the cross of Christ should be made void*} "Emptied" is the Greek verb *kenoô*, from *kenos*, to make empty.

18. {*For the word of the cross*} This is in contrast to human wisdom. {*To them that are perishing*} That is, those in the path to destruction (not annihilation (cf. 2 Thess. 2:10, also 2 Cor. 4:3). {*Foolishness*} (cf. 1 Cor. 1:18, 21, 23; 2:14; 3:19). "Saved" are in sharp contrast to those that are perishing. Salvation is: past (Rom. 8:24), present state (Eph. 2:5), as a process (1 Cor. 15:2), as a future result (Rom. 10:9). {*The power of God*} (cf. Rom. 1:16). No other message has this dynamite of God (1 Cor. 4:20). God's power is shown in the preaching of the Cross of Christ.

19. {*I will destroy*} (cf. Isa. 29:14 [LXX]). There is such a thing as the ignorance of the learned, the wisdom of the simple-minded. God's wisdom rises in the Cross above human philosophizing which scoffs at the Cross.

20. {*Where is the wise? Where is the scribe? Where is the disputer of this world?*} (cf. Isa. 33:18). "Wise man" refers to the Greek philosopher; "scholar" refers to the Jewish scribe and "philosopher" suits both the Greek and the Jewish disputant and doubter (Acts 6:9; 9:29; 17:18; 28:29). {*Hath not God made foolish? Has not God made foolish...world?*} "Not" is quite strong in the Greek syntax. "Made foolish" means "to prove foolish" (cf. Rom. 1:22). "World" means the non-Christian cosmos.

21. {*Knew not God*} Greek tense translates, "failed to know." This is a solemn dirge of doom on both Greek philosophy and Jewish theology that failed to know God. {*Through the foolishness of the preaching*} The focus is on the message or proclamation (cf. 1 Cor. 1:23). The metaphor is that of the herald proclaiming the approach of the king (Matt. 3:1; 4:17). The proclamation of the Cross seemed foolishness to the sophists then (and now), but it is consummate wisdom. {*To save them that believe*} This is the heart of God's plan of redemption, the proclamation of salvation for all those who trust Jesus Christ on the basis of his death for sin on the Cross.

22. {*Ask for signs...seek after wisdom*} Jews claimed to *possess* the truth: the Greeks were *seekers, speculators* (Vincent) (cf. Acts 17:23).

23. {*But we preach Christ crucified*} In contrast to verse 22, the proclamation is not a sign-shower nor a philosopher (Vincent). {*Stumbling block*} This is the Greek word *skandalon,* meaning elsewhere a trap or snare, which here tripped the Jews who wanted a conquering Messiah with a world empire (Matt. 27:42; Luke 24:21).

24. {*Christ...the wisdom of God*} Christ crucified is God's answer to both Jew and Greek and the answer is understood by those with open minds.

25. {*The foolishness of God*} This refers to the foolish act of God (the Cross as regarded by the world). {*Wiser than men*} (Matt. 5:20; John 5:36). Translate fully, "wiser than the wisdom of men."

26. {*After the flesh*} This includes all: wise, philosophers; men of dignity and power; the noble, of high birth; culture, power, birth.

27. {*God chose*} This is the Greek verb *eklegô,* to pick out, to choose, the middle for oneself. It expands the idea in "called" (v. 26). Three times this solemn verb occurs here with the purpose stated each time, "to shame."

29. {*That no flesh should glory before God*} This is the further purpose expressed by "so that" for variety and appeals to God's ultimate choice in all three instances.

30. {*Of him*} That is, God chose you. {*In Christ Jesus*} In the sphere of Christ Jesus the choice was made. This is God's wisdom. {*Who was made unto us wisdom from God*} The "becoming" was through the Incarnation, Cross, and Resurrection. Christ is the wisdom of God (Col. 2:2). All the treasures of wisdom and knowledge are in Christ Jesus. We are made righteous, holy, and redeemed in Christ Jesus. Redemption comes here last for emphasis though the foundation of the other two.

CHAPTER 2

1. {*Not with excellency of speech or of wisdom*} (cf. 1 Tim. 2:2). "Excellency" is the Greek word *huperochê,* from the verb *huperechô* (Phil. 4:7) and means preeminence, rising above. Here it means excess or superfluity, "not in excellence of rhetorical display or of philosophical subtlety" (Lightfoot).

2. {*For I determined not to know anything among you*} Lit. "For I did not decide to know anything among you." Paul means that he did not think it fit or his business to know anything for his message beyond this mystery of God. {*Save Jesus Christ and him crucified*} (cf. 1 Cor. 1:18). This is both the person (Jesus) and the office (Christ). This phrase was selected by Paul from the start as the center of his gospel message. He decided to stick to it even after Athens where he was practically laughed out of court.

3. {*I was with you...*} Paul had been in prison in Philippi, driven out of Thessalonica and Berea, politely bowed out of Athens. It is a human touch to see this shrinking as he faced the hard conditions in Corinth.

4. {*Not in persuasive words of wisdom*} This looks like a false disclaimer or mock modesty, for surely the preacher desires to be persuasive. Compare Colossians 2:4 for the specious and plausible Gnostic philosophers. Corinth put a premium on the veneer of false rhetoric and thin thinking. {*But in demonstration*} This is in contrast with the persuasion just mentioned.

5. {*That your faith should not stand*} The only secure place for faith to find a rest is in God's power, not in the wisdom of men.

6. {*Among the perfect*} Paul is here drawing the difference in teaching (of the Person of Christ) for babes [unable in spite of their years to digest solid spiritual food] (1 Cor. 3:1) and adults or grown men (cf. 1 Cor. 14:20; 3:15; Eph. 4:13; Heb. 5:14).

7. {*God's wisdom in a mystery*} "God" is the emphasis in the Greek syntax, in contrast to the wisdom of this age. God's wisdom is eternal and superior to the wisdom of any age or time. {*Foreordained before the worlds*} (1 Cor. 1:18-24). Christ crucified was no afterthought or change of plan (Robertson and Plummer).

8. {*Knoweth*} Lit. "has known, has discerned." They have shown amazing ignorance of God's wisdom. {*For had they known it*} This condition in the Greek is determined as unfulfilled. Peter in the great sermon at Pentecost commented on the ignorance of the Jews in crucifying Christ (Acts 3:17-19). {*The Lord of glory*} (cf. Jas. 2:1; Acts 7:2; Eph. 1:17; Heb. 9:5). Translate, "the Lord characterized by glory," bringing out the contrast between the indignity of the Cross (Heb. 12:2) and the majesty of the Victim (Luke 22:69; 23:43) (Robertson and Plummer).

9. {*But as it is written*} It is likely that Paul here combines freely Isaiah 64:4; 65:17; 52:15 in a free chain of quotations as he does in Romans 3:10-18. {*Heart*} The Greek word *kardia* here is more than emotion (cf. Rom. 1:21). The next verse shows that Paul uses this verse of what is now revealed and made plain, not of mysteries still unknown.

10. {*But unto us God revealed them*} Paul explains why what is prepared is no longer hidden. This revelation took place at the entry of the Gospel into the world, not at our personal salvation event. {*Through the Spirit*} The Holy Spirit is the agent of this definite revelation of grace, a revelation with a definite beginning or advent, an unveiling by the Spirit where human ability and research would not have sufficed. {*Searcheth all things*} (as in Rom. 1:21). This is the Greek verb *ereunaô*, (outside the NT) for a professional searcher's report and *eraunêtai*, searchers for customs officials. The Holy Spirit not merely investigates us, but he searches even the deep things of God (cf. Rom. 11:33).

11. {*Knoweth*} This is to know by personal experience, and the Greek tense has a focus "has come to know and still knows." {*The spirit of man that is in him*} That is, the self-consciousness of a human that resides in the man or woman (generic term for mankind). {*The Spirit of God*} (cf. 1 Cor. 2:6-10). God's Holy Spirit is amply qualified to make the revelation claimed. The Spirit of God is not the mere self-consciousness of God, but the personal Holy Spirit in his relation to God the Father.

12. {*That we might know*} Here is a distinct claim of the Holy Spirit for understanding (Illumination) the Revelation received. It is not a senseless rhapsody or secret mystery, but God expects us to understand the things that are freely given us by God.

13. {*Which things also we speak*} "Speak" is the Greek verb *laleô*; in the NT as here is used of the highest and holiest speech. Undoubtedly Paul employs the word purposely for the high utterance: of revelation (1 Cor. 2:10); of illumination (1 Cor. 2:12); of inspiration (1 Cor. 2:13). {*Not in words which man's wisdom teacheth*} (cf. Isa. 54:13). So then Paul claims the help of the Holy Spirit in the utterance of the words, which the Spirit teaches. Clearly Paul means that the help of the Holy Spirit in the utterance of the revelation extends to the words. {*Comparing spiritual things with spiritual*} Translate, "combining spiritual ideas with spiritual words."

14. {*Now the natural man*} This means "an unregenerate man." {*Receiveth not*} That is, "rejects, refuses to accept" (cf. Rom. 8:7). Here is clearly stated the inability of the mind of the flesh to receive the things of the Spirit untouched by the Holy Spirit. {*He cannot know them*} Greek tense translates, "he is not able to get a knowledge." His helpless condition calls for pity in place of impatience on our part, though such a one usually poses as a paragon of wisdom and feels sorry for the deluded followers of Christ. {*They are spiritually judged*} "Judged," means a sifting process to get at the truth by investigation as of a judge (cf. Acts 17:11).

15. {*Judgeth all things*} The spiritual man is qualified to sift, to examine, to decide rightly, because he has the eyes of his heart enlightened (Eph. 1:18) and is no longer blinded by the god of this world (2 Cor. 4:4).

16. {*For who hath known the mind of the Lord*} (cf. Isa. 40:13). The spiritual one is superior to others who attempt even to instruct God himself. {*But we have the mind of Christ*} (cf. 1 Cor. 2:6 to 13). All spiritual ones are superior to those who try to shake their faith in Christ, the mystery of God.

CHAPTER 3

1. {*But as unto carnal*} Lit. "fleshen, material of flesh." Paul wanted to speak the wisdom of God among the adults (1 Cor. 2:6), the spiritual (1 Cor. 2:15), but he was unable to treat them as spiritual ones in reality because of their seditions and immoralities. It is not culpable to a baby in Christ (1 Cor. 13:11), unless unduly prolonged (1 Cor. 14:20; Heb. 5:13).

2. {*I fed you with milk, not with meat*} Paul did not glory in making his sermons thin and watery. Simplicity does not require lack of ideas or dullness.

3. {*For ye are yet carnal*} (cf. 1 Cor. 3:1). Lit. "adapted to flesh, fitted for the flesh," The "worldly" in verse one has a focus of being babies, not adults; "worldly" here is in contrast to the spiritual, and means those who have given way to the flesh as if they were still unregenerate. { *Jealousy and strife*} Zeal (Greek *zêlos* from *zeô*, to boil) is not necessarily evil, but good if under control. It may be not according to knowledge (Rom. 10:2) and easily becomes jealousy and so quarreling follows jealousy; proof they walk according to men, not Christ.

4. {*Men*} That is, just mere human creatures, bringing home the argument of 1 Corinthians 3:1-4. Corinthians are acting *in* the flesh (v. 1), *like* the flesh (v. 3), not spiritual, as if still unregenerate.

5. {*Ministers*} (Col. 1:23, 25). Not leaders of parties or sects, but merely servants (general sense) through whom ye believed. The etymology of the word Thayer gives as the Greek parts *dia* and *konis* "raising dust by hastening." No mere servant (*diákonos*) has any basis for pride or conceit nor should be made the occasion for faction and strife.

6. {*But God gave the increase*} The Greek tense has a focus for the continuous blessing of God both on the work of Paul and Apollos, colaborers with God in God's field (cf. 1 Cor. 3:9).

7. {*So then neither—neither—but*} God is the whole and we are not anything.

8. {*Are one*} Paul expands the metaphor showing how the planter and the waterer work together. If no one planted, watering would be useless. If no one watered, what was planted would come to nothing.

9. {*God's fellow workers*}. God is the major partner in the enterprise of each life, but he lets us work with him. {*God's building*} God is the

Great Architect. We work under him and carry out the plans of the Architect.

10. {*As a wise masterbuilder*} (cf. Acts 18:1-18). Paul absolves himself and Apollos from responsibility for the divisions. Factions in the church were now a fact and Paul went to the bottom of the matter. This is the Greek word *architektôn,* in even wider senses than our use of architect. But Paul means through this metaphor to claim primacy as pastor of the church in Corinth. The successor to Paul did not have to lay a new foundation, but only to go on building on that already laid.

11. {*Other foundation*} Christ is the foundation here. Other is masculine because Paul has Christ in mind. {*Than that which is laid, which is Christ Jesus*} Lit. "alongside the one already laid." Clearly Paul means that on this one true foundation, Jesus Christ, one must build only what is in full harmony with the Foundation which is Jesus Christ.

12. {*Gold, silver, precious stones, wood, hay, stubble*} Note first three are durable materials (withstanding fire); next three perishable/burnable. This metaphor refers either to the persons as in God's building (cf. 1 Cor. 3:9) or to the character of the teaching (cf. 1 Cor. 3:13), or probably both ideas here.

13. {*The day*} This is the day of judgment (cf. 1 Thess. 5:4; Rom. 13:12; Heb. 10:25). Then the work of each will be made manifest. There is no escape from this final testing. {*It is revealed in fire*} (cf. 2 Thess. 1:8; 2:8). The "Day" is revealed with fire. This is a common Biblical metaphor (Dan. 7:9; Mal. 4:1; Matt. 3:12; Luke 3:16). This is not a purgatorial metaphor, but simple testing, as every fire tests the quality of the material used in the building.

14. {*If any man's work shall abide*} When the fire has done its work, what is left? That is the fiery test that our work must meet (cf. Matt. 20:8).

15. {*Shall be burned*} Again, an assumed true condition, lit. "to burn down" though "up" is also an acceptable translation. {*He shall suffer loss*} (cf. Matt. 16:26; Mark 8:36; Luke 9:25). This is not here total loss, but the man's work is burned up (sermons, lectures, books, teaching, all dry as dust). {*But he himself shall be saved*} His work is burned up completely and hopelessly, but he himself escapes destruction because he is really a saved man, a real believer in Christ. {*Yet so as through fire*} Clearly Paul means with his work burned down (cf. 1 Cor. 3:15). It is the tragedy of a fruitless, wasted life, whose work went up in smoke. The one who enters heaven by grace, as we all do who are saved, yet who brings no sheaves with him.

16. {*Ye are a temple of God*} Lit. "a sanctuary" the holy place and the most holy place of God. {*Dwelleth in you*} The Spirit of God makes his home in us, not in temples made with hands (Acts 7:48; 17:24).

17. {*Destroyeth...him shall God destroy*} There is warning enough here to make every pastor pause before he tears a church to pieces in order to vindicate himself. {*Holy*} The Corinthians themselves in their angry disputes had forgotten their holy heritage and calling, though this failing was no excuse for the ringleaders who had led them on.

18. {*Let no man deceive himself*} This is a warning that implied that some of them were guilty of doing it. Excited partisans can hypnotize themselves with their own supposed devotion to truth. {*Thinketh that he is wise*} This is a condition assumed to be true. This false wisdom of the world (cf. 1 Cor. 1:18-20, 23; 2:14) has led to strife and wrangling.

19. {*Foolishness with God*} (cf. Job 5:13). Whose standard does a church (temple) of God wish, that of this world or of God? The two standards are not the same. {*That taketh*} Lit. "to grasp with the hand," (cf. also Rom. 11:35). {*Craftiness*} Here this means versatile cleverness.

21. {*Wherefore let no one glory in men*} The spirit of glorying in party is a species of self-conceit and inconsistent with glorying in the Lord (cf. 1 Cor. 1:31).

22. All the words in this verse and the next are definite, even without the article in Greek. We must not think of the article as "omitted." The wealth of the Christian includes all things, all leaders, past, present, future, Christ, and God. There is no room for partisan wrangling here.

CHAPTER 4

1. {*Ministers of Christ*} Lit. "under-rowers," i.e., subordinate rowers of Christ (cf. Luke 4:20; Acts 13:5). {*Stewards of the mysteries of God*} The ministry is more than a mere profession or trade. It is a calling from God for stewardship.

2. {*That a man be found faithful*} Fidelity is the essential requirement in all such human relationships, in other words, plain honesty in handling money or in other positions of trust like public office.

3. {*That I should be judged of you...or of man's judgement*} Paul does not despise public opinion, but he denies "the competency of the tribunal" in Corinth to pass on his credentials with Christ as his Lord. {***Yea, I judge not mine own self***} "Indeed" is confirmatory, not adversative. Paul does not even set himself up as judge of himself.

4. {***For I know nothing against myself***} This is not a statement of fact, but an hypothesis to show the unreliability of mere complacent self-satisfaction (cf. Acts 5:2; 12:12; 14:6). {***Am I not hereby justified***} The Greek tense shows a state of completion. Failure to be conscious of one's own sins does not mean that one is innocent.

5. {***Judge nothing***} The Greek syntax translates, "stop passing judgment, stop criticizing" as they were doing. The censorious habit was ruining the Corinthian Church. {***Who will both bring to light***} This is the Greek verb *phaneroô* from *phaneros*. By turning on the light the counsels of all hearts stand revealed. {***His praise***} This is the praise due him from God (Rom. 2:29) that will come to each then, and not until then.

6. {***I have in a figure transferred***} (cf. 2 Cor. 11:13-15). This word here is clearly the rhetorical figure for a veiled allusion (to Paul and Apollos). {***That in us ye may learn***} Paul boldly puts himself and Apollos to the fore in the discussion of the principles involved. {***Not to go beyond the things which are written***} It is difficult to reproduce the Greek idiom in English, apparently a proverb or rule, and elliptical in form with no principal verb expressed. Lightfoot thinks that Paul may have in mind OT passages quoted in 1 Corinthians 1:19, 31; 3:19, 20. {***That ye be not puffed up***} This is the Greek verb *phusiaô, phusaô*, to blow up, to inflate, to puff up. *Phusioô* is from *phusis* (nature) and so meant to make natural, but it is used by Paul just like *phusaô* or *phusiaô* (from *phusa*, a pair of bellows), a vivid picture of self-conceit.

7. {***Maketh thee to differ***} That is, distinguishes you, separates you. All self-conceit rests on the notion of superiority of gifts and graces as if they were self-bestowed or self-acquired. {***Which thou didst not receive***} Pride of intellect, of blood, of race, of country, of religion, is thus shut out. {***As if thou hadst not received it***} This phrase punctures effectually the inflated bag of false pride. There is no foundation for pride and conceit.

8. {***Already are ye filled?***} (cf. Deut. 31:20; 32:15). It is keen irony, even sarcasm. Some Greek text editions make it a question and the rest of the sentence also (Westcott and Hort). {***Ye have reigned without us***} The Greek tense implies indecent haste (Lightfoot). They have a private millennium of their own, with all the blessings of the Messianic Kingdom (Luke 22:29; 1 Thess. 2:12; 2 Tim. 2:12) (Robertson and Plummer).

9. {*Hath set forth us the apostles last*} This is the Greek verb *apodeiknumi,* to show, to expose to view or exhibit (Herodotus), in technical sense (cf. 2 Thess. 2:4) for gladiatorial show (cf. 1 Cor. 15:32). In this grand pageant Paul and other apostles come last as a grand finale. {*As men doomed to die*} This word is used in Bel and the Dragon (31) for those thrown daily to the lions. This is in violent contrast to the kingly Messianic pretensions of the Corinthians (v. 8). {*A spectacle*} (cf. Heb. 11:33-40). This is the Greek word *theatron,* like our theater, means the place of the show (Acts 19:29, 31) and its spectacle event. The spectators include "the world, both to angels and men."

10. {*We...you*} The three antitheses refer respectively to teaching, demeanor, and worldly position. (Robertson and Plummer). The apostles were fools for Christ's sake (2 Cor. 4:11; Phil. 3:7). There is change of order (chiasm) in the third ironical contrast.

11. {*Even unto this present hour*} Lit. "this very minute." Ten verbs and four participles from verses 11 to 13 give a graphic picture of Paul's condition in Ephesus when he is writing this epistle: hunger, thirst, scant clothing, dealt blows, and vagabonds or spiritual hobos.

13. {*As the filth of the world*} Lit. sweepings, rinsings, cleansings around, dust from the floor, from the Greek verb *perikathairô,* to cleanse all around and so the refuse/garbage thrown off in cleansing. Outside the NT, *katharma* was the refuse of a sacrifice. {*The offscouring of all things*} (cf. Tob. 5:18). This word came to have a complimentary sense for the Christians who in a plague gave their lives for the sick. But it is a bold figure here with Paul of a piece with *perikatharmata.*

14. {*To shame you*} (cf. 2 Thess. 3:14). Lit. "shaming you," to turn one on himself. The harsh tone has suddenly changed.

15. {*Tutors*} This is the Greek word *paidagôgos.* This old word (*pais,* boy, *agôgos,* leader) was used for the guide or attendant of the child who took him to school (cf. Gal. 3:24), and also as a sort of tutor who had a care for the child when not in school. This is in contrast to Paul as the spiritual father in Christ.

16. {*Be ye imitators of me*} A command or plea, the Greek tense translates, "Keep on becoming imitators of me." Paul stands for his rights as their spiritual father.

19. {*If the Lord will*} (Jas. 4:15; Acts 18:21; 1 Cor. 16:7). A condition which is unfulfilled, but plausible. {*But the power*} The puffed up Judaizers did a lot of talking in Paul's absence. Paul was sensitive to their talk about his inconsistencies and cowardice (2 Cor. 1; 2; 10; 11; 12; 13).

21. {*Shall I come?*} Paul gives them the choice. They can have him as their spiritual father or as their pedagogue with a rod.

CHAPTER 5

1. {*Actually*} Lit. "wholly, altogether," like Latin *omnino* (cf. 1 Cor. 9:22). {*It is reported*} Lit. "it is heard," probably from the household of Chloe (1 Cor. 1:11). {*And such*} (cf. Acts 15:20, 29) This is a general sexual sin and not merely of the unmarried, whereas adultery is on the part of the married (Mark 7:21). {*That one of you hath his father's wife*} It was probably a permanent union (concubine or mistress) of some kind without formal marriage (cf. John 4:8). The woman probably was not the offender's mother (stepmother) and the father may have been dead or divorced.

2. {*And ye are puffed up*} The "you" is emphatic. It may be understood as a question. Decent self-respect should have compelled the instant expulsion of the man instead of pride in his rascality.

3. {*For I verily*} This is an emphatic statement of Paul's own attitude of indignation. He justifies his demand for the expulsion of the man. {*Have already judged*} Paul felt compelled to reach a conclusion about the case and in a sentence of much difficulty seems to conceive an imaginary church court where the culprit has been tried and condemned.

5. {*To deliver such an one unto Satan*} (cf. 1 Tim. 1:20, also 2 Cor. 12:7). Paul certainly means expulsion from the church (v. 2) and regarding him as outside of the commonwealth of Israel (Eph. 2:11). {*For the destruction of the flesh*} This refers to both physical suffering (Job 2:6) and for conquest of the fleshly sins, remedial punishment. {*That the spirit may be saved*} The goal is the reformation of the unknown offender.

6. {*Not good*} Lit. "not beautiful, not seemly," in view of this plague spot, this cancer on the church. {*A little leaven leaveneth the whole lump*} (cf. Gal. 5:9). The Greek word *zumê* (yeast/leaven) is a late word from *zeô,* to boil, as is *zumoô,* to leaven. Some of the members may have argued that one such case did not affect the church as a whole, a specious excuse for negligence that Paul here answers.

7. {*Purge out*} Lit. "to clean completely." The Greek tense shows urgency, "do it now before the whole church is contaminated." {*A new lump*} Make a fresh batch. That is, make a fresh start as a new community with the contamination removed (cf. also Col. 3:10; Eph. 4:22; 2 Cor. 5:17).

8. {*Wherefore let us keep the feast*} Greek tense translates, "let us keep on keeping the feast," a perpetual feast, and keep the leaven out (Lightfoot). {*With the unleavened bread of sincerity and truth*} "Sincerity" is the Greek word *eilikrinia,* some think it comes from *heilê* or *helê,* sunlight, and *krinô,* to judge by the light of the sun, holding up to the light.

9. {*I wrote unto you in my epistle*} (cf. 1 Cor. 5:11; 2 Thess. 3:14). This refers to a currently unknown epistle. {*To have no company with fornicators*} "Associate" is lit. "to mix up."

10. {*Not altogether*} That is, not absolutely, not in all circumstances; the limit is to members of the church, not outsiders. {*The covetous*} This word means "overreachers," those avaricious for more and more (cf. 1 Cor. 6:10; Eph. 5:5). {*Extortioners*} Here it is a robber or extortioner (cf. 1 Cor. 6:10). Bandits, hijackers, grafters they would be called today. {*For then must ye needs*} The premise of this condition is considered to be contrary to fact, from Paul's view.

11. {*If any man that is named a brother be*} This is offered as a hypothetical case, though not determined as true. What follows is a list found in 1 Corinthians 6:10 and also found in ancient social standards of the Romans. {*With such a one, no, not to eat*} Social contacts with such "a brother" are forbidden.

12. {*For what have I to do?*} Lit. "For what is it to me?" Outsiders are not within Paul's jurisdiction. God passes judgment on them.

CHAPTER 6

1. {*Having a matter against his neighbour*} This is a legal dispute, a case, a suit with his neighbor (1 Cor. 10:24; 14:17; Gal. 6:4; Rom. 2:1). {*Before the unrighteous*} The Jews held that to bring a lawsuit before a court of idolaters was blasphemy against the law. But the Greeks were fond of disputatious lawsuits with each other. Probably the Greek Christians brought cases before pagan judges.

2. {*Are ye unworthy to judge the smallest matters?*} Likely translate, "Are you unworthy of the smallest tribunals?" That is, of sitting on the smallest tribunals, of forming courts yourselves to settle such things?

3. {*How much more, things that pertain to this life?*} The question expects the answer "no," with an added sharp tone. "Life" is the Greek word for "manner of life" in contrast to the Greek *zôê*, the life principle.

5. {*I say this to move you to shame*} Shame is a translation of the Greek word *entropê* from *entrepô*, to turn in (1 Cor. 4:14). In NT only here and 1 Corinthians 15:34. {*One who...to decide between his brethren*} This question is expecting the answer "yes." Surely there is someone in the church to decide between two brothers (in the church); family in contrast to heathen judges should settle disputes between brothers in Christ.

7. {*Nay, already it is altogether a defect among you*} There is no victory; it is defeat for Christians to have lawsuits with one another. This was proof of the failure of love and forgiveness (Col. 3:13). {*Be defrauded*} Translate the Greek word and tense, "Allow yourselves to be robbed" (rather than have a lawsuit).

8. {*Nay, but ye yourselves do wrong and defraud*} "You" is emphatic.

9. {*Be not deceived*} Do not be led astray by plausible talk to cover up sin as mere animal behavior. Paul has two lists of sins. All those who practice these sins will fall short of the kingdom of God.

11. {*And such were some of you*} Lit. "And these things were some of you." Thank God the blood of Jesus does cleanse from such sins as these. But do not go back to them. {*But ye were washed*} This was their own voluntary act in baptism which was the outward expression of the previous act of God in cleansing and justifying before the baptism. The outward expression is usually mentioned before the inward change which precedes it (cf. Matt. 28:19).

12. {*Lawful...but not all things are expedient*} (cf. 1 Cor. 10:23). Paul limits the proverb to things not immoral, things not wrong *per se* (cf. 1 Cor. 6:9ff.). But even here liberty is not license. Many things, harmless in themselves in the abstract, do harm to others in the concrete. {*But I will not be brought under the power of any*} Paul is determined not to be a slave to anything harmless in itself. He will maintain his self-control.

13. {*Meats for the belly, and the belly for meats*} This saying had apparently been used by some in Corinth to justify sexual license (fornication and adultery). These Gentiles mixed up matters not alike at all (questions of food and sensuality). {*But the body is not for fornication, but for the Lord, and the Lord for the body*} Paul here boldly shows the fallacy in the parallel about appetite of the belly for food. The human body has a higher mission than the mere gratification of sensual appetite.

15. {*Members of Christ*} The body is not only adapted for Christ (v. 13), but it is a part of Christ, in vital union with him. {*God forbid*} Lit. "may it not happen!" The word "God" is not here.

16. {*One body*} (cf. Gen. 2:24; also Matt. 19:5). That union is for the harlot the same as with the wife.

17. {*One spirit*} This is the inner vital spiritual union with the Lord Jesus (Eph. 4:4; 5:30).

18. {*Flee*} The Greek tense translates abruptly, "have the habit of fleeing" (without delay or parley). {*Without the body*} Perhaps this means, fornication breaks the mystic bond between the body and Christ. Even gluttony, drunkenness, and the use of drugs are not within the body in the same sense as fornication. {*Sins against his own body*} The fornicator takes his body which belongs to Christ and unites it with a harlot. In fornication the body is the instrument of sin and becomes the subject of the damage wrought.

19. {*Your body is a temple*} (cf. 1 Cor. 3:16). Our spirits dwell in our bodies and the Holy Spirit dwells in our spirits. One's body is the very shrine for the Holy Spirit. In Corinth was the temple to Aphrodite in which fornication was regarded as consecration instead of desecration. Prostitutes were there as priestesses of Aphrodite, to help men worship the goddess by fornication.

20. {*For ye were bought with a price*} "Bought" is the Greek verb *agorazô,* to buy in the marketplace, related to a price (blood cf. 1 Pet. 1:19). Jesus life was a ransom (cf. Matt. 20:28). The Corinthians understood his meaning.

CHAPTER 7

1. {*Now concerning...*} The church had written Paul a letter in which a number of specific problems about marriage were raised. He answers them *seriatim* (in succession). The first is whether a single life is wrong. Paul pointedly says that it is not wrong, but good. Paul is not here opposing marriage. He is only arguing that celibacy may be good in certain limitations.

2. {*Because of fornications*} Here is one reason, but there are many: children; mutual love; family. Paul does not give a low view of marriage.

3. {*Render the due*} Marriage is not simply not wrong, but for many a duty. Both husband and wife have a mutual obligation to the other.

4. {*The wife*} The wife is mentioned first, but the equality of the sexes in marriage is clearly presented as the way to keep marriage undefiled (Heb. 13:4).

5. {*That ye may give yourselves unto prayer*} This means to have leisure for prayer. Note private devotions here. {*That Satan tempt you not*} Greek tense translates "that Satan may not keep on tempting you."

7. {*Yet I would*} This is Paul's personal preference under present conditions (cf. 1 Cor. 7:26). {*Even as I myself*} This clearly means that Paul was not then married (cf. also 1 Cor. 9:5).

8. {*To the unmarried and to the widows*} "Unmarried" may refer only to men since widows and virgins are separately treated (cf. 1 Cor. 7:25, 32); though it is hardly likely that Paul means only widowers and widows. Giving his preference, he does not say that it is *better* to be unmarried, but only that it is *good* for them to remain unmarried.

9. {*Better*} Marriage is better than continued sexual passion (using the metaphor of "burn (with passion)."

10. {*To the married*} Greek tense shows this is those still married. {*I give charge*} This is not a mere wish (cf. 1 Cor. 7:7, 8). {*Not I, but the Lord*} This refers to what Jesus had spoken to the married (husbands and wives) as in Matthew 5:31; 19:3-12; Mark 10:9-12; Luke 16:18. Paul reinforces his own inspired command by the command of Jesus (cf. Mark 10:9). {*That the wife depart not from her husband*} This means "divorce," though unusual then, was known (cf. Mark 10:12).

11. {*But and if she depart... let her remain unmarried*} That is, if (a condition not yet determined), in spite of Christ's clear prohibition, she get separated. Paul here makes no allowance for remarriage of the innocent party as Jesus does by implication. {*Or else be reconciled to her husband*} This is the Greek verb *katallassô*, old compound verb to exchange coins as of equal value, to reconcile (with a slight focus of completion or perfection). {*And that the husband leave not his wife*} (cf. Mark 10:11), lit. "to send away."

12. {*But to the rest say I, not the Lord*} Paul has no word about marriage from Jesus beyond the problem of divorce. This is no disclaimer of inspiration. He simply means that here he is not quoting a command of Jesus. {*An unbelieving wife*} The word here does not mean "unfaithful" to the spouse. This is a new problem, the result of work among the Gentiles, that did not arise in the time of Jesus. Paul has to deal with mixed marriages as missionaries do today in heathen lands.

14. {*Is sanctified in the wife*} Not eternal salvation; clearly, simply, Paul only means that the marriage relation is sanctified so that there is no need of a divorce. {*Else were your children unclean*} Translate, "since, accordingly, if it is otherwise, your children are illegitimate." If the relations of the parents be holy, the child's birth must be holy also (not illegitimate).

15. {*Is not under bondage...but God hath called us in peace*} This is the Greek verb *douloô*, to enslave, has been enslaved, does not remain a slave. The believing husband or wife is not at liberty to separate, unless the disbeliever or pagan insists on it. Willful desertion of the unbeliever sets the other free, a case not contemplated in Christ's words in Matthew 5:32; 19:9. God does not desire enslavement in the marriage relation between the believer and the unbeliever.

16. {*For how knowest thou?*} What does Paul mean? Is he giving an argument *against* the believer accepting divorce or *in favor* of doing so? Either is allowed in context. Likely Paul is saying, if it is a hopeless case, acquiescence to divorce is the only wise solution. But the believer ought to be sure that there is no hope before he breaks the bond.

17. {*Only*} Paul gives a general principle as a limitation to what he has just said in verse 15. In the verse, each has his lot from the Lord Jesus, has his call from God. He is not to seek a rupture of the marriage relation if the unbeliever does not ask for it.

18. {*Let him not become uncircumcized*} The point is that a Jew is to remain a Jew, a Gentile to be a Gentile. Both stand on an equality in the Christian churches.

21. {*Wast thou called being a bondservant? Care not for it*} Lit. "Let it not be a care to you." It was usually a fixed condition and a slave could be a good servant of Christ (Col. 3:22; Eph. 6:5; Titus 2:9), even with heathen masters. {*Use it rather*} Make use of what? Translate, "but if you can also become free, the rather use your opportunity for freedom." Probably this is in full harmony with the general principle above about mixed marriages with the heathen (see above).

23. {*Become not bondservants of men*} Lit. "stop becoming slaves of men." Paul here clearly defines his opposition to human slavery as an institution.

25. {*I have no commandment of the Lord...but I give my judgment*} It was quite possible for Paul to know this command of Jesus as he did other sayings of Jesus (Acts 20:35). Sayings of Jesus were passed on among the believers. But Paul had no specific word from Jesus on the subject of virgins. Paul had the command of Jesus concerning divorce to guide him. Here he has nothing from Jesus at all, only a deliberately formed decision from knowledge (2 Cor. 8:10), not a mere passing fancy. {*As one that hath obtained mercy of the Lord to be faithful*} This is far from being a disclaimer of inspiration. It is an express claim to help from the Lord in the forming of this duly considered judgment, which is in no sense a command, but an inspired opinion.

26. {*By reason of the present distress*} Probably, Paul has in mind the second coming of Jesus. Jesus had spoken of those calamities which would precede his coming (Matt. 24:8; also Luke 21:23) though Paul had denied saying that the advent was right at hand (2 Thess. 2:2).

27. {*Art thou bound to a wife? Seek not to be loosed*} Lit. "Are you bound to a wife? Do not be seeking release" i.e., release from the marriage bond (cf. Rom. 7:2).

28. {*But and if thou marry...thou hast not sinned*} A condition undetermined with prospect of being determined. {*Shall have tribulation in the flesh*} "Troubles" is in an emphatic position (cf. 2 Cor. 12:7). {*And I would spare you*} Greek tense translates, "I am trying to spare you."

29. {*The time is shortened*} Paul gives a new turn to the argument about the present necessity. "Is short" is the Greek verb *sustellô*, to place together, to draw together (cf. Acts 5:6). This word is found in the papyri for curtailing expenses. Apparently Paul pictures the foreshortening of time (opportunity) because of the possible nearness of and hope for the second coming (cf. 1 Cor. 3:20).

30. {*As though they possessed not*} In this entire verse and part of the next, Paul means that all earthly relations are to hang loosely about us in view of the second coming.

31. {*For the fashion of this world passeth away*} The Greek word *schêma* is the *habitus,* the outward appearance (cf. Phil. 2:7).

32. {*The things of the Lord*} This is the ideal state (so as to the widow and the virgin in verse 33), but even the unmarried let the cares of the world choke the word (Mark 4:19).

34. {*And there is a difference also between the wife and the virgin*} Paul's point is that the married woman is more disposed to care for the things of the world.

35. {*Not that I may cast a snare upon you*} The Greek word for snare is *brochon,* a noose or slipknot used to lasso animals. Paul does not wish to capture the Corinthians by lasso and compel them to do what they do not wish about getting married.

36. {*If she be past the flower of her age...if need so requireth*} Lit. "over [the] prime or bloom of life," past the bloom of youth. Apparently the Corinthians had asked Paul about the duty of a father towards his daughter old enough to marry, "it ought to happen." Paul has discussed the problem of marriage for virgins on the grounds of expediency. Now he faces the question where the daughter wishes to marry and there is no serious objection to it. The father is advised to consent.

37. {*To keep his own virgin daughter*} This means the case when the virgin daughter does not wish to marry and the father agrees with her.

39. {*For so long time as her husband liveth*} (cf. Rom. 7:2). This is the ideal and is pertinent today when husbands meet their ex-wives and wives meet their ex-husbands. There is a screw loose somewhere. Paul here treats as a sort of addendum the remarriage of widows. He will discuss it again in 1 Timothy 5:9-13.

40. {*I think*} He has inspired judgment on this difficult, complicated, tangled problem of marriage. But he has discharged his duty and leaves each one to decide for himself.

CHAPTER 8

1. {*Now concerning things sacrificed to idols*} The connection between idolatry and impurity was very close, especially in Corinth. The "things" were the meat left over after the heathen sacrifices; either eaten sacrificially, or taken home for private meals, or sold in the markets. Three questions about Christians eating these things are thus involved and Paul discusses them all in this dispute.

2. {*That he knoweth anything*} That is, "has acquired knowledge" (cf. 1 Cor. 3:18), has gone to the bottom of the subject. {*As he ought to know*} The really learned man knows his ignorance of what lies beyond. Shallow knowledge is like the depth of the mud hole, not of the crystal spring.

3. {*The same is known of him*} God knows those that are his (2 Tim. 2:19; Exod. 33:12). Those who know God are known of God (Gal. 4:9).

4. {*No idol is anything in the world*} (cf. Acts 7:41; 15:20; 1 Thess. 1:9). The idol was a mere picture or symbol of a god. If the god has no existence, the idol is a nonentity. {*No God but one*} This Christians held as firmly as Jews. The worship of Jesus as God's Son and the Holy Spirit does not recognize three Gods, but one God in three Persons (cf. Rom. 1:20).

6. {*Of whom...*} As the source of the universe (cf. Rom. 11:36; Col. 1:16) and also our goal is God (cf. Rom. 11:36); through Jesus Christ as the intermediate agent of creation (cf. Col. 1:15-20).

7. {*Howbeit in all men there is not that knowledge*} The knowledge of which Paul is speaking has to overcome inheritance and environment, prejudice, fear, and many other hindrances. {*Being used...*} This is the Greek word *sunêtheia* from *sunêthês* (*sun, êthos*), intimacy (cf. John 18:39; 1 Cor. 11:16). It is the force of habit that still grips them when they eat such meat. The idol taint clings in their minds to this meat. {*Conscience being weak*} This is the Greek word *suneidêsis* (*conscientia,* knowing together, conscience) (cf. Acts 23:1). Knowledge breaks down as a guide with the weak or unenlightened conscience.

8. {*Will not commend are we the worse are we the better*} Food will not give us an entree to God for commendation or condemnation, whether meat-eaters or vegetarians. Paul here disposes of the pride of knowledge (the enlightened ones) and the pride of prejudice (the unenlightened). Each was disposed to look down upon the other, the one in scorn of the other's ignorance, the other in horror of the other's heresy and daring.

9. {*This liberty of yours*} This means "grant, allowance, authority, power, privilege, right, liberty." It shades off easily. Personal liberty becomes a battle cry to those who wish to indulge their own whims and appetites regardless of the effect upon others. {*A stumbling block to the weak*} (cf. Rom. 14:13). The enlightened must consider the welfare of the unenlightened, else he does not have love.

10. {*If a man see thee which hast knowledge sitting at meat in an idol's temple*} This is a possible case. Here Paul considers only the effect of such conduct on the unenlightened brother. The weak will be emboldened to go on and do what he still believes to be wrong (eat sacrificial meat). Defiance is flung in the face of the unenlightened brother instead of loving consideration.

11. {*For whose sake Christ died*} The appeal to the death of Christ is the central fact that clinches Paul's argument.

12. {*Wounding their conscience*} This is the Greek verb *tuptô*, to smite with fist, staff, whip. The conscience is sensitive to a blow like that, a slap in the face. {*Ye sin against Christ*} They were overlooking this fact.

13. {*Maketh my brother to stumble*} This is the Greek verb *skandaliô*, to set a trap-stick (Matt. 5:29) or stumbling block (cf. 1 Cor. 8:9 and Rom. 14:13, 21). Small boys sometimes set snares for other boys, not merely for animals to see them caught. {*I will eat no flesh for evermore*} Referring to flesh offered to idols. This is Paul's principle of love (v. 1 Cor. 8:2) applied to the matter of eating meats offered to idols; better a vegetarian than to lead his weak brother to do what he considered sin.

CHAPTER 9

1. {*Am I not free?*} That is, free as a Christian from Mosaic ceremonialism (cf. 1 Cor. 9:19). {*Am I not an apostle?*} He has the exceptional privileges as an apostle to support from the churches and yet he foregoes these. {*Have I not seen Jesus our Lord?*} (cf. Acts 9:17, 27; 18:9; 22:14, 17; 2 Cor. 12:1). All these questions expect an affirmative answer.

3. {*My defence*} This is not "apologizing" but a regular sense of defense (cf. Acts 22:1; 25:16). {*To them that examine me*} (cf. 1 Cor. 2:15; 4:3). The critics in Corinth were "investigating" Paul to find faults.

4. {*Have we no right?*} This is a literary plural here. Translate the Greek syntax, "Do we fail to have the right?" expecting a "no" (you do have the right) answer to this negative question.

5. {*To lead about a wife that is a believer?*} Lit. "a sister a wife." This is a plea for the support of the preacher's wife and children.

6. {*Have we not a right to forbear working?*} Lit. "Do we not have the right not to do manual labor?" "Yes" is the expected answer.

7. {*What soldier ever serveth...at his own charges?*} "Expense" is the Greek word *opsônion* (from *opson*, cooked meat or relish with bread, and *ôneomai*, to buy) in the sense of rations or food, then for the soldiers' wages (often provisions) or the pay of any workman (cf. Rom. 6:23). Paul illustrates the proof that he has the right to receive pay for preaching (1 Cor. 9:7-13).

8. {*Do I speak these things after the manner of men?*} (1 Cor. 3:3; 9:8; 15:32; Gal. 1:11; 3:15; Rom. 3:5). "No" is the expected answer. {*The law also*} Perhaps objection was made that the Scripture does not support the practice of paying preachers.

10. {*Altogether*} Translate, "doubtless" or "assuredly." Note some versions put this in verse 9. {*In hope of partaking*} Lit. "he that threshes ought to thresh in hope of partaking." The point is that all the workers (beast or man) share in the fruit of the toil.

11. {*If...if*} These two phrases in the Greek are assumed to be true or fulfilled.

12. {*Do not we yet more?*} That is, because of Paul's peculiar relation to that church as founder and apostle. {*But we bear all things*} Paul deliberately declined to use his right to pay in Corinth. {*That we may cause no hindrance...*} "Hinder" is the Greek word *enkopê*, a cutting in (cf. *radio* or telephone) or hindrance from *enkoptô*, to cut in, rare word (like *ekkopê*).

14. {*Even so did the Lord ordain*} Just as God gave orders about the priests in the temple, so did the Lord Jesus give orders for those who preach the gospel to live out of the gospel (cf. Matt. 10:10; Luke 10:7).

15. {*For it were good for me to die, than that any man should make my glorying void*} Here Paul shows intense feeling on the subject (brought out by the complex Greek syntax).

16. {*For if I preach...woe is me...necessity*} This is an unfulfilled condition, though a conceivable case. Jesus had called him (Acts 9:6, 15; Gal. 1:15; Rom. 1:14). He could do no other than heed the call, and deserves no credit for doing it.

17. {*Of mine own will...willingly*} Paul's call was so clear that he certainly did his work *willingly* and so had a reward (Matt. 6:1); but the only *reward* that he had for his willing work was to make the gospel *free of expense* (cf. 1 Cor. 9:18). {*I have a stewardship intrusted to me*} Paul says, I have been entrusted with a stewardship and so would go on with my task like any steward even if unwilling.

20. {*Not being myself under the law*} He was emancipated from the law as a means of salvation, yet he knew how to speak to them because of his former beliefs and life with them (Gal. 4:21).

21. {*To them that are without law*} This refers to the heathen, those outside the Mosaic law (Rom. 2:14), not lawless (Luke 22:37; Acts 2:23; 1 Tim. 1:9).

22. {*I became weak*} This is the climax in his plea for the principle of love on the part of the enlightened [i.e., the knowledgeable] for the benefit of the unenlightened [i.e., the weak] (chapter 1 Cor. 8:1ff.). He thus brings home his conduct about renouncing pay for preaching as an illustration of love (1 Cor. 8:13). {*All things…by all means…that I may save some*} This is his goal and worth all the cost of adaptation. In matters of principle Paul was adamant as about Titus the Greek (Gal. 2:5). In matters of expediency as about Timothy (Acts 16:3) he would go half way to win and to hold. This principle was called for in dealing with the problem of eating meat offered to idols (Rom. 14:1; 15:1; 1 Thess. 5:14).

23. {*That I may be a joint partaker thereof*} Lit. "that I may become co-partner with others in the gospel." The point is that he may be able to share the gospel with others, his evangelistic passion.

24. {*In a race*} In most Greek cities, this is a racecourse for runners with a stated or fixed distance of 606 3/4 feet (cf. also Matt. 14:24; Luke 24:13).

25. {*That striveth in the games*} (1 Tim. 6:12; 2 Tim. 4:7). This is the Greek verb *agônizomai,* a common verb for contest in the athletic games (*agôn*). Probably, Paul often saw these athletic games. {*Is temperate in all things*} (cf. 1 Cor. 7:9). This is one who controls himself. The athlete then and now has to "control himself in all things." This is stated by Paul as an athletic axiom. Training for ten months was required under the direction of trained judges. {*A corruptible crown*} This is the Greek word *stephanos* (crown) from *stephô,* to put around the head, like the Latin *corona,* wreath or garland, badge of victory in the games. These were the most coveted honors in the whole Greek world, yet the elements of this vegetation crown withered and so not lasting (Findlay).

Another similar Greek word *diadêma* (diadem) was for kings (Rev. 12:3).

26. {*As not uncertainly*} Paul describes his own conduct as a runner in the race, Christ as the goal (Phil. 3:14). He kept his eye on Christ as Christ watched him. {*Fight…as not beating the air*} Paul changes to a boxer metaphor, swinging his fists, called "shadow fighting."

27. {*But I buffet my body*} Paul does not consider his flesh or body sinful and evil. But "it is like the horses in a chariot race, which must be kept well in hand by whip and rein if the prize is to be secured" (Robertson and Plummer). The boxers often used boxing gloves (*cestus,* of ox-hide bands) which gave telling blows. Paul was not willing for his body to be his master. He found good as the outcome of this self-discipline (2 Cor. 12:7; Rom. 8:13; Col. 2:23; 3:5). {*I myself should be rejected*} Paul means rejected for the *prize,* not for the entrance to the race. He will fail to win if he breaks the rules of the game (Matt. 7:22). What is the prize before Paul? Is it *reward* (cf. 1 Cor. 9:18)? Most writers take Paul to refer to the possibility of his rejection in his personal salvation at the end of the race. He does not claim absolute perfection (Phil. 3:12) and so he presses on. At the end he has serene confidence (2 Tim. 4:7) with the race run and won.

CHAPTER 10

1. {*All under the cloud*} This is the pillar of cloud (cf. Exod. 13:21; 14:19), which covered the host (Num. 14:14; Ps. 95:39). This mystic cloud was the symbol of the presence of the Lord with the people.

2. {*Were all baptized unto Moses in the cloud and in the sea*} The mystic cloud covered the people while the sea rose in walls on each side of them as they marched across. The immersion was complete for all of them in the sea around them and the cloud over them.

3. {*The same spiritual meat*} This refers to supernatural (hence "spiritual") manna (Exod. 16:13).

4. {*For they drank of a spiritual rock that followed them*} The Israelites were blessed by the water from the rock that Moses smote at Rephidim (Exod. 17:6) and at Kadesh (Num. 20:11) and by the well of Beer (Num. 21:16). The rabbis had a legend that the water actually followed the Israelites for forty years, in one form a fragment of rock fifteen feet high that followed the people and gushed out water. Possibly Paul alludes to this fancy and gives it a spiritual turn as a type of Christ in allegorical fashion (cf. Gal. 4:24). {*And the rock was Christ*} Christ was the source of the water which saved the Israelites from perishing as he is the source of supply for us today.

5. {*With most of them*} Only two (Caleb and Joshua) actually reached the Promised Land (Num. 14:30-32). {*Were overthrown*} (Num. 14:16). This is a powerful picture of the desolation wrought by the years of disobedience and wanderings in the desert.

7. {*Neither be ye idolaters*} Lit. "stop becoming idolaters, implying that some of them had already begun to be." Eating meat offered to idols might become a stepping stone to idolatry in some instances.

8. {*Neither let us commit fornication*} (Num. 14:16). Better, "let us cease practicing fornication as some were already doing" (1 Cor. 6:11; 7:2). The connection between idolatry and fornication was very close. Also Corinth had prostitution as part of the worship of Aphrodite.

9. {*Neither let us tempt the Lord*} Translate, "let us cease sorely testing the Lord by such conduct."

10. {*Neither murmur ye*} (cf. Num. 16:41). There is an implication that some of them were murmuring (cf. Matt. 20:11).

11. {*Now these things happened unto them*} Greek tense translates "happened from time to time." {*By way of example*} (cf. 1 Cor. 10:6). {*The ends of the ages have come*} Is this the Second Coming? (cf. Heb. 9:26, also Matt. 13:40). The plural seems to point out how one stage succeeds another in the drama of human history.

14. {*Wherefore*} Paul applies the example of the Israelites to the perilous state of the Corinthians about idolatry.

16. {*The cup of blessing*} This is the cup over which we pronounce a blessing as by Christ at the institution of the ordinance. {*A communion of the blood of Christ*} This is the Greek word *koinônia*, an old one from *koinônos*, meaning here partner (cf. Phil. 2:1; 3:10), and other meanings elsewhere. It refers to a spiritual participation in the blood of Christ which is symbolized by the cup.

17. {*One body*} This is here the mystical spiritual body of Christ as in 1 Corinthians 12:12, the spiritual kingdom or church of which Christ is head (Col. 1:18; Eph. 5:23).

18. {*After the flesh*} Lit. "Israel according to the flesh." This is the literal Israel, the Jewish people, not the spiritual Israel, composed of both Jews and Gentiles, the true children of faith (Rom. 2:28; 9:8; Gal.

3:7). {*Communion with the altar*} The Israelites who offer sacrifices have a spiritual participation in the altar.

19. {*A thing sacrificed to idols*} (cf. Acts 15:29; 1 Cor. 8:1, 4). {*Idol*} That is, an image of a god (cf. Acts 7:41; 15:20; 1 Cor. 8:4, 7).

20. {*To demons, and not to God*} Here it means an evil spirit (cf. Deut. 32:17 LXX). Likely, Paul means "to a no-god" (cf. Deut. 32:21). This is Paul's reply to the heathen who claimed that they worshipped the gods represented by the images and not the mere wood or stone or metal idols (cf. Acts 17:18).

21. {*Of the table of the Lord*} (cf. Luke 22:30; also Isa. 65:11; Jer. 7:18; Ezek. 16:18; 23:41; Mal. 1:7). Here "table" means, what is on the table. This refers plainly to the Lord's Supper (1 Cor. 11:20).

24. {*Let no man seek his own...his neighbour's good*} This is Paul's rule for social relations (1 Cor. 13:5; Gal. 6:2; Rom. 14:7; 15:2; Phil. 2:1) and is the way to do what is expedient and what builds up.

25. {*In the shambles*} A transliterated Latin word, *macellum.* We can imagine the poor Christians buying their modest pound of meat in the Corinthian *Macellum* (1 Cor. 10:25), with the same life-like reality with which the Diocletian maximum tariff called up the picture of the Galilean woman purchasing her five sparrows. {*Asking no questions for conscience sake*} (cf. 1 Cor. 8:4). Don't question whether a particular piece of meat had been offered to idols before put in the market. Only partially consumed at sacrifice, the rest was sold in the market. Do not be over-scrupulous.

28. {*But if any man say unto you...eat not*} This is a conceivable case, in which a weak believer points out that the meat has been offered to idols.

29. {*For why is my liberty judged by another conscience?*} Why conform a strong brother's conscience to that of the weak brother, about a piece of meat? The only reason is love, which builds up (cf. 1 Cor. 8:2; 13:1ff.).

31. {*To the glory of God*} This is the ruling motive in the Christian's life, not just having his own way about whims and preferences.

32. {*Give no occasion of stumbling*} (cf. Phil. 1:10; Acts 24:16). This has an active sense here, i.e., not tripping others by being a stumbling block (cf. Sirach 32:21).

33. {*That they may be saved*} (1 Cor. 9:22). This is the ruling passion of Paul in his dealings with men.

CHAPTER 11

1. {*Imitators of me*} (cf. 1 Cor. 8:1 to 10:33). That is, in the principle of considerate love; also Paul imitates Christ.

2. {*Hold fast the traditions*} (cf. Matt. 15:2). "Traditions" is the Greek word *paradosis* from *paradidômi*, something handed on from one to another: either bad (Mark 7:8) or good (as here).

4. {*Having his head covered*} Lit. "having a veil down from the head" ("veil" is not in the Greek, but still understood as there). The Greeks (both men and women) remained bareheaded in public prayer and this usage Paul commends for the men.

5. {*With her head unveiled*} (Num. 5:18). Courtesan prostitutes and lewd women went about unveiled; slave women wore the shaven head; also a punishment of the adulteress (cf. Isa. 7:20). This is public praying and prophesying. He does not here condemn the act, but the breach of custom which would bring reproach.

6. {*Let her also be shorn*} This is the Greek verb *keirô*, to shear (as sheep). Let her cut her hair close. A single act by the woman. {*If it is a shame*} This is a condition assumed to be true. Paul uses strong language because such behaviors proclaimed her a lewd woman.

7. {*The image and glory of God*} (cf. Gen. 1:28; 2:26). This refers to the moral likeness of God, not any bodily resemblance. Humanity (man and woman) is the glory of God as the crown of creation and as endowed with sovereignty like God himself.

10. {*To have a sign of authority*} This refers to the sign of authority (cf. subjection 1 Tim. 2:10) of the man over the woman. The veil on the woman's head is the symbol of the authority that the man with the uncovered head has over her. {*Because of the angels*} Though all kinds of conjectures, these are veiled angels (Isa. 6:2) present in worship (cf. 1 Cor. 4:9; Ps. 138:1) who would be shocked at the unveiled conduct of the women.

14. {*Nature itself?*} The Greek expects a "yes" to the question. "Nature" means native sense of propriety (cf. Rom. 2:14) in addition to mere custom.

15. {*For a covering*} This is the Greek word *peribolaion,* from *periballô* to fling around, as a mantle (Heb. 1:12) or a covering or veil as here. It is not in the place of a veil, but answering to as a permanent endowment.

18. {*First of all*} This is the primary reason for Paul's condemnation and the only one given. {*When ye come together in the church*} This is the Greek word *ekklêsia* and has the literal meaning of assembly. {*Divisions*} This is not formal cleavages into two or more organizations, but partisan divisions within one organization. {*I hear*} Lit. "I keep on hearing." The rumors of strife were so constant.

19. {*Must be*} That is, since moral conditions are so bad among you (cf. 1 Cor. 1 to 6, also Matt. 18:7). {*Parties*} (cf. 1 Cor. 1:11, also Acts 15:5). Heresy is theoretical schism, schism practical heresy (cf. Gal. 5:20; Titus 3:10; 2 Pet. 2:1).

20. {*To eat the Lord's Supper*} This Supper belongs to or pertains to the Lord. Possibly this refers both to the Lovefeast (a sort of church supper held in connection with, before or after, the Lord's Supper) and the Eucharist or Lord's Supper.

21. {*Taketh before*} It made the Lord's Supper a grab-game; one hungry and another drunk. Conduct like this led to the complete separation between the Lovefeast and the Lord's Supper.

22. {*What? Have ye not houses?*} Lit. "Do you fail to have houses?" expecting a no answer. Here Paul is not approving gluttony and drunkenness but only expressing horror at their sacrilege of the church.

23. {*For I received of the Lord*} This is a direct claim to revelation from the Lord Jesus on the origin of the Lord's Supper (cf. also Luke 22:17-20).

24. {*When he had given thanks*} This is the Greek verb *eucharisteô* from which comes our word *Eucharist* (cf. 1 Cor. 1:14). {*Which is for you*} (cf. John 19:36). The bread was broken, but not the body of Jesus.

26. {*Till he come*} (cf. Luke 22:18). The Lord's Supper is the great preacher of the death of Christ until his second coming (Matt. 26:29).

27. {*Shall be guilty*} (cf. Matt. 5:21). That is, shall be guilty of a crime committed against the body and blood of the Lord by such sacrilege (cf. Heb. 6:6; 10:29).

28. {*Let a man prove himself*} That is, test himself as he would a piece of metal to see if genuine.

29. {*If he discern not the body*} Eating the bread and drinking the wine as symbols of the Lord's body and blood in death probes one's heart to the very depths.

30. {*And not a few sleep*} Sufficient number are dead because of the desecration of the Lord's table. Paul evidently had knowledge of specific instances. A few would be too many.

31. {*But if we discerned ourselves*} The Greek condition assumes that they had not been judging themselves discriminatingly, else they would not be judged.

32. {*Ye are chastened of the Lord... with the world*} (Heb. 12:6). This is the Greek verb *paideuô*, from *pais,* child, to train a child by afflictions; though other forms of discipline also occurred. Afflictions are meant to separate us from the doom of the wicked world.

CHAPTER 12

1. {*Now concerning spiritual gifts*} (cf. 1 Cor. 7:1). Paul deals with this next question (cf. 1 Cor. 8:1) to the end of chapter 14.

2. {*Ye were led away*} (cf. Ps. 95:5-7) Lit. "without voice." Pagans were led astray by demons (1 Cor. 10:19). {*Howsoever ye might be led*} Rather, "as often as ye were led," with a notion of repetition.

3. {*Wherefore I give you to understand*} Lit. "I make known that." {*Speaking in the Spirit of God...*} There is no great distinction here between "utter sounds" (speaking) and "say." {*Jesus is anathema*} (cf. 1 Cor. 16:22; Gal. 1:8; Rom. 9:3). This blasphemous language against Jesus was mainly by the Jews (Acts 13:45; 18:6). It is even possible that Paul had once tried to make Christians say *Anathema* is Jesus (Acts 26:11).

4. {*Diversities*} This is the Greek word *diairesis,* distinctions, differences, distributions, from *diaireô,* to distribute, as *diairoun* (dividing, distributing) in verse 11. {*Of gifts*} (cf. Rom. 12:6; 1 Pet. 4:19). It means a favor bestowed or received without any merit (cf. Rom. 1:11).

6. {*Who worketh all things in all*} Paul is not afraid to say that God is the Energy and the Energizer of the Universe. Here Paul is speaking only of the workings of spiritual gifts and results as a whole, but he applies this principle to the universe (cf. Col. 1:16).

8. {*To one...*} There are nine manifestations of the Spirit's work (cf. 1 Cor. 12:8-10). {*The Word of wisdom*} Here it is speech full of God's wisdom (cf. 1 Cor. 2:7) under the impulse of the Spirit of God. This gift is placed first (revelation by the Spirit). {*The word of knowledge*} This gift is insight (illumination) according to the same Spirit.

9. {*Faith*} This is wonder-working faith (cf. 1 Cor. 13:2, also Matt. 17:20; 21:21). {*Gifts of healings*} It means acts of healing (cf. Luke 7:21; Acts 4:30; Jas. 5:14).

10. {*Workings of miracles*} Lit. "workings of powers" (cf. Gal. 3:5; Heb. 2:4). Some of the miracles were not healings such as the blindness on Elymas the sorcerer. {*Prophecy*} Lit. "to speak forth." This gift Paul will praise most (cf. 1 Cor. 14:1ff.). Not always prediction, but a speaking forth of God's message under the guidance of the Holy Spirit. {*Discernings of spirits*} (cf. Rom. 14:1; Heb. 5:14). This gift discerns between supernatural Spirit gifts or diabolical events (1 Tim. 4:1; 1 John 4:1), or merely strange, natural events. {*Divers kinds of tongues*} Placed lowest of all, this gift had become a source of confusion and disorder. Though there are kinds, this gift was essentially an ecstatic utterance of highly wrought emotion that edified the speaker (1 Cor. 14:4) and was intelligible to God (1 Cor. 14:2, 28). It was not always true that the speaker in tongues could make clear what he had said to those who did not know the tongue (1 Cor. 14:13). {*The interpretation of tongues*} (cf. 1 Cor. 14:26). When no one present understood the particular tongue, this gift was required, for any benefit to occur.

12. {*So also is Christ*} What Paul here means is Christ as the Head of the Church (cf. Col. 1:18, 24; Eph. 5:23, 30) has a body composed of the members who have varied gifts and functions like the different members of the human body. They are all vitally connected with the Head of the body and with each other.

13. {*Were we all baptized into one body*} This refers to a definite past event with each of them of different races, nations, classes, when each of them put on the outward badge of service to Christ. {*And were all made to drink of one Spirit*} This refers to a definite act in the past, probably to the inward experience of the Holy Spirit symbolized by the act of baptism.

15-16. {*It is not therefore not of the body*} Thinking or saying "I do not belong to the body" does not change the fact.

17. {*If the whole body were an eye*} The eye is the most wonderful organ: useful (Num. 10:31); the very light of the body (Luke 11:34). And yet how grotesque it would be if there were nothing else but a great round rolling eye! A big "I" surely!

18. {*But now hath God set*} That is, but as things are, in contrast to that absurdity. Why challenge God's will? (cf. Rom. 9:20).

19. {*One member*} (cf. 1 Cor. 12:17). The application to members of the church is obvious. It is particularly pertinent in the case of a "church boss."

22. {*Those members of the body which seem to be more feeble are necessary*} The vital organs (lungs, liver, etc.) are not visible, but life cannot exist without them.

23. {*We bestow*} Lit. "we place around as if a garland (Mark 15:17) or a garment" (Matt. 27:28).

24. {*Tempered the body together*} This is the Greek verb *sunkerannumi*, to mix together (cf. Heb. 4:2). Paul here gives a noble picture of the body with its wonderful organs planned to be the temple of God's Spirit (1 Cor. 6:19).

25. {*That there should be no schism*} Trouble in one organ affects the whole body.

26. {*Suffer with it*} This is the Greek verb *sunpaschô*, a medical term in this sense in other literature (cf. also Rom. 8:17). {*Rejoice with it*} One may tingle with joy all over the body thanks to the wonderful nervous system and to the relation between mind and matter.

28. {*Apostle*} This is the official title given the twelve by Jesus, and claimed by Paul though not one of the twelve. {*Prophets*} (cf. Acts 13:1). This is "for-speakers" for God and Christ. {*Teachers*} (cf. Luke 3:12; also John 3:10; 13:13; also 1 Tim. 2:7). {*Then miracles*} (cf. Rom. 12:7). Here a change is made from the concrete to the abstract. {*Helps*} Probably this refers to the work of the deacons, help rendered to the poor and the sick. {*Governments*} This is the Greek word *kubernêsis*, from *kubernaô* (cf. *kubernêtês* in Acts 27:11). Probably Paul has in mind bishops/overseers or elders, the outstanding leaders (cf. 1 Thess. 5:12; Rom. 12:8; Acts 15:22; Heb. 13:7, 17, 24).

29-30. {*Are all...?*} A "no" answer is expected to each of the questions.

31. {*And a still more excellent way*} (2 Cor. 4:17). "I show you a way *par excellence*" beyond all comparison. Already laid down in 1 Corinthians 8:1, this refers to the way of love (cf. 1 Cor. 13:1ff.).

CHAPTER 13

1. {*If...with the tongues*} This is a supposable case. The ecstatic gifts are comparably worthless in comparison to love. Lit. "with the tongues." This is mentioned first because really least and because the Corinthians put undue emphasis on this gift. {*But have not love*} This is the *crux* of the chapter. Love is the way *par excellence* of 1 Corinthians 12:31. In ancient literature, the rarity of the Greek word *agapê* made it easier for Christians to use this word for Christian love as opposed to *erôs* (sexual love). {*Clanging cymbal*} This is a hollow basin of brass, here ringing for any cause.

2. {*Prophecy…mysteries…all knowledge*} Not condemning, he simply places love above them.

3. {*Body…to be burned*} "Burned" is a variant to the true reading, "[If I surrender my body] that *I may glory.*"

4. Verses 4 to 7 picture the character or conduct of love in marvelous rhapsody. {*Suffereth long*} Lit. "long [from] passion [i.e., anger]" (cf. Jas. 5:7). {*Is kind*} This means gentle in behavior. {*Envieth not*} This is "zeal" in the bad sense here. Love is neither jealous nor envious (both ideas). {*Vaunteth not itself*} This is the Greek verb *perpereuomai,* from *perperos,* vainglorious, braggart. It means play the braggart. {*Is not puffed up*} Lit. "puffed up," to puff oneself out like a pair of bellows, i.e., arrogant (cf. 1 Cor. 4:6).

5. {*Doth not behave itself unseemly*} (cf. 1 Cor. 7:36; 12:23). That is, not indecent. {*Seeketh not its own*} That is, not seeking its own interests (1 Cor. 10:24, 33). {*Is not provoked*} (cf. Acts 17:16). This is irritation or sharpness of spirit. {*Taketh not account of evil*} Lit. "to count up, to take account" of as in a ledger or notebook.

6. {*But rejoiceth with the truth*} Not rejoicing in the triumph of evil, love is on the side of the angels.

7. {*Beareth all things*} (cf. 1 Cor. 9:12; 1 Thess. 3:1, 5). Love covers, protects, forbears (cf. 1 Pet. 4:8). {*Believeth all things*} Not gullible, but love has faith in men. {*Hopeth all things*} Love sees the bright side of things and does not despair. {*Endureth all things*} Love carries on like a stouthearted soldier.

8. {*They shall be done away*} This is the Greek verb *katargeô,* to make idle, inoperative. All these special spiritual gifts will pass. {*They shall cease*} The Greek voice translates, "they shall make themselves cease or automatically cease of themselves."

11. {*A child*} (cf. 1 Cor. 3:1). This is in contrast to the "perfect (adult)." {*spake…I thought…reasoned*} Translate the Greek tense for all three: I used to…. {*Now that I am become*} Translate the Greek tense, "I have become a man and remain so" (Eph. 4:14).

12. {*In a mirror*} Ancient mirrors were of polished metal, not glass, those in Corinth being famous. {*Darkly*} Lit. "in an enigma." This is true of all ancient mirrors.

13. {*Abideth*} The other gifts pass away, but these abide forever.

CHAPTER 14

1. {*Follow after love*} (cf. 1 Cor. 12:31). As if a veritable chase. Paul now proves the relative superiority of prophecy.

2. {*For no man understandeth*} Lit. "hears, gets the sense, understands." {*Mysteries*} (cf. 1 Cor. 2:7).

3. {*Edification...comfort...consolation*} That is, building up...calling to one's side...edification, cheer, incentive in these words, respectively.

5. {*Except he interpret*} Lit. "except if not" = "unless" (cf. also 1 Cor. 12:30; Luke 24:27; Acts 9:36).

7. {*Things without life*} Lit. "without a soul." {*Pipe...harp*} These are pipe and stringed instruments.

8. {*An uncertain voice*} Lit. "uncertain" = "not manifest." A military trumpet is louder than pipe or harp.

9. {*Unless ye utter speech easy to be understood*} "intelligible" = "well marked, distinct, clear." Good enunciation, a hint for speakers.

10. {*Without signification*} That is, without the faculty of speech (1 Cor. 12:2; Acts 8:32; 2 Pet. 2:16).

11. {*A barbarian*} The Greeks divided humanity into Greeks and Barbarians (all ignorant of Greek language and culture).

14. {*But my understanding is unfruitful*} That is, my intellect gets no benefit from rhapsodical praying that may even move my spirit.

15. {*With the understanding also*} Paul is distinctly in favor of the use of the intellect in prayer. Prayer is an intelligent exercise of the mind. {*And I will sing with the understanding also*} Paul prefers singing that reaches the intellect as well as stirs the emotions (cf. Eph. 5:19).

16. {*Else if thou bless with the spirit*} If one is praying and praising God (cf. 1 Cor. 10:16) in an ecstatic prayer, the one who doesn't understand the ecstatic language will not know when to say "amen" at the end of the prayer. (Neh. 5:13; 8:6; 1 Chr. 16:36; Ps. 106:48). {*He that filleth the place of the unlearned*} Lit. "the place of the unlearned." This is not a special part of the room, but the position of the uninitiated in the gift of tongues (cf. 1 Cor. 14:23).

19. {*Howbeit in church*} Private ecstasy is one thing (cf. 2 Cor. 12:1-9) but not in church worship, which has a focus on instruction.

20. {*Be not children in mind*} Lit. "Cease..." (what some evidently currently were) (cf. Heb. 5:11-14).

22. {*For a sign*} Lit. "tongues are *for* a sign," as in the Hebrew.

23. {*Will they not say that ye are mad?*} These unlearned unbelievers will say that the Christians are raving mad, lunatics (cf. Acts 12:15; 26:24).

24. {*He is reproved by all*} This is an old word for strong proof, is undergoing conviction. {*Is judged*} That is, is tested (cf. 1 Cor. 2:15; 4:3).

26. {*When ye come together*} Lit. "whenever" a normal repetition case in contrast with special case (cf. 1 Cor. 14:23).

28. {*Keep silence in church*} Greek tense shows he is not even to speak in a tongue once. He can indulge his private ecstasy with God.

29. {*By two or three...let the others discern*} (cf. 1 Cor. 14:27). That is, let two or three prophets speak. Others discern whether it is really of the Spirit (cf. 1 Cor. 12:10).

33. {*Not of confusion*} We need this reminder today. Orderly reverence is a common mark of the churches.

34. {*Keep silence in the churches*} (cf. 1 Tim. 2:12). First dress (cf. 1 Cor. 11:2-16), and now by their speech. In church the women are not allowed to speak nor even to ask questions. They are to do that at home.

37. {*The commandment of the Lord*} He claims inspiration for his position to the offenders.

40. {*Decently and in order*} That is surely a good rule for all matters of church life and worship.

CHAPTER 15

2. {*If we hold it fast*} This condition assumes that they are holding it fast. {*Except ye believed in vain*} Translate the Greek condition, "unless in fact you did believe to no purpose." Paul holds this peril over them in their temptation to deny the resurrection.

4. {*And that he was buried*} This item is an important detail as the Gospels show. {*And that he hath been raised*} The Greek tense emphasizes the permanence of the resurrection of Jesus. He is still risen.

5. {*And that he appeared to Cephas*} (John 21:14). Each "then" is considered chronological. "Appeared" is not a mere vision, but actual appearance. Peter was listed first among the Apostles (Matt. 10:2). Jesus

had sent a special message to him (Mark 16:7) after his resurrection.
{*To the twelve*} (John 20:24) Only ten were present, so this is a technical name.

6. {*To above five hundred brethren at once*} This refers to the prearranged meeting on the mountain in Galilee (Matt. 28:16), not over 25 years ago, and so many still living.

8. {*As unto one born out of due time*} (Num. 12:12; Job 3:16). Lit. "as to the miscarriage (or untimely birth)," Referring to the appearance of the ascended Jesus to Paul.

9. {*The least*} (cf. Eph. 3:8; 1 Tim. 1:15). Elsewhere, in response to attacks by the Judaizers, he defends his rank as equal to any apostle (2 Cor. 11:5, 23). {*Because I persecuted the church of God*} At times, a terrible fact that confronted Paul like a nightmare.

10. {*What I am*} Not, who, but what. His actual character and attainments. All "by the grace of God." {*I laboured more abundantly than they all*} (cf. Acts and Paul's Epistles). He had tremendous energy and used it.

12. {*How say some among you?*} That is, with proof of the resurrection (vv. 1 Cor. 15:1-11), and continual preaching of it, how can some question the resurrection? Some in Corinth (and the church) may have denied any and all miracles ever happening.

14. {*Vain*} Lit. "empty." referring to both Paul's preaching and their faith.

17. {*Vain*} That is, devoid of truth, a lie, stronger than "empty" (cf. 1 Cor. 15:14). {*Ye are yet in your sins*} Christ's death has no atoning value if he did not rise from the dead.

18. {*Then also...have perished*} An inevitable inference, the dead in Christ are delivered up to eternal misery (cf. 1 Cor. 8:11).

19. {*Most pitiable*} Paul makes morality turn on the hope of immortality.

20. {*But now*} This is emphatic in the Greek, esp. in light of the preceding argument. {*The first fruits*} (cf. 1 Cor. 15:23; 16:15; Rom. 8:23; Col. 1:18). Others raised from the dead died again, but not so Jesus. {*That sleep*} This is a beautiful picture of death.

21. {*By man also*} This refers to the first man (Adam) and the Godman, the Second Adam (Rom. 5:12), respectively.

22. {*Shall be made alive*} This is the Greek verb *zôopoieô*, here, to restore to life meaning general resurrection, some to eternal life or salvation, others to judgment.

23. {*At his coming*} The Greek word *parousia* was the technical word "for the arrival or visit of the king or emperor." Advent coins were struck after a *parousia* of the emperor.

26. {*The last enemy that shall be abolished is death*} Lit. "death is done away."

27. {*But when he saith*} Likely, "he" most naturally refers to "God," though it could be the future triumphant "Christ" as the subject.

28. {*That God may be all in all*} This is the final goal of all God's redemptive plans (cf. Rom. 11:36 and Col. 3:11).

30. {*Why do we also stand in jeopardy every hour?*} Paul's Epistles and Acts (especially chapter Acts 19:1ff.) throw light on Paul's argument. He was never out of danger from Damascus to the last visit to Rome.

31. {*I protest by that glorying in you*} (Gen. 42:15 LXX). Paul takes solemn oath (cf. also 2 Cor. 1:18, 23; 11:10, 31; Rom. 9:1). {*I die daily*} That is, I am in daily peril of death (2 Cor. 4:11; 11:23; Rom. 8:36).

32. {*If I fought with wild beasts at Ephesus*} Some think this is literal. But Paul was a Roman citizen and it was unlawful to punish a Roman citizen this way. Note that it is not mentioned in 2 Corinthians 11:23.

33. {*Be not deceived*} That is, do not be led astray by such a false philosophy of life. {*Evil company...*} That is, evil companionships. The line is from Menander, it may be a current proverb.

34. {*Awake up righteously*} That is, wake up as if from drunkenness and stop sinning.

35. {*But some one will say*} Paul knows what the skeptics were saying. He is a master at putting the standpoint of the imaginary adversary. {*How*} Paul answers: death itself is the way of resurrection as in the death of the seed for the new plant (cf. 1 Cor. 15:36). {*With what manner of body*} That is, will the first body that perishes be the raised body? Paul answers: It is a spiritual, not a natural, body that is raised (cf. 1 Cor. 15:38 to 54).

36. {*Except it die*} Death precedes life in plants; death of the seed and then the new plant. This answers how are the dead raised (cf. 1 Cor. 15:35).

37. {*Not the body which shall be*} The body of a plant is not yet in existence, but only the seed. We sow seeds, not plants (bodies). The butterfly comes out of the dying worm.

38. {*A body of its own*} This is shown even under the microscope the life cells may seem almost identical, yet be quite distinct.

39. {*The same flesh*} Paul takes up animal life to show the great variety there is as in the plant kingdom. Variety exists along with kinship (cf. the categories of God's creatures here) and progress (from flesh body to spirit body).

40. {*Earthly...celestial*} Paul now rises higher in argument: he indicates like differences to be seen in the heavens above us. Note that both kinds of bodies have their own kind of "glory."

42. {*It is sown in incorruption*} The resurrection body has undergone a complete change as compared with the body of flesh like the plant from the seed. It is related to it, but it is a different body of glory.

43. {*In weakness...in power*} Death can never conquer this new body (cf. Phil. 3:21).

44. {*A natural body*} Paul means to say that the "spiritual body" has some kind of germinal connection with the "natural body" though the new body is glorious beyond our comprehension.

45. {*The last Adam became a life-giving spirit*} God breathed a soul into Adam, Christ is the crown of humanity and has power to give us the new body.

46. {*Howbeit that is not first which is spiritual, but that which is natural*} This is the law of growth always.

47-49. {*Earthly...the second man from heaven*} This is a contrast of Adam's natural body and Christ's risen body.

50. {*Cannot inherit*} Death changes the natural body to the spiritual body, without regard to the special circumstances of the resurrection of Jesus.

51. {*We shall not all sleep...but we shall all be changed*} Paul means, "not all of us shall die." Some people will be alive when he comes. Both living and dead receive the resurrection body (cf. 1 Thess. 4:13-18).

52. {*In a moment*} This is the Greek word *atomos,* from *a* privative (negation) and *temnô,* to cut, indivisible: Scientific word for *atom* which was considered indivisible, but that was before the day of electrons and protons. {*In the twinkling of an eye*} "Twinkling" used by the Greeks for the flapping of a wing, the buzz of a gnat, the quivering of a harp, the twinkling of a star.

54. {*Is swallowed up*} (cf. Isa. 25:8). Lit. "to drink down, swallow down."

55. {*O death*} (cf. Hos. 13:14) Here Paul changes Sheol/Hades (Heb. and LXX) for "death." {*Thy sting*} This is the Greek word *kentron,* from *kentreô,* to prick, as in Acts 26:14. The serpent death has lost his poison fangs.

56. {*The power of sin*} (cf. Rom. 4:15; 5:20; 6:14; 7; Gal. 2:16; 3:1-5:4). In man's unrenewed state he cannot obey God's holy law.

57. {*But thanks be to God*} This is an exultant triumph through Christ over sin and death (cf. Rom. 7:25).

58. {*Be ye steadfast, unmovable*} Greek tense translates, "keep on becoming steadfast, unshaken."

CHAPTER 16

1. {*Now concerning the collection for the saints*} The introduction of this topic may seem sudden, but the Corinthians were behind with their part of it. {*So also do ye*} Corinthians had promised a long time before this to do something (2 Cor. 8:10; 9:1-5). Now do what you pledged.

2. {*Lay by him in store*} This means set aside by himself, in his home. Treasuring it (cf. Matt. 6:19). Have the habit of doing it. {*As he may prosper*} Lit. "to have a good journey, to prosper in general" (cf. Rom. 1:10; 2 John 2). This rule for giving occurs also in 2 Corinthians 8:12.

3. {*When I arrive*} That is, when*ever* I arrive, an indefinite period. {*Whomsoever ye shall approve by letters*} Lit. "by letters" to make it formal and regular and Paul would approve their choice of messengers to go with him to Jerusalem (2 Cor. 8:20). {*Bounty*} That is, gift, grace, as in 2 Corinthians 8:4-7. As a matter of fact, the messengers of the churches (2 Cor. 8:23) went along with Paul to Jerusalem (Acts 20:4).

5. {*When I shall have passed through Macedonia*} That is, "whenever I pass through," an indefinite period; though it is a definite plan.

6. {*Or even winter*} (cf. Acts 27:12; 28:11; Titus 3:12). He did stay in Corinth for three months (Acts 20:3), probably the coming winter. {*Whithersoever I go*} This is an indefinite local clause. As a matter of fact, Paul had to flee from a conspiracy in Corinth (Acts 20:3).

8. {*Until Pentecost*} He writes them in the spring before Pentecost. Apparently the uproar by Demetrius hurried Paul away from Ephesus (Acts 20:1).

9. {*For a great and effectual door is opened unto me*} The door stands wide open at last after his years there (Acts 20:31). Paul has a great opportunity for work in Ephesus. {*And there are many adver-*

saries} Translate, "and many are lying opposed to me," lined up against me. These Paul mentions as a reason for staying in, not for leaving, Ephesus (cf. Acts 19:1ff.).

10. {*That he be without fear*} Evidently he had reason to fear the treatment that Timothy might receive in Corinth (cf. 1 Cor. 4:17-21).

11. {*For I expect him*} Apparently, later Timothy had to return to Ephesus without much success before Paul left and was sent on to Macedonia with Erastus (Acts 19:22) and Titus sent to Corinth whom Paul then arranged to meet in Troas (2 Cor. 2:12).

12. {*And it was not at all his will to come now*} Apollos had left Corinth in disgust over the strife there which involved him and Paul.

13. {*Watch ye*} Lit. "Stay awake." {*Quit you like men*} Lit. "Play the man," show yourselves men. This verb is from the Greek word *anêr*, a man.

15. {*They have set themselves*} This noble family appointed themselves to be ministers to the saints that needed it (the poor and needy).

19. {*The churches of Asia*} This is the Roman province (Acts 10:10, 26; Col. 1:6; 2:1; 4:13, 16). The gospel spread rapidly from Ephesus. {*With the church that is in their house*} The churches had to meet where they could. Paul had labored and lived with this family in Corinth (Acts 18:2) and now again in Ephesus (Acts 18:19; 20:34). It was their habit wherever they lived (Rom. 16:5).

20. {*With a holy kiss*} In the synagogue men kissed men and women kissed women. This was the Christian custom at a later date and apparently so here (cf. 1 Thess. 5:26; 2 Cor. 13:12; Rom. 3:8; 1 Pet. 5:14). It seems never to have been promiscuous between the sexes.

21. {*Of me Paul with mine own hand*} (cf. 2 Thess. 3:17). Lit. "with the hand of me Paul." This is the sign in every Epistle; he dictated, but signed at the end.

22. {*Anathema*}. The word seems a bit harsh to us, but the refusal to love Christ on the part of a nominal Christian deserves anathema (see on 1 Cor. 12:3 for this word). {*Maranatha*} This Aramaic phrase means "Our Lord (*maran*) comes (*atha*) [or 'has come']." It seems to be a sort of watchword (cf. 1 Thess. 4:14; Jas. 5:7; Phil. 4:5; Rev. 1:7; 3:11; 22:20), expressing the lively hope that the Lord will come.

The Second Epistle to the Corinthians

Author: Apostle Paul
Recipients: Corinthian believers
Date: A.D. 54 or 55, after First Corinthians (likely in the autumn)
From: Macedonia (probably Philippi)
Occasion: Titus brings mixed news from Corinth of the Pauline majority and the minority in opposition; Paul sends a letter back to them and waits (2 Cor. 13:1-10).
Theme: Paul is trying to reestablish his relationship and authority with the Corinthian believers and deal with past issues as well as future ministry projects.

By Way of Introduction

Paul is the author, though some believe the text in its current state is a combination of an earlier letter (chapters 10 to 13 cf. 2 Cor. 2:3) attached to the first nine. There are in fact three obvious divisions: chapters 1-7, the report of Titus; chapters 8-9 the collection for the poor saints in Jerusalem (cf. 1 Cor. 16:1ff.); chapters 10-13 deal sharply with the Judaizing minority who still oppose Paul's leadership. These three subjects are in no sense inconsistent with each other. The letter is a unity.

This Epistle shows the grip of a great soul holding on to the highest ideals in the midst of manifold opposition and discouragements. Christ is Master of Paul at every turn.

It is not certain whether the letter mentioned in 2 Corinthians 2:3 is our First Corinthians or a lost letter (cf. 1 Cor. 5:9). If it is a lost one, we know of four Corinthian Epistles, assuming the unity of 2 Corinthians.

Chapter 1

1. {*In all Achaia*} The Romans divided Greece into two provinces (Achaia and Macedonia). Macedonia north, Achaia south (both Attica and the Peloponnesus). Corinth was the capital of Achaia where the pro-consul resided (Acts 18:12). {*Saints in the whole of Achaia*} This is likely the whole of the province, not merely the environs of Corinth.

3. {*The father of mercies... God of all comfort*} "Compassion" is characterized by mercies (emotions and acts of pity). "Comfort" is from the Latin *confortis* (brave together). The Holy Spirit is the Comforter (same word, John 14:16; 16:7).

4. {*In all our affliction...that we may be able to comfort*} *Affliction* is a translation of the Greek word *thlipsis,* from *thlibô,* to press (cf. Matt. 13:21 and 1 Thess. 1:6). {*Wherewith we can comfort*} The purpose of affliction in any Christian's life is to qualify him for ministry to others.

5. {*The sufferings of Christ*} The Greek syntax shows these are Christ's own sufferings. {*Abound unto us...through Christ*} Overflow to us so become fellow sufferers with Christ (2 Cor. 4:10; Rom. 8:17; Phil. 3:10; Col. 1:24). Partnership with Christ in suffering brings partnership in glory also (Rom. 8:17; 1 Pet. 4:13).

8. {*In Asia*} This is probably in Ephesus. Paul had many hardships (whether sickness or peril): trying to face a mob (Acts 20:30); a later plot to kill him (Acts 20:1); life threatening situations (cf. Rom. 16:4). It was beyond Paul's power to endure if left to himself. {*Of life*} The Greek have a focus of utter despair, lit. "at a complete loss of a way." There seemed no way out.

9. {*The answer of death*} In other literature, "sentence" has the sense of decision or judgment rendered. "Response" or "answer" is the best rendering, unless Paul conceives God as rendering the decision of death.

10. {*Delivered...will deliver*} This is the Greek verb *ruomai,* draw oneself, as out of a pit, rescue. So Paul faces death without fear. {*On whom we have set our hope*} The Greek syntax has a focus that we still have that hope.

11. {*Ye also helping together on our behalf*} Paul relied on God and felt the need of the prayer of God's people. {*By means of many*} Lit. "that out of many upturned faces [thanks may be given]."

12. {*Glorying*} This is the act of boasting, while in verse 14 the "boast" is the thing boasted of. {*Sincerity of God*} Greek syntax shows this as "the God-kind of sincerity" (cf. 1 Cor. 5:8).

13. {*Than what ye read...or even acknowledge*} "Read" in Greek (*anaginôskô*) is knowing again, recognizing (cf. Acts 8:30). "Read, understand" are a word play in the Greek (i.e., paronomasia = pun). Does he mean "read between the lines" as we say?

15. {*I was minded to come...before unto you*} The Greek tense translates, "I was wishing to come," picturing his former state of mind. This was his former plan while in Ephesus to go to Achaia directly from Ephesus (cf. v. 16).

16. {*And again*} This refers to the second benefit (v. 15). But he changed his plans and did not make that trip directly to Corinth, but came on to Macedonia first (Acts 19:21; 20:1; 1 Cor. 16:2; 2 Cor. 2:12). {*To be set forward by you*} (cf. Rom. 15:24) The anti-Pauline party took advantage of Paul's change of plans to criticize him sharply for vacillation and flippancy. So Paul has to explain his conduct.

17. {*Did I shew fickleness?*} An indignant "no" is the answer in Greek. "Light" is in the sense of levity.

18. {*Is not yea and nay*} That is, he is not a person saying 'Yes' and meaning or acting 'No.' Paul calls God to witness on this point.

20. {*In him is the yea*} Translate, "In him was the Yes come true." This applies to all God's promises.

21. {*Establishes*} This is the Greek verb *bebaioô*, from *bebaios*, firm. This is an apt metaphor in Corinth where confirmation of a bargain often took place (*bebaiôsis*) [cf. v. 22]. {*Anointed*} (cf. 1 John 2:20). Lit. "to consecrate," here with the Holy Spirit.

22. {*Sealed us*} This is the Greek verb *sphragizô*, common in LXX and papyri for setting a seal to prevent opening (Dan. 6:17), in place of signature (1 Kgs. 21:18). Papyri examples show a wide legal use to give validity to documents, to guarantee genuineness of articles as sealing sacks and chests. {*The earnest of the Spirit*} (2 Cor. 5:5; Eph. 1:14). Outside the NT, this was earnest money in a purchase for a cow or for a wife (a dowry); cf. our "earnest money." This earnest of the Spirit in our hearts is the witness of the Spirit that we are God's.

24. {*Helpers of your joy*} This refers to coworkers (1 Cor. 3:8) in your joy. This is a delicate correction to present misapprehension.

CHAPTER 2

1. {*That I would not come again to you with sorrow*} What does Paul mean by "another [lit. again]"? Had he paid another visit besides that described in Acts 18:1ff. which was in sorrow? Or does he mean that having had one joyful visit (that in Acts 18) he does not wish the second one to be in sorrow? Either is possible.

3. {*I wrote this very thing*} Does this refer to the present letter or another letter? Contextually not probably this letter or what we call "First Corinthians"; it may refer to 1 Corinthians 5:1ff. or to a lost letter.

4. {*With many tears*} He dictated that letter accompanied by tears. Paul was a man of heart (cf. also Phil. 3:18 and Acts 20:19, 31).

5. {*If any…*} This may refer either to the man of 1 Corinthians 5:1 or to the ringleader of the opposition to him. Either view is possible. It is notable that Paul does not name him.

6. {*Punishment*} This is the Greek word *epitimia,* for old Greek *to epitimion* (so papyri), from *epitimaô,* to show honor to, to award, to adjudge penalty.

7. {*Swallowed up*} (cf. 1 Cor. 15:54) Lit. "to drink down."

8. {*To confirm*} (Gal. 3:15). This is the Greek verb *kuroô,* to make valid, to ratify, from *kuros* (head, authority).

10. {*In the person of Christ*} Translate more exactly, "in the presence of Christ," before Christ, in the face of Christ.

11. {*That no advantage may be gained over us*} (cf. 1 Thess. 4:6; 2 Cor. 2:11; 7:2; 12:17). Translate, "that we may not be overreached by Satan." This is the Greek verb *pleonekteô,* from *pleonektês,* a covetous man (1 Cor. 5:10), to take advantage of, to gain, to overreach. {*His devices*} This means plans and purposes as here, denoting evil plans in context.

12. {*When a door was opened unto me*} (cf. 1 Cor. 16:9 and Col. 4:3). Here was an open door that he could not enter.

13. {*I had no relief*} The Greek tense shows a vivid dramatic recital. He still feels the shadow of that restlessness. He had no "relaxing or release" (Acts 24:34). {*Taking my leave of them*} This is the Greek verb *apotassô,* here, to separate oneself, to bid adieu to (cf. Mark 6:46).

14. {*But thanks be unto God*} Here is the finest exposition of all sides of the Christian ministry in existence, one that reveals the wealth of Paul's nature and his mature grasp of the great things in service for Christ. {*Leadeth in triumph*} Picture here is of Paul as captive in God's triumphal procession. {*The savour*} In a Roman *triumph* garlands of flowers scattered sweet odor and incense bearers dispensed perfumes. The knowledge of God is here the aroma, which Paul had scattered like an incense bearer.

15. {*A sweet savour of Christ*} (Phil. 4:18; Eph. 5:2). Lit. "well + to smell."

16. {*From death unto death*} That is, from one evil condition to another. Some people are actually hardened by preaching. {*And who is sufficient for these things?*} This is a rhetorical question. In himself no one is. But some one has to preach Christ and Paul proceeds to show that he is sufficient.

17. {*Corrupting*} This is the Greek verb *kapêleuô*, from *kapêlos*, a huckster or peddler, common in all stages of Greek for huckstering or trading. It is curious how hucksters were suspected of corrupting by putting the best fruit on top of the basket.

CHAPTER 3

1. {*To commend ourselves?*} Paul is sensitive over praising himself, though his enemies compelled him to do it. {*Epistles of commendation*} Here are NT examples of commending individuals by letters (Acts 15:25; 18:27; Rom. 16:1; 1 Cor. 16:10; 2 Cor. 8:22; Col. 4:10).

3. {*An epistle of Christ*} He turns the metaphor round and round. They are Christ's letter to men as well as Paul's. {*Of stone*} That is, composed of stone. {*Of flesh*} Lit. "fleshen" (cf. 1 Cor. 3:1; Rom. 7:14).

5. {*Of ourselves...as from ourselves*} Both phrases are saying, "*starting from*" ourselves. He has no originating power for such confidence.

7. {*Of death*} That is, a ministry marked by death in its outcome (cf. 1 Cor. 15:56; Gal. 3:10). The letter kills. {*Look steadfastly*} (cf. Luke 4:20; Acts 3:4). This is the Greek verb *atenizô,* from *atenês* (stretched, intent, *teinô* and *alpha* intensive).

9. {*Of condemnation*} This ministry brings condemnation because one is unable to obey the law. {*Is glory*} There is glory for the old dispensation.

10. {*In this respect*} The glory on the face of Moses was temporary, though real, and passed away (v. 7), a type of the dimming of the glory of the old dispensation by the brightness of the new. {*By reason of the glory that surpasseth*} Christ as the Sun of Righteousness has thrown Moses in the shade.

11. {*Passeth away*} That is, in process of disappearing before the gospel of Christ. {*Remaineth*} The new ministry is permanent. Christianity is still alive and is not dying.

14. {*But their minds were hardened*} Their thoughts literally made dull. This is the Greek verb *pôroô,* from *pôros,* hard skin, to cover with thick skin (callus), to petrify (cf. Mark 6:52; 8:17). {*Of the old covenant*} That is, in contrast to the new (cf. 2 Cor. 3:14). {*The same veil*} Not that identical veil, but one that has the same effect, that blinds their eyes to the light in Christ.

15. {*A veil lieth upon their heart*} With willful blindness the rabbis set aside the word of God by their tradition in the time of Jesus (Mark 7:8).

16. {*The veil is taken away*} (cf. Exod. 34:34). Moses' veil was taken from around his face whenever he went before the Lord.

17. {*Liberty*} That is, freedom of access to God without fear in contract with the fear seen in Exod. 34:30. We need no veil and we have free access to God.

18. {*Reflecting as in a mirror*} This is the Greek verb *katoptrizô*, from *katoptron*, mirror (*kata, optron*, a thing to see with). The word means beholding as in a mirror (cf. 1 Cor. 13:12). The point that Paul is making is that we shall not lose the glory as Moses did. But that is true if we keep on beholding or keep on reflecting. {*Into the same image*} That is, into the likeness of God in Christ (1 Cor. 15:48-53; Rom. 8:17, 29; Col. 3:4; 1 John 3:2).

CHAPTER 4

1. {*We faint not*} Paul speaks of himself in the literary plural. The Greek verb is *egkakeô*, late verb (*en, kakos*) to behave badly in, to give in to evil, to lose courage. It is the faint-hearted coward.

2. {*But we have renounced...*} They do attack the minister. His only safety is in instant and courageous defiance to all the powers of darkness. {*Handling deceitfully*} This is the Greek verb *doloô*, from *dolos*, deceit (from *delô*, to catch with bait), to ensnare, to corrupt with error. Used of adulterating gold or wine.

3. {*It is veiled in them that are perishing*} (cf. 2 Cor. 2:15). This entire clause is a condition assumed to be true in the Greek.

4. {*The god of this world*} Satan is "the god of this age"; he claimed the rule over the world in the temptations with Jesus. {*Blinded*} They refused to believe and so Satan got the power to blind their thoughts.

5. {*As your servants for Jesus' sake*} Translate "servant" as "bond-slave."

6. {*In the face of Jesus Christ*} The Christian who looks on the face of Jesus Christ as Moses looked upon the glory of God will be able to give the illumination of the knowledge of the glory of God.

7. {*This treasure*} (cf. Matt. 6:19-21). The treasure is the power of giving the illumination of the knowledge of the glory of God (v. 2 Cor. 4:6). {*In earthen vessels*} A jar was from baked clay, so many fragments of which are found in Egypt with writing on them. We are but earthen jars used of God for his purposes (Rom. 9:20) and so fragile.

8. {*Yet not straitened*} (2 Cor. 6:12). This is the Greek verb *stenochôreô*, (*stenochôros*, from *stenos*, narrow, *chôros*, space), to be in a narrow place, to keep in a tight place. {*Yet not unto despair*} Here is an effective play on words here, with similar word forms in the Greek and "despair" having a perfective element "lost, but not lost out."

9. {*Forsaken*} lit. "to leave behind, to leave in the lurch." {*Destroyed*} Was Paul referring to Lystra when the Jews stoned him and thought him dead?

12. {*Death worketh in us*} Physical death works in him while spiritual life (astonishingly) works in them.

14. {*Shall present us with you*} This shows that Paul was not certain that he would be alive when Jesus comes as has been wrongly inferred from 1 Corinthians 7:29; 10:11; 15:51.

15. {*Being multiplied through the many*} Lit. "making more through the more." One can think of Bunyan's *Grace Abounding*.

16. {*Our outward man...our inward man*} (cf. Rom. 7:22; Col. 3:9; Eph. 4:22). Here the decay of the bodily organism is set over against the growth in grace of the person (Bernard) (cf. also 1 Pet. 3:4).

17. {*Our light affliction which is for the moment...eternal weight of glory*} Note the careful balancing of words in contrast (affliction vs. glory; lightness vs. weight; moment vs. eternal).

Chapter 5

1. {*If...be dissolved*} This is a plausible case; "destroyed" is the very word used for striking down a tent. {*The earthly house of our tabernacle*} Translate rather, "If our earthly house of the tent." The house is the tent. {*We have a building from God*} We possess the title to it now by faith. "Faith is the title-deed to things hoped for" (Heb. 11:7).

{*Not made with hands*} (cf. Mark 14:58; also Col. 2:11). This is a spiritual, eternal home.

2. {*To be clothed upon with our habitation which is from heaven*} "Dwelling" is used here of the spiritual body as the abode of the spirit. It is a mixed metaphor (putting on as garment the dwelling place).

4. {*Not for that we would be unclothed*} Rather, "For that we do not wish to put off the clothing, but to put it on." Paul does not wish to be a mere disembodied spirit without his spiritual garment.

8. {*We are of good courage*} Good word for cheer. Cheer up. (cf. Matt. 9:2, 22). {*Are willing rather*} (cf. Phil. 1:21, also Luke 3:22). Rather, "We are well pleased, we prefer" if left to ourselves. {*To be at home with the Lord*} That is, to attain that goal is bliss for Paul.

9. {*We make it our aim*} This is the Greek verb *philotimouomai*, from *philotimos* (*philos, timê*, fond of honor), to act from love of honor, to be ambitious in the good sense (1 Thess. 4:11; 2 Cor. 5:9; Rom. 15:20).

10. {*Before the judgment seat of Christ*} This refers to a platform, the seat of the judge (Matt. 27:19).

11. {*The fear of the Lord*} Many today regard this a played-out motive, but not so Paul. He has in mind verse 10 with the picture of the judgment seat of Christ. {*That we are made manifest*} Greek tense translates, "stand manifested," i.e., a state of completion.

12. {*That ye may have wherewith to answer*} Lit. "That you may have something against (for facing those, etc.)." Paul wishes his champions in Corinth to know the facts. {*In appearance, and not in heart*} This refers to the Judaizers who were braggarts about their orthodox Judaism.

13. {*Whether we are beside ourselves*} This is the Greek verb *existêmi*, here, to stand out of oneself (intransitive) from *ekstasis*, ecstasy (cf. Mark 5:42). It is literary plural, for Paul is referring only to himself. Indicated by the Greek syntax, Paul assumes as true the charge that he was crazy (if I was crazy) for the sake of argument (which many did do, cf. Acts 26:24, also 1 Cor. 14:18 and 2 Cor. 12:1-6) which probably the Judaizers used against him.

14. {*The love of Christ*} That is, Christ's love for Paul (cf. 2 Cor. 4:15). {*Constraineth us*} This is the Greek verb *sunechô*, common verb, to hold together, to press the ears together (Acts 7:57), to press on every side (Luke 8:45), to hold fast (Luke 22:63), to hold oneself to (Acts 18:5), to be pressed (passive, Luke 12:50; Phil. 1:23). So here Paul's conception of Christ's love for him holds him together to his task whatever men think or say. {*One died for all*} This is the central tenet in Paul's theology and Christology. "For" is in the sense of substitution; that is, death in behalf so that the rest will not have to die. {*Therefore all died*} Logically, all died when Christ died, all the spiritual death possible for those for whom Christ died.

15. {*Should no longer live unto themselves*} The doctrine of Christ's atoning death carries a high obligation on the part of those who live because of him. Selfishness is ruled out by our duty to him.

16. {*According to the flesh*} That is, the fleshy way of looking at men. Worldly standards and distinctions of race, class, cut no figure now with Paul (Gal. 3:28). {*Even though we have known Christ after the flesh*} This refers to the fact that Paul had before his conversion known Christ, according to the standards of the men of his time, the Sanhedrin and other Jewish leaders. He had led the persecution against Jesus till Jesus challenged and stopped him at the crucial event of conversion (Acts 9:4).

17. {*The old things are passed away*} That is, the ancient way of looking at Christ among other things.

18. {*Who reconciled us to himself through Christ*} This is the great Greek verb *katallassô,* old word for exchanging coins (cf. also Matt. 5:24; Acts 7:26; Col. 1:20; Eph. 2:16 and also Rom. 5:11; 11:15). The point made by Paul here is that God needs no reconciliation, but is engaged in the great business of reconciling us to himself. {*And gave unto us the ministry of reconciliation*} The difficult, yet high and holy task is winning the unreconciled to God.

19. {*Not reckoning*} What Jesus did (his death for us) stands to our credit (Rom. 8:32) if we make our peace with God.

20. {*We are ambassadors therefore on behalf of Christ*} (cf. Eph. 6:20). This is the proper term in the Greek East for the Emperor's Legate in the inscriptions and papyri (Deissmann). So Paul has a natural pride in using this dignified term for himself and all ministers. The ambassador has to be *persona grata* with both countries (the one that he represents and the one to which he goes). {*Be ye reconciled to God*} The Greek distinct form translates, "get reconciled to God," and do it now.

21. {*Him who knew no sin*} Jesus made this claim for himself (John 8:46). {*He made to be sin*} This fact throws some light on the tragic cry of Jesus, "My God, My God, why have you forsaken me?" (Matt. 27:46).

CHAPTER 6

1. {*Working together with him*} We are coworkers, partners with God (1 Cor. 3:9), in this work of grace. {*In vain*} That is, into emptiness. The plan of God, the work of Christ on the Cross, the pleas of the ambassador may all be nullified by the recipient of the message.

4. {*But in everything commending ourselves*} Paul gives a marvelous summary of his argument about the dignity and glory of ministers of Christ as ministers of God under three aspects in verses 4 to 10. {*In distresses*} That is, in tight places (2 Cor. 12:10).

5. {*In stripes*} (cf. Luke 10:30; 12:48; Acts 16:23, 33). {*In tumults*} (cf. 1 Cor. 14:33). That is, instabilities, often from politics.

6. {*In love unfeigned*} This is the only love that is worthwhile (Rom. 12:9).

7. {*On the right hand and on the left*} Offensive weapons are on the right, defensive on the left (cf. 1 Thess. 5:8; Eph. 6:11).

8. {*As deceivers and yet true*} In the Clementines St. Paul is expressly described by his adversaries as an impostor or deceiver, and as disseminating deceit. Such slander from one's enemies is praise.

9. {*As unknown and yet well known*} Translate, "As ignored (as non-entities, obscure, without proper credentials cf. 2 Cor. 3:2) and yet fully recognized (by all who really matter as in 2 Cor. 11:6)."

10. {*Yet making many rich*} This is spiritual riches Paul has in mind (cf. 1 Cor. 1:5, also Matt. 5:37).

11. {*Our mouth is open unto you…our heart is enlarged*} Lit. "our mouth stands open to you." He has kept back nothing in his portrayal of the glory of the ministry as the picture of the open mouth shows.

12. {*Ye are not straitened in us*} (cf. 2 Cor. 4:8) There is no restraint in me (my heart). My adversaries may have caused some of you to tighten up your affections (cf. Jas. 5:11; 1 Pet. 3:8).

14. {*Be not unequally yoked with unbelievers*} No other example of this Greek verb has yet been found, though the adjective from which it is apparently formed, *heterozugos* (yoked with a different yoke) occurs in Leviticus 19:19 of the union of beasts of different kinds (cf. also

Deut. 22:10). Lit. "Stop becoming unequally yoked with unconverted heathen (unbelievers)." Some were already guilty of various unions, including marriage (cf. Eph. 5:7).

15. {*Belial*} The name is lit. "worthlessness," referring to Satan (*Book of Jubilees* 1.20). Paul graphically sums up the contrast between Christ and Satan, the heads of the contending forces of good and evil.

17. {*Unclean thing*} In the Greek, this could refer grammatically to an unclean person.

18. {*Saith the Lord Almighty*} (cf. 2 Sam. 7:8). "Almighty" is lit. "Ruler of all."

CHAPTER 7

1. {*Let us cleanse ourselves*} In other literature this is used of ceremonial cleansing; note that Paul includes himself. {*From all defilement*} This is the Greek *molusmos*, from *molunô*, to stain (cf. 1 Cor. 8:7), to pollute. In other literature, it includes all sorts of filthiness, physical, moral, mental, ceremonial, of flesh and spirit. {*Perfecting holiness*} Not merely negative goodness (cleansing), but aggressive and progressive (Greek present tense) holiness, not a sudden attainment of complete holiness, but a continuous process (1 Thess. 3:13; Rom. 1:4; 1:6).

2. {*We corrupted no man*} In response to Judaizers, this may refer to money, or morals, or doctrine. {*We took advantage of no man*} (cf. 1 Thess. 4:6 and 2 Cor. 2:11). That is, he got the best of no one in any evil way.

3. {*Not to condemn you*} Lit. "not for condemnation." {*To die together and live together*} Lit. "For the dying together and living together." You are in our hearts to share death and life.

4. {*I overflow with joy in all our affliction*} Lit. "my joy overflows (as in a flood)." This is a thoroughly Pauline sentiment.

5. {*Without were fightings*} This perhaps refers to pagan adversaries in Macedonia (cf. 1 Cor. 15:32).

6. {*The lowly*} (cf. Matt. 11:29). Lit. "low on the ground" (Ezek. 17:24), and a "low in condition" (Jas. 1:9; in 2 Cor. 10:1).

7. {*Mourning*} This is the Greek word *odurmos*, from *oduromai*, to lament.

8. {*I do not regret it*} This verb really means "repent" in the true sense of the English word's history of meaning (be sorry again). Paul is now glad that he made them sorry, though in a regretful mood at first.

9. {*Now I rejoice*} That is, now that Titus has come and told him the good news from Corinth (2 Cor. 2:12). This was the occasion of the noble outburst in 2 Corinthians 2:12 to 6:10. {*Unto repentance*} Note the sharp difference here between "sorrow" which is merely another form of "regret, remorse" (cf. 2 Cor. 7:8) and "repentance" "change of mind and life." Observe that the "sorrow" has led to "repentance" and was not itself the repentance.

11. {*Clearing of yourselves*} This is the Greek word *apologia,* in the old notion of *apologia* (self-vindication, self-defense) as in 1 Peter 3:15. {*Avenging*} This is a Greek word from *ekdikeô,* to avenge, to do justice (Luke 18:5; 21:22), vindication from wrong as in Luke 18:7, to secure punishment (1 Pet. 2:14).

13. {*For the joy of Titus*} Translate, "on the basis of the joy of Titus" (who was proud of the outcome of his labors in Corinth).

14. {*If...I have gloried*} This is a Greek condition assumed to be a fact or fulfilled (cf. 1 Cor. 3:21; 2 Cor. 5:12). {*I was not put to shame*} Paul had assured Titus, who hesitated to go after the failure of Timothy, that the Corinthians were sound and would come round all right if handled properly. Paul's joy is equal to that of Titus. {*In truth*} That is, in the sharp letter as well as in 1 Corinthians. He had not hesitated to speak plainly of their sins.

15. {*With fear and trembling*} Titus had brought a stern message (1 Cor. 5:5 from Paul) and they had trembled at his words (cf. Eph. 6:5; Phil. 2:12). Paul had himself come to the Corinthians at first with a nervous dread (1 Cor. 2:3).

CHAPTER 8

1. {*The grace*} Grace is manifested in the collection in the churches, poor as they were. The Romans had lacerated Macedonia.

2. {*Their deep poverty*} "Poverty" is the Greek word *ptôcheia,* from *ptôcheuô,* to be a beggar (cf. 2 Cor. 8:9) [from *ptôchos,* cowering in fear and poverty, as in Luke 14:13, but ennobled by Christ as in Matt. 5:3; 2 Cor. 8:9]. Poverty down deep, down to the bottom. {*Liberality*} Lit.

"single, simple" (Matt. 6:22), perhaps translate here "heartiness" (cf. 2 Cor. 9:11, 13).

3. {*Beyond their power*} Lit. "alongside power" (not likely "according to actual ability"). Paul commends this high pressure collection because of the emergency.

4. {*Beseeching us with much intreaty in regard of this grace*} (cf. Acts 24:27). Lit. "with much entreaty begging of us the favor...." Apparently Paul had been reluctant to press the Macedonians because of their manifest poverty. They demanded the right to have a share in it.

7. {*In this grace also*} This gifted church (1 Cor. 12:1-14:40) had fallen behind in the grace of giving. Kindly irony in this allusion.

8. {*The sincerity also of your love*} This is the Greek word *gnêsion*, an adjective, and contraction of *genesios* (*ginomai*), legitimately born, not spurious.

10. {*Judgment*} This is the Greek word *gnômê*. This is a deliberate opinion, but not a "command" (cf. 1 Cor. 7:25).

11. {*The readiness to will…the completion also*} (cf. Acts 17:11). They were quick to pledge. {*Out of your ability*} Lit. "Out of the having," and so, "out of what you can give" (cf. 2 Cor. 8:12).

12. {*According as a man hath*} Clearly God does not expect us to give what we do not have. {*Not according as he hath not*} The Greek tense has a focus, because a specific case is presented.

14. {*By equality*} This is the Greek word *isotês*, from *isos*, fair, equal (cf. Col. 4:1). {*Abundance*} (cf. 2 Cor. 8:2). {*Want*} (cf. 2 Cor. 9:12; Luke 21:4).

16. {*Which putteth*} The Greek tense of "put" translates "[God] who is continually giving [into the heart of Titus]." Hence, Titus is full of zealous care for you.

19. {*But who was also appointed*} This is the Greek verb *cheirotoneô*, to stretch out the hands (*cheir teinô*) and so to vote in public. The idea is that this brother was chosen by the churches, not by Paul.

20. {*Avoiding this*} Lit. "arranging for ourselves this." {*Bounty*} This is the Greek word *hadrotês*, from *hadros*, thick, stout, ripe, rich, great (cf. 1 Kgs. 1:9; 2 Kgs. 10:6).

21. {*We take thought*} Lit. "to plan beforehand" (cf. Rom. 12:17; 1 Tim. 5:8). {*But also in the sight of men*} It is not enough for one's financial accounts to be honorable as God sees them, but they should be so kept that men can understand them also.

23. {*About Titus*} Paul endorses Titus to the hilt: partner and fellow-worker. {*Messengers of the churches*} Lit. "apostle," but in the general sense of "sent ones" (from the Greek verb *apostellô,* to send) by the churches and responsible to the churches for the handling of the funds.

24. {*In the face of the churches*} A great host is pictured as watching how the Corinthians will treat these duly accredited agents in the collection (Titus and the other two brethren).

CHAPTER 9

2. {*I glory*} Greek tense translates, "I still am boasting," in spite of the poor performance of the Corinthians. {*Hath been prepared*} Greek tense translate, "stands prepared." {*Stirred up*} This is "to excite" in a good sense here, though bad sense in Colossians 3:21.

3. {*That ye may be prepared*} Greek tense translates, "that you may really be prepared." Paul's very syntax tells against them.

4. {*If there come with me any of Macedonia and find you unprepared*} The condition in Greek is considered undetermined, but stated as a lively possibility. {*Lest by any means we should be put to shame*} This is a literary plural. {*That we say not, ye*} A delicate syntactical turn occurs for what he really has in mind. He does wish that they become ashamed of not paying their pledges.

5. {*I thought...*} (cf. Phil. 2:25). Note the repetitive use of words showing preparation, "in advance...finish...promised [before]." In this verse he literally rubs it in that the pledge was overdue. {*And not of extortion*} Lit. "and not as covetousness." Some offerings exhibit mean, stingy, covetousness.

7. {*Not grudgingly*} Greek syntax so "not give reluctantly," or "not do reluctantly." That is, not give as out of sorrow. {*For God loveth a cheerful giver*} This is our word "hilarious" which comes from the Greek *hilaros,* which is from *hilaos* (propitious).

8. {*All sufficiency*} (1 Tim. 6:6). This is the Greek word *autarkeia,* from *autarkês* (Phil. 4:11). Paul takes this word of Greek philosophy and applies it to the Christian view of life as independent of circumstances.

10. {*Supplieth*} This is the Greek verb *epichorêgeô,* from *epi* and *chorêgeô* (cf. 1 Pet. 4:11). *Chorêgos* is old word for leader of a chorus (*choros, hêgeomai*) or chorus leader. The verb means to furnish a chorus at one's own expense, then to supply in general. (cf. 2 Cor. 9:10; Gal. 3:15; Col. 2:19; 2 Pet. 1:5).

11. {*Liberality*} (cf. 2 Cor. 8:2).

12. {*Service*} This is the Greek word *leitourgia,* from *leôs* (people, *laos*), *leitos* like *dêmosios,* public, and *ergon,* work. So, public service either in worship to God (Luke 1:23) or benefaction to others (2 Cor. 9:12; Phil. 2:30). Our word liturgy is this word.

13. {*Of your confession*} Lit. "to say together." It means either to declare openly (profess) or to declare fully (confess), to say the same thing as another; only the context can decide. The brethren in Jerusalem will know by this collection that Gentiles make as good Christians as Jews.

15. {*Thanks be to God for his unspeakable gift*} One of Paul's gems flashed out after the somewhat tangled sentence (vv. 10-14) like a gleam of light that clears the air. Words fail Paul to describe the gift of Christ to and for us.

CHAPTER 10

1. {*By the meekness and gentleness of Christ*} Paul had in the past spoken to the Corinthians about the character of Christ: the meekness of Jesus (cf. Matt. 11:29). "Gentleness" is the Greek word *epieikia,* some translate this, "sweet reasonableness" (cf. also Acts 24:4 and Phil. 4:5). In Greek Ethics the equitable man was called *epieikês,* a man who does not press for the last penny of his rights (Bernard). {*Lowly among you*} Probably Paul here is quoting one of the sneers of his accusers in Corinth about his humble conduct while with them (1 Cor. 2:23; 2 Cor. 7:6) and his boldness when away (1 Cor. 7:16).

3. {*In the flesh*} This is a very different thing from walking "according to the standards of the world/flesh" as his enemies charged. {*We war*} Paul fights only the devil and his agents, even if wearing the distinctive clothing of heaven.

4. {*To the casting down of strongholds*} "Casting down" is the Greek word *kathairesis,* from *kathaireô,* to take down, to tear down walls and buildings.

5. {*Casting down imaginations*} (Rom. 2:15). This is the same military figure (cf. v. 4). The reasonings or imaginations are treated as forts or citadels to be conquered. {*Every high thing that is exalted*} Paul aims to pull down the top-most perch of audacity in their reasonings against the knowledge of God. We need Paul's skill and courage today. {*Bringing every thought into captivity*} (cf. Luke 21:24). This is the Greek verb *aichmalôtizô,* from *aichmalôtos,* captive in war (*aichmê,* spear, *halôtos* verbal of *haliskomai,* to be taken).

6. {*Being in readiness*} Lit. "holding in readiness." {*When your obedience shall be fulfilled*} Paul expects that the whole church will become obedient to Christ's will.

7. {*Ye look*} Likely a statement of fact, though it could be a command in the Greek. {*Before your face*} They ought to look below the surface. If it is imperative, they should see the facts.

8. {*Somewhat abundantly*} This is comparative, "somewhat more abundantly" than I have, in order to show that he is as true a minister of Christ as his accusers are. Note there is no literary plural here.

10. {*They say*} Paul quotes directly the charge; attacking his looks and speech. {*Weighty and strong*} These words can be uncomplimentary and mean "severe and violent" instead of "impressive and vigorous." The adjectives bear either sense. {*His bodily presence*} Lit. "the presence of his body"; certainly uncomplimentary, accusers called his appearance unimpressive (lit. weak). It seems clear that Paul did not have a commanding appearance like that of Barnabas (Acts 14:12). He had some physical defect of the eyes (Gal. 4:14) and a thorn in the flesh (2 Cor. 12:7). {*His speech of no account*} (cf. 1 Cor. 1:28). The Corinthians (some of them) cared more for the brilliant eloquence of Apollos and did not find Paul a trained rhetorician (1 Cor. 1:17; 2:1, 4; 2 Cor. 11:6). Evidently Paul winced under this biting criticism of his looks and speech.

11. {*What we are*} This is a literary plural. Paul's quality is precisely the same; in his letters when absent, and in his deeds when present.

12. {*To number or compare ourselves...measuring themselves by themselves...are without understanding*} This is the keenest sarcasm. Setting themselves up as the standards of orthodoxy these Judaizers always measure up to the standard while Paul falls short. Paul is not keen to fall into the trap set for him. These men do not see their own picture so obvious to others (Eph. 5:17; 1 Tim. 1:7). Cf. Mark 8:17.

13. {*Beyond our measure*} Lit. "into the unmeasured things," "the unlimitable."

14. {*We stretch not ourselves overmuch*} Translate, "We do not stretch ourselves out beyond our rights."

18. {*Is approved*} This is the Greek word *dokimos,* accepted (from *dechomai*) by the Lord. The Lord accepts his own recommendation.

CHAPTER 11

1. {*Would that ye could bear with me*} "I hope," is lit. "I wish." It is said with a touch of irony here. {*In a little foolishness*} Lit. "Some little foolishness."

2. {*With a godly jealousy*} Lit. "with a jealousy of God." {*I espoused*} This is the Greek verb *harmozomai,* to join, to fit together, with a form that suggests personal involvement (from *harmos,* joint). Elsewhere from NT it is used for a betrothal. Paul treats the Corinthians as his bride.

4. {*Another Jesus*} Not necessarily a different Jesus, but any other "Jesus" is a rival and so wrong. {*A different spirit…a different gospel*} Here it is a different spirit and gospel, of another nature or kind (cf. "other" above).

5. {*That I am not a whit behind the very chiefest apostles*} "Super-apostles" is not referring to the pillar apostles (cf. Gal. 2:9), but likely speaking ironically of these Judaizers, who set themselves up to be such.

6. {*Rude in speech*} Paul admits that he is not a professional orator (cf. 2 Cor. 10:10), but denies that he is unskilled in knowledge; he knew his subject.

7. {*In abasing myself*} That is, humbling myself by making tents for a living while preaching in Corinth; again ironical.

8. {*I robbed…taking wages*} That is, he allowed other churches to do more than their share. He got his "rations" from other churches, not from Corinth while there.

9. {*I was not a burden to anyone*} This is the Greek verb *katanarkaô,* a medical term for growing quite stiff. *Narkaô* means to become numb, torpid, and so a burden. {*From being burdensome*} (cf. 1 Thess. 2:9). Lit. "not weight," free from weight or light. Paul kept himself independent.

11. {*God knoweth*} Whether or not they do, Paul knows that God understands his motives.

13. {*False apostles*} This is the Greek word *pseudapostolos,* from *pseudês,* false, and *apostolos.* Paul apparently made this word (cf. Rev. 2:2). {*Deceitful*} (cf. Rom. 16:18). This is the Greek word *dolios,* from *dolos* (lure, snare).

14. {*An angel of light*} The prince of darkness puts on the garb of light and sets the fashion for his followers in the masquerade to deceive the saints. This terrible portrayal reveals the depth of Paul's feelings about the conduct of the Judaizing (false brothers Gal. 2:4) leaders in Corinth.

16. {*Let no man think me foolish...receive me as a fool*} Paul feels compelled to boast of his career and work as an apostle of Christ after the terrible picture just drawn of the Judaizers. He feels greatly embarrassed in doing it. Some men can do it with complete composure.

17-18. {*Not after the Lord*} Paul knows Christ's example is meekness and gentleness (cf. 2 Cor. 10:1), but circumstances force Paul to do otherwise. He knows that it is a bit of foolishness of the world (lit. flesh) and not like Christ.

20. {*For ye bear with a man*} That is, "you tolerate tyranny, extortion, craftiness, arrogance, violence, and insult. This is sarcasm that cut to the bone, slapping the face is the climax of insult" (Plummer).

21. {*By way of disparagement*} Once again, this is intense irony (cf. 2 Cor. 6:8). After these prolonged explanations, this verse now changes in tone from irony to direct and masterful assertion.

23. {*As one beside himself*} This is the Greek verb *paraphroneô*, from *paraphrôn* (*para, phrên*), beside one's wits. Such open boasting is out of accord with Paul's spirit and habit. {*I more...*} He claims superiority now to these "super-apostles" (referring to Judaizers verse 2 Cor. 11:5; 12:11). {*In prisons*} This is plural in the Greek. Clement of Rome says that Paul was imprisoned seven times. We know of only five (Philippi, Jerusalem, Caesarea, twice in Rome). {*In deaths oft*} He had nearly lost his life, as we know, many times (cf. 2 Cor. 1:9; 4:11).

24. {*Five times received I forty stripes save one*} These are Jewish floggings (Matt. 27:36), not mentioned for Paul anywhere else in NT Thirty-nine lashes was the rule for fear of a miscount (Deut. 25:1-3).

25. {*Thrice was I beaten with rods*} A Roman/Gentile punishment. It was forbidden to Roman citizens by the *Lex Porcia*, but Paul endured it in Philippi (Acts 16:23, 37), the only one of the three named in Acts. {*Once was I stoned*} (cf. Acts 14:5-19). {*Thrice I suffered shipwreck*} (cf. 1 Tim. 1:19). We know nothing of these. The one told in Acts 27:1ff. was much later.

26. {*In perils...*} (cf. Rom. 8:35). This is effective repetition, without conjunctions (i.e., grammatical connectors "and, or, etc." called also asyndeton) presented in contrasting pairs.

27. {*In cold*} Cold from the elements (cf. Acts 28:2), or a Roman dungeon later (2 Tim. 4:9-18).

28. {*Besides those things that are without*} Probably this is meaning, "apart from those things beside these just mentioned." {*Anxiety for all the churches*} Paul had the shepherd's heart. As apostle to the Gentiles he had founded most of these churches.

31. {*I am not lying*} The list seems so absurd and foolish that Paul takes solemn oath about it (cf. 2 Cor. 1:23).

32. {*The governor under Aretas*} (cf. 2 Macc. 5:8). Though not certain, it is suggested that Caligula, to mark his dislike for Antipas, gave Damascus to Aretas (enemy of Antipas) during this time of which Paul speaks. It says in Acts 9:24 Jews kept watch, but there is no conflict as they cooperated with the guard set by Aretas at their request.

33. {*Through a window*} (cf. Acts 20:9). {*Was I let down*} This is the very Greek word Luke used in Acts 9:25. {*In a basket*} This was a humiliating experience for Paul in this oldest city of the world where he had started as a conqueror over the despised Christians.

CHAPTER 12

1. {*I must needs glory*} That is, he must go on with the glorying already begun, foolish as it is, though it is not expedient. {*Revelations of the Lord*} Paul had both repeated visions of Christ (Acts 9:3; 16:9; 18:9; 22:17; 27:23) and revelations. He claimed to speak by direct revelation (1 Cor. 11:23; 15:3; Gal. 1:12; Eph. 3:3, etc.).

2. {*I know a man*} Paul singles out one incident of ecstasy in his own experience that he declines to describe. He alludes to it in this indirect way as if it were some other personality. {*Caught up*} Lit. "to seize" (cf. Matt. 11:12). {*Even to the third heaven*} Paul seems to mean the highest heaven where God is, not some other reference (Plummer).

4. {*Into Paradise*} Here it apparently equals "third heaven" (cf. 2 Cor. 12:2 and Luke 23:43), which has some support in other sources.

6. {*I shall not be foolish*} This is an apparent contradiction to 2 Corinthians 11:1, 16. But he is here speaking of the Paul "caught up" in case he should tell the things heard.

7. {*A thorn in the flesh*} This is the Greek word *skolops,* used for splinter, stake, thorn. In the LXX it is usually thorn. This certainly referred to a persistent physical malady, here are some theories: malaria, eye trouble, epilepsy, insomnia, migraine or sick headache, etc. {*Messenger of Satan...buffet*} This is affliction personified. The Greek tense of the verb suggests that the messenger of Satan kept slapping Paul in the face and Paul now sees that it was God's will for it to be so.

9. {*He hath said*} The Greek tense suggests that this is "a final word." Paul probably still has the thorn in his flesh and needs this word of Christ. {*Is perfected*} Greek tense shows that the power is continually increased as the weakness grows (cf. Phil. 4:13). {*Most gladly rather...*} Translate, "most gladly will I boast in my weaknesses." Slowly Paul had learned this supreme lesson, but it will never leave him (Rom. 5:2; 2 Tim. 4:6-8). {*May rest upon me*} "Rest" is lit. "to fix a tent upon," here upon Paul himself by a bold metaphor, as if the power of the Lord was overshadowing him (cf. Luke 9:34).

10. {*Wherefore I take pleasure*} (cf. Matt. 3:17; 2 Cor. 5:8). The enemies of Paul will have a hard time now in making Paul unhappy by persecutions even unto death (Phil. 1:20-26). He is not courting martyrdom, but he does not fear it or anything that is for Christ's sake.

11. {*I am become foolish*} Paul feels that he has dropped back to the mood of 2 Cor. 11:1, 16. He has been swept on by the memory of the ecstasy.

14. {*Third time I am ready to come*} Had he been already twice or only once? He had changed his plans once when he did not go (2 Cor. 1:15). He will not change his plans now.

16. {*Crafty*} This word has a good or bad sense: skillful or cunning. Paul is quoting the word from his enemies. {*With guile*} Being ironical, this is the Greek word *dolos,* bait to catch fish with. The enemies of Paul said that he was raising this big collection for himself.

19. {*We are excusing ourselves*} This is the Greek verb *apologeomai;* he is not just "apologizing," but is in deadly earnest, as they will find out when he comes.

20. {*Lest by any means...*} With graphic pen pictures Paul describes what had been going on against him during his long absence. {*Whisperings*} This is the Greek word *psithurismos,* from *psithurizô,* to whisper into one's ear, and so gossip (cf. Eccl. 10:11).

21. {*Lest my God humble me*} This means a public humiliation as his fear. The conduct of the church had been a real humiliation whether he refers to a previous visit or not.

CHAPTER 13

2. {*If I come again*} This condition is a plausible, supposable case, though not determined or fulfilled.

4. {*But we shall live with him through the power of God*} So real is Paul's sense of his union with Christ.

5-6. {*Unless indeed ye be reprobate*} Paul challenged his opposers in Corinth to try and test themselves; whether or not they are in the faith is a much more vital matter than trying to prove Paul a heretic.

8. {*Against the truth*} He means in the long run. We can hinder and hold down the truth by evil deeds (Rom. 1:18), but in the end the truth wins.

9. {*For we rejoice*} Paul had far rather be weak in the sense of failing to exercise his apostolic power because they did the noble thing. He is no Jonah who lamented when Nineveh repented.

12. {*With a holy kiss*} In the Jewish synagogues where the sexes were separated, men kissed men, the women, women. This apparently was the Christian custom also. It was dropped because of charges made against the Christians by the pagans.

13. {*Grace...love...communion*} This benediction is the most complete of them all. It presents the persons of the Trinity in full form (cf. 2 Thess. 3:17).

The Epistle to the Galatians

Author: Paul, apostle
Recipients: The churches of Galatia
Date: possibly A.D. 56 or 57
From: possibly Corinth
Occasion: Paul responds to the damaging reports of Judaizers in Galatia.
Theme: A defense of Paul's Gospel

By Way of Introduction

This Epistle was written about seventeen years after Paul's conversion (cf. Gal. 1:18 and 2:1). Though not all scholars agree, it is clear that this was written *after* the Conference in Jerusalem (Acts 15:1-33); Galatians 2:1-14 (see commentary below on those verses) gives insight into that Acts event. The weight of the argument is for this placement. Also, it seems clear that it was written after the Epistles to the Thessalonians (A.D. 50-51) which were sent from Corinth.

Who are these Galatians? There is a northern and southern theory. The southern theory says this refers to churches of the Roman province (cf. Acts 16:6) such as Pisidia, Lycaonia, Phrygia. The northern theory says "Galatian" is an ethnographic use of the term and means the real Celts of North Galatia.

Galatians and Romans are epistles related in content. It is possible that when Paul reached Corinth in late autumn or early winter of A.D. 55 or 56 (Acts 20:1ff.), he received alarming reports of the damage brought by the Judaizers in Galatia. He had won his fight against them in Corinth (1 and 2 Cor.). So now he hurls this thunderbolt at them from Corinth (hence, the Epistle to the Galatians) and later, in a calmer mood, sends the fuller discussion to the church in Rome (hence, the Epistle to the Romans).

Chapter 1

1. {*Not from men, neither through men*} He was not an apostle by human authority. Judaizers had charged that Paul was not a genuine apostle, since he was not one of the twelve (as in 2 Cor. chapters 10 to

12). In chapters 1 and 2 Paul proves his independence of and equality with the twelve. {*But through Jesus Christ and God the Father*} (cf. 1 Cor. 9:1 and Acts 9:4-6; 22:7; 26:16). {*Who raised him from the dead*} Paul had seen the Risen Christ and was so qualified (1 Cor. 9:1; 15:8).

2. {*Unto the churches of Galatia*} This was a circular letter to all the churches (see also introduction).

4. {*Deliver*} This is the Greek word *exaireô*, to pluck out, to rescue (Acts 23:27). This "strikes the keynote of the epistle. The gospel is a rescue, an emancipation from a state of bondage" (Lightfoot). {*Out of this present evil world*} Lit. "out of the age the existing one being evil." Evil is emphasized in the Greek. {*According to the will of God*} This is not according to any merit in us.

6. {*Ye are so quickly removing*} Translate, "you are transferring yourselves". "Quickly" refers to either from the time of their conversion or most likely from the time when the Judaizers came and tempted them. {*Unto a different gospel*} (cf. 2 Cor. 11:4). Paul is vehement, for this is not mere difference in emphasis or spirit (cf. Phil. 1:18), this is a *different* gospel, a *different* Jesus.

7. {*Which is not another*} This is no "good news," but a yoke of bondage to the law and the abolition of grace. There is but one gospel and that is of grace, not works. {*Would pervert*} Lit. "wish to turn about," change completely (Acts 2:20; Jas. 4:9). The very existence of the gospel of Christ was at stake.

8. {*If we*} This is a literary plural, a condition considered not currently true, but plausible, "suppose we." The Jews termed Paul a renegade for leaving Judaism for Christianity. But it was before Paul had seen the Risen Christ that he clung to the law.

9. {*So say I now again*} Paul knows that he has just made what some will consider an extreme statement. He will stand by it to the end. He calls down a curse on any one who proclaims a gospel to them contrary to that which they had received from him.

11. {*Which was preached*} There is a word play, lit. "the gospel which was gospelized by me." {*It is not after man*} That is, not after a human standard and so he does not try to conform to the human ideal.

12. {*Nor was I taught it*} The source was not human, not any apostle, nor he taught it in the school of Gamaliel in Jerusalem or at the University of Tarsus. {*By revelation*} This is not limited to one revelation (unveiling) from Christ (cf. 1 Cor. 11:23). The Lord Jesus revealed his will to Paul.

13. {*Beyond measure*} Lit. "According to excess" (cf. throwing beyond, the Greek word *huperbolê*). {*I persecuted*} The Greek tense translates "I used to persecute" (cf. Acts chapters 7 to 9). {*Made havock of it*} This is the Greek verb *portheô,* to lay waste, to sack (cf. Gal 1:23) in Acts 9:21 Paul heard them use it of him and it stuck in his mind.

14. {*I advanced*} (cf. Rom. 13:12; 2 Tim. 2:16; 3:9, 13). Paul was a brilliant pupil under Gamaliel. See Philippians 3:4-6. Paul modestly claims that he went "beyond" his fellow-students in his progress in Judaism. {*More exceedingly zealous*} Lit. "more exceedingly a zealot" (cf. Acts 1:13; 21:20; 1 Cor. 14:12).

15. {*Who separated me*} This is the Greek verb *aphorizô,* from *apo* and *horos* to mark off from a boundary or line. The Pharisees were the separatists who held themselves off from others. Paul conceives himself as a spiritual Pharisee (cf. Rom. 1:1).

16. {*To reveal his Son in me*} Paul can mean to lay emphasis on his inward experience of grace or he may refer objectively to the vision of Christ on the way to Damascus, "in my case."

17. {*Before me*} The Jerusalem apostles were genuine apostles, but so is Paul. His call did not come from them nor did he receive confirmation by them. {*Into Arabia*} This visit to Arabia has to come between the two visits to Damascus which are not distinguished in Acts 9:22, 23.

18. {*Then after three years*} This is a round number to cover the period from his departure from Jerusalem for Damascus to his return to Jerusalem. {*Fifteen days*}, (cf. Acts 9:26-30). This refers to the two week period when Barnabas endorsed Paul to the suspicious disciples in Jerusalem and probably while he was preaching in the city.

19. {*Except James the brother of the Lord*} Paul is showing his independence of and equality with the twelve in answer to the attacks of the Judaizers.

21. {*Into the region of Syria and Cilicia*} (cf. Acts 9:30). Paul was not idle, but at work in Tarsus and the surrounding country.

22. {*Of Judea*} This is distinct from Jerusalem, for he had once scattered the church there and had revisited them before coming to Tarsus (Acts 9:26-31).

23. {*They only heard*} Translate the phrase, "They were only hearing from time to time."

CHAPTER 2

1. {*Then after the space of fourteen years I went up again*} The focus is on the points of contact with the apostles in Jerusalem. He did from time to time actually go into the city itself as is recorded in Acts. Paul here gives the inside view of this private conference in Jerusalem that came in between the two public meetings (Acts 15:2, 4, 6-29).

2. {*Before them who were of repute*} This refers to Peter, James the brother of the Lord, and John of Zebedee [Paul now makes the "Big Four"]. The decision reached by this group would shape the decision of the public conference in the adjourned meeting. It was of the utmost importance that they should see eye to eye. The Judaizers were assuming that the twelve apostles and James the Lord's brother would side with them against Paul and Barnabas.

4. {*But because of the false brethren privately brought in*} Evidently some of the Judaizers or sympathizers whom Paul had not invited had come in as often happens (cf. 2 Cor. 11:13 of the Judaizers in Corinth). {*To spy out*} This is the Greek verb *kataskopeô,* from *kataskopos,* a spy, to reconnoiter, to make a treacherous investigation. {*That they might bring us into bondage*} Lit. "to enslave completely." It was as serious a conflict as this. Spiritual liberty or spiritual bondage, which?

5. {*No, not for an hour*} This is a pointed denial that he and Barnabas yielded at all "in the way of subjection." The compromisers pleaded for the circumcision of Titus "because of the false brethren" in order to have peace. {*The truth of the gospel*} It was a grave crisis to call for such language. The whole problem of Gentile Christianity was involved in the case of Titus, whether Christianity was to be merely a modified brand of legalistic Judaism or a spiritual religion, the children of Abraham by faith. The case of Timothy later was utterly different, for he had a Jewish mother and a Greek father. Titus was pure Greek.

6. {*They, I say, imparted nothing to me*} Paul won his point, when he persuaded Peter, James, and John to agree with him and Barnabas in their contention for freedom for the Gentile Christians from the bondage of the Mosaic ceremonial law.

8. {*He that wrought for Peter unto the apostleship of the circumcision*} This is the Greek word *apostolên* for "apostleship" (cf. Acts 1:25; 1 Cor. 9:2). Paul recognizes Peter's apostleship (to Jews) and vice versa to

Paul and the Gentiles. This is a complete answer to the genuineness of Paul's apostleship, even though he was not one of the twelve.

9. {*They who were reputed to be pillars*} They had that reputation and Paul accepts them as such (1 Tim. 3:15). *Stuloi* is an old word for pillars, columns, as of fire (Rev. 10:1). These were the Pillar Apostles. {*Gave to me and Barnabas the right hands of fellowship*} This is the dramatic and concluding act of the pact for cooperation and coordinating independent spheres of activity. The compromisers and the Judaizers were brushed to one side when these five men shook hands as equals in the work of Christ's Kingdom.

11. {*I resisted him to the face*} This is the Greek verb *anthistêmi*, translated, "I stood against him face to face." In Jerusalem Paul faced Peter as his equal in rank and sphere of work. In Antioch he looked him in the eye as his superior in character and courage.

12. {*For before that certain came from James*} No doubt these brethren threatened Peter that they would tell James and the church about his conduct (cf. Acts 11:1-18). As a matter of fact the Jerusalem Conference did not discuss the matter of social relations between Jews and Gentiles though that was the charge made against Peter (Acts 11:1). {*He did eat with the Gentiles*} It was his habit to eat with the Gentiles, but then he began to separate himself just like a Pharisee and as if afraid of the Judaizers in the Jerusalem Church, perhaps half afraid that James might not endorse what he had been doing.

13. {*Insomuch that even Barnabas...was carried away with their dissimulation*} This can only mean hypocrisy in the bad sense (Matt. 23:28), not merely acting a part. It was a solemn moment when Paul saw the Jerusalem victory vanish and even Barnabas desert him as they followed the timid cowardice of Peter.

14. {*That they walked not uprightly*} This is the Greek verb *orthopodeô* (*orthos*, straight, *pous*, foot), Lit. "they are not walking straight." {*As do the Jews*} Really Paul charges Peter with trying to compel the Gentiles to live all like Jews, to Judaize the Gentile Christians, the very point at issue in the Jerusalem Conference when Peter so loyally supported Paul. It was a bold thrust that allowed no reply. But Paul won Peter back and Barnabas also (cf. 2 Pet. 3:15 and Acts 15:39; 1 Cor. 9:6).

16. {*Is not justified*} This is the Greek verb *dikaioô*, an old causative verb from *dikaios*, righteous (from *dike*, right), to make righteous, to declare righteous. It is one of the great Pauline words along with *dikaiosunê,* righteousness. The two ways of getting right with God are here set forth: by faith in Christ Jesus (objective genitive), by the works of the law (by keeping all the law in the most minute fashion, the way of the Pharisees). Paul knew them both (see Rom. 7:1ff.). {*Even we*} This means "we Jews" believed, had to believe, were not saved or justified till we did believe. This very point Peter had made at the Jerusalem Conference (Acts 15:10). He quotes Psalms 143:2. Paul uses *dikaiosunê* in two senses: (1) Justification, on the basis of what Christ has done and obtained by faith, thus we are set right with God (Rom. 1-5); (2) Sanctification, actual goodness as the result of living with and for Christ (Rom. 6-8). The same plan exists for Jew and Gentile.

17. {*A minister of sin*} This is an illogical inference. We were sinners already in spite of being Jews. Christ simply revealed to us our sin.

18. {*A transgressor*} Peter, by his shifts had contradicted himself helplessly as Paul shows by this condition. When he lived like a Gentile, he tore down the ceremonial law. When he lived like a Jew, he tore down salvation by grace.

20. {*I have been crucified with Christ*} This is one of Paul's greatest mystical sayings. Paul uses the same word in Rom. 6:6 for the same idea. In the Gospels it occurs of literal crucifixion of Christ and the two thieves (cf. Mark 15:32). Paul uses often the idea of dying with Christ (Gal. 5:24; 6:14; Rom. 6:8; Col. 2:20) and burial with Christ also (Rom. 6:4; Col. 2:12). {*No longer I*} So complete has become Paul's identification with Christ that his separate personality is merged into that of Christ (cf. Rom. 7:25). {*For me*} Paul has the closest personal feeling toward Christ. He appropriates to himself the love which belongs equally to the whole world.

21. {*Then Christ died for nought*} This is assumed to be a true condition. If one man apart from grace can win his own righteousness, any man can and should. Hence Christ died gratuitously, unnecessarily.

CHAPTER 3

1. {*Who did bewitch you?*} Translate, "Somebody 'fascinated' you." This refers to some aggressive Judaizer [man or woman] (Gal. 5:7). This is the Greek verb *baskainô,* kin to *phaskô* (*baskô*), to speak, then to bring evil on one by feigned praise or the evil eye, to lead astray by evil arts.

2. {*This only*} Paul strikes at the heart of the problem. He will show their error by the point that the gifts of the Spirit came by the hearing of faith, not by works of the law.

3. {*Are ye now perfected in the flesh?*} Lit. "perfected in the flesh?" There is a double contrast, between "having begun/Spirit" and "finishing/flesh" (cf. 2 Cor. 8:6; Phil. 1:6).

4. {*Did ye suffer?*} Here it means to suffer ill. We have records of persecution in South Galatia (Acts 14:2, 5, 19, 22).

5. {*Worketh miracles*} (cf. 1 Thess. 2:13; 1 Cor. 12:6). "Works" is a great word for God's activities (Phil. 2:13).

6. {*It was reckoned unto him for righteousness*} (cf. Gen. 15:6 and Rom. 4:3). Note that James (Jas. 2:23) quotes it for emphasis on obedience to God. Paul and James are discussing different episodes in the life of Abraham. Both are correct.

7. {*The same are sons of Abraham*} Paul writes that the real sons of Abraham are those who believe which springs out of faith, not out of blood.

8. {*Would justify*} The Greek tense translates "does justify." {*Preached the gospel beforehand*} (cf. Gen. 12:3; 18:18). This Scripture announced beforehand the gospel on this point of justification by faith, and included all the nations of the earth.

10. {*Under a curse*} (cf. Rom. 3:9). This is a picture of the curse hanging over them like a Damoclean blade. The Greek word *katara* is an old one (*kata,* down, *ara,* imprecation).

11. {*In the sight of God*} Lit. "by the side of God," as God looks at it, for the simple reason that no one except Jesus has ever kept *all* the law, God's perfect law.

13. {*Redeemed us*} The Greek verb is *exagorazô,* to buy from, to buy back, to ransom; such as slaves (cf. 1 Cor. 6:20; 7:23); and so Christ's purchase (cf. Gal. 4:5; Col. 4:5; Eph. 5:16). {*Having become a curse for us*} We were under a curse. Christ became a curse over us and so between us and the overhanging curse which fell on him instead of on us. Thus he bought us out and we are free from the curse which he took on himself. {*That hangeth on a tree*} (cf. Deut. 21:23). The allusion was to exposure of dead bodies on stakes or crosses (Josh. 10:26). *Xulon* means wood, not usually tree, though so in Luke 23:31 and in later Greek.

14. {*That we might receive*} So in Christ we all (Gentile and Jew) obtain the promise of blessing made to Abraham, through faith.

15. {*Though it be but a man's covenant, yet when it hath been confirmed*} Lit. "Yet a man's covenant ratified." "Covenant" is the Greek *diathêkê*. It can be translated as both covenant and will (Matt. 26:28; 1 Cor. 11:25; 2 Cor. 3:6; Heb. 9:16). "Established" is the Greek verb *kuroô*, to ratify, to make valid; here a state of completion, authoritative confirmation.

16. {*But as of one…which is Christ*} But the promise to Abraham uses "seed" as a collective substantive and applies to all believers (both Jews and Gentiles). Here Paul uses a rabbinical refinement which is yet intelligible. The people of Israel were a type of the Messiah and he gathers up the promise in its special application to Christ. He does not say that Christ is specifically referred to in Genesis 13:15 or 17:7.

17. {*Four hundred and thirty years after*} This is the date in Exodus 12:40 for the sojourn in Egypt (cf. Gen. 15:13).

18. {*The inheritance*} (cf. Matt. 21:38; Acts 7:5). This came to Israel by the promise to Abraham, not by the Mosaic law.

19. {*What then is the law?*} Translate, "why then the law?" A pertinent question if the Abrahamic promise antedates it and holds on afterwards. {*It was added because of transgressions*} (cf. Gal. 3: 15). In Paul's mind the law is no part of the covenant, but a thing apart, in no way modifying its provisions (Burton). "Because" here is "not in order to create transgressions," but rather "to make transgressions palpable," (Ellicott) thereby pronouncing them to be from that time forward transgressions of the law. {*Till the seed should come*} This refers to Christ (cf. Gal. 3:16). {*By the hand of a mediator*} This refers to Moses here, but also of Christ (1 Tim. 2:5; Heb. 8:6; 9:15; 12:24).

20. {*Is not a mediator of one*} A middleman comes in between two parties. The law is in the nature of a contract between God and the Jewish people with Moses as the mediator or middleman. {*But God is one*} There was no middleman between God and Abraham. He made the promise directly to Abraham.

21. {*Which could make alive*} (cf. 1 Cor. 15:22). This is the Greek verb *zôopoieô*, late compound (*zôos*, alive, *poieô*, to make). He means spiritual life, here and hereafter.

22. {*Hath shut up*} Lit. "did shut together," shut on all sides, completely as a shoal of fish in a net (Luke 5:6). {*Under sin*} It is as if the lid closed in on us over a massive chest that we could not open or as prisoners in a dungeon (cf. Rom. 3:10-19; 11:32).

23. {*Before faith came*} (cf. Gal. 3:22). Lit. "before the coming as to the Faith." This is the faith in Christ as Savior.

24. {*Our tutor unto Christ*} (cf. 1 Cor. 4:15). This was a common word for the slave employed in Greek and Roman families of the better class in charge of the boy from about six to sixteen. The *paedagogue* watched his behavior at home and attended him when he went away from home as to school. Christ is our Schoolmaster and the law as *paedagogue* kept watch over us till we came to Christ.

25. {*Under a tutor*} Now that faith has come, the pedagogue is dismissed. We are in the school of the Master.

26. {*For ye are all sons of God*} This is "sons of God" in the full ethical and spiritual sense (cf. Gal. 3:14), through faith.

27. {*Were baptized into Christ*} Better translated, "were baptized unto Christ," that is in reference to Christ. {*Did put on Christ*} Clothed as a badge or uniform of service like that of the soldier. This verb is common in the sense of putting on garments, metaphorically here (cf. Rom. 13:14; Col. 3:9; Eph. 4:22-24; 6:11, 14).

28. {*One man*} In Christ there is but one moral personality, distinctions and differences disappear: racial, national, class, economic distinctions; sex rivalry disappears.

29. {*If ye are Christ's*} There is only one meaningful test, not the distinctions of verse 28.

CHAPTER 4

1. {*A child*} This is the Greek word *nêpios,* a child that that does not talk (*nê, epos,* word). That is a minor, an infant, immature intellectually and morally in contrast with a full grown person (1 Cor. 3:1; 14:20; Phil. 3:15; Eph. 4:13).

2. {*Under guardians*} This is used commonly as the guardian of an orphan minor. {*Stewards*} This is used of a manager of a household whether freeborn or slave (cf. Luke 12:42; 1 Cor. 4:2). Papyri show it as manager of an estate and also as treasurer like Romans 16:23. {*Until the time appointed of the father*} Under Roman law the *tutor* had charge of the child till he was fourteen when the curator took charge of him till he was twenty-five.

3. {*When we were children*} This is before the epoch of faith came. {*We were held in bondage*} The Greek tense has a focus of enslaving in a permanent state of bondage. {*Under the rudiments of the world*} Probably here Paul has in mind the rudimentary character of the law. The Greek word *stoicheion* is any first thing in a *stoichos* like the letters of the alphabet, the material elements in the universe (2 Pet. 3:10), the heavenly bodies.

4. {*The fulness of the time*} God sent forth his preexisting Son (Phil. 2:6) when the time for his purpose had come (cf. Gal. 4:2). {*Born of a woman under law*} This refers to true humanity and Jewish race, with no direct reference here to the Virgin Birth of Jesus; though his deity is affirmed.

6. {*The Spirit of his Son*} This is the Holy Spirit, called the Spirit of Christ (Rom. 8:9), the Spirit of Jesus Christ (Phil. 1:19). The Holy Spirit proceeds from the Father and from the Son (John 15:26). {*Crying, Abba, Father*} Abba is the Aramaic word for father (cf. John 20:28). It is possible that the repetition here (since Abba = Father) and in Romans 8:15 may be "a sort of affectionate fondness for the very term that Jesus himself used" (Burton) in the Garden of Gethsemane (Mark 14:36). Others think it shows the bilingual culture that Paul and Jesus came out of.

7. {*No longer a bondservant*} The spiritual experience (Gal. 3:2) has set each one free. Each is now a son and heir.

8. {*To them which by nature are not gods*} This refers to idols (Acts 17:29) and the demons which they represent (cf. 1 Cor. 8:5; 10:20).

9. {*Now that ye have come to know God*} This has a focus of "come to know by experience through faith in Christ."

10. {*Ye observe*} Lit. "to stand beside and watch carefully," here with great care. It hurt Paul to the quick after his own merciful deliverance to see these Gentile Christians drawn into this spider web of Judaizing Christians, once set free, now enslaved again.

11. {*I am afraid of you*} He shudders to think of it. Shown by the Greek syntax, Paul fears that the worst has happened.

12. {*Be as I am*} Greek tense translates "Keep on becoming as I am."

13. {*Because of an infirmity of the flesh*} Known to the Galatians, this generally refers to a sickness of some kind: eye trouble? (Gal. 4:15); thorn in flesh? (2 Cor. 12:7); an attack of malaria? (cf. travel in marshlands suggested in Acts 13; 14); we do not know.

14. {*Nor rejected*} The Greek word is *ekptuô,* to spit out, to spurn, to loathe. {*As Christ Jesus*} He was received, in spite of his illness and repulsive appearance, whatever it was. This is not the event of Acts 14:12.

15. {*That gratulation of yourselves*} Lit. "to pronounce happy," (cf. Rom. 4:6, 9). {*Ye would have plucked out your eyes and given them to me*} This is strong language and is saved from hyperbole by "if possible." Did Paul not have at this time serious eye trouble?

16. {*Your enemy*} They looked on Paul now as an enemy to them. So the Pharisees and Judaizers generally now regarded him.

19. {*I am in travail*} I am in birth pangs, a powerful picture of pain (cf. Gal. 4:27; Rev. 12:2). {*Until Christ be formed in you*} This figure is the embryo developing into the child. Paul boldly represents himself as again the mother with birth pangs over them. This is better than to suppose that the Galatians are pregnant mothers by a reversal of the picture (cf. 1 Thess. 2:7).

20. {*I am perplexed*} Paul is saying, "I am at a loss and know not what to do" or "I am lost at this distance from you."

21. {*That desire to be under the law*} Lit. "under law" (cf. Gal. 3:23; 4:4), That is, a legalistic system. Paul makes direct reference to these so disposed to "hear the law." He makes a surprising turn, but a legitimate one for the legalists by an allegorical use of Scripture.

22. {*By the handmaid*} (cf. Gen. 16:1) This is a common word for damsel which came to be used for female slave or maidservant (Luke 12:45) or doorkeeper like Matthew 26:29. So in the papyri.

24. {*Which things contain an allegory*} Lit. "which things are allegorized." Paul does not deny the actual historical narrative, but he simply uses it in an allegorical sense to illustrate his point for the benefit of his readers who are tempted to go under the burden of the law.

25. {*This Hagar*} "This" is neuter in Greek, and so referring to the word Hagar (not to the woman) as applied to the mountain. The Arabians are descendants of Abraham and Hagar (her name meaning wanderer or fugitive). {*Answereth to*} Paul shows opposing principles: Hagar/Sarah, Ishmael/Isaac, old/new covenant, earthly/heavenly Jerusalem).

26. {*The Jerusalem that is above*} Paul uses the rabbinical idea that the heavenly Jerusalem, the Kingdom of God, corresponds to the one here to illustrate his point without endorsing their ideas (cf. Rev. 21:2). He uses the city of Jerusalem to represent the whole Jewish race (Vincent).

27. {*The desolate*} The prophet refers to Sarah's prolonged barrenness and Paul uses this fact as a figure for the progress and glory of Christianity (the new Jerusalem of freedom) in contrast with the old Jerusalem of bondage (the current Judaism).

30. {*Cast out*} This quotation is from Genesis 21:10 (Sarah to Abraham) and confirmed in Genesis 21:12 by God's command to Abraham. Paul gives allegorical warning thus to the persecuting Jews and Judaizers. "The law and the gospel cannot coexist. The law must disappear before the gospel" (Lightfoot).

31. {*But of the free woman*} We are children of Abraham by faith (Gal. 3:7).

CHAPTER 5

1. {*With freedom*} This is the freedom that belongs to us children of the free woman (Gal. 4:31). {*Stand fast therefore*} Translate, "keep on standing therefore," or "stay free since Christ set you free." {*Be not entangled again*} The Greek tense translates, "*Stop* being entangled by a yoke of bondage." The Judaizers were trying to lasso the Galatians for the old yoke of Judaism.

2. {*If ye receive circumcision*} This is a supposable case, but with terrible consequences, for they will make circumcision a condition of salvation. In that case Christ will help them not at all.

3. {*A debtor*} This is the Greek word *opheiletês,* a common word from *opheilô,* to owe for one who has assumed an obligation (cf. Gal. 3:10). He takes the curse on himself.

4. {*Ye are severed from Christ*} Translate, "You did fall out of grace," or "you left the sphere of grace in Christ and took your stand in the sphere of law" as your hope of salvation. Paul does not mince words and carries the logic to the end of the course. He is not, of course, speaking of occasional sins, but he has in mind a far more serious matter, that of substituting law for Christ as the agent in salvation.

6. {*Availeth anything*} Lit. "to have strength" (cf. Matt. 5:13). Neither Jew nor Greek has any advantage in his state (cf. Gal. 3:28). All stand on a level in Christ.

7. {*Who did hinder you?*} Someone "cut in" on the Galatians as they were running the Christian race and tried to trip them or to turn them.

8. {*This persuasion*} This is "the art of persuasion," the effort of the Judaizers to persuade you.

9. {*A little leaven leaveneth the whole lump*} (cf. 1 Cor. 5:6). It is merely the pervasive power of leaven, not evil, that is the focus.

11. {*Why am I still persecuted?*} Some of the Judaizers even circulated the slander that Paul preached circumcision in order to ruin his influence.

12. {*Cut themselves off*} This means here to mutilate.

13. {*Only use not*} Translate better as "turn not your liberty into an occasion for the flesh," as a spring board for license (cf. 2 Cor. 5:12).

14. {*Love neighbor...*} (cf. Lev. 19:18). Paul uses here a striking paradox by urging obedience to the law against which he has been arguing, but this is the moral law as proof of the new love and life (cf. Rom. 13:8).

15. {*If ye bite and devour one another*} This condition is assumed as true. Two common and old Greek verbs often used together of wild animals, or like cats and dogs.

16. {*Ye shall not fulfil...the lust of the flesh*} The "not" is emphatic. "Lust" is just craving or longing, lit. "yearning after."

17. {*Lusteth against*} This verse is like a tug of war, lined up against one another face to face. Christ and Satan long for the possession of the city of Man Soul as Bunyan shows.

18. {*Under the law*} (cf. Gal. 3:2-6) Instead of "under the flesh" as one might expect. The flesh made the law weak (Rom. 8:3; Heb. 9:10, 13). They are one and the same in result.

21. {*Practise*} This is the Greek verb *prassô* for habitual practice (our very word, in fact), not *poieô* for occasional doing. The habit of these sins is proof that one is not in the Kingdom of God and will not inherit it.

22. {*The fruit of the Spirit*} Paul changes the figure from works in verse 19 to fruit as the normal outcropping of the Holy Spirit in us. It is a beautiful tree of fruit that Paul pictures here with nine luscious fruits on it. {*Love*} This is first (cf. 1 Cor. 13:1ff.); {*Joy*} (cf. 1 Thess. 1:6); {*Peace*} (cf. 1 Thess. 1:1); {*Long-suffering*} (cf. 2 Cor. 6:6); {*Kindness*} (cf. 2 Cor. 6:6); {*Goodness*} (cf. 2 Thess. 1:11); {*Faithfulness*} (cf. Matt. 23:33; 1 Cor. 13:7, 13); {*Meekness*} (cf. 1 Cor. 4:21; 2 Cor. 10:1); {*Temperance*} (cf. Acts 24:25).

25. {*By the Spirit let us also walk*} Translate the Greek tense, "Let us also go on walking by the Spirit." Let us make our steps by the help and guidance of the Spirit.

26. {*Provoking one another*} This is the Greek verb *prokaleô,* to call forth, to challenge to combat, here in a bad sense.

CHAPTER 6

1. {*If a man be overtaken*} The Greek verb is *prolambanô,* to take beforehand, to surprise, to detect. {*Trespass*} Lit. "a falling aside, a slip or lapse" in the papyri rather than a willful sin. {*Ye which are spiritual*} (cf. 1 Cor. 3:1). This is the spiritually led (Gal. 5:18), the spiritual experts in mending souls.

2. {*Bear ye one another's burdens*} Greek tense translates, "keep on bearing." It is when one's load (cf. Gal. 6:5) is about to press one down. Then give help in carrying it.

5. {*Each shall bear his own burden*} "Load" is an old word for ship's cargo (Acts 27:10). Christ calls his "load" light (Matt. 11:30) but that of the Pharisees is heavy (Matt. 23:4).

7. {*Be not deceived*} Translate the Greek syntax, "stop being led astray." {*God is not mocked*} Lit. "the nose cannot be turned up at God." That is done towards God, but never without punishment. {*Whatsoever a man soweth...reap*} This is one of the most frequent of ancient proverbs (Job 4:8; 2 Cor. 9:6 also cf. Matt. 7:16; Mark 4:26).

8. {*Corruption*} This word here plainly means the physical and moral decay or rottenness that follows sins of the flesh as all men know.

9. {*Let us not be weary in well-doing*} Lit. "let us not keep on giving in to evil while doing the good." {*If we faint not*} Lit. "not loosened out," relaxed, exhausted as a result of giving in to evil.

10. {*As we have opportunity*} Translate, "As we have occasion at any time." {*Let us work that which is good*} Lit. "Let us keep on working the good deed."

13. {*They who receive circumcision*} The Greek tense translates, "those who are having themselves circumcised."

14. {*Hath been crucified unto me*} This is one of the great sayings of Paul concerning his relation to Christ and the world in contrast with the Judaizers (cf. Gal. 2:19; 3:13; 4:4; 1 Cor. 1:23; Rom. 1:16; 3:21; 4:25;

5:18). {***World***} A definite reference, this is Paul's old world of Jewish descent and environment that is dead to him (Phil. 3:3).

17. {***The marks of Jesus***} This is the Greek word *stigma,* from *stizô,* to prick, to stick, to sting. Slaves had the names or stamp of their owners on their bodies. There were devotees also who stamped upon their bodies the names of the gods whom they worshipped. Paul gloried in being the slave of Jesus Christ. This is probably the image in Paul's mind since he bore in his body brand marks of suffering for Christ received in many places (2 Cor. 6:4-6; 11:23), probably actual scars from the scourgings (thirty-nine lashes at a time).

The Epistle to the Ephesians

Author: Apostle Paul
Recipients: Believers of the Roman Province of Asia
Date: Probably A.D. 63 (cf. Colossians and Philemon)
From: Rome (though some suggest other places)
Occasion: To confront the Gnostic heresy
Theme: The Dignity of the Church as the Body of Christ, the Head

By Way of Introduction

If Colossians is Pauline, there is little or nothing to be said against the Pauline authorship of this Epistle. Though Colossians was written first, Ephesians is a fuller treatment of the same general theme in a more detached and impersonal manner than Colossians.

The only mention of Ephesus (Eph. 1:1) is not original, but Colossians 4:16 mentions "the letter from Laodicea" to find the probable explanation. After writing the stirring Epistle to the Colossians Paul dictated this so-called Epistle to the Ephesians as a general or circular letter for the churches in Asia (Roman province).

Like Colossians, the same Gnostic heresy is met but with this difference. Colossians emphasizes the Dignity of Christ as the Head of the Church, while Ephesians stresses the Dignity of the Church as the Body of Christ the Head.

Chapter 1

3. {*Blessed*} The Greek verb is *eulogeô,* common in the LXX for Hebrew *baruk* (Vulgate *benedictus*) and applied usually to God, sometimes to men (Gen. 24:31), but in NT always to God (Luke 1:68). There is no "to be" verb in Greek and could be a wish, command, or declarative statement.

4. {*Even as he chose us in him*} Lit. "to pick out, to choose." This is a definitive statement of God's elective grace concerning believers in Christ. {*Before the foundation of the world*} Lit. "the laying of a foundation." This very phrase with *pro* in the Prayer of Jesus (John 17:24) of love of the Father toward the Son. It occurs also in 1 Peter

1:20. Paul in summary fashion gives an outline of his view of God's redemptive plans for the race.

5. {*Having foreordained us*} This is the Greek verb *proorizô*, late and rare compound to define or decide beforehand (cf. Acts 4:28; 1 Cor. 2:7; Rom. 8:29, also Eph. 1:11). {*According to the good pleasure of his will*} "Pleasure" means "purpose" rather than "good pleasure" here.

7. {*Sins*} This is trespasses, not the more general word for "sins." Clearly Paul makes the blood of Christ the cost of redemption, the ransom money (Matt. 20:28; Mark 10:45; 1 Tim. 2:6; Col. 1:9).

8. {*According to the riches of his grace*} A thoroughly Pauline phrase, riches of kindness (Rom. 2:4), riches of glory (Col. 1:27; Eph. 3:16; Phil. 4:19), riches of fullness of understanding (Col. 2:7), riches of Christ (Eph. 3:8), and in Ephesians 2:7 "the surpassing riches of grace."

10. {*Unto a dispensation of the fulness of the times*} (cf. Col. 1:25 and Gal. 4:4). {*To sum up*} This is the Greek verb *anakephalaioô*, to head up all things [in Christ], a literary word. In NT only here and Romans 13:9.

11. {*We were made a heritage*} The Greek verb is *klêroô*, an old word, to assign by lot (*klêros*), to make a *klêros* or heritage (cf. Acts 17:4). {*Purpose*} Lit. "a setting before" (Acts 11:23; 27:13).

12. {*Who had before hoped in Christ*} Probably the reference is to those who like Paul had once been Jews and had now found the Messiah in Jesus.

13. {*Ye were sealed*} This is the Greek verb *sphragizô*, old verb, to set a seal on one as a mark or stamp, sometimes the marks of ownership or of worship of deities like *stigmata* (Gal. 6:17). Marked and authenticated as God's heritage as in Ephesians 4:30. See 2 Corinthians 1:22 for the very use of the metaphor here applied to the Holy Spirit even with the word *arrabôn* (earnest).

14. {*An earnest*} (cf. 2 Cor. 1:22) This verse emphasizes that the Gentiles are also included in God's promise of salvation. {*Of our inheritance*} God's gift of the Holy Spirit is the pledge and first payment for the final inheritance in Christ. {*Of God's own possession*} (cf. 1 Pet. 2:9; Heb. 10:39). "God's possession" is supplied in context. God has purchased us back to himself.

17. {*The Father of glory*} This means "the God characterized by glory" (the *Shekinah*, Heb. 9:5) as in Acts 7:2; 1 Corinthians 2:8; 2 Corinthians 1:3; James 2:1. {*A spirit of wisdom and revelation*} Though it is possible to translate this "a spirit" (small "s"), it is open to question if it is possible to obtain this wisdom and revelation apart from the Holy Spirit (cf. Gal. 6:1; Rom. 8:15).

18. {*Having the eyes of your heart enlightened*} Translate, "the eyes of your heart having been enlightened." This is a beautiful figure, the heart regarded as having eyes looking out toward Christ. But the grammar is difficult.

20. {*Made him to sit*} (cf. 1 Cor. 6:4). This is a metaphorical local expression.

21. {*Far above all rule*} (cf. Heb. 9:5, also Col. 1:16). Paul claims primacy for Jesus Christ above all angels, *aeons,* what not. These titles all were used in the Gnostic speculations with a graduated angelic hierarchy. {*World*} Lit. "age, present time" (Matt. 12:32 and Gal. 1:4; 1 Tim. 6:17) and the future life (Eph. 2:7; Luke 20:35).

23. {*The fulness of him that filleth all in all*} All things are summed up in Christ (cf. Eph. 1:10), who is the *plêrôma* of God (Col. 1:19), and in particular does Christ fill the church universal as his body.

CHAPTER 2

1. {*When ye were dead*} Their former state was spiritually dead.

2. {*According to the course of this world*} This is a curious combination of "a period of time" and "the world in that period" (cf. 1 Cor. 1:20 and 1 Cor 3:9). {*The prince of the power of the air*} "Air" was used by the ancients for the lower and denser atmosphere, and another word for the higher and rarer. Satan is here pictured as ruler of the demons and other agencies of evil, "the prince of this world" (John 6:11). {*That now worketh*} Those who deny the existence of a personal devil cannot successfully deny the vicious tendencies in modern men.

3. {*The desires*} This is plural here "the wishes," "the wills" of the flesh like the cravings just mentioned. Gentiles had no monopoly of such sinful impulses. {*Were by nature children of wrath*} Paul is insisting that Jews as well as Gentiles are the objects of God's wrath because of their lives of sin, a rather unpalatable truth (cf. Rom. 2:1-3:20). The implication of original sin is here, but not in the form that God's wrath rests upon little children before they have committed acts of sin.

5. {*Quickened us together with Christ*} (cf. Col. 2:13). It is literal resurrection in the case of Jesus, spiritual in our case as pictured in baptism. {*By grace have ye been saved*} As a parenthesis, this is by the instrument of grace. The whole process is all of grace because we were dead.

8. {*For by grace*} Paul now gives the explanatory reason, the grace previously mentioned. {*Through faith*} This phrase he adds in repeating what he said in verse 5 to make it plainer. "Grace" is God's part, "faith" ours. {*And that*} Note "that" refers to the act of being saved by grace conditioned on faith on our part. Paul shows that salvation does not have its source in men, but from God.

9. {*That no man should glory*} It is all of God's grace.

10. {*Workmanship*} This is the Greek word *poiêma*. Old word from verb *poieô* with the ending "*ma*" meaning result (cf. Rev. 1:20). {*Created*} This is not the original creation (cf. Col. 1:16; Eph. 3:9), but the moral and spiritual renewal in Christ, the new birth, as in Ephesians 2:15; 4:24. {*Afore prepared*} Lit. "to make ready beforehand" (cf. Rom. 9:23). Good works by us were included in the eternal foreordination by God.

11. {*Uncircumcision...circumcision*} This refers to Gentiles and Jews (cf. Gal. 5:6; Rom. 2:27).

12. {*Separate from Christ*} This describes their former condition as heathen. {*Alienated from the commonwealth of Israel*} (cf. Col. 1:21, also Phil. 1:27). This refers to the spiritual Israel or Kingdom of God and Acts 22:28 as citizenship. {*Having no hope*} This is no hope of any kind (cf. Gal. 4:8 and 1 Thess. 4:5). {*Without God*} This is atheists in the original sense of being without God and also in the sense of hostility to God from failure to worship him (cf. Rom. 1:18-32).

13. {*Afar off...are made nigh*} That is, once far from the citizenship of spiritual Israel and its hope in God in Christ, and now near. {*In the blood of Christ*} An essential comment (Eph. 1:7), particularly in view of the Gnostic denial of Christ's real humanity.

14. {*For he is our peace*} To Jew and Gentile now one (John 10:16), this is not just what he did, but who he was and is. {*Both one*} This has a focus on oneness, unity, identity (cf. Gal. 3:28). Race and national distinctions vanish in Christ. {*Brake down the middle wall of partition*} In the temple courts a partition wall divided the court of the Gentiles from the court of Israel with an inscription forbidding a Gentile from going further. This also was a figurative wall of the enmity between Jew and Gentile as the middle wall of partition.

15. {*Having abolished*} Lit. "to make null and void." {*The twain*} Lit. "the two men" referring to Jew and Gentile. {*One new man*} Lit. "into one fresh man" (Col. 3:9-11). {*Making peace*} Christ is the peacemaker between men, nations, races, classes.

17. {*Preached peace*} Lit. "He gospelized peace" to near/Jew and far/Gentile. By the Cross Christ could preach that message.

18. {*Through him…we both*} Jew and Gentile receive the work of redemption through the Trinity (cf. Eph. 1:13).

20. {*Christ Jesus himself being the chief corner stone*} The Greek word is *akrogôniaios*; and here is the primary foundation-stone at the angle of the structure by which the architect fixes a standard for the bearings of the walls and cross-walls throughout.

21. {*Each several building*} Lit. "every building," perhaps referring to the various parts of the temple, without a definition of each part but the whole framing into a temple (1 Pet. 2:5).

22. {*Ye [Gentiles] also are builded together*} The Greek verb is *sunoikodomeô*, here meaning "to build together out of varied materials" (cf. 1 Pet. 2:5). {*For a habitation*} (cf. Eph. 3:17). Possibly each of us is meant here to be the "habitation of God in the Spirit" and all together growing "into a holy temple in the Lord," a noble conception of the brotherhood in Christ.

CHAPTER 3

1. {*For this cause*} The Greek phrase is *toutou charin.* Use of *charin* (accusative of *charis* [grace]) as a preposition with the genitive and referring to the preceding argument about God's elective grace.

2. {*If so be that ye have heard…stewardship*} This condition is assumed to be true (cf. Eph. 1:9; 3:9; Col. 1:25).

3. {*By revelation*} (cf. Gal. 1:12). Revelation was Paul's qualification for preaching "the mystery" (cf. Eph. 1:9).

5. {*In other generations*} Revelation has come not only to Paul, but all apostles and prophets of God.

6. Here are three "together" words in the verse: fellow-heirs (cf. Rom. 8:17); members (cf. Col. 1:7); sharers (like joint owners of a house).

8. {*Unto me who am less than the least of all saints*} This was not mock humility (15:19), for on occasion Paul stood up for his rights as an apostle (2 Cor. 11:5). {*The unsearchable riches of Christ*} Lit. "not + to track out," (cf. Job 5:9; 9:10, also Rom. 11:33).

10. {*Might be made known*} The mystery was made known to Paul (cf. Eph. 3:3) and now he wants it blazoned forth to all powers (Gnostic *aeons* or what not). {*The manifold wisdom of God*} Lit. "much-variegated, with many colors" (cf. Matt. 4:24).

13. {*That ye faint not*} Lit. "to behave badly in, to give in to evil" (cf. Luke 18:1; 2 Thess. 3:13; 2 Cor. 4:1, 16; Gal. 6:9) Paul uses all his apostolic authority to keep the readers from giving in to evil because of his tribulations for them.

14. {*I bow my knees*} He now prays whether he had at first intended. Kneeling was a common position as an attitude in prayer (Luke 22:41; Acts 7:40; 20:36; 21:5), though standing is also frequent (Mark 11:25; Luke 18:11, 13).

15. {*Every family*} Paul seems to mean that all the various classes of men on earth and of angels in heaven get the name of family from God the Father of all.

16. {*That he would grant you*} This is the greatest of all Paul's prayers. With five petitions in this letter: (1) Ephesians 1:16-23; (2) he may give strength; (3) You may give dwelling to Christ (v. 17); (4) you may have power to grasp (v. 18); (5) you may have power to know (v. 19).

17. {*That Christ may dwell…being rooted and grounded in love*} Lit. "to make one's home, to be at home." Christ is asked to make his home in our hearts. Paul piles up metaphors (dwelling, rooted, grounded).

18. {*That ye may be strong*} Lit. "to have full strength." {*With all the saints*} There is no isolated privilege. Fellowship open to all. Paul gives a rectangular (four dimension) measure of love (breadth, length, height, depth).

20. {*That is able to do*} Paul is fully aware of the greatness of the blessings asked for, but the Doxology ascribes to God the power to do them for us.

21. {*In the church*} This is the church universal, the body of Christ. {*And in Christ Jesus*} He is the Head of the glorious church.

CHAPTER 4

3. {*In the bond of peace*} (cf. Col. 3:14). But there is no peace without love (Eph. 4:2).

4. {*One body...one Spirit...in one hope*} This refers: (1) the mystical body of Christ, the spiritual church or kingdom (cf. Eph. 1:23; 2:16). (2) Holy Spirit. (3) The same hope for both Jew and Greek.

5. {*One Lord...one faith...one baptism*} This refers: (4) The Lord Jesus Christ and he alone (no series of *aeons*). (5) One act of trust in him for Jew and Greek. (6) There is only one act of baptism for all (Jews and Gentiles) who confess Christ by means of this symbol, not that they are made disciples by this one act, but merely so profess him, put Christ on publicly by this ordinance.

6. {*One God and Father of all*} This refers to the fact that there is not a separate God for each nation or religion. One God for all men. {***Who is over all and through all and in all***} Thus by three prepositions Paul has endeavored to express the universal power of God in human lives.

8. {***Wherefore he saith***} (cf. Ps. 68:18). This is a quote of a Messianic Psalm of victory which Paul adapts and interprets for Christ's triumph over death.

9. {***Into the lower parts of the earth***} If "ascended" is the Ascension of Christ, then this is the Incarnation (the Descent) to earth (cf. v. 10); also possible is the reference to the descent into Hades of Acts 2:31.

11. {***And he gave***} (cf. 1 Cor. 12:28). There are four groups here, we will deal with the meaning of the last. A pastor is a shepherd with an essential function of protection. Only here are preachers termed shepherds (cf. John 21:16). Here Paul groups "shepherds and teachers" together. All these gifts can be found in one man, though not always. Some have only one.

12. {***For the perfecting***} Translate, "for the mending (repair) of the saints" (cf. Matt. 4:21; Gal. 6:1). {***Unto the building up***} (cf. Eph. 2:21). This is the ultimate goal in all these varied gifts, "building up."

13. {***Till we all attain***} (cf. Phil. 3:11). "The whole" including every individual. Hence the need of so many gifts. {***Unto the unity of the faith***} (cf. Eph. 4:3). Lit. "Oneness of faith" (of trust) in Christ which the Gnostics were disturbing. {***And of the knowledge of the Son of God***} This is "full knowledge," in opposition to the Gnostic vagaries.

{*Unto a full-grown man*} (cf. Eph. 2:15; 4:14) This is in the sense of adult as opposed to infants. {*Unto the measure of the stature*} (cf. Eph. 3:19). Here is a picture of boys rejoicing in gaining the height of a man.

14. {*Tossed to and fro*} This is like in waves (cf. Jas. 1:6). {*Carried about*} Lit. "to carry round, whirled round." If not anchored by full knowledge of Christ, people are at the mercy of these squalls. {*By the sleight...in craftiness...after the wiles of error*} Paul has covered the whole ground in this picture of Gnostic error.

15. We are the body and Christ is the Head. We are to grow up to his stature.

16. {*Unto the building up of itself*} Modern knowledge of cell life in the human body greatly strengthens the force of Paul's metaphor. This is the way the body grows by cooperation under the control of the head and all "in love."

17. {*In vanity of their mind*} Lit. "In emptiness of their intellect" (cf. Rom. 8:20).

18. {*Being darkened...in their understanding*} This is the Greek verb *skotoô,* old verb from *skotos* darkness (cf. Rev. 9:2; 16:10). Understanding includes the emotions as well as the intellect. {*Hardening*} This is a late medical term (Hippocrates) for callous hardening (cf. Mark 3:5; Rom. 11:25).

19. {*Being past feeling*} This is the Greek verb *apalgeô,* to cease to feel pain. {*To lasciviousness*} This is unbridled lust (cf. 2 Cor. 12:21; Gal. 5:19). {*To work all uncleanness*} This perhaps refers to prostitution, "for a trading (or work) in all uncleanness." Certainly Corinth and Ephesus could qualify for this charge.

20. {*But ye did not so learn Christ*} This is in sharp contrast to pagan life.

21. {*If so be that*} Lit. "if indeed." This a condition assumed to be true. {*Even as truth is in Jesus*} Cerinthian Gnostics did distinguish between the man Jesus and the *aeon* Christ. So there may be significance that Paul flatly affirms that there is "truth in Jesus."

24. {*The new man*} (cf. Eph. 2:15; Col. 3:10). This is the brand-new man. {*After God*} This is after the pattern God, the new birth, the new life in Christ, destined to be like God in the end (Rom. 8:29).

26. {*Be ye angry and sin not*} (Ps. 4:4). Paul is giving a permission to be angry, not a command. But there is a prohibition against sinning as the peril in anger. {*Let not the sun go down upon your wrath*} There is danger in settled mood of anger.

27. {*Neither give place to the devil*} (Rom. 12:19). The Greek syntax means either, "stop doing it" or "do not have the habit."

28. {*Steal no more*} This means "cease stealing."

29. {*Corrupt*} This is what is rotten, putrid, like fruit (Matt. 7:17), fish (Matt. 13:48), here the opposite of "good."

30. {*Grieve not the Holy Spirit of God*} The Greek syntax means either "cease grieving" or "do not have the habit of grieving." {*Ye were sealed*} (cf. Eph. 1:13-14). This is until the day when final redemption is realized.

31. {*Clamour*} (cf. Col. 3:8). This is the Greek word *kraugê,* an old word for outcry (Matt. 25:6; Luke 1:42).

32. {*Be ye kind to one another*} (cf. Col. 3:12). Greek syntax translates, "keep on becoming kind" (cf. Rom. 2:4).

CHAPTER 5

2. {*An offering and a sacrifice to God*} Christ's death was an offering to God "in our behalf" not an offering to the devil (Anselm), a ransom as Christ himself said (Matt. 20:28), Christ's own view of his atoning death.

4. {*Jesting*} This is the Greek word *eutrapelia,* from *eutrapelos,* nimbleness of wit, quickness in making repartee, but in low sense as here ribaldry, scurrility.

5. {*Ye know of a surety*} There are two Greek words for "knowing" here. Why? Probably this means, "you know recognizing by your own experience."

6. {*With empty words*} (cf. Col. 2:4; Eph. 2:2). Probably Paul has in mind the same Gnostic praters.

7. {*Partakers with them*} This refers to being partners with these Gnostics.

11. {*Unfruitful*} (cf. Eph 5:9). Now a mixing of metaphor of fruit and darkness. {*Reprove*} This means to convict by turning the light on the darkness.

13. {*Are made manifest by the light*} Turn on the light. Often the preacher is the only man brave enough to turn the light on the private sins of men and women or even those of a community.

14. {*Shall shine*} (cf. Job 25:5; 31:26). The last line suggests the possibility that we have here the fragment of an early Christian hymn (cf. 1 Tim. 3:16).

17. {*Be ye not foolish*} The Greek syntax translates, "Stop becoming foolish."

18. {*Be not drunken with wine...but be filled with the Spirit*} This is the Greek verb *methuskô*, to intoxicate. The syntax means to be forbidden as a habit and to stop it also if guilty. Spirit filling is in contrast to a state of intoxication with wine.

19. {*To the Lord*} (cf. Col. 3:16). This verse shows varieties of praise, another proof of the deity of Christ.

20. {*In the name of our Lord Jesus Christ*} Jesus had told the disciples to use his name in prayer (John 16:23).

21. {*Subjecting yourselves to one another*} This is an old military figure to line up under (Col. 3:18). It is possible to start a new paragraph here.

25. {*Even as Christ also loved the church*} This is the wonderful new point not in Colossians 3:19 that lifts this discussion of the husband's love for his wife to the highest plane.

26. {*That he might sanctify it*} Jesus stated this as his longing and his prayer (John 17:17-19). This was the purpose of Christ's death (Eph. 5:25). {*By the washing of water*} (cf. 1 Cor. 6:11; Titus 3:5). This can mean either "bathing" or "washing." The reference here seems to be to the baptismal bath (immersion) of water, "in the bath of water."

27. {*That he might present...glorious*} (cf. Col. 1:22; also 2 Cor. 11:2). As if in splendid clothing, this is Christ's goal, for purity, being holy and blameless, and not being wrinkled and spotted.

31. {*For this cause*} (Gen. 2:24) Lit. "answering to this." This whole verse is a practical quotation and application of the language to Paul's argument here (cf. Matt. 19:5).

32. {*This mystery is great*} (cf. Eph. 1:9). Clearly Paul means to say that the comparison of marriage to the union of Christ and the church is the mystery.

33. {*Nevertheless*} Lit. "Howbeit," not to dwell unduly on the matter of Christ and the church. {*Let the wife see that she fear*} Lit. "fear" but here it means "reverence."

CHAPTER 6

2. {*The first commandment with promise*} (cf. Exod. 20:12). Some take it to be "first" because it was taught first to children.

4. {*Provoke not to anger*} (cf. Rom. 10:19; also Col. 3:21). These are quotations from the LXX. The active, as here, has a causative sense. Paul touches the common sin of fathers. {*In the chastening and admonition of the Lord*} This may be general instruction and culture of the child (and adults in 2 Tim. 3:16); though it can be in a narrower sense of "chastening" (Heb. 12:5, 7, 11). {*Instruction*} This word does have the idea of correction (cf. 1 Cor. 10:11; Titus 3:10).

6. {*But as servants of Christ*} (cf. Phil. 1:1). {*Doing the will of God*} This is even while slaves of men.

8. {*Whatsoever good thing each one doeth*} Lit. "each one if he do anything good."

9. {*And forbear threatening*} Lit. "Letting up on threatening." {*Both their Master and yours*} He says to "the lords" of the slaves. Paul is not afraid of capital or labor.

10. {*Finally*} Lit. "in respect of the rest" (cf. 2 Thess. 3:1; Phil. 3:1; 4:8).

11. {*The whole armour*} Compare our word "panoply" (cf. Luke 11:22; Eph. 6:11, 13). Complete armor in this period included "shield, sword, lance, helmet, greaves, and breastplate." Paul adds belt and shoes to the list, not armor but necessary for the soldier. {*The wiles of the devil*} (cf. Eph. 4:14). He is a crafty foe and knows the weak spots in the Christian's armor.

12. {*Our wrestling is not*} The Greek word is *palê*, from *pallô*, to throw, to swing, a contest between two until one hurls the other down and holds him down. We sorely need the full armor of God.

14. {*Stand therefore*} Translate the Greek tense, "Take your stand therefore" (in view of the arguments made). {*Having girded your loins with truth*} Greek action translates, "having girded your own loins."

15. {*Having shod*} Lit. "Having bound under" (sandals) (Mark 6:9; Acts 12:8, only other NT example). {*With the preparation*} Readiness of mind that comes from the gospel whose message is peace.

16. {*The shield of faith*} "Shield" is a late word in this sense a large stone against the door in Homer, from the Greek word *thura*, door, large and oblong. {*To quench*} (cf. Matt. 12:20). {*All the fiery darts*}

These darts were sometimes ablaze in order to set fire to the enemies' clothing or camp or homes.

17. {*Which is the word of God*} The sword given by the Spirit to be wielded as offensive weapon (the others defensive) by the Christian is the word of God. See Hebrews 4:12 where the word of God is called "sharper than any two-edged sword."

18. {*At all seasons*} Prayer is needed in this fight "on all occasions."

20. {*For which I am an ambassador in chains*} (cf. 2 Cor. 5:20). Paul is now an old man (*presbutês,* Phlm. 9) and feels the dignity of his position as Christ's ambassador.

23. {*Love and faith*} This is love of the brotherhood accompanied by faith in Christ and as an expression of it.

24. {*In uncorruptness*} Lit. "never diminishing" referring to love (cf. 1 Cor. 15:42).

The Epistle to the Philippians

Author: Paul, servant of Christ
Recipients: Christians of Philippi
Date: About A.D. 61
From: Rome
Occasion: From prison, Paul gives thanks to the Philippians for their gift and seeks to clear up any quarrels in the church.
Theme: Joy in the new life in Christ, in all circumstance

By Way of Introduction

Philemon, Colossians, Ephesians were written close to the time of this epistle, before or afterwards. But there was time for Epaphroditus to come to Rome, to fall sick, for the news to reach Philippi and for Epaphroditus to hear of their concern about him. The church in Philippi was Paul's joy and pride and they had helped him before as they did this time.

The Epistle is a beautiful expression of gratitude for the love and gifts of the Philippian saints. For Paul, death looms, but still he has a note of joy running through the epistle. He hopes to be set free and to see them again.

Chapter 1

1. {*With the bishops*} The Greek word is *episkopos,* singled out from "all the saints," which is equal to and "elder" (cf. Acts 20:17, 28). The plural is here employed because there was usually one church in a city with several pastors (bishops, elders). {*And deacons*} Here it is the church officer (1 Tim. 3:8-13), not a general "servant" (cf. Matt. 22:13).
4. {*With joy*} Paul is a happy prisoner as in Philippi when he and Silas sang praises at midnight though in prison (Acts 16:25).
5. {*For your fellowship*} Translate, "On the basis of your contribution" (cf. 2 Cor. 8:4; 9:13; Acts 2:42), a particular kind of partnership.
6. {*Being confident*} The Greek verb is *peithô,* to persuade. {*This very thing*} Translate the full Greek "this thing itself." {*Will perfect it*} Lit. "fully finish." God began and God will consummate it but not without their cooperation and partnership (2 Cor. 8:6; Gal. 3:3).

7. {*Because I have you in my heart*} Lit. "because of the holding me (or you) in the heart as to you (or me)." The idea is love begets love. {*In the defence*} This is our word "apology," but not our idea of apologizing (cf. Acts 22:1; 25:16, also Phil. 1:16).

8. {*My witness*} This is a solemn oath (cf. Rom. 1:9). {*In the tender mercies*} Lit. "in the bowels" as the seat of the affections.

9. {*May abound*} This is the Greek verb *perisseuô,* may keep on overflowing, a perpetual flood of love, "yet more and more."

10. {*Approve the things that are excellent*} Originally, "test the things that differ" (cf. Rom. 2:28). The verb "approve" was used for assaying metals. The first step is to distinguish between good and evil and that is not always easy in our complex civilization. {*Sincere*} Lit. "to judge by sunlight" or "to sift by rapid rolling." At any rate it means pure, unsullied. {*Void of offence*} Probably, lit. "not stumbled against."

12. {*The things which happened unto me*} Lit. "The things concerning me" = "my affairs." {*Unto the progress*} It is a technical term in Stoic philosophy for "progress toward wisdom" and it appears also in the papyri and the LXX (cf. Phil. 1:25; 1 Tim. 4:15).

13. {*Throughout the whole praetorian guard*} Lit. "praetorian guard" These picked soldiers, concentrated in Rome by Tiberius, had double pay and special privileges and became so powerful that emperors had to court their favor. Paul had contact with one after another of these soldiers. In the NT it means the palace of the provincial governor either in Jerusalem or Caesarea (Matt. 27:27; Mark 15:16; John 18:28, 33; 19:9; Acts 23:35). Some take it to mean the camp or barracks of the praetorian guard. The Greek, "in the whole praetorium," allows this meaning, though there is no clear example of it. At any rate Paul, chained to a soldier, had access to the soldiers and the officials.

16. {*Of love*} Lit. "out of love" to Paul as well as to Christ (cf. 1 Cor. 13:1ff.).

17. {*Of faction*} That is, out of partisanship. This is the Greek word *eritheuô,* to spin wool, and that from *erithos,* a hireling (cf. 2 Cor. 12:20; Gal. 5:20). {*Not sincerely*} "Not purely," that is with mixed and impure motives. {*To raise up affliction for my bonds*} Now that Paul is down they jump on him in mean and nagging ways.

18. {*What then?*} This is a sharp problem put up to Paul by the conduct of the Judaizers. {*Whether in pretence...*} (cf. Acts 27:30). Paul sees clearly through the pious pretense of these Judaizers and rejoices that people get some knowledge of Christ. Some knowledge of Christ is better than no knowledge of him. {*Yea, and will rejoice*} Paul is determined to rejoice in spite of the efforts of the Judaizers to prod him to anger.

19. {*To my salvation*} This may refer to his release from prison as he strongly hopes to see them again (Phil. 1:26), or eternal salvation (cf. Phil. 1:20). Does it refer to both?

20. {*Shall be magnified*} Lit. "to make great" (Acts 19:17). {*In my body*} (cf. Rom. 12:1). It is harder often to make Christ great in the body than in the spirit.

21. {*To live is Christ*} Living is coextensive with Christ. {*Gain*} This is the Greek word *kerdos*. This is an old word for any gain or profit, interest on money (Phil. 3:7; Titus 1:11). {*To die*} This is to cash in both principal and interest and so to have more of Christ than when living. So Paul faces death with independence and calm courage.

22. {*I wot not*} (cf. Luke 2:15; Rom. 9:22). That is, "I know not." This may mean more than just "to know"; it very well may mean to make known, "to declare." Translate the entire phrase, "I do not declare what I shall choose."

23. {*I am in a strait*} Lit. "I am held together." Translate "I am hemmed in on both sides" (Luke 8:45). {*Betwixt the two*} Lit. "From the two (sides)." Pressure to live on, pressure to die and be with Christ. {*To depart*} (cf. Luke 12:36). Used in other non-biblical contexts "to break up camp, to weigh anchor and put out to sea, to depart" (cf. taking down a tent; cf. 2 Cor. 5:1).

27. {*Let your manner of life*} (cf. Acts 23:1) This the Greek verb *politeuomai*, from *politês*, citizen, and that from *polis*, city, to be a citizen, to manage a state's affairs, to live as a citizen. Philippi as a colony possessed Roman citizenship and Paul was proud of his own possession of this right. Better render, "Only do you live as citizens."

28. {*Affrighted*} The metaphor is of a timid or scared horse. Translate, "not startled in anything." {*By the adversaries*} (cf. 2 Thess. 2:4) These men who were lined up against may have been Jews or Gentiles or both. {*Evident token*} This is an old term for "proof," "an Attic law term" (Kennedy) (cf. 2 Cor. 8:24; Rom. 3:25).

29. {*In the behalf of Christ*} Lit. "the in behalf of Christ." But Paul divides the idea and uses the article "to" again both with "believe" and with "suffer." Suffering in behalf of Christ is one of God's gifts to us.

CHAPTER 2

1. {*Fellowship*} This is the Greek word *koinônia*, a partnership in the Holy Spirit "whose first fruit is love" (Gal. 5:22). {*Any tender mercies*} This word is used for the nobler viscera and so for the higher emotions.

2. {*Fulfil*} Better to translate here, "fill full." Paul's cup of joy will be full if the Philippians will only keep on having unity of thought and feeling. {*Being of one accord*} Lit. "harmonious in soul"; these are souls that beat together, in tune with Christ and with each other. {*Of one mind*} Lit. "thinking the one thing." Like clocks that strike at the same moment. Identity of ideas and harmony of feelings.

3. {*Through vainglory*} This is empty pride (cf. Gal. 5:26). {*In lowliness of mind*} Though a false humility exists (cf. Col. 2:18, 23), here it is an ennobled and dignified virtue (cf. Acts 20:19; Matt. 11:29 and 1 Pet. 3:8).

4. {*Looking*} Not keeping an eye on the main chance for number one, but for the good of others.

5. {*Have this mind in you*} The Greek tense translate, "keep on thinking this in you which was also in Christ Jesus." This refers to humility. Paul presents Jesus as the supreme example of humility.

6. {*Being*} Translate "existing." {*The form of a servant*} "Form" is the Greek word *morphê* means the essential attributes as shown in the form. In his preincarnate state Christ possessed the attributes of God and so appeared to those in heaven who saw him. {*A prize*} Paul means a prize to be held on to rather than something to be won ("robbery"). {*To be on an equality with God*} Lit. "the being equal with God" (cf. Rev. 21:16). {*Emptied himself*} Christ gave up his environment of glory. He took upon himself limitations of place (space) and of knowledge and power, though still on earth retaining more of these than any mere man.

7. {*In the likeness of men*} It was a likeness, but a real likeness, no mere phantom humanity as the Docetic Gnostics held.

8. {*He humbled himself*} It is a voluntary humiliation on the part of Christ and for this reason Paul is pressing the example of Christ upon the Philippians, this supreme example of renunciation. {*Obedient*} Lit. "giving ear to" (cf. Acts 7:39; 2 Cor. 2:9). {*Unto death... Yea, the death of the cross*} The bottom rung in the ladder from the Throne of

God. Jesus came all the way down to the most despised death of all, a condemned criminal on the accursed cross.

9. {*Highly exalted*} God lifted him above or beyond the state of glory which he enjoyed before the Incarnation. Christ's humanity was the glory taken back to heaven, returning now as both Son of God and Son of Man.

10. {*That in the name of Jesus every knee should bow*} These are not perfunctory genuflections whenever the name of Jesus is mentioned, but universal acknowledgment of the majesty and power of Jesus who carries his human name and nature to heaven (cf. Rom. 8:22; Eph. 1:20-22 and in particular Rev. 5:13).

12. {*Work out*} Lit. "work on to the finish." This exhortation assumes human free agency in carrying on the work of one's salvation. {*With fear and trembling*} That is, not slavish terror, but wholesome, serious caution. This is a nervous and trembling anxiety to do right (Lightfoot). Paul makes no attempt to reconcile divine sovereignty and human free agency, but boldly proclaims both.

13. {*Which worketh in you*} God is the Energy and the Energizer of the universe. {*Both to will and to work*} God does it all, then. Yes, but he puts us to work also and our part is essential.

15. {*That ye may be*} Translate, "that ye may become." {*Harmless*} This means "unmixed, unadulterated" (cf. Rom. 16:19). {*Without blemish*} Lit. "without spot," and so unblemished in reputation and in reality. {*Perverse*} Lit. "to distort, to twist, to turn to one side" (Matt. 17:17; Acts 13:10).

16. {*As lights in the world*} This refers to luminaries like the heavenly bodies. Christians are the light of the world (Matt. 5:14) as they reflect the light from Christ (John 1:4; 8:12).

17. {*And if I am offered*} (cf. 2 Tim. 4:6). Paul pictures his lifeblood as being poured upon the sacrifice and service of the faith of the Philippians in mutual service and joy.

22. {*The proof*} This is "the test" as of metals (2 Cor. 2:9; 9:13). Three times they had seen Timothy (Acts 16:13; 19:22; 20:3).

23. {*How it will go with me*} Lit. "The things concerning me," that is, the outcome of the trial (cf. 1 Cor. 4:17, 19).

25. {*Messenger*} Lit. "apostle" in non-technical sense of messenger [missionary] (cf. 2 Cor. 8:23).

26. {*Was sore troubled*} This is the Greek word *adêmoneô* either from an unused *adêmôn* (*a* "not" + *dêmos,* "away from home, homesick") or from *adêmôn, adêsai* ("discontent, bewilderment"). In any case the distress of Epaphroditus was greatly increased when he knew that the Philippians (the homefolks) had learned of his illness. {*He was sick*} The Greek tense translates "he did become sick."

29. {*In honour*} Lit. "prized, precious" (Luke 7:2; 14:8; 1 Pet. 2:4, 6). This is a noble plea in behalf of Christ's minister.

30. {*Hazarding his life*} This is the Greek word *paraboleuô* (from the adjective *parabolos*), to place beside. Its meaning here is "exposing himself to danger."

CHAPTER 3

2. {*Beware*} Three times in this verse for urgency and with different epithet for the Judaizers each time. {*The dogs*} Paul here turns the phrase on the Judaizers themselves. {*The concision*} This is "incision, mutilation" in contrast with circumcision (cf. Lev. 21:5; 1 Kgs. 18:28).

3. {*For we*} We believers in Christ, the children of Abraham by faith, whether Jew or Gentile, the spiritual circumcision in contrast to the merely physical (Rom. 2:25-29; Col. 2:11; Eph. 2:11). {*In the flesh*} This is a technical term in Paul's controversy with the Judaizers (2 Cor. 11:18; Gal. 6:13). External privileges beyond mere flesh.

5. {*Thinketh to have confidence*} Translate, "seems to himself to have confidence." {*I yet more*} That is, "I have more ground for boasting than he" (cf. Phil. 3:5-6). {*Circumcised the eighth day*} Ishmaelites were circumcised in the thirteenth year, proselytes from Gentiles in mature age, Jews on the eighth day (Luke 2:21). {*Of the stock of Israel*} That is, not a proselyte. {*Benjamin*} (cf. Judg. 5:14). King Saul was from this little tribe and it was Paul's own Hebrew name. {*A Hebrew of the Hebrews*} He was not a Hellenized Jew, with its distinct language and customs (cf. Acts 6:1) though he knew the Greek language (Acts 21:40; 22:2). {*A Pharisee*} (cf. Gal. 1:14) Not a Sadducee, Paul continued a Pharisee in many essential matters like the doctrine of the resurrection (Acts 23:6). Cf. 2 Cor. 11:22.

6. {*As touching zeal*} He was a zealot against Christianity, and ringleader in the persecution from the death of Stephen until his own conversion (Acts 8:1-9:9). {*Found blameless*} (cf. Gal. 1:14). He knew and practiced all the rules of the rabbis. A marvelous record, scoring a hundred in Judaism.

7. {*Were gain to me*} Lit. plural "Were gains." Paul had natural pride in his Jewish attainments. He was the star of hope for Gamaliel and the Sanhedrin.

8. {*Yea, verily, and*} This Greek phrase shows the force and passion of his conviction (cf. Phil. 2:3). {*Dung*} This is the Greek word *skubalon*. This is a late word of uncertain etymology, either connected with *skôr* (dung) or from *es kunas ballô*, to fling to the dogs and so refuse of any kind. {*That I may gain Christ*} Paul was never satisfied with his knowledge of Christ and always craved more fellowship with him.

10. {*That I may know him*} This means to have personal acquaintance or experience with. This is Paul's major passion, to get more knowledge of Christ by experience. {*The power of his resurrection*} Power in the sense of assurance to believers in immortality (Lightfoot) (1 Cor. 15:14; Rom. 8:11), in the triumph over sin (Rom. 4:24), in the dignity of the body (1 Cor. 6:13; Phil. 3:21), in stimulating the moral and spiritual life (Gal. 2:20; Rom. 6:4; Col. 2:12; Eph. 2:5). {*The fellowship of his sufferings*} This is partnership in his sufferings, an honor prized by Paul (Col. 1:24). {*Becoming conformed to his death*} This is the Greek verb *summorphizô*, from *summorphos* (cf. Rom. 6:4).

11. {*If by any means I may attain*} This is not an expression of doubt, but of humility (Vincent), a modest hope (Lightfoot). {*Resurrection*} Apparently, Paul is thinking here only of the resurrection of believers out from the dead, yet not denying a general resurrection.

12. {*I have already obtained*} Translates, "I did already obtain," summing up all his previous experiences as a single event. {*Or am already made perfect*} Paul has made great progress in Christ-likeness, but the goal is still before him, not behind him.

13. {*To have apprehended*} Lit. "to grasp completely." {*Forgetting the things which are behind*} Paul can mean either his old pre-Christian life, his previous progress as a Christian, or both (all of it). {*Stretching forward*} This is the Greek verb *epekteinô*, stretching myself out towards. This is a metaphor of a runner leaning forward as he runs.

14. {*Toward the goal*} Lit. "Down upon the goal," who is Jesus himself to whom we must continually look as we run (Heb. 12:2). The word means a watchman, then the goal or mark.

15. {*Let us be thus minded*} The Greek tense translates, "Let us keep on thinking this," namely, that we have not yet attained absolute perfection.

17. {*An ensample*} The Greek word is *tupon,* originally the impression left by a stroke (John 20:25), then a pattern (mold) as here (cf. 1 Thess. 1:7; 1 Cor. 10:6, 11; Rom. 5:14; 6:17).

18. {*Even weeping*} This shows deep emotion as he dictated the letter and recalled these apostate followers of Christ (cf. 2 Cor. 2:4). {*The enemies of the cross of Christ*} This refers to either: (1) Judaizers who denied the value of the cross of Christ (Gal. 5:11; 6:12, 14); or (2) Epicurean antinomians whose loose living gave the lie to the cross of Christ (1 John 2:4).

19. {*Whose god is their belly*} This refers to sensuality in food, drink, sex then as now, which has mastered some people.

20. {*Our citizenship*} (cf. Phil. 1:27) Paul was proud of his Roman citizenship and found it a protection. The Philippians were also proud of their Roman citizenship. But Christians are citizens of a kingdom not of this world (John 18:36). {*We wait for*} This word vividly pictures Paul's eagerness for the second coming of Christ.

21. {*According to the working*} Lit. "according to the energy." If any one doubts the power of Christ to do this transformation, Paul replies that he has power "even to subject all things unto himself."

CHAPTER 4

1. {*So stand fast*} (cf. Phil. 1:27). They were tempted to defection. Standing firm is difficult when a panic starts.

2. {*Euodia...Syntyche*} Possibly each of these rival women (possibly of rank or deaconesses) had church assemblies in their homes, one a Jewish-Christian church, the other a Gentile-Christian church. Or "it may have been accidental friction between two energetic Christian women" (Kennedy).

3. {*True yokefellow*} Some have suggested this peacemaker refers to a proper name though it is not found in the inscriptions; some suggest this is a title for Epaphroditus.

4. {*Rejoice...rejoice*} As a command, "keep on rejoicing," repeated for emphasis in spite of discouragements.

5. {*Your forbearance*} Some translate, "your sweet reasonableness" and "your moderation" (cf. Jas. 3:17; 1 Tim. 3:3). {*The Lord is at hand*} Near in time (cf. *Maran atha* 1 Cor. 16:22); or near in space.

6. {*In nothing be anxious*} The Greek tense translates, "stop being anxious" (cf. Matt. 6:31).

7. {*Shall guard*} (cf. Acts 9:24; 2 Cor. 11:32). Translate, "shall garrison." God's peace as a sentinel mounts guard over our lives.

8. {*Honourable*} This means, "revered, venerated" (1 Tim. 3:8). {*Pure*} This refers to things clean: thoughts, words, deeds. {*Lovely*} This means "pleasing, winsome." {*Of good report*} Lit. "fair-speaking, attractive." {*Virtue*} (cf. Isa. 42:12; 43:21 [LXX]; Phil. 4:8; 1 Pet. 2:9; 2 Pet. 1:3, 5). This is the Greek word *aretê*, possibly from *areskô*, to please, used very often in a variety of senses by the ancients for any mental excellence or moral quality or physical power. {*Think on these things*} This is a command, and the Greek tense has a focus of habit of thought. We are responsible for our thoughts and can hold them to high and holy ideals.

9. {*In me*} Paul dares to point to his life in Philippi as an illustration of this high thinking. {*These things do*} The Greek tense has a focus of practicing as a habit.

10. {*I rejoice*} The Greek tense has a timeless focus, "I did rejoice, I do rejoice." {*Ye have revived*} This is the Greek verb *anathallô*, to sprout again, to shoot up, to blossom again, referring to their thinking as renewing.

11. {*I have learned*} This is simply "I did learn." Paul is looking at his long experience as a unit. {*To be content*} This is the Greek word *autarkês* (cf. 2 Cor. 9:8; 1 Tim. 6:6). Paul is contented with his lot and he learned that lesson long ago.

12. {*Have I learned the secret*} Similar to our word "mystery," this means "to instruct in secrets." Paul draws this metaphor from the initiatory rites of the pagan mystery religions.

13. {*In him that strengtheneth me*} (cf. 1 Tim. 1:12). Paul has such strength so long as Jesus keeps on putting power into him.

14. {*That ye had fellowship*} Translate, "you did well contributing for my affliction."

15. {*In the matter*} Lit. "As to an account." No other church opened an account with Paul.

17. {*I seek for*} The apostle has nervous anxiety to clear himself of wanting more gifts.

19. {*According to his riches in glory*} God has an abundant treasure in glory and will repay the Philippians for what they have done for Paul.

22. {*They that are of Caesar's household*} This is not members of the imperial family, but some connected with the imperial establishment, ranging from slaves to even to the highest functionaries. Christianity has begun to undermine the throne of the Caesars. Some day a Christian will sit on this throne.

THE EPISTLE TO THE COLOSSIANS

AUTHOR: Apostle Paul
DATE: Probably A.D. 63
FROM: Rome
OCCASION: To fight false teachings about the deity of Christ
THEME: The Dignity of Christ as the Head of the Church and the deity of Christ

BY WAY OF INTRODUCTION

There is every mark of Paul's style and power in this Epistle, written at the same time as Ephesians and Philemon. This was written between the time of Acts 28 and the burning of Rome in A.D. 64

The Epistle itself gives it as being due to the arrival of Epaphras from Colossae (Col. 1:7-9; 4:12ff.). He is probably one of Paul's converts while in Ephesus who in behalf of Paul (Col. 1:7) evangelized the Lycus Valley (Colossae, Hierapolis, Laodicea) where Paul had never been himself (Col. 2:1; 4:13-16). Since Paul's departure for Rome, the "grievous wolves" whom he foresaw in Miletus (Acts 20:29ff.) had descended upon these churches and were playing havoc with many and leading them astray much as new cults today mislead the unwary.

Gnosticism was a world-view that sought to explain everything on the assumption that matter was essentially evil and that the good God could only touch evil matter by means of a series of *aeons* or emanations so far removed from him as to prevent contamination by God and yet with enough power to create evil matter.

Paul had won his fight for freedom in Christ against the Judaizers, now he must fight philosophic speculation found in the cults of the Gnostics (Docetic and Cerinthian), Eleusinian mysteries, and Mithraism.

In particular, there were false teachings about the person of Christ: Docetics held that Jesus did not have a real human body, but only a phantom body and no real humanity; Cerinthians admitted the humanity of the man Jesus, but claimed that the Christ was an *aeon* that came on Jesus at his baptism in the form of a dove and left him on the Cross so that only the man Jesus died (cf. Phil. 2:5-11).

So then Colossians seems written expressly for our own day when so many are trying to rob Jesus Christ of his deity, as did the Gnostics then. Knowledge of Gnosticism is one of the keys to understanding Colossians.

CHAPTER 1

2. {*At Colossae*} Colossae was a city of Phrygia on the Lycus River; Hierapolis and Laodicea are some ten or twelve miles away.

4. {*Having heard of* } This is a literary plural unless Timothy is included. {*Which ye have*} The love is directed towards all the saints, not in the sphere of all the saints.

5. {*Because of the hope*} (cf. Rom. 8:24). This phrase is more likely linked to "the love" of verse four. Note "faith, love, and hope" are loosely grouped here. {*Laid up*} Lit. "laid away or by" (cf. 1 Tim. 6:19; also Matt. 6:20, 1 Pet. 1:4). {*In the word of the truth of the gospel*} (cf. Gal. 2:5, 14). They heard the pure gospel from Epaphras before the Gnostics came.

6. {*In all the world*} The gospel was spreading all over the Roman Empire. {*Is bearing fruit...increasing*} As the Greek emphasizes, the growing and the fruit bearing go on simultaneously as always with Christians (inward growth and outward expression). {*Ye heard and knew*} They heard the gospel from Epaphras and at once recognized and accepted. They fully apprehended the grace of God and should be immune to the shallow vagaries of the Gnostics.

7. {*Of Epaphras*} Lit. "from Epaphras," the source of their knowledge of Christ.

8. {*Who also declared*} This is the Greek verb *dêloô*, to make manifest. Epaphras told Paul about their "love in the Spirit."

9. {*That ye may be filled with...the knowledge of his will*} "Full knowledge" is the keynote of Paul's reply to the conceit of Gnosticism. The cure for these intellectual upstarts is not ignorance, not obscurantism, but more knowledge of the will of God. {*In all spiritual wisdom and understanding*} (cf. Eph. 1:8). Paul faces Gnosticism with full front and wishes the freest use of all one's intellectual powers in interpreting Christianity.

10. {*In the knowledge of God*} Translates, "by means of the full knowledge of God." This is the way for fruit bearing and growth to come (cf.

Col 1:6). {*Unto all pleasing*} In order to please God in all things
(1 Thess. 4:1). The Greek word is *areskia,* from *areskeuô,* to be complai-
sant, and usually in bad sense (obsequiousness); here in a good sense.
11. {*Strengthened...power*} Lit. " empowered with all power" (cf. Heb.
11:34). {*According to the might of his glory*} "Might" is an old word
for perfect strength, in NT it is applied only to God. Here his might is
accompanied by glory (*Shekinah*).
12. {*Who made us meet*} (cf. 2 Cor. 3:6). Translates, "who made us fit
or adequate for." {*To be partakers*} Lit. "For a share in" (cf. Acts 8:21;
16:12; 2 Cor. 6:15). {*Of the inheritance*} Lit. "of the lot," "for a share
of the lot." First a pebble or piece of wood used in casting lots (Acts
1:26), then the allotted portion or inheritance as here (Acts 8:21).
13. {*Delivered*} The Father's redemptive work marks the transition to
the wonderful picture of the person and work of Christ in nature and
grace in Colossians 1:14 to 20, a full and final answer to the Gnostic
depreciation of Jesus Christ (see also Introduction). {*Translated*} (cf.
1 Cor. 13:2). He has changed us from the kingdom of darkness to the
kingdom of light. {*Of the Son of his love*} Probably, "the Son who is
the object of the Father's love" (cf. Matt. 3:17). Paul here rules out the
whole system of *aeons* and angels that the Gnostics placed above Christ.
14. {*Our redemption*} (cf. Rom. 3:24). Lit. "buying back." This is a
release on payment of a ransom for slave or debtor (Heb. 9:15). {*The
forgiveness of our sins*} Lit. "sending away" of sins (cf. Eph. 1:7), and
so he buys us back, and then sends away the sin.
15. {*The image*} The Greek word is *eikôn* (2 Cor. 4:4; 3:18; Rom. 8:29;
Col. 3:10). Jesus is the very stamp of God the Father as he was before
the Incarnation (John 17:5) and is now (Phil. 2:5-11; Heb. 1:3). {*Of the
invisible God*} But the one who sees Jesus has seen God (John 14:9,
cf. Rom. 1:20). {*The first born*} The Greek word is *prôtotokos* (cf. John
1:1-18; Heb. 1:1-4; Phil. 2:5-11). By using this word, Paul did not regard
Christ as a creature like "all creation." It is rather the comparative (superlative) force of *prôtos* (cf. Col. 1:18; Rom. 8:29; Heb. 1:6; 12:23; Rev.
1:5). "Image" shows the relationship to the Father; "firstborn" shows
the relationship to the universe.
16. {*In him were created*} (cf. John 1:3; Heb. 1:2). The whole of creative activity is summed up in Christ including the angels in heaven
and everything on earth, and is a complete denial of the Gnostic philosophy.

17. {*Before all things*} Clearly, Christ is before both in time and pre-eminence as Creator. Jesus is eternal (John 8:58, 17:5; Rev. 22:13; 2 Cor. 8:9; Phil. 2:6). {*Consist*} The Greek verb is *sunistêmi,* to place together and here to cohere, to hold together (cf. Col. 1:16). Christ is the controlling and unifying force in nature. The Gnostic philosophy that matter is evil and was created by a remote *aeon* is thus swept away.

18. {*The head of the body*} Jesus is first not only over nature, but spiritual (1 Cor. 11:3; 12:12, 27; Rom. 12:5. See further Col. 1:24: 2:19; Eph. 1:22; 4:2, 15; 5:30). Body is but one figure of the kingdom of Christ. {*The beginning*} Christ has priority in time and in power (cf. in creation Rev. 3:14; first in resurrection 1 Cor. 15:20, 23). {*That in all things he might have the preeminence*} Lit. "to hold the first place." Christ is first in time and in rank.

19. {*For it was the good pleasure of the Father*} "Father" supplied in the context (Matt. 3:17; 1 Cor. 10:5). {*All the fulness*} (cf. Col. 2:9) This is a recognized technical term in theology, denoting the totality of the Divine powers and attributes. The Gnostics distributed the divine powers among various *aeons.* Paul gathers them all up in Christ.

20. {*Through him...*} He is the sufficient and chosen agent in the work of complete reconciliation for the universe (cf. Col. 1:22; Eph. 2:16, also 2 Cor. 5:18-20; Rom. 5:10). {*Through the blood of his cross*} Paul speaks this for the benefit of the Docetic Gnostics who denied the real humanity of Jesus and as clearly stating the *causa medians* of the work of reconciliation to be the Cross of Christ, a doctrine needed today.

21. {*Being in time past alienated*} The Greek verb is *apallotrioô,* to estrange, to render *allotrios* (belonging to another), alienated from God, a vivid picture of Heathenism as in Romans 1:20-23, also Ephesians 2:12; 4:18.

22. {*Yet now*} "Now" being not at the present moment, but in the present order of things in the new dispensation of grace in Christ. {*In the body of his flesh*} (cf. Col. 2:11; Eph. 2:14). Apparently Paul combines both "body" and "flesh" to make plain the actual humanity of Jesus against incipient Docetic Gnostics who denied it. {*Through death*} (cf. Col. 1:20). The reconciliation was accomplished by means of Christ's death on the cross and not just by the Incarnation. {*To present*} Lit. "to place beside in many connections" (cf. Acts 23:33; Col. 2:28; see also 2 Cor. 11:2; 4:14).

23. {*Grounded*} This is to be "laid down as a foundation" (cf. 1 Cor. 3:11). This is a picture of the saint as a building (cf. Eph. 2:20). {*Steadfast*} (cf. 1 Cor. 7:37; 15:58). This is a metaphor of seated in a chair. {*In all creation*} The Greek word *ktisis* is the act of founding (Rom. 1:20) from *ktizô* (v. Col. 1:16), then a created thing (Rom. 1:25), then the sum of created things as here and Revelation 3:14. It is hyperbole, to be sure, but Paul does not say that all men are converted, but only that the message has been heralded abroad over the Roman Empire in a wider fashion than most people imagine.

24. {*That which is lacking*} "The leftovers," (cf. Luke 21:4; 1 Thess. 3:10; 2 Cor. 8:14; 9:12). {*For his body's sake*} As Paul showed in his exultation in suffering in 2 Corinthians 11:16-33, though not in the same sense in which Christ suffered and died for us as Redeemer.

25. {*According to the dispensation of God*} Lit. "According to the economy of God," "economy" from the verb, "to be a house steward" (cf. Luke 16:2-4; 1 Cor. 9:17; Eph. 1:9; 3:9). It was by God's stewardship that Paul was made a minister of Christ.

26. {*The mystery*} (cf. 1 Cor. 2:7). The Gnostics talked much of "mysteries." Paul takes their very word (already in common use, Matt. 13:11) and uses it for the gospel.

27. {*God was pleased*} "God willed" this change from hidden mystery to manifestation. {*To make known*} This is the crowning wonder to Paul that God had included the Gentiles in his redemptive grace (Eph. 3:1-2). He feels the high honor keenly and meets the responsibility humbly. {*Which*} Addressing Gentiles, this refers back to "mystery" and connects to "Christ *in* [not among] you the hope of glory." It is the personal experience and presence of Christ in the individual life of all believers (cf. Eph. 3:17).

28. {*We proclaim*} This refers to Paul, Timothy and all like-minded preachers against the Gnostic depreciation of Christ. {*Perfect*} Spiritual adults in Christ, no longer babes in Christ (Heb. 5:14), mature and ripened Christians (Col. 4:22; Eph. 4:13). The Gnostics used "perfect" of the one fully initiated into their mysteries.

29. {*Striving*} (cf. Col. 2:1). Lit. "to contend in athletic games, to agonize," a favorite metaphor with Paul who is now a prisoner.

CHAPTER 2

1. {*How greatly I strive*} Lit. "how great a contest I am having." Here it is an inward contest of anxiety (cf. 2 Cor. 11:28). Paul's concern extended beyond Colossae to Laodicea (Col. 4:16) and to Hierapolis (Col. 4:13), the three great cities in the Lycus Valley where Gnosticism was beginning to do harm.

2. {*Being knit together*} Lit. "to make go together, to coalesce in argument" (Acts 16:10), in spiritual growth (Col. 2:19), in love (cf. Col. 3:14) as here. {*Of the full assurance of understanding*} (cf. 1 Thess. 1:5; Col. 2:2; Heb. 6:11; 10:22). Paul desires the full use of the intellect in grasping the great mystery of Christ and it calls for the full and balanced exercise of all one's mental powers. {*That they may know*} Lit. "Unto full knowledge." This use "full, additional knowledge" is Paul's reply to the Gnostics with the limited and perverted knowledge.

3. {*All the treasures of wisdom and knowledge*} (cf. Matt. 2:11; 6:19-21). "Treasures" is our "thesaurus" for coffer, storehouse, treasure. Paul confronts these pretentious intellectuals (Gnostics) with the bold claim that Christ sums up all wisdom and knowledge. These treasures are hidden (Mark 4:22) whether the Gnostics have discovered them or not. They are there (in Christ) as every believer knows by fresh and repeated discovery.

4. {*May delude*} Lit. "to count aside" and so wrong, to cheat by false reckoning, to deceive by false reasoning.

5. {*Your order*} This is the military line (from Greek verb *tassō*), unbroken, intact. A few stragglers had gone over to the Gnostics, but there had been no panic, no breach in the line. {*Steadfastness*} This is probably the same military metaphor as in "orderly" just before. The solid part of the line which can and does stand the attack of the Gnostics.

6. {*Christ Jesus the Lord*} This phrase occurs nowhere else by Paul. Hence it is plain that Paul here meets the two forms of Gnostic heresy about the Person of Christ (the recognition of the historical Jesus in his actual humanity against the Docetic Gnostics, the identity of the Christ or Messiah with this historical Jesus against the Cerinthian Gnostics, and the acknowledgment of him as Lord). {*Walk in him*} Translate the Greek tense, "Go on walking in him." Stick to your first lessons in Christ.

8. {*Take heed*} This is a common verb for warning like our "look out," "beware." {*That maketh spoil of you*} This is the Greek verb *sulagôgeô,* late and rare (found here first) verb (from *sulê,* booty, and *agô,* to lead, to carry), to carry off as booty a captive, slave, maiden. There was some one outstanding leader who was doing most of the damage in leading the people astray. {*Tradition*} Tradition may be good (2 Thess. 2:15; 3:6) or bad (Mark 7:3). Here it is worthless and harmful, merely the foolish theories of the Gnostics. {*Rudiments*} This refers to the specious arguments of the Gnostic philosophers as here with all their *aeons* and rules of life. {*And not after Christ*} Christ the Creator and Sustainer is the yardstick by which to measure philosophy and all phases of human knowledge.

9. {*For in him dwelleth all the fulness of the Godhead bodily*} Here Paul states the heart of his message about the Person of Christ. There dwells (at home) in Christ not one or more aspects of the Godhead (the very essence of God) not merely the *quality* of God (cf. Rom. 1:20). The fullness of the God-head was in Christ before the Incarnation (John 1:1, 18; Phil. 2:6), during the Incarnation (John 1:14, 18; 1 John 1:1-3). It was the Son of God who came in the likeness of men (Phil. 2:7).

10. {*The head*} All rule and authority comes after Christ whether angels, *aeons,* kings, what not.

11. {*In the putting off*} As if an old garment, i.e., the fleshly body (cf. Col. 2:15).

12. {*Having been buried with him in baptism*} (cf. Rom. 6:4). For all who in the rite of baptism are plunged under the water, thereby declare that they put faith in the expiatory death of Christ for the pardon of their sins.

13. {*Being dead through your trespasses*} This is moral death (cf. Rom. 6:11; Eph. 2:1, 5). The "trespass" is a lapse or misstep (Matt. 6:14; Rom. 5:15-18; Gal. 6:1). {*And the uncircumcision of your flesh*} This means "Dead in your trespasses and your alienation from God, of which the uncircumcision of your flesh was a symbol." {*Did he quicken together with him*} (cf. Eph. 2:4, 5). This word was apparently coined by Paul for this passage.

14. {*Having blotted out*} The Greek verb is *exaleiphô,* to rub out, wipe off, erase (cf. Acts 3:19 [LXX]; Rev. 3:5; Col. 2:14). Here the word explains "forgiven" and is simultaneous with it. {*And he hath taken it* *out of the way*} (cf. John 1:29). The Greek perfect tense emphasizes the permanence of the removal of the bond which has been paid and canceled and cannot be presented again. {*Nailing*} Cf. 3 Macc. 4:9 with the very word *staurôi*. The victim was nailed to the cross as was Christ. "When Christ was crucified, God nailed the Law to His cross" (Peake).

15. {*Having put off from himself*} (cf. Col. 3:9). This expresses complete removal. Did God or Christ disarm? Likely God is the referent. {*Powers and authorities*} Likely this refers to angels such as the Gnostics worshipped. In the Cross of Christ God showed his power openly without aid or help of angels. {*He made a show of them*} That is, he made an open, public example of them (cf. Matt. 1:19). {*Triumphing over them on it*} (cf. 2 Cor. 2:14). The Greek verb is *thriambeuô* here to celebrate a triumph in the usual sense. It is derived from *thriambos,* a hymn sung in festal procession and is kin to the Latin *triumphus* (our triumph), a triumphal procession of victorious Roman generals. God won a complete triumph over all the angelic agencies.

16. {*Let no one judge you*} The Greek syntax has a focus of forbidding the habit of passing judgment in such matters. Paul has here in mind the ascetic regulations and practices of one wing of the Gnostics, possibly Essenic or even Pharisaic influence (cf. 1 Cor. 8-9; Rom. 14; 15).

18. {*Rob you of your prize*} (cf. Col. 3:15). Here it means to decide or give judgment against. The judge at the games is called *brabeus* and the prize *brabeion* (1 Cor. 9:24; Phil. 3:14). {*And worshipping of the angels*} Humility is a virtue (cf. Col. 3:12), but it is linked with worship of the angels which is idolatry and so is probably false humility. They may have argued for angel worship on the plea that God is high and far removed and so took angels as mediators as some men do today with angels and saints in place of Christ.

19. {*Not holding fast the Head*} The Greek suggests this is an actual case of deserting Christ as the Head. The Gnostics dethroned Christ from his primacy (Col. 1:18) and placed him below a long line of *aeons* or angels. {*Through the joints...and bonds*} Lit. "joints and bonds." Both words picture well the wonderful unity in the body by cells, muscles, arteries, veins, nerves, skin, glands, etc. It is a marvelous machine working together under the direction of the head.

20. {*If ye died*} This condition is assumed as true, "since..."; this is alluding to the picture of burial in baptism (Col. 2:12). {*Why do ye subject yourselves to ordinances?*} The bond of decrees (Col. 2:14) was removed on the Cross of Christ. Paul still has in mind the rules of the ascetic wing of the Gnostics (Col. 2:16).

21. {*Handle not, nor taste, nor touch*} These are specimens of Gnostic prohibitions. The Pharisees, Essenes, Gnostics made piety hinge on outward observances instead of inward conviction.

23. {*Which things*} Lit. "Which very things," referring to these ascetic regulations. {*Have indeed a show of wisdom*} Lit. "word of wisdom" is probably "the repute of wisdom" (Abbott). {*In will-worship*} This word occurs nowhere else and was probably coined by Paul, to describe the voluntary worship of angels (cf. Col 2:18). {*And humility*} This is clearly here the bad sense, "in mock humility." {*And severity to the body*} Ascetics often practice flagellation and other harsh treatment to the body.

CHAPTER 3

1. {*If then ye were raised together with Christ*} The Greek assumes a true condition, "since then..." (cf. Col. 2:20). {*The things that are above*} Lit. "the upward things" (cf. Phil. 3:14), the treasure in heaven (Matt. 6:20). Paul gives this ideal and goal in place of merely ascetic rules.

2. {*Set your mind on*} Greek tense translates, "Keep on thinking about." {*Not on the things that are upon the earth*} Paul does not mean that we should never think the things upon the earth, but that these should not be our aim, our goal, our master.

3. {*For ye died*} This is a definite event, aorist active indicative, died to sin (Rom. 6:2). {*Is hid*} The Greek tense shows that this remains concealed, locked together with Christ, in God.

5. {*Mortify*} Lit. "to put to death, to treat as dead." Paul does not go to the other Gnostic extreme of license on the plea that the soul is not affected by the deeds of the body. Paul's idea is that the body is the temple of the Holy Spirit (1 Cor. 6:19).

6. {*Cometh the wrath of God*} Paul does not regard these sins of the flesh as matters of indifference.

7. {*Walked aforetime*} Referring to their previous pagan state and their former way of life.

8. {*Put ye also away*} Lit. "to put away," lay aside like old clothes, as a metaphor of clothing. {*All these*} Rid yourself of the whole bunch of filthy rags (moral failures and filthy talk): wrath, malice, slander, shameful speaking (cf. Col. 3:5; Gal. 5:20; Eph. 4:29-31).

9. {*Lie not to another*} Paul focuses on another similar sin; translates either "stop lying" or "do not have the habit of lying." {*The old man*} Here Paul brings in another metaphor (mixes his metaphors as he often does), that of the old life of sin regarded as "the ancient man" of sin already crucified (Rom. 6:6; cf. Eph. 4:22).

10. {*And have put on*} The Greek verb is *endunô*, old and common verb (Latin *induo*, English endue) for putting on a garment. Used of putting on Christ (Gal. 3:27; Rom. 13:14). {*The new man*} (cf. Eph. 4:24). {*Which is being renewed*} Paul apparently coined this word, a continual refreshment of the new (young) person in Christ Jesus. {*Unto knowledge*} This is full (additional) knowledge (one of the keywords in this Epistle).

11. {*There cannot be*} Lit. "There does not exist." This is the ideal which is still a long way ahead of modern Christians. All distinctions disappear in Christ and the new man in Christ. {*Slave...freeman*} Class distinctions vanish in Christ. In the Christian churches were found slaves, freedmen, masters. Perhaps Paul has Philemon and Onesimus in mind. {*But Christ is all...and in all*} "Christ occupies the whole sphere of human life and permeates all its developments" (Lightfoot). Christ has obliterated the words barbarian, master, slave, all of them and has substituted the word *adelphos* (brother).

12. {*Put on therefore*} This is the figure of "the new man" as "the new garment." With old clothing taken off (Col. 3:8), Paul now gives in contrast garments to put on.

13. {*Forbearing one another*} Lit. "holding yourselves back from one another." {*Forgiving each other...*} Christ's forgiveness of us is here made the reason for our forgiveness of others.

14. {*Put on love*} (cf. Luke 3:20). The verb has to be supplied from Colossians 3:12. {*The bond of perfectness*} (cf. Col. 2:19). Here it is apparently the girdle that holds the various garments together. In a succinct way Paul has here put the idea about love set forth so wonderfully in 1 Cor. 13:1ff.

15. {*The peace of Christ*} This means, "the peace that Christ gives" (John 14:27). {*Rule*} The Greek word is *brabeuô,* to act as umpire (*brabeus*) (cf. 1 Cor. 7:15). {*Be ye thankful*} Lit. "Keep on becoming thankful."

16. {*With psalms*} This is the Psalms in the OT originally with musical accompaniment. {*Hymns*} This is praises to God composed by the Christians (1 Tim. 3:16). {*Spiritual songs*} This is a general description of all whether with or without instrumental accompaniment. The same song can have all three words applied to it. {*Singing with grace...in your hearts*} Without this there is no real worship "to God." Whether with instrument or with voice or with both it is all for naught if the adoration is not in the heart.

18. {*Wives*} This first class is dealt with. {*Be in subjection to your husbands*} (cf. Eph. 5:22). The Greek verb *hupotassomai* has a military air, common in the *Koiné* for such obedience. Obedience in government is essential as the same word shows in Romans 13:1, 5. {*As is fitting in the Lord*} Wives have rights and privileges, but recognition of the husband's leadership is essential to a well-ordered home.

19. {*Husbands*} Now the second class is dealt with. {*Love your wives*} The Greek tense of this command translates "keep on loving." That is precisely the point. {*Be not bitter*} Greek syntax translates, "Stop being bitter" or "do not have the habit of being bitter." This is the sin of husbands. The bitter word rankles in the soul.

20. {*Children*} Now the third class is dealt with. {*Obey your parents*} Lit. "to listen under (as looking up)," to hearken, to heed, to obey. {*In all things*} This is the hard part for the child, not occasional obedience, but continual.

21. {*Fathers*} Again, another class is dealt with. {*Provoke not*} Here it means to nag and as a habit.

22. {*Slaves*} Still another class is dealt with. {*Your masters according to the flesh*} Christ is their lord, but even so they were to obey their lords in the flesh, fearing the Lord. {*Not with eye service*} (cf. Eph. 6:6). This is service while the master's eye was on the slave and no longer. {*In singleness of heart*} (cf. Eph. 6:5). Lit. "simple, without folds" (cf. 2 Cor. 11:3).

23. {*Heartily*} Lit. "From the soul" and not with mere eye service (cf. Eph. 6:7). {*As unto the Lord*} Even when for men. This is the highest test of worthwhile service. If it were only always true!

24. {*Ye serve the Lord Christ*} As his slaves and gladly so. Perhaps better as commands, translates, "keep on serving."

CHAPTER 4

1. {*Masters*} Yet another class is dealt with by Paul. {*That which is just and equal*} If employers always did this, there would be no labor problem. {*A Master in heaven*} A wholesome reminder to the effect that he keeps his eye on the conduct of masters towards their employees.

3. {*The mystery of Christ*} Translate, "the mystery which is Christ" (cf. Col. 2:2), one that puts out of comparison the foolish "mysteries" of the Gnostics. {*For which I am also in bonds*} Paul is always conscious of this limitation, this chain. At bottom he is a prisoner because of his preaching to the Gentiles.

5. {*Toward them that are without*} A Pauline phrase for those outside the churches (1 Thess. 5:12; 1 Cor. 5:12). It takes wise walking to win them to Christ.

6. {*Seasoned with salt*} This is the Greek verb *artuô* (old verb from *airô,* to fit, to arrange) about salt in Mark 9:50; Luke 14:34. Nowhere else in the NT Not too much salt, not too little. Plutarch uses salt of speech, the wit which flavors speech (cf. Attic salt). Our word *salacious* is this same word degenerated into vulgarity. Grace and salt (wit, sense) make an ideal combination.

7. {*All my affairs*} Lit. "all the things relating to me" (cf. Acts 25:14; Phil. 1:2).

8. {*That ye may know*} Translates, "that ye may come to know." {*Our estate*} Lit. "the things concerning us."

9. {*Together with Onesimus*} This is the co-bearer of the letter with Tychicus and praised on a par with him, runaway slave though he is. {*Who is one of you*} Said not as a reproach to Colossae for having such a man, but as a privilege to the church in Colossae to give a proper welcome to this returning converted slave and to treat him as a brother as Paul argues to Philemon.

10. {*Aristarchus*} He was from Thessalonica and accompanied Paul to Jerusalem with the collection (Acts 19:29; 20:4) and started with Paul to Rome (Acts 27:2; Phlm. 1:24). {*My fellow prisoner*} (cf. Phlm. 1:23) It is unknown whether this refers to an actual voluntary imprisonment or of spiritual imprisonment (cf. Phil. 2:25; Phlm. 1:2). {*Mark*} Once rejected by Paul for his defection in the work (Acts 15:36-39), but now cordially commended because he had made good again. {*If he come unto you, receive him*} Paul's commendation of Mark is hearty and unreserved as he does later in 2 Timothy 4:11. The Greek verb *dechomai* (welcome) is the usual one for hospitable reception (Matt. 10:14; John 4:45; Phil. 2:29; Luke 10:38).

11. {*Jesus which is called Justus*} This is another illustration of the frequency of the name Jesus (Joshua). The surname Justus is the Latin *Justus* for the Greek *Dikaios* and the Hebrew *Zadok* and very common as a surname among the Jews. The name appears for two others in the NT (Acts 1:23; 18:7). {*A comfort unto me*} The Greek word *parêgoria* is an old word (here only in NT) from *parêgoreô,* to make an address and means solace, relief. A medical term. Curiously enough, our word *paregoric* comes from it.

12. {*Epaphras who is one of you*} He is the one who brought news from Colossae (cf. Col. 1:7).

13. {*And for them in Hierapolis*} This is the third of the three cities in the Lycus Valley which had not seen Paul's face (Col. 2:1). It was across the valley from Laodicea. Probably Epaphras had evangelized all three cities and all were in peril from the Gnostics.

14. {*Luke, the beloved physician*} (cf. Phlm. 1:24; 2 Tim. 4:11). The author of the Gospel and the Acts. Both Mark and Luke are with Paul at this time, possibly also with copies of their Gospels with them. The article here (repeated) may mean "my beloved physician." It would seem certain that Luke looked after Paul's health and that Paul loved him.

16. {*And the epistle from Laodicea*} The most likely meaning is that the so-called Epistle to the Ephesians was a circular letter to various churches in the province of Asia, one copy going to Laodicea and to be passed on to Colossae as the Colossian letter was to be sent on to Laodicea.

17. {*Take heed*} Translates, "keep an eye on." {*Thou hast received in the Lord*} The Greek verb is *paralambanô,* used by Paul of getting his message from the Lord (1 Cor. 15:3). {*That thou fulfil it*} The Greek tense translates, "that you keep on filling it full." It is a life-time job.

18. {*Of me Paul with mine own hand*} It is more precisely, "with the hand of me Paul" (cf. 2 Thess. 3:17; 1 Cor. 16:21). {*My bonds*} The chain (cf. Eph. 6:20) clanked afresh as Paul took the pen to sign the salutation. He was not likely to forget it himself.

The First Epistle to the Thessalonians

Author: Paul
Recipients: Thessalonian believers
Date: A.D. 50 to 51
From: Corinth
Occasion: To correct gross misapprehension and misrepresentation of his preaching about the Second Coming of Christ
Theme: Thanksgiving to God and exhortation to right living in the midst of persecution

By Way of Introduction

We cannot say that this is Paul's first letter to a church (cf. 2 Thess. 2:2). But this is the earliest one that has come down to us and it may even be the earliest NT book, unless the Epistle of James antedates it or even Mark's Gospel. Paul was in Corinth and Timothy and Silas had just arrived from Thessalonica (1 Thess. 3:6; Acts 18:5). They had brought supplies from the Macedonian churches to supply Paul's need (2 Cor. 11:9), as the church in Philippi did once and again while Paul was in Thessalonica (Phil. 4:15ff.).

Some of the disciples in Thessalonica had misunderstood Paul's preaching about the second coming of Christ and had quit work and were making a decided disturbance on the subject, and drew their own inferences for idleness and fanaticism as some do today. Undoubtedly Paul had touched upon eschatological matters while in Thessalonica. Clearly Paul had said also that Jesus was going to come again according to his own promise before his ascension.

Undoubtedly Paul hoped for the early return of Jesus as most of the early Christians did, but that is a very different thing from setting a time for his coming.

That hope of Christ's return should serve as a spur to increased activity (not make idle) for Christ in order to hasten his coming.

Chapter 1

1. {*Unto the church of the Thessalonians*} "Church" means here a local assembly that is an organization for worship whether assembled or unassembled. {*In God the Father and the Lord Jesus Christ*}. This church is grounded in and exists in the sphere and power of the Father and Lord Jesus. Paul did not get his view of Jesus the full "Lord Jesus Christ" from current views of Mithra or of Isis or any other alien faith. The Risen Christ became at once for Paul the Lord of his life. {*Grace to you and peace*} "Grace" is one of the great words of the NT (cf. John 1:16). Perhaps no one word carries more meaning for Paul's messages than this word Grace (Greek word *charis* from *chairô*, rejoice). {*Peace*} This Greek word *eirênê* is more than the Hebrew *shalôm* so common in salutations (cf. John 14:27 and Phil. 4:7).

2. {*We give thanks*} "The plural implies that all three missionaries prayed together" (Moffat). {*For you all*} "All" means the church as a whole and each person in the whole church. {*Making mention*} (cf. Rom. 1:9; Eph. 1:16; Phlm. 1:4). Did Paul have a prayer list of the Thessalonian disciples which he read over with Silas and Timothy?

3. {*Remembering*} This is the Greek word *mnêmoneuô* from adjective *mnêmôn* (mindful) and so to call to mind, to be mindful of. {*Without ceasing*} Lit. "not + to leave off." {*Your work of faith*} "Work" is the general term for work or business, employment, task. This work is marked by, characterized by, faith. Note that we are justified by faith, but faith produces works (Rom. 6-8). {*Labour of love*} Translate, "the labor that love prompts." Originally a quite common word, *agapê* (love) is one of the great words of the NT. When Christianity first began to think and speak in Greek, it took up *agapê* investing it and related words with the new glow with which the NT writings make us familiar, a content which is invariably religious (Moffatt). {*Patience of hope...in Christ*} This is patience marked by hope, the endurance inspired by hope (Frame). Here it is a distinctly Christian virtue. Jesus is the object of this hope, the hope of his second coming which is still open to us (cf. also 1 Thess. 1:1). {*Before our God and Father*} The picture here is the day of judgment when all shall appear before God.

4. {*Knowing*} Translate the Greek syntax, "since we know." {*Beloved by God*} The Greek verb is *agapaô*, the verb so common in the NT for the highest kind of love; the whole phrase is quite affectionate (cf. 2 Thess. 2:13, Deut. 33:12). {*Your election*} That is, the election of you by God (cf. Eph. 1:4). This Greek word for choice is always of God's choice of men (Acts 9:15; 1 Thess. 1:4; Rom. 9:11; 11:5, 7; 2 Pet. 1:10).

5. {*Our gospel*} Paul had a definite, clear-cut message of grace that he preached everywhere including Thessalonica. In its origin Paul's gospel is of God (1 Thess. 2:2, 8, 9), in its substance it is Christ's (1 Thess. 3:2; 2 Thess. 1:8), and Paul is only the bearer of it (1 Thess. 2:4, 9; 2 Thess. 2:14). Paul and his associates have been entrusted with this gospel (1 Thess. 2:4) and preach it (Gal. 2:2). {*Not only—but also*} Not miracles, this is a sharp contrast of word and power (cf. 1 Cor. 2:4; 4:20). {*In the Holy Spirit and much assurance*} It means the full confidence which comes from the Holy Spirit. {*For your sake*} It was all in their interest and for their advantage, however it may have seemed otherwise at the time.

6. {*Imitators of us and of the Lord*} The Greek word is *mimêtês* from *mimeomai,* to imitate and that from *mimos* (mimic, actor). This is more than "followers," in the NT only six times (1 Thess. 1:6; 2:14; 1 Cor. 4:16; 11:1; Eph. 5:1; Heb. 6:12). It is a daring thing to expect people to "imitate" the preacher, but Paul adds "and of the Lord." {*In much affliction*} Lit. "pressure." Tribulation has the idea of pressing hard on an object. {*With joy of the Holy Spirit*} The Holy Spirit gives the joy in the midst of the tribulations as Paul learned (Rom. 5:3).

7. {*So that ye became…an ensample*} The result of the above is expressed. "Example" is the Greek word *tupos* from *tuptô,* to strike, and so the mark of a blow, print as in John 20:25. It is an example or pattern to be imitated (cf. Acts 7:44; Phil. 3:17).

8. {*From you hath sounded forth*} This means to sound out of a trumpet or of thunder, to reverberate like our echo. {*Is gone forth*} It is a graphic picture with a pardonable touch of hyperbole (Moffatt) for Thessalonica was a great commercial and political center for disseminating the news of salvation (on the Egnation Way). {*Your faith to God-ward*} Lit. "the faith of you that toward the God." Clearly, their faith is now directed toward the true God and not toward the idols from which they had turned (cf. 1 Thess. 1:10).

9. {*Report*} Greek tense translates, "keep on reporting." {*What manner of entering in*} Translate, "what sort of entrance." {*To turn*} This is the Greek verb *epistrephô,* an old verb for turning and is common in the Acts for Gentiles turning to God, as here from idols, though not by Paul again in this sense. {*From these vain things to the living God*} This is an image of a heathen god (cf. *idol*). Common in the

LXX in this sense and also cf. Acts 14:15, no longer dead like the idols from which they turned, but alive and genuine as the God they serve. **10.** {*To wait for his Son from heaven*} Greek tense translates, "to keep on waiting for." The hope of the second coming of Christ was real and powerful with Paul. {*Whom he raised from the dead*} Paul having personal witness, this fact is the foundation stone for all his theology and it comes out in this first chapter. { *Jesus which delivereth us from the wrath to come*} It is the historic, crucified, risen, and ascended Jesus Christ, God's Son, who delivers from the coming wrath. As his very name, he is our Savior (Matt. 1:21); our Rescuer (Rom. 11:26, cf. Isa. 59:20). It is eschatological language, this coming wrath of God for sin (1 Thess. 2:16; Rom. 3:5; 5:9; 9:22; 13:5). Paul is certain that God's wrath in due time will punish sin.

CHAPTER 2

1. {*That it hath not been found vain*} Lit. "has not become empty or hollow [as a completed state]."
2. {*But having suffered before*} "But" is in strong contrast to the "failure" above. The church here has personal knowledge of these events. {*And been shamefully entreated in Philippi*} This was "more than the bodily suffering; it was the personal indignity that had been offered to him as a Roman citizen" (Milligan) (cf. Acts 16:16-40). Paul shows that the memory still rankled in his bosom. {*We waxed bold in our God*} The Greek word is *parrêsiazomai,* old deponent verb from *parrêsia* (full story, *pan, rêsia*) [cf. Acts 26:26]. The insult in Philippi did not close Paul's mouth, but had precisely the opposite effect. {*The gospel of God in much conflict*} Lit. "much struggle." This figure is of the athletic games and may refer to outward conflict like Philippians 1:30 or inward anxiety (Col. 2:1). He had both in Thessalonica.
3. {*Exhortation*} This is persuasive discourse, calling to one's side, for admonition, encouragement, or comfort. {*Nor in guile*} The Greek word is *dolôs* from *delô,* to catch with bait. Paul is keenly sensitive against charges against the correctness of his message and the purity of his life.
4. {*But even as we have been approved by God*} The Greek word is *dokimazô,* to put to the test, but here the tense for completed state means tested and proved and so approved by God.

5. {*Using words of flattery*} This was the selfish conduct (that is "flattery") of too many of the rhetoricians of the day; such conduct extremely repugnant to Paul. {*Nor a cloke of covetousness*} Translate, "pretext of greediness." This is the charge of self-interest rather than the mere desire to please people. Paul feels so strongly his innocence of this charge that he calls God as witness in a solemn oath (cf. 2 Cor. 1:23; Rom. 9:1; Phil. 1:8).

6. {*Nor seeking glory of men*} First greed is repudiated, now worldly ambition (cf. Acts 20:19; 2 Cor. 4:5; Eph. 4:2). Paul and his associates had not tried to extract praise or glory out of men. {*When we might have been burdensome, as apostles of Christ*} This "burdensome" can have a double sense: either in matter of finance or of dignity. {*As Christ's apostles*} This clearly means as missionaries, whether in the technical sense or not (cf. Acts 14:4, 14; 2 Cor. 8:23; 11:13; Rom. 16:7; Phil. 2:25; Rev. 2:2). They were entitled to pay, though they did not invoke it.

7. {*But we were gentle in the midst of you*} Though many prefer the Greek text here as "gentle," "Babes" is the clearly correct reading. Paul is fond of the Greek word *nêpioi* (babes). {*As when a nurse cherishes her own children*} The picture here is that of the mother-nurse who suckles and nurses her own children, a use found in Spohocles, and a picture of Paul's tender affection for the Thessalonians. *Thalpô* is an old word to keep warm, to cherish with tender love.

8. {*Even so, being affectionately desirous of you*} Lit. "to long for," derived from the language of the nursery. {*To impart...souls*} Lit. "souls." Paul and his associates held nothing back. {*Because ye were become very dear to us*} The Greek is *agapêtos,* beloved and so dear. A beautiful picture of the growth of Paul's affection for them.

9. {*Travail*} This is difficult labor, harder than mere toil (cf. 2 Thess. 3:8; 2 Cor. 11:27). {*Night and day*} Translate, "both by day and by night," perhaps beginning before dawn and working after dark (cf. 1 Thess. 3:10). {*That we might not burden any of you*} Lit. "not laying a burden on one" (cf. 2 Thess. 3:8; 2 Cor. 2:5.) Paul boasted of his financial independence where he was misunderstood as in Thessalonica and Corinth (2 Cor. 9 to 12), though he vindicated his right to remuneration.

10. {*How holily and righteously and unblameably*} With three adverbs, Paul calls the Thessalonians and God as witnesses to his life toward you the believers. All this argues that Paul spent a considerable time in Thessalonica, more than the three Sabbaths mentioned by Luke.

12. {*To the end that...walk worthily of God*} These are the three phases of the minister's preaching, to the end that they will walk worthily (cf. Phil. 1:27; Eph. 4:1). {*Kingdom*} Here, the kingdom is the future consummation because of glory (cf. 2 Thess. 1:5; 1 Cor. 6:9; 15:50; Gal. 5:21; 2 Tim. 4:1, 18), but Paul uses it for the present kingdom of grace also as in 1 Corinthians 4:20; Romans 14:17; Colossians 1:13.

13. {*Worketh in you*} The idea is that the word of God is set in operation in you that believe.

14. {*Imitators of the churches of God which are in Judea*} (cf. 1 Thess. 1:5). This passage implies Paul has admiration for the Jewish Churches, and so there is no feud existing between St. Paul and the Twelve, a distortion by extension of Galatians 2:1ff. (Lightfoot). {*Countrymen*} This is their fellow-countrymen or tribesmen. This word refers primarily to Gentiles who no doubt joined the Jews in Thessalonica who instigated the attacks on Paul and Silas.

15. {*Who both killed the Lord Jesus and the prophets*} The Jews killed the prophets before the Lord Jesus who reminded them of their guilt (Matt. 23:29). Paul, as Peter (Acts 2:23), lays the guilt of the death of Christ on the Jewish leaders. {*And drove us out*} This is an old verb to drive out or banish, to chase out as if a wild beast. This likely refers to when the rabbis and the hoodlums from the marketplace chased him out of Thessalonica by the help of the politarchs (cf. also Acts 17:5). {*And are contrary to all men*} Jews did have a reputation among Roman leadership as hostile. It seems like a bitter word about Paul's countrymen whom he really loved (Rom. 9:1-5; 10:1-6), but Paul knew only too well the middle wall of partition between Jew and Gentile.

16. {*Forbidding us*} They show their hostility to Paul at every turn. Right here in Corinth, where Paul is when he writes, they had already shown venomous hostility toward Paul as Luke makes plain (Acts 18:6). {*To fill up their sins alway*} It may either be God's conceived plan to allow the Jews to go on and fill up or it may be the natural result from the continual sins of the Jews. {*Is come*} Likely translate, "But the wrath has come upon them at last." Paul vividly foresees and foretells the final outcome of this attitude of hate on the part of the Jews.

17. {*Being bereaved of you*} Lit. "being orphaned from you." Paul changes the figure again from babies to nursing mothers, to fathers, now orphans referring to a period of separation from them (cf. 1 Thess. 2:7, 11). {*For a short season*} Lit. "for a season of an hour." It has seemed long to Paul, some months at any rate. {*In presence, not in heart*} Lit. "in face." Paul's heart was with them, though they no longer saw his face. {*Heart*} The Greek word is lit. "heart" *kardia*. This is the inner man, the seat of the affections and purposes, not always in contrast with intellect. Paul was out of sight, though not "out of mind."

18. {*We desired to come to you. I Paul*} Here this is a literary plural, not literal. Paul uses his own name elsewhere (2 Cor. 10:1; Gal. 5:2; Col. 1:23; Eph. 3:1; Phl. 1:19) {*And Satan hindered us*} This Greek verb was used long before NT times to cut in a road, to make a road impassable. So Paul charges Satan with cutting in on his path (cf. Acts 24:4; Gal. 5:7, also Rom. 15:22; 1 Pet. 3:7).

19. {*Crown of glorying*} When a king or conqueror came on a visit he was given a wreath of glorying. Paul is answering the insinuation that he did not really wish to come. {*At his coming*} The Thessalonians, Paul says, will be his crown, glory, joy when Jesus comes.

CHAPTER 3

1. {*When we could no longer forbear*} The Greek verb is *stegô* to cover from *stegê*, roof (Mark 2:4), to cover with silence, to conceal, to keep off, to endure (cf. also 1 Cor. 9:12; 13:7).

3. {*That no man be moved*} The Greek verb is *sainô*, to wag the tail, to flatter; "beguile" here suits the sense.

4. {*We told you beforehand*} Translate the Greek tense, "we used to tell you beforehand."

5. {*Lest by any means the tempter had tempted you*} It is a fear that the thing may turn out to be so about the past.

6. {*Even now*} Timothy has come. Why Silas is not named is not clear, unless he had come from Berea or elsewhere in Macedonia. {*Glad tidings of*} This verb is sometimes translated evangelizing (gospelizing). {*Longing to see us*} Lit. "to long after [in the directions of a particular object]."

7. {*Distress…physical necessity*} Lit. "choking and crushing."

9. {*Render again unto God*} Lit. "to give back in return for" (cf. 2 Thess. 1:6). {*For you*} Lit. "Around (concerning) you." (cf. 1 Thess. 3:2 "concerning your faith").

10. {*Exceedingly*} (cf. 1 Thess. 3:10; 5:13) Lit. "more than out of bounds (overflowing all bounds)." {*And perfect*} This is the Greek verb *katartizô*, to mend nets (Matt. 4:21) or men (Gal. 6:1) repair.

11. {*Our God and Father himself…and our Lord Jesus*} Note one article with both substantives for one person. Elsewhere there is one article, treating "our God and Savior Jesus Christ" as one just like "our Lord and Savior Jesus Christ" in 2 Peter 1:11; 2:20; 3:18. {*Direct our way*} The Greek mood communicates a wish (1 Thess. 3:11,12; 5:23; 2 Thess. 2:17; 3:5, 16; Rom. 15:5, 13). The Greek verb is *kateuthunô*, to make a straight path.

12. {*Make you to increase to superabound*} The Greek mood is a wish for future. It is hard to see much difference between the two verbs.

13. {*To the end he may stablish*} (cf. 1 Thess. 3:2). The Greek verb is *stêrizô*, from *stêrigx*, a support. {*Unblameable*} This word is rare in the NT. Each chapter ends with a verse on the second coming of Christ.

CHAPTER 4

1. {*We beseech*} This means to make an urgent request of one, not "question" (1 Thess. 5:12; 2 Thess. 2:1; Phil. 4:3).

2. {*What charge*} This is plural: charges or precepts, command (Acts 16:24), prohibition (Acts 5:28), right living (1 Tim. 1:5).

3. {*Your sanctification*} The Greek word is *hagismos* from the verb *hagiazô* and both to take the place of the old words *hagizô*, with the Christian meaning having taken over the older meanings of consecration to a god or goddess. {*That ye abstain from fornication*} Pagan religion did not demand sexual purity of its devotees, the gods and goddesses being grossly immoral. Priestesses were in the temples for the service of the men who came.

4. {*To possess himself of his own vessel*} It means either his own body or his own wife. Paul demands sexual purity on the part of men (married as well as unmarried). There is no double standard here. When the husband comes to the marriage bed, he should come as a chaste man to a chaste wife.

5. {*Not in the passion of lust*} Plain picture of the wrong way for the husband to come to marriage. {*That know not God*} The heathen knew gods as licentious as they are themselves, but not God.

6. {*And wrong his brother*} This means to take more, to overreach, to take advantage of, to defraud. {*In the matter*} The delicacy of Paul makes him refrain from plainer terms and the context makes it clear enough as in 2 Corinthians 7:11. {*An avenger*} This is a regular term in the papyri for legal avenger. God is the avenger for sexual wrongs both in this life and the next.

7. {*Not for uncleanness, but in sanctification*} God has "called" us all for a decent sex life consonant with his aims and purposes.

8. {*He that rejecteth*} Lit. "to not place" and so "to proscribe a thing, to annul it."

9. {*Concerning love of the brethren*} This means the love of brothers or sisters; though outside the NT it could mean love of actual kin, it is always the kinship in the love of Christ as here in the NT. {*Are taught by God…to love one another*} Only those taught of God keep on loving one another, love neighbors and even enemies as Jesus taught (Matt. 5:44).

11. {*That ye study to be quiet*} This is ambition to do good, not evil (cf. 1 Thess. 4:11; 2 Cor. 5:9; Rom. 5:20). There was a restless spirit in Thessalonica because of the misapprehension of the second coming. So Paul urges an ambition to be quiet or calm, to lead a quiet life, including silence (Acts 11:18). {*To do your own business*} Greek syntax translates, "to have the habit of attending to their own affairs." (cf. 2 Thess. 3:11). This restless meddlesomeness here condemned. {*To work with your own hands*} Paul gave a new dignity to manual labor by precept and example. "Pious" idlers in the church in Thessalonica were promoting trouble.

13. {*Concerning them that fall asleep*} The Greek tense gives idea of repetition, from time to time fall asleep. Greeks and Romans used this figure of sleep for death as Jesus does (John 11:11) and NT generally. Somehow the Thessalonians had a false notion about the dead in relation to the second coming. {*Even as the rest which have no hope*} This picture of the hopelessness of the pagan world about the future life is amply illustrated in ancient writings and particularly by inscriptions on tombs.

15. {*By the word of the Lord*} We do not know to what word of the Lord Jesus Paul refers, probably Paul meaning only the point in the teaching of Christ rather than a quotation. Or he may be claiming a direct revelation (cf. the Lord's Supper in 1 Cor. 11:23). {*Ye that are* *alive*} Paul here includes himself, but this by no means shows that Paul knew that he would be alive at the Parousia of Christ. He was alive, not dead, when he wrote. {*Shall in no wise precede*} The "not" is strong. Hence, there was no ground for uneasiness about the dead in Christ.

16. {*With a shout*} As if with a military command, Christ will come as Conqueror. {*The dead in Christ shall rise first*} The dead in Christ will rise before those still alive are changed.

17. {*Then*} This is the next step, not the identical time, but immediately afterwards. {*Shall be caught up*} This is the Greek verb *harpazô*, to seize, to carry off like Latin *rapio* (cf. *rap*ture). {*To meet the Lord in the air*} This rapture of the saints (both risen and changed) is a glorious climax to Paul's argument of consolation. {*And so*} This is the outcome, to be forever with the Lord, whether with a return to earth or with an immediate departure for heaven Paul does not say.

CHAPTER 5

1. {*But concerning the times and the seasons*} "Dates" is a definite space of time, not a rather extended period of time.

2. {*Know perfectly*} Accurately know, not "the times and the seasons," but their own ignorance. {*As a thief in the night*} This means suddenly and unexpectedly.

3. {*When they are saying peace and safety*} These false prophets will say this (cf. Ezek. 13:10) {*They shall in no wise escape*} The "not" is strong (as in 1 Thess. 4:15).

5. {*Sons of light...sons of day*} This is chiefly a translation Hebraism (cf. Luke 16:8 and Eph. 5:9).

6. {*Let us not sleep*} Translate the Greek tense, "let us not go on sleeping." {*Be sober*} Originally meaning "to not be drunk," here it is in the figurative sense, "to be calm, sober-minded" (cf. also 1 Thess. 5:8).

7. {*They that be drunken are drunken in the night*} There is a slight difference in the Greek (the first verb is inceptive [get]), translate, "those who *get* drunk *are* drunk" at night, the favorite time for drunken revelries.

8. {*Putting on the breastplate of faith and love...for a helmet, the hope of salvation*} (cf. Eph. 6:14, 17, also Isa. 59:17). The idea of watch-

fulness brings the figure of a sentry on guard and armed to Paul's mind (cf. Rom. 13:12).

9. {*But unto the obtaining of salvation through our Lord Jesus Christ*} "Receive" may be passive (God's possession as in 1 Pet. 2:9), or active (obtaining, as in 2 Thess. 2:14). The latter is probably the idea here. Salvation here is in the sense of our final victory and its hope.

10. {*Whether we wake or sleep...that we should live together with him*} This is used here of life and death, not as metaphor, covering all life (now and hereafter) together with Jesus.

12. {*Them that labour among you...over you...and admonish you*} The same article connects all three participles, different functions of the same leaders in the church. "Work hard" is an old word for toil even if weary. "Over you" is lit., "those who stand in front of you," your leaders in the Lord, the presbyters or bishops and deacons. "Admonish" is lit. "Putting sense into the heads [minds] of people."

13. {*And to esteem them*} The idlers in Thessalonica had evidently refused to follow their leaders in church activities. We need wise leadership today, but still more wise following.

14. {*Admonish the disorderly*} Like keeping order in military sense, this means to put sense into the unruly mob who break ranks. {*Encourage the fainthearted*} (cf. John 11:31) "Timid" is lit. "small-souled, little-souled." Conditions often cause some to lose heart and wish to quit. These must be held in line. {*Support the weak*} Lit. "to cling to, to hold on to [the weak]." The weak are those tempted to sin (immorality, for instance). {*Be long-suffering toward all*} These disorderly elements try the patience of the leaders. Hold out with them.

18. {*In everything give thanks*} It is God's will that we find joy in prayer in Christ Jesus in every condition of life.

19. {*Quench not the spirit*} The Greek syntax here means to stop doing it or not to have the habit of doing it. It is a bold figure. Some of them were trying to put out the fire of the Holy Spirit, probably the special gifts of the Holy Spirit as verse 20 means. But even so the exercise of these special gifts (1 Cor. 12-14; 2 Cor. 12:2-4; Rom. 12:6-9) was to be done decently (1 Thess. 4:12) and in order (1 Cor. 14:40) and for edification (1 Cor. 14:26).

20. {*Despise not prophesyings*} Greek syntax means "stop counting as nothing." Here this is "forth-telling" rather than "fore-telling" (1 Cor. 14:1ff.) and evidently depreciated in Thessalonica as in Corinth later.

21. {*Prove all things*} Even the gift of prophecy has to be tested (1 Cor. 12:10; 14:29) to avoid error. Paul shows fine balance here.

22. {*Abstain from every form of evil*} Though "kind/form" can mean the appearance or look. But, if so taken, it is not semblance as opposed to reality. Here it is in the sense of class or kind. Evil had a way of showing itself even in the spiritual gifts including prophecy.

23. {*Sanctify you*} This is a new verb in LXX and NT for the old *hagizô*, to render or to declare holy (hagios), to consecrate, to separate from things profane. {*Wholly*} Here it means the whole of each of you, every part of each of you, through and through qualitatively rather than quantitatively. {*Your spirit and soul and body*} Not necessarily trichotomy (three essential parts to a human) as opposed to dichotomy (two essential parts to a human) as elsewhere in Paul's Epistles. Both believers and unbelievers have an inner man (soul, mind, heart) and the outer man (body). But the believer has the Holy Spirit of God, the renewed spirit of man (1 Cor. 2:11; Rom. 8:9-11). {*Be preserved entire*} Note singular verb and singular adjective showing that Paul conceives of the man as "an undivided whole" (Frame). {*At the coming*} This is the Second Coming which was a sustaining hope to Paul.

24. {*Faithful*} God is faithful: he calls and will carry through (Phil. 1:6).

26. {*With a holy kiss*} A customary salutation for rabbis, this is a token of friendship and love (1 Cor. 16:20; 2 Cor. 13:12; Rom. 16:16).

27. {*That this epistle be read unto all the brethren*} Clearly Paul wrote for the church as a whole and wished the epistles read aloud at a public meeting.

28. {*The grace*} Paul prefers this noble word to the customary "Farewell, be strong" (cf. 2 Thess. 3:18 and also 1 Cor. 16:23; Rom. 16:20 and Col. 4:18; 1 Tim. 6:21; Titus 3:15; 2 Tim. 4:22). The full Trinitarian benediction we find in 2 Corinthians 13:13.

The Second Epistle to the Thessalonians

Author: Paul
Recipients: Thessalonian believers
Date: A.D. 50 to 51
From: Corinth
Occasion: Paul writes to calm excitement and to make it plain that he had not said that the Second Coming was to be right away.
Theme: Paul commends the Thessalonians for their growth in Christ. He corrects a false teaching that the Second Coming is imminent and rebukes those who have used this false teaching as an excuse to quit working.

By Way of Introduction

First Thessalonians did not settle all the difficulties in Thessalonica. There was some opposition to Paul's authority and even defiance (cf. 2 Thess. 3:6, 10, 14). Paul finds it necessary to warn the Thessalonians against the zeal of some deceivers who even invent epistles in Paul's name to carry their point in the church (2 Thess. 2:1ff.). He calls attention to his own signature at the close of each genuine letter. As a rule he dictated the epistle, but signed it with his own hand (2 Thess. 3:17).

This Epistle is a bit sharper in tone than the First and also briefer. The bearer of the first letter brought back news that made a second necessary. It was probably sent within the same year as the first.

Chapter 1

3. {*We are bound*} From the divine view, Paul feels a sense of obligation to keep on giving thanks to God because of God's continued blessings on the Thessalonians (cf. 2 Thess. 2:13). {*Even as it is meet*} From the human view, "right" is the Greek word *axios*, appropriate. {*Aboundeth*} This is the fulfillment of a prayer made in the first epistle (cf. 1 Thess. 3:12), one proof that 2 Thessalonians is later than 1 Thessalonians.

4. {*In all your persecutions*} This is a more specific term than "tribulations"; these are chasings and pursuings (cf. 2 Cor. 12:10). Their patience and faith had already attracted Paul's attention (1 Thess. 1:3) and their tribulations (1 Thess. 1:6).

5. {*A manifest token of the righteous judgment of God*} "Evidence" is the Greek word *endeigma* from *endeiknumi,* to point out, result reached, a thing proved.

6. {*If so be that it is a righteous thing with God*} This is a condition determined as fulfilled, assumed as true. This is from God's standpoint. This is as near to the idea of absolute right as it is possible to attain. {*To recompense affliction to them that afflict you*} This is in a bad sense here (cf. good sense 1 Thess. 3:9). Paul is certain of this principle, though he puts it conditionally, "on the whole" or "provided that."

7. {*Rest with us*} Lit. "let up, release" (cf. 2 Cor. 2:13; 7:5; 8:13). {*At the revelation of the Lord Jesus*} This is the Parousia (1 Thess. 2:19; 3:13; 5:23). This is a revelation of the Messiah (1 Cor. 1:7, 1 Pet. 1:7, 13 [cf. Luke 17:30]). A recompense to the persecutors and the rest from the persecutions; the angels are the attendants.

8. {*To them that know not God*} Apparently chiefly Gentiles in mind (1 Thess. 4:3; Gal. 4:8; Rom. 1:28; Eph. 2:12), though Jews are also guilty of willful ignorance of God (Rom. 2:14). {*And to them that obey not the gospel of our Lord Jesus*} This looks like another class and so refers to Jews (Rom. 10:16). Both Jews as instigators and Gentiles as officials (politarchs) were involved in the persecution in Thessalonica (Acts 17:5-9; 2 Thess. 1:6).

9. {*Shall suffer punishment*} Lit. "to pay a penalty of justice/right" (cf. Phlm. 19). This is the regular phrase in classic writers for paying the penalty. {*Eternal destruction*} (cf. 4 Macc. 10:15). Destruction (cf. 1 Thess. 5:3) does not mean here annihilation, but, as Paul proceeds to show, separation from the face of the Lord and separation from the glory of his might, for an eternity (lit. "age-long") in the coming age, in contrast to this age (cf. Matt. 25:46).

10. {*That believed*} The Greek tense has a focus that Paul thus reassures those who believed his message when there (1 Thess. 1:6; 2:13) (Frame). {*On that day*} The day of Christ's coming (2 Tim. 1:12, 18; 4:8).

11. {*To which end*} Probably referring to the contents of verses 2 Thessalonians 1:5 to 10. {*Of your calling*} "Calling" can apply to the beginning as in 1 Corinthians 1:26; Romans 11:29, but it can also apply to the final issue as in Philippians 3:14; Hebrews 3:1. Both ideas may be here. It is God's calling of the Thessalonians. {*Work of faith*} (cf. 1

Thess. 1:3). Paul prays for rich fruition of what he had seen in the beginning. Work marked by faith, springs from faith, sustained by faith. {**With power**} Lit. "in power": God's power (Rom. 1:29; Col. 1:4); Christ (1 Cor. 1:24); Holy Spirit (1 Thess. 1:5).

12. {**The name**} The OT (LXX) uses "name" embodying the revealed character of Jehovah; so here the Name of our Lord Jesus means the Messiahship and Lordship of Jesus (cf. Acts 1:15). {**In you, and ye in him**} This reciprocal glorying is Pauline, but it is also like Christ's figure of the vine and the branches in John 15:1-11. {**Of our God and the Lord Jesus Christ**} This can be translated "according to the grace of our God and the Lord Jesus Christ," (two entities/persons) though he may also mean "according to the grace of our God and Lord, Jesus Christ" (one entity/person cf. Titus 2:13; 2 Pet. 1:1).

CHAPTER 2

1. {**Touching the coming of our Lord Jesus Christ**} This is the Parousia, which lays emphasis on the presence of the Lord with his people (2 Thess. 2:1). {**And our gathering together unto him**} Here Paul is referring to the rapture, and the being forever with the Lord thereafter (cf. 1 Thess. 4:15-17, also Matt. 24:31; Mark 13:27).

2. {**Ye be not quickly shaken**} The Greek is *saleuô,* to agitate, to cause to totter like a reed (Matt. 11:7), the earth (Heb. 12:26); used with the mind (Greek *nous*), "keep their heads, keep a sober sense." {**Nor yet be troubled**} The Greek verb for troubled is an old work meaning to cry aloud, to be in a state of nervous excitement, "a continued state of agitation following the definite shock (unsettling) received" (Milligan). {**As that the day of the Lord is now present**} Paul hoped for the return of Christ but did not claim that Christ's return was imminent. {**Let no man beguile you in any wise**} Paul broadens the warning to go beyond conversation and letter. He includes "tricks" of any kind. {**Except the falling away come first**} The second coming not only is not "imminent," but will not take place before certain important things take place, a definite rebuff to the false enthusiasts of verse 2. "Falling" is the Greek word *apostasia,* the late form of *apostasis* and is our word apostasy. It seems clear that the word here means a religious revolt. Paul had spoken to the Thessalonians about it earlier. {**And the man of sin be revealed**} Since he is "revealed," this is likely a superhuman character of the event (Milligan); he is hidden somewhere who will be suddenly manifested just as false apostles pose as angels of light (2 Cor. 11:13), whether the crowning event of the apostasy or another name for the same event. He seems to be the Antichrist of 1 John 2:18. {*The son of perdition*} Lit. "the son of perdition," is applied to Judas in John 17:12, but here to the lawless one, who is not Satan, but one definite person who is doing the work of Satan.

4. {*He that opposeth and exalteth himself*} Like John's Antichrist this one opposes Christ and exalts himself. {*So that he sitteth in the temple of God*} Gaius Caligula had made a desperate attempt to have his statue set up for worship in the Temple in Jerusalem. This incident may lie behind Paul's language here. {*Setting himself forth as God*}. Caligula claimed to be God. In 1 John 2:18 we are told of "many antichrists" some of whom had already come. Hence it is not clear that Paul has in mind only one individual or even individuals at all rather than evil principles.

5. {*I used to tell you these things*}. So Paul recalls their memory of his words and leaves us without the clue to his idea. We know that one of the charges against him was that Jesus was another king, a rival to Caesar (Acts 17:7). That leads one to wonder how far Paul went when there in contrasting the kingdom of the world of which Rome was ruler and the kingdom of God of which Christ is king.

7. {*For the mystery of lawlessness doth already work*} This *mystery* means here the *secret purpose* of lawlessness already at work, the only instance of this usage in the NT.

8. {*And then*} Emphatic note of time, i.e., when the restraining one is taken out of the way, *then* the lawless one, the man of sin, the man of perdition, will be revealed. {*Whom the Lord [Jesus] shall slay*} (cf. Isa. 11:4) This is a picture of the triumph of Christ over this adversary. It is a powerful picture how the mere breath of the Lord will destroy this archenemy. {*And bring to naught by the manifestation of his coming*} "Destroy" is lit. "to render useless." It will be a grand fiasco, this advent of the man of sin. The mere appearance of Christ destroys the adversary (Vincent).

9. {*Whose coming is*} The Antichrist has his *parousia* (coming) also. So the two Epiphanies coincide. {*Lying wonders*} Lit. "in wonders of a lie." Note here the three words for the miracles of Christ (Heb. 2:4), power, signs, wonders, but all according to the working of Satan; just as Jesus had foretold (Matt. 24:24), wonders that would almost lead astray the very elect.

10. {***With all deceit of unrighteousness***} This past-master of trickery will have at his command all the energy and skill of Satan to mislead and deceive. {***The love of the truth***} That is the gospel in contrast with *lying* and *deceit*.

11. {***And for this reason God sendeth them***} Here is the definite judicial act of God (Milligan) who gives the wicked over to the evil which they have deliberately chosen (Rom. 1:24, 26, 28).

12. {***That they all might be judged***} Condemnation is involved in the fatal choice made, final judgment. These victims of the man of sin did not believe the truth and found pleasure in unrighteousness.

14. {***Whereunto***} The goal, that is the final salvation. Through our gospel, God called the Thessalonians through Paul's preaching as he calls men now through the heralds of the Cross as God chose. {***Of glory***} This is the *shekinah,* glory of Jesus).

15. {***Hold the traditions***} "Teaching" is lit. "tradition," from the Greek word *paradosis* for what is handed over to one. {***By word***} Paul draws here no distinction between oral tradition and written tradition as was done later. The worth of the tradition lies not in the form but in the source and the quality of the content.

17. {***Comfort and stablish***} God is the God of comfort (2 Cor. 1:3-7) and strength (Rom. 1:11; 16:25).

CHAPTER 3

1. {***Pray***} Greek tense translates, "keep on praying." {***That the word of the Lord may run and be glorified***} Greek tense translates, "may keep on running and keep on being glorified." Paul probably derived this metaphor from the stadium (1 Cor. 9:24; Gal. 2:2; Rom. 9:16; Phil. 2:16; 2 Tim. 4:7).

2. {***And that we may be delivered***} This is a second and more personal petition (Milligan), conceived as an event in a point of time (not on-going). {***From unreasonable and evil men***} Paul had a plague of such men in Corinth as he had in Thessalonica.

3. {***From the evil one***} (cf. Matt. 6:13) Probably grammatically masculine; either a reference to the Devil, or merely the evil man (cf. v. 2). Perhaps Paul has in mind the representative of Satan, the man of sin, pictured in 2 Thessalonians 2:1-12, by the phrase here without trying to be too definite. It might also be grammatical neuter and so not refer to an entity at all.

5. {*Direct*} The Greek word is *kateuthunô,* used of guiding the feet (Luke 1:79; 1 Thess. 3:11). The grammatical mood is one of a wish for the future (cf. 2 Thess. 2:17; 1 Thess. 5:23). {*Into the love of God*} Some believe this is not only as an objective attribute of deity, but as a ruling principle in our hearts. Most scholars take it here as subjective, the characteristic of God. {*Into the patience of Christ*} Usually this is taken to mean, "the patience shown by Christ," rather than "the patient waiting for Christ" (objective genitive).

6. {*That ye withdraw yourselves*} The Greek verb is *stellô,* to place, arrange, make compact or shorten as sails, to move oneself from or to withdraw oneself from.

7. {*How ye ought to imitate us*} Lit. "how it is necessary to imitate us" (cf. 2 Thess. 3:9; Heb. 13:7; 3 John 11). Paul knew that he had to set the new Christians in the midst of Jews and Gentiles a model for their imitation (Phil. 3:17). {*For we behaved not ourselves disorderly among you*} The Greek verb is *atakteô,* to be out of ranks of soldiers. This is a specific denial on Paul's part (cf. 2 Thess. 3:6, 17).

8. {*For nought*} Lit. "as a gift, giftwise" (cf. 2 Cor. 11:7). He lodged with Jason, but did not receive his meals *gratis,* for he paid for them. Paul had to make his financial independence clear to avoid false charges.

9. {*Not because we have not the right*} Paul is sensitive on his right to receive adequate support (1 Thess. 2:6; 1 Cor. 9:1-27, esp. 4). He did allow churches to help him where he would not be misunderstood (2 Cor. 11:7-11; Phil. 4:45).

10. {*If any will not work, neither let him eat*} As a condition determined as true or fulfilled, this is apparently a Jewish proverb based on Genesis 3:19, and also found elsewhere.

11. {*That work not at all, but are busy-bodies*} Lit. "doing nothing but doing around" also rendered "doing no business but being busy bodies." "The first persecution at Thessalonica had been fostered by a number of fanatical loungers (Acts 17:5)" (Moffatt). These theological deadbeats were too pious to work, but perfectly willing to eat at the hands of their neighbors while they frittered away the time in idleness.

12. {*That with quietness they work, and eat their own bread*} Lit. "that working with quietness they keep on eating their own bread." This is the precise opposite of their conduct (cf. 2 Thess. 3:11).

13. {*But ye, brethren, be not weary in well doing*} The "ye" is emphatic in contrast to the piddlers, with a grammatical focus of not starting such an act (cf. 2 Cor. 13:7; Gal. 6:9; Rom. 7:21, also 1 Tim. 6:18).

14. {*Note that man*} Put a tag on that man. This Greek verb is regularly used for the signature to a receipt or formal notice (Moulton and Milligan). {*To the end that he may be ashamed*} The idea is to have one's thoughts turned in on oneself.

15. {*Not as an enemy*} This is always the problem in such ostracism as discipline. Few things in our churches are more difficult of wise execution than the discipline of erring members.

16. {*Give you peace*} The Lord Jesus whose characteristic is peace, can alone give real peace to the heart and to the world. (John 14:27).

17. {*The token in every epistle*} This is a mark and proof of the genuineness of each epistle, Paul's signature. Already there were spurious forgeries (2 Thess. 2:2). Thus each church was enabled to know that Paul wrote the letter.

The First Epistle to Timothy

Author: Paul an Apostle
Recipient: Timothy in Ephesus
Date: Probably A.D. 65
From: Macedonia (Philippi)
Occasion: With personal touches, Paul wishes to help Timothy meet the problems of doctrine (against the Gnostics), discipline, and church training which are increasingly urgent.
Theme: Personal and corporate dimensions of church leadership and administration

Chapter 1

1. {*According to the commandment*} (cf. 1 Cor. 7:6; 2 Cor. 8:8; Rom. 16:26; 1 Tim. 1:1; Titus 1:3). Paul is saying that he is an apostle under orders.

3. {*To tarry*} (cf. Acts 13:43). {*That thou mightest charge*} This Greek word is *paraggellô,* "to transmit a message along from one to another (2 Thess. 3:4, 6, 10). {*Certain men*} (cf. 1 Tim. 1:20) This is vague though Paul doubtless has certain persons in Ephesus in mind.

4. {*To fables*} The Greek word is *muthois,* "speech, narrative, story, fiction, falsehood," (2 Pet. 1:16; 1 Tim. 1:4; 4:7; Titus 1:14; 2 Tim. 4:4). {*Genealogies*} (cf. Titus 3:9). {*Endless*} Lit. "not + to go through." Used here for describing the Gnostic emphasis on *aeons* (ages). {*Questionings*} Lit. "seekings out" (cf. Rom. 3:11, also cf. Acts 15:2; 1 Tim. 6:4; Titus 3:9; 2 Tim. 2:23).

6. {*Having swerved*} Lit. "having missed the mark" (cf. 1 Tim. 6:21; 2 Tim. 2:18). {*Have turned aside*} Lit. "to turn or twist out or aside" (cf. Heb. 12:13 and as metaphor in 1 Tim. 1:6; 6:20; 2 Tim. 4:4).

10. {*For abusers of themselves with men*} The Greek word is *arsenokoitais* for sodomites (cf. 1 Cor. 6:9). {*Men-stealers*} Lit. man + to catch by the foot, to enslave (whether stealing free men into slavery or stealing existing slaves). By the use of this word Paul deals a blow at the slave trade (cf. Philemon). {*The sound doctrine*} "Sound" is lit. "healthful" doctrine in a figurative sense (cf. 2 Tim. 4:3), from a verb for being well (cf. Luke 5:31; 3 John 2).

13. {*Before*} Lit. "formerly, as to the former time" (cf. Gal. 4:13). {*Persecutor*} Paul knew well enough what he was (Acts 22:4, 7; 26:14; Gal. 1:13, 23; Phil. 3:6; 2 Tim. 3:12). {*Injurious*} "An insolent man" (cf. Rom. 1:30). {*I obtained mercy*} (cf. 2 Cor. 4:1; Rom. 11:30). {*Ignorantly*} Lit. "not knowing," as in a blindness of heart (cf. Rom. 2:4).

14. {*Abounded exceedingly*} The Greek is a compounded word for emphasis of above and beyond (cf. Rom. 5:20; 6:1).

15. {*Faithful is the saying*} This phrase is used five times in the Pastorals (1 Tim. 1:15; 3:1; 4:9; Titus 3:8; 2 Tim. 2:11). This is probably a definite saying or quotation inferring knowledge of John's writings (cf. also 2 Tim. 2:11; for the content of the saying cf. John 9:37; 11:27; 16:28; 18:37). {*Chief*} Though on par with the Twelve (cf. Gal. 2:6-10), Paul also calls himself the least of the apostles (1 Cor. 15:9); and the less than the least of all saints (Eph 3:8). It is not mock humility here, but sincere appreciation of the sins of his life (cf. Rom. 7:24) as a persecutor of the church of God (Gal. 1:13), of men and even women (Acts 22:4; 26:11). He had sad memories of those days.

16. {*In me as chief*} Paul becomes the "specimen" sinner as an encouragement to all who come after him. {*Long-suffering*} (cf. 2 Cor. 6:6). {*For an ensample*} Lit. "a sketch, rough outline," derived from the Greek verb *hupotupoô,* "to outline." Paul is a sample of the kind of sinners that Jesus came to save (cf. 2 Pet. 2:6).

18. {*I commit*} Lit. (as a banking figure) "to place beside" [as food on table] and in the Greek middle voice "to entrust" (Luke 12:48; Luke 23:46). {*According to the prophecies which went before on thee*} When Timothy first comes before us (Acts 16:2) "he was testified to" by the brethren. He began his ministry rich in hopes, prayers, predictions. {*That by them thou mayest war the good warfare*} (cf. 2 Cor. 4:4). This pictures fighting as if in defensive armor (cf. 1 Cor. 9:7; 2 Cor. 10:3).

19. {*Holding faith and a good conscience*} The picture may be as a shield (Eph. 6:16) or at any rate possessing (Rom. 2:20). {*Made shipwreck*} This Greek verb is *nauageô,* derived from *naus,* ship, and *agnumi,* to break (cf. 2 Cor. 11:25).

20. {*Hymenaeus*} (cf. in 2 Tim. 2:17). {*Alexander*} Probably the same as the one in 2 Timothy 4:14 (likely not that of Acts 19:33). {*I delivered unto Satan*} (cf. 1 Cor. 5:5). It is a severe discipline of apostolic authority, apparently exclusion and more than mere abandonment (1 Thess. 2:18; 1 Cor. 5:11; 2 Cor. 2:11), though it is an obscure matter.

CHAPTER 2

2. {*For kings*} Note that Nero had already set fire to Rome and laid it on the Christians whom he was also persecuting. {*Life*} This is the Greek word *bios,* for the course of life in contrast to *zôê* (cf. Luke 8:14). {*Gravity*} (cf. Phil. 4:8; 1 Tim. 3:4; Titus 2:7).

4. {*To the knowledge*} Lit. "The full knowledge" (cf. Col. 1:6; Eph. 4:13, also 2 Tim. 3:7). Paul is anxious as in Colossians and Ephesians that the Gnostics may not lead the people astray. They need the full intellectual apprehension of Christianity.

5. {*One God*} This is standard Pauline argument for a universal gospel (Gal. 3:20; Rom. 3:30; Eph. 4:6). {*One mediator*} Lit. "a middle man" (cf. Gal. 3:20; Heb. 8:6; 9:15; 12:24).

6. {*A ransom for all*} (cf. Matt. 20:28 = Mark 10:45). The "for" in Greek is the notion of substitution where benefit is involved. The Greek word for "ransom" *antilutron* has a focus on the idea of exchange (cf. Gal. 1:4).

8. {*I desire*} (cf. Phil. 1:12). {*The men*} This is men in contrast to women (cf. 1 Tim. 2:9). It is public worship, of course, and in every place for public worship. Many modern Christians feel that there were special conditions in Ephesus as in Corinth which called for strict regulations on the women that do not always apply now. {*Lifting up holy hands*} This is standing to pray. The point here is that only men should lead in public prayer who can lift up "clean hands" (morally and spiritually clean). See Luke 24:50. {*Without wrath and disputing*} (cf. Phil. 2:14).

9. {*In like manner that women*} This is likely not instruction limited to prayer (cf. 1 Tim. 2:11-15). {*Adorn themselves*} This verb is derived from the Greek word *kosmos* "arrangement, ornament, order, world" (cf. Luke 21:5; Titus 2:10. See 1 Cor. 11:5). {*With shamefastness*} This is a word for shame, reverence (cf. Heb. 12:28).

10. {*Becometh*} The Greek word is *prepei,* "seemly." Paul wishes women to wear "becoming" clothes, but godliness is part of the "style" desired. Only here in NT good dress and good works combined.

12. {*I permit not to teach*} (cf. 1 Cor. 16:7). Paul speaks authoritatively. This refers to in the public meeting clearly. And yet all modern Christians allow women to teach Sunday school classes. One feels somehow that something is not expressed here to make it all clear. {*Nor to have dominion over a man*} The Greek word is *authenteô*, derived from *authentes*, a self doer, a master, autocrat.

14. {*Being beguiled*} This may mean in the Greek a perfective state, "completely deceived," though it is not certain (cf. 2 Thess. 2:3; 1 Cor. 3:18; 2 Cor. 11:3; Rom. 7:11; 16:18; 1 Tim. 2:14). {*Hath fallen*} The Greek tense indicates an active, permanent state (cf. 1 Cor. 11:7).

15. {*Through the childbearing*} "Through here" does not mean "by means of," rather by "function of." Though possibly referring to the birth of the Savior as glorifying womanhood, Paul may have mostly in mind that childbearing, not public teaching, is the peculiar function of woman with a glory and dignity all its own.

CHAPTER 3

2. {*The bishop*} Used in common Greek, it is applied to communal officials in Rhodes. For relation to Biblical elders (without any monarchical sense as in the Church Fathers) see Acts 20:28 (cf. also Acts 20:17; Titus 1:5, 7; Phil. 1:1). {*Without reproach*} Lit. "not to be taken hold of," irreproachable (cf. 1 Tim. 5:7; 6:14). {*Of one wife*} This clearly means one at a time. {*Temperate*} Lit. "to be sober," (cf. 1 Tim. 3:11; Titus 2:2 and also 1 Thess. 5:6, 8). {*Orderly*} (cf. 1 Tim. 2:9). This means here to be seemly, decent in conduct. {*Apt to teach*} This means qualified to teach (1 Tim. 3:2; 2 Tim. 2:24).

3. {*No brawler...nor striker*} Lit. "one who sits long at [beside] his wine," (cf. Titus 1:3). {*Not contentious*} Lit. "not a fighter," (cf. Titus 3:2). {*No lover of money*} Lit. "not lover of silver," (cf. Heb. 13:5).

5. {*Shall he take care of*} Lit. "direction of care towards (cf. Luke 10:34). {*The church of God*} As a parenthesis to the above discussion, this is the local church belonging to God (cf. Acts 20:28; also 1 Tim. 3:15, elsewhere with article 1 Cor. 10:32; 15:9; 2 Cor. 1:1; Gal. 1:13).

6. {*Not a novice*} Cf. the English "neophyte," lit. "newly planted." {*Being puffed up*} This is from the Greek word *tuphoomai*, old word (from *tuphos*, smoke, pride), to raise a smoke or mist (a smoke screen of pride, cf. 1 Tim. 6:4; 2 Tim. 3:4). {*The condemnation of the devil*} (cf. Rom. 3:8) The Greek syntax translates "[the condemnation] *passed on or received by* the devil."

7. {*From them that are without*} Paul cares about the witness of outsiders (cf. 1 Thess. 4:12; 1 Cor. 10:32; Col. 4:5). There are, of course, two sides to this matter. {*Reproach*} (cf. Rom. 15:3). {*The snare of the devil*} This is a snare set by the devil. Used as a snare for birds (Luke 21:35), any sudden trap (Rom. 11:9), of sin (1 Tim. 6:9), of the devil (1 Tim. 3:7; 2 Tim. 2:26). Ancients used it of the snares of love.

8. {*Deacons*} (cf. Phil. 1:1). Now another class of church officers: first, bishops or elders; now, deacons. {*Not double tongued*} This is one placed between two persons and saying one thing to one, another to the other. Like Bunyan's Parson "Mr. Two-Tongues." {*Not given to much wine*} Lit. "Not holding [the mind] on much wine." The vocabulary choice in Greek implies that the mind is involved. That attitude leads to over-indulgence (cf. 1 Tim. 1:4).

9. {*The mystery of the faith*} Lit. "The inner secret of the faith," the revelation given in Christ (cf. 2 Thess. 2:7; 1 Cor. 2:7; Rom. 16:25; Col. 1:26; Eph. 3:9). {*In a pure conscience*} (cf. 1 Tim. 1:19).

10. {*First be proved*} Lit. "to test as metals, etc." (cf. 1 Thess. 2:4). How the proposed deacons are to be "first" tested before approved Paul does not say. See Philippians 1:10 for the two senses (test, approve) of the word. {*If they be blameless*} Lit. "being blameless" (cf. 1 Cor. 1:8; Col. 1:22).

11. {*Women*} Apparently this is "women as deacons" (Rom. 16:1 about Phoebe) and not women in general or just "wives of deacons." {*Not slanderers*} This is the original meaning of the Greek word *diabolos,* the devil being the chief slanderer (Eph. 6:11). "She-devils" in reality (Titus 2:3). {*Faithful in all things*} Perhaps referring to distribution of alms, the deaconesses had special temptations.

13. {*A good standing*} In the inscriptions it means a good foothold or standing. It is doubtful if Paul means a higher ranking here.

15. {*To behave themselves*} It is conduct as members of God's family that Paul has in mind. This is the Greek word *anastrephô,* to turn up and down (cf. 2 Cor. 1:12; Eph. 2:3). {*In the house of God*} This is the family of God rather than the house or temple of God. Christians as yet had no separate houses of worship. Christians are: a sanctuary (1 Cor. 3:16; 2 Cor. 6:16); and conversely a family (Eph. 2:19). {*Which*} This relative pronoun connects "house of God," with church. {*The church* *of the living God*} Probably here it refers to the general church or kingdom, though the local church in 1 Timothy 3:5. {*The pillar and ground of the truth*} Paul changes the metaphor again as he often does. Those words are in apposition to "church" and "household." On "pillar" Galatians 2:9; Revelation 3:12. "Ground" probably means "stay" or "support" rather than "foundation" or "ground" (cf. Col. 1:23; 2 Tim. 2:19 for similar idea. See also Matt. 16:18).

16. {*The mystery of godliness*} Here the phrase explains "a pillar and ground of the truth" (v. 15, cf. also Col. 1:27). The revealed secret of true religion, the mystery of Christianity. {*Was manifested*} The Greek word is *phaneroô*, to manifest. Here used to describe the incarnation "in the flesh" of Christ (an answer also to the Docetic Gnostics). The verb is used by Paul elsewhere of the incarnation (Rom. 16:26; Col. 1:26) as well as of the second coming (Col. 3:4). {*Preached among the nations*} "Nations" may mean "all creation" (Col. 1:23) and not just Gentiles as distinct from Jews. Paul had done more of this heralding of Christ among the Gentiles than any one else. It was his glory (Eph. 3:1, 8; cf. 1 Tim. 2:7). {*Received up in glory*} This refers to the ascension. This verse has six Greek verbs in the same voice and tense in succession, making a rhythmic arrangement like a hymn (cf. Rom. 8:29).

CHAPTER 4

1. {*Expressly*} This refers to the Holy Spirit: either in OT prophecy (Acts 1:16) or in Christian utterance (2 Thess. 2:2; 1 Cor. 14:1; cf. also Matt. 24:10, 24). {*In later times*} This is relative time from the prediction, now coming true (a present danger). {*From the faith*} This refers not to a creed, but faith in God through Christ. {*Seducing spirits*} The Greek word is *plane*, wandering. This is probably some heathen or the worst of the Gnostics.

2. {*Through the hypocrisy of men that speak lies*} (cf. Gal. 2:13). The classical Greek word for "liars" carries the sense of liars on a large scale. {*Branded in their own conscience as with a hot iron*} The Greek verb is *kausteriazô*, a rare verb only here and once in Strabo. Branded with the mark of Satan (2 Tim. 2:26) as Paul was with the marks of Christ (Gal. 6:17).

3. {*Forbidding to marry*} (cf. Col. 2:16, 21). Paul condemns the ascetic practices of the Gnostics. The Essenes, Therapeutae and other oriental sects forbade marriage. In 1 Corinthians 7:1ff. Paul does not condemn marriage.

4. {*Creature*} The Greek word *ktisma* has a focus on the result of creating (cf. Gen. 1:31; Mark 7:15; Rom. 14:14). {*To be rejected*} Lit. "to throw away." {*If it be received*} Lit. Greek tense is "Being received," in conditional sense, "with thanksgiving."

5. {*It is sanctified*} Here "is" has a focus of being "rendered holy" rather than "declared holy" (cf. 1 Tim. 4:4). {*Through the word of God and prayers*} "Word and prayers" are a figure almost of two elements as one, so translate, "by the use of Scripture in prayer."

6. {*If thou put the brethren in mind of these things*} Translate, "suggesting these things to the brethren." {*Nourished in*} The Greek word is *entrephô*, "to nourish in," used by Plato of "nourished in the laws." {*The words of the faith*} This is the right diet for babes in Christ. {*Which thou hast followed*} Lit. "to follow beside," of persons (often in old Greek) or of ideas and things (Luke 1:3; 1 Tim. 4:6; 2 Tim. 3:10).

7. {*Refuse*} The Greek verb is *paraiteô*, old verb, to ask of one and then to beg off from one as in Luke 14:18; Acts 25:11; 1 Timothy 4:7; 5:11; Titus 3:10; 2 Timothy 2:23. {*Old wives' tales*} (cf. 1 Tim. 1:4). Tales such as old women tell to children like the Gnostic *aeons*. {*Exercise thyself*} This Greek work was originally to exercise naked (Greek word *gumnos*, cf. also Heb. 5:14; 12:11).

10. {*Saviour of all men...specially of them that believe*} (cf. 1 Tim. 1:1). Not that all men "are saved" in the full sense, but God gives life (cf. 1 Tim. 6:13) to all (Acts 17:28); while God is potentially Savior of all, He is actually Savior of believers. In this sense Jesus is the "Savior of the World" (John 4:42). Cf. Galatians 6:10.

12. {*Despise*} Lit. "To think down on, despise," (cf. Rom. 2:4). {*Be thou*} A command in the Greek, with the tense translating, "Keep on becoming." {*In purity*} This has a focus on the sinlessness of life. Used of a Nazirite (Num. 6:2, 21, cf. also 1 Tim. 5:2).

13. {*Till I come*} Translate, "While I am coming." {*Give heed*} Translate, "keep on putting thy mind on."

14. {*Neglect not*} Lit. "not to care." (cf. Matt. 22:5; 1 Tim. 4:14; Heb. 2:3; 8:9). {*The gift that is in thee*} Here it is God's gift to Timothy as in 2 Timothy 1:6. {*By prophecy*} This was accompanied by prophecy (1 Tim. 1:18), not bestowed by prophecy. {*With the laying on of the hands of the presbytery*} (cf. Barnabas and Saul, Acts 13:2), There is no way to tell when and where it was done, whether at Lystra when Timothy joined Paul's party or at Ephesus just before Paul left Timothy there (1 Tim. 1:3)

15. {*Be diligent in these things*} (cf. Acts 4:25). Translate Greek tense, "keep on practicing these things." {*Thy progress*} The Greek word is *prokopê,* from *prokoptô,* to cut forward, to blaze the way (cf. Phil. 1:12, 25).

16. {*Take heed to thyself…continue in these things*} (cf. Phil. 2:1, 16). Translate, "Keep on paying attention to yourself." "Persevere" translates, "stay by them," "stick to them," "see them through." Stick to the business of framing your own life and your teaching on right lines (Parry). {*Thou shalt save*} This means to finally, in the future, save (cf. 1 Cor. 9:27; John 10:9).

CHAPTER 5

1. {*Rebuke not an elder*} This is not the office of a minister (cf. 1 Tim. 3:2). The Greek syntax is the prohibition against committing an act. Lit. "to strike upon," here in figurative sense with words rather than with fists. Respect for age is what is here commanded, an item appropriate to the present time.

3. {*That are widows indeed*} (cf. Mark 12:40, 42; Acts 6:1; 1 Cor. 7:8). Verses 3 to 8 are widows who are in distress; 9 to 16 are those who are in the employment of the local church for certain work. In spite of arising trouble, all classes of widows in Ephesus (cf. Acts 6:1-6) were to be properly respected (lit. honored).

4. {*Let them learn*} Greek tense translates as a command, "Let them keep on learning." {*First*} This means "before anything else." No "corban" business here (cf. Mark 7:11). No acts of "piety" toward God will make up for impiety towards parents. {*Their own family*} Only duty to Christ is greater (Luke 14:26). {*To requite*} Lit. "to give back," (Rom. 2:6), to keep on giving back. {*Their parents*} Lit. "one who comes before, ancestor" (cf. 2 Tim. 1:3).

5. {*Desolate*} This means without husband, children, or other close kin.

6. {*She that giveth herself to pleasure*} (cf. Jas. 5:5). This is the Greek verb *splatalaô,* from *spatalê* riotous, luxurious living.

8. {*Provideth not for his own*} Lit. "to think beforehand" (cf. 2 Cor. 8:21; Rom. 12:7). {*He hath denied the faith*} His act of impiety belies (Titus 1:16) his claim to the faith (Rev. 2:13). {*Worse than an unbeliever*} That is, the unbeliever makes no profession of piety.

9. {*He hath denied the faith*} This is the Greek verb *katalegô*, "to set down in an official list." This list of genuine widows (vv. 1 Tim. 5:3, 5) apparently had some kind of church work to do (care for the sick, the orphans, etc.).

10. {*If she hath brought up children…if she hath used hospitality to strangers*} Here are two qualifications of leadership (cf. 1 Tim. 3:2). The whole verse is filled with conditions assumed to be true or fulfilled. {*If she hath relieved the afflicted*} This is the Greek word *eparkeô*, to give sufficient aid (cf. 1 Tim. 5:16). Experience that qualified her for the work of showing mercy. {*If she hath diligently followed*} Lit. "to follow close upon," (cf. 1 Tim. 5:24; 1 Pet. 2:21). In summary, a widow must show her qualifications for leadership as with bishops and deacons.

11. {*But younger widows refuse*} Lit. as a command "Beg off from." They lack experience as above and they have other ambitions. {*When they have waxed wanton*} Lit. "to feel the impulse of sexual desire," (cf. Rev. 18:7, 9). Some render as "exercise youthful vigor against Christ."

12. {*Their first pledge*} It is like breaking the marriage contract. Evidently one of the pledges on joining the order of widows was not to marry.

13. {*And withal…they learn to be idle*} Such young enrolled widows have other perils also, see below (cf. also Titus 1:12). {*Going about…from house to house*} This is a vivid picture of idle tattlers and gossips strolling about. {*But gossips*} This is the Greek word *phluaros,* from *phluô* to boil up, to throw up bubbles, like blowing soap bubbles (cf. 3 John 10).

14. {*The younger widows*} "Widows" strictly not in Greek, though needed for the idea. {*Rule the household*} Note that the wife is here put as ruler of the household, proper recognition of her influence; a new and improved position.

15. {*After Satan*} Lit. as a preposition "behind Satan." Used by Jesus of disciples coming behind (follow after) him (Matt. 16:24).

16. {*That believeth*} The "believer" is one of the household rulers (cf. 1 Tim. 5:14); the "widows" refer to the widows dependent on her and who are considered as candidates to be enrolled in the list.

17. {*Of double honour*} (cf. 1 Tim. 6:1) The Greek word *timês* suggests "remuneration" (pay) rather than "honor." Others say it means "honorarium" (both honor and pay and so "double"). Still others, suggest twice the pay given the enrolled widows. Double pay for special service was known among soldiers. {*Especially those who labor in word and teaching*} (cf. 2 Tim. 2:6). "Labor," can mean either: the amount of effort as intense (cf. 1 Tim. 5:18), or actually doing in contrast to presiding (cf. Titus 1:8; 1 Thess. 5:12). The former is more likely.

18. {*The laborer is worthy of his hire*} (cf. Luke 10:7, also Matt. 10:10). 1 Corinthians 9:14 clearly shows that Jesus had said this saying. Yet two things are not clear: is Paul quoting the Gospel of Luke (possible if dated about A.D. 62 or 63) or some other source?; second, does "Scripture" in this verse refer to this saying as well as the first saying of not muzzling the ox?

20. {*Them that sin*} This refers to the elders who continue to sin. {*In the sight of all*} Lit. "in the eye of all." This refers to the elders or even of the church (cf. 1 Tim. 5:21; Gal. 1:20). This is public rebuke when a clear case, not promiscuous gossip. {*May be in fear*} Lit. "may keep on having fear" (of exposure). Possibly this refers to the rest of the elders.

22. {*Lay hands hastily*} Laying hands is in the sense of approval for ordination (cf. Acts 6:6; 13:3). {*Keep thyself pure*} The Greek tense translates, "Keep on keeping thyself pure."

23. {*Be no longer a drinker of water*} Not complete asceticism, but only the need of some wine urged in Timothy's peculiar physical condition (a sort of medical prescription for this case). {*But use a little wine*} The emphasis here is on a *little* wine. {*Thine often infirmities*} Lit. "weaknesses, lack of strength" (cf. Luke 5:33; Acts 24:26; Rom. 8:26). Timothy was clearly a semi-invalid.

24. {*Evident*} Lit. "openly plain," or "plain before all" (cf. Heb. 7:24). {*And some men also they follow after*} These sins dog their steps (cf. 1 Pet. 2:21). The sins are not clearly manifest at first, but come out plainly at last. How true that is of secret sins.

CHAPTER 6

1. {*Their own masters*} That is always where the shoe pinches. Our "despot" is this very Greek word; "lord" in Greek has a wider outlook (of humans Titus 2:9; 2 Tim. 2:21; 1 Pet. 2:18; of God Luke 2:29; Acts 4:24, 29; of Christ 2 Pet. 2:1).

2. {*Let not despise them*} Lit. "to think down on" (cf. 1 Tim. 4:12). He must not presume on the equality of Christian brotherhood not allowed by the state's laws. Some of these Christian slaves might be pastors of churches to which the master belonged.

3. {*Teacheth a different doctrine*} (cf. 1 Tim. 1:3). This is assumed to be a true or fulfilled condition. {*The words of our Lord Jesus Christ*} "Of" can mean either: (1) the words *from* the Lord Jesus, a collection of his sayings (cf. 1 Tim. 5:18; Acts 20:35); or (2) words *about* Jesus (cf. 2 Tim. 1:8; 1 Cor. 1:18).

4. {*Doting*} The Greek word is *noseô*, to be sick, to be morbid over. {*Disputes of words*} Lit. "logomachy" to fight over words (2 Tim. 2:14). {*Surmisings*} Lit. "to surmise, to suspect" (Acts 25:18). All these are the product of an ignorant, conceited mind.

5. {*Wranglings*} Lit. "mutual irritations or rubbings alongside." {*Bereft of the truth*} (cf. 1 Cor. 6:8).

8. {*Food*} Lit. in plural "supports or nourishments." {*Covering*} Lit. in plural "coverings."

9. {*Desire to be rich*} This is the will to be rich at any cost and in haste (Prov. 28:20). Possibly Paul still has teachers and preachers in mind. {*Drown*} The Greek word is *buthizô* from *buthos* (bottom), to drag to the bottom (cf. Luke 5:7 of the boat). {*Destruction and perdition*} This is not annihilation, but eternal punishment (cf. 1 Thess. 5:3; 2 Thess. 1:9; 1 Cor. 5:5 and also 2 Thess. 2:3; Phil. 3:19).

10. {*The love of money*} (cf. 2 Tim. 3:12). This refers back to "want to get rich" in verse 9. {*A root of all kinds of evil*} Here a metaphorical root (Rom. 11:11-18). Undoubtedly Paul quotes a similar proverb attributed to Bion and to Democritus, roughly, "the love of money is the 'metropolis' of all evil." {*Have pierced themselves through*} The Greek word has a perfective focus "to *completely* pierce."

12. {*Lay hold on*} Lit. "get a grip on" (cf. 1 Tim. 6:19). {*The good confession*} This is the public confession in baptism which many witnessed (cf. 1 Tim. 6:13 of Jesus).

13. {*Witnessed*} Christ gave his evidence as a witness to the Kingdom of God. Evidently Paul knew some of the facts that appear in John 18:1ff.

14. {*Until the appearing*} This is second epiphany (coming) of Christ (cf. 2 Thess. 2:18, also Titus 2:13; 2 Tim. 1:10; 4:1, 8).

15. {*Who is the blessed and only Potentate*} Translate as "The happy and alone Potentate" (cf. Luke 1:52). {*The King of kings*} Translate, "the King of those who rule as kings." This is a title of the Ancient Near East; cf. "Lord of lords" (Rev. 10:16).

16. {*Who only hath immortality*} (cf. 1 Cor. 15:53). Emperor worship may be behind the use of "alone" here. {*Amen*} This marks the close of the doxology as in 1 Timothy 1:17.

17. {*In this present world*} Lit. "In the now age," which is in contrast with the future. {*But on God*} He alone is stable, not wealth. {*Richly all things to enjoy*} This is a lavish emphasis to the generosity of God.

19. {*Laying up in store*} (cf. Matt. 6:19). Ironically, a treasure is gathered by giving it away. {*Which is life indeed*} This life is merely the shadow of the eternal reality to come.

20. {*Guard that which is committed unto thee*} The Greek tense shows a certain urgency. "Entrusted" is lit. "to place beside as a deposit," 2 Timothy 2:2. This is a banking figure. {*Babblings*} Lit. "uttering emptiness" (cf. 2 Tim. 2:16).

THE SECOND EPISTLE TO TIMOTHY

AUTHOR: Paul
RECIPIENT: Timothy (in Ephesus)
DATE: Autumn of A.D. 67 or Spring of A.D. 68
FROM: Rome
OCCASION: Paul, a prisoner facing death, urges Timothy to come as soon as possible to him.
THEME: A passionate reminder of the basics for living the Christian life and being a minister of Jesus Christ

CHAPTER 1

1. {*According to the promise of the life which is in Christ Jesus*} Translate, "With a view to the fulfillment of the promise" (cf. Gal. 3:29; 1 Tim. 4:8). Here this is life that is in Christ Jesus including both the present and the future.

3. {*I thank*} Translate, "I have gratitude" (cf. 1 Tim. 1:12, also Luke 17:9; Acts 2:47). {*Whom I serve from my forefathers*} The Greek tense translates "I have been serving." For forefathers see 1 Timothy 5:4. Paul claims a pious ancestry as in Acts 24:14; Acts 26:5; Galatians 2:14; Philippians 3:4-7. {*Unceasing*} (cf. Rom. 9:2). Translate, "how I hold the memory concerning you unceasing." The use of the Greek *adialeiptôs* (adverb) is a sort of epistolary formula (1 Thess. 1:2; 2:13; 5:17; Rom. 1:9).

4. {*Night and day*} Translate, "by night and by day" (cf. 1 Thess. 2:9; 3:10). {*Remembering thy tears*} (cf. 1 Cor. 11:2). This is probably an allusion to the scene at Miletus (Acts 20:37, cf. Acts 20:19).

5. {*Having been reminded*} Lit. "having received a reminder" (1 Pet. 1:13, also Rom. 7:8, 11). This is likely a reminder by another. {*I am persuaded*} Greek tense translates "I stand persuaded" (cf. 1 Tim. 1:12 and Rom. 8:38).

6. {*That thou stir up*} Lit. "to rekindle, to stir into flame," and the Greek tense translates "to keep blazing," (cf. 1 Thess. 5:19 for the figure of fire concerning the Holy Spirit; also Luke 12:49).

7. {*A spirit of fearfulness*} "Timidity" is always in a bad sense of cowardice. {*Of love*} (a fruit Gal. 5:22; which drives out fear 1 John 4:18). {*Of discipline*} Lit. "control," this is self-control (cf. 1 Tim. 2:9).

8. {*Be not ashamed of*} (cf. Rom. 1:16; 6:21). The Greek tense translates "Do not become ashamed" (as he had not). {*The testimony of our Lord*} (cf. 1 Cor. 1:6; 2:1). Paul probably has in mind the saying of Jesus preserved in Mark 8:38 (Luke 9:26; cf. also 2 Tim. 2:12). {*Suffer hardship with*} Paul challenges Timothy by this verb for the purpose to a joint suffering with the Lord Jesus and Paul "for the gospel." {*According to the power of God*} This is power given by God (2 Cor. 6:7).

9. {*Called us with a holy calling*} The calling is apparently not the invitation, but the consecrated service (cf. Phil. 3:14). God calls men (1 Thess. 2:12; 1 Cor. 1:9; Gal. 1:6; Rom. 8:20; 9:11).

10. {*By the appearing*} This refers to the Incarnation (Titus 2:11; 3:4). {*Brought to light*} One might say, "to turn the light on" (cf. 1 Cor. 4:5; Eph. 1:18). {*Life and incorruption*} This is the opposite of "death," and means an unchangeable life.

12. {*That which I have committed unto him*} "Entrusted," literally, "my deposit," as in a bank, the bank of heaven which no burglar can break (Matt. 6:19, also 2 Tim. 1:14). {*Against that day*} The day of Christ's second coming (cf. 2 Tim. 1:18; 4:8; 2 Thess. 1:10).

14. {*Guard*} (cf. 1 Tim. 6:20). God has also made an investment in Timothy (cf. 2 Tim. 1:12). Timothy must not let that fail.

15. {*Are turned away from me*} It is not known to what incident Paul refers, whether the refusal of the Christians in the Roman province of Asia to help Paul on his arrest (or in response to an appeal from Rome) or whether the Asian Christians in Rome deserted Paul in the first stage of the trial (cf. 2 Tim. 4:16). Two of these Asian deserters are mentioned by name, perhaps for reasons known to Timothy.

16. {*Grant mercy*} This Greek form shows this is a wish about the future. {*Unto the house of Onesiphorus*} (cf. 2 Tim. 4:19). Apparently Onesiphorus is now dead (cf. also 2 Tim. 1:18). {*For he oft refreshed me*} Lit. "to cool again" (cf. Acts 3:20). In the first imprisonment or the second. If he lost his life for coming to see Paul, it was probably recently during this imprisonment.

17. {*He sought me diligently and found me*} He did it at the risk of his own life apparently.

18. {*Grant unto him to find mercy*} The Greek form expresses this as a wish for the future (cf. 2 Tim. 1:16). This is that he find mercy from the Lord (Jesus) as he found me. {*Thou knowest very well*} Lit. "you know better (than I)," for he did those things in Ephesus where you are.

CHAPTER 2

1. {*Be strengthened*} Greek tense translates "keep on being empowered," "keep in touch with the power" (cf. 1 Tim. 1:12; Rom. 4:20;
Phil. 4:13; Eph. 6:10). {*In the grace that is in Christ Jesus*} This is
where the power is located. Christ is the *dynamo* for power only when
and while we keep in touch with him.

2. {*From me*} (cf. 2 Tim. 1:13). Paul was Timothy's chief teacher of
Christ. {*Among many witnesses*} These are not mere spectators, but
testifiers in some legal sense. Paul in 1 Corinthians 15:1-8 gives many
witnesses of the resurrection of Christ. {*Commit thou*} Lit. "to deposit" as a command (cf. 1 Tim. 1:12, 14, 18). {*Others also*} This is
"others" not in the sense of "different," but "others *in addition.*" This is
the way to pass on the torch of the light of the knowledge of God in
Christ. Paul taught Timothy who will teach others who will teach still
others.

3. {*As a good soldier*} Paul does not hesitate to use this military metaphor (this word only here for a servant of Christ) with which he is so
familiar (cf. 1 Cor. 9:7; 2 Cor. 10:3; 1 Tim. 1:18).

4. {*Entangleth himself*} Lit. "to inweave" (cf. Matt. 27:29 and 2 Pet.
2:20). {*In the affairs of this life*} This is "business, occupation," (cf.
Luke 19:13). The Greek word *bios* is the "course of life" (cf. 1 Tim. 2:2)
not the other Greek word for life *zôê* as "existence."

5. {*If also a man contend in the games...have contended*} The Greek
tense of the first "contends" is to "engage in a contest in general" while
the second "contends" Greek tense is to "engage in a particular contest." {*Is not crowned*} (cf. Heb. 2:7, 9). The victor in the athletic
contests was crowned with a garland.

6. {*The husbandman that laboreth*} Translates, "The toiling tiller of
the soil" (cf. 1 Cor. 3:9 and also 1 Cor. 9:7).

7. {*Consider*} As a command, lit. "to put your mind" (cf. Eph. 3:4 and
1 Cor. 10:15). {*Understanding*} This is "comprehension" (from the
Greek *suniêmi*, to send together, to grasp).

8. {*Risen from the dead*} The Greek tense translates "still risen" (cf.
1 Cor. 15:4, 12-20). This is the cardinal fact about Christ that proves his
claim to be the Messiah, the Son of God. {*According to my gospel*}
(cf. Rom. 2:16; 16:25). This is not a written gospel, but my message.

See also 1 Corinthians 15:1; 2 Corinthians 11:7; Galatians 1:11; 2:2; 1 Timothy 1:11.

9. {*I suffer hardship*} Lit. "I suffer evil" (cf. 2 Tim. 4:5; Jas. 5:13). {*Unto bonds*} Lit. "up to bonds." This is a common experience with Paul (2 Cor. 11:23; Phil. 1:7, 13, 14; Col. 4:18). {*As a malefactor*} Lit. "doer of evil" (cf. Luke 23:32 [of the robbers]). One of the charges made against Paul. {*Is not bound*} Paul is bound with a chain, but no fetters are on the word of God (cf. 1 Thess. 2:13; 1 Cor. 14:36; 2 Cor. 2:17; Phil. 1:14; Titus 2:5).

10. {*For the elect's sake*} Lit. "Because of the elect" (Rom. 8:33; Col. 3:12; Titus 1:1) for whom Paul suffered so much (Col. 1:6; 12:15; Phil. 2:17; Eph. 3:1, 13). {*The salvation*} This refers to the final salvation "with eternal glory." This phrase only here and 1 Peter 5:10, but in 2 Corinthians 4:17 we have "eternal weight of glory."

14. {*That they strive not about words*} This Greek word *logomacheô* is apparently coined by Paul from *logomachia* (1 Tim. 6:4 which see), a back formation in that case. A mere war of words displeases Paul (Titus 3:9).

15. {*To present*} (cf. Col. 1:22, 28). {*Approved unto God*} (cf. 1 Cor. 11:19; 2 Cor. 10:18). {*Handling aright*} Lit. "cutting straight." It occurs in Proverbs 3:6; 11:5 for making straight paths. Some suggesting a straight plowing or stone laying metaphor. Since Paul was a tent maker and knew how to cut straight the rough camel-hair cloth, why not let that be the metaphor? Certainly plenty of exegesis is crooked enough (crazy-quilt patterns) to call for careful cutting to set it straight.

17. {*Will eat*} Lit. "Will have pasturage or increase." {*As doth gangrene*} This Greek word is derived from *graô* or *grainô*, to gnaw, to eat, an eating, spreading disease. Hymenaeus is probably the one mentioned in 1 Timothy 1:20. Nothing is known of Philetus.

19. {*Let every one depart*} (This is a paraphrase of Num. 16:27; Isa. 26:13; 52:11; Jer. 20:9). Lit. "Let every one stand off from." This is probably another echo of the rebellion of Korah.

20. {*In a great house*} This is a metaphor of a palace. He doubtless has the Kingdom of God in mind, but he works out the metaphor of a great house of the rich. {*Of earth*} This is baked clay (cf. 2 Cor. 4:7).

21. {*If a man purge himself*} Paul drops the metaphor of the house and takes up the individual as one of the "vessels/articles." {*Prepared*} The Greek shows a state of readiness (cf. 1 Cor. 2:9 [LXX]).

22. {*Youthful*} There are lusts peculiar to flaming youth. {*Follow after*} Be in a steady pursuit as if in a chase of virtues (cf. 1 Thess. 5:15, also Gal. 5:22).

23. {*Ignorant*} Lit. "Untrained, uneducated," as the speculations of a half-educated mind. {*Refuse*} (cf. 1 Tim. 4:7).

24. {*Must not strive*} Lit. "it is not necessary for him to fight" (in such verbal quibbles). {*Forbearing*} This is the Greek word *anexikakos* from *anexô* and *kakon,* putting up with evil.

25. {*Correcting*} This implies "schooling" (Parry) (cf. Titus 2:12). {*Repentance*} This is the Greek word *metanoia,* change of mind (2 Cor. 7:10; Rom. 2:4). {*Unto the knowledge of the truth*} This is "full knowledge" (cf. Col. 1:9).

26. {*They may recover themselves*} Lit. "to be sober again," (cf. 1 Thess. 5:6). {*Out of the snare of the devil*} They have been caught while mentally intoxicated in the devil's snare (1 Tim. 3:7). See Romans 11:9 for "snare." {*By him unto his will*} The best way to understand this is "captive by him [Devil] to do his [God's] will [when they have come back to their senses]."

CHAPTER 3

2. {*Boastful*} This is an old word for empty pretender (cf. Rom. 1:30).

4. {*Headstrong*} This is an old word lit. "falling forward," (cf. Ac. 19:36).

5. {*A form of godliness*} (cf. Rom. 2:20). This has the outward shape without the reality.

6. {*That creep*} Here it means "to enter," to slip in by insinuation, as here (cf. Jude 4; 2 Pet. 2:1; Gal. 2:4). These stealthy "creepers" are pictured also in Titus 1:11. {*Take captive*} The Greek tense translates, "taking captive" (cf. 2 Cor. 10:5; Rom. 7:23). {*Silly women*} Lit. "little women," it is used contemptuously here. Ramsay suggests "society ladies." {*Laden with sins*} This is the Greek word *sôreuô,* from *sôros,* a heap) to heap up (cf. Rom. 12:20). {*Divers*} Lit. "many colored" (cf. Titus 3:3). Modern examples abound to illustrate how Gnostic cults led women into licentiousness under the guise of religion or of liberty. The priestesses of Aphrodite and of Isis were illustrations ready to hand. {*Led away*} The Greek tense translates, "continually led astray" or "from time to time."

7. {*Never able to come to the knowledge of the truth*} This is a pathetic picture of these hypnotized women without intellectual power to cut through the fog of words and, though always learning scraps of things, they never come into the full knowledge of the truth in Christ.

8. {*Jannes and Jambres*} These are the traditional names of the magicians who withstood Moses (cf. Exod. 7:11). {*Withstood*} Lit. "they stood against." Paul here pictures the seducers of the "weak-willed women" above. {*Reprobate*} (cf. 1 Cor. 9:27; Titus 1:16). They had renounced their trust in Christ.

11. {*What things befell me*} This refers to actual experiences of Paul (cf. 2 Cor. 11:30-33 as even in the book of Acts 13-14; also Gal. 2:11). {*What persecutions I endured*} This is the Greek word *hupopherô*, to bear under (cf. 1 Cor. 10:13).

12. {*That would live godly shall suffer persecution*} Paul does not regard his experience as peculiar, but only part of the price of loyal service to Christ.

13. {*Impostors*} This is an old word from wailers (Greek *goaô*, to bewail), professional mourners, deceivers, jugglers. Modern impostors know all the tricks of the trade.

14. {*But abide thou*} The "you" is an emphatic contrast. {*Knowing from whom*} The list included the OT prophets, Paul, Eunice, Lois. There ought to be moral authority in such personages.

15. {*From a babe*} Only here in the Pastorals. This teaching from the fifth year, covering the whole of Timothy's recollections. {*Thou has known*} This is reaching from a babe until now (in the letter). Would that Christian parents took like pains today. {*The sacred writings*} This is "Sacred writings" or "Holy Scriptures."

16. {*Every scripture inspired of God is also profitable*} Is this "every scripture" or "all scripture?" One can render it here either way. A second concern is where to insert the understood "to be" verb in the sentence. Is it "All scripture (or every scripture) *is* inspired of God and profitable"; or "All scripture (or every scripture), inspired of God, *is* also profitable"? {*Inspired of God*} Lit. "God-breathed." Perhaps this is in contrast to the commandments of men in Titus 1:14. {*Profitable*} The Greek word is *ôphelimos* (cf. 1 Tim. 4:8. See Rom. 15:4); there are four things for which the Scriptures are profitable: teaching, reproof, correction (lit. to set straight in addition cf. Titus 1:5), and instruction (cf. Eph. 6:4).

CHAPTER 4

2. {*Be instant in season, out of season*} "Prepared," lit. "take a stand," "stand upon it or up to it," "carry on," "stick to it." There are all sorts of seasons (lit. "times" see next verse), some difficult (cf. 2 Tim. 3:1), some easy (cf. 1 Cor. 16:12). {*Reprove*} Translate, "bring to proof" (Eph. 5:11). {*Rebuke*} Lit. "to give honor (or blame) to, to chide" (Luke 17:3).
3. {*A time when*} This is one of the "out of season" times. {***Will not endure***} Lit. "will not hold themselves back from" (Col. 3:13). {***Having itching ears***} The Greek word is *knêthô*, late and rare form of the Attic *knaô,* to scratch, to tickle. Clement of Alexandria tells of speakers tickling the ears of those who want to be tickled. This is the temptation of the merely "popular" preacher, to furnish the latest tickle.
4. {*Myths*} They prefer myths to the truth as some today turn away to any fads that will give a new momentary thrill to their itching ears and morbid minds.
5. {*Do the work of an evangelist*} This is a gospelizer (cf. 1 Cor. 1:17; Eph. 4:11). {*Fulfil*} This verb means to fill full (cf. Col. 4:12, 17).
6. {*I am already being offered*} Lit. "to pour out a libation or drink offering" (cf. Phil. 2:17). What was then a possibility is now a certainty. The sacrifice of Paul's life-blood has begun. {*Of my departure*} Lit. "to loosen up or back, to unloose," (cf. Phil. 1:23 for the metaphor of death). {*Is come*} (cf. 1 Thess. 5:3; Luke 21:34). The Greek tense has a focus that the hour has struck. The time has come.
7. {*I have fought the good fight*} (cf. 1 Cor. 9:25; Col. 1:29 and also Phil. 1:27, 30, etc.). The "fight" is the athletic contest of his struggle for Christ. {*I have finished the course*} He had used this metaphor also of himself to the elders at Ephesus (Acts 20:24). Then the "course" was ahead of him. Now it is behind him. {*I have kept the faith*} Paul has not deserted. He has kept faith with Christ (cf. Rev. 14:12).
8. {*Crown of righteousness*} This is the victor's crown (cf. 1 Cor. 9:25). {*At that day*} This refers to that great and blessed day (cf. 2 Tim. 1:12, 18). {*The righteous judge*} This is the umpire who makes no mistakes who judges us all (2 Cor. 5:10).
10. {*Forsook me*} This is willful desertion (cf. Col. 4:14 and Phlm. 24). {*Titus to Dalmatia*} Titus had been asked to rejoin Paul in Nicopolis where he was to winter, probably the winter previous to this one (Titus 3:12). He came and has been with Paul.

11. {*Only Luke is with me*} Luke is with Paul now in Rome as during the first Roman imprisonment (Phlm. 1:24; Col. 4:14). {*Take Mark*} Lit. "to pick up," (cf. Eph. 6:13, 16). {*He is useful to me*} (cf. 2 Tim. 2:21). Paul had long ago changed his opinion of Mark (Col. 4:10) because Mark had changed his conduct and had made good in his ministry.

13. {*The books*} These are probably papyrus rolls. {*Especially the parchments*} The dressed skins were first made at Pergamum and so termed "parchments." These in particular would likely be copies of OT books, parchment being more expensive than papyrus, possibly even copies of Christ's sayings (Luke 1:1-4).

14. {*Alexander the coppersmith*} (cf. 2 Tim. 1:20). This is not the one in Acts 19:33 unless he afterwards became a Christian.

16. {*At my first defence*} This is the original sense of "apology" as in Philippians 1:7, 16. Either the first stage in this trial or the previous trial and acquittal at the end of the first Roman imprisonment. Probably the first view is correct, though really there is no way to decide.

17. {*But the Lord stood by me*} Lit. "took his stand by my side" (cf. Rom. 16:2). Clearly Jesus appeared to Paul now at this crisis and climax as he had done so many times before. {*Strengthened me*} Translate, "poured power into me" (cf. Phil. 4:13).

18. {*Will deliver me*} One should recall the Lord's Prayer. Paul is not afraid of death. He will find his triumph in death (Phil. 1:21). {*Unto his heavenly kingdom*} (cf. 1 Cor. 15:24, 50). He will save me there finally and free from all evil. {*To whom be the glory*} This is Paul's final doxology, his swan song, to Christ as in Romans 9:5; 16:27.

21. {*Before winter*} This is a pathetic item if Paul was now in the Mamertine Dungeon in Rome with winter coming on and without his cloak for which he asked. How long he had been in prison this time we do not know. He may even have spent the previous winter or part of it here. {*The Lord be with thy Spirit*} Let us hope that Timothy and Mark reached Paul before winter, before the end came, with the cloak and with the books. Our hero, we may be sure, met the end nobly. He is already more than conqueror in Christ who is by his side and who will welcome him to heaven and give him his crown. Luke, Timothy, Mark will do all that mortal hands can do to cheer the heart of Paul with human comfort. He already had the comfort of Christ in full measure.

The Epistle to Titus

Author: Paul
Recipient: Titus (cf. Tit. 1:4)
Date: Probably A.D. 66 or 67
From: Apparently Nicopolis
Occasion: Paul gives Titus direction for putting church leaders in place in the churches on Crete.
Theme: Holy living as individuals and as churches

Chapter 1

1. {*According to the faith of God's elect*} "According to" expresses the aim of Paul's apostleship, not the standard by which he was chosen (cf. Phil. 3:14). {*The knowledge*} This means "full knowledge" (cf. 1 Tim. 2:4). The combination of faith and full knowledge of the truth is to bring godliness on the basis of the hope of life eternal.

2. {*Before times eternal*} Not to God's purpose before time began (Eph. 1:4; 2 Tim. 1:9), but to definite promises (Rom. 9:4) made in time.

3. {*In the message*} (cf. 1 Cor. 1:21; 2:4). This is the human proclamation (preaching) of God's word. {*Of God our Savior*} (cf. Titus 1:4 of salvation in Christ). In Titus 2:13 he applies both "God and Savior" to Christ.

4. {*My true child*} Titus is not mentioned in Acts, possibly because he is Luke's brother. But one can get a clear picture of him by turning to 2 Corinthians 2:13; 7:6-15; 8:6-24; 12:16-18; Galatians 2:1-3; Titus 1:4; 3:12; 2 Timothy 4:10. He had succeeded in Corinth where Timothy had failed. Paul had left him in Crete as superintendent of the work there. Now he writes him from Nicopolis (Titus 3:12).

5. {*Left I thee in Crete*} The Greek word *apoleipô* (left) possibly suggests a more temporary stay. Paul had apparently stopped in Crete on his return from Spain about A.D. 65. {*That thou shouldest set in order*} Lit. "to set straight thoroughly in addition; a clean job of it." {*The things that were wanting*} Lit. "The things that remain" (cf. Titus 3:13; Luke 18:22). Either things left undone or things that survive. {*And appoint*} This is the same word used in Acts 6:13 about the deacons. The word does not preclude the choice by the churches. This was what was to be "straightened out." {*Elders*} The Greek word is *presbuteros* (cf. 1 Tim. 3:2; 4:17). {*As I gave thee charge*} This is a clear reference to previous personal details given to Titus on previous occasions.

7. {*The bishop*} (cf. "elder" in Titus 1:5). Elder is the title, oversight is the function. {*Not self-willed*} Lit. "self-pleasing," and so arrogant (cf. 2 Pet. 2:10). {*Not greedy of filthy lucre*} Lit. "Not greedy of shameful gain"; used of deacons (1 Tim. 3:8), and elders (1 Tim. 3:3).

8. {*Temperate*} Lit. "in strength," so having power over, controlling, here only in NT. Picture of self-control.

9. {*Holding to*} Lit. "to hold back," (in middle voice) "to hold oneself face to face with, to cling to," (cf. 1 Thess. 5:14). {*The faithful word*} (cf. 1 Tim. 1:15; 6:3; Rom. 16:17). Some would see a reference here to Christ as the Personal *Logos* (Word). {*The gainsayers*} Lit. "The talkers back." This is from an old word, "to answer back," (cf. Rom. 10:21).

10. {*Vain talkers*} Lit. "empty talkers," (cf. 1 Tim. 1:6). {*Deceivers*} Lit. "Mind deceivers," (cf. Gal. 6:3). {*Specially they of the circumcision*} (cf. Acts 11:2; Gal. 2:12; Col. 4:11). Jews are mentioned in Crete in Acts 2:11. Apparently Jewish Christians of the Pharisaic-type tinged with Gnosticism.

11. {*Whose mouths must be stopped*} Lit. "whom it is necessary to silence by stopping the mouth." This is to stop the mouth either with bridle or muzzle or gag. {*Overthrow*} Lit. "to turn up, to overturn," (cf. 2 Tim. 2:18). In papyri to upset a family by perversion of one member. {*For filthy lucre's sake*} The Cretans are given a bad reputation for itinerating prophets for profit.

12. {*A prophet of their own*} Their self-styled "prophet" (or poet), and so accepted by the Cretans and by Cicero and Apuleius, that is Epimenides who was born in Crete at Cnossos. It is a hexameter line and Callimachus quoted the first part of it in a Hymn to Zeus. It is said that Epimenides suggested to the Athenians the erection of statues to "unknown gods" (Acts 17:23). {*Liars*} (cf. 1 Tim. 1:10). The Cretans had a bad reputation on this line, partly due to their claim to having the tomb of Zeus. {*Idle gluttons*} This is blunt and forceful language (cf. Phil. 3:19). Both words give the picture of the sensual glutton.

13. {*Testimony*} Referring to the poet Epimenides. Paul endorses it from his recent knowledge. {*Sharply*} (cf. 2 Cor. 13:10). Here it means "curtly," "abruptly." It is necessary to appear rude sometimes for safety, if the house is on fire and life is in danger.

14. {*Not giving heed to Jewish fables*} (cf. 1 Tim. 1:4). Perhaps this is a reference to the oral traditions condemned by Christ in Mark 7:2-8 (cf. also Col. 2:22, apparently Pharisaic type of Gnostics). {*Who turn away from the truth*} Lit. "men turning *themselves* away from the truth" (truth = gospel 1 Tim. 4:3, cf. Eph. 4:21).

15. {*To them that are defiled*} The Greek verb is *miainô,* to dye with another color, to stain (cf. Jude 8; Heb. 12:15).

CHAPTER 2

1. {*But speak thou*} This is in contrast to these Pharisaic Gnostics in Crete. {*Sound*} Lit. "healthful" (cf. Titus 1:13; 2:2; 1 Tim. 1:10).

2. {*Aged men*} (cf. Phlm. 9). For discussion of family life see also Colossians 3:18-4:1; Ephesians 5:22-6:9; 1 Timothy 5:1-6:2. For the adjectives here see 1 Timothy 3:2, 8; for the substantives see 1 Timothy 6:11.

3. {*Reverent*} (cf. 1 Tim. 2:10). Like people engaged in sacred duties. {*Nor enslaved to much wine*} (cf. 1 Tim. 3:8). {*Teachers of that which is good*} This is teaching good and beautiful things.

4. {*That they may train*} This is a purpose clause. The Greek word is *sôphronizô,* to make sane, to restore to one's senses, to discipline. {*To love their husbands...children*} Though lit. "men," it is husbands in context.

5. {*Workers at home*} Lit. "keepers at home" (cf. 1 Tim. 5:13). "Keepers at home" are usually "workers at home."

8. {*He that is of the contrary part*} "The one on the opposite side" (your opponent). Cf. verse 9; 1 Timothy 5:14. {*May be ashamed*} Lit. "to turn one on himself" and so be ashamed (to blush) as in 2 Thessalonians 3:14; 1 Corinthians 4:14. {*Evil*} Lit. "easy (easy morals)," so worthless; bad, as in 2 Corinthians 5:10.

9. {*Not gainsaying*} Lit. "Not answer back" (cf. Rom. 10:21).

10. {*Not purloining*} Lit. "to set apart for oneself," so to embezzle or steal (cf. Acts 5:2). {*That they may adorn*} This is the Greek word *kosmeô* (cf. 1 Tim. 2:9). Paul shows slaves how they may "adorn" the teaching of God as being attractive.

11. {*Worldly lusts*} This is the Greek word *kosmikos* (from *kosmos*). Here it means the evil of this present age (cf. 1 John 2:16).

13. {*Looking for*} This verb was used of Simeon (Luke 2:25) and others (Luke 2:38) who were looking for the Messiah. {*The blessed hope and appearing of the glory*} This refers to the second Epiphany of Christ or the second coming as in 1 Timothy 6:14; 2 Timothy 4:1, 8. {*Of our great God and Savior Jesus Christ*} This is one person (cf. 2 Pet. 1:1, 11).

15. {*Let no man despise thee*} Literally, "let no man think around you," and so despise you (cf. 1 Tim. 4:12). The best way for the modern minister to command respect for his "authority" is to do thinking that will deserve it.

CHAPTER 3

2. {*Not to be contentious*} Lit. "To be nonfighters" (1 Tim. 3:3). {*Gentle*} (cf. 1 Tim. 3:3).

4. {*His love toward man*} The Greek is *philanthrôpia*. "The *philanthrophy* of God our Savior" (cf. Acts 28:2).

5. {*Through the washing of regeneration*} "Washing," (cf. Eph. 5:26), here as there, the laver or the bath. Probably in both cases there is a reference to baptism, but, as in Romans 6:3-6, the immersion is the picture or the symbol of the new birth, not the means of securing it. {*And renewing of the Holy Spirit*} (cf. renew Rom. 12:2). Here, as often, Paul has put the objective symbol before the reality. The Holy Spirit does the renewing, man submits to the baptism after the new birth to picture it forth to men.

6. {*Which...*} The reference is to the great Pentecost (Acts 2:33) as foretold by Joel (Joel 2:28). {*Richly*} Then and to each one in his own experience (cf. Rom. 10:12; 1 Tim. 6:17).

9. {*Fightings about the law*} These are "legal battles" (cf. 1 Tim. 6:4; 2 Tim. 2:23). Wordy fights about Mosaic and Pharisaic and Gnostic regulations. {*Shun*} This is the Greek word *periistêmi*, step around, stand aside (2 Tim. 2:16). {*Unprofitable*} Lit. "not good, not gainful" (cf. Heb. 7:18).

10. {*Heretical*} Possibly a schism had been started here in Crete. {*Refuse*} Lit. "to ask from, to beg off from." Possibly an allusion here to Christ's directions in Matthew 18:15-17.

11. {*Is perverted*} Lit. "to turn inside out, to twist," so to pervert.

12. {*Or Tychicus*} Paul's well-known disciple (Col. 4:7; Eph. 6:21; 2 Tim. 4:12). {*To Nicopolis*} Probably in Epirus, a good place for work in Dalmatia (2 Tim. 4:10).

13. {*Zenas the lawyer*} He may be one of the bearers of the Epistle with Apollos. Probably an expert in the Mosaic law as the word means in the Gospels. {*Apollos*} Paul's friend (Acts 18:24-19:1; 1 Cor. 1:12).

14. {*Let learn*} Greek tense translates "keep on learning how." {*Unfruitful*} (cf. 1 Cor. 14:14; Eph. 5:11).

THE EPISTLE TO PHILEMON

AUTHOR: Paul the Apostle
RECIPIENT: Philemon, a slave owner
DATE: A.D. 63
FROM: Rome
OCCASION: The return of a converted run-away slave, Onesimus; and issues of restitution are dealt with.
THEME: Paul applies the spirit of Christianity to the problem of slavery in words that have ultimately set the slaves free from bondage to men.

BY WAY OF INTRODUCTION

This brief letter was sent with Ephesians and Colossians to Philemon by Onesimus, along with Tychicus who is going to Colossae with Onesimus (Col. 4:7-9; cf. Eph. 6:21ff.). Unique from the other two, Paul wrote it himself without dictation, rather by his own manacled hand (cf. Phlm. 19).

1. {***To Philemon***} A resident of Colossae and a beloved convert of Paul's (Phlm. 19), perhaps coming to Ephesus while Paul was there (Acts 19:9, 26; 1 Cor. 16:19). He was active in the church in Colossae, described as a "co[fellow]-worker."

2. {***To Apphia our sister***} She was apparently the wife of Philemon, and "sister" in the Christian sense. {***To the church in thy house***} House churches were common in the NT times, both Palestine and outer lands. Special church buildings for worship came later, and house churches were common (cf. Acts 12:12 Mary's house; 1 Cor. 16:19; cf. Rom. 16:1 Aquila/ Prisca; Col. 4:15 Nympha).

5. {***Hearing***} Through Epaphras or possibly Onesimus (Col. 1:7, 8; 4:12). Some understand "Love and faith" is toward the Lord Jesus, though it carries over to all saints. Others translate as chiasm "Faith [to] Jesus, Love [for] saints."

6. {***The fellowship of thy faith***} That is, a partnership (cf. Phil. 1:5). {***Effectual***} Found only here and 1 Corinthians 16:9; Hebrews 4:12. Papyri uses "effective" of a mill in working order, of plowed land, etc.

7. {*I had*} A point in time with an on-going focus, so Paul refers to his joy when he first heard the good news about Philemon's activity (Phlm. 5). {*The hearts*} Here means the "emotional nature" for the nobler viscera like heart, lungs, liver (cf. Phil. 1:8). {*Have been refreshed*} (cf. also Matt. 11:28), a relief whether temporary (Mark 6:31) or eternal (Rev. 14:13).

8. {*That which is befitting*} Means "to come up to requirements" and so to be befitting (cf. Col. 3:18; Eph. 5:4). {*I rather beseech*} A request rather than a "command," which he has a perfect right to do.

9. {*Paul the aged*} Once called "young" (Acts 7:58), Paul was perhaps a bit under sixty at the letter's writing (cf. elder men Titus 2:2 or Zacharias Luke 1:18). Hippocrates calls an "elder man" from 49 to 56 and "old man" after that. Some translate as "ambassador" (cf. Eph. 6:20), with some evidence from the LXX, though there is no real reason why Paul should not term himself properly here as "Paul the aged."

10. {*For my child*} A tender and affectionate reference to Onesimus as his spiritual child. {*Whom I have bonds*} This figurative fatherhood through the gospel (1 Cor. 4:15). Paul is evidently proud of winning him to Christ though a prisoner himself.

11. {*Onesimus*} A common name among slaves. The name is from Greek meaning "profit, help." {*Who was aforetime unprofitable to thee but now is profitable to thee and to me*} A play (pun) on the meaning of the name Onesimus. "Useful" in the verse has a strong emphasis of being *quite* useful.

12. {*I have sent back*} This is a point in time, as it will look when Onesimus arrives, with a focus on the very person of Onesimus.

13. {*I would fain have kept*} Lit. "I was wishing to hold back," again from the standpoint of the arrival of Onesimus.

14. {*Without thy mind*} Lit. "without your judgment, purpose" (1 Cor. 1:10; 7:25). {*Thy goodness*} Meaning here a "good deed." {*But of free will*} Lit. "According to what is voluntary," not forced (Num. 15:3).

15. {*That thou shouldst have him*} Lit. "that you might keep on having him back," is the conclusion of why he had left. {*For ever*} Onesimus is both here (for good) and hereafter (eternal). Surely a noble thing for Paul to say and a word that would touch the best in Philemon.

16. {*No longer as a servant*} Here, as always, "slave" not "servant." The converted runaway slave is to be treated now as a brother in Christ by his legal master, Philemon. {*But more than a servant*} Lit. "but beyond [better than] a slave."

17. {*If then thou countest me a partner*} The "if" really means "since" in the sense that Paul assumes that he does. {*Receive him as myself*} With Paul's surpassing delicacy and consummate tact, these words sound the death knell of human slavery wherever the spirit of Christ is allowed to have its way.

18. {*But if he hath wronged thee at all*} The "if" really means "since" in the sense that Paul assumes that Onesimus did wrong Philemon. He had probably robbed Philemon before he ran away. {*Or oweth*} Delicate way of putting the stealing. {*Put that to mine account*} It means to set to one's account.

19. {*Write with mine hand*} Paul is both noting his personal writing and that this is a personal note for collection of the obligation (cf. 2 Thess. 3:17; 1 Cor. 16:21; Col. 4:18). This is Paul's promissory note, common in papyri writings concerning debts. {*That I say not*} (cf. 2 Cor. 9:4). Paul is tactfully reminding Philemon that Paul had led him also to Christ. {*Thou owest to me even thine own self besides*} He uses every available argument to bring Philemon to see the higher ground of brotherhood in Christ about Onesimus.

20. {*Let me have joy of thee*} This is the regular construction for a wish or desire about the future.

21. {*Obedience*} "Compliance" seems less harsh to us in the light of Philemon 9. {*Even beyond what I say*} Paul "knows" that Philemon will set Onesimus free. He prefers that it come as Philemon's idea and wish rather than as a command from Paul.

22. {*But withal*} Along with your kindly reception of Onesimus (cf. Acts 24:26; 27:40).

23. {*Epaphras*} The Colossian preacher who apparently started the work in Colossae, Hierapolis, and Laodicea, and who had come to Rome to enlist Paul's help in the fight against incipient Gnosticism in the Lycus Valley. {*My fellow prisoner*} Used metaphorically here, though some hold that Epaphras became a prisoner with Paul in Rome.

25. {*Grace*} This great word occurred in the greeting (cf. Phlm. 3) as it does in the farewell.

The Epistle to the Hebrews

Author: Possibly Apollos, though not certain
Recipients: Jewish (Hebrew) Christians in a local church somewhere, even possibly Rome; we do not know for sure where.
Date: About A.D. 69
From: Apparently from Italy (Heb. 13:24)
Occasion: The author is battling to stop a departure from Christ back to Judaism.
Theme: Hold fast the confession in Jesus as Messiah and Savior.

By Way of Introduction

In spite of unsolved matters and problems, Hebrews takes high rank for its intellectual grasp, spiritual power, and its masterful portrayal of Christ as High Priest. It is much briefer than the Fourth Gospel, but it carries on further the exalted picture of the Risen Christ as the King-Priest who reigns and pleads for us now.

In Hebrews we find the Person of Christ as superior to the prophets of the Old Testament because he is the Son of God through whom God has spoken in the new dispensation (Heb. 1:1-3). This Son is God's Agent in the work of creation and of grace as we see it stated in Phil. 2:5-11; Col. 1:13-20; John 1:1-18. This high doctrine of Jesus as God's Son with the glory and stamp of God's nature is never lowered, for as God's Son he is superior to angels (Heb. 1:4-2:4), though the humanity of Jesus is recognized as one proof of His glory (Heb. 2:5-18). Jesus is shown to be superior to Moses as God's Son over God's house (Heb. 3:1-4:13).

But the chief portion of the Epistle is devoted to the superiority of Jesus Christ as priest to the work of Aaron and the whole Levitical line (Heb. 4:14-12:3). Here the author with consummate skill, though with rabbinical refinements at times, shows that Jesus is like Melchizedek and so superior to Aaron (Heb. 4:14-7:28), works under a better covenant of grace (Heb. 8:1-13), works in a better sanctuary which is in heaven (Heb. 9:1-12), offers a better sacrifice which is his own blood (Heb. 9:13-10:18), and gives us better promises for the fulfillment of his task (Heb. 10:19-12:3).

In style, Hebrews begins like a treatise, proceeds like a sermon, and concludes like a letter. It is, in fact, more like a literary composition than any other New Testament work. The eleventh chapter reveals a studied style and as a whole the Epistle belongs to the literary *Koiné* rather than to the vernacular. Some think that the author did not know Hebrew but follows the Septuagint throughout in his abundant use of the Old Testament.

Who is the author? Some think Paul, through the hand of various copyists like Luke. But no early writer attributes it to Paul. Other authors suggested are Apollos, Barnabas, Priscilla. For myself I should with Luther guess Apollos as the most likely author of this book which is full of the Spirit of God.

The traditional view is that the author is addressing Jewish Christians in a definite locality, whether a large church or a small household church. The author seems clearly to refer to a definite church (cf. Heb. 10:32-34). The church in Jerusalem had undergone sufferings like these, but we really do not know where the church was.

Any date offered must include the fact that the Temple is still standing. If it was already destroyed, it is hard to understand how the author could have written Heb. 10:1f. On the other hand, the mention of Timothy in Heb. 13:23 as being "set free" raises an inquiry concerning Paul's last plea to Timothy to come to him in Rome (2 Tim. 4:11-13).

Apparently Timothy came and was put in prison. If so, since Paul was put to death before Nero's own death (June 8, A.D. 68), there is left only the years A.D. 67 to 69 as probable or even possible.

It is thus the last of the New Testament books before the Johannine writings, all of which come towards the close of the century and after the destruction of Jerusalem.

Paul fought Judaizers and Gnostics; but in Hebrews, these Jews argued that the prophets were superior to Jesus, the law came by the ministry of angels, Moses was greater than Jesus, and Aaron than Jesus. The author turns the argument on the Jews and boldly champions the glory of Jesus as superior at every point to all that Judaism had, as God's Son and man's Savior, the crown and glory of the Old Testament prophecy, the hope of mankind. It is the first great apologetic for Christianity and has never been surpassed. It is a profound homily.

CHAPTER 1

1. {*Having spoken*} Greek word shows this is the highest form of speech. {*By divers portions...in divers manners*} The Old Testament revelation came at different times and in various stages, and ways, as a progressive revelation of God to men. God spoke by dream, by direct voice, by signs, in different ways to different men (Abraham, Jacob, Moses, Elijah, Isaiah, etc.). The two "manys" are a literary device meaning "variously."

2. {*At the end of these days*} Cf. "long ago," in verse 1. {*Hath spoken*} Greek tense translates "did speak" in a final and full revelation. {*In his Son*} "The OT slopes upward to Christ" (J. R. Sampey). Here the idea is not merely what Jesus said, but what he is (Dods) (cf. John 1:18). {*Heir of all things*} (cf. Mark 12:6). The idea of sonship easily passes into that of heirship (Gal. 4:7; Rom. 8:17). {*Through whom*} The heir is also the intermediate agent in creation (cf. Col. 1:16; John 1:3). {*The worlds*} Lit. "The ages" but means the "world" or "universe" (cf. Heb. 1:3; Rom. 11:36; Col. 1:16).

3. {*The effulgence of his glory*} The Greek *apaugasma,* derived from *apaugazô,* "to emit brightness" (cf. 2 Cor. 4:4, 6; Wisdom 7:26). This can mean either a reflection of light, or a light ray from a source, the latter more likely. {*The very image of his substance*} *Charactêr* is an old word from *charassô,* to cut, to scratch, to mark. It was the agent or tool that did the marking, then the mark or impress made the exact reproduction, a meaning clearly expressed by *charagma* (Acts 17:29; Rev. 13:16). The word occurs in the inscriptions for "person" as well as for "exact reproduction" of a person. {*Purification of sins*} Lit. "to cleanse," referring to the priestly work of Christ (cf. Matt. 8:3; Heb. 9:14), here the cleansing from sins (cf. also 2 Pet. 1:9; Job 7:21). {*Sat down*} Lit. "took his seat," a formal and dignified act. {*Of the Majesty on high*} (cf. Deut. 32:3; 2 Sam. 7:23; Ps. 93:4 and Heb. 1:3; 8:1; Jude 25). Christ resumed his original dignity and glory (John 17:5). Jesus is here pictured as King (Prophet and Priest also) Messiah seated at the right hand of God.

4. {*Name*} This is in the sense of "rank." Having proven Jesus superior to prophets (Heb. 1:2) now proceeds to prove, through Scripture, the Son superior to angels (Heb. 1:4-2:18).

5. {*Unto which*} Translate, "To which individual angel." As a class angels are called sons of God (*Elohim*) (Ps. 29:1), but no single angel is called God's Son like the Messiah in Psalm 2:7.

6. {*And when he again bringeth in*} This can refer to the Incarnation, Second Coming, or merely introduce the quotation, depending on which words you attach it to.

7. {*Of the angels*} "Of" translates "With reference to (on the one hand)." The quotation is from Psalm 104:4. See Verse 8 for the completion of the argument "on the other hand." {*Winds*} The meaning apparently is one that can reduce angels to the elemental forces of wind and fire (Moffatt).

8. {*O God*} This fifth quotation is from (Messianic) Psalm 45:7. This can be translated as the case of address "O God," or simple subject/object translated "God is thy throne" or "Thy throne is God." Either makes good sense. {*Sceptre*} Old word for walking stick, staff (Heb. 11:21).

9. {*Oil of gladness*} Perhaps this refers to the festive anointing on occasions of joy (cf. Heb. 12:2, also Luke 1:44). {*Fellows*} Greek word *metochous,* derived from *metechô,* partners, sharers (cf. Luke 5:7).

10. {*Lord*} Sixth quotation from Psalm 102:26-28. "You" is emphatic here and next two verses. This Messianic Psalm pictures the Son in his Creative work and in his final triumph.

11. {*But thou continuest*} "You" is emphatic. This is what matters most, the eternal existence of God's Son as Creator and Preserver of the universe.

12. {*A mantle*} Greek word is *peribolaion* "covering," derived from *pariballô,* to fling around, as a veil in 1 Colossians 11:15. {*Shall not fail*} Lit. "to leave out, to fail," used of the sun (cf. Luke 23:45).

13. {*Hath he said*} This seventh quotation is proof of the Son's superiority as the Son of God (his deity) to angels and is from (Messianic) Psalm 110:1. {*Sit thou*} (cf. Matt. 22:44; Jas. 2:3).

14. {*Ministering spirits*} Greek word is *leitourgika.* It occurs in the papyri for "work tax" (money in place of service) and for religious service also. The word is made from *leitourgia* (Luke 1:23; Heb. 8:6; 9:21). {*Sent forth*} Greek tense translates, "sent forth repeatedly, from time to time as occasion requires." {*That shall inherit*} Translate as "That are going to inherit," or "destined to inherit" (Matt. 11:14).

CHAPTER 2

1. {*To give heed*} (cf. Acts 8:6). {*More earnest*} This is comparative adverb, "more earnestly," "more abundantly," (cf. 1 Thess. 2:7). {*Lest haply we drift away*} The Greek verb *pararreô*, old verb "to flow by or past, to glide by," Xenophon uses it of the river flowing by. Here the metaphor is that "of being swept along past the sure anchorage which is within reach," (Westcott) a vivid picture of peril for all.

2. {*For if...proved steadfast*} This is a condition assumed as true.

3. {*So great salvation*} "So great" is a correlative pronoun of age, but used of size in the NT (Jas. 3:4; 2 Cor. 1:10). {*Which*} Referring to "salvation," before described, now summarized. {*Having at the first been spoken*} Lit. "having begun to be spoken." {*Through the Lord*} This is the Lord Jesus who is superior to angels. Jesus was God's full revelation and he is the source of this new and superior revelation. {*By them that heard*} Those who heard the Lord Jesus. Only one generation between Jesus and the writer. Paul (Gal. 1:11) got his message directly from Christ.

4. {*God also bearing witness with them*} The Greek verb is *sunepimartureô*, lit. "to join + in giving additional + testimony." {*Both by signs and wonders and by manifold powers and by gifts of the Holy Ghost*} These are the instruments of God's witness (cf. Acts 2:22). Each word adds an idea about the works of Christ.

5. {*For not unto angels*} The author now proceeds to show (Heb. 2:5-18) that the very humanity of Jesus, the Son of Man, likewise proves his superiority to angels. {*The world to come*} This is the new order, the salvation just described. {*Whereof we speak*} The author is discussing this new order introduced by Christ which makes obsolete the old dispensation of rites and symbols.

6. {*Hath testified*} Lit. "to testify vigorously" (Acts 2:40). {*The son of man*} This is not the Messiah "*The* Son of Man" but lit. "son of man" like the same words so often in Ezekiel. {*Visited*} Lit. "to look upon, to look after, to go to see." (Matt. 25:36). From this verb we get the Greek word *episcopos*, "overseer, bishop."

7. {*Thou madest him a little lower*} Lit. "to lessen, to decrease, to make less," here of degree or time. {*Than the angels*} (cf. Heb. 1:4, 9). The Hebrew here has *Elohim* which word refers to judges in Psalm 82:1, 6 (John 10:34). Here it is certainly not "God" in our sense. In

Psalm 29:1 the LXX translates *Elohim* by *huoi theou* (sons of God). {*Thou crownedst*} (cf. 2 Tim. 2:5). The Psalmist refers to God's purpose in creating man with such a destiny as mastery over nature.

8. {*Nothing that is not subject to him*} "Not subject," here in passive sense, active sense in 1 Timothy 1:9. Man's sovereignty was meant to be all-inclusive including the administration of "the world to come."

9. {*Even Jesus*} We do not see man triumphant, but we do see Jesus, who is human and is realizing man's destiny. But this is not all. Death has defeated man, but Jesus has conquered death. {*Because of the suffering of death*} Jesus in his humanity was put lower than the angels for a little while (cf. Phil. 2:9-11). There is more glory to come to Jesus surely, but he is already at God's right hand (Heb. 1:3). {*That by the grace of God he should taste death for every man*} This phrase is purpose, not result. The author interprets and applies the language of the Psalm to Jesus and here puts Christ's death "instead of" every man, as the motive for his incarnation and death on the Cross. His death was in behalf of every one, and was sufficient for all, efficient for some.

10. {*It became him*} Lit. "to stand out, to be becoming or seemly." The voluntary humiliation or incarnation of Christ the Son a little lower than the angels was a seemly thing to God the Father as the writer now shows in a great passage (Heb. 2:1-18) worthy to go beside Philippians 2:5-11. {*Through whom*} This is a direct repudiation of the Gnostic view of intermediate agencies between God and the creation of the universe. {*The author*} Lit. "one leading off, leader or prince." Jesus is the author of salvation, the leader of the sons of God, the Elder Brother of us all (Rom. 8:29). {*To make perfect*} The writer does not say that Jesus was sinful (cf. Heb. 4:15), but simply that "by means of sufferings" God perfected his Son in his human life and death for his task as Redeemer and Savior. There was no moral imperfection in Jesus, but he lived his human life in order to be able to be a sympathizing and effective leader in the work of salvation.

11. {*He is not ashamed*} (cf. Rom. 1:16). Because of the common Father, Jesus is not ashamed to own us as "brothers," unworthy sons though we be.

12. {*Unto my brethren*} To prove his point the writer quotes Psalm 22:22 when the Messiah is presented as speaking to the brothers.

13. {*I will put my trust in him*} This is a quotation from Isaiah 8:17, 18. The author represents the Messiah as putting his trust in God as other men do (cf. Heb. 12:2). Certainly Jesus did this constantly.

14. {*That he might bring to nought*} The purpose of the incarnation is clearly stated here, the means being his own death. {*Power of death*} Not only human's fear of death, but also Satan's sway over the realm of death (Zech. 3:5). {*The Devil*} Death is the devil's realm, for he is the author of sin.

15. {*Through fear of death*} The ancients had great fear of death though the philosophers like Seneca argued against it. There is today a flippant attitude towards death with denial of the future life and rejection of God. But the author of Hebrews saw judgment after death (Heb. 9:27). Hence our need of Christ to break the power of sin and Satan in death.

16. {*Doth he take hold*} Lit. "to lay hold of, to help," (cf. Heb. 2:18). {*The seed of Abraham*} This is the spiritual Israel (Gal. 3:29), children of faith (Rom. 9:7).

17. {*In all things*} Except yielding to sin (Heb. 4:15) and yet he knew what temptation was. Jesus fought through to victory over Satan. {*To be made like unto his brethren*} Christ, our Elder Brother, resembles us in reality (Phil. 2:7 "in the likeness of men") as we shall resemble him in the end. Jesus was like his brethren in actual human nature. {*Merciful and faithful high priest*} Jesus as the priest-victim is the chief topic of the Epistle. These two adjectives (merciful and faithful) touch the chief points in the function of the high priest (Heb. 5:1-10), to God not human government. {*To make propitiation for*} This idea occurs in the LXX (Ps. 65:3), but only here in NT, though in Luke 18:13 the passive form occurs as in 2 Kings 5:18. In 1 John 2:2 we have the Greek word *hilasmos* used of Christ (cf. Heb. 7:25). The inscriptions illustrate the meaning in Hebrews 2:17 as well as the LXX.

18. {*Being tempted*} The temptation to escape the shame of the Cross was early and repeatedly presented to Christ (cf. Matt. 4:8-11; 16:22; 26:39; Luke 22:44; Heb. 5:8). {*He is able*} This word strikes the heart of it all. Christ's power to help is due not merely to his deity as God's Son, but also to his humanity without which he could not sympathize with us (Heb. 4:15). {*Them that are tempted*} These Jewish Christians were daily tempted to give up Christ, to apostatize from Christianity. Jesus understands himself their predicament and is able to help them to be faithful.

CHAPTER 3

1. {*The Apostle and High Priest of our confession*} This syntax of the Greek article show this is one person. This is the only time in the NT that Jesus is called Greek *apostolos* (though cf. "sent" John 17:3). It may mean "not a mere envoy, but an ambassador or representative sent with powers." The author has already termed Jesus high priest (Hebrews 2:17). These Hebrew Christians had confessed Jesus as their Apostle and High Priest. They do not begin to understand what Jesus is and means otherwise they wouldn't even consider giving him up. "Confession" runs through Hebrews with an urgent note for fidelity (cf. Heb. 4:14; 10:23).

2. {*As also was Moses*} No deprecatory remarks are made here about Moses as he did not about the prophets and the angels. He cheerfully admits that Moses was faithful "in all [God's] house" (cf. Num. 12:7). This is "family," not a building, (1 Tim. 3:15) in which God is the Father.

3. {*Than the house*} The architect is superior to the house just as Sir Christopher Wren is superior to St. Paul's Cathedral. The point in the argument calls for Jesus as the builder. But it is God's house, existing before Moses (Heb. 11:2, 25). Jesus as God's Son founded and supervised this house of God.

5. {*And Moses*} (cf. Num. 12:7). This Greek word is kin to the verb *therapeuô*, to serve, to heal, and *therapeia*, service (Luke 9:11) and a group of servants (Luke 12:42). {*For a testimony of those things which were afterward to be spoken*} Is this witness to Moses or God and whether it points on to Christ? (cf. Heb. 9:9). {*As a son*} Cf. that this is not a servant.

6. {*Whose house are we*} We Christians (Jew and Gentile) looked at as a whole, not as a local organization. {*If we hold fast*} This note of contingency and doubt runs all through the Epistle. We are God's house if we do not play the traitor and desert. {*And glorying*} The author makes no effort to reconcile this warning with God's elective purpose. He is not exhorting God, but these wavering Christians. All these are Pauline words.

8. {*As in the provocation*} Lit. "embitterment, exasperation." (cf. Col. 3:19). The reference is to *Meribah* (Exod. 17:1-7). {*As in the provocation*} The reference is to *Massah* which took place at Rephidim.

9. {*Tempted me by proving me*} They were not content with God's promise, but demanded objective proof (deeds) of God.

10. {*I was displeased*} This is a word for extreme anger and disgust (cf. Heb 3:17). {*They did not know*} In spite of God's works and loving patience the Israelites failed to understand God's ways with them.

11. {*As I sware*} The oath relates to the above disobedience (cf. Heb. 6:13). {*Into my rest*} (cf. Heb. 4:8, also Acts 7:49; Heb. 3:11 to 4:11). Primarily the rest in Canaan and then the heavenly rest in which God dwells.

12. {*Take heed*} Solemn warning to the Jewish Christians from the experience of the Israelites as told in Psalm 95:1ff. {*An evil heart of unbelief*} The Greek word is *kardia* and is common in the LXX (about 1,000 times), but "evil heart" only twice in the OT (Jer. 16:12; 18:12). {*Unbelief*} This is rather the active disbelief, refusal to believe. {*In falling away*} Lit. "to stand off from, to step aside from."

13. {*By the deceitfulness of sin*} Lit. "trick, fraud," as is always the case with sin (Rom. 7:11; 2 Thess. 2:10). Apostasy (Heb. 12:4) is their peril and it is a trick of sin.

14. {*For we are become partakers of Christ*} (cf. Heb. 1:9; 3:1; 6:4). We have become partners with Christ and hence should not be tricked into apostasy.

16. {*Did provoke*} (cf. Heb. 3:15 to which it points), exasperating the anger of God. {*Nay, did not all*} This phrase is a favorite device of the diatribe style, (Moffatt) i.e., to answer one rhetorical question with another (Luke 17:8, cf. also Heb. 3:17, 18). There was a faithful minority mentioned by Paul (1 Cor. 10:7).

17. {*Carcasses*} Old word for members of the body like the feet, in LXX a dead body (Num. 14:29), here only in NT.

CHAPTER 4

1. {*A promise being left*} God's promise still holds good for us in spite of the failure of the Israelites. {*Should seem to have come short of it*} The Greek word is *hustereô,* old verb from *husteros* "to be too late, to fail to reach the goal" (cf. Heb. 11:37; 12:15).

2. {*For indeed we have had good tidings preached unto us*} (cf. Heb. 4:6 of the Israelites). We have the promise of rest as the Israelites had. The parallel holds as to the promise, the privilege, the penalty.

3. {*Do enter*} We are sure to enter in, we who believe. {*He hath said*} This word shows permanent value of God's word as in Hebrews 1:13; 4:4; 10:9, 13; 13:5; Acts 13:34. God has spoken. That is enough for us. {*From the foundation of the world*} The Greek word *katabolê,* late word from *kataballô,* usually laying the foundation of a house in the literal sense. In the NT usually with Greek preposition *apo* (Matt. 25:44) or *pro* (John 17:24) about the foundation of the world.

4. {*Somewhere on this wise*} This is a quotation of Genesis 2:2 (cf. Exod. 20:11; 31:17). This a literary style for an indefinite allusion to an OT quotation (cf. Heb. 2:6). {*Rested*} It is not, of course, absolute rest from all creative activity as Jesus shows in John 5:17. But the seventh day of God's rest was still going on (clearly not a twenty-four hour day).

6. {*It remaineth*} Lit. "to leave behind, to remain over," (cf. Heb. 4:9; 10:26). This leftover promise is not repeated, though not utilized by the Israelites under Moses nor in the highest sense by Joshua and David.

7. {*He again defineth a certain day*} "Set," lit. "to set a limit" (cf. Acts 17:26; Rom. 1:4). {*In David*} Attributing the Psalm to David or in the Psalter at any rate. {*After so long a time*} The time between Joshua and David.

8. {*He would not have spoken*} Translate as "he would not speak" (be speaking), in the passage in David.

9. {*A Sabbath rest*} (cf. Exod. 16:30). Lit. "to keep the Sabbath," apparently coined by the author (cf. Rev. 14:13). {*For the people of God*} The syntax shows a blessed personal interest to the true Israel by God (Gal. 6:16).

10. {*As God did from his*} It is not cessation of work, but rather of the weariness and pain in toil. The writer pictures salvation as God's rest which man is to share.

11. {*Let us therefore give diligence*} The exhortation has a warning like that in Hebrews 4:1. {*After the same example of disobedience*} "An example" means "a copy" (John 13:15; Jas. 5:10). The Israelites set a terrible example and it is so easy to copy the bad examples.

12. {*The word of God*} This refers to that just quoted about the promise of rest and God's rest, but true of any real word of God. {*Living*} (cf. the Living God, Heb. 3:12). {*Active*} Energetic, powerful (John 1:12; Phil. 3:21; Col. 1:29). {*Two-edged*} Lit. "Two-mouthed." {*Piercing*} Lit. "to partition." {*Of both joints and marrow*} This surgeon goes into and through the joints and marrow, not cleaving between them. {*Quick to discern*} The Greek word is *kritikos,* derived from *krinô,* skilled in judging, as the surgeon has to be and able to decide on the instant what to do. So God's word like his eye sees the secret lurking doubt and unbelief.

13. {*That is not manifest*} God's microscope can lay bare the smallest microbe of doubt and sin. {*Naked…laid open*} God's eyes see all the facts in our inmost hearts.

14. {*A great high priest*} The author now takes up the main argument of the Epistle, already alluded to in Hebrews 1:3; 2:17; 3:1, the priestly work of Jesus as superior to that of the Levitical line (Heb. 4:14-12:3). Jesus is superior to the prophets (Heb. 1:1-3), to angels (Heb. 1:4-2:18), to Moses (Heb. 3:1-4:13), he has already shown. {*Who hath passed through the heavens*} This is a completed state. Jesus has passed through the upper heavens up to the throne of God (Heb. 1:3) where he performs his function as our high priest. {*Let us hold fast our confession*} Greek tense translates "Let us keep on holding fast." This keynote runs all through the Epistle, the exhortation to the Jewish Christians to hold on to the confession (cf. Heb. 3:1) of Christ already made. Before making the five points of Christ's superior priestly work ([1] better priest than Aaron, Heb. 5:1-7:25; [2] under a better covenant, Heb. 8:1-13; [3] in a better sanctuary, Heb. 9:1-12; [4] offering a better sacrifice, Heb. 9:13-10:18; [5] based on better promises, Heb. 10:19-12:3).

15. {*Without sin*} This is the outstanding difference that must never be overlooked in considering the actual humanity of Jesus. He did not yield to sin. Satan used his strongest weapons against Jesus, did it repeatedly, and failed. Jesus remained "undefiled" in a world of sin (John 8:46). This is our ground of hope, the sinlessness of Jesus and his real sympathy.

16. {*Let us therefore draw near*} Greek tense translates "Let us keep on coming to." This verb in Hebrews means reverent approach for worship (Heb. 7:25; 10:1, 22; 11:6). {*Unto the throne of grace*} A kingly seat but marked by grace because Jesus is there (Matt. 19:28). {*To help us in time of need*} *Eukairos* is an old word (*eu,* well, *kairos,* opportunity), only here in the NT "For well-timed help," "for help in the nick of time," before too late.

CHAPTER 5

1. {*In things pertaining to God*} The two essential points about any high priest are human sympathy (Heb. 5:1-3) and divine appointment (Heb. 5:4). He is taken from men and appointed in behalf of men. {*That he may offer*} Greek tense translates, "that he keep on offering (from time to time)." {*For sins*} Normal priests included their own sins (Heb. 7:27) except in the case of Jesus.

2. {*Who can bear gently*} The Greek word is *metriopatheô*, lit. "moderate + to feel or suffer." It is a philosophical term used by Aristotle to oppose the *apatheia* (lack of feeling) of the Stoics. Philo ranks it below *apatheia.*

3. {*For himself*} This means "in behalf of" as does another Greek preposition (Matt. 26:28).

4. {*Taketh the honor unto himself*} The priest was called of God. This is the ideal and was true of Aaron. The modern minister is not a priest, but he also should be a God-called man.

5. {*So Christ also*} Just as with Aaron. Jesus had divine appointment as high priest also. {*But he that spake unto him*} God did glorify Jesus in appointing him priest as we see in Psalm 2:7 quoted already as Messianic (Heb. 1:5). Jesus himself repeatedly claimed that the Father sent him on his mission to the world (John 5:30, 43; 8:54; 17:5, etc.).

6. {*In another place*} (cf. Ps. 110:4). It is this crucial passage by which the author will prove the superiority of Jesus to Aaron as high priest. Only the word "priest" occurs here which the author uses as synonymous with "high priest." {*Melchizedek*} (cf. Heb. 5:10-7:28).

7. {*In the days of his flesh*} In verses 7 to 9 the author turns to the other requirement of a high priest, human sympathy; on all points but experience of sin. {*Supplications*} (cf. Job 40:22) Lit. "to come to one," and suggests one coming with an olive branch. {*With strong crying and tears*} This alludes to Gethsemane (cf. Luke 22:44), or secondarily, other shedding of tears of Jesus (John 11:35; Luke 19:41). {*Having been heard for his godly fear*} Fine picture of Christ's attitude toward the Father in the prayer in Gethsemane and in all his prayers.

8. {*Yet learned obedience*} Succinct and crisp statement of the humanity of Jesus (cf. Luke 2:40, 52 and with Heb. 2:10). {*By the things which he suffered*} He always did his Father's will (John 8:29), but he

grew in experience as in wisdom and stature and in the power of sympathy with us.

9. {*Having been made perfect*} This is the completion of the process of training (cf. Heb. 2:10). {*The author of eternal salvation*} "Author," lit. "causing," often in Greek with "salvation" (cf. Luke 23:4, 14, 22; Acts 19:40 and Heb. 2:10 or even Isa. 45:17).

11. {*Of whom*} This refers to likeness of Jesus as high priest to Melchizedek that the author has in mind. {*Dull of hearing*} Lit. " no push in the hearing, slow and sluggish in mind as well as in the ears."

12. {*Of the first principles of the oracles of God*} These beginnings are the ABC's of Christian teaching like Hebrews 6:1. {*Of milk*} Still babes (1 Cor. 3:2), they are without intellectual and spiritual teeth, unable to chew.

13. {*Without experience*} This means "inexperienced," from the metaphor of the infant not able to chew.

14. {*For full-grown men*} This is adults (relative perfection) in contrast with babes (cf. 1 Cor. 2:6; 3:1; 13:11; Phil. 3:15; Eph. 4:4), not absolute perfection (Matt. 5:48).

Chapter 6

1. {*Of the first principles of Christ*} Translate, "teachings *about* Christ (cf. Heb. 5:12). {*And press on*} The precise sense here is to go on to a higher stage of instruction. {*Unto perfection*} (cf. Heb. 5:14; Col. 3:14). Let us go on to the stage of adults, not babes, able to masticate solid spiritual food.

2. {*Baptisms*} The plural by itself does not mean specifically Christian baptism, but rather ablutions or immersions such as the mystery religions and the Jewish *cultus* required for initiates, proselytes, and worshippers in general (Moffatt). {*Laying on of hands*} This was a common sign of blessing (Matt. 19:13), of healing (Mark 7:32), in the choice of the Seven (Acts 6:6), in the bestowal of the Holy Spirit (Acts 8:17; 19:6), in separation for a special task (Acts 13:3), in ordination (1 Tim. 4:14; 5:22; 2 Tim. 1:6), and other uses as well.

4. {*As touching those who were once enlightened*} This is the metaphorical sense here (cf. John 1:9; Eph. 1:18; Heb. 10:32). "Once," means "once for all," not "once upon a time" (cf. Heb. 9:7, 26, 27, 28; 12:26, 27).

6. {*It is impossible to renew them again*} (cf. Heb. 6:18; 10:4; 11:6). "Impossible to renew," bluntly denies the possibility of renewal for apostates from Christ (cf. Heb. 3:12-4:2). It is a terrible picture and cannot be toned down. The one ray of light comes in Heb. 6:8-12. {*Seeing they crucify to themselves afresh*} "Again" is not "afresh" but "up." This is the reason why renewal for such apostates is impossible. They crucify Christ. {*And put him to an open shame*} This is to make an example of, and in a bad sense to expose to disgrace.

8. {*Thorns and thistles*} (cf. Matt. 7:16). Roman soldiers scattered balls with sharp iron spikes, one of which was called *tribulus* (meaning "thistles" here) to hinder the enemy's cavalry. {*Rejected*} The Greek word is *adokimos* (cf. 1 Cor. 9:27; Rom. 1:28; Gal. 3:10).

9. {*Better things*} Better than those pictures in Hebrews 6:4-8. {*That accompany salvation*} Lit. "Things holding on to salvation" (Mark 1:38), a common Greek phrase.

11. {*And we desire*} He is not wholly satisfied with them as he had already shown (Heb. 5:11-14). They have not given up Christ (Heb. 6:4-8), but many of them are still babes and not adults (Heb. 5:13, 14).

12. {*That ye be not sluggish*} Possibly translate "dull of hearing" as some already were (Heb. 5:11). {*Imitators*} (cf. 1 Thess. 1:6; 2:14). This is "mimic" in good sense. The writer wishes to hold and develop these sluggards through those who inherit the promises (cf. Heb. 10:19-12:3).

15. {*Having patiently endured*} Lit. "long spirit." (cf. Heb. 6:12). {*He obtained*} God was true to his word and Abraham was faithful.

16. {*In every dispute*} (cf. Heb. 6:16; 7:7; 12:3). Talking back, face to face, in opposition.

17. {*The immutability of his counsel*} Translate, "the unchangeableness of his will." {*Interposed*} (cf. Heb. 8:6). Lit. "to act as mediator or sponsor or surety," intransitively to pledge one's self as surety.

18. {*By two immutable things*} That is, the oath and promise of God, which bring encouragement (cf. Heb. 6:17). {*Have encouragement*} Greek syntax translates "that we may keep on having." {*Who have fled for refuge*} (cf. Acts 14:6). The word occurs for fleeing to the cities of refuge (Deut. 4:42; 19:5; Josh. 20:9). {*Set before us*} Hope is placed before us as the goal (cf. "joy" set before Jesus [Heb. 12:2]).

19. {*As an anchor of the soul*} Cf. lit. anchor (Acts 27:29), figuratively here an anchor of hope firm and immovable. The ancient anchors were much like the modern ones with iron hooks to grapple the rocks and so hold on to prevent shipwreck (1 Tim. 1:19). {*That which is within the veil*} This is the Holy of Holies, "the inner part of the veil" (the space behind the veil). The anchor is out of sight, but it holds. That is what matters.

20. {*As a forerunner*} This is an old word used for a spy, a scout, only here in NT. Jesus has shown us the way, has gone on ahead, and is the surety (cf. Heb. 7:22) and guarantor of our own entrance later.

CHAPTER 7

1. {*This Melchizedek*} (cf. Gen. 14:18-20; Ps. 110:1). It is a daring thing to put Melchizedek above Aaron, but the author does it. The writer is now explaining "forever" of Hebrews 6:20. Melchizedek is the only one in his line and stands alone in the record in Genesis. {*Priest of God Most High*} This title "Most High" was applied to God by the Canaanites, Phoenicians, Hebrews, and Greeks.

2. {*A tenth*} It was common to offer a tenth of the spoils to the gods. So Abraham recognized Melchizedek as a priest of God. {*King of righteousness*} The author gives in Greek the meaning of the Hebrew words Melchizedek (King of righteousness, cf. Heb. 1:8) and Salem (peace).

3. {*Without father, without mother, without genealogy*} The entire phrase means "devoid of any genealogy." The record in Genesis tells nothing of any genealogy. Melchizedek stands alone. He is not to be understood as a miraculous being without birth or death. {*Abideth a priest*} According to the record in Genesis, the only one in his line just as Jesus stands alone, but with the difference that Jesus continues priest in fact in heaven.

4. {*How great*} Geometrical magnitude in contrast to arithmetical, translate "how distinguished." {*Out of the chief spoils*} Lit. "top + a heap," the top of the pile. {*Patriarch*} (cf. Acts 2:29).

7. {*Dispute*} The Greek word is *antilogia* (cf. Heb. 6:16). The writer makes a parenthetical generalization.

8. {*Here...there*} The former refers to the Levitical system, the latter the case of Melchizedek. {*That he lives*} The Genesis record tells nothing of his death.

10. {*In the loins of his father*} Levi was not yet born. The reference is to Abraham, the forefather of Levi. This is a rabbinical imaginative refinement appealing to Jews.

11. {*Perfection*} This is more the act than the quality or state (cf. Heb. 6:1). The Levitical priesthood failed to give men a perfectly adequate relation to God. {*Received the law*} Lit. "to enact law," here specifically, "to furnish with law" (cf. Heb. 8:6). {*Another priest*} That is, a priest of a different line, not just one more of the same line.

12. {*The priesthood being changed*} This is an old word "to transfer" (Gal. 1:6). {*A change*} (Heb. 7:12; 11:5; 12:27). God's choice of another kind of priesthood for his Son, left the Levitical line off to one side, forever discounted, passed by the order of Aaron.

15. {*Ariseth another priest*} Now assumed to be a fact (cf. Heb. 7: 11).

16. {*Carnal*} ("Fleshen" as in 1 Cor. 3:1, not "fleshlike," 1 Cor. 3:3). The Levitical priests became so merely by birth. {*Of an endless life*} Lit. "not + to dissolve," (cf. 2 Cor. 4:1), indissoluble. Jesus as priest lives on forever. He is Life.

18. {*A disannulling*} (cf. Heb. 9:26). This Greek word is common in the papyri in a legal sense of making void. {*Unprofitableness*} Lit. "not useful," useless (cf. Titus 3:9).

19. {*Made nothing perfect*} Here is another parenthesis. And yet law is necessary. {*Of a better hope*} This better hope (cf. Heb. 6:18-20) does bring us near to God as we come close to God's throne through Christ (cf. Heb. 4:16).

22. {*The surety*} The Latin Vulgate translates *sponsor;* this is one who gives a pledge or guarantee. It is not clear whether the author means that Jesus is God's pledge to man, or man's to God, or both. He is both in fact, as the Mediator (cf. Heb. 8:6) between God and man (Son of God and Son of man).

24. {*Unchangeable*} Lit. "Not + valid or inviolate," (cf. Heb. 7:3). God placed Christ in this priesthood and no one else can step into it (cf. also Heb. 7:11).

25. {*To the uttermost*} (cf. Luke 13:10). Latin Vulgate renders it *in perpetuum* (temporal idea). This is possible, but the common meaning is completely, utterly in degree.

26. {*Became us*} "Such" refers to the Melchizedek character of Jesus as high priest and in particular to his power to help and save (cf. Heb. 2:17, also 7:24). {*Holy*} Saintly, pious (cf. Acts 2:24; 13:35). {*Guileless*} Without malice, innocent (cf. Rom. 16:18). {*Undefiled*} Untainted, stainless, real ethical cleanness; not merely ritual purity (Lev. 21:10-15).

27. {***When he offered up himself***} (cf. Heb. 9:14) This is an old verb for sacrifice to place on the altar (1 Pet. 2:5, 24).

28. {***Perfected***} (cf. Heb. 2:10). Imperfect and sinful as we are we demand a permanent high priest who is sinless and perfectly equipped by divine appointment and human experience (Heb. 2:17; 5:1-10) to meet our needs, and with the perfect offering of himself as sacrifice.

CHAPTER 8

1. {***The chief point***} Lit. "belonging to the head." This is the main matter, "the pith." {***Such an high priest***} Such as the one described in Hebrews 4:16 to 7:28 and in particular 7:26 to 28. {***Sat down***} (cf. Heb. 1:3). This phrase prepares the way for the next point.

2. {***Of the sanctuary***} Lit. "of the holy places" (cf. Heb. 9:8; 10:19; 13:11). This is the area between the holy place and the most holy place as in Hebrews 9:2. {***Of the true tabernacle***} This is the anti-type or archetype of the tabernacle in the wilderness in which Aaron served, the ideal tabernacle in heaven of which the earthly tabernacle was a symbol and reproduced in the temple which merely copied the tabernacle. {***Pitched***} (cf. Num. 24:6).

4. {***He would not be a priest at all***} Translate, "Not even would he be a priest." {***Seeing there are those***} Jesus was not of the tribe of Levi and so could not serve here.

5. {***Is warned of God***} The Greek verb is *chrêmatizô*, old verb (from *chrêma,* business) for which see on Matthew 2:12, 22; Luke 2:26. {***The pattern***} The very word used in Exodus 25:40 and quoted also by Stephen in Acts 7:44 (cf. also John 20:25; Rom. 6:17). The tabernacle was to be patterned after the heavenly model.

6. {***But now***} This is the logical use of *nun,* as the case now stands, with Jesus as high priest in heaven. {***Hath he obtained***} Lit. "to hit the mark, to attain." {***A ministry the more excellent***} Lit. "A more excellent ministry." This remark applies to all the five points of superiority over the Levitical priesthood. {***The mediator***} Lit. "middle man (arbitrator)." Already in Galatians 3:19 and 1 Timothy 2:5. See also Hebrews 9:15; 12:24. {***Of a better covenant***} Also called a "new" covenant (cf. Heb. 9:15; 12:24). {***Upon better promises***} That is, "Upon the *basis* of." But how "better" if the earlier were also from God? This idea, alluded to in Hebrews 6:12-17, will be developed in Hebrews 10:19-12:3 with great passion and power.

7. {*Faultless...for a second*} (cf. Luke 1:6; Phil. 2:15). The condition assumes that the old covenant was not "blameless," apparently a serious charge which he hastens to explain.

8. {*Finding fault with them*} The covenant was all right, but the Jews failed to keep it. Hence God made a new one of grace in place of law. {*A new covenant*} (cf. Heb. 12:24; 1 Cor. 11:25). "New" is fresh, on new lines as opposed to the old as in 2 Corinthians 3:6, 14; "new" is young or not yet old.

9. {*To lead them forth*} Translate "For the purpose of leading...." {*For they continued not*} (cf. Acts 14:22). The Israelites broke the covenant. Then God annulled it. {*I regarded not*} Translate, "I neglected" as in Hebrews 2:3. The covenant was void when they broke it.

10. {*That I will make*} Lit. "that I will covenant." {*Into their mind*} Their intellect, their moral understanding, all the intellect as in Aristotle (Col. 1:21; Eph. 4:18). {*On their heart*} The Greek word is *kardia* which is the seat of man's personal life, the two terms covering the whole of man's inward nature.

11. {*They shall not teach*} The "not" is emphatic. {*Know the Lord*} In the new covenant all will be taught of God (Isa. 54:13; John 6:45), whereas under the old only the educated scribe could understand the minutiae of the law (cf. 2 Cor. 3:7-18).

12. {*Merciful*} (cf. Luke 18:13). {*Will I remember no more*} Greek has the emphatic double negative.

13. {*He hath made the first old*} This is fresh, new in contrast to old and out of date. {*That which is becoming old and waxeth aged*} "Aging" refers to the decay of old age (cf. an old man) so that both ideas appear here in opposition to "fresh and new" above.

CHAPTER 9

1. {*And its sanctuary, a sanctuary of this world*} (cf. Exod. 36:3; Num. 3:38 and Heb. 8:2). The Greek word *kosmikon* is a late adjective from *kosmos*, relating to this world.

2. {*A tabernacle the first*} (cf. Heb. 8:2). Large tents usually had two divisions (the outer and the inner or the first and the second). The large outer tent was entered first and was called "Holy," the first division of the tabernacle. The two divisions are here termed two tabernacles.

3. {*After the second veil*} The first veil opened from outside into the Holy Place, the second veil opened from the Holy Place into the Most Holy Place.

4. {*Having a golden censer*} It is not certain whether the Greek word *thumiatêrion* here means censer or altar of incense. In the LXX (2 Chr. 26:19; Exod. 8:11; 4 Macc. 7:11) it means censer and apparently so in the inscriptions and papyri. But in Philo and Josephus it means altar of incense (Exod. 30:1-10). Apparently the altar of incense was in the Holy Place, though in Exodus 30:1-10 it is left quite vague. {*The ark of the covenant*} A box or chest four feet long, two and a half broad and high (Exod. 25:10).

5. {*Cherubim of glory*} Hebrew word (dual form), paired (two in number), made of gold (Exod. 25:18-22). They are called living creatures in the LXX (Isa. 6:2; Ezek. 1:5-10; 10:5-20). {*The mercy seat*} The pinions [wings] of the Cherubim spread over the rectangular gold slab on top of the ark termed the mercy seat. The Greek word *hilastêrios* has to mean mercy seat, the place, not the propitiatory gift or propitiation, as in Romans 3:25.

7. {*Once in the year*} That is, "once for each year (not at any time)." {*Not without blood*} (cf. Lev. 16:14). Not even he could enter the second tent (Holy of Holies) without blood. {*The errors of the people*} These are "errors" (cf. Gen. 43:12) not "crimes" as willful sins (cf. Heb. 10:26).

8. {*The way into the Holy place*} This is used for the very Presence of God (cf. Heb. 8:2). {*While as the first tabernacle is yet standing*} Translate, "the first tabernacle still having a place." The veil at the entrance kept the people out of the first tent as the second veil (cf. Heb. 8:3) kept the priests out of the Holy of Holies.

9. {*A parable*} Lit. "parable," this is like a type or shadow of "the heavenly reality" (Moffatt) (cf. also Heb. 9:9; 11:19); see also Matthew 13:3. {*For the time now present*} Better translated, "For the present crisis," this is the age in which they lived, not the past, not the future (cf. 1 Cor. 3:22; Rom. 8:38). This age of crisis, foreshadowed by the old tabernacle, pointed on to the richer fulfillment still to come.

10. {*Only with meats and drinks and divers washings*} What ritual value these Levitical sacrifices had was confined to minute regulations

about diet and varied ceremonial cleansing, i.e., the clean and unclean (cf. Mark 7:4; Exod. 29:4; Lev. 11:25, 28; Num. 8:7; Rev. 6:2). {*Imposed*} Lit. "be laid upon (cf. 1 Cor. 9:16). {*Until a time of reformation*} Definite statement of the temporary nature of the Levitical system already stated in Hebrews 7:10-17; 8:13 and argued clearly by Paul in Galatians 3:15 to 22. This Greek word *diorthôsis* is used by Hippocrates for making straight misshapen limbs (cf. Heb. 12:12). Christianity itself is the great Reformation of the current Judaism (Pharisaism) and the spiritual Judaism foreshadowed by the old Abrahamic promise (see Gal. 3:1; Rom. 9:1ff).

11. {*Through the greater and more perfect tabernacle*} Christ as High Priest employed in his work the heavenly tabernacle (cf. Heb. 8:2) after which the earthly was patterned (Heb. 9:24). {*Not of this creation*} (cf. 2 Cor. 4:18; Heb. 8:2). This greater and more perfect tabernacle is heaven itself (Heb. 9:24).

12. {*Through his own blood*} This is the great distinction between Christ as High Priest and all other high priests. They offer other victims' blood (v. 7), but he offered his own blood. He is both victim and High Priest (cf. Heb. 13:12; Acts 20:28). {*Once for all*} In contrast to the yearly entrances of the Levitical high priests (cf. Heb. 9:7). {*Having obtained*} The value of Christ's offering consists in the fact that he is the Son of God as well as the Son of man, that he is sinless and so a perfect sacrifice with no need of an offering for himself, and that it is voluntary on his part (John 10:17). {*Redemption*} The Greek word *lutrôsis* (from *lutroô*) is a late word for the act of ransoming (cf. *lutron*, ransom), in OT only here and Luke 1:68; 2:38. But *apolutrôsis* elsewhere (as in Luke 21:28; Rom. 3:24; Heb. 9:15; 11:35). The author now turns to discuss the better sacrifice (Heb. 9:13-10:18) already introduced.

13. {*Ashes*} (cf. Matt. 11:21; Luke 10:13). {*Of a heifer*} This is a red heifer whose ashes mingled with water and were sprinkled on the contaminated or defiled ones (Num. 19:1) as the blood of bulls and goats was offered for sins (Lev. 16:1). {*Sanctify*} This ceremonial ritual does serve "for the cleansing of the flesh," but not for the conscience (cf. v. 9). The cow was unblemished, the individual clean.

14. {*How much more*} By the measure of the superiority of Christ's blood to that of goats and bulls and the ashes of a heifer. {*Through the eternal Spirit*} This refers to Christ's own spirit which is eternal as he is. There is thus a moral quality in the blood of Christ not in that of other sacrifices. {*Offered himself*} The voluntary character of Christ's death is again emphasized.

15. {*A death having taken place*} This refers to Christ's death. {*Of the transgressions*} (cf. Heb. 9:12 redemption). {*Under the first covenant*} Here there is a definite statement that the real value in the typical sacrifices under the OT system was in the realization in the death of Christ. It is Christ's death that gives worth to the types that pointed to him. So then the atoning sacrifice of Christ is the basis of salvation.

16. {*A testament*} Also translated "covenant," here "testament." This double sense of the word is played upon also by Paul in Galatians 3:15. We say today "The NT" (*Novum Testamentum*) rather than "The New Covenant." Both terms are pertinent. {*Of force*} The Greek word is *bebaia*, stable, firm (cf. Heb. 3:6, 14). {*Where there hath been death*} A will is only operative when there is death. {*For doth it ever avail while he that made it liveth?*} This could be translated a question expecting a "no" answer; or a positive statement of fact.

18. {*Has been dedicated*} Lit. "stands dedicated," (cf. Heb. 10:20). It means to renew, to inaugurate.

19. {*When every commandment had been spoken*} (cf. allusions in Exod. 24:3). It had become the custom to mingle water with the blood and to use a wisp of wool or a stem of hyssop for sprinkling (Num. 10:2-10). {*Both the book itself*} There is nothing in Exodus about sprinkling the book of the covenant, though it may very well have been done. He omits the use of oil in Exodus 40:9 and Leviticus 8:10 and applies blood to all the details.

21. {*In like manner with the blood*} The use of the article does not necessarily refer to the blood mentioned in verse 19. In Exodus 40:9 Moses sprinkled the tabernacle with oil. It had not been erected at the time of Exodus 24:5. Josephus gives a tradition that blood was used also at this dedication. Blood was used annually in the cleansing rites on the day of atonement.

22. {*Apart from shedding of blood*} Lit. "pouring out of blood," (cf. Matt. 26:28). The blood is the vital principle and is efficacious as an atonement. The blood of Christ sets aside all other plans for pardon.

24. {*Like in pattern to the true*} (cf. 1 Pet. 3:21). Here it is the "counterpart of reality" (Moffatt). Moses was shown a model of the heavenly realities and he made a "copy" on that model.

25. {*That he should offer himself often*} This phrase expresses purpose, translate also the Greek tense "keep on offering himself" (cf. Heb. 5:1, 3). {*With blood not his own*} The Greek word *allotrios* means "belonging to another," "not one's own" (Luke 16:12).

26. {*Since the foundation of the world*} (cf. Heb. 4:3). The one sacrifice of Christ is of absolute and final value (1 Pet. 1:19; Rev. 13:8). {*To put away sin*} (cf. Heb. 7:18). "The sacrifice of Christ dealt with sin as a principle: the Levitical sacrifices with individual transgressions" (Vincent).

27. {*It is appointed*} (cf. Luke 19:20; Col. 1:5; 2 Tim. 4:8 (Paul's crown). {*Once to die*} Once for all to die, as once for all to live here. No reincarnation here. {*After this cometh judgement*} Death is not all. Man has to meet Christ as Judge as Jesus himself graphically pictures (Matt. 25:31-46; John 5:25-29).

28. {*Shall appear a second time*} Blessed assurance of the Second Coming of Christ, but this time "apart from sin." {*Unto salvation*} Final and complete salvation for "them that wait for him (cf. Phil. 3:20).

CHAPTER 10

1. {*Shadow*} The Greek is *skian*. The contrast here between *skia* (shadow, shade caused by interruption of light as by trees, Mark 4:32) and Greek *eikôn* (image or picture) is striking. The law gives only a dim outline of the good things to come (Heb. 9:11).

2. {*Having been once cleansed*} Translate, "if they had once for all been cleansed."

5. {*When he cometh into the world*} This refers to the Incarnation of Christ (Ps. 40:79, LXX text with slight text changes, yet same sense. So the writer of Hebrews "argues that the Son's offering of himself is the true and final offering for sin, because it is the sacrifice, which, according to prophecy, God desired to be made" (Davidson).

6. {*Thou hadst no pleasure*} (cf. Matt. 3:17). God took no pleasure in the animal, grain, burnt-offering, or the sin-offering.

7. {*Lo, I am come*} Referring to Messiah offering himself to God's will. {*In the roll of the book it is written of me*} This "stands written." Scroll is lit. "roll [head] of the book." Here it refers "to the OT as a prediction of Christ's higher sacrifice" (Moffatt).

9. {*He taketh away the first*} The Greek word is *anaireô*, to take up, to abolish, (of a man) to kill (Matt. 2:16). "First" refers to the system of animal sacrifices (cf. Heb. 10:8). {*That he may establish the second*} "To" marks a purpose; "second" refers to doing God's will (cf. Heb. 10:8-9). This is the author's exegesis of the Psalm.

10. {*We have been sanctified*} The Greek word is *hagiazô*, to set apart, to sanctify. The divine will, unfulfilled in animal sacrifices, is realized in Christ's offering of himself.

11. {*Ministering and offering*} The Greek tense and syntax graphically describes the priest and places the reader in the scene of constant, repetitive action. {*Take away*} The Greek word is *periaireô*, to take from around, to remove utterly (cf. Acts 27:20).

12. {*When he had offered*} Greek tense shows this as a single act in contrast to verse 11. {*One sacrifice*} This the main point. The one sacrifice does the work that the many failed to do.

13. {*Henceforth expecting*} Translate, "for the rest" or "for the future." The expectant attitude of Christ here is that of final and certain victory (John 16:33; 1 Cor. 15:24-28).

14. {*He hath perfected*} He has done what the old sacrifices failed to do (cf. Heb. 10:1). {*Them that are sanctified*} The Greek tense shows either: the process still going on, or because of the repetition in so many persons (cf. Heb. 2:11).

15. {*And the Holy Ghost also beareth witness to us*} The author confirms his interpretation of Psalm 40:7-9 by repeating from Jeremiah (Jer. 31:31) what he had already quoted (Heb. 8:8-12).

18. {*There is no more offering for sin*} This is the logical and triumphant conclusion concerning the better sacrifice offered by Christ (Heb. 9:13-10:18). As Jeremiah had prophesied, there is actually remission (removal) of sins. Repetition of the sacrifice is needless.

19. {*Having therefore*} The author now gives a second (the first in Heb. 8:1-6) résumé of the five arguments concerning the superior priestly work of Christ (Heb. 10:19-25) coupled with an earnest exhortation like that in Hebrews 4:14-16, with which he began the discussion, before he proceeds to treat at length the fifth and last one, the better promises in Christ (Heb. 10:26-12:3). {*Boldness*} This is the dominant note all through the Epistle (cf. Heb. 3:6; 4:16; 10:19, 35). They were tempted to give up Christ, to be quitters. {*Into the holy place*} That is, the heavenly sanctuary where Jesus is (Heb. 6:18-20). This is the better sanctuary (Heb. 9:1-12).

20. {*By the way which he dedicated for us*} Jesus opened (dedicated) for us by his Incarnation and Death for us. Thus he fulfilled God's promise of the "New Covenant" (Heb. 8:7-13) in Jeremiah. Because of the coming of Christ in the flesh we have the new way opened for access to God (Heb. 2:17; 4:16).

22. {*With a true heart*} With loyalty and fidelity. {*Having our hearts sprinkled from an evil conscience*} This is an evident allusion to the sprinkling of blood in the old tabernacle (Heb. 9:18-22) and the shedding of Christ's blood for the cleansing of our consciences (Heb. 10:1-4, cf. also 1 Pet. 1:2).

23. {*Let us hold fast*} Translate Greek tense, "keep on holding fast," (cf. Heb. 3:6, 14). {*That it waver not*} Lit. "unwavering, not leaning"; it is a confession of hope, not of despair. {*That promised*} This is the argument remaining to be discussed (Heb. 10:26-12:3) and already alluded to (Heb. 6:13; 8:6). The ministry of Jesus rests upon "better promises."

24. {*Let us consider one another*} Greek tense translates "keep on doing so..." (cf. Heb. 3:1). {*To provoke*} The Greek word is *paroxusmos,* sharpened, stimulated, incited (cf. English "paroxysm"). So here in good sense "for incitement to," but negative in Acts 15:39; and elsewhere the word is used of disease, irritation, or contention. {*Unto love and good works*} So Paul seeks to stir up the Corinthians by the example of the Macedonians (2 Cor. 8:1-7).

25. {*Not forsaking*} Translate, "Not leaving behind, not leaving in the lurch" (2 Tim. 4:10). {*The assembling of yourselves together*} Lit. "to gather together besides (cf. Matt. 23:37; Luke 17:27, also 2 Thess. 2:1). {*As the custom of some is*} (cf. Luke 22:39; John 19:40). Already some Christians had formed the habit of not attending public worship, a perilous habit then and now. {*The day drawing nigh*} This refers to the Second Coming of Christ.

26. {*After that we have received*} Translate lit. "After the receiving." {*Knowledge*} This is "full knowledge," (cf. Heb. 6:4). {*There remaineth no more*} Lit. "No longer is there left behind" for one has renounced the one and only sacrifice for sin that can remove sin (Heb. 10:1-18).

27. {*Expectation*} This sense is usually "reception," or "interpretation," but this sense of expectation is coined by the writer (cf. Heb.

11:10, also Rom. 8:19, 23, 25). {*A fierceness of fire*} This is anger marked by fire (cf. Isa. 26:11; Zeph. 1:19; Ps. 79:5 and also 2 Thess. 1:8-10). {*Devour*} Lit. "to (figuratively) eat."

28. {*Hath set at naught*} Lit. "not + to place, put," to render null and void, to set aside (cf. Mark 7:9 and also Heb. 7:18; 9:26). {*On the word of two or three*} This translates, "On the basis of two or three...."

29. {*How much*} This is an argument from the lesser to the greater, "the first of Hillel's seven rules for exegesis" (Moffatt). {*Think ye*} This is an appeal to their own sense of justice about apostates from Christ. {*Who hath trodden under foot the Son of God*} The Greek word is *katapateô* (cf. Matt. 5:13) for scornful neglect like Zechariah 12:3. See same idea in Hebrews 6:6. {*Wherewith he was sanctified*} It is an unspeakable tragedy that should warn every follower of Christ not to play with treachery to Christ (cf. Heb. 6:4-8). {*An unholy thing*} This is the Greek word *koinos,* lit. "common" in the sense of uncleanness (cf. Acts 10:14).

31. {*A fearful thing*} (cf. Heb. 10:27, 31; 12:21). The sense is not to be explained away. The wrath of God faces wrongdoers. {*To fall*} Lit. "the falling." We are not dealing with a dead or an absentee God, but one who is alive and alert (cf. Heb. 3:12).

32. {*Call to remembrance*} It is a definite experience of people in a certain place. Jerusalem Christians had had experiences of this nature, but so had others.

33. {*Being made a gazing-stock*} Late verb to bring upon the stage, to hold up to derision (cf. 1 Cor. 4:9).

34. {*Ye had compassion on*} Lit. "to have a feeling with, to sympathize with." {*Prisoners*} Lit. "the bound ones," (cf. Eph. 3:1; 2 Tim. 1:8). {*A better possession*} (cf. Acts 2:45). In place of their plundered property they have treasures in heaven (Matt. 6:20). {*Abiding*} No oppressors (legal or illegal) can rob them of this (Matt. 6:19).

35. {*Cast not away therefore your boldness*} Figurative verb here to throw away from one as worthless; and literal in Mark 10:50. The Jewish Christians in question were in peril of a panic and of stampeding away from Christ.

36. {*Of patience*} Lit. "remaining under" trial (Luke 8:15). This was the call of the hour then as now. {*Having done the will of God*} This is an essential prerequisite to the exercise of patience and to obtain the promised blessing. There is no promise to those who patiently keep on doing wrong.

38. {*If he shrink back*} Lit. "to draw oneself under or back, to withdraw," (cf. Acts 20:20, 27; Gal. 2:12 and Rom. 1:17).

39. {*But we*} In contrast to renegades who do flicker and turn back from Christ. {*Unto the saving of the soul*} Lit. "to reserve, to preserve (Luke 17:33) to purchase (Acts 20:28)." So here preserving or saving one's life as in Plato, but "possession" in Ephesians 1:14, "obtaining" in 1 Thessalonians 4:9. Papyri have it in sense of preservation.

CHAPTER 11

1. {*The assurance of things hoped for*} (cf. also Heb. 1:3; 3:14; 2 Cor. 9:4). Yet here is the essential meaning common in the papyri in business documents as the basis or guarantee of transactions. "We venture to suggest the translation 'Faith is the *title-deed* of things hoped for'" (Moultan and Milligan).

3. {*By faith*} This is repeated with rhetorical skill most of the rest of the chapter. After that only a summary is given. {*Have been framed*} Lit. "to mend, to equip, to perfect," (Luke 6:40). {*So that*} This expresses result.

4. {*Through which*} This refers to the sacrifice. {*Through it*} This second pronoun refers to his faith as shown by his sacrifice. Precisely why Abel's sacrifice was better than that of Cain apart from his faith is not shown. {*Being dead*} Lit. "having died." {*Yet speaketh*} Cf. Genesis 4:10; Hebrews 12:24. Speaks still through his faith.

5. {*Was translated*} Lit. "to change" (cf. Heb. 7:12; Acts 7:16). {*That he should not see death*} This expresses result here. {*He was not found*} (cf. Gen. 5:24). Greek tense translates "was still not found." {*Translation*} Lit. "change," (cf. Heb. 7:12; 12:27). Our very word "metathesis." {*That he had been well-pleasing unto God*} (cf. Heb. 11:5; 13:16). The word is common of a servant pleasing his master.

6. {*Impossible*} This is a strong word (cf. Heb. 6:4, 18, also Rom. 8:8; Gal. 1:10). {*Must believe*} Moral necessity to have faith (trust). This is true in business also (banks, for instance). {*That he is*} The very existence of God is a matter of intelligent faith (Rom. 1:19) So that men are left without excuse. {*He is a rewarder*} Lit. "reward + to pay back," (cf. Heb. 10:35; 11:26).

7. {*Being warned of God*} "Warned" is an old word for oracular or divine communications as already in Hebrews 8:5 (cf. Matt. 2:12, 22, etc.). {*Moved with godly fear*} Lit. "to take hold well or carefully," and so to show oneself godly, to act circumspectly or with reverence. {*Heir*} He himself believed his message about the flood. Like Enoch he walked with God (Gen. 6:9).

8. {*Not knowing whither he went*} Abraham is a sublime and graphic example of faith. He did not even know where the land was that he was going to receive "as an inheritance."

10. {*He looked for*} The Greek tense shows his steady and patient waiting in spite of disappointment. {*The foundations*} Not just "tents" (Heb. 11:9). Abraham set his steady gaze on heaven as his real home, being a mere pilgrim (*paroikos*) on earth.

11. {*Since she counted him faithful who had promised*} Sarah herself, old as she was, believed God who had promised.

12. {*And that as good as dead*} Lit. "to make dead, to treat as dead," (Rom. 4:19), here by hyperbole. {*By the sea shore*} Lit. "Along the lip of the sea" (from Gen. 22:17). {*Innumerable*} Lit. "not + to number.

13. {*In faith*} Lit. "According to faith." {*Greeted them*} Lit. "to salute" (Matt. 5:47). Abraham rejoiced to see Christ's day in the dim distance (John 8:56). {*Strangers*} A word with societal stigma in the host country (Gen. 23:4; 47:9).

14. {*A country of their own*} Lit. "land of the fathers," one's native land (John 4:44). Cf. our patriotic, patriotism.

15. {*Had been mindful...would have had*} Translate the phrase "If they had continued mindful, they would have kept on having [opportunity].

16. {*They desire*} This is an old word for stretching out after, yearning after as in 1 Timothy 3:1.

17. {*Being tried*} The Greek tense shows the test was still going on. {*Offered up*} The act was already consummated so far as Abraham was concerned when it was interrupted and it stands on record about him (cf. Gen. 22:1-18).

18. {*To whom it was said*} (cf. Gen. 21:12). God's very words were in the heart of Abraham now about Isaac "his only son" (cf. Luke 7:12).

19. {*Accounting*} Abraham had God's clear command that contravened God's previous promise. This was his solution of his difficult situation. {*God is able*} God had given him Isaac in his old age. God can raise him from the dead. It was Abraham's duty to obey God.

22. {*When his end was nigh*} (cf. Matt. 2:19), "finishing his life." {*Of the departure*} Here this is a figure for "death" (Luke 9:31; 2 Pet. 1:15).

23. {*A goodly child / no ordinary child*} Lit. "the child was goodly," meaning "of polished manners, genteel," (cf. Exod. 2:2; Acts 7:20).

24. {*When he was grown up*} Lit. "Having become great" (cf. Exod. 2:11). {*Refused*} Lit. "to deny, to refuse." He was of age and made his choice not from ignorance.

25. {*To be entreated with*} Lit. "to treat ill with" (cf. also Heb. 11:37; 13:3). {*To enjoy the pleasures of sin for a season*} Lit. "to have temporary pleasure of sin." To have been disloyal to God's people would have brought enjoyment to Moses in the Egyptian Court for a short while only.

27. {*He endured*} The Greek word is *kartereô*, old word from *karteros*, strong, here only in NT. Moses had made his choice before slaying the Egyptian. He stuck to it resolutely. {*As seeing him who is invisible*} This is the secret of his choice and of his loyalty to God and to God's people.

28. {*He kept*} Greek tense emphasizes the permanent nature of the feast. {*The sprinkling of the blood*} Translate, "the pouring of the blood" (cf. Exod. 12:7, 22 and also Exod. 24:6; 29:16; Deut. 16:6).

29. {*Which assaying to do*} Lit. "of which taking trial." The idiom occurs in Deuteronomy 28:56 and Hebrews 11:36. {*Were swallowed up*} Lit. to drink down, to swallow down (Matt. 23:24).

31. {*Having received the spies with peace*} Lit. "to welcome" (Luke 10:8, 10).

32. {*And what shall I more say?*} It is both a literary and an oratorical idiom here. He feels helpless to go on in the same style as he has done from Abel to Rahab (Heb. 11:4-31). {*Will fail me if I tell about*} Lit. "will leave me telling about." This is a vivid and picturesque description of the author's embarrassment of riches as he contemplates the long list of the heroes of faith during the long years in Palestine.

33. {*Subdued/conquered kingdoms*} The author has here (vv. 33, 34), "nine terse clauses" (Moffatt) with no connective words, with great rhetorical and oratorical force (sledge-hammer style).

35. {*Were tortured*} The Greek word is *tumpanizô*, late verb from *tumpanon* (kettledrum, drumstick), to beat the drum, to beat to death

(cf. 2 Macc. 7 about Eleazar and the Mother and the seven sons), once in LXX (1 Sam. 21:13). {*That they might obtain a better resurrection*} This expresses a purpose. This is better because it is not temporary.
37. {*They were stoned*} Cf. Zechariah son of Jehoiada (2 Chr. 24:20). "A characteristic Jewish punishment" (Vincent) (cf. John 10:31). {*They were sawn asunder*} This is a cruel Jewish punishment (Amos 1:3) said to have been inflicted on Isaiah. {*With the sword*} This is the fate of unpopular prophets (1 Kings 10:10; Jer. 26:23). {*Went about in sheepskins*} Here the sufferings of the living; this is the rough garment of prophets as Elijah (1 Kings 19:13, 19; cf. also Paul, 2 Cor. 11:9).
38. {*Of whom the world was not worthy*} This is a graphic picture in a short parenthetical relative clause, a phrase to stir the blood of the readers. {*Wandering*} They went like lost sheep, hunted by wolves.
39. {*Received not the promise*} This refers to the Messianic promise they did not live to see (Heb. 11:13), though they had individual special promises fulfilled as already shown (Heb. 11:33).
40. {*Some better thing*} This refers to the better promises (cf. Heb. 8:6). {*That apart from us they should not be made perfect*} This glorious and gracious purpose (foresight) of God is not due to any special merit in us. It is simply the fullness of the time in God's dispensation of grace of which we are the beneficiaries.

CHAPTER 12

1. {*Cloud of witnesses*} The metaphor refers to the great amphitheater with the arena for the runners and the tiers upon tiers of seats rising up like a cloud. The martyrs here are not mere spectators, but testifiers (witnesses) who testify from their own experience (cf. Heb. 11:2, 4, 5, 33, 39) to God's fulfilling his promises as shown in Hebrews 11. {*Laying aside*} The runners ran in the stadium nearly naked. {*Every weight*} Here every encumbrance that handicaps like doubt, pride, sloth, anything. No trailing garment to hinder or trip one. {*The sin which doth so easily beset us*} Lit. "the easily besetting sin." Likely best rendered, "the sin standing around us" (Vulgate). In this case apostasy from Christ was that sin. {*Let us run*} The Greek tense translates, "let us keep on running."
2. {*Looking unto*} Lit. "looking away to Jesus" (cf. Phil. 2:23). Fix your eyes on Jesus, after a glance at "the cloud of witnesses," for he is

the goal (cf. Heb. 11:26). {*The author*} (cf. Heb. 2:10) "The pioneer of personal faith." {*For the joy*} At the end of the race lay the joy "set before him" while here was the cross at this end (the beginning of the race) which he endured. {*Despising shame*} The cross at his time brought only shame (most shameful of deaths, "yea, the death of the cross" Phil. 2:8). But Jesus despised that, in spite of the momentary shrinking from it, and did his Father's will by submitting to it. {*Hath sat down*} Greek tense emphasizes he is still there (cf. Heb. 1:3).

3. {*Consider*} Lit. "to reckon up, to compare, to weigh." Understanding Jesus is the key to the whole problem, the cure for doubt and hesitation. {*Not grow weary*} This is an old verb to be weary as here or sick as in James 5:15.

4. {*Resisted*} This is an old verb to stand in opposition against in line of battle, intransitively "to stand face to face against." {*Unto blood*} Shedding blood was true of Jesus and many of the other heroes of faith in Hebrews 11.

5. {*Ye have forgotten*} Lit. "to cause to forget." {*Reasoneth with you*} This is an old verb to ponder different things, to converse (cf. Acts 19:8. {*Regard not lightly*} The Greek syntax translates, "Stop regarding...." {*Chastening*} The Greek word is derived from *paideuô*, to train a child (pais), instruction (2 Tim. 3:16), which naturally includes correction and punishment as here (cf. also Eph. 6:4).

6. {*Scourgeth*} This is the Greek verb *mastigoô,* from *mastix* (whip). This is a hard lesson for God's children to learn and to understand (cf. also Heb. 5:7 about Jesus).

9. {*We had*} Greek tense translates, "we used to have." {*To chasten us*} Lit. "as chasteners [an agent of such]." Old word from Greek derived from *paideuô*. Only once in LXX (Hos. 5:2) and twice in NT (here and Rom. 2:20). {*We gave them reverence*} Lit. "we turned ourselves to" as in Matthew 21:37, habitual attitude of reverence. {*Unto the father of spirits*} Lit. "To the Father of our spirits," as God is.

10. {*Chastened*} Translate, "used to chasten." {*As seemed good to them*} Lit. "to bear together," (cf. 1 Cor. 12:7).

11. {*For the present*} A classical phrase (Thucydides), lit. "to be beside." {*Peaceable fruit*} (cf. Jas. 3:17). Peaceable after the chastening is over. {*Exercised thereby*} This word is picturing the discipline as a gymnasium (cf. Heb. 5:14; 1 Tim. 4:17).

12. {*Lift up*} This is the Greek word *anorthoô,* to make straight (cf. Luke 13:13; Acts 15:16), in reference to the feeble and palsied extremities.

13. {*Straight paths*} "Paths," is lit. "track of a wheel (cf. Jas. 3:6 from Greek *trechô,* to run); translate, "Straight wheel tracks." {*Be not turned out of the way/disabled*} This is an old verb "to turn out, to twist, to put out of joint," (cf. 1 Tim. 1:6). Vivid picture of concern for the lame (cf. Matt. 11:5). Graphic picture of concern for the weak.

15. {*Looking carefully*} Lit. to have oversight (cf. 1 Pet. 5:2); cf. Greek *episcopos* (bishop). {*Springing up*} Lit. to sprout." It is pictured here as a quick process (cf. also Deut. 29:18). {*Trouble*} This is an old verb to trouble with a crowd, to annoy (cf. Luke 6:18). {*Be defiled*} The Greek word is *mianô,* old verb to dye, to stain, to defile as in Titus 1:15 (the conscience). The contagion of sin is terrible as any disease.

16. {*For one mess of meat*} This is the idea of exchange, "for one act of eating" (1 Cor. 8:4). {*His own birthright*} This is from Genesis also and in Philo, only here in NT. From *prôtotokos* (first born, Heb. 1:6).

17. {*He was rejected*} This is an old verb "to disapprove," (Matt. 21:42). {*Place of repentance*} This is the Greek word *metanoia,* a change of mind and purpose, not sorrow though he had tears (cf. Gen. 27:38). Esau is a tragic example of one who does a willful sin which allows no second chance (Heb. 6:6; 10:26). The author presses the case of Esau as a warning to the Christians who were tempted to give up Christ.

19. {*Unto blackness*} This is the Greek word *gnophos* kin to *nephos,* cloud (cf. Exod. 10:22). {*Tempest*} Lit. "to boil, to rage" (cf. Exod. 10:22). {*Intreated*} Lit. "to ask from alongside," (Mark 15:6), then to beg away from oneself, to depreciate as here, to decline (Acts 25:11), to excuse (Luke 14:18), to avoid (1 Tim. 4:7).

20. {*For they could not endure*} Translate the Greek tense, "for they were not enduring (bearing)." {*That which was enjoined*} Lit. "to distinguish, to dispose, to order."

21. {*The appearance*} The Greek word is *phantazô,* old verb from *phainô,* to make visible, here only in NT "The manifestation." {*I exceedingly fear and quake*} (cf. Deut. 9:19).

22. {*City*} (cf. Heb. 11:10, 16). Heaven is termed thus a spiritual mountain and city. {*Innumerable hosts of angels*} Lit. "Myriads of angels," (cf. 1 Cor. 4:15 as in Luke 12:1).

23. {*To the general assembly*} This is used in Isaiah 66:10 for keeping a festal holiday. Possibly to be connected with "angels," though not certain. {*Church of the firstborn*} Probably this is an additional item besides the angelic host as the people of Israel are called firstborn (Exod. 4:22). The Greek word *ekklêsia* (church) here has the general sense of all the redeemed, as in Matthew 16:18; Colossians 1:18; Ephesians 5:24-32, and equivalent to the kingdom of God. {*Who are enrolled in heaven*} Lit. "to write off, to copy, to enroll" (cf. Luke 2:1, 3, 5). Enrolled as citizens of heaven even while on earth (Luke 10:20; Phil. 1:27; 3:20; 4:3; Rev. 13:8, etc.).

24. {*To Jesus*} This great fact is not to be overlooked (Phil. 2:10). He is there as Lord and Savior and still "Jesus." {*The mediator of a new covenant*} (cf. Heb. 7:22; 8:6, 8, 9, 10; 9:15) and now gloriously consummated. {*Better*} Abel's blood still speaks (Heb. 11:4), but it is as nothing compared to that of Jesus.

25. {*See*} The Greek word *blepô* is an earnest word (cf. Heb. 3:12). Driving home the whole argument of the Epistle by this powerful contrast between Mount Zion and Mount Sinai. The consequences are dreadful to apostates now, for Zion has greater terrors than Sinai, great as those were. {*Much more we*} Again, an argument from the less to the greater. "We shall not escape." Our chance to escape is far less, "we who turn away the one from heaven," God speaking through his Son (Heb. 1:2).

26. {*Will I make to tremble*} (cf. Matt. 21:10). The author applies this "yet once more" and the reference to heaven to the second and final "shaking" at the Second Coming of Jesus Christ for judgment (cf. Heb. 9:28).

27. {*That those things which are not shaken may remain*} The Kingdom of God is not shaken, fearful as some saints are about it.

28. {*Let us have grace*} Greek tense translates, "Let us keep on having grace" (cf. Heb. 4:16), though it can mean "Let us keep on having gratitude" (cf. Luke 17:9). {*With reverence and awe*} (cf. Heb. 5:7; 11:7). "Awe" is the apprehension of danger as in a forest. When the voice and tread of a wild beast are distinctly heard close at hand the "awe" becomes "fear" (Vincent).

CHAPTER 13

1. {*Brotherly love*} The Greek word is *philadelphia* (cf. 1 Pet. 3:8; 1 Thess. 4:9). It is always in order in a church.

2. {*Have entertained angels unawares*} This refers to Abraham and Sarah doing so (cf. Gen. 18:1ff.). Translate, "some escaped notice when entertaining angels."

4. {*Let marriage be*} This Greek word *gamos* elsewhere in the NT, means the wedding or wedding feast (Matt. 22:29; John 2:1). {*Undefiled*} (cf. Heb. 7:26). "Defile the bed" is a common expression for adultery. {*Fornicators*} These are the unmarried who are impure. {*Adulterers*} Impure married persons. God will judge both classes.

5. {*Be ye free from the love of money*} Translate, "Let your manner of life be without love of money" (cf. 1 Tim. 3:3). {*Content with such things as ye have*} (cf. Luke 3:14 and Phil. 4:11). Translate, "Contented with the present things." {*For himself has said*} The quotation is a free paraphrase of Genesis 28:15; Deuteronomy 31:8; Joshua 1:5; 1 Chronicles 28:20. Note the five negatives in Greek *ou* and *mê,* strengthening each other "*never* leave...*nor never* forsake."

7. {*Remember*} This is an old verb to be *mindful,* translate, "Keep in mind" (cf. Heb. 11:22). {*And considering the issue of their life*} The Greek word *ekbasis* is an old word from *ekbainô,* to go out (Heb. 11:15), originally way out (1 Cor. 10:13), but here in sense of end or issue. {*Imitate their faith*} (cf. 2 Thess. 3:7, 9; 3 John 11). Translate the Greek tense, "Keep on imitating the faith of the leaders."

8. {*Jesus Christ is the same yesterday and today, yea and forever*} "Yesterday" refers to the days of Christ's flesh (Heb. 2:3; 5:7) and to the recent work of the leaders (Heb. 13:7). "Today" refers to the crisis which confronts them. "Forever" is eternity as well as the Greek can say it. Jesus Christ is eternally "the same" (cf. Heb. 1:12) and the revelation of God in him (Heb. 1:1) is final and never to be superseded or supplemented (Moffatt). Hence the peril of apostasy from the only hope of man.

9. {*By divers and strange teachings*} The Greek word *xenos* meaning "unheard of" (1 Pet. 4:12). The new is not always wrong any more than the old is always right (Matt. 13:52). But the air was already full of new and strange teachings that fascinated many by their very novelty. The warning here is always needed (cf. Gal. 1:6-9; 2 Tim. 3:16). {*That the heart be established by grace*} Lit. "to make stable." How true it is that in the atmosphere of so many windy theories only the heart is stable that has an experience of God's grace in Christ. {*Were not profited*} Mere Jewish ceremonialism and ritualism failed to build up the spiritual life. It was sheer folly to give up Christ for Pharisaism.

11. {*Of those beasts whose blood*} Lit. "the blood of which beasts" (cf. Lev. 4:12, 21; 16:27). See also Exodus 29:14; 32:26 for burning without the camp.

12. {*Wherefore Jesus also*} The parallel is drawn between the OT ritual and the better sacrifice of Jesus already discussed (Heb. 9:13-10:18).

13. {*Let us therefore go forth to him*} Translate, "Let us keep on going out there to him." If a separation has to come between Judaism and Christianity, let us give up Judaism, and go out to Christ "outside the camp" and take our stand with him there on Golgotha, bearing his reproach as Jesus himself endured the Cross despising the shame (Heb. 12:2).

14. {*An abiding city*} Jerusalem has lost its charm for followers of Christ. The Epistle must have been written before the destruction of Jerusalem else a reference to that event could hardly have been avoided here (Vincent). We are now where Abraham was once (Heb. 11:10).

15. {*Let us offer up*} Lit. "let us keep on offering up." Jesus is living and let us go to him. {*Which made confession to his name*} This is in the sense of praise, in the sense of gratitude.

16. {*To communicate*} This is the Greek word *koinônia* (cf. 2 Cor. 9:13). This is in the sense of "contribution, beneficence." Here are three great definitions of worship and religious service in the NT (Moffatt) (here, Rom. 12:1; Jas. 1:27), all inward and ethical.

17. {*As they that shall give account*} These leaders as good shepherds recognize keenly their responsibility for the welfare of the flock. {*And not with grief*} Lit. "And not groaning" (cf. Rom. 8:23). {*Unprofitable*} Lit. "not + to pay + tax, useful or profitable (cf. Luke 17:2), not profitable, not advantageous, By the figure of understatement (*litotes*) means "hurtful, pernicious."

20. {*Who brought again from the dead*} This is the only direct mention of the resurrection of Jesus in the Epistle, though implied often (Heb. 1:3, etc.). {*With the blood of the eternal covenant*} (cf. Zech. 9:11). The language reminds us of Christ's own words in Mark 14:24 (Matt. 26:28; Luke 22:20; 1 Cor. 11:25) about "my blood of the covenant."

21. {*Make you perfect*} (cf. Heb. 10:5). A wish for the future. See 1 Corinthians 1:10; 2 Corinthians 13:11; 2 Timothy 3:17. This is one of the noblest doxologies in the NT.

22. {*Bear with*} Translate, "hold yourselves back from" (cf. Col. 3:13).

24. {*They of Italy*} Either those with the author in Italy or those who have come from Italy to the author outside of Italy.

THE EPISTLE OF JAMES

AUTHOR: James, son of Joseph and Mary, the half brother of Jesus
RECIPIENTS: The twelve tribes which are of the Dispersion (Jas. 1:1),
likely referring to Christian and Non-Christian Jews
DATE: Before A.D. 50, earliest of all NT books
OCCASION: This is a letter and a brief sermon.
THEME: Christian principles for living as individuals and as members
of the church

BY WAY OF INTRODUCTION

THE AUTHOR

This writer is likely not James of Zebedee (died, Acts 12:2), but
James of Joseph and Mary, related to Jesus legal family, active in
the Christian movement (Gal. 1:19): leader of the church in Jerusalem
(Acts 12:17); presiding over the Conference in Jerusalem (Acts 15:13-21
and devout friend of Paul (Acts 21:18-25). James was not one of the
Twelve (Apostles), but an apostle in the general sense of that term like
Barnabas (Acts 14:14), perhaps Silas and Timothy (1 Thess. 2:7), cer-
tainly not on a *par* with Paul, who claimed equality with the twelve.

Later he was called "James the Just." A devout Jew, he was strictly
the half brother of Jesus, since Joseph was not the actual father of Jesus.
He was won to Christ by a special vision of the Risen Christ (1 Cor.
15:7), and was in the upper room before the great Pentecost (Acts 1:14).
He was married (1 Cor. 9:5). Sources agree that he died a martyr.

The tone and content makes it reasonable to assume an early date.
There is no allusion to Gentile Christians in the epistle. There is no
mention of issues in Rome of the faith/works debate and no mention
of the Jerusalem Conference, so the date is before A.D. 50.

"Twelve tribes" refers to Jews in general. It is probable also that
James is addressing chiefly the Eastern Dispersion in Syria,
Mesopotamia, and Babylonia as Peter writes to five provinces in the
Western Dispersion in Asia Minor. He may have in mind merely Chris-
tian Jews outside of Palestine, of whom there were already many scat-
tered since the great Pentecost.

The letter is a picture of early Christian life in the midst of difficult social conditions between capital and labor which also exist today. So then it is a very modern message even if it is the earliest NT book. James is concerned mainly with the ethical and social aspects of the gospel that Jewish followers of Christ may square their lives with the gospel which they believe and profess.

Faith and works is a major theme in the letter. We shall see that, though James and Paul use the same words (faith, works, justify), they mean different things by them.

James writes in the easy and accurate *Koiné* Greek of a cultivated Jew (literary *Koiné*, not the vernacular). Though Classical Greek parallels are sometimes made, the style of James is even more kin to that seen in the Jewish wisdom literature like Proverbs, the Wisdom of Solomon, etc.

Thus James is both an Epistle and a brief Christian sermon on a high plane for a noble purpose. The author shows acquaintance with the LXX, but there are few Hebraisms in the language, though the style is Hebraic, as is the whole tone of the book (Hebraic and Christian). "The style is especially remarkable for constant hidden allusions to our Lord's sayings, such as we find in the first three Gospels" (Hort).

CHAPTER I

1. {*James*} Greek for Hebrew "Jacob," a common name. {*To the twelve tribes*} This means "Israel in its fullness and completeness" (Acts 26:7) (Hort). {*Which are of the Dispersion*} (cf. Deut. 28:25 [LXX]). Christian Jews are chiefly, if not wholly, in view. Palestinian Jews were farmers; while Jews of the Dispersion were city dwellers and traders. James writes thus in cultural *Koiné* but in the Hebraic tone.

2. {*Count it*} Greek tense has idea "[Consider] it now and once for all." {*All joy*} This is "whole joy," "unmixed joy," not just "some joy" along with much grief (cf. Phil. 2:29). {*Ye fall into*} It is the picture of being *surrounded* by trials. {*Manifold temptations*} The Greek word *peirasmos* (temptations) can mean either a good (John 6:6) or bad sense (Matt. 16:1). Here it is in the good sense of "trials." Trials rightly faced are harmless, but wrongly met become temptations to evil.

3. {*Knowing*} This is experimental knowledge, the only way of getting this view of "trials" as "all joy." {*The proof*} The Greek word *dokimion* here and in 1 Peter 1:7, clearly means "the genuine element in your faith," not "crucible" nor "proving." Your faith like gold stands the test of fire and is approved as standard. {*Patience/perseverance*} Lit. "remaining under," this is "staying power" (Ropes) (Col. 1:11).

4. {*Let have*} Greek tense translates "let it keep on having." {*Perfect*} (cf. Rom. 5:3; also John 17:4). {*Perfect and entire*} Perfected at the end of the task (mature) and complete in all parts.

5. {*Lacketh wisdom*} "If any one falls short of wisdom." "Lacks" is a banking figure, to have a shortage of wisdom (practical knowledge). {*Let him ask*} Greek tense translates "let him keep on asking." {*Liberally*} See Isaiah 55:1 for the idea of God's gracious giving and the case of Solomon (1 Kgs. 3:9-12; Prov. 2:3). {*Upbraideth not*} Greek verb *oneidizô* means "to reproach, to cast in one's teeth," Matthew 5:11. The evil habit of giving stinging words along with the money is illustrated in Sirach 41:22, also Hebrews 4:16. {*And it shall be given him*} (cf. Matt. 7:7, 11; Luke 11:13), meaning here not only "wisdom," but referring to all good gifts, including the Holy Spirit.

6. {*Nothing doubting*} Lit. "to separate + between," i.e., to discriminate as shown clearly in Acts 11:12, 15:9. It is a vivid picture of internal doubt. {*Driven by the wind...tossed*} It is a vivid picture of the sea whipped into white-caps by the winds (cf. Eph. 4:14).

7. {*That man*} "That" is emphatic, the doubting person.

8. {*Double minded*} Apparently James coined this term, lit. "twice + soul," and so "double-souled, double-minded," Bunyan's "Mr. Facing-both-ways." (cf. also Matt. 14:31). {*Unstable*} (cf. Isa. 54:11 and Jas. 3:8). It means unsteady, fickle, staggering, reeling like a drunken man. Surely to James such "doubt" is no mark of intellectuality.

9. {*Of low degree*} This is outwardly humble in situation (cf. Luke 1:52 and Ps. 9:39; Prov. 30:14), not the spiritually humble as in Matthew 11:29; James 4:6. Already the rich and the poor in the churches had their occasion for jealousies. {*Glory in his high estate*} Ironic, but true. In his low estate he is "in his height" (cf. Luke 1:78; Eph. 3:1; etc.).

10. {*Rich...in that he is made low*} The Cross of Christ lifts up the poor and brings down the high. It is the great leveler of men. {*Flower of the grass*} (cf. Isa. 40:6, also Jas. 1:11; 1 Pet. 1:24). It is true of all, though here applied to "the rich brother." {*He shall pass away*} Greek tense translates "shall pass completely away [from earth]."

11. {*Ariseth…withereth…falleth*} All three verbs have a timelessness, as when in a known saying. Grass and flowers are often used to picture the passing nature of human life. The flower dries up and is destroyed. The beautiful rose is pitiful when withered.

12. {*When he hath been approved*} Greek tense translates "Having become approved," (cf. Jas. 1:3, also Rom. 5:4 and 1 Tim. 6:9). {*The crown of life*} (cf. Rev. 2:10). This crown is "an honorable ornament" (Ropes) not a victor's garland of leaves as with Paul in 1 Corinthians 9:25; 2 Timothy 4:8, the linen fillet diadem of royalty in Psalms 21:3.

13. {*Let no one say*} Greek has a focus of prohibiting such a habit. {*I am tempted of God*} Here the temptation has no origin nor does it spring from God. {*Cannot be tempted with evil*} Ancient writer had a proverb, "free from evils." That is possible here, but the context calls for "untemptable" rather than "untempted."

14. {*When he is drawn away by his own lust*} "Desire" in Greek is *epithumia,* an old word for craving: good (Phil. 1:23) or evil (Rom. 7:7) as here. Like a fish drawn out from his retreat. {*Enticed*} Greek is derived from *delear* (bait), and so the verb is "to catch fish by bait or to hunt with snares," allured by definite bait (cf. 2 Pet. 2:14, 18).

15. {*The lust*} This is the desire which one has, a definite focus (cf. Jas. 1:14). {*When it hath conceived*} Here the Greek has the picture of the lust as a woman, "having conceived." The will yields to lust and conception takes place. {*Beareth sin*} Lit. "to bring forth as a mother or fruit from seed," Sin is the union of the will with lust (cf. Ps. 7:14). {*When it is full grown*} It means here completeness of parts or functions as opposed to rudimentary state: illustrated as when the winged insect (full-grown) in contrast with the chrysalis or grub (inception). The sin at birth is fully equipped for its career (Rom. 6:6; Col. 3:5). {*Bringeth forth death*} Lit. "to give birth to," this is a medical term, not literary. The child of lust is sin, of sin is death, powerful figure of abortion. The child is dead at birth.

16. {*Be not deceived*} This is the way of sin to deceive and to kill (Rom. 7:7-14). The devil is a master at blinding men's eyes about sin (2 Cor. 4:4; Rom. 1:27; Eph. 4:14; etc.).

17. {*From the Father of lights*} For this use of Greek *patêr* see Job 38:28 (Father of rain); 2 Corinthians 1:3; Ephesians 1:17. God is the Author of light and [heavenly] lights. {*Variation*} Greek word is *parallagê* derived from *parallassô,* "to make things alternate." James here is comparing God (Father of the lights) to the sun (Mal. 4:2), which does have periodic variations.

18. {*Of his own will*} God as Father acted deliberately of set purpose. {*He brought us forth*} Regeneration, not birth of all men, though God is the Father in the sense of creation of all men (Acts 17:28). {*By the word of truth*} This refers to the gospel message of salvation (2 Cor. 6:7; Col. 1:5; Eph. 1:13; 2 Tim. 2:15).

19. {*Ye know this*} This form can be a command, or a statement of fact, in context this is probably the latter. {*Swift to hear*} The picture points to listening to the word of truth (cf. Jas. 1:18) and is aimed against violent and disputatious speech (Jas. 3:1-12). The Greek moralists often urge a quick and attentive ear. {*Slow to anger*} Here he probably means that slowness to speak up when angry will tend to curb the anger.

20. {*The wrath of man*} The Greek apparently means a male in contrast to a woman. This man's anger is a kind of settled indignation in contrast with boiling rage or fury.

21. {*Putting away*} Lit. "to put off," a metaphor of removing clothing (cf. Rom. 13:12; Col. 3:8; Eph. 4:22, 25; 1 Pet. 2:1). {*Overflowing of wickedness*} This can mean either general evil or special kind of "malice." But any of either sense is some kind of immodesty or excessive behavior. {*The implanted word*} This is inborn, ingrown and not engrafted. It is "the rooted word" (cf. Jas. 1:18), sown in the heart as the soil or garden of God (Matt. 13:3-23; 15:13; 1 Cor. 3:6). {*Able to save*} This is ultimate salvation (cf. 1 Pet. 1:9; Jas. 2:14; 4:12; 5:20; Rom. 1:16).

22. {*But be ye*} Greek tense translates, "But keep on becoming." {*Deluding yourselves*} Lit. "to reckon aside" and a reflexive pronoun; such a man does not delude anyone but himself.

23. {*In a mirror*} (cf. 1 Cor. 13:12). The mirrors of the ancients were not of glass, but of polished metal of silver or usually of copper and tin (cf. also 2 Cor. 3:18).

24. {*He beholdeth himself*} The tenses in this verse present a vivid and lifelike picture of the careless listener to preaching (Christ's wayside hearer). Translate thusly, "He *glanced* at himself and off he *has gone* and immediately *forgot* what sort of a man *he was*."

25. {*He that looketh into*} Greek word is *parakuptô*, "to stoop and look into" (John 20:5, 11), "to gaze carefully by the side of, to peer into or to peep into" (1 Pet. 1:12). {*The perfect law*} James here refers to the word of truth (Jas. 1:18), the gospel of grace (Gal. 6:2; Rom. 12:2). {***The law of liberty***} This law rests on the work of Christ, whose truth sets us free.

26. {***Thinketh himself to be religious***} This Greek word *thrêskos* is found nowhere else except in lexicons. It likely refers to the external observances of public worship, such as church attendance, almsgiving, prayer, fasting (Matt. 6:1-18). It is the Pharisaic element in Christian worship. {***While he bridleth not his tongue***} (cf. Jas. 1:19 and 3:12). The picture is that of a man putting the bridle in his own mouth, not in that of another (cf. "muzzle" Matt. 22:12). {***Religion***} This Greek word *thrêskeia* means religious worship in its external observances, religious exercise or discipline.

27. {***Pure religion and undefiled***} This is not a definition of religion or religious worship, but only a pertinent illustration of the right spirit of religion which leads to such acts. {***To visit***} This explains the "this" in the prior phrase. The Greek verb *episkeptomai*, "to go to see, to inspect," and the tense has a focus of being in the habit of going to see (cf. Matt. 25:36, 43). {***The fatherless and widows***} These two are "the natural objects of charity in the community" (Ropes). "Orphan" is one without either a father or mother or both. {***To keep***} Greek tense translates, "to keep on keeping oneself un-specked from the world." A world (Greek *kosmos*) full of dirt and slime bespatters the best of men.

CHAPTER 2

1. {***The Lord of Glory***} James thus terms "our Lord Jesus Christ" the *Shekinah* Glory of God (cf. Heb. 9:5, also Rom. 9:4; 2 Cor. 4:6; Eph. 1:17; Heb. 1:3. Cf. 2 Cor. 8:9; Phil. 2:5-11). {***With respect of persons***} Do not show partiality. This is a Hebrew idiom for *panim nasa*, "to lift up the face on a person," to be favorable and so partial to him.

2. {***If there come in***} This is a supposable case, a contrast of rich and poor classes. {***A man with a gold ring***} Lit. "A gold-fingered man." {***In fine clothing...vile clothing***} This is bright (brilliant, glossy, fine) clothing (c. Luke 23:11; Acts 10:30; Rev. 18:41). In contrast with "vile clothing" means "filthy, dirty (clothing)" (cf. Rev. 22:11).

3. {***And ye have regard to***} Lit. "to gaze upon," (cf. Luke 1:48; 9:38). {***And say***} Again, a continuing supposable case. {***Sit thou here in a good place***} "You" is emphatic; a good seat was a place of honor (cf.

Matt. 23:6). {***Stand thou there***} "You" is again emphatic. {***Or sit under my footstool***} Conquerors often placed their feet on the necks of the victims (Luke 20:43).

4. {***Are ye not divided in your own mind?***} Greek syntax expects a yes answer (cf. 1 Cor. 7:28 and Jas. 1:6; Matt. 21:21). {***Judges with evil thoughts***} They are guilty of partiality (a divided mind) as between the two strangers. Lit. "reasoning" (Rom. 1:21).

5. {***Did not God choose?***} Greek syntax expects a "Yes" answer (cf. 1 Cor. 1:27). {***The poor***} Here James does not affirm that God chose all the poor, but only that he did choose poor people [as a class] (Matt. 10:23-26; 1 Cor. 1:26-28). {***Rich in faith***} The poor are rich because of their faith (cf. Jas. 1:9).

6. {***But ye have dishonoured the poor man***} The act of partiality is pictured in James 2:3. {***Oppress you***} There are examples in papyri of harsh treatment by men in authority. {***Drag you***} A focus on violent treatment (cf. Acts 16:19; 21:30, and Luke 12:58; Acts 8:3). {***Before the judgment seats***} This is the place where judgment is given by a judge (cf. 1 Cor. 6:2, 4).

7. {***Blaspheme***} Lit. "speaking evil," (cf. Luke 22:65). {***The name***} What name is that? Almost certainly the name of Christ (cf. Acts 11:26; 26:28; 1 Pet. 4:14, 16). It was blasphemy/slander to speak against Christ as some Jews and Gentiles were doing.

8. {***The royal law***} This can mean a law fit to guide a king, or such as a king would choose, or even the king of laws. Jesus had said that on the law of love hang all the law and the prophets (Matt. 22:40; cf. the Golden Rule Matt. 7:12). This is probably the royal law which is violated by partiality (Jas. 2:3; cf. Lev. 19:18 and Luke 10:28).

9. {***But if ye have respect of persons***} Again, this is assumed as a true condition of discrimination (cf. Jas. 2:8). {***Ye commit sin***} Lit. "You work a sin." A serious charge, apparently, for what was regarded as a trifling fault (cf. Matt. 7:23 and Ps. 6:8). {***Being convicted***} Lit. "to convict by proof of guilt" (John 3:20; 8:9, 46; 1 Cor. 14:24).

10. {***Whosoever shall keep***} The Greek word *têreô*, "to guard" (cf. Matt. 27:36). {***And yet stumble in one point***} It is just beginning to fall (cf. Jas. 3:2; Rom. 11:11). {***Guilty of all***} To be a lawbreaker one does not have to violate all the laws, but he must keep all the law to be a law-abiding citizen, even laws that one does not like (cf. Matt. 5:18). James is urging obedience to all God's laws.

11. {*A transgressor of the law*} (cf. Jas. 2:9). Murder springs out of anger (Matt. 5:21-26). People free from fleshly sins have often made their condemnation of fleshly sins an excuse for indulgence in spiritual sins.

12. {*So speak ye, and so do*} These are commands that are as a habit (cf. Jas. 1:19-21, 22-25, 26, 27). {*By a law of liberty*} (cf. Jas. 1:25) This is not individual caprice of "personal liberty."

13. {*Glorieth against*} Lit. "to exult over (down)" (cf. Jas. 3:14; Rom. 11:18). Only mercy can triumph over justice with God and men.

14. {*What doth it profit?*} Rhetorical question, almost of impatience. It "was a common expression in the vivacious style of a moral diatribe" (Ropes). {*If a man say*} A possible scenario for the whole verse, Greek tense translates "if one keep on saying." {*But have not works*} Greek tense translates "but keeps on not having works." It is the spurious claim to faith that James here condemns. {*Can that faith save him?*} "No" answer is expected.

15. {*If a brother or sister be naked*} It does not here mean absolutely naked, but without sufficient clothing (cf. Matt. 25:36; John 21:7; Acts 19:16).

16. {*And one of you say unto them*} Again, a possible scenario in the verse, not assumed to be a fact. {*Be ye warmed and filled*} Likely translate "warm yourselves" and fill yourselves. Instead of warm clothes and satisfying food they get only empty words to look out for themselves. {*What doth it profit?*} Here is the conclusion of the long "if" condition begun in James 2:15.

17. {*If it have not works*} Greek tense translates "if it keep on not having works." It is a dead faith.

18. {*Yea, a man will say*} James introduces an imaginary objector who speaks one sentence: "You have faith and I have works." {*Show me thy faith apart from thy works*} This is the reply of James to the objector, with a Greek tense of urgency. {*And I by my works will shew thee my faith*} It is not faith *or* works, but proof of real faith (live faith *vs.* dead faith). The mere profession of faith with no works or profession of faith shown to be alive by works. James is not here discussing "works" as a means of salvation but works as proof of faith.

19. {*Thou believest that God is one*} An example of mere creed (though fundamental) apart from works, belief that God exists. Good as far as it goes. {*The demons also believe*} They go that far, they never doubt the fact of God's existence, yet they bristle in horror.

20. {*But wilt thou know?*} James here introduces a new argument (cf. Rom. 13:3). {*O vain man*} This man is empty and deficient, like a fool (1 Cor. 15:36 and Rom. 2:1; 9:20). {*Barren*} (cf. 2 Pet. 1:8) Some think "inactive" as the idea here, like money with no interest and land with no crops.

21. {*Justified by works*} This is the phrase that is often held to be flatly opposed to Paul's statement in Romans 4:1-5, where Paul pointedly says that it was the faith of Abraham (Rom. 4:9) that was reckoned to Abraham for righteousness, not his works. But Paul is talking about the faith of Abraham before his circumcision (Jas. 4:10) as the basis of his being set right with God, which faith is symbolized in the circumcision. James makes plain his meaning also. {*In that he offered up Isaac his son upon the altar*} James points to the offering of Isaac on the altar (Gen. 22:16) as *proof* of the faith that Abraham already had. Paul discusses Abraham's faith as the basis of his justification, that and not his circumcision. There is no contradiction at all between James and Paul.

24. {*Is justified*} James is discussing the proof of faith, not the initial act of being set right with God (Paul's idea in Rom. 4:1-10). {*And not only by faith*} This phrase clears up the meaning of James. Faith (live faith) is what we must all have (Jas. 2:18), only it must show itself also in deeds as Abraham's did.

26. {*Apart from the spirit*} Lit. "apart from breath (of life)." It is not easy to tell when one is dead, but the absence of a sign of breath on a glass before the mouth and nose is proof of death. Startling picture of dead faith in our churches and church members with only a name to live (Rev. 3:2).

CHAPTER 3

1. {*Be not many teachers*} Greek syntax translates, "stop becoming teachers (so many of you)." There is thus a clear complaint that too many of the Jewish Christians were attempting to teach what they did not clearly comprehend. Teachers are necessary, but incompetent and unworthy ones do much harm.

2. {*In word*} This means "in speech." The teacher uses his tongue constantly and so is in particular peril on this score. {*A perfect man*} This can mean "a perfect husband" or generic "male." The wife is at liberty to test her husband by this rule of the tongue. {*To bridle the whole body also*} As horses are led by the mouth, so a man follows his own mouth whether he controls the bridle therein (Jas. 1:26) or someone else holds the reins. James apparently means that the man who bridles his tongue does not stumble in speech and is able also to control his whole body with all its passions.

3. James now gives an example assumed to be true, showing the power of the tongue. {*The horses' bridles*} Here is the first illustration (cf. Rev. 14:20). The body of the horse follows the bridle.

4. {*The ships also*} Here is a second metaphor. {*By a very small rudder*} There is a focus that this is a quite small blade device. {*The impulse*} A Greek word for a motion, this refers to the hand that worked the rudder, who keeps the boat straight with intention.

5. {*A little member*} This is the member of the human body (1 Cor. 12:12, etc.; Rom. 6:13, etc.). {*How much…how small*} A double question in Greek, "What-sized fire kindles what-sized forest?" (cf. Luke 12:49).

6. {*The tongue is a fire*} This metaphor of fire is applied to the tongue (cf. Prov. 16:27; 26:18-22; Sirach 28:22). {*The world of iniquity*} James means to say that the tongue can play havoc in the members of the human body. {*Which defileth the whole body*} Lit. "to stain, spot" (cf. Eph. 5:27; 2 Pet. 2:13, also Judg. 1:23, even Jas. 1:27).

7. {*Beasts and birds, of creeping things and things of the sea*} These four classes of animals (in two pairs) come from Genesis 9:2: quadrupeds, flying animals, crawling things (snakes), creatures from the sea. {*Hath been tamed*} The Greek tense shows the continuous process through the ages of man's lordship over the animals (cf. Gen. 1:28).

8. {*A restless evil*} The tongue is evil when set on fire by hell, not evil necessarily. {*Full of deadly poison*}Greek word *thanatêphoros*, "death + to bear or bring," death-bringing. Here only in NT, like the restless death-bringing tongue of the asp before it strikes.

9. {*We bless*} Lit. "good word" (cf. Luke 1:64). "This is the highest function of speech" (Hort). {*The Lord and Father*} Both terms applied to God. {*Which are made after the likeness of God*} Lit. "to make like," so making like, (Gen. 1:26; 9:6, cf. resemblance Phil. 2:7). It is this image of God which sets man above the beasts.

10. {*Ought not*} It is a moral incongruity for blessing and cursing to come out of the same mouth.

11. {*The fountain*} This is a fissure in the earth with water (cf. John 4:14). {*The sweet and the bitter*} This is presenting a quality "sweet" (Rev. 10:9); "bitter" is lit. "sharp, harsh," (cf. Jas. 3:14).

12. {*Can?*} No is the expected answer (cf. Matt. 7:16).

13. {*Who*} James here returns to the standpoint of James 3:1 about many teachers. Speech and wisdom are both liable to abuse (1 Cor. 1:5, 17; 2:1-3:20). {*By his good life*} (cf. Gal. 1:13). Actions speak louder than words even in the case of the professional wise man (cf. 1 Pet. 1:15). {*In meekness of wisdom*} a quality of a listener (Jas. 1:21) and Messiah (cf. Matt. 5:5; 11:29 and Zech. 9:9 [Matt. 21:5]).

14. {*Bitter jealousy*} (cf. Acts 5:17; Heb. 12:14; Eph 4:31). Pride of knowledge is evil (1 Cor. 8:1) and leaves a bitter taste. {*Faction*} This is a pushing forward for personal ends, partisanship (cf. Phil. 1:16). {*Glory not*} (Jas. 2:13). Wisdom is essential for the teacher. Boasting arrogance disproves the possession of wisdom.

15. {*This wisdom*} All talk and disproved by the life; this is counterfeit wisdom, not real wisdom (cf. Jas. 1:5; 3:17). {*Earthly...sensual...devilish*} (cf. John 3:12). Wisdom of this kind has earthly limitations (Phil. 3:19); sensuous or animal life; demon-like.

16. {*Vile*} Kin to German *faul,* first slight, ordinary, then bad. The steps are cheap, paltry, evil. Opposed to Greek *agatha* (good) in John 5:39.

17. {*First pure*} First in rank and time. The Greek *hagnos* is from the same root as *hagios* (holy), old adjective, pure from fault, not half-good and half-bad, like that above. {*Then peaceable*} (cf. Heb. 12:11). But clearly great as peace is, purity (righteousness) comes before peace and peace at any price is not worth the having. {*Without variance*} "Unhesitating," not doubting (cf. Jas. 1:6). Here only in NT. This wisdom does not put a premium on doubt.

18. {*Is sown in peace*} The seed which bears the fruit is sown, but James catches up the metaphor of fruit (cf. Jas. 3:17). Only in peace is the fruit of righteousness found. {*For them that make peace*} (cf. Matt. 5:9; Eph. 2:15; Col. 1:20). Only those who act peaceably are entitled to peace.

CHAPTER 4

1. {*Wars...fightings*} This covers the chronic state or campaign to separate conflicts or battles in the war. So James covers the whole ground by using both words. The origin of a war or of any quarrel is sometimes hard to find, but James touches the sore spot here.

2. {*Ye lust*} The Greek word is *epithumeô*, "to have yearning passion for." Coveting what a man or nation does not have is the cause of war according to James. {*Ye have not, because ye ask not*} Make the service of God your supreme end, and then your desires will be such as God can fulfill in answer to your spirit of prayer (Ropes) (cf. Matt. 6:31-33, also 7:7).

3. {*That ye may spend it in your pleasures*} Lit. "to squander" (Luke 15:14). God does not hear prayers like this.

4. {*Ye adulteresses*} Is this literal (Rom. 7:3), or figuratively for all unfaithful followers of Christ like an unfaithful bride [to Him] (cf. 2 Cor. 11:1; Eph. 5:24-28); likely the former. {*Maketh himself*} This is a passive, not middle voice and is so translated "is constituted."

5. {*The Scripture*} Personification as in Galatians 3:8 and James 2:23. But no OT passage is precisely like this although it is "a poetical rendering" of Exodus 20:5 (cf. Gen. 6:3-5; Isa. 63:8-16 and even Gal. 5:17, 21; Rom. 8:6, 8).

6. {*God resisteth the proud*} "Resists" is an old military term, to range in battle against, with dative case (Rom. 13:2) as in James 5:6. "Proud" is like our vernacular "stuck-up folks" (Rom. 1:30), "haughty persons."

7. {*Be subject therefore unto God*} The Greek tense and grammatical mood has a note of urgency (cf. 1 Pet. 2:23; 5:5). There are 10 such commanding verbs in James 4:7-10. {*But resist the devil*} "Take a stand against." Result of such a stand is that the devil will flee.

8. {*Cleanse your hands*} This is lit. "to cleanse," from dirt in a ritual sense (Exod. 30:19-21; Mark 7:3, 19). Here it is figurative, as in Hosea 1:16; Psalms 24:4. {*Ye sinners*} A sharp term to strike the conscience; this is a "reproach meant to startle and sting" (Ropes). {*Purify your hearts*} (cf. Jas. 3:17). Elsewhere this is ceremonial (Acts 21:24, 26), but here morally (cf. 1 Pet. 1:22; 1 John 3:3).

9. {*Be afflicted*} Lit. "to endure toils" (cf. Jas. 5:1). {*Mourn...weep*} Often together in NT (Mark 16:10; Luke 6:25). A call to the godly sorrow spoken of in 2 Corinthians 7:10, like an OT prophet. {*Heavi-*

ness} Greek word *katêpheia,* "a downcast eyes [look]"; cf. the hanging down of the eyes like the publican in Luke 18:13.

10. {*Humble yourselves*} Though Greek action is formally passive, it has almost the middle or reflexive sense, hence *yourselves* (cf. 1 Pet. 5:6). {*He shall exalt you*} Used by Jesus in contrast with humility (cf. Matt. 23:12; Luke 14:11; 18:14).

11. {*Speak not one against another*} Greek syntax tells this is a prohibition against such a habit or a command to quit doing it. James returns to the subject of the tongue as he does again in 5:12 (twice before, 1:26; 3:1-12). {*Not a doer of the law, but a judge*} This tone of superiority to law is here sharply condemned. James has in mind God's law, of course, but the point is the same for all laws under which we live. We cannot select the laws which we will obey unless some contravene God's law, and so our own conscience (Acts 4:20).

12. {*One only*} This "one" excludes all others but God. {*And to destroy*} Cf. the picture of God's power in Matthew 10:28, a common idea in the OT (Deut. 32:39; 1 Sam. 2:16; 2 Kgs. 5:7). {*But who art thou?*} In this rhetorical question, "You" is emphatic and anticipatory (cf. Rom. 9:20; 14:4).

13. {*Into this city*} One would point out the city on the map as he made the proposal. {*And spend a year there*} Lit. "We will do a year there." {*And trade*} The Greek verb *emporeuomai* derived from *emporos* (a merchant or trader, a drummer, one going in and getting the trade, Matt. 13:45), a vivid picture of the Jewish merchants of the time.

14. {*Whereas ye know not*} Translate as "who indeed do not know." {*What is your life?*} The Greek has a focus to translate, "What is the *character* or *quality* of your life?" {*As vapor*} This is the answer. This is a vapor or mist, *atmos,* from which we get our word "atmosphere" (cf. Joel 2:30; Acts 2:19). {*That appeareth and then vanisheth away*} There is play on the two verbs (cf. Matt. 6:19 and Heb. 4:13).

15. {*If the Lord will*} This verse is not assumed to be a fact. It is the proper attitude of mind (Acts 18:21; 1 Cor. 4:19; 16:7; Rom. 1:19; Phil. 2:19, 24; Heb. 6:3), not to be uttered always in words like a charm.

17. {*To him that knoweth to do good*} Translate, "to one knowing how to do a good deed." {*And doeth it not*} (cf. "not a doer" Jas. 1:23 and Matt. 7:26). {*Sin*} Unused knowledge of one's duty is sin, the sin of omission (cf. Matt. 23:23).

CHAPTER 5

1. {*Come now, ye rich*} This is an exclamatory interjection (cf. Jas. 4:13). Direct address to the rich as a class as in 1 Timothy 6:17. Apparently here James has in mind the rich as a class, whether believer, as in James 1:10, or unbeliever (cf. Jas. 2:1, 6). The plea here is not directly for reform, but a warning of certain judgment (Jas. 5:1-6). {*Weep and howl*} Greek tense translates "Burst into weeping" (cf. Matt. 5:38). {*That are coming upon you*} The Greek tense form is present, but the meaning is in the futuristic prophetic sense.

2. {*Riches*} (cf. 2 Cor. 8:2) derived from the Greek word *pleotos* "fullness." {*Are corrupted*} Lit. "to corrupt, to destroy." On the worthlessness of mere wealth see Matthew 6:19, 24. {*Were moth-eaten*} (cf. Job 13:28). Rich robes as heirlooms, but moth-eaten is a vivid picture.

3. {*Rust*} Silver does corrode and gold will tarnish. {*Your flesh*} The plural is used for the fleshy parts of the body like pieces of flesh (Rev. 17:16; 19:18, 21). Rust eats like a canker, like cancer in the body. {*As fire*} Does this go back to "eat (the flesh)," that is the eternal fire of Gehenna which awaits them (Matt. 25:41; Mark 9:44); or does it relate to "hoarded wealth"? (cf. Matt. 6:19 and see Prov. 16:27). It is more natural to take it with "eats."

4. {*Laborers*} This is anyone who works, especially agricultural workers (Matt. 9:37). {*Who mowed*}This mowing strongly implies the gathering together, to reap. {*Fields*} These are estates or farms (Luke 12:16). {*Which is of you kept back by fraud*} The Greek verb *aphustereô*, "to be behind-hand from, to fail of, to cause to withdraw, to defraud." Pitiful picture of earned wages kept back by the rich addressed in the Epistle. {*The cries*} This refers to the stolen money, the workers cry out for vengeance. {*That reaped*} Lit. "to reap, to harvest while summer allows" (Matt. 6:26). {*Of the Lord of Sabaoth*} This is the "Lord of Hosts," (cf. Isa. 5:9 as in Rom. 9:29). In Hebrew "Hosts" is *Sabaoth*, a title of the omnipotence of God (cf. Rev. 4:8). God hears the cries of the oppressed workmen even if the employers are deaf.

5. {*Ye have lived delicately*} (cf. Luke 7:25) "to lead a soft life." {*Taken your pleasure*} A late and rare verb to live voluptuously or wantonly (cf. 1 Tim. 5:6). {*Ye have nourished*} (cf. Matt. 6:26). They are fattening themselves like sheep or oxen all unconscious of "the day of slaughter" (cf. Rom. 8:36).

6. {*Ye have condemned*} (cf. Acts 25:15). The rich controlled the courts of justice. {*Ye have killed the righteous one*} (cf. Jas. 2:11; 4:2). There is probably no direct reference to one individual who is righteous, though it does picture well the death of Christ and also the coming death of James himself, who was called "the Just."

7. {*Be patient therefore*} The appeal is to the oppressed brethren. Catch your wind for a long race (long-tempered as opposed to short-tempered). See already the exhortation to patience in James 1:3, 12 and repeated in James 5:11. {*Until the coming of the Lord*} This means the second coming of Christ (cf. Jas. 4:8 and Matt. 24:3, 37, 39; 1 Thess. 2:19). {*The husbandman*} This is the worker in the ground (cf. Matt. 21:33). {*Waiteth for*} The Greek verb *ekdechomai* is an old verb for eager expectation (cf. Acts 17:16). {*Being patient over it*} The Greek verb *makrothumeô* (just used in the exhortation), picturing the farmer longing and hoping over his precious crop (cf. Luke 18:7 of God).

8. {*Stablish*} Lit. "to make stable," (Luke 22:32; 1 Thess. 3:13). {*Is at hand*} In 1 Peter 4:7 the same word appears to have an eschatological sense as apparently here. How "near" or "nigh" did James mean? Clearly, it could only be a hope, for Jesus had distinctly said that no one knew when he would return.

9. {*Murmur not*} Greek syntax translates "Stop groaning against one another," as some were already doing in view of their troubles. In view of the hope of the Second Coming lift up your heads. {*Standeth before the doors*} Greek tense translates "is standing now." Again like the language of Jesus (cf. Matt. 24:33; Mark 13:29). Jesus the Judge is pictured as ready to enter for the judgment.

10. {*For an example*} The Greek word is *hupodeigma*, "to copy under, to teach" (Luke 6:47), here for copy to be imitated as in John 13:15, as a warning (Heb. 4:11). {*Of suffering*} Lit. "suffering evil," (cf. Jas. 5:13; 2 Tim. 2:3, 9). {*Of patience*} (cf. 2 Cor. 4:6; Col. 1:11) "Patience" is restraint from retaliating, "endurance," is not easily succumbing.

11. {*We call blessed*} The Greek verb *makarizô* is derived from *makarios* happy (cf. Luke 1:48). "We felicitate" (cf. Jas. 1:3, 12; Dan. 12:12). {*Of Job*} Job did complain, but he refused to renounce God (Job 1:21; 2:10; 13:15; 16:19; 19:25). He had become a stock illustration of loyal endurance. {*The end of the Lord*} This is the conclusion wrought by the Lord in Job's case (Job 42:12).

12. {*Above all things*} This means here "especially." No connection with what immediately precedes. Probably an allusion to the words of Jesus (Matt. 5:34-37). {*Swear not*} Greek syntax and tense are a prohibition of the habit (or to quit doing it if guilty). The various oaths (profanity) are forbidden. The Jews split hairs in their use of profanity, and by avoiding God's name imagined that they were not really guilty of this sin. {*Let be*} "Your yes be yes" and no more (cf. Matt. 5:37).

13. {*Is any suffering?*} (cf. Jas. 5:10, also 2 Tim. 2:3, 9; 4:5). The lively interrogative is common in the diatribe rhetoric and suits the style of James. {*Let him pray*} Greek tense translates the command or exhortation "let him keep on praying" (instead of cursing as in Jas. 5:12). {*Let him sing praise*} This Greek word is *psallô*, originally to twang a chord as on a harp, to sing praise to God whether with instrument or without (cf. 1 Cor. 14:15; Rom. 15:9; Eph. 5:19). Greek tense translates "Let him keep on making melody."

14. {*Let him call for elders*} Care for the sick is urged in 1 Thessalonians 5:14 ("help the sick"). {*Let them pray over him*} Prayer for the sick is clearly enjoined. {*Anointing him with oil*} The use of olive oil was one of the best remedial agencies known to the ancients. They used it internally and externally. It is clear both in Mark 6:13 and here that medicinal value is attached to the use of the oil and emphasis is placed on the worth of prayer. At bottom in James we have God and medicine, God and the doctor, and that is precisely where we are today. The best physicians believe in God and want the help of prayer.

15. {*The prayer of faith*} Cf. James 1:6 for prayer marked by faith. {*Shall save*} No reference here to salvation of the soul. The medicine does not heal the sick, but it helps nature (God) do it. {*The Lord shall raise him up*} This is a precious promise, but not for a professional "faith-healer" who scoffs at medicine and makes merchandise out of prayer. {*And if he have committed sins*} This is not an assumed fact, but here supposing that he has committed sins as many sick people have (Mark 2:5; John 5:14; 9:2; 1 Cor. 11:30). {*It shall be forgiven him*} (cf. Matt. 7:2, 7; Rom. 10:10). Not in any magical way, not because his sickness has been healed, not without change of heart and turning to God through Christ.

16. {*Confess therefore your sins one to another*} Confession of sin to God is already assumed. But public confession of certain sins to one another in the meetings is greatly helpful in many ways. This is not

confessing to one man like a priest in place of the public confession. One may confess to the pastor without confessing to God or to the church. {***Pray for one another***} Greek tense translates "Keep this up." {***That ye may be healed***} This is probably of bodily healing (cf. Jas. 5:14), though it is used also of healing of the soul (Matt. 13:15; 1 Pet. 2:24; Heb. 12:13).

17. {***He prayed fervently***} The phrase shows intensity, and is particularly frequent in the LXX (Gen. 2:17; 31:30) in imitation of the Hebrew infinitive absolute (cf. also Luke 22:15; John 3:29; Acts 4:17).

18. {***Gave rain***} This idiom is in the LXX of God as here of heaven (1 Sam. 12:17; 1 Kgs. 18:1) and also in Acts 14:17. {***Brought forth***} Lit. "to sprout [crops]."

19. {***If any one among you do err***} This is not an assumed fact, but is a supposed case; "err" is lit. "to go astray, to wander" (Matt. 18:12), figuratively (Heb. 5:2).

20. {***From the error***} Lit. "out of the wandering" (cf. Jas. 5:19). See 1 John 4:6 for contrast between "truth" and "error." {***A soul from death***} This is the soul of the sinner won back to Christ. It is ultimate and final salvation here meant by the future Greek tense. {***Shall cover a multitude of sins***} This phrase here means "love refuses to see faults," as in Proverbs 10:12. Whose sins are covered, those of the converter or the converted? Some take it to mean the sins of the converter, who thus saves himself by saving others. The language here will allow that, but not NT teaching in general.

THE FIRST EPISTLE OF PETER

AUTHOR: Simon Peter (Cephas), an apostle of Jesus Christ
RECIPIENTS: Believers in five Roman provinces: Pontus, Galatia, Cappadocia, Asia, and Bithynia
DATE: About A.D. 65
FROM: Either actual Babylon, or mystical Babylon (Rome), likely the latter
OCCASION: Evidently Peter's objective is to cheer and strengthen the Christians in these five provinces who are undergoing fiery trials (1 Pet. 1:7ff.).
THEME: Christians are born to a living hope that makes a difference in the details of life.

BY WAY OF INTRODUCTION

"There is no book in the NT which has earlier, better, or stronger attestation, though Irenæus is the first to quote it by name" (Bigg). Eusebius places it among the acknowledged books, those accepted with no doubt at all.

We know a great deal about the life of Peter from the Gospels and Acts. He had personally escaped death at the hands of Herod Agrippa I (Acts 12:3ff.). But he also is rebuked by Paul for cowardice because of the Judaizers (Gal. 2:11-21). He traveled with his wife (1 Cor. 9:5) and went to Asia Minor (1 Pet. 1:1) as far as Babylon or Rome (1 Pet. 5:13). John Mark and Silvanus Silas were apparently both his secretaries for writing Greek, since Peter was not expert in the Greek (Acts 4:13). The details of the end of his life are not as well known.

The date of A.D. 65 assumes Nero's persecution, and the death of Peter about A.D. 67 or 68.

Peter and Paul's writings are related. Their relationship was not one of extreme antithesis producing a Jewish and Gentile Christianity (cf. Gal. 2:11-21).

The other extreme is to deny any Pauline influence on Peter or of Peter on Paul. Paul was friendly to Peter (Gal. 1:18), but was independent of his ecclesiastical authority (Gal. 2:1-10) and Peter championed Paul's cause in the Jerusalem Conference (Acts 15:7-13).

Peter was familiar with some of Paul's Epistles (2 Pet. 3:15ff.). There is some indication of Peter's use of Romans and Ephesians in this Epistle. Peter may have read James, but not the Pastoral Epistles.

When Rome had a persecution, the provinces easily imitated the capital city. Paul's life in the Acts and his Epistles abundantly show how early persecution arose in Asia Minor. We know too little of the history of Christianity in Asia Minor from A.D. 60 to 70 to deny the fiery trials and suffering as a Christian (1 Pet. 4:16).

Peter states that he is in Babylon (1 Pet. 5:13), apparently with his wife (1 Cor. 9:5). The Christians were called "evil-doers" (1 Pet. 2:12) in the time of Nero. So we can think of Rome as the place of writing and that Peter uses "Babylon" to hide his actual location from Nero.

Probably the readers are mainly Jewish Christians, but not to the exclusion of Gentiles. Peter has clearly Paul's idea that Christianity is the true Judaism of God's promise (1 Pet. 2:4-10). There is no reason to not think Peter did work in similar regions to Paul in Asia Minor.

Paul's long imprisonment in Caesarea and Rome had removed him from his accustomed activities and travel, and so Peter was writing as a leader, especially among the Jewish believers.

The Epistle is mainly exhortation, advice, and encouragement; with a minimum of argument and little of the closely knit reasoning seen in Romans. There is frequent use of the LXX and the Greek is decent *Koiné* Greek.

CHAPTER 1

1. {*An apostle of Jesus Christ*} This is his official title, also Peter terms himself *sunpresbuteros* (fellow elder) in 1 Peter 5:1. {*To the elect*} Greek syntax emphasizes this is viewed as a group. Some translate the phrase to modify the next word, "to elect sojourners." {*Who are sojourners*} Greek term *parepidêmos,* lit. "to sojourn by the side of natives," so strangers sojourning for a while in a particular place (cf. Heb. 11:13). The picture in the metaphor is that heaven is our native country and we are only temporary sojourners here on earth. {*Of the Dispersion*} Lit. "scattered abroad," (Acts 8:1; Jas. 1:1) Jews outside of Palestine, then included Gentile Christians.
2. {*The foreknowledge*} From Greek term *proginôskô* (cf. 1 Pet. 1:20), lit. "to know beforehand." {*Of God the Father*} (cf. 1 Pet. 1:3, 17 and

Rom. 1:7). Peter here presents the Trinity (God the Father, the Spirit, Jesus Christ). {***Unto obedience***} Lit. from Greek verb "to hear under, to hearken" to the Lord Jesus as in 1 Peter 1:22. {***And sprinkling of the blood of Jesus Christ***} This refers to the death of Christ on the cross (cf. Heb. 9:13), a word used in the LXX of the sacrifices (Num. 19:9, 13, 20, cf. Heb. 12:24).

3. {***The God and Father of our Lord Jesus Christ***} (cf. John 20:17; 2 Cor. 1:3; Eph. 1:3; and part of it in 2 Cor. 11:31; Romans 15:6). {***Unto a living hope***} Peter is fond of the word "living" (1 Pet. 1:23; 2:4, 5, 24; 4:5, 6). The Pharisees cherished the hope of the resurrection (Acts 23:6), but the resurrection of Jesus gave it proof and permanence (1 Cor. 15:14, 17). It is no longer a dead hope like dead faith (Jas. 2:17, 26). This revival of hope was wrought "by the resurrection of Jesus Christ."

4. {***Unto an inheritance***} From Greek term *klēronomos,* "heir" for the property received by the heir (Matt. 21:38), here a picture of the blessedness in store for us pilgrims (Gal. 3:18). {***Undefiled***} Lit. "without defect or flaw in the title" (cf. Jas. 1:27; Heb. 13:4). {***That fadeth not away***} Lit. "not + to dry up, to wither" (cf. Jas. 1:11), late and rare word in several inscriptions on tombs, here only in NT. These inscriptions will fade away, but not this inheritance in Christ.

5. {***Are guarded***} A military term (Acts 9:24; 2 Cor. 11:32), used of God's love (Phil. 4:7) as here. "The inheritance is kept; the heirs are guarded" (Bengel). {***Unto a salvation***} Deliverance is the goal of the process and final salvation here, consummation as in 1 Thessalonians 5:8. {***In the last time***} This is a unique phrase usually thought to refer to the Day of Judgment (cf. John 6:39; Acts 2:17; Jas. 5:3; 2 Tim. 3:1; Heb. 1:2; Jude 1:18; 1 John 2:18).

6. {***Though ye have been put to grief***} Lit. "to be made sorrowful" (cf. 2 Cor. 6:10). {***In manifold temptations***} "Trials" is a better translation (cf. Jas. 1:2).

7. {***Being more precious...that perisheth***} Lit. "of great price." Even gold just wears away. {***Though it is proved by fire***} The Greek *dokimazō* is a common verb for testing metals. Faith stands the test of fire better than gold, but even gold is refined by fire. {***At the revelation of Jesus Christ***} Referring to the second coming of Christ as the Judge and Rewarder (cf. 1 Pet. 1:13; 4:13; 2 Thess. 1:7; 1 Cor. 1:7; Luke 17:30).

8. {***Not having seen***} It is possible that Peter here has in mind the words of Jesus to Thomas as recorded in John 20:29 ("Happy are those not seeing and yet believing"). {*Unspeakable*} From Greek verb lit. "not + to speak out." Compare Paul's "indescribable" gift (cf. 2 Cor. 9:15). {*Full of glory*} This is a "glorified joy," like the glorified face of Moses (cf. Exod. 34:29; 2 Cor. 3:10).

9. {*The end of your faith...salvation*} Lit. "end" of faith, this is the conclusion, the culmination of faith (2 Cor. 3:13; Rom. 2:21; 10:4; cf. Heb. 12:2 of Jesus as Pioneer and Perfecter of Faith).

10. Verses 3-12 in this chapter are really one long sentence connected by connector words. Here, Peter lingers over the Greek word *sôtêria* (salvation) with something new to say each time. Here it is the general sense of the gospel of grace. {*Searched diligently*} (cf. 1 Macc. 9:26).

11. {*The Spirit of Christ which was in them*} Peter definitely asserts here that the Spirit of Jesus Christ (the Messiah) was in the OT prophets, the Holy Spirit called the Spirit of Christ and the Spirit of God (Rom. 8:9), who spoke to the prophets as he would speak to the apostles (John 16:14). {*Did point unto*} Greek tense translates "did keep on pointing to," though they did not clearly perceive the time. {*When he testified beforehand*} Though grammatically a neuter, it should be rendered "he" (and so as to Acts 8:15). Here we have predictive prophecy concerning the Messiah, though some modern critics fail to find predictions of the Messiah in the OT. {*The glories that should follow them*} The plural "glories" is rare, but occurs in Exodus 15:11; Hosea 9:11. The glories of Christ followed the sufferings as in 1 Peter 4:13; 5:1, 6.

12. {*It was revealed*} The Greek term *apokaluptô,* lit. "to reveal, to unveil." Here is revelation about the revelation already received, revelation after research. {*Did they minister*} Greek tense translates "they were ministering." {*To look into*} Lit. "peer into" (cf. Luke 24:12; John 20:5, 11; Jas. 1:25). Angels had interest in the Incarnation (cf. Luke 2:13).

13. {*Girding up...the loins...mind*} This is a vivid metaphor for habit of people of that time, who quickly gathered up their loose robes with a girdle when in a hurry or starting on a journey. {*The loins*} Lit. "for the part of the body where the girdle was worn," but here a metaphor (Luke 12:35; Eph. 6:14). {*Mind*} Greek term is *dianoia,* lit. "see through," as the faculty of understanding, Matthew 22:37.

14. {*As children of obedience*} This is a common Hebraism of those of a class or kind (cf. Eph. 2:2 and 1 Pet. 1:2), these are "children marked by obedience." {*Not fashioning yourselves*} This is the outward pattern in contrast with the inward change (cf. Rom. 12:2, also Phil. 2:6). {*According to your former lusts*} These are desires in the bad sense (cf. 1 Pet. 4:2; 2 Pet. 1:4; Jas. 1:14).

17. {*Without respect of persons*} This Greek word is found nowhere else except later Christian writings, though related words are (cf. Acts 10:34; Jas. 2:9; 1 Pet. 1:1). {*According to each man's work*} God judges just as Christ judges also (2 Cor. 5:10). {*Of your sojourning*} From the Greek *paroikeô*, lit. "to dwell beside (in one's neighborhood)," and so of pilgrims or strangers (cf. Acts 7:6) as of Jews away from Palestine or of Christians here on earth (cf. dispersion 1 Pet. 1:1). {*In fear*} This is in the emphatic position at the beginning of the clause with *anastraphête* at the end.

18. {*Knowing*} The appeal here is to an elementary Christian belief, the holiness and justice of God with the added thought of the high cost of redemption. {*Ye were redeemed*} From Greek *lutron* (ransom for life as of a slave, Matt. 20:28), to set free by payment of ransom. The ransom is the blood of Christ. {*Not with corruptible things*} Slaves were set free by silver and gold (cf. 1 Pet. 1:23; 1 Cor. 9:25; 15:53; Rom. 1:23.) {*Handed down from your fathers*} The Jews made a wrong use of tradition (Matt. 15:2), but the reference here seems mainly to Gentiles (1 Pet. 2:12).

19. {*As of a lamb*} This is of the lamb prescribed for the Passover sacrifice (Exod. 12:5; cf. also Lev. 12:8; Num. 15:11; Deut. 14:4). John the Baptist applies it to Jesus (John 1:29, 36). It occurs also in Acts 8:32 quoted from Isaiah 53:7. Undoubtedly both the Baptist and Peter have this passage in mind. Elsewhere in the NT *arnion* is used of Christ (Rev. 5:6, 12). Jesus is the Paschal Lamb.

20. {*Who was foreknown indeed*} Lit. "to know beforehand" (cf. Rom. 8:29; 2 Pet. 3:17 and 1 Pet. 1:2). {*Before the foundation of the world*} The Greek word *katabolê* was originally laying the foundation of a house (Heb. 6:1). The Savior had a preincarnate state with the Father as here and in John 17:24; cf. also Ephesians 1:4. {*For your sake*} Proof of God's love, not of their desert or worth (Acts 17:30; Heb. 11:39).

21. {*Gave glory to him*} See Peter's speech in Acts 3:13 about God glorifying (*edoxasen*) Jesus and also the same idea by Peter in Acts 2:33-36; 5:31. {*So that your faith and hope might be in God*} "So that" is a result, more probable than design, though it could be a purpose.

22. {*Seeing ye have purified*} From the Greek *hagnos* (pure), but of the internal person: here souls, in James hearts (Jas. 4:8 cf. 1 John 3:3) of moral cleansing also. {*Unfeigned*} (cf. Jas. 3:17; 2 Cor. 6:6). No other kind of brotherly love (Greek *philadelphia*) is worth having (1 Thess. 4:9; Heb. 13:1; 2 Pet. 1:7).

24ff. {*For all flesh is as grass...withereth...falleth*} Quotation from Isaiah 40:6-8 (partly like the LXX, partly like the Hebrew). See a free use of this imagery about the life of man as grass and a flower in James 1:11.

CHAPTER 2

1. {*Putting away therefore*} This is a common verb, in metaphorical sense either to cleanse defilements (1 Pet. 3:21; Jas. 1:21) or to put off clothing (Rom. 13:12; Col. 3:5; Eph. 4:22). Either sense suits here. {*Guile*} From the Greek verb *delô*, "to catch with bait," hence capture by deceit. {*Hypocrisies*} (cf. 1 Pet. 1:22 "sincere"). Christ denounced hypocrites which the disciples did not understand, including Peter (Mark 7:6ff.; Matt. 15:16ff.).

2. {*As newborn babes*} The Greek word *brephos*, old word, originally unborn child (Luke 1:41, 44), then infant (Luke 2:12), here figuratively. "Newborn" probably means that they were recent converts, possibly slight proof that the Epistle written before Romans by Paul. {*The spiritual milk which is without guile*} (cf. 1 Cor. 9:7 and as metaphor in 1 Cor. 3:2). "Pure" lit. "not + deceit," unadulterated milk, which, alas, is so hard to get. "Spiritual" is a derivative from Greek *logos* meaning "reason, speech," (cf. Rom. 12:1). Paul uses *logikon* in the sense of "rational" or "spiritual," and that idea is possible here. {*That ye may grow thereby*} (cf. Col. 2:19; Eph. 4:15). Peter uses the word of God as the food for growth, especially for babes in Christ, not emphasizing the distinction from solid food made in 1 Corinthians 3:2; Hebrew 5:13.

3. {*If ye have tasted*} This phrase assumed to be a fact. "Taste" is in the figurative sense as in Hebrew 6:4. {*Gracious*} This is a quotation from Psalm 34:8. The Hebrew for the LXX Greek *chrêstos* is simply *tobh* (good). Plato used the word for food also, and Peter carries out the metaphor in *gala* (milk) as in Luke 5:39.

4. {*A living stone*} Note the apparent intentional contradiction between "living" and "stone." Cf. also "living hope" in 1 Peter 1:3 and "living word" in 1 Peter 1:23. {*Rejected...elect*} The Greek word *apodokimazô,* "to repudiate after test" (Luke 9:22). "Chosen and precious" is from Isaiah 28:6, not merely approved as fit, and this "stone" has a pre-eminence of position with God (Hart).

5. {*Ye also as living stones*} Peter applies the metaphor about Christ to the readers. {*Are built up a spiritual house*} (cf. Matt. 16:18). If the metaphor of a house of living stones seems "violent" (Vincent), it should be remembered that Jesus employed the figure of a house of believers. Peter just carried it a bit farther. This "spiritual house" includes believers in the five Roman provinces of 1 Peter 1:1 and shows clearly how Peter understood the metaphor of Christ in Matthew 16:18 to be not a local church, but the church general (the kingdom of Christ). {*To be a holy priesthood*} The verb of this word is lit. "to serve as priest" (Luke 1:8; cf. Exod. 19:6); it is either the office, order, or body of priests. Peter has the same idea of Revelation 1:6 that all believers are priests (Heb. 4:16) and can approach God directly.

6. {*Contained in Scripture*} This is Isaiah 28:16 with some changes. "Chief cornerstone" is a word apparently invented by Isaiah. Paul in Ephesians 2:20 uses the same word, making Christ the chief cornerstone (the only other NT example). In Isaiah the metaphor is rather a foundation stone.

7. {*Was made the head of the corner*} This verse is from Psalm 118:22 with evident allusion to Isaiah 28:16. See Matthew 21:42; Mark 12:10; Luke 20:17, where Jesus himself quotes Psalm 118:22 and applies the rejection of the stone by the builders to the Sanhedrin's conduct toward him.

8. {*And*} Peter now quotes Isaiah 8:14 and gives a new turn to the previous quotation. To the disbelieving, Christ was indeed "a stone of stumbling and rock of offense," quoted also by Paul in Romans 9:32, which see for discussion. The first stone of stumbling is Greek *proskomma* an obstacle against which one strikes by accident; the second "rock" is Greek *skandalon,* a trap set to trip one.

9. {*An elect race*} From Isaiah 43:20. The blood relation of the spiritual Israel (not the Jewish race) through the new birth (1 Pet. 1:23). {*A royal priesthood...holy nation*} Christian officials are "elders" not "priests." We are all *hiereis* (priests). {*A holy nation*} Here applied, it is not to the national Israel, but to the spiritual Israel of believers (both Jews and Gentiles). {*A people for God's own possession*} The idea here occurs in Exodus 19:5; Deuteronomy 7:6; 14:2; 26:18; Malachi 3:17; Ephesians 1:14; Titus 2:14. {*Darkness*} = Heathenism.

10. {*Which had not obtained mercy*} (cf. Hos. 1:1; 2:1ff. in Rom. 9:25), which may have been known to Peter or not. {*But now have obtained mercy*} Tense has a focus of being a single event which ended "not receiving mercy."

11. {*As sojourners and pilgrims*} (cf. Gen. 33:4; Ps. 39:13). The Christian's fatherland is heaven. {*To abstain from*} (cf. 1 Thess. 4:3). In indirect command, the Greek tense translates "to keep on abstaining from." {*War against the soul*} Greek tense translates "to carry on a campaign" (Jas. 4:1). See this struggle between the flesh and the spirit vividly pictured by Paul in Galatians 5:16-24.

12. {*Seemly*} The Gentiles are on the watch for slips in moral conduct by the Christians. {*By your good works*} Out of (as a result of) your good (beautiful) deeds.

13. {*Every ordinance of man*} Peter here approves no special kind of government, but he supports law and order as Paul does (Rom. 13:1-8) unless it steps in between God and man (Acts 4:20). {*As supreme*} Lit. "to stand out above (to have it over)" (cf. Rom. 13:1). It is not the divine right of kings, but the fact of the king as the outstanding ruler.

14. {*As sent by him*} "Him" is God, as Jesus made plain to Pilate; even Pilate received his authority ultimately "from above" (John 18:11).

15. {*Silence*} Greek verb derived from Greek noun *phimos,* muzzle (cf. Matt. 22:12).

16. {*For a cloke of wickedness*} This Greek word *epikalumma* (cf. Rom. 4:7) is here with a figurative sense for pretext to do wickedness under, a thing, alas, that sometimes happens.

17. {*Honor...love...fear...honor*} These are all commands in the verse, and the last three verbs translate the Greek tense "keep on...." {*Love the brotherhood*} This is in the collective sense, meaning all Christians (cf. 1 Macc. 12:10; 4 Macc. 10:3).

18. {*Servants*} This is a domestic slave (*oiketês*), a house servant, in contrast to the more general Greek word for slave, *doulos. Oiketês* in NT occurs only here, Luke 16:13; Acts 10:7; Romans 14:4. {*Be in subjection*} This has the force of a command, though the form is not strictly an imperative (1 Pet. 3:1, 7). {*To your masters*} An absolute owner of a possession such as a slave. It is used also of God (Luke 2:29; Acts 4:24, 29) and of Christ (2 Pet. 2:1; Jude 1:4). The Greek *kurios*

(Lord or lord) has a wider meaning and not necessarily suggesting absolute power. {*To the good and gentle*} There were slave-owners (masters) like this as there are housekeepers and employers of workmen today. This is no argument for slavery, but only a sidelight on a condition bad enough at its best. {*To the froward*} Lit. "the crooked," (cf. Luke 3:5; Acts 2:40; Phil. 2:15). Unfortunately there were slave-holders as there are employers today, like this group. The test of obedience comes precisely toward this group.

19. {*For this is acceptable*} Lit. "For this thing is grace/thanks" (Rom. 7:25), referring to obedience to crooked masters. {*If a man endureth griefs*} Greek word is *hupopherô*, "to bear up under," (cf. 1 Cor. 10:13; 2 Tim. 3:11). Note plural of "pains." {*For conscience toward God*} Suffering is not a blessing in and of itself, but, if one's duty to God is involved (Acts 4:20), then one can meet it with gladness of heart (cf. Acts 23:1; 1 Cor. 8:7; 1 Pet. 3:16).

20. {*When ye sin*} Greek aspect has a continued repetition. {*And are buffeted for it*} This verb is derived from the Greek word *kolaphos* "fist," only in NT (cf. Matt. 26:67) and ecclesiastical writers. Repeated action again. {*This is acceptable with God*} Translate this phrase as "This thing (neuter) is thanks (cf. 1 Pet. 2:19) as God looks at it [lit. by the side of]."

21. {*For hereunto were ye called*} They were called to suffer without flinching (Hort), if need be. {*Leaving you an example*} "Example" is the Greek *hupogrammos,* also a late and rare word, meaning a writing-copy for one to imitate. {*That ye should follow his steps*} Peter does not mean that Christ suffered only as an example (1 Pet. 1:18), but he did leave us his example for our copying (1 John 2:6).

22. {*Who did no sin*} Quotation from Isaiah 53:9. He has already expressed the sinlessness of Christ in 1 Peter 1:19. The next phrase is a combination of Isaiah 53:9; Zephaniah 3:13.

23. {*Reviled not again*} The Greek tense tells of repeated incidents. {*But committed himself*} Translate the Greek tense, "kept on entrusting himself"; Jesus thus handed himself and his cause over to the Father who judges righteously.

24. {*Bare our sins*} The Greek word *anapherô* is a common verb of bringing sacrifice to the altar (cf. Isa. 53:12; Deut. 21:23). Jesus is the perfect sin offering (Heb. 9:28), with the Cross in the place of an altar (Bigg). {*Upon the tree*} Better translated "wood" (1 Cor. 3:12); not tree here as in Luke 23:31. Peter uses this word for the Cross in Acts 5:30; 10:39. {*By whose stripes ye were healed*} (cf. Isa. 53:5). "Wounds," is a rare word for a bruise or bloody wound, here only in NT (cf. 1 Pet. 1:18). Writing to slaves who may have received such stripes, Peter's word is effective.

25. {*Unto the Shepherd and Bishop of your souls*} Jesus also is our Apostle (cf. Heb. 3:1) and he deserves all other titles of dignity that we can give him.

CHAPTER 3

1. {*To your own husbands*} "Own" emphasized in both the words and the grammar. Wives are not enjoined to be in subjection to the husbands of other women. {*Even if any obey not the word*} I.e., remain heathen, the Greek syntax assumes that such a condition exists or is a fact (cf. 1 Pet. 1:23, 25; 2:8). {*Without the word by the behavior of their wives*} Here "word" means "talk" not "word of God." Won by pious living, not by nagging. Many a wife has had this blessed victory of grace.

3. {*Whose adorning*} Referring to the wives, this adorning is from the Greek word *kosmos* "ornament" (cf. our *cosmetics*). It can also mean "world" (John 17:5) considered as an orderly whole. {*Let it be*} A command of exhortation. "Braid" has the idea of "weave or interweave" (cf. 2 Tim. 2:4; 2 Pet. 2:20). {*Of wearing*} (cf. Matt. 27:28), to put around, a placing around. Ornaments of gold were worn round the hair as nets and round the finger, arm, or ankle. {*Or of putting on*} Peter is not forbidding the wearing of clothes and ornaments by women, but the display of finery by contrast (cf. 1 Tim. 2:9-13; Isa. 3:16).

4. {*But the hidden man of the heart*} Here "man," is in contrast with "adorning" just before. There is an inner/outer and old/new man (2 Cor. 4:16; Rom. 7:22; Col. 3:9; Eph. 3:16; 4:22, 24). {*In the incorruptible apparel of a meek and quiet spirit*} Spirit here is "disposition" or "temper" unlike any other use in the NT. While in 1 Peter 3:18, 19; 4:6 it means the whole inner man as opposed to "flesh" or "body."

6. {*Obeyed Abraham*} Translate the Greek tense, "used to obey." {*Calling him lord*} (cf. Gen. 18:12). {*Whose children ye now are*} Translate the Greek word and tense as "whose children you became."

7. {*Ye husbands likewise*} Here refers to honoring all men (1 Pet. 2:17), not "likewise" of 1 Peter 3:1. {*Dwell with*} Greek has a focus of domestic association (cf. 1 Pet. 2:18; 3:1). {*According to knowledge*} That is, "with an intelligent recognition of the nature of the marriage relation" (Vincent). {*Giving honor unto the woman as unto the weaker vessel*} "Vessel" is Greek word *skeuos* "furniture, utensil" (Matt. 12:29; 2 Tim. 2:20). Here both husband and wife are termed vessels or parts of the furniture of God's house (cf. also 2 Cor. 4:7 for minister as a vessel). She is termed "the weaker," not for intellectual or moral weakness, but purely for physical reasons, which the husband must recognize with due consideration for marital happiness. {*To the end that your prayers be not hindered*} (cf. Rom. 15:22). "Hinder" means "to interrupt, cut in." Husbands surely have here cause to consider why their prayers are not answered.

8. {*Finally*} This is the conclusion, not of the Epistle, but only of the addresses to various classes. {*Compassionate*} (cf. Rom. 12:15). This is our "sympathetic" in original sense.

9. {*Not rendering evil for evil*} (cf. Rom. 12:17 and 1 Thess. 5:15). Peter may have obtained it from Paul or both from Proverbs 17:13; 20:22. This is an approximation to Christ's repeal of the law of just retribution *lex talionis* (Hort) (Matt. 5:38; cf. also 1 Pet. 2:23). {*That ye should inherit a blessing*} "That" translates "For this purpose." The blessing is a plain reference to Esau (cf. Heb. 12:17) after he had sold his birthright. Christians are the new Israel (both Gentiles and Jews) and are the spiritual descendants of Isaac (Gal. 4:22).

11. {*Let him turn away*} (cf. Rom. 3:12; 16:17). Peter adapted the passage all through to his own construction and use.

12. {*Upon*} The Greek preposition *epi* is a positive "on" or "upon" for the Lord's care, but then the second "on" *epi* evildoers changes to "against."

13. {*That will harm you*} (cf. Acts 7:6, 19). Any real hurt, either that wishes to harm you or that can harm.

14. {*But and if ye should suffer*} The Greek syntax shows that this is an undetermined condition with less likelihood. For righteous suffering, cf. also Matthew 5:10.

15. {*Sanctify*} Do this instead of being afraid. {*To give answer*} Greek *apologia,* in the old sense of *apologia,* an answer back, a defense, not an excuse or "apology" as in saying you're sorry or some such (cf. Acts

22:1). {*A reason concerning the hope that is in you*}. Be ready with a spoken defense of the inward hope. This attitude calls for an intelligent grasp of the hope and skill in presenting it.

16. {*Wherein ye are spoken against*} Peter may be recalling his own experience at Pentecost when the Jews first scoffed and others were cut to the heart (Acts 2:13, 37). {*In Christ*} Paul's common mystical phrase that Peter has three times (here, 1 Pet. 5:10, 14).

17. {*Better*} Patient endurance not only silences slander (1 Pet. 3:16) and is Christ-like (v. 18), but it has a value of its own (v. 17).

18. {*Because Christ also died*} The example of Christ should stir us to patient endurance. {*The righteous for the unrighteous*} Lit. "just for unjust" (no articles). See 1 Peter 2:19 for the sinlessness of Christ as the one perfect offering for sin. This is what gives Christ's blood value. He has no sin himself. {*That he might bring us to God*} This is to present us to God on the basis of his atoning death for us, which has opened the way (Rom. 3:25; Heb. 10:19). {*But quickened in the spirit*} The Greek grammar makes clear that the spirit of Christ did not die when his flesh did, but was endued with new and greater powers of life (cf. 1 Cor. 15:22). But the use of the word "Spirit" in contrast with "flesh" starts Peter's mind off in a long comparison by way of illustration that runs from verses 19 to 22.

19. {*In which also*} Referring to Spirit above. Some conjecture that the text read "Noah," or "Enoch." Some reject such a reading as inconsistent with the context, though it would relieve the difficulty greatly. Many agree that this event recorded took place between Christ's death and his resurrection and holds that Peter is alluding to Christ's descent into hell in Acts 2:27 (with which he compares Matt. 27:52; Luke 23:34; Eph. 4:9). If Christ did offer this group another chance, is this a one time event or do other groups get another chance? One can only say that it is a slim hope for those who neglect or reject Christ in this life to gamble with a possible second chance after death which rests on very precarious exegesis of a most difficult passage in Peter's Epistle. {*Unto the spirits in prison*} The language is plain enough except that it does not make it clear whether Jesus did the preaching to spirits in prison at the time or to people whose spirits are now in prison.

20. {*Waited*} Lit. "to wait out to the end," as for Christ's Second Coming (Phil. 3:20). A hundred years apparently after the warning (Gen. 5:32; 6:3; 7:6) Noah was preparing the ark, and Noah as a preacher of righteousness (2 Pet. 2:5) forewarned the people, who disregarded it. {*Were saved*} Lit. "to bring safe through" (cf. Acts 27:44). {*Through water*} Translate "by means of water" as the intermediate agent. They came through the water in the ark and so were saved by the water in spite of the flood around them. Peter lays stress on the water rather than on the ark (Heb. 11:7).

21. {*Baptism*} (cf. Matt. 3:7). So here baptism is presented as corresponding to (prefigured by) the deliverance of Noah's family by water. It is only a vague parallel, but not over-fanciful. {*Doth now save you*} The saving by baptism which Peter here mentions is only symbolic (a metaphor or picture as in Rom. 6:2-6), not actual as Peter hastens to explain. {*Not the putting away of the filth of the flesh*} "Filth" (cf. Jas. 2:2; Rev. 22:11), here only in NT (cf. Isa. 3:3; 4:4). Baptism, Peter explains, does not wash away the filth of the flesh either in a literal sense, as a bath for the body, or in a metaphorical sense of the filth of the soul. {*But the interrogation of a good conscience toward God*} This is avowal of consecration to God after inquiry, having repented and turned to God and now making this public proclamation of that fact by means of baptism (the symbol of the previous inward change of heart). {*Through the resurrection of Jesus Christ*} For baptism is a symbolic picture of the resurrection of Christ as well as of our own spiritual renewal.

CHAPTER 4

1. {*For as much then as Christ suffered in the flesh*} This connects and applies the main lesson of 1 Peter 3:18-22, the fact that Christ suffered for us. {*Hath ceased from sin*} Temptation has lost its appeal and power with such a person.

3. {*May suffice*} This is apparently referring to Christ's words in Matthew 6:34 (possibly as an axiom or proverb). {*The desire*} Jews sometimes fell in with the ways of Gentiles (Rom. 2:21-24; 3:9-18; Eph. 2:1-3) as today some Christians copy the ways of the world. {*In lasciviousness*} This is walking in unbridled lustful excesses (2 Pet. 2:7; 2 Cor. 12:21). {*Revellings*} Greek word *kōmois* derived from *keimai*, "to lie down", this is wild drinking parties (cf. Gal. 5:21; Rom. 13:13). {*Carousings*} This is lit. "Drinking." In the light of these words it seems strange to find modern Christians justifying their "personal liberty" to drink and carouse. {*Abominable idolatries*} (cf. Acts 10:28). Jews in the OT often fell into idolatrous practices.

4. {*They think it strange*} That is "They are surprised or astonished" (cf. Acts 17:20; 1 Pet. 4:12). {*That ye run not with them*} Lit. "to run together" like a crowd or a mob as here (just like our phrase, "running with certain folks").

6. {*Even to the dead*} Does Peter here mean preached to men after they are dead or to men once alive but dead now or when the judgment comes? Some take this to mean spiritually dead [as in sins, etc.] (cf. Col. 2:13; Eph. 2:1), which is possible contextually. Others take it to mean that all men who did not hear the gospel message in this life will hear it in the next before the final judgment.

7. {*But the end of all things is at hand*} (cf. Matt. 3:2; Jas. 5:8). How near Peter does not say, but he urges readiness (1 Pet. 1:5; 4:6) as Jesus did (Mark 14:38).

8. {*Being fervent*} From the Greek word *ektenê* derived from *ekteinô*, to stretch out, so translate "holding intent you love among yourselves."

9. {*Using hospitality*} Lit. "friendly to strangers" (cf. 1 Tim. 3:2; Titus 1:8). {*Without murmuring*} Complaint spoils hospitality. Jesus enjoined the entertainment of strangers (Matt. 25:35). Inns were rare and very poor. Hospitality made mission work possible (3 John 5).

10. {*As good stewards*} Lit. "house-manager" (cf. Luke 16:1; 1 Cor. 4:1) used by Paul of himself and of any bishop (Titus 1:7), but here of any Christian. {*Of the manifold grace of God*} "Varied," lit. "many-colored" (cf. 1 Pet. 1:6 and Jas. 1:2).

11. {*If any man speaketh*} This phrase in Greek is assumed as a fact. {*Speaking as it were oracles of God*} This means here of the utterances of God through Christian teachers. {*If any one ministereth*} Again assumed to be a fact. See Acts 6:2-4 for the twofold division of service involved here.

12. {*Think it not strange*} Meaning here, "be not amazed/surprised." {*Concerning the fiery trial among you*} Lit. "by the among you burning," here a metaphorical sense of fire burning (cf. 1 Pet. 1:7; Rev. 18:9, 18, only other NT examples). It occurs in Proverbs 27:21 for the smelting of gold and silver and so in Psalm 56:10 (LXX 65:10).

13. {*Ye are partakers of*} Greek word derived from *koinônos*, partner, "to share in." {*That ye may rejoice with exceeding joy*} See 1 Peter 1:6

to 8 for this same idea associated with the second coming of Christ as here.

14. {*If ye are reproached*} This phrase is assumed to be true in the syntax (cf. also Jas. 1:5). {*For the name of Christ*} Translate "In the matter of the name of Christ" (cf. Matt. 5:11; 19:29; Acts 5:41; 9:16; 21:13). {*The Spirit of glory and the Spirit of God*} The reference is to the Holy Spirit, who is the Spirit of Glory and of God.

15. {*As*} "As" means "charged as and being so." The first two are specific crimes, the third a general term "evildoer," (cf. 1 Pet. 2:12, 14), lastly "meddler" is a term apparently coined by Peter, lit. "belonging to another + overseer, inspector." The idea is apparently one who spies out the affairs of other men (cf. 1 Thess. 4:11; 5:13; 2 Thess. 3:11).

16. {*But if as a Christian*} This word occurs only three times in the NT (Acts 11:26; 26:28; 1 Pet. 4:16). It is a word of Latin formation coined to distinguish followers of Christ from Jews and Gentiles (Acts 11:26).

17. {*House of God*} can mean the same as the "spiritual house" (cf. 1 Pet. 2:5) or a local church, or even the family.

18. {*And if the righteous is scarcely saved*} Quotation is from Proverbs 11:31. See 1 Peter 3:12, 14; Matthew 5:20. But the Christian is not saved by his own righteousness (Phil. 3:9; Rev. 7:14).

19. {*Commit their souls*} The Greek word *paratithêmi,* old word, a banking figure, to deposit, as in 1 Timothy 1:18; 2 Timothy 2:2, the word used by Jesus as he died (Luke 23:46).

CHAPTER 5

1. {*Who am a fellow-elder*} (cf. Acts 11:30; 20:17). It is noteworthy that here Peter the Apostle (1 Pet. 1:1) calls himself an elder along *with* the other "elders."

2. {*Tend*} Peter remembers Jesus' very words to him (cf. John 21:16) and Peter doubtless has this fact in mind here (cf. Acts 20:28). {*Exercising the oversight*} (cf. Heb. 12:15). {*Willingly*} The opposite of compulsion (cf. Heb. 10:26). {*Nor yet for filthy lucre*} (cf. 1 Tim. 3:8; Titus 1:7, 11). Clearly the elders received stipends, else there could be no such temptation.

3. {*The charge allotted to you*} (cf. Acts 1:17, 25). Here meaning the charges assigned (cf. Acts 17:4). {*Making yourselves ensamples*} Lit.

"types, models" (cf. 1 Thess. 1:7). The Greek tense has the idea "Continually becoming [examples]."

4. {*The crown of glory that fadeth not away*} (cf. Jas. 1:12; 1 Cor. 9:25; 2 Tim. 4:8; Rev. 2:10; 3:10; 4:4). Here it is a crown of victory. "Unfading," (cf. 1 Pet. 1:4) the Greek is derived from the flower *amaranth* (so called because it never withers and revives if moistened with water and so used as a symbol of immortality).

5. {*Unto the elder*} This refers here to age, not to office as in 1 Peter 5:1 (cf. 1 Tim. 5:1, 17). {*All*} This refers to all ages, sexes, classes, etc. {*Gird yourselves with humility*} The Greek word *egkomboomai* is a command, derived from the Greek *egkombôma* was the white scarf or apron of slaves. It is quite probable that Peter here is thinking of what Jesus did (John 13:4) when he girded himself with a towel and taught the disciples the lesson of humility.

6. {*That he may exalt you*} Greek syntax translates "For the purpose..." (cf. Luke 14:11; Phil. 2:9).

7. {*Casting*} An allusion from Psalm 55:22. Lit. "to throw upon," as when casting their clothes on the colt.

8. {*Your adversary*} This is an old word for opponent in a lawsuit (Matt. 5:25). {*The devil*} The devil is a slanderer (cf. Matt. 4:1). {*As a roaring lion*} Jesus is the Lion (Rev. 5:5). But Satan *roars* at the saints (cf. Ps. 22:13). {*Whom he may devour*} Lit. "to drink down," and so "to devour some one." The devil's purpose is the ruin of men. He is a "peripatetic" on the prowl; Satan wants all of us and sifts us all (Luke 22:31).

9. {*Whom withstand*} Cowardice never wins against the devil (2 Tim. 1:7), but only courage. {*Steadfast in your faith*} "Firm" has the idea of being solid like a foundation (2 Tim. 2:19).

10. {*In Christ*} A Pauline phrase (2 Cor. 5:17-19), but Petrine also. For God's "calling" us, see 1 Thessalonians 5:23; 1 Corinthians 1:8; Romans 8:29.

11. {*To him*} This refers to God. Note "power" (Greek *kratos*) in the doxology as in 1 Timothy 6:16 and briefer than the doxology in 1 Peter 4:11, to Christ.

12. {*By Silvanus*} Probably this postscript (1 Pet. 5:12-14) is in Peter's own handwriting, as Paul did (2 Thess. 3:17; Gal. 6:11-18). If so, Silvanus (Silas) was the amanuensis and the bearer of the Epistle. {*That this is the true grace of God*} Peter includes the whole of the Epistle by God's

grace (1 Pet. 1:10) and obedience to the truth (John 1:17; Gal. 2:5; Col. 1:6).

13. {*She that is in Babylon*} This refers either to actual Babylon in the East, or mystical Babylon (Rome) as in the Apocalypse. {*Elect together with you*} This may refer either to Peter's wife (1 Cor. 9:5) or the church in "Babylon" (Rome?). The natural way to take it is for Peter's wife. (cf. 2 John 1:1, 13). {*Mark my son*} So this fact agrees with the numerous statements by the early Christian writers that Mark, after leaving Barnabas, became Peter's "interpreter" and under his influence wrote his Gospel. We know that Mark was with Paul in Rome some years before this time (Col. 4:10).

14. {*That are in Christ*} This is the greatest of all secret orders and ties, one that is open to all who take Christ as Lord and Savior.

THE SECOND EPISTLE OF PETER

AUTHOR: Simon Peter (Cephas)
RECIPIENTS: Believers in five Roman provinces in Asia Minor (2 Pet. 3:1; cf. 1 Pet. 1:1)
DATE: About A.D. 66 or 67, before the death of Peter
FROM: unknown (see also First Peter)
OCCASION: This epistle deals with heresies of that general region in Asia Minor, as with Paul (cf. Acts 20:29ff.). First Peter deals with persecutions, but here with the heretics that threaten to lead them astray.
THEME: The truths of the faith are the foundation for growing to maturity.

BY WAY OF INTRODUCTION

It is true that more modern scholars deny the genuineness of 2 Peter than that of any single book in the canon, even those scholars who are followers of Christ as Lord and Savior. Second Peter has problems of peculiar difficulty that call for careful consideration and balanced judgment. It is easy to take an extreme position for or against it without full knowledge of all the evidence.

The epistle has a mixed history of acceptance in the Church: some rejecting (as the Peshito, or Erasmus), others accepting (as Augustine or Clement), and still others placing it among disputed books (as Eusebius or Calvin). When one considers the brevity of the Epistle, the use of it is really as strong as one can expect. It may be said for it that it won its way under criticism and was not accepted blindly.

The epistle claims Simon Peter as author. Symeon is another Jewish spelling of Simon. Though the name could be added to the text and so be a false epistle. In favor of the epistle being genuine, there is no heresy in this epistle, no startling new ideas that would lead one to use the name of Simon Peter. It is rather full of edifying and orthodox teaching.

Though many consider it suspect, the writer makes use of his own contact with Jesus, especially at the Transfiguration of Christ (Mark 9:2-8; Matt. 17:1-8; Luke 9:28-36); but silence would also have been criticized. In 2 Peter 1:15 Peter speaks of his own plan for preserving the knowledge of Jesus when he is gone (possibly by Mark's Gospel). All this is in perfect keeping with Peter's own nature.

The first and second are different, yet is exaggerated by some scholars; for there are many points of similarity, such as the repetitions of certain vocabulary. Both letters appear to know and use the OT Apocrypha. Both are fond of the plural of abstract substantives. Both make sparing use of Greek particles. Both use the article similarly, idiomatically, and sometimes not using it. There are some 361 words in 1 Peter not in 2 Peter, 231 in 2 Peter not in 1 Peter. There are 686 *hapax legomena* (single occurrence words) in the NT, 54 in 2 Peter instead of the average of 62, a large number when the brevity of the epistle is considered. There are several ways of explaining these variations. One way is to say that they are written by different men, but difference of subject has to be borne in mind, as well as different secretaries.

The writer accepts Paul as Scripture (2 Pet. 3:15ff.). Though some consider this evidence of non-Petrine authorship, since Paul rebuked Peter (Gal. 2:11ff.). But neither Peter nor Paul cherished a personal grudge where the Master's work was involved (cf. 1 Cor. 9:5). Some say Peter would never put Paul's writings with OT Scripture. But Paul claimed the help of the Holy Spirit in his writings and Peter knew the marks of the Holy Spirit's power.

Though some place this epistle after A.D. 100, the writer's use of "thousand years" (2 Pet. 3:8) suits the first century, not the second. As a matter of fact, the false teachers described in 2 Peter suit the first century precisely if one recalls Paul's troubles with the Judaizers in Galatia and Corinth and with the Gnostics in Colossae and Ephesus. Every feature in the description of the false teachers and mockers is to be found in the apostolic age.

Concerning who 2 Peter is written to, there is nothing in 2 Peter to differentiate its first readers from those of 1 Peter.

Though not without difficulty, I agree with those who say that the epistle is what it professes to be by Simon Peter. It is more like NT books than pseudepigraphic literature.

CHAPTER 1

1. {*To them that have obtained*} Lit. "to obtain by lot" (Luke 1:9). {*Like precious*} Lit. "equal + honor, price" likely referring to honor and privilege (with that of Peter or any of the apostles). {*In the righteousness*} Greek syntax suggests a definite righteousness, in the OT

sense applied to God (Rom. 1:17) and here to Christ. {*Of our God and Savior Jesus Christ*} The Greek syntax teaches, really demands, that this is one person, not two (cf. 2 Pet. 1:11; 2:20; 3:2, 18).

2. {*Be multiplied*} Greek expresses a wish for the future (cf. 1 Pet. 1:2; Jude 1:2). {*In the knowledge*} The Greek has a focus on *full* knowledge (cf. 2 Pet. 1:8). As in Colossians, so here full knowledge is urged against the claims of the Gnostic heretics to their special "knowledge."

3. {*Seeing that his divine power hath granted unto us*} God has given as a gift (cf. Mark 15:45). {*His divine power*} Refers to Christ, since he is "God" (2 Pet. 1:1). "Divine" commonly had an imperial connotation. {*All things that pertain unto life and godliness*} The new life in Christ who is the mystery of godliness (1 Tim. 3:16). Lit. "well" [good] + "to worship."

4. {*His precious and exceeding great promises*} "Great" is one step below a true superlative, "greatest" to the quite heightened elative "very great." {*Partakers*} From the Greek *koinônos* (cf. 1 Pet. 5:1). {*Of the divine nature*} Though the phrase is found in other ancient philosophies and religions, Peter is referring to the new birth (cf. 1 Pet. 1:23).

5. {*All diligence*} From an old verb which means "to hasten." {*In your faith*} Faith as the foundation of all in the list finishing with Christian love, this is faith as a strong conviction (cf. Heb. 11:1, 3); the root of the Christian life (cf. Eph. 2:8). {*Supply*} Lit. "chorus-leader," i.e., to fit out the chorus with additional (complete) supplies. {*Virtue*} This is moral power, moral energy, vigor of soul (Bengel) (cf. 2 Pet. 1:3). {*Knowledge*} Insight, understanding (1 Cor. 16:18; John 15:15).

6. {*Temperance*} Lit. "one holding himself" and so not greedy (cf. Titus 1:8, cf. also Acts 24:25; Gal. 5:23).

7. {*Love*} This is an act by deliberate choice (Matt. 5:44). Love for Christ as the crown of all (1 Pet. 1:8) and so for all men. Love is the climax as Paul has it (1 Cor. 13:13).

8. {*Knowledge*} Greek word for "full (additional) knowledge" (cf. 2 Pet. 1:2).

9. {*Seeing only what is near*} This derives from a word Aristotle used to refer to a near-sighted man. He screws up his eyes because of the light. {*Having forgotten*} Lit. "having received forgetfulness," (cf. 2 Tim. 1:5). {*The cleansing*} Christ is the expiatory sacrifice of Christ for our sins (Heb. 1:3; 1 Pet. 1:18; 2:24; 3:18). If this is a reference to baptism, it is only symbolic.

10. {*Wherefore*} Because of the exhortation and argument in verses 2 Peter 1:5-9. {*Give the more diligence*} Enter into a condition of diligence, and so command in the Greek (cf. 2 Tim. 2:15; 2 Pet. 1:15). {*Calling and election*} The first has a focus of the "invitation," the second the "actual acceptance" (cf. 1 Thess. 1:4; Rom. 9:11). {*Ye shall never stumble*} A very strong negative—*never* stumble or fall (cf. Jas. 2:10; 3:2).

11. {*Into the eternal kingdom*} The believer's inheritance (cf. 1 Pet. 1:4). This is the spiritual reign of God in men's hearts here on earth (1 Pet. 2:9) and in heaven.

12. {*Wherefore*} Since they are possessed of faith that leads to godliness which they are diligently practicing now he insists on the truth and proposes to do his part by them about it. {*To put you in remembrance*} Greek tense translates "to keep on reminding you of those things." {*In the truth which is with you*} This is "the truth present to you." The readers are firmly established in the truth, but Peter is eager to make them stronger.

13. {*Tabernacle/tent*} Used in a literal sense in Deuteronomy 33:18 (cf. Acts 7:46; Mark 9:5), here in this metaphorical sense of life as a pilgrimage (1 Pet. 1:1; 2:11). Peter feels the nearness of death and the urgency upon him. {*To stir you up*} Greek tense and form translates "to wake out of sleep" [thoroughly] (Mark 4:39), "to keep on rousing you up [to full alertness]."

14. {*Cometh swiftly*} It is not clear whether *tachinos* here means "soon" or "speedy" (cf. Isa. 59:7; Jas. 1:19); or "sudden." Either sense agrees with the urgent tone of Peter here, whether he felt his death to be near or violent or both.

15. Peter may also have had an intimation by vision of his approaching death, as Paul often did (Acts 16:9; 18:9; 21:11; 23:11; 27:23). {*After my decease*} Lit. "exodus, way out" here meaning death (cf. Luke 9:31), and for departure from Egypt (cf. Heb. 11:22), possibly alluding to the Transfiguration. {*To call these things to remembrance*} It is possible, as Irenæus (iii. I. I) thought, that Peter had in mind Mark's Gospel, which would help them after Peter was gone. Mark's Gospel was probably already written at Peter's suggestion.

16. {*We did not follow*} Lit. "to follow out." The *not* is emphatic in Greek. It is used of death following for any Gentile in the temple violating the barrier. {*Cunningly devised fables*} "Fables" is an old term for "word, narrative, story, fiction, fable, falsehood" (cf. 1 Tim. 1:4).

Lit. "to play the sophist, to invent cleverly" and so also in the old writers and in the papyri. Some of the false teachers apparently taught that the Gospel miracles were only allegories and not facts (Bigg). {***The power and coming***} This can refer to the incarnation of Christ, or his second coming (cf. 2 Cor. 7:6; 1 Tim. 6:14; 2 Tim. 1:10). It was a technical term in the papyri for the coming of a king or other high dignitary, when used of Christ, refers to his second coming (2 Pet. 3:4, 12). {***Of his majesty***} *His* is emphatic in the phrase (cf. 2 Tim. 2:26). Peter clearly felt that he and James and John were lifted to the highest stage of initiation at the Transfiguration of Christ.

17. {***When there came such a voice to him***} (cf. 1 Pet. 1:13). "Voice" (*phônê*) is used also of Pentecost (Acts 2:6). {***From the excellent glory***} "Majestic" used several times in OT, this is probably a reference to the bright cloud [*shekinah*] in Matthew 17:5.

18. {***In the holy mount***} Made holy by the majestic glory (cf. Ezek. 28:14), probably referring to one of the lower slopes of Hermon. Peter's account is independent of the Synoptic narrative, but agrees with it in all essentials.

19. {***Made more sure***} The Transfiguration scene confirmed the Messianic prophecies and made clear the deity of Jesus Christ as God's Beloved Son. {***In a dark place***} Lit. "parched, squalid, dirty, dark, murky," here only in NT, though in Aristotle and on tombstone for a boy. {***The day-star***} Lit. "to bring light," so, light-bringing, light-bearer (Lucifer) applied to Venus as the morning star.

20. {***Of private interpretation***} Better translated, "No prophecy of Scripture comes out of private '*disclosure*.'" Though it can be translated "explanation," its related verb can mean "disclose" in relationship to parables (Mark 4:34). It is the prophet's grasp of the prophecy, not that of the readers that is here presented.

21. {***Moved by the Holy Ghost***} Note the passive voice in Greek, "moved from time to time." Peter is not here warning against personal interpretation of prophecy, but against the folly of upstart prophets with no impulse from God.

CHAPTER 2

1. {***Shall privily bring in***} Lit. "to bring in by the side as if secretly" (cf. Gal. 2:4). {***Denying***} This the Gnostics did, the very thing that

Peter did, alas (Matt. 26:70) even after Christ's words (Matt. 10:33). {*Even the Master*} Lit. "absolute master," (with no evil connotation) referring here to Christ (Jude 4), and elsewhere of God (Acts 4:24).

2. {*The way of truth*} Greek *hodos* (way) occurs often in NT for Christianity (Acts 9:2; 16:17; 18:25; 22:4; 24:14). This phrase is in Genesis 24:48 as "the right road," and that is what Peter means here.

3. {*In covetousness*} As did Balaam (cf. 2 Pet. 2:15). These licentious Gnostics made money out of their dupes. A merely intellectual Gnosticism had its fruit in immorality and fraud. {*Shall make merchandise of you*} (from Greek *emporos,* a traveling merchant); cf. our word "emporium" (John 2:16, market house). {*Slumbereth not*} From the Greek verb "to nod," (cf. Matt. 25:5). Note the Greek word *apôleia* (destruction) three times in 2 Peter 2:1 to 3.

4. {*For if God spared not*} There are a series of "if" statements, which culminate in verse 10 with the "then" conclusion. Here, the first instance of certain doom, that of the fallen angels. {*Cast them down to hell*} This Greek verb is from *tartaros,* the dark and doleful abode of the wicked dead like the *Gehenna* of the Jews) (cf. Enoch 20:2 as the place of punishment of the fallen angels, while *Gehenna* is for apostate Jews).

5. {*The ancient world*} The second instance, the deluge, called Noah's Flood (Matt. 24:38; Luke 17:27; 2 Pet. 2:5). {*A preacher of righteousness*} Here a "herald" (cf. 1 Tim. 2:7; 2 Tim. 1:11). It is implied in 1 Peter 3:20 that Noah preached to the men of his time during the long years. {*Upon the world of the ungodly*} The whole world was "ungodly" (cf. 1 Pet. 4:18) save Noah's family of eight.

6. {*Turning into ashes*} From the Greek *tephra,* "ashes" used in the ancient world of an eruption of Vesuvius.

7. {*Sore distressed*} Lit. "to work down, to exhaust with labor, to distress," (cf. Acts 7:24). {*By the lascivious life of the wicked*} "Wicked" means here rebels against law of nature and conscience (cf. 1 Pet. 4:3).

8. {*From day to day*} This can be translated "day in day out." (cf. Ps. 96:2). {*Vexed*} Greek tense translates "kept on tormenting." This is the Greek verb *basanizô,* lit. "to test metals, to torment" (Matt. 8:29).

9. {*The Lord knoweth how*} This is the culmination or conclusion of all the "ifs" begun in verse 4. God can deliver his servants as shown by Noah and Lot and he will deliver you. {*The godly*} Lit. "well [good], to worship," in NT only here and Acts 10:2, 7. {*Under punishment*} Greek tense emphasizes continuity of the punishment (cf. Matt. 25:46). **10.** {*Chiefly*} He turns now to the libertine heretics (2 Pet. 2:2, 7). {*Despise dominion*} The Greek *kuriotês* is late word for lordship, perhaps God or Christ (cf. Col. 1:16; Eph. 1:21; Jude 1:8). {*Self-willed*} Lit. "self-pleasing," (cf. Titus 1:7). {*They tremble not to rail at dignities*} Lit. "glories" (cf. Jude 8). Perhaps these dignities are evil angels. **12.** {*But these*} This refers to the false teachers of 2 Peter 2:1. {*Without reason*} Brute beasts like wild animals (cf. Jude 10; Acts 25:27). {*And destroyed*} "And for destruction" just like a beast of prey caught (cf. 2 Pet. 1:4). {*In matters whereof they are ignorant*} A picture of loud ignoramuses posing as experts.

13. {*As the hire of wrong-doing*} The idea here may be one of being defrauded. Peter plays on words again here as often in 2 Peter. {*Count it pleasure*} The picture proceeds now with participles like *hêgoumenoi* (counting). {*Spots*} Greek for a disfiguring spot (cf. Eph. 5:27). {*Revelling*} This means "living in luxury."

14. {*Of adultery*} Rather, "of an adulteress," (cf. Jas. 4:4). Vivid picture of a man who cannot see a woman without improper sexual thoughts toward her (cf. Matt. 5:28). {*Exercised*} From the Greek word *gumnazô*, precisely as in Hebrews 5:14. Rhetorical metaphor from the gymnasium. {*Children of cursing*} Hebraism meaning those of the class or kind of "accursed" (cf. 1 Pet. 1:14).

15. {*The way of Balaam*} These false teachers, as shown in 2 Peter 2:13, followed the way of Balaam, "who loved the hire of wrong-doing."

16. {*A dumb ass*} The animal is lit. "being under a yoke," and is applied to the ass as the common beast of burden (cf. Matt. 21:5). "Speechless" is lit. "without voice," old word for idols and beasts. {*Spake*} Lit. "to utter a sound" (cf. 2 Pet. 2:18, Acts 4:18). {*Madness*} Lit. "being beside one's wits."

18. {*Great swelling words*} That is, boasting words (cf. Jude 16).

19. {*Liberty*} Greek term is *eleutheria*. Promising "personal liberty," that is license, after the fashion of advocates of liquor today, not the freedom of truth in Christ (John 8:32; Gal. 5:1, 13). {*Themselves bondservants*} Controlled by corruption and sin as Paul has it in Romans 6:20. {*Is brought into bondage*} (cf. Rom. 6:16, 18; 8:21).

20. {*The defilements*} Greek term is *miasmata*, from *miainô* (cf. the English word "miasma"). The body is sacred to God (cf. also 2 Pet.

2:10). {*They are again entangled*} Lit. "to inweave (noosed, fettered)" (cf. 2 Tim. 2:4). {*Overcome*} Greek tense translates, "are repeatedly worsted" (cf. 2 Pet. 2:19). It is not clear whether the subject here is the deluded victims (Bigg) or the false teachers themselves (Mayor) (cf. Heb. 10:26).

21. {*It were better*} This is a phrase of possibility, propriety, obligation (Matt. 26:24; 1 Cor. 5:10; Rom. 7:7; Heb. 9:26). {*Not to have known*} Lit. "to know fully." {*To turn back*} Lit. "to turn back, to return." {*From*} The Greek case has a focus of separation from a source (cf. Acts 12:25) {*Holy commandment*} (cf. Rom. 7:12 and 1 Tim. 6:14). Second Peter strikes a high ethical note (2 Pet. 1:5).

22. {*The sow that had washed*} This is a female hog. This proverb does not occur in the OT, probably from a Gentile source because about the habit of hogs. {*To wallowing*} Lit. "To rolling," (for the verb, see Mark 9:20). {*In the mire*} Lit. "dung, mire." There is a story about a hog that went to the bath with people of quality, but on coming out saw a stinking drain and went and rolled himself in it.

CHAPTER 3

1. {*Beloved*} Greek term is *agapêtos*. With this vocative verbal (four times in this chapter), Peter "turns away from the Libertines and their victims" (Mayor). {*This is now the second epistle that I write unto you*} This apparently refers to the Epistle of First Peter. {*I stir up*} Perhaps this is to be translated "I *try* to stir up" (cf. 2 Pet. 1:13). {*Mind*} Here the Greek word means "understanding" (cf. 1 Pet. 1:13). {*Sincere*} Supposed lit. rendering "sunlight + to judge by it."

2. {*Of the Lord and Savior through your apostles*} "Your" does not necessarily mean Peter did not write the epistle, this a needless inference. The meaning is that they should remember the teaching of their apostles and not follow the Gnostic libertines.

3. {*Knowing this first*} The "power" of Christ has been discussed in the epistle above, and Peter now takes up the *parousia*, the second coming (cf. 2 Pet. 1:16).

4. {*Where is the promise of his coming?*} This is the only sample of the questions raised by these mockers. Peter had mentioned this subject of the Greek *parousia* in 2 Peter 1:16. Now he faces it squarely. Peter, like Paul (1 Thess. 5:1; 2 Thess. 2:1), preached about the second coming (2 Pet. 1:16; Acts 3:20), as Jesus himself did repeatedly (Matt. 24:34) and as the angels promised at the Ascension (Acts 1:11). Both Jesus and Paul (2 Thess. 2:1) were misunderstood on the subject of the time and the parables of Jesus urged readiness and forbade setting dates for his coming, though his language in Matthew 24:34 probably led some to believe that he would certainly come while they were alive.

5. {*For this they wilfully forget*} Literally, "for this escapes them being willing." "Forget," lit. "to escape notice of, to be hidden from" (cf. Acts 26:26). {*Compacted*} (cf. Col. 1:17) "consist." Grammatically bound to "earth" not "heavens." Though "heaven" is plural, there is no need to make Peter mean the Jewish mystical "seven heavens" because of the plural which was used interchangeably with the singular (Matt. 5:9). {*Out of water and amidst water*} Creation was out of the primeval watery chaos (Gen. 1:2). "By water" may mean the condition or state of being (cf. Heb. 12:1). The reference may be to Genesis 1:9, the gathering together of the waters.

7. {*Have been stored up*} Greek word is *thêsaurizô* (cf. Matt. 6:19; Luke 12:21). {*For fire*} The destruction of the world by fire is here pictured as in Joel 2:30; Psalm 50:3.

8. {*Do not forget this one thing*} Rather, "let not this one thing escape you." Peter applies the language of Psalm 90:4 about the eternity of God and shortness of human life to "the impatience of human expectations" about the second coming of Christ. "The day of judgment is at hand (1 Pet. 4:7). It may come tomorrow; but what is tomorrow? What does God mean by a day? It may be a thousand years" (Bigg). Precisely the same argument applies to those who argue for a literal interpretation of the thousand years in Revelation 20:4-6. It may be a day or a day may be a thousand years. God's clock does not run by our timepieces. The scoffers scoff ignorantly.

9. {*Is not slack concerning his promise*} Lit. "to be slow in, to fall short of" (cf. 1 Tim. 3:15). {*Slackness*} God is not impotent nor unwilling to execute his promise. {*Not wishing any...to perish*} Some will perish (2 Pet. 3:7), but that is not God's desire. God wishes "all to come" lit. "all to make room" (cf. Acts 17:30; Rom. 11:32; 1 Tim. 2:4; Heb. 2:9 for God's provision of grace for all who will repent).

10. {*The day of the Lord*} This great day will certainly arrive, but in God's own time. {*As a thief*} That is suddenly, without notice. This very metaphor Jesus had used (Luke 12:39; Matt. 24:43) and Paul after him (1 Thess. 5:2) and John will quote it also (Rev. 3:3; 16:15). {*With a great noise*} Greek term is *roizêdon*. This is an onomatopoetic word [i.e., its sounds are like the designative meaning], a whizzing sound of rapid motion through the air like the flight of a bird, or thunder, or even fierce flame. {*With fervent heat*} From the Greek term *kausos* (usually medical term for fever), and nearly always employed for fever temperature. So it may be a conflagration from internal heat, though others think it merely means "to burn."

12. {*Earnestly desiring*} Lit. "to hasten (like our speed)" (cf. Luke 2:16), but it is sometimes transitive as here either (preferably so) to "hasten on the second coming" by holy living (cf. 1 Pet. 2:12), with which idea compare Matthew 6:10; Acts 3:19ff., or to desire earnestly (Isa. 16:5). {*Shall melt*} Greek term is *têkô*, "to make liquid." The repetitions here make "an effective refrain" (Mayor).

13. {*Wherein dwelleth righteousness*} Certainly "righteousness" (*dikaiosunê*) is not at home in this present world either in individuals, families, or nations.

15. {*Longsuffering of our Lord is salvation*} Lord here is Christ; "longsuffering" here is an opportunity for repentance (cf. 1 Pet. 3:20). {*Our beloved brother Paul*} Paul often uses this term of others. It is not surprising for Peter to use it of Paul in view of Galatians 2:9, in spite of Galatians 2:11-14. {*Given to him*} Peter claimed wisdom for himself, but recognizes that Paul had the gift also. His language here may have caution in it as well as commendation.

16. {*As also in all his epistles*} We do not know to how many Peter here refers. There is no difficulty in supposing that Peter "received every one of St. Paul's epistles within a month or two of its publication" (Bigg). And yet Peter does not here assert the formation of a canon of Paul's epistles. {*Hard to be understood*} We know that the Thessalonians persisted in misrepresenting Paul on this very subject of the second coming as Hymenaeus and Philetus did about the resurrection (2 Tim. 2:17). Paul's teaching about grace was twisted to mean moral laxity like Galatians 3:10; Romans 3:20, 28; 5:20. Peter does not say that he himself did not understand Paul on the subject of faith and freedom. {*Unlearned*} Lit. "not...to learn." {*The other scriptures*} There is no doubt that the apostles claimed to speak by the help of the Holy Spirit (1 Thess. 5:27; Col. 4:16) just as the prophets of old did (2 Pet. 1:20). Note "other" means "the rest." Peter thus puts Paul's epistles on the

same plane with the OT, which was also misused (Matt. 5:21-44; 15:3-6; 19:3-10).

17. {***Knowing these things beforehand***} (*proginôskontes*). Hence they are without excuse for misunderstanding Peter or Paul on this subject. {***Beware***} Lit. "to guard." {***Being carried away***} Lit. "to carry away together with" (cf. Gal. 2:13). {***With the error***} The Greek syntax suggests "by the instrument of error." The Greek word *planê* is lit. "the wandering." {***Ye fall from***} Lit. "to fall out of."

18. {***But grow***} Greek tense translates "but keep on growing," cf. the fate of the others in verse 17. {***In the grace and knowledge***} Grow in both. Keep it up. {***For ever***} Lit. "to the day of eternity." (cf. Sirach 18:9ff.). One of the various ways of expressing eternity (cf. John 6:5; 12:34).

THE FIRST EPISTLE OF JOHN

AUTHOR: The Apostle John, the beloved disciple, author of the fourth gospel and three epistles, and many say Revelation as well
RECIPIENT: It is not clear to whom the Epistle is addressed. The Epistle was clearly sent to those familiar with John's message, possibly to the churches of the Province of Asia (cf. the Seven Churches in Revelation).
DATE: A.D. 85 to 95
FROM: Ephesus
OCCASION: An underlying concern that the subtle danger of Gnosticism might permeate a false teaching about the true nature of the person of Christ
THEME: Fellowship with God and with other believers is inseparable.

BY WAY OF INTRODUCTION

This epistle and the Gospel of John are by the same writer, the Apostle of Love or Thunder (as the occasion required). In the whole of the First Epistle there is hardly a single thought that is not found in the Gospel. One imitates the other, but which came first is a matter of debate. But a close examination shows they quite likely have the same author. Westcott suggests that one compare John 1:1-18 with 1 John 1:1-4 to see how the same mind deals with the same ideas in different connections. "No theory of conscious imitation can reasonably explain the subtle coincidences and differences in these two short crucial passages."

This epistle is not a polemic primarily, yet the errors of the Gnostics are constantly before John's mind. John, like Paul in Colossians, Ephesians, and the Pastoral Epistles, foresaw this dire peril of Gnosticism to Christianity. Gnostics threatened to undermine the Gospel message by deifying the devil along with dethroning Christ. There were two kinds of Gnostics, both agreeing in the essential evil of matter: Docetic and Cerinthian. Some Gnostics practiced asceticism, some licentiousness. John opposes both classes in his Epistles. Nine times John gives tests for knowing the truth and uses the verb *ginôskô* (know) each time (1 John 2:3, 5; 3:16, 19, 24; 4:2, 6, 13; 5:2).

Westcott thinks that the Fourth Gospel was written to prove the deity of Christ, assuming his humanity, while 1 John was written to prove the humanity of Christ, assuming his deity. Certainly both ideas appear in both books.

The tone of the author is that of an old man. His urgent message that the disciples, his "little children," love one another is like another story about the aged John, who, when too feeble to stand, would sit in his chair and preach "Little children, love one another."

CHAPTER 1

1. {*That which*} Note fourfold repetition of *ho* (that which) without connectives (asyndeton). {*That which we have heard*} "We" throughout here is likely a literary plural. The perfect tense stresses John's equipment to speak on this subject so slowly revealed. {*Handled*} The very verb used by Jesus to prove that he was not a mere spirit (Luke 24:39). "Hearing, sight, touch" combine to show the reality of Christ's humanity against the Docetic Gnostics.

2. {*Was manifested*} With the clause as a parenthesis, the Greek means to make known what already exists, whether invisible (B. Weiss) or visible, "intellectual or sensible" (Brooke). This parenthesis emphasizes the reality of the Incarnation using "seen" and "witness" and "message."

3. {*That which we have seen and heard, declare we*} (cf. 1 John 1:1, 2, 3), a resumption after the parenthesis in verse 2. Emphasis by repetition is a thoroughly Johannine trait. {*That ye also may have*} Translate "For the purpose that." {*Fellowship with us*} "Fellowship" a common word in this Epistle, from *koinônos,* partner (Luke 5:10), and *koinôneô,* to share, in (1 Pet. 4:13), *with* emphasizing mutual relationship (Acts 2:42); *with* the believers and *with* God the Father and Son.

4. {*May be fulfilled*} Remain full (cf. John 16:24). The passive stresses the state of completion in the purpose (the "to" of the clause).

5. {*And*} The connector word to the verse in Greek shows that mutual fellowship depends on mutual knowledge. {*Message*} (cf. 1 John 3:11) from verb "to announce, to disclose," (cf. John 4:25).

7. {*If we walk*} Translate as "keep on walking in the light with God." {*As he*} God is light (cf. 1 John 1:5; 1 Tim. 6:16). {*And the blood of Jesus his Son cleanseth us from all sin*} This phrase coordinates with the preceding one. Walking in the light with God makes possible fellowship with one another and is made possible also by the *real* (not phantom) atoning blood of Jesus; this action was not a mere example. Atoning blood does cleanse the conscience and life and nothing else does (Heb. 9:13; Titus 2:14; cf. also 1 John 1:9; 3:3).

8. {*We have no sin*} (cf. John 9:41; 15:22, 24). That is, we have no personal guilt, no principle of sin. This some of the Gnostics held, since matter was evil and the soul was not contaminated by the sinful flesh, a thin delusion which is still taught today by some.

9. {*If we confess*} The Greek verb is *homologeô,* translate tense as "if we keep on confessing." Confession of sin to God and to one another (Jas. 5:16) is urged throughout the NT. {*Faithful*} Jesus made confession of sin necessary to forgiveness. It is God's promise and he is "righteous" (*dikaios*).

10. {*We have not sinned*} This is a denial of any specific acts of sin, while in verse 8 we have the denial of the principle of sin. Personal perfectionism has two causes: one the stifling of conscience in making God a liar (John 8:44), and the other ignorance of God's word, which is not in us, else we should not make such a claim (Smith).

CHAPTER 2

1. {*That ye may not sin*} Translate "for the purpose to..." {*We have*} The tense focuses on a present reality (cf. 2 Cor. 5:1). {*An advocate*} The Greek word *paraklêton* (cf. John 14:16, 26; 15:26; 16:7). The Holy Spirit is God's Advocate on earth with men, while Christ is man's Advocate with the Father (cf. same idea in Rom. 8:31-39; Heb. 7:25).

2. {*And he*} This is a personal emphasis. He himself in his own person, both priest and sacrifice (Heb. 9:14). {*The propitiation*} Greek word is *hilasmos* (cf. verb Luke 18:13; Heb. 2:17, cf. also 1 John 4:10). {*For the whole world*} Possibly just regard this as "the whole world" as a mass of sin (1 John 5:19). At any rate, the propitiation by Christ provides for salvation for all (Heb. 2:9) if they will only be reconciled with God (2 Cor. 5:19-21).

3. {*If we keep his commandments*} Translate the Greek tense, "if we keep on keeping." {*Know that we know him*} Translate Greek tense, "Know we that we have come to know and still know [him.]" The Gnostics boasted of their superior knowledge of Christ, and John here challenges their boast by an appeal to the testable knowledge of Christ which is shown by keeping Christ's commandments.

4. {*I know him*} This is one of the pious platitudes, cheap claptrap of the Gnostics, who would bob up in meetings with such explosions. John punctures such bubbles with the sharp addition {*And keepeth not*} Greek tense translates, "The one who keeps on saying: 'I have come to know him,' and keeps on not keeping his commandments is a liar" (cf. John 8:44; 1 John 1:8, 10). There is a whip-cracker effect in John's words.

5. {*But whoso keepeth*} Greek tense translates, "whoever keeps on keeping." {*Hath the love of God been perfected*} Probably translate "love *for* God," which is realized in obedience.

6. {*Himself also to walk*} Greek tense translates "keep on walking," a continuous performance, not a spasmodic spurt. {*Even as he walked*} Greek tense a focus of summing up the life of Christ on earth (cf. 1 John 3:3, 5, 7, 16; 4:17; John 7:11; 9:12, 28; 19:21).

7. {*Which ye had*} Greek tense has focus of reaching back to the beginning of their Christian lives (cf. John 13:34).

8. {*Is passing away*} Night does pass by even if slowly. See this verb in verse 1 John 2:17 of the world passing by like a procession.

10. {*Occasion of stumbling*} From the Greek *skandalon* (cf. Matt. 13:41; 16:23). It is a stumbling block or trap either in the way of others (its usual sense Matt. 18:7); or in one's own way (the likely contextual meaning, cf. 1 John 2:11).

11. {*Blinded*} This Greek word is used of the god of this age to keep men from beholding the illumination of the gospel of the glory of Christ who is the image of God (cf. 2 Cor. 4:4).

12. {*I write*} Here repeated three times in present tense, referring to this Epistle.

13. {*Young men*} (*neaniskoi*). The younger element in contrast to the fathers, full of vigor and conflict and victory. {*Ye have overcome*} The Greek tense shows a permanent victory after conflict.

14. {*I have written*} Repeated three times in epistolary aorist, referring to this Epistle, not to a previous Epistle. This tense change is quite in John's style to repeat himself with slight variations.

15. {*Love not the world*} The Greek grammar has a focus of (1) either stop doing it or (2) do not have the habit of doing it. This use of "world" (Greek *kosmos*) is common in John's Gospel (John 1:10; 17:14; cf. 1 John 5:19). {*If any man love*} Greek tense translates, "if any keep on loving the world." {*The love of the Father*} Translate Greek case as "love for the Father." (cf. 1 John 2:5). In antithesis to love of the world.

16. {*The lust of the flesh*} Greek case translates, "lust *felt by* the flesh" (cf. Mark 4:19; Gal. 5:17). {*Vain glory of life*} (cf. Jas. 4:16, also Rom. 1:30; 2 Tim. 3:2.) "Life" here is the external aspect (Luke 8:14), not the inward principle (Greek *zôê*). These three sins include all possible sins: of Eve (Gen. 3:1-6) and the temptations of Jesus (Matt. 4:1-11).

17. {*Passeth away*} Greek tense translates "is passing by." There is consolation in this view of the transitory nature of the conflict with the world. Even the lust which belongs to the world passes also.

18. {*It is the last hour*} "Hour" can be used for a crisis, the Greek syntax marks the character of the "hour" (John 2:4; 4:21, 23; 5:25, 28, etc.). {*Antichrist cometh*} (Cf. Mark 13:6, 22; Matt. 24:5, 15, 24; Mark 13:22; Acts 20:30; 2 Thess. 2:3). The Greek *Anti* can mean substitution or opposition, but both ideas are identical in the word *antichristos*.

20. {*Anointing*} Greek word is *chrisma,* from *chriô,* to anoint, perhaps suggested by the use of *antichristoi* in verse 1 John 2:18. Christians are "anointed ones," (Ps. 105:15). Followers of Christ do have "the oil of anointing" = the Holy Spirit (cf. Exod. 29:7; 1 John 2:27).

24. {*As for you*} "You" is in sharp grammatical, emphatic contrast with the antichrists.

26. {*Concerning them that would lead you astray*} The Greek syntax translates "*trying* to lead you astray." John is doing his part to rescue the sheep from the wolves, as Paul did (Acts 20:29).

28. {*That we have boldness*} Greek syntax translates "that we may get boldness." {*Before him*} Lit. "From him," as if shrinking away from Christ in guilty surprise.

29. {*If ye know*} That is, if you know by intuitive or absolute knowledge that Christ is righteous, then you "know" by experimental knowledge.

CHAPTER 3

1. {*That we should be called*} "Call" in Greek is *kaleô,* "to call or name," (cf. Matt. 2:23).

3. {*Purifieth himself*} Greek verb from *hagnos* (pure from contamination), used of ceremonial purifications (John 11:55; Acts 21:24, 26 as in Exod. 19:10) and then of personal internal cleansing of heart (Jas. 4:8), soul (1 Pet. 1:22), self (here). Cf. Philippians 2:12 the work of both God and man.

4. {*Sin is lawlessness*} Sin and lawlessness are interchangeable here, and antithetical to righteousness. "Doing" of sin has a grammatical focus of being in the *habit* of sin.

5. {*He*} (*ekeinos*). Again referring to Jesus (cf. 1 John 3:3; John 1:18). {*To take away sins*} Translate the Greek syntax "for the purpose of..." (cf. John 1:29); Christ bore our sins (cf. Isa. 53:11), and so the Greek has several terms for "bearing, lifting, taking away" of sins. {*And in him is no sin*} "There was no sinful principle in him," as the NT teaches (John 7:18; 8:46; 2 Cor. 5:21; Heb. 4:15; 7:26; 9:13).

6. {*Sinneth not*} Translate the Greek tense, "does not keep on sinning." {*Whoever sinneth*} Here the Greek tense has a focus of one who lives a life of sin, not mere occasional acts of sin, as another tense might show.

7. {*Let no man lead you astray*} Translate the Greek tense, "keep on leading you astray." (See 1 John 1:8; 2:26).

8. {*Sinneth from the beginning*} Greek tense translates, "he has been sinning from the beginning" of his career as the devil. This is his normal life and those who imitate him become his spiritual children.

9. {*And he cannot sin*} This does not mean "and he cannot commit sin." The Greek tense translates "and he cannot *go on* sinning." A great deal of false theology has grown out of a misunderstanding of the tense of "to sin." Paul has precisely John's idea in Romans 6:1, cf. 15.

10. {*Doeth not righteousness*} Greek tense translates "is not in the habit of doing..."

12. {*Of the evil one*} This refers to the Devil. {*Slew*} Lit. "to slay, to butcher, to cut the throat" (Latin *jugulare*) like an ox in the meat market (cf. Rev. 5:6, 9, 12, etc.).

13. {*Marvel not*} The Greek syntax translates "cease wondering, stop being surprised."

14. {*We know*} "We" is emphatic in contrast to the unregenerate world, the Christian consciousness shared by writer and readers.

15. {*A murderer*} Lit. "man-killer," (cf. John 8:44 [of Satan]). {*No*} Lit. "not all" according to Hebraistic idiom = "no one" as in 1 John 2:19, 21.

16. {*Know we*} Greek tense translates "we have come to know and still know." {*Love*} Here translate, "the thing called love" {*We ought*} "We" is emphatic here. Of course, our laying down our lives for the brethren has no atoning value in our cases as in that of Christ, but is a supreme proof of one's love (John 13:37; 15:13), as often happens.

17. {*The world's goods*} Lit. "the life of the world." This is the living or livelihood, *zôê*, the principle of life (1 John 2:16) of the world. *Bios* is not in the sense of evil or wicked, but simply this mundane sphere. {*Shutteth up*} Lit. "shuts up the bowels." The Greek verb translates "to close like the door." The tense gives graphic slamming the door of his compassion (*splagchna*), the nobler viscera, the seat of the emotions, as in Philippians 2:11; Colossians 3:12.

20. {*Whereinsoever our heart condemn us*} This Greek word occurs only three times in the NT: here, 1 John 3:21, Galatians 2:11. It means to know something against one, to condemn. {*Because God is greater than our heart*} Just so Peter replied to Jesus in spite of his denials (John 21:17). God's omniscience is linked with his love and sympathy. God knows every secret in our hearts. This difficult passage strikes the very center of Christian truth.

21. {*If our heart condemn us not*} The converse of the preceding, but not a claim to sinlessness, but the consciousness of fellowship in God's presence. {*Boldness toward God*} We have boldness, even in prayer (Heb. 4:16; cf. also 1 John 2:28).

22. {*Whatsoever we ask*} In form no limitations are placed here save that of complete fellowship with God, which means complete surrender of our will to that of God our Father. See the clear teaching of Jesus on this subject in Mark 11:24; Luke 11:9; John 14:12; 16:23 and his example (Mark 14:36; Matt. 26:39; Luke 22:42). The answer may not always be in the form that we expect, but it will be better. {*Because*} Here is a twofold reason why we receive regularly the answer to our prayers (1) "we keep on keeping" (1 John 2:3) his commandments and (2) "we do" (practice regularly) "the things that are pleasing."

23. {*Name of...Jesus*} (1) The "name" of Jesus Christ here stands for all that he is, "a compressed creed" (Westcott) (cf. 1 John 1:3). But (2) "we should love one another," as he has already urged (1 John 2:7; 3:11) and as he will repeat (1 John 4:7, 11; 2 John 1:5). There are frequent points of contact between this Epistle and the words of Jesus in John 13 to 17.

24. {*Abide*} We abide in God and God abides in us through the Holy Spirit (John 14:10, 17, 23; 17:21). Therefore let God be a home to you, and be you the home of God: abide in God, and let God abide in you (Bede). {*By the Spirit*} It is thus that we know that God abides in us.

It is by the Holy Spirit, first mentioned in this Epistle and "Holy" not used with "Spirit" in this Epistle or the Apocalypse.

CHAPTER 4

1. {*Believe not every spirit*} Greek syntax translates, "Stop believing," as some were clearly carried away by the spirits of error rampant among them, both Docetic and Cerinthian Gnostics. Credulity means gullibility and some believers fall easy victims to the latest fads in spiritualistic hoaxes and deception. {*Prove the spirits*} Put them to the acid test of truth as the metallurgist does his metals. If it stands the test like a coin, it is acceptable (2 Cor. 10:18), otherwise it is rejected (1 Cor. 9:27; 2 Cor. 13:5-7). {*Many false prophets*} Jesus had warned people against them (Matt. 7:15), even when they as false Christs work portents (Matt. 24:11, 24; Mark 13:22). It is an old story (Luke 6:26) and recurs again and again (Acts 13:6; Rev. 16:13; 19:20; 20:10) along with false teachers (2 Pet. 2:1).

2. {*That Jesus Christ is come in the flesh*} John 9:22 (cf. 2 John 1:7) describes Jesus as already come in the flesh (his actual humanity, not a phantom body as the Docetic Gnostics held). There are similar tests in the NT: by Paul for confessing the deity of Jesus Christ in 1 Corinthians 12:3, and for the Incarnation and Resurrection of Jesus in Romans 10:6-10.

6. {*He that knoweth God...hears us*} The Greek tenses translates, "the one who keeps on getting acquainted with God, growing in his knowledge of God."

7. {*Every one that loveth*} The Greek tense has a focus of persistence in loving.

8. {*He that loveth not*} Greek tense translates "keeps on not loving."

10. {*He*} The *he* is emphatic in the phrase about love, referring to God. {*To be the propitiation*} The Greek word is *hilasmon* (cf. 1 John 2:2; Rom. 3:25).

11. {*If God so loved us*} The *if* here could be better translated *since* (it is a fact, cf. John 3:16).

12. {*If we love one another*} Greek tense translates "if we keep on loving one another."

16. {*We know*} Greek tense translates, "we have come to know and still know" (cf. John 6:9).

17. {*As he is*} That is Christ as in 1 John 2:6; 3:3, 5, 7, 16. Same tense (present) as in 1 John 3:7.

18. {*Fear*} This is a kind of dread, opposite of boldness, like a bond-slave (Rom. 8:15), not the reverence of a son (Heb. 5:7) or the obedience to a father (1 Pet. 1:17). {*Perfect love*} There is such a thing, perfect because it has been perfected (1 John 4:2, 17, cf. Jas. 1:4). {*Casteth out fear*} So that fear does not exist in real love (cf. John 6:37; 9:34; 12:31; 15:6) "to turn out-of-doors," a powerful metaphor. Perfect love harbors no suspicion and no dread (1 Cor. 13).

19. {*He first*} (cf. John 20:4, 8). God loved us *before* we loved him (John 3:16). Our love is in response to his love for us, as a simple statement of what is actual.

20. {*If a man say*} "Suppose one say" (cf. 1 John 1:6). {*I love God*} John is quoting an imaginary disputant (cf. 1 John 2:4). {*And hateth*} Greek tense translates, "and keep on hating," (cf. also 1 John 2:9; 3:15). {*A liar*} Blunt and to the point (cf. 1 John 1:10; 2:4). {*Cannot love*} Greek tense translates, "Is not able to go on loving," (cf. 1 John 2:9).

21. {*From him*} The "him" refers either to God or Christ (cf. Mark 12:29-31; 1 John 2:7).

CHAPTER 5

1. {*Him also that is begotten of him*} The Greek has a focus that this is the brother or sister by the same father. So then we prove our love for the common Father by our conduct towards our brothers and sisters in Christ.

2. {*Hereby*} John's usual phrase for the test of the sincerity of our love (cf. 1 John 3:14; 5:2). {*And do*} Greek tense translates, "and whenever we keep on doing his commandments," (cf. 1 John 1:6).

3. {*Are not grievous*} Lit. "Not heavy," the adjective in Matthew 23:4 with *burdens,* with *wolves* in Acts 20:29, of Paul's letters in 2 Corinthians 10:10, of the charges against Paul in Acts 25:7. Love for God lightens his commands.

4. {*Whatsoever is begotten of God*} This is stated in the grammatical neuter gender to express sharply the universality of the principle (cf. John 3:6, 8; 6:37, 39). {*Overcometh the world*} Greek tense translates a continuous victory because a continuous struggle "keeps on conquering the world." This is "the sum of all the forces antagonistic to the spiritual life" (Smith). {*That overcometh*} Difficult to express in English, the Greek tense here singles out an individual experience when one believed or when one met temptation with victory. Jesus won the victory over the world (John 16:33) and God in us (1 John 4:4) gives us the victory.

5. {*And who is he that overcometh?*} This is not here a mere rhetorical question (1 John 2:22), but an appeal to experience and fact. Greek tense translates, "the one who keeps on conquering the world," (cf. 1 Cor. 15:57).

6. {*By water and blood...Spirit*} This refers to the water (as at the baptism) and blood (as on the Cross). These two incidents in the Incarnation are singled out because at the baptism Jesus was formally set apart to his Messianic work by the coming of the Holy Spirit upon him and by the Father's audible witness, and because at the Cross his work reached its culmination ("It is finished," Jesus said). There are other theories that do not accord with the language and the facts. It is true that at the Cross both water and blood came out of the side of Jesus when pierced by the soldier, as John bore witness (John 19:34), a complete refutation of the Docetic denial of an actual human body for Jesus and of the Cerinthian distinction between Jesus and Christ. There is thus a threefold witness to the fact of the Incarnation, but he repeats the twofold witness before giving the third, the Holy Spirit, a chief witness at Jesus' baptism and all through his ministry.

7. {*For there are three who bear witness*} The rest of the verse is an addition found in older English versions with the underlying Greek Textus Receptus. This addition to the verse is found in no Greek MS. save two late [i.e., very long after the first century] cursives (manuscript 162 in the Vatican Library of the fifteenth century, and manuscript 34 of the sixteenth century in Trinity College, Dublin). Jerome did not have it. Cyprian applies the language of the Trinity and Priscillian has it. Erasmus did not have it in his first edition, but rashly offered to insert it if a single Greek MS. had it and 34 were produced with the insertion, as if made to order. The fact and the doctrine of the Trinity do not depend on this spurious addition. Some Latin scribe caught up Cyprian's exegesis and wrote it on the margin of his text, and so it got into the Vulgate and finally into the Textus Receptus by the stupidity of Erasmus.

8. {*The Spirit and the water and the blood*} (cf. 1 John 5: 6, 7). {*Agree in one*} Lit. "Are for the one thing," i.e., to bring us to faith in Jesus as the Incarnate Son of God, the very purpose for which John wrote his Gospel (John 20:31).

9. {*If we receive*} The phrase in Greek is assumed as true.

11. {*That God gave*} The Greek tense of "gave" has a focus on the great historic fact of the Incarnation (John 3:16), but the Greek tense in 1 John 3:1 is to emphasize the abiding presence of God's love.

13. {*That ye may know*} This means "to know with settled intuitive knowledge."

14. {*Toward him*} Fellowship face to face with Christ. For boldness see 1 John 2:28. {*If we ask anything*} Such asking can have personal interest as in James 4:3, though the point is not to be pressed too far, see Matt. 20:20, 22; John 16:24, 26. {*According to his will*} This is the secret in all prayer, even in the case of Jesus himself. For the phrase, see 1 Peter 4:19; Galatians 1:4; Ephesians 1:5, 11. {*He heareth us*} Even when God does not give us what we ask, in particular then (Heb. 5:7).

15. {*Whatsoever we ask*} This means "our petitions." The Greek noun is from the verb *aiteô*, "requests," here only in John, elsewhere in NT Luke 23:24; Philippians 4:6.

16. {*Not unto death*} Most sins are not mortal sins, but clearly John conceives of a sin that is deadly enough to be called "unto death." This distinction is common in the Rabbinic writings and in Numbers 18:22 the LXX has "to incur a death-bearing sin" as many crimes then and now bear the death penalty. There is a distinction in Hebrews 10:26 between sinning willfully after full knowledge and sins of ignorance (Heb. 5:2). Jesus spoke of the unpardonable sin (Mark 3:29; Matt. 12:32; Luke 12:10), which was attributing to the devil the manifest work of the Holy Spirit. It is possible that John has this idea in mind when he applies it to those who reject Jesus Christ as God's Son and set themselves up as antichrists.

17. {*All unrighteousness is sin*} Unrighteousness is one manifestation of sin as lawlessness (1 John 3:4) is another. The world today takes sin too lightly, even jokingly as a mere animal inheritance. Sin is a terrible reality, but there is no cause for despair. Sin not unto death can be overcome in Christ.

18. {*Sinneth not*} Greek tense translates "does not keep on sinning," (cf. 1 John 3:4-10). {*The evil one*} (*ho ponêros*). Probably referring to

Satan, not just any evil man (cf. 1 John 2:13; Matt. 6:13). {***Touchest him not***} Lit. "to lay hold, grasp" rather than a mere superficial touch (cf. Col. 2:21). Here the idea is to touch to harm.

20. {***This***} This can refer to God or Jesus Christ. It is a bit tautological to refer it to God, but that is probably correct, God in Christ, at any rate. God is eternal life (John 5:26) and he gives it to us through Christ.

21. {***Guard yourselves***} The reflexive pronoun accents the need of effort on their part. Idolatry was everywhere and the peril was great.

The Second Epistle of John

Author: The Apostle John, the beloved disciple, author of the fourth gospel and three epistles, and many say Revelation as well
Recipient: Likely, "the chosen lady," a title referring to a loyal woman (Kyria?), or possibly to a church (in Pergamum?).
Date: A.D. 85 to 90
From: Ephesus
Occasion: To confront the Gnostic heresies
Theme: Christians are characterized by both love and loyalty to sound teaching.

By Way of Introduction

The author terms himself "the elder." Some hold that it is the mythical "presbyter John" of whom Papias may speak, but this is not likely the author of this epistle. There is no way of deciding whether "the elect lady" is a woman or a church. It is not certain that 2 John was written after 1 John, though probable. Origen rejected it and the Peshitta Syriac does not have 2 and 3 John.

1. {*And her children*} This may be understood literally (cf. 1 Tim. 3:4) or spiritually (cf. Gal. 4:19, 25; 1 Tim. 1:2 and also 1 John 2:1, 12). If literal, the grammatical neuter embraces both sexes. {*That know*} The Greek tense can be translated, "those that have come to know and still know."

3. {*Grace, mercy, peace*} This salutation is like that in the Pastoral Epistles: Grace, the wellspring in the heart of God; mercy, its outpourings; peace, its blessed effect. {*And from Jesus Christ*} The repetition of "from" "serves to bring out distinctly the twofold personal relation of man to the Father and to the Son" (Westcott).

4. {*I have found*} Here with its usual force, it is a continued discovery. {*Certain of thy children*} Probably members of the church (from Pergamum?) cut off here in Ephesus. {*We received*} (cf. John 10:18; Acts 17:15; Col. 4:10). Perhaps the reference here is to 1 John 2:7; 3:23.

5. {*Beseech*} This means "pray" as in 1 John 5:16. {*Lady*} (cf. 2 John 1). {*We had*} This is not a literary plural, rather John is identifying all Christians with himself in this blessing.

6. {*That we should walk*} Greek tenses emphasizes "that we *keep on* walking."

7. {*Deceivers*} Lit. "wandering, roving" (cf. 1 Tim. 4:1; 1 John 2:26). Here it is a noun, of Jesus (Matt. 27:63), of Paul (2 Cor. 6:8), and here, referring to the Gnostic deceivers. {*That Jesus Christ cometh in the flesh*} The Greek tense is treating the Incarnation as a continuing fact which the Docetic Gnostics flatly denied. {*The deceiver and the antichrist*} This refers to one individual, not two. This one is *par excellence* in popular expectation (1 John 2:22), though many in reality (1 John 2:18; 3 John 7).

9. {*Whosoever goeth onward*} Lit. "to go on before," (Mark 11:9) here in a bad sense {*And abideth not in the teaching of Christ*} Not the teaching *about* Christ, but that of Christ which is the standard of Christian teaching as the walk of Christ is the standard for the Christian's walk (1 John 2:6). See John 7:16; 18:19. These Gnostics claimed to be the progressives, the advanced thinkers, and were anxious to relegate Christ to the past in their onward march. This struggle goes on always among those who approach the study of Christ. Is he a "landmark" merely or is he our goal and pattern? Progress we all desire, but progress toward Christ, not away from him. Reactionary obscurantists wish no progress toward Christ, but desire to stop and camp where they are. "True progress includes the past" (Westcott). Jesus Christ is still ahead of us all calling us to come on to him.

10. {*This teaching*} (cf. 2 John 9 and 7). {*Into your house*} John does not refer to entertaining strangers (Heb. 13:2; 1 Tim. 5:10), but to the deceiving propagandists who were carrying dissension and danger with them. {*Receive him not*} (cf. John 1:12; 6:21; 13:20) {*Give him no greeting*} This is usually greeting when first meeting (Acts 15:23; 23:26; Jas. 1:1), though it can be at the end of a meeting (2 Cor. 13:11). It can very well be understood of the peril of allowing these Gnostic propagandists to spread their pernicious teachings (cf. Mormons or Communists) in home and church (usually meeting in the home). This is assuming that the men were known and not mere strangers.

11. {*Partaketh in his evil works*} It is to be understood that the churches often met in private homes (Rom. 16:5; Col. 4:15), and if these traveling deceivers were allowed to spread their doctrines in these homes and then sent on with endorsement as Apollos was from Ephesus to Corinth (Acts 18:27), there was no way of escaping responsibility for the harm wrought by these propagandists of evil. It is not a case of mere hospitality to strangers.

12. {*With paper and ink*} The "paper" was a leaf of papyrus prepared for writing by cutting the pith into strips and pasting together (cf. Jer. 43:23); "ink" is an old adjective for black (Matt. 5:36; Rev. 6:5, 12). Apparently John wrote this little letter with his own hand. {*Face to face*} Lit. "Mouth to mouth," (cf. 1 Cor. 13:12; 3 John 14; and Num. 12:8).

THE THIRD EPISTLE OF JOHN

AUTHOR: John, the last of the apostles
RECIPIENT: Gaius, a dependable, loyal layman of the local church.
DATE: A.D. 85 to 90
FROM: Ephesus
OCCASION: The same Gnostic deceivers are at work as in the other Johannine Epistles.
THEME: Contrast between warm hospitality and arrogance

BY WAY OF INTRODUCTION

Addressed to Gaius (possibly from Pergamum, cf. Rev. 2:13), though which one we do not know. Paul is friend of three with this name (Acts 19:29; 20:4; 1 Cor. 1:14). It is possible that Second and Third Epistles of John are connected: here to a loyal man, the other to a loyal woman. Three persons are sharply sketched in Third John (Gaius, Diotrephes, Demetrius). Gaius is the dependable layman in the church, Diotrephes the dominating official, Demetrius the kindly messenger from Ephesus with the letter, a vivid picture of early church life and missionary work.

2. {*Thou mayest prosper*} This is an old verb lit. "prosperous in a journey, to have a good journey, to prosper," (1 Cor. 16:2; Rom. 1:10; cf. also LXX).

3. {*Bare witness*} Greek tense denotes repetition, from time to time.

6. {*Before the church*} Greek lack of article indicates a public meeting (cf. 1 Cor. 14:19, 35). {*Thou wilt do well*} This is a common polite phrase in letters (papyri) like our "please." (cf. Acts 10:33; Jas. 2:19; 1 Cor. 7:37; Phil. 4:14; 2 Pet. 1:19). {*Worthily of God*} (cf. 1 Thess. 2:12; Rom. 16:2; Phil. 1:27; Col. 1:10; Eph. 4:1). "Since they are God's representatives, treat them as you would God" (Holtzmann). From Homer's time, it was customary to speed the parting guest, sometimes accompanying him, sometimes providing money and food. Rabbis were so escorted and Paul alludes to the same gracious custom in Romans 15:24; Titus 3:13.

9. {*I wrote somewhat unto the church*} An allusion to a brief, introductory (unimportant?) letter of commendation (Acts 18:27; 2 Cor.

3:1; Col. 4:10) sent along with the brethren in 3 John 5 to 7 or to some other itinerant brethren. {*Diotrephes*} An ambitious leader and sympathizer with the Gnostics would probably prevent the letter referred to being read to the church. Hence he sends Gaius this personal letter warning against Diotrephes. {***Who loveth to have the preeminence among them***} This ambition to be first of Diotrephes does not prove that he was a bishop over elders, as was true in the second century. He may have been an elder (bishop) or deacon, but clearly desired to rule the whole church.

10. {*Prating against us*} Lit. "to babble," cf. 1 Timothy 5:13, to accuse idly and so falsely, here only in NT. {***Casteth them out of the church***} Lit. "casts out" (cf. out of temple or synagogue, John 2:15; 9:34).

11. {*Imitate not*} "Do not have the *habit* of imitating" (cf. 2 Thess. 3:7, 9; Heb. 13:7).

12. {*Yea we also*} This is a literary plural, referring to John himself.

13. {*With ink and pen*} "by means of black (ink) and reed" (used as pen, cf. 2 John 12). This was for papyrus and parchment, not a sharp stylus for wax tablets.

15. {*Peace to thee*} Cf. Latin *Pax tibi* like the Jewish greeting *shalom* (Luke 10:5; 24:36; John 20:19, 21). {*By name*} A common idiom in the papyri, as the good shepherd calls his sheep by name, so does John (John 10:3).

THE EPISTLE OF JUDE

AUTHOR: Possibly Judas, half brother of the Lord Jesus and brother of James (Matt. 13:55); some think it is the Apostle Judas (not Iscariot cf. John 14:22; Luke 6:16?), though it is most unlikely. Clement of Alexandria thinks that, like James, he deprecated being called the brother of the Lord Jesus as claiming too much authority. Judas has several referents in the NT.

RECIPIENT: Of this we know nothing at all. The readers were probably both Jewish and Gentile Christians.

DATE: A.D. 65 to 67, though it is merely a conjecture.

FROM: Jerusalem and Alexandria are urged as the place of composition, but of that we have no real information.

OCCASION: To warn against the Gnostics, as is true of 2 Peter and elsewhere in the NT.

THEME: Contending for the faith in difficult situations.

BY WAY OF INTRODUCTION

Beyond a doubt Jude and Second Peter are connected (cf. Jude 3-18 and 2 Pet. 2:1-18). The probability is that not much time elapsed between them, with Jude just before Second Peter. This is an option that is all so subjective that I have no desire to urge the point unduly.

Jude uses and even quotes apocryphal books. Jude (v. 14) quotes from "Enoch" by name and says that he "prophesied." What he quotes is a combination of various passages in the Book of Enoch as we have it now. Tertullian wanted to canonise Enoch because of what Jude says, whereas Chrysostom says that the authenticity of Jude was doubted because of the use of Enoch. "Prophesied" might be used here in Jude in a lesser sense. Jude (v. 9) also alludes to the "Assumption of Moses."

The style of Jude is terse and picturesque, with a fondness for triplets, often with a poetic ring. The use of the OT is very much like that in 2 Peter. Bigg remarks on the stern and unbending nature of the author, with no pathos and a harsh view of things and with frequent use of Pauline phraseology.

1. {*To them that are called*} or possibly translated "being called" (cf. 1 Pet. 1:1). {*Kept for Jesus Christ*} "Kept *by* Jesus Christ" is quite possibly an interpretation.

3. {*I was constrained*} "I had necessity" (cf. Luke 14:18; Heb. 7:27). {*To contend earnestly*} A strong word (cf. 1 Tim. 6:12). {*For the faith*} Here not in the original sense of trust, but rather of the thing believed (cf. Jude 20; Gal. 1:23; 3:23; Phil. 1:27).

4. {*Are crept in*} Compound literally "beside-in-to sink or plunge," so to slip in secretly as if by a side door, here only in NT. {*Set forth*} "to write of beforehand" (see also Gal. 3:1; Rom. 15:4). {*Ungodly men*} A key word in the (Jude 15 cf. 2 Pet. 2:5; 3:7). {*Turning*} "To change," (cf. Gal. 1:6). {*Our only Master and Lord*} Both titles refer to the one person, Jesus Christ (cf. 2 Pet. 1:1).

5. {*The Lord*} Usually this word is understood to mean the Lord Jesus Christ (cf. 1 Cor. 10:4, 9; Heb. 11:26 for references to Jesus in the OT). {*Afterward*} Lit. "the second time." {*Destroyed them that believed not*} This reference is to when all the people rescued from Egypt perished except Caleb and Joshua (Num. 14:27-37). This first example by Jude is not in 2 Peter, but is discussed in 1 Corinthians 10:5-11; Hebrews 3:18-4:2.

6. {*And angels*} The second example in Jude, the fallen angels. {*Kept not*} The tense has play on "he has kept" later in same verse. {*Principality*} Lit. "beginning, rule," i.e., the first place of power (cf. 1 Cor. 15:24; Rom. 8:38), which can refer to evil angels (Eph. 6:12; cf. Deut. 32:8). {*Their own proper habitation*} A dwelling-place [of spirit] used only here and 2 Corinthians 5:2. {*In everlasting bonds*} "In" can also be "by, with." {*Eternal*} used only here and Romans 1:20 (of God's power and deity).

7. {*Even as*} The third instance, cities of the plain, Sodom, Gomorah, also including Admah and Zeboiim (cf. Deut. 29:23; Hos. 11:8). Zoar, the other city, was spared. {*Having given themselves over to fornication*} That which is outside the moral law, this word is only here in NT, but in LXX (Gen. 38:24; Exod. 34:15). {*Strange flesh*} Horrible immorality of all kinds, including even unnatural uses (Rom. 1:27), called "sodomy" (cf. Gen. 19:4-11).

9. {*Contending with the devil*} Lit. "to separate, to strive with" (cf. Acts 11:2). {*Concerning the body of Moses*} Some refer this to Zechariah 3:1, others to a rabbinical comment on Deuteronomy 34:6. There is a similar reference to traditions in Acts 7:22; Galatians 3:19; Hebrews 2:2; 2 Timothy 3:8. But this explanation hardly meets the facts. {*A railing accusation*} Lit. "charge of blasphemy" (cf. 2 Pet. 2:11). {***The Lord rebuke thee***} These words occur in Zechariah 3:1-10 where the angel of the Lord replies to the charges of Satan. Some say this is an allusion to the *Assumption of Moses,* one of the apocryphal books.

11. {***In the way of Cain***} Cain is Jude's fourth example (cf. Heb. 11:4; 1 John 3:11; also Gen. 4:7). {***Ran riotously***} Lit. "they were poured out," vigorous metaphor for excessive indulgence; but it is used also of God's love for us (Rom. 5:5). {***In the error of Balaam***} The fifth example in Jude (cf. 2 Pet. 2:15). {***In the gainsaying of Korah***} The sixth example uniquely in Jude, the word "rebellion" is originally "answering back" (Heb. 6:16).

12. {***Hidden rocks***} Lit. "rocks in the sea (covered by the water)." For disorder at the Lord's Supper (and love-feasts?) see 1 Corinthians 11:17-34. The Gnostics made it worse, so that the love-feasts were discontinued. {***Clouds without water***} This is a powerful picture of disappointed hopes (cf. also 2 Pet. 1:8). {***Twice dead***} That is fruitless (once dead) and having died (twice dead).

13. {***Wandering stars***} Lit. "Stars wanderers." Some refer this to comets or shooting stars. See Isa. 14:12 for an allusion to Babylon as the day-star who fell through pride.

14. {***Enoch the seventh from Adam***} The genealogical order occurs in Genesis 5:4-20, with Enoch as seventh. He is so termed in Enoch 60:8; 93:3. {***Prophesied***} If the word is given its ordinary meaning as in 1 Peter 1:10, then Jude terms the Book of Enoch an inspired book.

15. {***Hard things***} Harsh, rough things as in John 6:60.

16. {***Showing respect of persons***} "to admire, to wonder at" a Hebraism (in Lev. 19:15; Job 13:10; cf. also Matt. 22:16; Luke 20:21; Jas. 2:9). {***For the sake of advantage***} See also Jude 11. The covetousness of these Gnostic leaders is plainly shown in 2 Peter 2:3, 14.

19. {***They who make separations***} Lit. "boundary, to make a horizon," rare word, in Aristotle for making logical distinctions (cf. Lev. 20:24, also Matt. 25:32). {***Sensual***} That which is opposed to spiritual (cf. 1 Cor. 2:14; 15:44; Jas. 3:15). {***Having not the Spirit***} Probably refers to the Holy Spirit, as is plain in verse 20. Cf. Romans 8:9.

20. {***Building up***} Used as a metaphor of building a house, common in Paul (1 Cor. 3:9-17; Col. 2:7; Eph. 2:20). {***On your most holy faith***}

For the spiritual temple see also 1 Peter 2:3-5, "most holy" a true superlative.

21. {*Keep yourselves*} A sense of urgency here in the grammar and the context (cf. v. 1, 5; see also Jas. 1:27).

23. {*Snatching them out of the fire*} (*ek puros harpazontes*) Quotation from Amos 4:11 and Zechariah 3:3. cf. Psalm 106:18.

24. {*From stumbling*} Used in Xenophon—of sure-footed as of a horse that does not stumble, and so of a good man (Jas. 3:2; 2 Pet. 1:10). {*Before the presence of his glory*} Its form suggests a presence "right down before the eye" of his glory (cf. Eph. 1:4).

25. {*To the only God our Savior*} (cf. Rom. 16:27). "Savior" is used of God eight times in the NT, six of them in the Pastoral Epistles. Doxa (glory) to God or Christ in all the doxologies except 1 Timothy 6:16.

THE REVELATION OF JOHN

AUTHOR: Apostle John
RECIPIENTS: Seven churches in Asia (Rev. 1:4), with a special message to each
DATE: About A.D. 95
FROM: Patmos, a small island for exiles
OCCASION: Christians (and Jews) were being persecuted by the Roman government because they would not worship the emperor (many of which were unstable at best) as another god. Christians were often blamed unfairly and slandered for Roman troubles, and so were persecuted severely.
THEME: Christ cares and watches constantly the suffering saints; there is doom to his enemies, and final triumph and bliss for the faithful.

BY WAY OF INTRODUCTION

Perhaps no single book in the NT presents so many and so formidable problems as the Apocalypse of John. These difficulties concern the authorship, the date, the apocalyptic method, the relation to the other Johannine books, the purpose, the historical environment, the reception of the book in the NT canon, the use and misuse of the book through the ages, etc. In the eastern churches the recognition of the Apocalypse of John was slower than in the west.

Some early in the Church rejected the book. Others accepted it but attributed the authorship to others than the Apostle John. But finally the book was accepted in the east as the book of Hebrews was in the west after a period of doubt.

The Greek text of the Revelation is not as well attested as other parts of the NT. It may be characterized as "poor" on that basis of comparison. The result of this poor state is that the versions are of special importance for the text of the book. In no single or group of manuscripts do we have a fairly accurate text, though a few are better than others.

Apocalypse is a prophecy of a special type; it is an unveiling. Here it is the revelation of Jesus Christ. Revelation is similar in style to Ezekiel, Zechariah, and Daniel in the OT. One reason for this style of writing is severe persecution and the desire to deliver a message in symbolic form, and to cheer the persecuted. In this case, the context was likely persecution that was motivated by emperor worship in Rome.

Historically, there were two persecuting emperors who were mainly responsible for many martyrs for Christ: Nero and Domitian. But emperor worship began before Nero. For the most part the emperors were tolerant of Christians, save the two mentioned above. An emperor was titled *Dominus ac Deus noster* (Our Lord and God), certainly at odds with Christian titles for Jesus Christ and God the Father. The worship of the emperor did not disturb the worshippers of other gods except the Jews and the Christians, and in particular the Christians were persecuted after the (false) accusation of the burning of Rome, when they were distinguished from the Jews. After Nero it was a crime to be a Christian (cf. 2 Thess. 2:3ff.; also 1 John 2:18, 22; 4:3; 2 John 7).

Though highly disputed by some sources, this John (Rev. 1:1) is likely the Apostle John (not one commonly called Presbyter John), also the author of the Fourth Gospel and the three Epistles bearing his name (Rev. 1:1, 4, 9; 22:8). The rule with apocalypses is to give fictitious names, and so this identification would be an exception (as with the Shepherd of Hermas). A respectable number of modern scholars still hold to the ancient view that the Apocalypse of John is the work of the Apostle and Beloved Disciple, the son of Zebedee.

Though notable, the differences in the Greek grammar, vocabularies, and styles of the Epistles, Gospel, and Revelation are often explained by good, reasonable, and historical arguments; and so the assertion of the same author of all the books stands. For example, John the Apostle was termed one of two "unlettered and unofficial men" (Acts 4:13). Therefore the Fourth Gospel underwent careful scrutiny and possibly by the elders in Ephesus (John 21:24), and so had a different style. On the other hand, if John wrote the Apocalypse while in Patmos and so away from Ephesus, it seems quite possible that here we have John's own style more than in the Gospel and Epistles, different and "uncorrected" from the view of the elders of Ephesus (or others). Maybe the level of excitement of the vision made John revert to an old style. And in favor of both being the same author, there are numerous coincidences in vocabulary and style between the Fourth Gospel and the Apocalypse.

Again, though disputed, the entire Revelation is a unity; and not a series of Jewish and Christian apocalypses pieced together in a more or less bungling fashion. Many of the Jewish apocalypses do show composite authorship, but this is not so here. There are no differences in language (vocabulary or grammar) that argue for varied sources. The essential unity of the book has stood the test of the keenest criticism. Most ancient writers agree John lived to an old age, to at least A.D. 98. This long life makes possible two chief theories for the date of the Revelation: (1) soon after Nero's death (after A.D. 68); (2) in the reign of Domitian (reigned A.D. 81-96). Both dates are supported by modern and ancient scholars. A date in the reign of Domitian is best supported overall (and not much later than the Fourth Gospel), with possibly allusions to Nero and some of the revival myths surrounding him, and events from his time.

He likely wrote down the visions, with some reflection, before he left the exile from Patmos to Ephesus. There is a note of sustained excitement all through the book, combined with high literary skill in the structure of the book in spite of the numerous grammatical lapses.

Though not likely a chronological panorama, the series of sevens bear a relation to one another, like a kaleidoscope. There is progress and power in the arrangement and the total effect.

There is constant use of OT language and imagery, almost a mosaic, but without a single formal quotation. There is constant repetition of words and phrases in true Johannine style. In fact there is genuine artistic skill in the structure of the book, in spite of the deflections from ordinary linguistic standards. In the visions and all through the book there is constant use of symbols, as is the fashion in apocalypses like the beasts, the scorpions, the horses, etc. These symbols probably were understood by the first readers of the book, *though the key to them is lost to us.* Even the numbers in the book (3½, 7, 3, 4, 12, 24, 1000) cannot be pressed, though some do so.

There are literally many theories of interpretation. Something can be said for each view but none satisfies the whole picture by any means. Here are just a few. (1) The events of the Revelation are continuous (one after another), charting history to its end. Often in this view specific identifications of person and events in history are made. (2) The events of the Revelation are synchronous (many events occurring parallel or at the same time) charting history to its end. (3) The events of the Revelation are preterist (the events are taken as historical, as all over and done, either in the era of Nero or Domitian). Roman Catholic scholars have been fond of the preterist view, often for theological anti-Protestant reasons. (4) The events of the Revelation are futurist, which keeps the fulfillment all in the future and which can be neither proved nor disproved. (5) There is also the purely spiritual theory which finds no historical allusion anywhere. Some take the millennium literally as a thousand years (with variations within that frame). Others take it as a symbol, with doubt about any numerical value (cf. 2 Pet. 3:8).

There seems abundant evidence to believe that this apocalypse, written during the stress and storm of Domitian's persecution, was intended to cheer the persecuted Christians with a view of certain victory at last, but with no scheme of history in view. So considered, this vision of the Reigning Christ in heaven with a constant eye on the suffering saints and martyrs is a guarantee of certain triumph in heaven and ultimate triumph on earth. The picture of Christ in heaven is a glorious one. He is the Lamb that was slain, the Lion of the tribe of Judah, the Word of God, the Victor over his enemies, worshipped in heaven like the Father, the Light and Life of men. Instead of trying to fit the various symbols on particular individuals, one will do better to see the same application to times of persecution from time to time through the ages.

All Scripture is God's true word, but undoubtedly one should bear in mind that apocalyptic symbolism has its own methods and laws of interpretation, and by these the student must be guided (cf. Rev. 19:9). The same Christ who was the Captain of salvation in the time of Domitian is the Pioneer and Perfecter of our faith today. The Apocalypse of John gives glimpses of heaven as well as of hell. Hope is the word that it brings to God's people at all times.

The seven churches that were written to had a message suited to the peculiar needs of each church and with a direct reference to the geography and history of each church and city. There were other churches in the Province of Asia besides these seven, but these form a circle from Ephesus where John had lived and wrought. They do present a variety of churches, not necessarily all types, and by no means a chart of seven dispensations of Christian history.

CHAPTER 1

1. {*The Revelation*} (cf. Luke 2:32; 2 Thess. 1:7). This the Greek word *apokalupsis,* from *apokaluptô,* to uncover, to unveil: used for insight into truth (cf. Eph. 1:17); or for the revelation of God or Christ at the second coming of Christ (2 Thess. 1:7; 1 Pet. 1:7). {*Of Jesus Christ*} The Greek syntax translates, "[a revelation] about Jesus Christ."

2. {*The testimony of Jesus Christ*} That is, "to the testimony by Jesus Christ."

4. {*From him which is...was...is to come*} "Who is" is purposely constructed in the Greek to call attention to the eternity and unchangeableness of God (cf. of God, Exod. 3:14). The entire phrase reminds one of a phrase also in pagan Greek religion, "Zeus was, Zeus is, Zeus will be."

5. {*Who is the faithful witness*} Lit. "The witness the faithful." Jesus here is the witness (*martus*) who is faithful in relationship to this book (cf. Rev. 1:1 and 22:16), not to the witness of Jesus before Pilate (1 Tim. 6:13). {*Unto him that loveth us...loosed*} Greek tense shows he loosed us once for all, but loves us always.

8. {*The Lord God*} Lit. "The Lord the God." (cf. Ezek. 6:3, 11; 7:2 and Rev. 4:8; 11:17; 15:3; 16:7; 19:6; 21:22). {*The Almighty*} This is the Greek word *pantokratôr,* made from *pas* [all] and *krateô* [power, might] (cf. 2 Cor. 6:18 [from Jer. 38:35] and Rev. 1:8; 4:8; 11:17; 15:3; 16:7, 14; 19:6, 15; 21:22).

13. {*One like unto a son of man*} Not Christ "*the* Son of man" but is like "a son of man," but not a man. {*At the breasts*} This is the Greek word *mastos,* here referring to the nipples of a man. High girding like this was a mark of dignity as of the high priest.

16. {*A sharp two-edged sword*} This is the long sword (not a defensive dagger like sword) (cf. Luke 2:35; Rev. 1:16; 2:12; Heb. 4:12).

CHAPTER 2

2. {*I know*} This is the Greek verb *oida,* not *ginôskô,* and so "emphasizes better the absolute clearness of mental vision which photographs all the facts of life as they pass" (Swete) (cf. also Rev. 2:9, 13, 19; 3:1, 8, 15). {*Works and thy toil and patience*} This is endurance in hard toil.

{*And didst try*} This is the Greek verb *peirazô*, to test, a reference to a recent crisis when these Nicolaitans (v. 6) were condemned.

5. {*And repent...and do*} The Greek word and syntax is an urgent appeal for instant change of attitude and conduct before it is too late. Do it at once!

7. {*To him that overcometh*} This is the Greek verb *nikaô*, to have victory, overcome. It is a common Johannine verb (cf. John 16:33; 1 John 2:13; 4:4; 5:4; Rev. 2:7, 11, 17, 26; 3:5, 12, 21; 5:5; 12:11; 15:2; 17:14; 21:7).

9. {*Thy tribulation and thy poverty*} Greek syntax emphasizes each of the two items. Persecution was their affliction, which helped to intensify the poverty of the Christians (Jas. 2:5; 1 Cor. 1:26; 2 Cor. 6:10; 8:2). In contrast with the wealthy church in Laodicea (Rev. 3:17).

10. {*Be thou faithful*} Lit. "*Keep on* becoming faithful" (cf. Heb. 12:4), as the martyrs have done (Jesus most of all).

17. {*A white stone...a new name written*} "Stone" is the Greek word *psêphos,* pebble, from *psaô,* to rub. Though with many uses, in context the white stone may mean an amulet or charm, referring as a figure of speech to the Christian person. The name written upon this "white stone" is not the person's own name, but that of Christ (cf. Rev. 3:12). The person then may be the "white stone" on which the new name is written.

22. {*I do cast*} Lit. "I do cast" the Greek tense makes judgment imminent. {*Into a bed*} Lit. "into bed" with the meaning of "a bed of sickness in contrast with the bed of adultery" (Beckwith).

23. {*Searcheth the hearts and reins*} (cf. Jer. 17:10). "Reins" lit. is "kidneys" but in the same area of meaning as the "heart" in context, hence the translation "mind."

25. {*Hold fast...till I come*} "Hold on" is a command with an aspect of the event as being "holding" as a point in time. Either the meaning is "get a grip on..." or "hold on" (as a single decisive effort).

27. {*He shall rule with a rod of iron*} (cf. Ps. 2:8). Lit. "I will shepherd them with a rod of iron" (cf. Rev. 7:17; 12:5; 19:15). This "rod" here is a royal scepter and indicates rigorous rule.

28. {*The morning star*} Lit. "The star the morning one." In Revelation 22:16 Christ is the bright morning star. The victor will have Christ himself.

CHAPTER 3

2. {*Be thou watchful; stablish the things that remain*} Lit. "keep on becoming watchful, make stable remaining things." Note that he does not say "Arise from the dead" (Eph. 5:14), for there are vestiges of life. Those still alive are addressed through the angel of the church. They are not actually dead, but in grave peril (cf. Titus 1:5). {*For I have found no works of thine*} Lit. "For I have not found any works of yours fulfilled." The church's works as a whole have not measured up to God's standard.

3. {*Remember*} (cf. Rev. 2:5). {*If therefore thou shalt not watch, I will come as a thief*} The Greek condition shows it is a plausible case that they will not wake up and keep watch.

4. {*A few names*} Lit. "few names," but meaning persons in this context (cf. Acts 1:15; Rev. 11:13). {*Did not defile*} This is the Greek verb *molunô*, pollution or defilement (cf. 1 Cor. 8:7; 1 Pet. 1:4). {*They are worthy*} This is a relative sense of "worth" not in an absolute God and Christ (Rev. 4:11; 5:9)

7. {*The holy, he that is true*} Lit. "the holy, the genuine." It is a recognized title of the Messiah as the consecrated one set apart (cf. God, Rev. 4:8 6:10, to Christ, Mark 1:24; Luke 4:34; John 6:69; Acts 4:27, 30; 1 John 2:20).

8. {*I have set*} Lit. "I have given," a gift of Christ, this open door.

10. {*Patience*} This is "perseverance" (cf. Rev. 13:10; 14:12; also 2 Thess. 3:5).

14. {*The beginning of the creation of God*} "Ruler" can be translated "beginning" but the sense is not that he is *the first* of created things (as in a series) as the Arians held and Unitarians do now; but the beginning in the sense of being the *originating source* of creation through whom God works (Col. 1:15, 18, a passage probably known to the Laodiceans, John 1:3; Heb. 1:2, as is made clear by Rev. 1:18; 2:8; 3:21; 5:13).

17. {*I am rich...have gotten riches*} Laodicea was a wealthy city and the church "carried the pride of wealth into its spiritual life" (Swete). This church has only imagined spiritual riches which in reality the church did not possess. This was just the opposite of church in Smyrna (poor in wealth, rich in grace). This church was in a rich city and was rich in pride and conceit, but poor in grace and ignorant of its spiritual poverty. {*Miserable*} They were actually pitiable (cf. 1 Cor. 15:19) in their extreme (naked) spiritual poverty (cf. Rev. 2:9). Perhaps there was some local example of self-complacency is in mind. {*Blind*} (cf. salve, Rev. 3:18). The remedies to these pitiful conditions are found in the next verse.

18. {*That thou mayest clothe thyself...eye salve*} Here are the remedies to verse 17. "Salve" is the Greek word *kollourion,* a form of *kollura* (coarse bread of cylindrical shape), object of *agorasai,* a name for a famous Phrygian powder for the eyes made in Laodicea, Latin *collyrium* (used for eye salve by Horace and Juvenal). It was applied by rubbing in the eyes.

19. {*As many as I love...*} (cf. Prov. 3:12 [in Heb. 12:6]). {*Be zealous...repent*} The Greek tenses here are a graphic picture of these commands, "*keep on* being zealous; and *begin* to repent." Note the earnestness is like a burning hot zeal in contrast to the lukewarm of verse 16.

CHAPTER 4

1. {*Speaking...saying*} "Speaking" is grammatically different than "saying" but this is because the first relates to the feminine "trumpet" and the second relates to the sense of who is talking, and so is grammatically masculine (the one sitting).

2. {*Straightway I was in the Spirit*} But John had already "come to be in the Spirit" (Rev. 1:10, the very same phrase). The first time the Greek tense may show the "entrance" into the Spirit "I came to be in the Spirit"; and here the Greek tense shows sequel or result "At once I found myself in the Spirit."

5. {*Seven lamps of fire*} (cf. Ezek. 1:13; Zech. 4:12). Here this means "torch" (cf. Rev. 8:10), and is identified with the Holy Spirit (the Seven Spirits of God) as in Revelation 1:4; 3:1.

6. {*As it were a glassy sea*} Old adjective (from *hualos,* glass, 21:18, 21), in the NT only here and 15:2. Possibly from *heui* (it rains), like a raindrop. This is its appearance, not the material.

7. {*Like a lion...calf...man...flying eagle*} Again differing in appearance from Ezekiel's vision (cf. Ezek. 1:6, 10). "The four forms represent whatever is noblest, strongest, wisest, and swiftest in nature;" the likeness in each instance extended only to the face (Swete). But it is not

necessary to try to find a symbolism in each face here like the early baseless identification with the Four Evangelists (the lion for Mark, the man for Matthew, the calf for Luke, the eagle for John).

8. {*Six wings*} (cf. Isa. 6:2, but not like Ezek. 1:6). {*Round about and within*} Lit. "and within" but meaning "under the wings."

9-10. {*When the living creatures shall give...shall fall down*} The Greek syntax has the notion of repetition "whenever."

11. {*Our Lord and our God*} (cf. John 20:28). {*Thou didst create*} The Greek tense shows this as a point in time, as a summary picture of the whole (not as a process) [cf. Col. 1:16].

CHAPTER 5

1. {*In the right hand*} Lit. "upon the right hand," that is, the open palm (cf. Ezek. 2:9).

4. {*I wept much*} Lit. "I *kept on* weeping much" (Rev. 1:12; 2:14; 5:4, 14; 6:8, 9; 10:10; 19:14; 21:15).

6. {*A Lamb*} Standing either close to the throne or in the space between the throne and the elders, this is Christ (John 1:29, 36; Acts 8:32; 1 Pet. 1:19, like Isa. 53:7). In Revelation, "lamb" occurs for the Crucified Christ 29 times in twelve chapters. {*As though it had been slain*} "as if" is used because the Lamb is now alive, but (in appearance) with the marks of the sacrifice. The Christ as the Lamb is both sacrifice and Priest (Heb. 9:12; 10:11). {*Seven horns...seven eyes...seven spirits*} Seven horns is a common symbol in the O.T. for strength and kingly power (1 Sam. 2:10; 1 Kgs. 22:11; Ps. 112:9; Dan. 7:7, 20) and often in Revelation (Rev. 12:3; 13:1; 17:3, 12). Fullness of power (the All-powerful one) is symbolized by seven. Seven eyes (cf. Zech. 3:9; 4:10) denotes omniscience. Here they are identified with the seven Spirits of Christ, which is also the Holy Spirit (cf. Rev. 1:4). The Holy Spirit is both Spirit of God and of Christ (Rom. 8:9).

9. {*They sing*} This means to chant with lyrical emotion (Col. 3:16). {*A new song*} (cf. Col. 3:16; Eph. 5:19). It is a *fresh* song for new mercies (Isa. 42:10; Ps. 33:3; 40:3, etc.), here in praise of redemption to Christ (Rev. 14:3) like the new name (cf. Rev. 2:17; 3:12), the new Jerusalem (cf. Rev. 3:12; 21:2), the new heaven and the new earth (cf. Rev. 21:1), not the old song of creation (cf. Rev. 4:8, 11) to God. {*Didst purchase unto God...men*} That is, purchased from sin by Christ (cf.

1 Cor. 6:20; 7:23; Gal. 3:13; 4:5; 2 Pet. 2:1; cf. 1 Pet. 1:18). {**With thy blood**} The blood of Christ as the price of our redemption runs all through the Apocalypse. This is the reason why Christ is worthy to "take the book and open its seals." That is, he is worthy to receive adoration and worship (cf. Rev. 4:11) as the Father does. {**Men of every...**} All these are grouping of words for all mankind, representatives of all races and nations (cf. Rev. 7:9; 13:7; 14:6).

11. {**And I saw**} Now enters a new element to the throne and inner circle, an outer and vaster circle of angels who enter the refrain of the new song of redemption in antiphonal singing, answering the song of the four living creatures and the twenty-four elders. All efforts at numbering this group ultimately fail, they are countless myriads, innumerable hosts of the angels (cf. I Enoch 40:1. See Dan. 7:10).

14. {**Amen**} The four living creatures give their approval to the doxology *after* the antiphonal songs. Now is a reverent silence. {**Fell down and worshipped**} In silent adoration that closes the whole service of praise to the One upon the throne and to the Lamb. The representatives of the redeemed bow in silent worship (cf. Rev. 4:10). Just as God is worshipped, so Christ is here worshipped by the universe (Phil. 2:10ff.).

CHAPTER 6

4. {**A great sword**} Not a dagger, this is a long sword in battle. (cf. Rev. 1:16; 2:12, 16; 6:8; 19:15, 21).

6. {**Of wheat...for a penny...of barley...**} These are normal prices. This proclamation forbids famine prices for food (solid and liquid). The prohibition is addressed to the nameless rider who represents Famine and Lack. Wheat and barley, oil and the vine, were the staple foods in Palestine and Asia Minor. Actually, the Greek measure here is less than a quart with us. This was enough wheat to keep a man of moderate appetite alive for a day. {**Of barley**} Barley was the food of the poor and it was cheaper even in the famine and it took more of it to support life. Here the proportion is three to one (cf. 2 Kgs. 7:18).

8. {**A pale horse**} (cf. Zech. 6:3). This is a greenish-yellow color, yet when referring to a normal horse color, it is a sorrel horse or light bright chestnut coloring (not a green horse). It may be a color in the vision of a surreal horse pale as in the ashen color of a face blanched by fear (pallid) and so the pale horse is a symbol of death and terror. {**His**

name was Death} Unlike the other three riders, Death is named as this fourth rider (so personified) and there is with Death his inseparable comrade, Hades (cf. Rev. 1:16; 20:13). Hades, the unseen place, the abode of the dead, the keys of which Christ holds (Rev. 1:18). {*Over the fourth part of the earth*} Wider authority was given to this rider than to the others, though what part of the earth is included in the fourth part is not indicated. The four scourges of Ezekiel 14:21 are here reproduced: sword, famine, plague, beasts.

9. {*Under the altar...of the slain*} (cf. Rev. 8:3, 5; 9:13; 11:1; 14:18; 16:7). The blood of the sacrifices was poured at the bottom of the altar, hence "under" (Lev. 4:7). The altar of sacrifice (Exod. 39:39; 40:29), not of incense. The Lamb was slain (Rev. 5:6, 9, 12) and these martyrs have followed the example of their Lord. Christians were slain during the Neronian persecution and now again under Domitian. A long line of martyrs has followed (cf. Rev. 5:6). {*For the word of God*} (cf. Rev. 1:9). This is the confession of loyalty to Christ as opposed to emperor worship.

10. {*O Master*} This is the Greek title *despotês*. In context here, it is addressing God (cf. Luke 2:29; Acts 4:24), but elsewhere to Christ (cf. Jude 4; 2 Pet. 2:1).

12. {*There was a great earthquake*} (cf. Rev. 8:5; 11:13, 19; 16:18). Jesus spoke of earthquakes (cf. Mark 13:8, also Matt. 24:29). The reference here is not to some local earthquake like those so common in Asia Minor. {*As sackcloth of hair*} (cf. Isa. 50:3). This is a coarse garment of black hair clinging to one like a sack; used by mourners, suppliants, prophets leading austere lives (Matt. 3:4; 11:21; Luke 10:13). A celestial phenomena following earthquakes, this is something like an eclipse of the sun (cf. Joel 2:10; Ezek. 32:7; Isa. 13:10; Mark 13:24). {*As blood*} (cf. Acts 2:20). Peter interpreting the apocalyptic eschatological language of Joel 2:31, is pointing to the events of the day of Pentecost as also the great day of the Lord. Peter's interpretation of Joel should make us cautious about too literal an exegesis of these grand symbols.

13. {*Her unripe figs*} The base meaning is figs that grow in winter and fall off in the spring without getting ripe (Song 2:11). Here is a figure for a sign of the end of the world's long winter (cf. Isa. 34:4; Nah. 3:12).

14. {*When she is shaken of a great wind*} Here is a vivid picture of the expanse of the sky rolled up and away as a papyrus roll (Luke 4:17). {*Was removed...as a scroll when it is rolled up*} (cf. Rev. 16:20). It is a picture for violent displacements in the earth's crust (cf. Nah. 1:5; Jer. 4:24).

15. {*The kings...princes...chief captains...rich...strong*} Five classes (plurals) all the powerful, strong, self-satisfied, and complacent of the earth who normally scoff will be terror-stricken and hide. {*Every bond-man and freeman*} The last two show the two extremes of society (note the singulars). These are unbelievers all.

16. {*They say...fall on us*} The Greek tense has a sense of urgency, "Fall *now!*...hide us *now!*" "What sinners dread most is not death, but the revealed Presence of God"(Swete) (cf. Gen. 3:8).

CHAPTER 7

1. {*Four angels...that no wind should blow*} The four winds (cf. Matt. 24:31) are held prisoner by angels at each of the four corners. Some Jews held the winds from due north, south, east, west to be favorable, while those from the angles (see Acts 27:14) were unfavorable. There is an angel of the fire (cf. Rev. 14:18) and an angel of the waters (cf. Rev. 16:5).

2. {*The seal of the living God*} This seal means the signet ring, like that used by an Oriental monarch, to give validity to the official documents.

3. {*Till we shall have sealed...upon their foreheads*} (cf. Ezek. 9:4). "Forehead" is the space above or between the eyes (cf. Rev. 7:3; 9:4; 13:16; 14:1, 9; 17:5; 20:4; 22:4).

4-8. {*A hundred and forty and four thousand*} He did not see the sealing or count them himself, but only heard. This is a symbolical number connoting perfection. It is not to be taken literally. {*Out of every tribe of the children of Israel*} There are two views here. One view is that this number is referring *only to Jews* (by race, whether as a remnant of Judaism or just Jewish Christians). The other view is it refers to Gentiles as well as Jewish Christians (the true Israel, Rev. 2:9; 3:9 and like Paul in Galatians and Romans). The latter view is more probable. The list is not geographical, since Levi is included, but Dan is omitted and Manasseh put in his place, though he as the son of Joseph is included in Joseph. There are various lists of the tribes in the OT (Gen. 35:22; 46:8; Exod. 1:1; Num. 1:2; 13:4; 26:34; Deut. 27:11; 33:6; Josh. 13-22; Judg. 5; 1 Chr. 2-8; 12:24; 27:16; Ezek. 48) and given in various orders. In 1 Chronicles 7:12 both Dan and Zebulun are omitted. Joseph is given here in place of Ephraim. The distribution is equal (12,000) to each tribe.

14. {*My lord...thou knowest*} After a question from one of the elders of the vision, John gives "an address of reverence to a heavenly being" (Vincent), not an act of worship on John's part. {*They which come out of the great tribulation*} In the vision, "the martyrs are still arriving from the scene of the great tribulation" (Charles). Apparently some great crisis is contemplated (Matt 13:19; 24:21; Mark 13:10), though the whole series may be in mind and so may anticipate final judgment. {*And they washed...made them white*} (cf. Gen. 49:11 and Exod. 19:10, 14). For the cleansing power of Christ's blood see also Romans 3:25; 5:9; Colossians 1:20; Ephesians 1:7; 1 Peter 1:2; Hebrews 9:14; 1 John 1:7 Revelations 1:5; 5:9; 22:14. They were cleansed at a point in time, looking back when on the earth. {*In the blood of the Lamb*} There is power alone in the blood of Christ to cleanse from sin (1 John 1:7), not in the blood of the martyrs themselves. The result is white, not red, as one might imagine.

CHAPTER 8

1. {*There followed a silence about the space of half an hour*} Lit. "There came silence." There is a dramatic effect by this profound stillness with no elder or angel speaking, no chorus of praise nor cry of adoration, no thunder from the throne, but a temporary cessation in the revelations (cf. Rev. 10:4).

2. {*The seven angels...seven trumpets*} "The" in the Greek seems to point to seven well-known angels. In Enoch 20:7 the names of seven archangels are given (Uriel, Raphael, Raguel, Michael, Sariel, Gabriel, Remiel) and "angels of the Presence" is an idea like that in Isaiah 63:9. We do not know precisely what is John's idea here.

3. {*Much incense*} "Incense" actually means here the live coals on which the incense falls, thus burning the incense into smoke.

11. {*Wormwood*} When not a proper name, this is grammatically feminine, a species of bitter plant which grows in the land of Israel and Palestine. Here the name is grammatically masculine, in agreement with "star." The "star" made some of the water poisoned (lit. bitter).

13. {*An eagle*} Lit. "One eagle," with the numeral "one" as an indefinite article (cf. Rev. 9:13; 18:21; 19:17). See Revelation 4:7 also for the flying eagle, the strongest of birds, sometimes a symbol of vengeance (cf. Deut. 28:49; Hos. 8:1; Hab. 1:8).

CHAPTER 9

1. {*Of the pit of the abyss*} This is the Greek word *abussos,* from an *alpha* privative [not] *bussos* [depth], hence place *without depth,* the bottomless place. It occurs in Romans 10:7 for the common receptacle of the dead for Hades (Sheol), but in Luke 8:31 a lower depth is sounded, (Swete) for the abode of demons, and in this sense it occurs in Revelation 9:1, 2, 11; 11:7; 17:8; 20:1, 3.

3. {*Locusts*} (cf. v. 7 and Matt. 3:4; Mark 1:6.) The Israelites were permitted to eat them, but when the swarms came like the eighth Egyptian plague (Exod. 10:13ff.) they devoured every green thing. The smoke was worse than the fallen star and the locusts that came out of the smoke were worse still, a swarm of hellish locusts. {*The scorpions*} Old name for a little animal somewhat like a lobster that lurks in stone walls in warm regions, with a venomous sting in its tail (cf. Luke 10:19; 11:12; Rev. 9:3, 5, 10). The scorpion ranks with the snake as hostile to man.

7. {*The shapes...unto horses*} This imagery of warhorses is like that in Joel 2:4. The likeness of a locust to a horse, especially to a horse equipped with armor, is so striking that the insect is named in German *Heupferd* (hay horse), and in Italian *cavalett* a little horse. {*As it were crowns*} These are not actual crowns, but what looked like crowns of gold, as conquerors, as indeed they were (cf. Rev. 4:4; 6:2; 12:1; 14:14). These locusts of the abyss have another peculiar feature, human-looking faces. It had this face on these demonic locusts to give added terror, also "suggesting the intelligence and capacity of man" (Swete).

10. {*Tails*} (cf. Rev. 9:10, 19; 12:4). {*Like unto scorpions...stings*} "Sting" is the Greek word *kentra,* from *kentrew,* to prick, to sting (cf. Paul, Acts 26:14 and death, 1 Cor. 15:55). It is used of the spur of a rooster, the quill of the porcupine, and the stings of insects (Vincent). It was the goad used for oxen (Prov. 26:3; Acts. 26:14).

11. {*Abaddon...Apollyon*} This is Hebrew and Greek respectively for "Destroyer" as a symbolic name of the creature. Does this refer to Death or Satan?

15. {*Which had been prepared*} The Greek tense shows they are in a state of readiness prepared by God (cf. Rev. 12:6; 16:12; Matt. 25:34).

17. {*Breastplates as of fire and of hyacinth and of brimstone*} This probably is referring to the riders rather than to the horses. The breastplates and their intense, deep colors are descriptions which are only metaphors. Both rider and war horse are terrible, fearful creatures.

18. {*By these three plagues*} (cf. Exod. 11:1 also Rev. 9:20; 11:6; 15:1, 6, 8; 16:9; 18:4, 8; 22:18). The three plagues refer to fire, smoke, and brimstone which proceed from the mouths of the horses (v. 17).

20. {*Repented not*} The two-thirds of mankind still spared did not change their creed or their conduct (repent). {*Of the works*} This refers to idolatries, as the next verse shows. {*Devils*} (cf. O.T., Deut. 32:17; Ps. 96:5; 106:37 and N.T. 1 Cor. 10:21). The worship of idols is called the worship of unclean spirits. The idols here represented demons (cf. Dan. 5:23). {*Idols*} The helplessness of these idols is often seen in the O.T. (cf. Ps. 113:1, 2; Ps. 115:4).

CHAPTER 10

1. {*Another strong angel*} But note that the seventh trumpet does not sound until Revelation 11:15. This angel is not one of the seven or of the four, but like the other strong angel in Revelation 5:2; 18:21 or the other angel in Revelation 14:6, 15. The opening of the seventh seal was preceded by two visions (chapter Rev. 7:1ff.) and so here the sounding of the seventh trumpet (Rev. 11:15) is preceded by a new series of visions (Rev. 10:1 to 11:14). {*Arrayed with a cloud*} The language of the verse suggests Christ (cf. sun, pillar of fire Rev. 1:15-16). Also, Christ will come on the clouds (Rev. 1:7) as he ascended on a cloud (Acts 1:9). Is this "angel" Christ? Likely it is not (cf. v. 6). God's chariot is in the clouds (Ps. 104:3), but this angel is a special messenger of God. All of this is still no proof that this angel is Christ.

4. {*I was about to write*} Greek tense translates, "I was on the point of beginning to write" (cf. Rev. 1:11, 19). {*Seal up*} The Greek tense of this command means "seal up at once." The content of the utterances is not known (cf. 2 Cor. 12:4).

7. {*According to the good tidings which he declared*} Lit. "As he gospelized to...prophets." It was the OT prophets who hoped for a cleaning up of all mysteries in the last days (cf. Amos 3:7; Jer. 7:25; 25:4).

8. {*Again speaking and saying*} This is the voice mentioned in Revelation 10:4.

9. {*Take it and eat it up*} Lit. "eat it down." (cf. Ezek. 3:1-3; Jer. 15:6). The book was already open and was not to be read aloud, but to be digested mentally by John.

10. {*I took—and ate it up*} The order of the results is here changed to the actual experience (sweet in the mouth, bitter in the belly).

11. {*They say*} Lit. "then, they say to me." The plural may show it is an indefinite statement (cf. Rev. 13:16; 16:15). It is possible that the allusion is to the heavenly voice (Rev. 10:4, 8) and to the angel (Rev. 10:9), and so the plural is an actual plural.

CHAPTER 11

1. {*A reed*} Such reed plants grew in immense brakes in the Jordan valley; used for a writer's reed (3 John 7), a measuring rod (here, 21:15ff.; Ezek. 40:3-6; 42:16-19). {*Rise and measure*} Ezekiel also measures the temple (cf. Ezek. 42:2). But modern scholars do not know how to interpret this interlude (Rev. 11:1-13) before the seventh trumpet (Rev. 11:15). However understood, there are three points in the interlude: (1) the chastisement of Jerusalem or Israel (cf. Rev. 11:1-2); (2) the mission of the two witnesses (cf. Rev. 11:3-12); (3) the rescue of the remnant (v. 13).

2. {*The court*} Here this refers to the outer court of the temple that was a place of prayer for the Gentiles (cf. Mark 11:17), but now John is to cast it out and leave to its fate (given to the Gentiles in another sense) to be profaned by them. {*They shall tread under foot*} This trampling is in a show of contempt (cf. Luke 21:24), even the holy city (Matt. 4:5; Isa. 48:2; Neh. 11:1). {*Forty and two months*} (cf. Dan. 7:25; 12:7). This time period occurs in three forms in the Apocalypse: (1) 42 months (cf. Rev. 13:5); (2) 1260 days (cf. Rev. 11:3; 12:6); (3) "3 & ½ years" (lit. "time, times and half a time" Rev. 12:14, also Dan. 7:25). This period, however its length may be construed, covers the duration of the triumph of the Gentiles, of the prophesying of the two witnesses, of the sojourn of the woman in the wilderness.

3. {*Unto my two witnesses*} The Greek syntax shows these are two well-known characters, like Elijah, Elisha, but there is no possible way to determine who they refer to. All sorts of identifications have been attempted.

4. {*The two olive trees*} (cf. Rom. 11:17, 24, also Zech. 4:2, 3, 14). Again the Greek syntax shows these are familiar known entities, which are identical to each other, not different references.

9. {*To be laid in a tomb*} Lit. "to be placed in a tomb."

11. {*After...the breath of life from God*} Clearly this is an allusion where the dead bones lived again. (cf. Ezek. 37:5, 10, also 2 Kgs. 13:21). The spectators of this event were panic-stricken.

13. {*Earthquake*} Earthquakes are often given as a symbol of great upheavals in social and spiritual order (cf. Ezek. 37:7; 38:19; Hag. 2:6; Mark 13:8; Heb. 12:26; Rev. 6:12; 16:18). {*Were affrighted...gave glory*} Here is a picture of "a general movement toward Christianity, induced by fear or despair-a prediction fulfilled more than once in ecclesiastical history" (Swete). They gave recognition of God's power (cf. John 9:24; Acts 12:23; Rom. 4:20).

15. {*Great voices*} Perhaps these are the great voices of the living creatures of Revelations 4:6; 5:8. {*The kingdom of our Lord and of his Christ*} This is the certain and glorious outcome of the age-long struggle against Satan, who wields the kingdom of the world which he offered to Christ on the mountain for one act of worship. But Jesus scorned partnership with Satan in the rule of the world, and chose war, war up to the hilt and to the end. Now the climax has come with Christ as Conqueror of the kingdom of this world for his Father. *This is the crowning lesson of the Apocalypse.* {*He shall reign*} God shall reign, but the rule of God and of Christ is one as the kingdom is one (1 Cor. 15:27). Jesus is the Lord's Anointed (Luke 2:26; 9:20).

17. {*O Lord God*} (cf. Rev. 1:8; 4:8). {*The One who is...*} (cf. Rev. 1:4, 8; 4:8; 16:5). {*Thou hast taken*} The Greek tense of "taken" is emphasizing the permanence of God's rule, "you have assumed your power."

18. {*Were wroth*} Lit. "became angry." This is the culmination of wrath against God (cf. Rev. 16:13; 20:8, also Pss. 2:1, 5, 12; 99:1; Acts 4:25).

CHAPTER 12

1. {*A great sign*} This is the first of the visions to be so described (cf. Rev. 13:3; 15:1), and it is introduced by a form of the Greek verb *horaô*, used to introduce heavenly appearances.

3. {*Seven diadems*} This is the Greek word *diadêma*, (cf. English diadem), a royal band to bind a tiara on the head; this is not a *stephanos*, chaplet or wreath like the Latin *corona* (cf. 13:1; 19:12). If Christ as Conqueror has many diadems, it is not strange that Satan should wear seven (ten in Rev. 13:1).

5. {*Who is to rule all the nations with a rod of iron*} (cf. Rev. 2:27 and Ps. 2:9). Here is a direct reference to the birth of Jesus from Mary, who thus represented in her person this ideal woman (God's people). This is elsewhere applied there to the victorious, triumphant Christian (cf. Rev. 19:15). {*Was caught unto God*} This refers to the ascension of Christ, with omission of the ministry, crucifixion, and resurrection of Christ because he is here simply showing that the Dragon's vigilance was futile. "The Messiah, so far from being destroyed, is caught up to a share in God's throne" (Beckwith).

7. {*There was war in heaven*} Lit. "There came to be war in heaven."

9. {*Was cast down*} The Greek tense shows he was cast down for good and once for all, a glorious, complete consummation (cf. Luke 10:18; John 12:31).

11. {*They overcame him because of the blood of the Lamb*} (John 16:33 and Rev. 3:21; 5:5). "The victory of the martyrs marks the failure of Satan's endeavors" (Swete). The blood of Christ is here presented as the ground for the victory and not the means (cf. Rev. 1:5; 5:9). Christ conquered Satan, and so makes our victory possible (Luke 11:21; Heb. 2:18). {*They loved not their life even unto death*} (cf. Heb. 12:4). They did not put their own lives before loyalty to Christ (cf. John 12:25, also Mark 8:35; Matt. 10:39; 16:25; Luke 9:24; 17:33). Jesus himself had been obedient to death (Phil. 2:8). These martyrs seem to be still alive on earth, but their heroism is proleptically pictured.

14. {*The two wings of the great eagle*} Not the eagle of Revelation 8:13, but the generic use of the article.

17. {*Waxed wroth*} The Dragon went off to make war with the scattered followers of the Lamb not in the wilderness, perhaps an allusion to Genesis 3:15. The devil carries on relentless war with all those which keep the commandments of God and hold the testimony of Jesus. These two marks excite the wrath of the devil then and always (cf. Rev. 1:9; 6:9; 14:12; 19:10; 20:4).

CHAPTER 13

1. {*Out of the sea*} (cf. Rev. 12:3). The imagery comes from Daniel 7:3 (cf. Rev. 17:8). This wild beast from the sea (cf. Dan. 7:17, 23) is a vast empire used in the interest of brute force. The Roman Empire seems to be meant here (Rev. 17:9, 12). {*Names of blasphemy*} (cf. Rev. 17:3). The meaning is made plain by the blasphemous titles assumed by the Roman emperors in the first century.

2. {*Like unto a leopard*} also called a panther. The leopard was considered a cross between a panther and a lioness. {*As the feet of a bear...as the mouth of a lion*} (cf. Dan. 7:4). This beast combines features of the first three beasts in Daniel 7:2. The strength and brutality of the Babylonian, Median, and Persian empires appeared in the Roman Empire. The catlike vigilance of the leopard, the slow and crushing power of the bear, and the roar of the lion were all familiar features to the shepherds in Palestine. The dragon works through this beast. The beast is simply Satan's agent. Satan claimed this power (Matt. 4:9; Luke 4:6) and Christ called Satan the prince of this world (John 12:31; 14:30; 16:11). So the war is on.

3. {*As though it had been smitten...and his deathstroke was healed*} (cf. the Lamb, Rev. 5:6). This apparently refers to the death of Nero in June A.D. 68 by his own hand. But after his death pretenders arose claiming to be Nero *redivivus* (revived) even as late as A.D. 89 John seems to regard Domitian as Nero over again in the persecutions carried on by him. The distinction is not always preserved between the beast (Roman Empire) and the seven heads (emperors), but in Revelation 17:10 the beast survives the loss of five heads. Here it is the deathstroke of one head, while in verses 12, 14 the beast himself receives a mortal wound. All the earth wondered at and followed after this Antichrist, represented by Domitian as Nero *redivivus* (revived).

8. {*Whose*} This is in the singular in the Greek, thus calling attention to the responsibility of the individual in emperor worship.

11. {*Another beast*} (cf. Rev. 13:1). The Greek makes clear this is another beast *of the same* kind, like the first beast of verse 1; though having some different features and origination.

14. {*That they should make an image to the beast*} (cf. Rev. 13:14, 15; 14:9, 11; 15:2; 16:2; 19:20; 20:4). This image of the emperor could be his head upon a coin (Mark 12:16), an *imago* painted or woven upon a standard, a bust in metal or stone, a statue, anything that people could be asked to bow down before and worship. This kind of test the priests in the provinces pressed as it was done in Rome itself. Emperor worship is really devil worship. {*The stroke of the sword...and lived*} This can refer to the death of Nero by his own sword or perhaps a reference to Domitian as a second Nero in his persecution of Christians.

15. {*To give breath to it*} (cf. Rev. 11:11). This "beast" probably refers to a world system like the first beast (not a mere person), was endowed with the power to work magical tricks. {*As many as should not worship*} This is ventriloquism like that in Acts 16:16. {*As many as should not worship*} It is clear that refusal to worship the image of the emperor carried with it capital punishment in Trajan's time.

16-18. {*A mark*} (Rev. 13:16, 17; 14:9, 11; 16:2; 19:20; 20:4). This is the Greek word *charagma,* from *charassô,* to engrave. In Revelation it refers to the brand of the beast on the right hand or on the forehead or on both. In the papyri, official business documents often have the name and image of the emperor, with the date as the official stamp or seal and with *charagma* as the name of this seal. Animals and slaves were often branded with the owner's name, as Paul (Gal. 6:17) bore the *stigmata* of Christ. {*Even the name or the number*} The stamp (the mark) may bear either the name or the number of the beast. The name and the number are one and the same. They could write the name in numerals, for numbers were given by letters. This may be according to a sort of *gematria* (code) known to the Apocalyptist and his Asian readers, but not generally intelligible; rather it is a puzzle (cf. 17:9). {*Six hundred and sixty-six*} All sorts of solutions are offered for this conundrum: These are Hebrew letters for Nero Caesar.

CHAPTER 14

1. {*The Lamb*} (cf. Rev. 5:6; 7:17; 12:11; 13:8) This future vision is after the visions of the two beasts. Mount Zion is the site of the new city of God (Heb. 12:22), the Jerusalem above (Gal. 4:26), the seat of the Messianic Kingdom whether heaven or the new earth (Rev. 21; 22). These victors have the name of the Lamb and God upon their foreheads (cf. Rev. 3:12; 22:4; mark of the beast Rev. 13:16; 14:11). This seal protects them (cf. Rev. 9:4). {*A hundred and forty and four thousand*} Some details of the scene of the 144,000 are different (cf. Rev. 7:4-8).

4. {*Were not defiled with women*} This is the Greek word *molunô,* to stain (cf. Rev. 3:4). The use of this word rules out marriage, which was not considered sinful. If taken literally, the words can refer only to adultery or fornication.

5. {*Was found no lie*} (cf. Isa. 53:9; 1 Pet. 2:23). {*Without blemish*} As

8. {*Fallen, fallen*} Lit. "fell, fell." Tense marks a point in time. The words are repeated as a solemn dirge announcing the certainty of the fall. The English rendering is more musical and rhythmical than the literal (cf. Isa. 21:9).

10. {*He also shall drink*} If they worship and meet the conditions of the warning, the Greek tense shows it is certain they will drink. {*Prepared unmixed*} Lit. "the mixed unmixed." This is strong wine (undiluted with water) mixed with spices to make it still stronger (cf. Ps. 75:9). {*With fire and brimstone*} (cf. Gen. 19:24; Isa. 30:33; Ezek. 38:22). Also translated "fire and brimstone" (cf. Rev. 9:17 and also Rev. 19:20; 20:10; 21:8).

12. {*The faith of Jesus*} Lit. "the faith in Jesus." He is the object of our faith (cf. Rev. 2:13; Mark 11:22; Jas. 2:1).

15. {*Send forth...and reap*} Both commands urging Christ to action, the Greek tense shows to send forth the sickle and reap *now.*

17. {*He also*} Distinct from the Reaper on the cloud (cf. vv. 15-16), this is the fifth angel who is God's messenger from heaven (temple where God dwells). This fifth angel with his sharp sickle is to gather the vintage (vv. 18-20) as Christ did the wheat.

19. {*The vintage of the earth*} Lit. "the vine of the earth." The vine refers here to the collective enemies of Christ.

20. {***Blood from the winepress***} (cf. Isa. 63:3). The image of treading out the grapes is a familiar one in the East, blood and grape juice are of similar colors. Joel pictures the valley of Jehoshaphat as the place of the slaughter of God's enemies (cf. Joel 3:12, also Zech. 14:4). {***As far as a thousand and six hundred furlongs***} This is literally about the distance of 3,200 American football fields (roughly 180 miles), and such a distance would cover the length of Palestine. But it is more likely the metaphor for the whole earth, an exuberant apocalyptic symbolism (Swete).

CHAPTER 15

1. {***Another sign in heaven***} This statement is looking back to Revelation 12:1, 3, after the series intervening. {***Which are the last***} Here is another "seven" series (seven is a number of finality and completeness): Seven Seals (cf. Rev. 6:1 ff.); Seven Trumpets (cf. chapters 8-11); Seven Bowls [seven last plagues] (cf. Rev. 15:1ff., 7ff.). But there is an even closer connection with chapters 12-14, that is, the drama of the long conflict between the church and the world (Swete). Here is the final cycle of such visitations (cf. Rev. 21:9).

3-4. {***The song of Moses and the song of the Lamb***} (cf. Exod. 14:31; 15:1-19). This is a single victory song, with one note to Moses (the crossing of the Red Sea) and a separate note of victory to the Lamb (the Glorified Messiah). Old and New thus are combined in Hebraic tone and expressions. This martyr's song has the ring of great poetry.

6. {***With precious stone pure and bright***} Lit. "with stone pure bright"; note that some Greek texts read "linen" pure bright (cf. Rev. 17:4; 18:16; Ezek. 28:13, also Rev. 19:8, 14).

7. {***Seven golden bowls***} These are golden saucers, but not full of incense as in Revelation 5:8, but full of the wrath of God. Portents of dreadful events.

8. {***Was filled with smoke***} Smoke is here the symbol of God's presence (cf. Exod. 19:18; Isa. 6:5). The symbolic smoke "screen" also keeps all out of the sanctuary for the time being.

CHAPTER 16

1. {*The seven bowls*} Lit. "these bowls" referring back to verse 7 (anaphoric article).

2. {*A noisome and grievous sore*} Lit. "bad and malignant sore." This is like the sixth Egyptian plague (Exod. 9:10; Deut. 28:27, 35) and Job 2:7.

3. {*Even the things that were in the sea*} Lit. "every soul of life," that is, all that is marked by life (cf. Gen. 1:21); it is complete destruction, not partial (cf. Rev. 8:9).

5. {*The angel of the waters*} Angels have charge of various nature powers (cf. winds, Rev. 7:1; fire Rev. 14:18). The rabbis spoke also of an angel with power over the earth and another over the sea. {*Which art and which wast*} This is an idiom for God's eternity (cf. Rev. 1:4, 8; 4:8, also 11:17). {*Thou Holy One*} (cf. Rev. 3:1; 15:3).

9. {*They blasphemed the name of God*} (cf. Rev. 13:6; Jas. 2:7; Rom. 2:24; 1 Tim. 6:1). {*They repented not*} They blamed God for the plagues. This phrase is like a refrain of a funeral dirge (cf. Rev. 9:20; 16:11). In Revelation 11:13 some did repent because of the earthquake. Even deserved punishment may harden the heart.

12. {*That come from the sunrising*} Lit. "those from the rising of the sun," that is, the kings from the east (cf. Matt. 2:2) in their march against Rome.

13-14. {*Of the dragon*} That is, Satan (cf. Rev. 12:3, 9). {*Of the beast*} That is, the brute force of the World power represented by the Roman Empire (Swete). He is called first beast (cf. Rev. 13:1, 12) and then just the beast (cf. Rev. 13:14; 14:9, 11; 15:2; 16:2, 10). {*Of the false prophet*} (cf. Matt. 7:15; Acts 13:6; 1 John 2:22; 4:3; 2 John 7). This is the second beast (cf. Rev. 13:11-14 and 19:20; 20:10). So the sixth bowl introduces the dragon and his two subordinate beasts of chapters Revelation 12-13 (the two beasts). {*Three unclean spirits*} (cf. Zech. 13:2). Out of the mouths of each (Satan, the beast [first beast] and the false prophet [second beast]) comes an evil spirit. The mouth was the seat of influence. {*As it were frogs*} These are demons [v. 14, also 1 Tim. 4:1] (cf. loathsome things Exod. 8:5; Lev. 11:10). {*To gather them together unto war*} (cf. Joel 2:11; 3:4). Not a war between nations (cf. Mark 13:8), but it is more likely war against God and the reckoning of the nations (cf. Ps. 2:2) and probably the battle pictured in Revelation 17:14; 19:19 (cf. 2

Pet. 3:12). Paul terms it the Parousia of the Lord Jesus (cf. 1 Thess. 5:2; 2 Thess. 1:10; 2:2; 1 Cor. 1:8; 2 Cor. 1:14; Phil. 1:6; 2:16; 2 Tim. 1:12, 18; 4:8).

16. {*Har-Magedon*} Lit. Hebrew "Har-Magedon." Perhaps meaning "the mountains of Megiddo" though not certain.

19. {*Babylon*} This refers to Rome (cf. Rev. 17:18); it was not overlooked. God was simply biding his time with Rome. {*The cup of the wine of the fierceness of his wrath*} (cf. Jer. 30:24).

21. {*Every stone about the weight of a talent*} This is pertaining to the Greek unit of measure *talantiaios,* from *talanton* (cf. Exod. 9:24, also Josh. 10:11; Isa. 28:2; Ezek. 38:22). A *talanton* ranged in weight in NT literature from 57 to 80 American pounds; and in the LXX from 108 to 130 American pounds. So, "*about* a hundred pounds" is an approximation in translating this word.

CHAPTER 17

1. {*I will show thee*} One of the seven angels with the seven bowls explains the judgment on Babylon (the Prostitute) in the next two chapters (cf. Rev. 14:8; 16:19). {*That sitteth upon many waters*} (cf. Jer. 51:13). Babylon got its wealth by means of the Euphrates and the numerous canals for irrigation. Rome does not have such a system of canals, but this item is taken and applied to the New Babylon in Revelation 17:15. Other cities in the OT are also called harlots (cf. Nineveh, Nah. 3:4 and Tyre Isa. 23:16).

2. {*The kings of the earth*} (cf. Rev. 16:14). This refers either to human rulers in general, or the vassal kings absorbed by the Roman Empire (cf. 1:5; 6:15; 17:18; 18:3, 9; 19:19; 21:24). {*Committed fornication*} This is a figure for purchasing the favor of Rome by accepting her suzerainty (lordship) and with it her vices and idolatries.

3. {*He carried me away*} That is, carried away in a vision of ecstasy, in his own spirit (cf. Rev. 21:10). Some interpret "spirit" as the Holy Spirit and not John's spirit (cf. Rev. 1:10; 4:2; 21:10). {*Into a wilderness*} (cf. Isa. 14:23). John may here picture this to be the fate of Rome or it may be that he himself, in the desert this side of Babylon, sees her fate. In Revelation 21:10 he sees the New Jerusalem from a high mountain. {*Sitting...upon a scarlet-coloured beast*} She (the harlot city of Rome) is sitting on this beast with seven heads and ten horns. Crimson is the color of splendor. {*Full of names of blasphemy*} (cf. Rev. 13:1) Here the names cover the whole body of the beast (first beast, Rev. 13:1; 19:20). {*Seven heads and ten horns*} This personified beast refers to Roman world power.

5. {*Upon her forehead a name written*} Roman harlots wore a label with their names on their brows, as here. There is undoubtedly a contrast between this woman here and the woman in chapter Revelation 12:1ff. Others in the book have names on their bodies (cf. Rev. 14:1; 22:4, also 19:16). {*Mystery*} The name Babylon is to be interpreted mystically or spiritually for Rome (cf. Rev. 11:8). Rome, the Metropolis of the Empire, is the mother of harlotry and of the world's idolatries.

9. {*Here is the mind which hath wisdom*} (cf. Rev. 13:18). {*Seven mountains*} Rome was known as the city on seven hills. {*Seven heads*} Each head is a symbol for a king (cf. v. 10). Here the woman (Rome) riding the beast has seven heads (cf. beast with seven heads Rev. 13:1).

10. {*Seven kings*} This is another change in the symbolism. The identification of these seven kings is one of the puzzles of the book. {*The five are fallen*} (cf. 2 Sam. 3:38). This is a common expression for the downfall of kings (Ezek. 29:5; 30:6; Isa. 21:9). {*The one is*} That is, the one when this vision is dated. {*The other is not yet come*} This may refer to Domitian, even though some argue it cannot. The difficulty about counting these emperors is that Galba, Otho, Vitellius reigned so briefly that they hardly merit being included. {*He must continue a little while*} Some think this refers to Titus, who died September 13, A.D. 81, after a short reign.

13. {*They give their power and authority unto the beast*} The new powers are allies of the beast. Just as the dragon gave both power and authority to the beast (cf. Rev. 13:2), so they are wholly at the service of the beast.

16. {*These shall hate the harlot*} The downfall of Rome will come from the sudden change in subject peoples. {*Shall burn her utterly with fire*} John wrote before the days of Alaric, Genseric, Ricimer, Totila, with their hordes which devastated Rome and the west in the fifth and sixth centuries. "No reader of the *Decline and Fall* can be at a loss for materials which will at once illustrate and justify the general trend of St. John's prophecy" (Swete).

18. {*The woman*} She is now explained to be the city of Rome, after the beast has been interpreted (cf. v. 9). Rome followed Babylon, and other cities may follow in their train.

CHAPTER 18

1. {*Was lightened*} Lit. "by reason of his glory." "So recently has this angel come from the Presence, that in passing he flings a broad belt of light across the dark earth" (Swete).

2. {*Fallen, fallen is Babylon the great*} (cf. Rev. 14:8). Lit. "Did fall, did fall Babylon the great." It is repeated like a solemn dirge of the damned.

5. {*Have reached*} This is the Greek verb *kollaô,* from *kolla,* gluten, glue, to cleave to, to join one another in a mass here up to heaven (cf. Jer. 51:9; Zech. 14:5).

10. {*Standing afar off*} This verse is the dirge of the kings. It is a vivid picture of the terrible scene, fascinated by the lurid blaze (cf. Nero's delight in the burning of Rome in A.D. 64), and yet afraid to draw near. There is a weird charm in a burning city. They feared the same fate.

12-13. {*Of ivory*} (cf. 1 Kgs. 22:39). Elephant tusk as a precious item, this is the Greek word *elephantinos,* from *elephas* (compare English "elephant"). {*Slaves*} Lit. "bodies," the meaning of this Greek word *sôma* is "slave" (cf. Gen. 34:29; Tobit 10:11; also 2 Macc. 8:11).

14. {*All things that were dainty and sumptuous*} "Riches" is the Greek word *liparos,* from *lipos* (grease) and so fat, about food; "splendor" is the Greek word *lampros,* bright and shining (Jas. 2:2), about clothing. {*Are perished from thee*} The Greek is a *doubled* double negative, as emphatic a negation as the Greek language can make.

17. {*Shipmaster*} This is the Greek word *kubernêtês* (from *kubernô,* to steer); this is the helmsman, sailing master (cf. pilot Acts 27:11 [subordinate to the "owner of the ship"]). {*Gain their living by the sea*} Lit. "work the sea." This idiom is as old as Hesiod for sailors, fishermen (cf. vv. 10, 15).

21. {*A strong angel*} Lit. "one mighty angel" but the meaning is the indefinite article, not "one" as a numeral. {*As it were a great millstone*} This is not a small millstone turned by women (Matt. 24:41), but one requiring a beast of burden to turn it (Mark 9:42), and so a large (lit. "great") one. Like a boulder hurled into the sea, Rome is destroyed; already the old Babylon was a desert waste. (Notice that "never" in vv. 21 to 23 is used five times which is an emphatic double negative in the Greek.)

23. {*With thy sorcery*} This is the Greek word *pharmakia,* from *pharmakeuô,* to prepare drugs, from *pharmakon,* sorcery (cf. Rev. 9:21); so here meaning sorcery and magical arts.

24. {*In her*} That is, in Rome. {*Was found*} (cf. Rev. 16:6; 17:6). Rome butchered to make a Roman holiday. They killed not merely gladiators, but prophets and saints from Nero's massacre A.D. 64 to Domitian and beyond (cf. Jerusalem, Matt. 23:35).

CHAPTER 19

1. {*Hallelujah*} This is Hebrew for "praise the Lord" (cf. Rev. 19:1, 3, 4, 6). The Great *Hallel* (a title for Pss. 104 to 109) is sung chiefly at the feasts of the Passover and tabernacles (cf. Rev. 12:10).

2. {*For*} Here it means "because." The reason for God's judgments is given in Revelation 15:3; 16:7. The doom of Babylon seen in Revelation 14:7 is now realized.

3. {*Goeth up*} (cf. Rev. 18:21, also Isa. 34:9). Lit. "*keeps on* going up." This describes Babylon's utter collapse.

5. {*A voice from the throne*} This is an angel of the Presence, not God nor the Lamb (cf. though Rev. 16:17). This angel summons all the servants of God to join in the antiphonal praise to God (cf. 1 Chr. 16:36).

6. {*The Lord our God, the Almighty*} (cf. Rev. 1:8; 4:8; 11:17; 15:3; 16:7, 14; 19:15; 21:22). Compare the Latin phrase *deus et dominus noster* used of the Roman emperor. But "God became king" in fullness of power on earth with the fall of the world power.

7. {*The marriage of the Lamb*} In the O.T. God is the Bridegroom of Israel (cf. Hos. 2:16; Isa. 54:6; Ezek. 16:7). In the N.T. Christ is the Bridegroom of the Kingdom (the universal spiritual church as seen by Paul, 2 Cor. 11:2; Eph. 5:25, and by John in Rev. 3:20; 19:7, 9; 21:2, 9; 22:17). In the Gospels Christ appears as the Bridegroom (Mark 2:19; Matt. 9:15; Luke 5:34; John 3:29). Three metaphors of women appear in the Apocalypse: Mother (chapter 12); Harlot (chapters 17-19); Bride (Rev. 19:7 to end). "The first and third present the Church under two different aspects of her life, while the second answers to her great rival and enemy" (Swete). {*Made herself ready*} There is something for the Bride to do (1 John 3:3; Jude 21; 2 Cor. 7:1), but the chief preparation is the act of Christ (Eph. 5:25).

10. {*To worship him*} John either felt that the angel represented God or he was beside himself with excitement over the glorious consummation. He was tempted to worship an angel (cf. Col. 2:18). But the angel refuses worship from John on this ground. All Christians (cf. Rev. 6:11) and angels are God's servants (Heb. 1:4-14). {*Worship God*} And worship Christ, who is the Son of God (cf. Rev. 5:13). {*The spirit of prophecy*} The possession of the prophetic spirit shows itself in witness to Jesus (cf. illustrations in Mark 1:10; Matt. 3:16; Luke 3:21; John 1:51; Rev. 4:1; 10:1; 11:19; 14:17; 15:5; 18:1; 19:1, 7-9).

13. {*In a garment sprinkled with blood*} Note that some Greek manuscripts have "dipped," but "sprinkled" is probably the correct reading (cf. Isa. 63:3). But whether dipped or sprinkled, this is the blood of Christ's enemies, not the blood of Calvary (cf. Rev. 1:5; 5:9; 7:14; 12:11).

15. {*That he should smite and he shall rule them with a rod of iron*} He will rule (lit. "shepherd") them with a rod of iron (cf. 2:27; 12:5; also Christ as Shepherd (cf. 1 Pet. 2:25; Heb. 13:20).

18. {*The flesh of kings...*} Lit. "fleshes of kings" which in the Greek plural means "pieces of flesh."

20. {*The false prophet*} Possibly this is the second beast of Revelation 13:11-17; 16:13; 20:10. Some identify him as the priesthood of the Imperial cult, which practiced all kinds of magic and imposture to beguile men to worship the Beast. {*The mark of the beast*} (cf. Rev. 13:15-16; 14:9; 16:2; 20:4). {*That burneth with brimstone*} (cf. Rev. 20:10; 21:8). Just as there is a water lake (cf. Luke 5:1) there is a *Gehenna* like lake (cf. Matt. 5:22). It is a different figure from the abyss (cf. Rev. 9:1; 20:1). This is the final abode of Satan, the beast, the false prophet, and wicked men. The fact of hell is clearly taught here, but the imagery is not to be taken literally any more than that of heaven is to be so understood (cf. Rev. 4; 5; 21; 22). Both fall short of the reality.

CHAPTER 20

2. {*The dragon*} (cf. Rev. 12:9). Now seized, Satan has been behind the beast and the false prophet from the start. All the different names given here for the dragon some call a parenthesis. {*For a thousand years*} In this book of symbols, how long is a thousand years? All sorts of theories are proposed, none of which fully satisfy one. Perhaps Peter has given us the only solution open to us: one day with the Lord is as a thousand years and a thousand years as one day (cf. 2 Pet. 3:8). God's clock does not run by ours. Times, seasons, and programs are *his* timing. This wonderful book was written to comfort the saints in a time of great trial, not to create strife among them.

3. {*Into the Abyss*} (cf. Rev. 9:1 and Luke 8:31). Satan already has been cast out of Heaven (cf. Rev. 12:9), now he is cast out of the earth, and returns to his own place, the Abyss. {*That he should deceive no more*} This is glorious relief after the strain of the previous visions of conflict. Small wonder that Christians today cherish this blessed hope whatever the actual meaning may be. {*For a little time*} Whatever the thousand years means, it is here said plainly that after it is over the devil will again have power on earth for a little time.

4. {*And they lived*} This can also be translated simply as a point in time "they lived." If a certain kind of Greek tense it means "came to life" (as here translated) or "lived again" (cf. Rev. 2:8 and 20:5). If another kind of the same tense, then it could mean "*increased* spiritual life." See John 5:21-29 for the double sense of life and death (now literal, now spiritual) precisely as we have the second death in Revelations 2:11; 20:6, 14.

5. {*The rest of the dead*} Some say this refers to all except the martyrs, both the righteous and the unrighteous. But some take this to mean only the wicked. {*Lived not until the thousand years should be finished*} Though some interpret this as bodily resuscitation, apocalyptic method of interpreting prophecy may require that this be treated as symbolic. I comment and confess my own ignorance therefore as to the meaning of the symbolism without any predilections for post-millennialism or premillennialism. {*This is the first resurrection*} Theologically speaking, this first resurrection may be a special incident in the present life before the Parousia (the Coming of [King] Christ). It has no parallel with 1 Thessalonians 4:16, where the dead in Christ are raised before those living are changed. (cf. "Regeneration" of Matt. 19:28 and the "Restoration" of Acts 3:21). No effort is here made to solve this problem (but cf. Rev. 20:12 and John 5:29; Acts 24:15).

9. {*The camp of the saints*} This is the Greek word *parembolê*, military camp, and can refer to Israelites group (Exod. 29:14) or Roman barracks (Acts 24:34, 37) and for an army in line of battle (Heb. 11:34; Rev. 20:9).

11. {*A great white throne*} (cf. Rev. 4:4; 20:4 also Matt. 25:31-46; Rom. 14:10; 2 Cor. 5:10). "The absolute purity of this Supreme Court is symbolized by the color of the Throne" (cf. Dan. 7:9; Pss. 9:1; 97:2). The Almighty Father sits upon the throne (cf. Rev. 4:2, 9; 5:1, 7, 13; 6:16; 7:10, 15; 19:4; 21:5), and the Son sits there with him (Heb. 1:3) and works with the Father (John 5:19-21; 10:30; Matt. 25:31; Acts 17:31; 2 Cor. 5:10; 2 Tim. 4:1). {*From whose face the earth and the heaven fled away*} The non-eternity of matter is a common teaching in the OT (Pss. 97:5; 102:27; Isa. 51:6) as in the NT (Mark 13:31; 2 Pet. 3:10). All is now spiritual. Even scientists acknowledge the fact that the material universe had a beginning and will eventually cease to exist.

12. {*The dead, the great and the small*} The general resurrection of verse 13 is pictured by anticipation as already over. No living are mentioned after the battle of verses 7-10, though some will be living when Jesus comes to judge the quick and the dead (2 Tim. 4:1; 1 Thess. 4:13). All classes and kinds are standing before the throne (Rev. 11:18; 13:16; 19:5, 18). {*Books were opened*} (cf. Dan. 7:10). The record of each human being has been kept in God's books. The sentence upon each rests upon written evidence. {*Another book which is the book of life*} (cf. Rev. 3:5; 13:8; 17:8). "It is the roll of living citizens of Jerusalem," (Swete) "the church of the first born enrolled in heaven" (Heb. 12:23). We are saved by grace, but character at last (according to their works) is the test as the fruit of the tree (Matt. 7:16, 20; 10:32; 25:31-46; John 15:6; 2 Cor. 5:10; Rom. 2:10; Rev. 2:23; 20:12; 22:12).

14. {*Were cast*} First were cast the two beasts (cf. Rev. 19:20); then the devil (cf. Rev. 20:10); now Death personified and is disposed of in victory (the last enemy, 1 Cor. 15:26, 54; Hos. 13:14); in the next verse all "out of Christ" are cast. Hades has no more terrors, for the saints are in heaven. There is no more fear of death (Heb. 2:15), for death is no more (Rev. 21:4). The second death (cf. Rev. 2:11; 20:6; 21:8) is here identified as in Revelation 21:8 with the lake of fire.

15. {*If any was not found written in the book of life*} (cf. Dan. 12:2, also John 5:29; Acts 24:15). All "out of Christ" now follow those of verse 14. There is no room here for: (1) soul sleeping; (2) an intermediate state; (3) a second chance; (4) annihilation of the wicked.

CHAPTER 21

1. {*A new heaven and a new earth*} (cf. Isa. 65:17; 66:22; Ps. 102:25). This new vision is the picture of the bliss of the saints. {*And the sea is no more*} The sea had given up its dead (cf. Rev. 20:13). There were great risks on the sea (cf. Rev. 18:17). The old physical world is gone in this vision. It is not a picture of renovation of this earth, but of the disappearance of this earth and sky (not heaven where God dwells). It is a glorious picture here in Revelation 21:1-8 in sharp contrast to the lake of fire in Revelation 20:11-15. The symbolism in neither case is to be pressed too literally, but a stern and a glorious reality exists behind it all.

2. {*The holy city, new Jerusalem*} "The New Earth must have a new metropolis, not another Babylon, but another and greater Jerusalem" (Swete), and not the old Jerusalem which was destroyed A.D. 70. It was called the Holy City in a conventional way (Matt. 4:5; 27:53), but now in reality because it is new and fresh, this heavenly Jerusalem of hope (Heb. 12:22), this Jerusalem above (Gal. 4:26) where our real citizenship is (Phil. 3:20). One must not manipulate the symbolism too much. It is better to see the glorious picture with John and let it tell its own story. {*As a bride adorned*} New Jerusalem here as a bride adorned is a figure of the *abode of God*, not the figure of bride as the *people of God* as in Revelation 19:7.

3. {*The tabernacle of God is with men*} It is one of the angels of the Presence speaking (cf. Rev. 16:17; 19:5). {*And he shall dwell with them*} (cf. Rev. 7:15 from Ezek. 37:27; Zech. 2:10; 8:8 and John 1:14), now a blessed reality of the Father. The metaphor stands for the Shekinah Glory of God in the old tabernacle (cf. Rev. 7:15; 13:6; 15:5), the true tabernacle of which it was a picture (Heb. 8:2; 9:11). God is now Immanuel in fact, as was true of Christ (Matt. 1:23).

4. {*Shall wipe away every tear from their eyes*} A figure like a tender mother as in Revelation 7:17 (Isa. 25:8). There is peace and bliss: no death, mourning, pain, or any other cause to tear.

5. {*Behold, I make all things new*} (cf. Isa. 43:18). This is the first time since Revelation 1:8 that God speaks directly. Though in the story voices have come out of the throne and sanctuary (cf. Rev. 21:3 and Rev. 16:1, 17), likely angels. {*And he saith*} Now, probably, an angel begins speaking, has happened before in the story (cf. Rev. 14:13; 19:9). {*Faithful* *and true*} That is, they are reliable and genuine (cf. God, Rev. 19:11; Christ, 3:14).

6. {*I am the Alpha and Omega*} He is the First Cause and the Finality (cf. Rev. 22:13, also Isa. 44:6). Such titles as these apply to both Christ (cf. Col. 1:18; Rev. 3:14) and God (cf. Rom. 11:36; Eph. 4:6). {*Of the fountain*} God is the bountiful Giver (Jas. 1:5, 17) of the Water of Life (cf. Rev. 7:17; 22:1, 17 and Isa. 55:1).

7. {*He that overcometh*} This is a common phrase in chapters two and three of the end of each of the Seven Letters. {*I will be his God*} (cf. Gen. 17:7 and Rev. 21:3). {*He shall be my son*} This was made first of Solomon (2 Sam. 7:14) and applied to David later in Psalm 89:26.

8. {*Their part shall be*} This verse is in contrast to the state of the blessed (cf. vv. 3 to 7). It is the state of those who have disfranchised themselves from the Kingdom of God. They are with Satan and the two beasts, and are the same with those not in the book of life (cf. Rev. 20:15) in the lake of fire and brimstone (cf. Rev. 19:20; 20:10, 14), that is the second death (cf. Rev. 2:11; 20:6, 14). It is a list of eight classes of the doomed and damned. {*Abominable*} That is, those who have become defiled by the impurities of emperor worship (Rev. 7:4; 21:27; Rom. 2:22; Titus 1:16). {*Fornicators*} (cf. 1 Cor. 5:10; 1 Tim. 1:9). {*Sorcerers*} This word is closely connected with idolatry and magic (cf. Rev. 9:21; 13:13). {*Idolaters*} (cf. 1 Cor. 5:10; 10:7; Eph. 5:5; Rev. 22:15).

9. {*The bride the wife of the Lamb*} (cf. Rev. 17:1ff.). This is shown by one of the group of seven angels because of the contrasts: (1) harlot city (Babylon) there (chapter 17) and the heavenly city (New Jerusalem) here; (2) Bride in sharp contrast with the Harlot. The New Jerusalem was briefly presented in verse 2, but now is pictured at length (cf. Rev. 21:9-22:5) in a nearer and clearer vision. {*The bride, the wife of the Lamb*} (cf. Rev. 19:7; 21:2). "Wife" anticipates the reality of the marriage to come.

10. {*He carried me away in the Spirit*} (cf. Rev. 17:7). It is the same language when John received a vision of the Harlot City in a wilderness. {*Mountain*} (cf. Ezek. 40:2). Apparently this is not Mount Zion, for the New Jerusalem is seen from this mountain (cf. Rev. 14:1).

11. {*Having the glory of God*} This verse is a parenthesis describing the radiance of the dazzling splendor of God (cf. Isa. 60:1; Ezek. 43:5). God's very presence is in the Holy City (the Bride).

12. {*Having a wall great and high*} John now continues with the description of the structure. There is one gate each for the twelve tribes, having its tribal name on it (cf. Ezek. 48:31 and Rev. 7:1-8). {*Twelve angels*} These angels act as guards or gatekeepers (cf. Isa. 62:6; 2 Chr. 8:14).

13. {*Three gates...*} The east is mentioned first as the direction of orientation (cf. Ezek. 42:16).

14. {*Twelve foundations*} (cf. Isa. 28:16; Heb. 11:10). That is, twelve foundation stones (cf. 1 Cor. 3:11; 2 Tim. 2:19). There are twelve, because of the twelve apostles as foundation stones (Eph. 2:20). Jesus had spoken of twelve thrones for the apostles (Matt. 19:28); names of all twelve are here written. One may wonder if the name of Judas is on that stone or that of Matthias.

15. {*For a measure a golden reed*} The rod of gold was in keeping with the dignity of the service of God (cf. Rev. 1:12; 5:8; 8:3; 9:13; 15:7).

16. {*Lieth foursquare*} (cf. Ezek. 48:16, 20). Actually, it is cube, with the base a tetragon (Rev. 21:12). According to Herodotus, Babylon was a square, each side being 120 *stadia* (about 240 American football fields). Diodorus Siculus says that Nineveh was also foursquare. {*Twelve thousand furlongs*} This is about 1500 miles. But is it the sum total of the four sides, or the measurement of each of the four sides? Some of the rabbis argued that the walls of the New Jerusalem of Ezekiel would reach to Damascus and the height would be 1500 miles high. It is a perfect cube like the Holy of Holies in Solomon's temple (1 Kgs. 6:19). Do not reduce the measurements to literal interpretations; this is highly symbolic language. The meaning is that heaven will be large enough for all (cf. John 14:1).

17. {*A hundred and forty and four cubits*} "Thick" is not strictly in the Greek. It is not clear whether it is the height or the breadth of the wall that is meant. The wall may be 144 cubits "high" though it is not as likely. A wall of 216 feet is not enormous in comparison with the 7,000,000 feet (1500 miles) height of the city. Hence, it is contextually probable that breadth (thickness) is meant. This number was used before (cf. Rev. 7:4; 14:1). Though measured by an angel, a human standard was employed.

18. {*The building of the wall*} The Greek of this phrase makes clear that the wall had jasper *built into* it (v. 11). {*Was pure gold*} The city shone like a mass of gold in contrast with the jasper luster of the wall.

19-20. {*Were adorned*} (cf. Rev. 4:3). Though some hold no mystical meaning to the list of the twelve stones, the twelve gems do correspond closely (only eight in common) with the twelve stones on the high priest's breastplate (Exod. 28:17-20; 39:10; Ezek. 28:13; Isa. 54:11). The exact identification and/or hue and/or brilliancy of the stones is in some cases difficult to establish with certainty. Here are broad categories: blues (sapphire, jacinth, amethyst); greens (jasper, chalcedony, emerald, beryl, topaz, chrysoprase); reds (sardonyx, carnelian); yellow (chrysolite). Possibly this variety of kinds and colors illustrates the variety of gifts and graces in the twelve apostles.

21. {*Twelve pearls*} (cf. Isa. 54:12). These are gate towers (cf. v. 12). Pearl is one of the commonest of jewels (Matt. 7:6; 13:46; 1 Tim. 2:9). {*Street*} Though singular in the Greek, yet this includes all the streets.

22. {*I saw no temple therein*} The whole city is a temple in one sense (v. 16), but it is something more than a temple even with its sanctuary and Shekinah Glory in the Holy of Holies. {*For the Lord God the Almighty, and the Lamb are the temple thereof*} (cf. Rev. 1:8). In 2 Corinthians 6:16 believers are the sanctuary of God, but now God and the Lamb is our Sanctuary (cf. chapters 4-5).

23. {*To shine upon it*} (cf. Isa. 60:19). If the sun and moon did shine, they would give no added light in the presence of the Shekinah Glory of God. The splendor of the sun and moon is simply put to shame by the glory of God Himself. {*And the lamp thereof is the Lamb*} Christ is one lamp *for all* in contrast with the many lampstands of the churches on earth (cf. Rev. 1:12, 20). "No words could more clearly demonstrate the purely spiritual character of St. John's conception of the New Jerusalem" (Swete).

24-25. {*Amidst the light thereof*} (cf. Isa. 60:3, 11, 20). Is this a picture of heaven itself or some gracious purpose of God towards humanity which has not yet been revealed (Swete) (cf. Rev. 22:2)? This looks like the former, a continued picture of heaven.

26. {*They shall bring*} Lit. "they will bring to it." Rome gathered the merchandise of the world (cf. Rev. 18:11). The City of God will have the best of all the nations (Isa. 60:5, 11), an expansion of Revelation 21:24.

CHAPTER 22

1. {*He shewed me*} (cf. Rev. 21:9, 10 and 1:1; 4:1). Now is shown the interior of the city. {*A river of water of life*} (cf. Rev. 7:17; 21:6; 22:17; John 4:14). There was a river in the Garden of Eden (cf. Gen. 2:10). The metaphor of river reappears in Zechariah 14:8; Ezekiel 47:9, and the fountain of life in Joel 3:18; Jeremiah 2:13; Proverbs 10:11; 13:14; 14:27; 16:22; Psalm 36:10. The river was shimmering like mountain water over the rocks. {*Proceeding out of the throne of God and of the Lamb*} (cf. Ezek. 47:1; Zech. 14:8). Already in Revelation 3:21 Christ is pictured as sharing the Father's throne (cf. Heb. 1:3, also Rev. 22:3). This phrase has no bearing on the doctrine of the Procession of the Holy Spirit.

2. {*The tree of life*} (cf. Gen. 1:11 and Rev. 2:7; 22:14). {*For the healing of the nations*} That is, spiritual healing, of course. Leaves are often used for obtaining medicines. Here again the problem occurs whether this picture is heaven before the judgment or afterwards. Reliance on chronology is precarious here.

4. {*They shall see his face*} This vision of God was withheld from Moses (Exod. 33:20, 23), but promised by Jesus to the pure in heart (Matt. 5:8) and mentioned in Hebrews 12:14 as possible only to the holy, and promised in Psalm 17:15. Even here on earth we can see God in the face of Christ (2 Cor. 4:6), but now in the New Jerusalem we can see Christ face to face (1 Cor. 13:12), even as he is after we are made really like him (2 Cor. 3:18; Rom. 8:29; 1 John 3:2). It is anthropomorphic language, to be sure, but it touches the essential reality of religion. "The supreme felicity is reached, immediate presence with God and the Lamb" (Beckwith). {*His name on their foreheads*} (cf. Rev. 3:12; 7:3; 14:1).

5. {*Shall be night no more*} (cf. Rev. 21:25). {*Shall give them light*} (cf. Rev. 21:23). {*They shall reign*} That is, reign eternally in contrast with the limited millennial reign of Revelation 20:4, 6. This glorious eternal reign with Christ occurs repeatedly in the book (cf. Rev. 1:6; 3:21; 5:10) as in Luke 22:30. Christ's Kingdom is spiritual (John 18:36). "The visions of the Apocalypse are now ended; they have reached their climax in the New Jerusalem" (Swete). Now John gives the parting utterances of some of the speakers, and it is not always clear who is speaking.

7. {*And behold, I come quickly*} (cf. Rev. 1:2; 2:5, 16; 3:11; 16:15). Christ is the speaker, either through this angel or more probably directly from Christ without introduction as in verses 12 and 16. Once more we must recall that "soon" is according to God's time, not ours (cf. 2 Pet. 3:8). {*Blessed*} This is the sixth beatitude, like the first (cf. Rev. 1:3). This book is here called a "prophecy" (cf. Rev. 22:10, 18, 19). It is Christ's revelation from God, a direct message from God. Part of it is prediction of doom on Christ's enemies, but most of it is a comforting picture of final triumph and bliss for the faithful in a time of great distress and persecution.

11. {*Let him do unrighteousness still*} The language here is probably ironical, with a reminder of Daniel 12:10, in no sense a commendation of their lost estate. It is the time when Christ has shut the door to those outside who are now without hope (Matt. 25:10; Luke 13:25). The states of both the evil and the good are now fixed forever. There is no word here about a "second chance" hereafter.

12. {*My reward is with me*} It is Christ speaking again, and he repeats his promise of coming quickly (cf. v. 7). He speaks now as the Rewarder (cf. Heb. 11:6, also Rev. 11:18; Isa. 40:10; 62:11). Each will receive the reward according to his own work (Rev. 2:23; 2 Cor. 5:10; Rom. 2:26).

13. {*I am the Alpha and the Omega*} This phrase is applied to God in Revelation 1:8; 21:6, and here alone to Christ, crowning proof in this book of Christ's deity. Compare "Beginning and End" used of God in Revelation 21:6 (cf. Heb. 12:2) and here of Christ. "First and Last" is applied only to Christ (Rev. 1:17; 2:8). These title thus show Christ is qualified to be the Judge and Rewarder (cf. v. 12). Christ was the Creator of the universe for the Father. So now he is the Consummation of redemption.

14. {*Blessed*} This is the last (seventh) beatitude of the book and "deals with the issues of the higher life" (Swete). {*That they may have the right to come to the tree of life*} (cf. Rev. 2:7; 22:2).

15. {*Without*} That is, outside the holy city (cf. Rev. 21:8, 27). All outside the holy city are in the lake that burns with fire and brimstone, the second death (symbolic language of hell, the eternal absence from fellowship with God). Compare also figures outside of lighted house, i.e., outer darkness (cf. Matt. 8:12; 22:13; 25:30), as the abode of the damned. Another symbol is the worm that does not die (cf. Mark

9:48). {*The dogs*} This refers to the morally impure (cf. Deut. 23:18; 2 Kgs. 8:13; Ps. 22:17, 21; Matt. 7:6; Mark 7:27; Phil. 3:3). Dogs in Middle Eastern cities are the scavengers and excite unspeakable contempt. {*Every one that loveth and maketh a lie*} Satan is the father of lying (cf. John 8:44) and Satan's home is a congenial place for those who love and practice lying (cf. 2 Thess. 2:12, also John 1:6; Rom. 1:25; Eph. 4:25).

16. {*I Jesus*} This is the last and most solemn attestation to the book that is from Jesus (the historic Jesus known to the churches), in harmony with Revelation 1:1. It is the Jesus of history here speaking, who is also the Christ of theology and the Lamb of God. {*For the churches*} (cf. Rev. 10:11; John 12:16). It is not just for the seven churches (Rev. 1:4), but for all the churches in the world then and now. {*I am the root and the offspring of David*} (cf. Rev. 5:5; Matt. 22:42-45). {*The bright, the morning star*} The Davidic King is called a star (cf. Num. 24:17; Luke 1:78). This "daystar" is interpreted as Christ (cf. 2 Pet. 1:19). In Revelation 2:28 the phrase "the morning star" occurs in Christ's words, which is here interpreted.

17. {*The Spirit and the bride*} This refers to the prophets and the saints. The Holy Spirit, speaking through the prophets or the Spirit of prophecy (cf. Rev. 2:7; 16:4; 18:24), joins with the bride (cf. Rev. 21:2), the people of God, in a response to the voice of Jesus just heard. After the picture of heaven in Revelation 22:1-5 there is intense longing (cf. Rev. 19:7) of God's people for the consummation of the marriage of the Lamb and the Bride. {*Let him come*} (cf. Isa. 55:1). The thirsty man is bidden to come himself before it is too late (cf. Rev. 5:6, also John 6:35; 7:37). {*He that will*} He can come even if not yet eagerly thirsting. {*Let him take*} This gracious and wide invitation is cheering after the gloomy picture of the doomed and the damned. The warnings of doom are meant to deter men from falling victims to all the devil's devices then and now. The door of mercy still stands wide open today, for the end has not yet come. The series of panoramas is over, with the consummation pictured as a reality. Now we drop back to the standpoint before we saw the visions through John's eyes. In verse 17 we hear the voice of the Spirit of God inviting all who hear and see to heed and to come and drink of the water of life freely offered by the Lamb of God.

18-19. {*I testify*} These verses are from Jesus himself, still bearing solemn witness to this book, with warning against willful perversion of its teachings. {*If any man shall add...if any man shall take away*} This warning is directed against perversions of this book, not about the NT or the Bible as a whole, though it may be true there also.

20. {*He which testifieth*} That is, Jesus (cf. Rev. 1:2) who has just spoken (cf. Rev. 22:18). {*Yea: I come quickly*} (cf. Rev. 22:7, 12). {*Come, Lord Jesus*} John expresses his absolute belief in the Lord's promise (cf. 1 Cor. 16:22, also Titus 2:13; 2 Tim. 4:8).

21. {*The grace of the Lord Jesus be with the saints*} John's own benediction, an unusual ending for an apocalypse, but suitable for one meant to be read in the churches (cf. Rev. 1:3). It is a good word for the close of this marvelous picture of God's gracious provision for his people in earth and heaven.